Praise for *Give and Take*

"An outstanding achievement. Tillotson's book is a full-scale treatment of modern taxation in Canada. Her findings and methodology bring tax history onto a new plane. Not many books generate the intellectual force to reshape a subject. *Give and Take* is one that does."
  – Romain Huret, author of *American Tax Resisters*

"Taxes are the price we pay for civilization. But the social contract underpinning our (sometimes grudging) willingness to pay them is complex, fragile, and should never be taken for granted. Shirley Tillotson's rollicking history of Canadian tax debates reveals precisely how that social contract was constructed – and why Canada is a much better place for it."
  – Jim Stanford, Harold Innis Industry Professor of Economics,
    McMaster University

"Shirley Tillotson's brilliant book rescues the history of taxation from the grip of technical, abstract detail and gives it a human face. Here is cultural and social history at its best, written in an engaging style. She shows how tax payers and collectors held conversations over whether to comply or resist and how they debated the nature of democracy and citizenship. This book is a major contribution to the history of Canada with wider implications for understanding other twentieth-century societies."
  – Martin Daunton, professor emeritus of economic history,
    Cambridge University

"Rather than relying on ministerial statements and Department of Finance documents, Tillotson delves into the archives and studies 'the conversation' between tax authorities and tax payers, revealing emotion as well as logic. In other words, this is a very human history."
  – Joe Martin, director of Canadian Business and Financial History,
    Rotman School of Management

"This colourful, convincing portrait of Canadian tax culture masterfully illustrates how tax policy decisions reflected larger political and social currents of change, and the power of taxation to define the meaning of citizenship and the role of government. Tillotson has a talent for depicting key characters and the emotions aroused by debates over taxation. She brings a delightful humour and wit to the telling of these stories."
– Lisa Philipps, professor of taxation law, Osgoode Hall Law School

"Those interested in future reform will welcome this detailed and fascinating history of the Canadian tax system from the introduction of the national income tax in 1917 to the Carter Commission and the 1971 federal budget."
– Michael Veall, editor, *Canadian Public Policy*

"Canadians urgently need 'good tax talk,' and Shirley Tillotson delivers in this brilliant and deeply researched history of taxation, society, and democracy in Canada. This important book raises the level of an old and continuing conversation about taxation, citizenship, and the nation-state – a conversation that resounds through the many chambers of the nation's past and embraces all of us."
– Eric Sager, professor emeritus, History, University of Victoria

"Oliver Wendell Holmes said, 'I like to pay taxes. With them, I buy civilization.' Shirley Tillotson says, 'With taxes, we try to buy democracy, too.' In *Give and Take*, she documents the what and when of twentieth-century-Canadian income tax, but she also explores how taxes redefined Canadians' relationship with government and with citizenship. The results? 'Well,' she says, 'mixed.'"
– Christopher Moore, author of *Three Weeks in Quebec City: The Meeting That Made Canada*

"*Give and Take* is the very best history we have of Canadian taxation in the twentieth century, one that provides a wonderful model for studying the relationship between public finance and society in a modern liberal democracy. Tillotson's brilliant use of primary sources sets a high bar for future explorations of the complex and intertwined roles of civic culture and class identity in shaping tax policy."
– W. Elliot Brownlee, research professor of history, University of California, Santa Barbara

Give and Take

The Citizen-Taxpayer and the Rise of Canadian Democracy

Shirley Tillotson

$ ¢ $

UBCPress · Vancouver · Toronto

26 25 24 23 22 21 20 19 18 17   5 4 3 2 1

Printed in Canada on FSC-certified ancient-forest-free paper (100% post-consumer recycled) that is processed chlorine- and acid-free.

Library and Archives Canada Cataloguing in Publication

ISBN 9780774836722 (hardback)
ISBN 9780774836746 (pdf)
ISBN 9780774836753 (epub)
ISBN 9780774836760 (mobi)

Cataloguing-in-publication data for this book is available from Library and Archives Canada.

Canadä

UBC Press gratefully acknowledges the financial support for our publishing program of the Government of Canada (through the Canada Book Fund), the Canada Council for the Arts, and the British Columbia Arts Council.

This book has been published with the help of a grant from the Canadian Federation for the Humanities and Social Sciences, through the Awards to Scholarly Publications Program, using funds provided by the Social Sciences and Humanities Research Council of Canada.

Printed and bound in Canada by Friesens

Set in ITC Garamond Std by Marquis Interscipt
Copy editor: Dallas Harrison
Indexer: Susan Brown
Cover designer: David Drummond

UBC Press
The University of British Columbia
2029 West Mall
Vancouver, BC V6T 1Z2
www.ubcpress.ca

Contents

Give and Take

1
Talking Tax

Income taxes require a high level of taxpayer morale and cooperation if they are to be collected cheaply or adequately.
— Henry Simons, American economist[1]

Over the years, there has been scarcely any relationship between government and people which has been more sensitive than taxation, and, indeed, which has caused more civil bloodshed. If you people [Americans] had not been so supersensitive to a tax on tea, I would not now be speaking to you from a foreign land.
— Kenneth LeM. Carter, Canadian accountant[2]

BIRDS DO IT. BEES DO IT. Even chimpanzees do it. They all "pay taxes."[3] Everywhere I look there are stories of non-humans stumping up a share of their favourite foodstuff (or some other valuable commodity) for use by their group. What these reports usually fail to say, though, is whether there is a bailiff chimp ready to seize property or a chimp leader making a pitch for tax compliance. In these "Just So" stories, no one points out how hard chimp governments have to work to raise revenue or how often chimps debate what is "fair" taxation.

We Canadians scarcely know more about our tax history than we know about the tax practices of chimps in the wild. In a 1959 interview, the dean of Canadian economic and political history, Donald Creighton, blithely affirmed in his Red Tory way that Canadians were cheerful collectivists, historically happy to carry a heavy tax burden for the sake of their independent national life.[4] In 2006, the Fraser Institute's Mark Milke called on Canadians to throw off their "serfdom": in describing our tax history, he chose the Chinese head tax (hardly a typical one) to illustrate his view that taxation is oppressive.[5] Neither Creighton nor Milke provided an accurate picture of our tax history. But such simplistic stories still circulate because Canadian historians have provided commentators with little else to work with. Our research-based scholarly tax history, especially for the period that I cover in this book, the first fifty-five years of the federal income tax, is a remarkably small body of literature. Canadian historians working on this period have sometimes written about tax as part of their work on federalism and regionalism.[6] But for tax history as such we have only a few works by economists, tax law scholars, sociologists, and political scientists.[7] Whatever the good qualities of that literature, and there are many, it treats taxpayers (if they are discussed at all) as abstractions.

I want to put real human beings into our tax history and, in the process, show how dramatic, engaging, and sometimes amusing this history can be. Why should taxation not be interesting? Taxation is about how we take on the problems of collective life, figuring them out in light of our times and concocting solutions to them, sometimes ad hoc and foolish, occasionally far-sighted and even brilliant. Tax history need not be a dense and abstract account of technical adjustments and electoral calculations. It involves police raids and trials, impassioned orations, and cunning tax dodges. Taxation is not simply something done by the powerful to the weak: although taxes have sometimes been collected at gun point, even in Canada, and some sort of force always backs the tax collector's demands, governments in modern Canada know that levying a productive tax, with modest collection costs, requires negotiation. The tax laws themselves are negotiated, of course, but even those of us who never get close to the legislative process still make decisions about taxpaying. If a tax can be evaded or avoided, then anyone who pays it has decided to pay it, more or less deliberately. We might notice arriving at that decision when we fill in an honest income tax return. But we also decide, usually out of prudence, to pay less obviously self-assessed taxes, such as a sales tax or customs tariff. For example, smugglers, participants in cash transactions, and purchasers of dubious second-hand goods have decided not to pay certain taxes. Our taxpaying or -dodging decisions become routine. But there are turning points, moments of change, when the normal give and take is unsettled. And that is where we find our history as taxpayers.

At those moments, governments and their tax collectors have worked hard to persuade Canadians to pay their taxes. They haven't always succeeded. As in any other area of law, compliance with tax laws is sometimes motivated by fearful prudence, and weak enforcement means less compliance. But compliance has also been motivated by honour, respect for order, commitment to community values, or just herd mentality. Canada's tax policy makers and revenue agents have thought about taxpayer psychology, and in seeking compliance they have invoked not only cowardice and carefulness but also other motivations. I explore the history of that engagement between tax collectors and taxpayers. Which blend of persuasion and policing worked or failed? How did the political resources of governments and citizens change over the turbulent times between 1917 and 1971? Did negotiations on taxpaying play out differently in, say, Vancouver and Saint John? To answer such questions, I investigate the social and cultural contexts that shaped Canadians as taxpayers and the political culture that Canadian politicians and administrators share with the public.

This history is not primarily about economic policy or high politics or legislative drafting, though each appears in glimpses and as background. Tax history as I write it is a conversation rather than a monologue enunciated by ministers of finance. And it's a conversation in which the participants – ministers and deputy ministers as well as taxpayers and protesters – are human beings with emotions, ideas, and identities and not just "interests" narrowly, abstractly, and ahistorically defined. Self-interest is always foundational to human choice, but of historical interest are changes in how we understand both "self" and "interest." Our tax history is less predictable than left-wing or right-wing ideology would suggest when taxpayers are included in the story. Their ideas about what it is to be free, to be honourable, to participate in politics, and to be secure help to build both a particular tax system and a political culture. That culture is historical, and it is both broadly human and specifically Canadian.

By learning more about our tax history from this angle, we can also learn more about the history of democracy in this country. It's a more recent history than you might think. In 1917, when this book's story begins, Canada was still something of a British colony – in fiscal terms as much as in many other ways. By themselves, the limits set by Westminster on our freedom of fiscal choice meant that we were not quite self-governing, and those limits were at least as important as the better-known fact that Canada did not make its own foreign policy. If democracy consists of institutions and cultural norms that allow all to participate in deciding matters that matter, then not being fully our own decision makers about tax and war meant that Canadians during the First World War were not yet enjoying the full measure of democratic public life. Even in areas where we did have more national autonomy, politics was far from completely democratic: most Canadian residents could not vote in national elections, and the provincial and municipal franchises were a hodgepodge of exclusions and privileges. By the standard of "no taxation without representation," there was still a long way to go in 1917. Over the course of the next six decades, the right to vote lost its links to sex, race, and property ownership. By 1971, Canada had become more genuinely democratic. "Voters" and "taxpayers" were not yet exactly the same set of people, but the overlap was almost complete. In addition, political action (never limited simply to voting) had expanded well beyond the vote. Canadians had created hundreds of interest groups and other types of broadly political movements, multiplying the mechanisms of democratic action in the process. And by 1971 our national sovereignty, though incomplete in economic terms and still internally contested by Quebec *indépendentistes,* was strongly asserted. Over the decades between 1917 and 1971, there were two crucial points, one during the 1940s and the other during the 1960s, when taxation issues added momentum to the overall trend of democratization. Tax was good for democracy.

A Strangely Entertaining Social History of Taxation

One might imagine that studying tax would be all about poring over tedious policy documents, statistical reports, and statutes. And I have done a lot of that. But in order to make this book a study of conversations, negotiations, and politics of all kinds, low as well as high, I have made a point of looking for sources in which I could see humans doing a variety of things with words, not only presenting expert opinions or making laws. I sought out sources that would allow me to hear the voices from below as well as those from above. This goal led me to approach the records of the Department of Finance and the Department of National Revenue in a particular way. In these records and in the papers of prime ministers, finance ministers, opposition leaders, and tax officials, both local and national, I found and used many policy studies and reports. But what I especially looked for – and found – were letters. There is a treasure trove of letters in these files, from all sorts of Canadians, about tax and debt and related topics. These letters explain, they advise, they implore, and they protest. They provide a remarkably revealing window into a wide variety of subjects – from family budgets to views on the Constitution. The letters also include frank discussions among political allies. Equally fascinating are the exchanges between civil servants and politicians, professors, journalists, and businesspeople (from the president of Dominion Steel to the local druggist and many in between).

These letters are a gold mine for social history. Their accounts of daily life and descriptions of power are fascinating. But they also present some problems as evidence. First, were these letters written by odd or otherwise exceptional people? In general, no. There was not one file for serious letters from important people and another for ignorable letters from nobodies. Letters from high-status men and women, political friends, and confidential advisers appear in many of the filing systems next to letters from the general public.[8] As the researcher flips through files, letters from former prime ministers and university presidents appear unpredictably before or after letters from poor widows and labour union secretaries. This is true of all the different archival collections, but it is especially noticeable in the Second World War finance ministry's correspondence files on tax questions, organized by last name of the writer. It is also true in the "Budget Proposals from the Public," covering 1956–68. It is possible that similar files covering earlier years once existed but were thrown out, as operational records often are. We know that the correspondence in these proposals from the public was organized as a normal part of the budget process, in ways that I will describe in more detail in Chapter 10. Although a few letter writers in every period are identified as obsessive or unreasonable by comments in the files, the vast majority of writers speak in recognizably ordinary voices, though not always cool-tempered ones. The Department of Finance's tax specialist between 1934 and 1958, A. Kenneth (Ken) Eaton, emphasized in 1966 the value placed on such letters: "Let no sceptic suggest that along the route there [was] any channelling off of outside requests [for tax changes] into a waste paper basket. That just [did] not happen."[9] Writing a letter to the minister of finance or the prime minister was not the behaviour of green-ink-wielding weirdos, though by the 1960s one sees more correspondents themselves worrying that they might be read as "crank[s]."[10]

Second, do these letters matter as evidence of policy impact? Reading these files as a social and cultural historian, I wasn't looking only for letters that I knew to be from influential people. Nor did it matter particularly to me whether the letters had been read by ministers or only by their staff members. I read the letters simply as evidence of various attitudes toward tax and democracy in the world where politicians and policy makers lived and acted. Juxtaposing the contents of these letters with the statements of politicians in Parliament, with letters to editors and editorials, with magazine features, with opinion polls, and with records of social organizations makes the letters a thread in the tapestry of public opinion that I have tried to weave. Often they confirm what the more public documents say but in more vivid personal voices. Before public opinion polling began in the 1940s, these letters provided policy makers with a way of knowing what voters thought and felt. Many of the letters are the archival equivalent of conversations on the politicians' summer picnic circuit, though perhaps, because more private, these letters are less polite and more personally revealing. Some of the letters are more like conversations in the Mount Royal Club or in the lobby of the Chateau Laurier, the voices of politicians' peers offering reading suggestions, conveying serious political intelligence, making known their financial power. Letters from both ordinary and elite Canadians offer colour and detail to the picture of tax culture. More than the preprocessed responses to pollsters' questions, they tell us about the thoughts behind the views, the connections between tax ideas and other frameworks of meaning. To understand how political life connects to daily life, how experiences of taxation and democratization were connected, these letters, in all their variety, are invaluable, and often surprising.[11]

In addition to politicians' and officials' papers, and citizens' letters in them, I used other types of archives to deal with specific themes. To investigate tax evasion, for example, beyond allegations in letters, I examined the previously unstudied (and well-hidden) tax case dockets of the Exchequer Court of Canada in the interwar years. I also sampled municipal police court registers in Vancouver, Halifax, Charlevoix County (Quebec), and various Ontario communities, and I sought out newspaper coverage related to particular court cases. This was by no means a method aimed at high-level tax jurisprudence, of which Canada, in any case, has only a small amount before 1949. It was rather a means to get a sense of how big a part prudence played in tax compliance. Who would have had reason to think that evasion was risky? How much did tax collectors rely on citizens' willingness to comply and how much on fear of effective enforcement? To understand the work of persuasion involved in tax legitimation and resistance, I read budget speeches, the opposition's responses, and other discussions of taxation in the records of the House of Commons debates. Comparing these sources to the letters in the politicians' files, the parliamentarians appear in a good light, representing many, though not all, of Canadians' widely held views. The public relations publications of the Department of National Revenue, as well as advertisements by the government, also give the terms in which Finance and Revenue officials believed that tax could be made understandable and acceptable.

I also made an effort to get closer to local sources (both municipal and provincial) and particular communities to avoid treating "Canada" as a homogeneous thing. There was relevant historical work on many of these areas and communities, but there is much more to do, even in the areas that I examined. The records of the Department of Indian Affairs contain letters from "Indians" – members of Indigenous nations – as well as reports from Indian agents and correspondence among officials. These sources come from many parts of Canada. I explored the records of premiers and Departments of Finance in British Columbia, Ontario, and Quebec and municipal records in Toronto, Vancouver, Halifax, and Saint John. I benefited from the ever-expanding databases of digitized newspapers to follow tax talk in the prairie provinces, Montreal, Prince Edward Island, small-town Ontario, and, predominantly, the Toronto *Globe,* the *Toronto Daily Star,* and their successor papers. But I also consulted microfilms for other papers on particular stories. And, of course, I drew on other historians' work. My goal was at least to hint at Canada's regional diversity of tax cultures, without denying the political weight that urban central Canada has carried since the 1920s.

The period that I cover is set by the creation of the national income tax in 1917 and its reform in the 1971 budget, but I don't discuss the federal income tax alone. I also tell stories about customs collection and episodes in provincial and municipal tax history. The more local taxes have been extremely important in Canadians' experience of taxation. The more local the tax, it seems, the more open and flexible the negotiation of payment. Being a national taxpayer was quite a different experience than being a local one, especially after 1942. Across these jurisdictional levels, the identity of the taxpayer sometimes matched, but more often it didn't. A host of attitudes toward privacy, honour, authority, and community was involved in making and remaking the local, provincial, and national systems of assessment and collection. The federal income tax did not simply land in 1917 like a space ship on an empty field. It was bolted to an existing Rube Goldberg machine of a fiscal federation in which, at every level, decades of expedience, political competition, and economic change had created a messy, and specifically Canadian, tax culture. The history of that tax culture before 1917 has been written by my colleague and collaborator Elsbeth Heaman. In that history, municipal taxation plays a central part and helps to explain the origins of the federal income tax. But even though that local level recedes gradually in political importance over the period that I discuss, its legal and cultural legacy continues well into the 1950s, over the life span of the late Victorians.

To understand the cultural context of tax policy, I have drawn on sources that reveal the beliefs and practices of daily life. In doing so, I have not just followed a fashion in policy studies, though indeed many policy scholars now integrate ideas about emotion and narrative into their analyses of policy change.[12] In 1953, the executive director of the Canadian tax practitioners' professional organization, the Canadian Tax Foundation, pointed to the importance of such an approach in an essay on taxable capacity: he wrote that how effectively a given kind of tax can be collected depends not only on its rate, high or low, but also on deeply cultural aspects such as "the attitudes and motives of taxpayers[,] which extend far beyond direct reactions to the tax itself."[13] Tax collectors inevitably keep such matters in mind as they deal with taxpayers. For that reason alone, the history of taxation requires social and cultural history.

To think about how tax history is part of a social change as broad as twentieth-century democratization requires that we put taxes into a cultural context. That context is part of what historian Martin Daunton has called the "relations of extraction": the political processes that shape who pays, how much, and by which methods and the administrative processes that invoke as "the regular taxpayer" specific classes and types of people.[14] The relations of extraction can include party politics, statute law, and the institutions of government, but they also include sociological assumptions, ideas about property rights, community norms, standards of reliable economic knowledge, and a whole host of other cultural aspects. I cast a wide net here, including geography, time period, type of tax, and aspects of politics. But I do not pretend to have written the comprehensive and complete book of Canadian tax history in the mid-twentieth century. I hope to have left interesting gaps for others to explore. Nor have I written a book of policy history. Instead, I explore the cultural vocabularies on which governors and governed, tax collectors and taxpayers, both draw. Not all popular perspectives influenced the inside world of lawmaking. But politicians and tax administrators sought and often found common ground with taxpayers as they harvested votes and collected taxes. Emphasizing tax legitimation over economics and the view from outside rather than inside policy making, I have tried to sketch the big picture of how things fiscal helped to make modern Canada's democratic culture. Our practice of democracy is still imperfect, but it was better in 1971 than in 1917, in part because more Canadians had become federal income tax payers.

Getting beyond Tax Clichés

The standard narrative in twentieth-century Anglo-American tax history centres on debates about income taxation.[15] The story has been somewhat modified in recent years, and some elements cannot easily be stated in the ideologically neutral terms that I would prefer, but I will attempt to sketch it without gestures to either the right or the left. Its main claim is that taxing income was the result of war emergencies (nineteenth-century ones in the United States and Britain, twentieth-century ones in these countries and in Canada). Income tax later developed into a means for managing the economy and financing the welfare state. In the process, the story goes, income taxation changed its nature. In its earlier forms, the tax on income reached only the wealthy, because those with lower incomes were exempt, and rates were constant (what we now call a "flat tax," what was then called a "proportionate" rather than a "progressive" one). It was a simple tax. Over time, it became more complex. Different kinds of income (e.g., from wages or investments) were taxed at different rates ("differentiation"). Lower incomes began to be taxed (the move from "class tax" to "mass tax") during the Second World War. Higher incomes were taxed at progressively higher rates (a "graduated" rate structure) or subjected to surtaxes, making income tax "progressive" in the technical sense as well as the political sense. Partly through differentiation and partly through exemption of some kinds of income or exemption of income earned by some kinds of people or activities, income tax law became more complex. In Canada, more than elsewhere, historical narratives about income taxation emphasize that, during the 1950s and 1960s, widespread agreement on the value of social security and the viability of macroeconomic management helped to keep tax questions out of the partisan fray. Taxpaying was widely understood to be part of a fair bargain between responsible citizen and responsive state.[16] Only in the early 1980s did intense opposition to taxation begin to move tax-cutting promises into the centre of party politics.[17]

Much in that narrative is correct: certainly, the movement of income taxation from the margin to the centre of taxation is the headline story of the mid-twentieth century. But as with all choices about headlines, emphasis on a particular theme can be distorting. All twentieth-century tax history becomes the hazy background of a story about the modern income tax. Progressive (in the political sense) historians tell their variant of the story in triumphalist terms, seeing the creation of a modern income tax (in the 1940s in Canada and the United States) as essential to the development of a successful welfare state. Conservative thinkers see this as a story of mob democracy, the creation of a discriminatory tax regime driven by populist governments' opportunistic use of antipathy toward the "rich."[18] Neither pays much attention to the whole tax story. Both miss the history of sales taxes, poll taxes, land taxes, customs duties, excise taxes, resource rents, and estate or inheritance taxes. They also miss the larger public finance story, including lotteries, and especially the relationship between taxation and public credit (the ability to borrow). Without a better sense of these other sources of public revenue, it is impossible to appreciate the politics and broader social meanings of the history of income taxation. Although I, too, have left out some important taxes – succession duties, resource rents, and (largely) corporate income taxes – I have added enough of this broader fiscal context, I hope, to show how income tax borrowed from and changed in relation to other revenue sources. To focus only on the modern income tax shines a bright beam on some questions but makes it hard to see, in the shadows, the surrounding terrain of tax culture.

Bringing that larger terrain to light makes the tax bargains of the twentieth century look less like an unambiguous victory for the welfare state. From my point of view, the story is a sadder one in which people who feared change and saw their self-interest in narrow terms held back the development of an effective income tax in the 1920s and a well-funded national welfare state in the 1950s and 1960s. Tax resistance, especially resistance to income tax, was one tool of opposition to better social security. And it was not only the rich and their allies or narrowly provincialist governments that mounted that opposition. Elements of the voting public more generally took positions about tax driven by fears about smaller amounts of money and more personal losses of autonomy. The enormous crises and conflicts of the twentieth century repeatedly revealed, at increasing levels of specificity, that evocations of community and common interest (often rhetorical tools of party politics) are either naively blinkered or troubled by legitimate (though often unheard) challenges. I have tried to amplify some of these challenges, not to stir up hatreds and resentments, and not because I think that these voices should necessarily have carried the day, but to highlight that tax compliance was and always is made amid conflict. Canadians were neither uniquely quiescent nor supremely consensual. The conflicts over fair taxation that erupted in the late 1960s and continued through the 1970s and 1980s were old struggles in new contexts. In producing a tax history that gives a past to these conflicts, and to others since them, I do not mean to say that Canada has failed to develop a democratic politics. Quite the contrary. It is to say that taxation has been central to the history of our common life, including our political history, and, as in all complex matters of justice, knowing that history helps us to let go of ideological simplicities and to approach present problems realistically. If we want Canadians to act out of a strong commitment to community, then we need to think about how to build that commitment. It doesn't occur, fully developed, in nature.

The evidence that I present tells us that Canadian tax culture is more like that of the United States, in having a history of conflict over taxes, than Canadian popular culture (and some history and sociology) would have us think. But I also want to challenge a concept of national culture that emphasizes broadly shared ideas and values.[19] Canada has such strong regional cultures, deeply grounded in different constitutional histories, that free-floating ideas don't root equally well in every part of the country. To see Canadian specificity in a less homogenizing way than through a national culture lens, I used a quasi-anthropological conception of tax culture in designing the research. In that conception, culture is not only about ideas, even though ideas are important. Culture is also found in the practices of tax paying and revenue raising. Culture lies in ways of doing things, formed by interactions among human beings who themselves live within certain kinds of institutions – parliaments and courts, shopping malls and rooming houses, reserves and suburbs – that school the imagination, making some kinds of taxation normal and others unthinkable. For example, in some of the cash-poor districts of Canada's prairie west, the roads that everyone needed were still being built and maintained with statute labour in the 1920s; in urban Ontario, long after that way of maintaining roads had passed, paying a poll tax (sometimes called a statute labour tax) was a vestigial reminder that being a citizen meant contributing something for collective purposes.[20] Tax culture in Canada is a conversation among regions, and, though becoming payers of national income taxes generated some shared national vocabulary, even the income tax began as an aspect of regional politics. And when differences between Canada and the United States emerged on the national scale, and they did, their origins included regional cultures and politics.

The differences among political communities within a nation are as important in shaping tax history as are the differences among nations. Conflicts between neighbouring colonies were among the problems of public finance that prompted the formation of Canada (and many other federal states). The British North American colonies that joined Confederation in the mid-nineteenth century, and those that joined it later, all hoped to benefit from the improvement in public credit that belonging to a bigger country (with more natural resources and a coordinated tariff policy) would provide. But as all students of such federations know, federal nations are economically regionalized and fiscally complex. Canada's Constitution Act recognizes this fact, in section 36(2), by guaranteeing that all parts of the country will enjoy "reasonably comparable levels of public services at reasonably comparable levels of taxation." How we arrived at that arrangement is a well-known story, but the relative role of tax expertise and political pressure in making those judgments is less well known. The story's tax aspects provide an excellent window into not only the intellectual history of economics but also the political cultures that shaped fiscal federalism.

Beyond the practices of elite accommodation, the regional and provincial variations in tax culture include popular constitutionalisms, an element of public opinion that politicians address. Here I draw on the work of constitutional scholars such as Jeremy Webber and Roderick Macdonald.[21] They point out that the meaning of the Constitution Act does not lie in the text but comes from a continuing and stable set of concerns, a political tradition or "constitutive conversation" whose main themes endure, even while related themes evolve over time. Ordinary Canadians might never have been able to recite verbatim sections 91 through 93 of the British North America Act, nor might they ever have cared much about which level of government delivered the public services that they wanted. But in the broader sense of what "provincial rights" and "regional disparity" mean, or more recently what the significance of "genuine consultation" and "multiculturalism" might be, my research suggests that constitutional questions were bound up, in tax talk, with emotions, identities, and the concerns of daily life.

To be more specific: views on rum running or land taxes or the proper level of personal exemptions in the income tax were not positions on "the role of the state" or "the division of powers" in the abstract. People who talked about such tax questions were talking about the standing of one political community's norms, their own, in relation to those of another. Ponder this bit of public finance rhetoric from one William Rand of Canning, Nova Scotia, in 1931: "For sixty years Nova Scotia has been bled to build railways and canals for Canada, then bled again to maintain them so that the Canadian may have them free of tolls, while a wharf on the coast of Nova Scotia can be used only by paying [a] toll to Canada." That's why, he thundered, "that to call a Nova Scotian a Canadian provokes only a bitter anger or actual resentment."[22] Surprised by Rand's rhetoric? You probably haven't lived in Nova Scotia for any length of time. One political community's touchstone terms are not those of another; that's part of what defines a political community. Tax culture historically has done some of the work of constituting those diverse political communities within Canada.

Beyond what it tells us about political cultures, a history of tax culture can draw our attention to some key terms in tax debates, some with continuing relevance, others that tell us how much our world has changed. For example, opponents of progressive taxation of income charge that this method expresses a morally unattractive envy, and its supporters charge the flat-taxers with unethically allowing super-consumption in a world where many are deeply in need. In this conflict, there is at play the profoundly cultural question of which kinds or levels of consumption are basic and which kinds constitute luxury. Many kinds of taxation have taken aim at "extravagant" spending, and tax resistance has often consisted of disputing the idea of luxury embedded in such taxation. Studying the letters that Canadians wrote to their leaders about the strains imposed by taxation makes it possible to see historical changes in the meanings of luxury: for example, the change from a time when owning a car was an extraordinary luxury to one when a car became nearly a necessity whose sacrifice, in order to pay a tax bill, came close to being an intolerable hardship. Discussion of consumption taxes and poll taxes and their role in family budgets reveals how

Canadians weighed the return on taxpaying compared with other expenditures. When was paying for household servants considered a basic necessity, recognized in the income tax law, and when and why did that end? How was saving factored into the list of basic necessities, both in personal life and as public policy? All of these questions relate to a more fundamental change in culture. How has common sense about what is "economic" behaviour changed over time? When did tax talk begin to invoke a larger system, "the economy"? When did it come to seem that a state is justified in setting tax policy in ways that control these arguably personal practices of thrift and indulgence in order to manage that system?

Often bound up in definitions of subsistence and appropriate spending are notions among taxpayers of whom they are obliged to support. Mostly, these notions are linked to family relationships, another central category of culture. Personal income tax laws incorporate many and varied ideas about appropriate family relationships. Dependent children are usually recognized as requiring expenditures that belong within subsistence. But how long children can be considered dependent is culturally and historically contingent. The nature of dependency entailed by various kinds of physical and mental disability is another area where family relations, medical science, and labour market considerations intersect in the tax code. Equally cultural is the question of whether all support relations that seem to be required morally can also be regarded as legally recognized dependencies. What about a taxpayer who provides for the abandoned wife of the taxpayer's deadbeat son? Wives (more often in the past than today) appear as a cost against a married man's income, but single women (and especially single mothers) have often pointed out that wives provide valuable services that might be described as non-market income, so that having a spouse is a form of income and not an expense. Exactly which relationship a wife has to her husband's income is a matter both of culture and of tax law. All of these and many more debates about family and tax make this aspect of culture a particularly rich history to explore. And for Canadians it is one of the more striking dimensions of our income tax history that our tax law treats families differently than American tax law treats families in the United States.

Finally, norms of democratic participation are a cultural phenomenon central to this book. In 1921, suffragist Ella Murray asserted that, "until women understand taxation, they are not in a position to undertake public life."[23] Which things should an adult man know about politics and public life? Have they always been the same? Have they changed over time for adult women? Do they vary by class or racialized identity? In the process of democratization that I trace, changes in tax practices produced changes in the norms of political engagement and even in the norms of business competence. The tax system helped to define the kind of person you needed to appear to be in order to be a respectable citizen. Different levels of government addressed people as taxpayers in ways that changed over time. In the 1950s, some towns were still trying to charge a head tax on anyone coming "from away" to work in the town. Such poll taxes spoke to an older view of citizenship as having a narrow basis in residency. More commonly, by the 1950s, the national identity embedded in paying income tax dominated in defining the link between tax and citizenship.

Ordinary knowledge, political community, family relationships, thrift, and extravagance – these are the kind of tax culture topics that I explore. They are interesting for what they add to our understanding of economic culture and political culture. In addition, tax culture topics illuminate how taxation, and especially the modern income tax, shaped what the national state in Canada is and does and what is democratic or not in all that. In the end, I hope that you'll see quasi-voluntary taxpaying as a means of building democracy, engaging people in necessary political conversations. Historians of economic development note that resource-funded states tend not to develop vigorous democratic institutions. In the Anglo-American tradition, these institutions – parliaments, congresses – had their historical origins in tax bargaining.[24] In mid-twentieth-century Canada, developments in taxation brought Canadians into political activism, and in that sense taxation built democracy. This general process had its own Canadian history, and we will be better citizen-taxpayers if we understand it at the grassroots and not just in the legislature.

Tax and the Development of Mass Democracy

The argument I make in this book puts a lot of weight on a hyphen, the one that connects "citizen" and "taxpayer." Setting up these two as opposites, one socially minded, the other selfish, is a convention of contemporary debate.[25] But the story that I found in my research suggests that the two ideas are not simply opposites. Talking about taxes draws people into public life. In the nineteenth century, as historian Elsbeth Heaman shows in *Tax, Order, and Good Government*, taxation was arranged to protect property.[26] To speak as a citizen was usually to speak as a property owner, someone who had a "stake in the country." During the period I examine, however, late-nineteenth-century challenges to that narrow notion of citizenship bore fruit. Different kinds of people insisted that the taxes they paid entitled them to a more weighty political voice. Self-interest always played a part in those claims. But the more varied the range of interests expressed in tax talk, the more tax questions have forced us to think about how interests intersect. In the tax administration of the interwar years, a lot was hidden from public view, and that secrecy limited the quality of citizen engagement possible on tax questions. But the new tax publics of the '50s and '60s brought to light serious questions of how tax fairness and a just social order might be created and combined. In the sometimes fierce conflicts of those decades, taxpayers became citizen-taxpayers engaged in tough conversations about how to define and pay for our collective life. The work of democracy lies in such conversations.

2
We, the Taxpayers

CHEESE MIGHT EXPLAIN A LOT. In the summer of 1917, Britain needed $40 million worth of Canadian cheese but had no way of paying for it.
Suddenly, Canada's finance minister decided to create a federal tax on income. Since 1914, Sir Thomas White had resisted the calls for an income
tax, saying that it made more sense to borrow or to use other kinds of taxation to pay for the war. In June 1917, however, he learned that, if Canadian
farmers wanted Britain to buy their cheese – or hay or flour – Canada
would have to extend further credit to Britain.[1] So the Canadian government would have to pay the farmers for their cheese and collect from
Britain later. And to do that, given the state of the Canadian government's
own revenues, Canada would have to tap some new sources beyond the
borrowing and taxing already planned. In other words, for Canadians to
earn income while producing for Britain, there would have to be a new
income tax.

Until about a month before introducing federal income tax legislation
on July 25, 1917, White regularly argued that Canada should not have a
federal income tax. Some provinces had provincial income taxes or municipal ones or both, he pointed out. To duplicate them would be burdensome and open to constitutional objection. To tax incomes at a higher rate
than that in the United States would cost Canada both immigrants and
capital. Administering an income tax in Canada would be expensive and
difficult, hard to make fair because easy to evade. Finally, income tax assessment and collection would take time, and funds were needed now. For

all of these reasons, White told Parliament that borrowing and more limited forms of taxation would be better ways to pay for the war. If he was honestly committed to these views in 1915 and 1916, then why did he decide in 1917 that the time for a federal income tax had come? Selling cheese to Britain was only part of the explanation.

One thing is certain: the pressures on White's decisions were fierce. Late in 1917, the normally robust fifty-one-year-old finance minister suffered a "temporary physical breakdown" brought on by the "stupendous anxieties" of the previous months.[2] However, if we understand the contexts in which he made his 1917 decision, then both his delay in taxing income and his concession on that measure make sense. Scholars have pointed to a cluster of causes. First, tax competition with the United States was less of a worry after the wartime taxation of income became heavier there. And then the promise of a progressive income tax helped to support the political alliances that Prime Minister Robert Borden sought with the English-speaking Liberals who favoured conscription.[3] But to understand what creating a federal income tax meant in Canada, in the broad cultural terms of its time, we need to see it in two other contexts, both of them about popular understandings of public finance. One of those contexts is the debate about taxation that had begun before the war and continued after it.[4] The other is the history of the federal government's borrowing and the new place that this borrowing came to occupy in public opinion during the First World War. Borrowing and taxing are always connected in public finance, but ideas about obligation, community, and identity connect them in culture, too.

The Frameworks of War Finance

Finance ministers make tax choices in conditions not of their own choosing, with an eye to what is possible. In theory, any tax is possible, but in reality the only useful tax is one reasonably inexpensive to collect. It helps if the means of collection already exist, and it is essential that most of the prospective taxpayers be willing to pay. That willingness can come from fear, but enforcement based only upon prudential compliance is expensive. The tax authority's cheaper alternative is to inspire a conviction that the tax is reasonably light and apparently fair.

White's first steps in war finance illustrate these ideas perfectly. In the first war budget in 1915, all that White did by way of new taxation was create the Special War Revenue Act (SWRA) and hike the rates of existing customs duties. The SWRA taxes and the new customs duties could be collected by the trained hands of the tens of thousands of staff members already toiling away in the Departments of Inland Revenue and Customs and Excise. Merchants knew how to complete customs declarations and how to obtain excise stamps. Customers dreamed of cheaper goods but could only imagine how much less they might pay if the tariff were different. The prices hid the tax. With the new SWRA tax on matches, for example, lighting the stove became more expensive. But such tiny increments weighed ever so lightly. Critics expressed concerns about the SWRA's use of consumption taxes. They wanted only "fancy" matches to be taxed. They suggested alternatives, among them the income tax. Supporters of the government thought the range of new taxes nicely broad, however.[5] In spite of what the opposition said, not all of the taxes fell on consumers. Included in the SWRA measures was a 1 percent tax on the premium income of insurance firms and on the general income of trust and loan companies.[6] The burden was light, familiar in form, and widely spread.

In confining itself to these kinds of taxes, White's 1915 budget respected not only existing collection practices but also Canadian fiscal federalism. Federal taxation was mostly of the indirect sort: merchants or importers or manufacturers who wrote a cheque to the receiver general to cover these excises or customs duties built the amount of the cheque into the price of goods sold. Many people paid "the tariff tax" in the form of higher prices, but it was impossible for them to know exactly how much of the price of a blanket or cigar was tax. The federal government issued no tax assessment to any Canadian. The dominion specialized in hidden, indirect taxation. Provinces and municipalities, in contrast, were direct tax collectors. Cities, towns, and organized districts of all sorts sent out tax bills. They depended for their revenues on such direct taxation: they assessed, billed and, if necessary, sent a sheriff to hunt down tax delinquents. As Elsbeth Heaman has pointed out, to tax in this way meant having a vulnerable revenue.[7] Finance Minister White knew this well. Early in his working life, he was on the staff of the City of Toronto assessment office.[8] He knew how difficult it was to assess direct taxes fairly and to collect them reliably. Income taxes (along with poll taxes and personal property taxes) were among the most contested of municipal direct taxes. While few Canadian cities and only one Canadian province (British Columbia) relied heavily on income taxation, those governments would not have welcomed another tax on income.[9] To introduce a federal income tax would have meant double taxation for the well-to-do of Toronto and British Columbia, among other places. The political cost to the federal government would have been high and the likelihood of full compliance with a federal income tax low, unless other options truly had been exhausted. White's steering clear of income taxation was not just a constitutional scruple but also a realistic appraisal of his options.

By the end of the war, White had introduced nearly all of the forms of tax that his critics had suggested in 1915. Cautiously, with a sense that the government's war expenditures were in advance of public support for the war (keeping in mind the whole country and not just Toronto and anglophone Montreal), White and Borden's Conservatives followed, rather than led, public opinion in their means of war taxation.[10] White's first concession to his critics was an excess profits tax (in 1916, retroactive to 1915 profits, and revised in 1917 to higher rates). White also added more stamp taxes and luxury taxes as the war went on. The income tax in 1917 was the last in a series of concessions. Yet taxation contributed only a small (though essential) part of war finance. At the end of the 1918–19 fiscal year, with peace only four months old, federal war tax revenues were paying for nothing except the interest owed on money borrowed in the 1915–16 war loans and the Victory Loans of 1917, 1918, and 1919.[11] In effect, Canada's war finance plan consisted entirely of borrowing, and the wartime taxes served merely to pay interest charges on the new debt. To understand the tax conversation about the war, it is essential to see taxes in relation to government borrowing.

Canada was not alone among the belligerent nations in borrowing rather than taxing for war. But in a young nation, as Canada was in the 1910s, even peacetime public spending relied heavily on borrowing, with taxation only a means of backing the loans. Current tax revenue could not pay for the many railways, bridges, and other such development expenses whose ultimate effects would be to generate tax revenues. Like a private firm, a government that issued a bond to finance development spending had to convince lenders that the "enterprise" would generate a revenue stream from which tax-funded interest payments on that bond would reliably flow. Being an importing nation with a reasonably steady customs revenue helped to make Canada's credit good on international markets. A good customs revenue meant that the national government could avoid the political costs of direct taxation and rely on borrowing.

It also helped Canada's credit to have Britain's backing. In the 1910s, Canada's bonds were still safeguarded by the United Kingdom under its Colonial Stock Act. This statute empowered the imperial government in London to disallow any Canadian legislation deemed injurious to Canada's creditors, an arrangement that made Canada's debt less risky.[12] Foreign lenders scrutinized the public accounts, and Canadian finance ministers attempted to dress up those accounts to add lustre to the nation's credit-worthiness.[13] As a trust company president lamented in 1915, the idea that foreign lenders were an infinite source of revenue for development spending made life easy for the federal government.[14] The national taxman could afford to have a gentle touch.[15]

It was not a lack of *national* taxation but a lack of national *direct* taxation and the abundance of credit that framed the finance minister's choices before 1917. The norms of fiscal federalism and the credit of a young country meant, as economists of the 1930s and 1940s agreed, that for White to have begun war finance with a lot of new taxation would have been "revolutionary" or "impossible."[16] In this, they echoed White's 1921 *Story of Canada's War Finance*: Canadians in 1915 and 1916 were willing cheerfully to pay familiar taxes to finance the war, but other kinds of tax would have been deeply resisted.[17] They thought that White's preference for borrowing was in line with public opinion.[18] Closer to the war years, in 1918, Toronto newspaper editor John Lewis would write complacently that, in 1915 and 1916, alternative revenue proposals of a "radical kind" – income tax and land tax – had been made only "outside Parliament." Lewis, like many relieved Canadians, was in a mood for celebration in 1918: he depicted Canadians as having been cooperative taxpayers, compliant even to the dangerous point of encouraging extravagance.[19] But Lewis and the economists of the interwar years misrepresented the array of opinion that confronted White both outside and inside Parliament, even from the beginning of the war.

The Larger Tax Conversation

Although borrowing was the main source of war finance, many proposals circulated in 1915 and 1916 about taxing citizens to pay for the war. From the first, in the emergency ways and means debate of August 1914, opposition members advocated taxing income. Liberals Michael Clark, a doctor and farmer from Alberta, and Frank Carvell, a businessman and lawyer from rural New Brunswick, both called for a "good stiff" graduated income tax.[20] A Liberal lawyer from Cape Breton, William Carroll, pointed out that rich men were asking to contribute large sums to the war and suggested that an income tax would allow them to do so.[21] Such proposals inside Parliament reflected ideas that had circulated outside it at least since the Farmers' Platform of 1910. Income taxation as a permanent replacement for customs revenue was part of the vocabulary of low-tariff Liberalism in the 1890s and 1910s.[22] It is true that, in August 1914, a senior banker privately advised Conservative Finance Minister White that income taxation would be "unpopular."[23] But there were Liberals among the rich, and whether for partisan reasons or not some of them advocated a war income tax at the beginning of the war. In 1918, one of Canada's richest men, Izaac Walton Killam, a financier with significant interests in pulp, paper, and hydro power, deplored the fact that introducing a graduated income tax "had been delayed three years" (introduced in 1917 rather than in 1914), with the result that this "vitally important, fair, and effective means of securing war revenue" had failed to become productive during the war.[24] Here was one of the richest men in Canada, not someone whom the western farmers would normally have seen as an ally, calling the federal income tax an excellent thing, a measure that should have been in place from the beginning of the war. There was in fact debate from its outset, both inside and outside Parliament, about alternative methods of paying for the war. Some of these methods were radical, others not obviously so.

Far more alarming than income taxation or business war profits taxation was real "conscription of wealth." Confusingly, proponents of income taxation often used the phrase as their slogan. But income taxation or excess profits taxation meant only the extraction of wealth-in-the-making. A more radical proposal to conscript actual wealth was made in Britain in 1915 and 1916. That was the proposal of a "capital levy," not a tax on income, year by year, but the conscription of savings. British trade unionists on the left would have preferred simply to conscript rather than to borrow wealth and proposed the capital levy as an alternative to the war loans. In 1916, they criticized the borrowing of capital through war loans as merely a welfare scheme for the rich: the interest on war loans would end up supporting the owners of war bonds for decades to come. If the government needed money to fight the war, unionists argued, then it should impose a capital levy.[25] According to one proud Canadian socialist, all socialists should vote against war loans.[26] In 1917, it was reported in a Toronto newspaper that British "financial authorities and politicians and officials" were actually considering a capital levy.[27] In contrast, when Canadians called for the conscription of wealth, and when White acknowledged the fairness of the moral claim thus expressed, they were usually talking about income and profit taxation or at most taxation of inheritances and speculative land holdings.[28]

But some wealthy Canadians who followed British politics thought that White meant the more alarming possibility proposed in Britain. "In consequence of the publicity given the expression [conscription of wealth]," Sir Thomas recalled in 1921, "there were 'runs' [on the banks] in certain parts of Canada [in 1917]" as people sought to save their bank deposits from confiscation. He quickly rose in Parliament during the summer income tax debate to calm those fears and to distinguish wealth taxation from income taxation.[29] In spite of his attempts to allay concerns, the idea of a capital levy still swirled around as a truly radical alternative later in 1917. Income tax advocate Michael Clark was still telling people on the eve of the December 1917 election that he (and his fellow Liberal-Conservative coalition candidates) differed from "socialists and Laurierites" (Liberals outside the coalition) in that he opposed the "conscription of money" (the capital levy). He carefully distinguished that kind of tax from the less radical and, to him, thoroughly desirable war income tax.[30] At the end of the war, in discussions on dealing with the war debt, the capital levy would again be proposed.[31] The threat of a capital levy was part of the context that made income taxation seem, comparatively, almost desirable.

The other radical tax that John Lewis claimed was discussed only outside Parliament was land tax. But even the idea of a national land value tax was discussed enthusiastically both inside and outside Parliament during the war, and had some serious political and business supporters, including the electorally significant farmers. Unlike income tax, land value taxation no longer packs a political punch. It is now a nearly dead option, but it was very much alive during the Great War. In fact, the values that underpinned the land tax had a lot to do with those that inspired prewar advocates of progressive rate income taxation: equity across class lines and the social (rather than the individual) basis of most wealth.[32]

Land value taxation was another name for what was more controversially called the "single tax." Many jurisdictions taxed land: municipalities relied heavily on land taxes, variously assessed. In England, taxing land value as opposed to taxing income or consumption or forms of wealth other than land was well established as a Liberal reform measure since before the war, and retained influential supporters into the 1920s, including Chancellor of the Exchequer Phillip Snowden. The core idea of the single tax movement was that wealth created by overall community economic growth should revert to the community for general use. That kind of wealth was represented by the increased market value of undeveloped lands in areas of new settlement, profits made in sales of such land, or increased land rents charged to tenants on such land. Single taxers called these forms of income "unearned increments." An unearned increment, in single tax thinking, was the fit target of 100 percent taxation. In Canada, association of the land value tax with the organized farmers gave it the coloration of a sectional protest in the west, where farming dominated.[33] But it was not just a farmers' tax, nor was it only a matter for municipal governments.

During the war, the single tax movement rose to the national level. In 1916, single taxers organized the Canadian League for Taxation of Land Values (CLTLV). They worried about the ballooning national debt and the heavy bill for veterans' pensions soon to come. They disputed the merits of other taxes: not only the tariff tax had to go, but also new taxes proposed in 1915 and 1916 were equally inferior to the land tax. They argued that there would have to be a confusing maze of income taxes, sales taxes, and excise taxes if such taxes were truly to reach all Canadians in as fair a way as the land value tax would. And most of these taxes would trigger capital flight or inhibit business investment. Not so with the land value tax, they argued. It rewarded making land productive, and, best of all, land could not leave the country.[34]

Even though the CLTLV's program entailed root and branch reform, its advocates were not marginal figures arguing against capitalism. In partisan terms, and indeed in ideological terms, land tax enthusiasts tended to be Liberals. They wanted a fairer market, not the end of private property. In 1916, they were not fringe folk. Founding members included future federal cabinet ministers T.A. Crerar and Charles Dunning (Saskatchewan's provincial treasurer in 1916). One among them, E.C. Drury, would soon be the premier of Ontario. A considerable number of the other founders were current or future MPs, MLAs, or MPPs. There was a senator and several lawyers who were or soon would be KCs. These were solid citizens, albeit ones with big ideas.[35] Perhaps most surprisingly, if you think that idealistic tax reformers are never "practical men," their president was W.M. Southam, the owner of a large printing firm, the publisher of the *Ottawa*

Citizen, and an executive, with his brother H.S., of the Southam family's newspaper empire, just emerging as a heavyweight actor in the Canadian business scene.[36] The Southams would write to Prime Minister Borden in 1918 urging him (as their newspapers had been doing "for some years") to consider land value taxation at the national level. Along with putting their own prestige in the service of their cause, they referred to the Great War Veterans' Association as a supporter of their tax proposals.[37]

With prompting from Borden, White took the Southams' letter seriously. He had Parliamentary Counsel F.H. Gisborne report to him on every form of land tax assessment in the country's provinces and municipalities. Along with this information, Gisborne offered two pieces of advice that would effectively kill the single tax as a federal revenue source. Although practical men had proposed it, it was not a practical proposal. First, it would be "very costly" to develop a national land tax assessment system. Second, in a British civil servant sort of understatement, Gisborne suggested that introducing land value taxation would present a "very considerable difficulty" for any government hoping to get re-elected. Rural ridings dominated the seats in the House of Commons, and, in spite of what the organized farmers believed, the impact of the CLTLV proposals would be higher taxes for rural landowners, not lower ones.[38] But as early as the 1915 budget debate, the land tax, along with the income tax, was part of spirited debate inside the House as well as outside it.[39]

Another voice for direct taxation at the national level emerged over the course of the war from the mouths of men and women who initially thought that giving rather than loaning or taxpaying could finance at least part of the war. These were the organizers of the Canadian Patriotic Fund (CPF), the war charity organized to support soldiers' families, when the soldier's assigned pay fell short. As Desmond Morton has shown, the CPF deployed modern fundraising methods to mobilize voluntary contributions to the war effort. Giving to the CPF was supposed to be truly voluntary, with no motive other than patriotism and compassion. However, these purely altruistic motives were not sufficient. Especially in rural Canada, the donation quotas set for each community turned out to be too high. In response, some provinces and municipalities began to levy a Patriotic Fund tax or even to borrow on their municipal credit to meet the needs of the fund. New Brunswick, Ontario, Saskatchewan, and Alberta began levying such a tax early in the war. Toronto and Saint John, and perhaps other cities, voted to pay into the Patriotic Fund from general city revenue.

By 1916, Herbert Ames, the fund's leader, was willing to acknowledge that the limits of charity were drawing near. The organization had attempted to ensure that everyone not fighting was making some other sacrifice for the war, but the concern arose, predictably, that not all were contributing their fair share. The appeal of taxation was that there would be legal recourse, not just moral suasion, in collecting for the fund and hunting down the free riders.[40]

We see in the case of the Patriotic Fund an early example of a process that took place later, during the 1950s, as I showed in an earlier book, *Contributing Citizens*.[41] In the 1950s, some charity fundraisers, like Ames in 1916, argued that charity needed to be supplemented or even replaced by taxation. Exhausted fundraisers, frustrated by free riders, began to see some compulsion as the means to fairness and effectiveness. Similarly, in 1917, fair-minded people among the wealthy, and not just the working poor, saw progressive income taxation as a reasonable way to finance the war. And, when British statesmen were considering outright confiscation of capital, even the less community-minded among the rich could see that national income taxation would be prudent. Any tax measures that would protect invested wealth, including mortgages on western lands, against the predations of the flourishing single tax movement were also of interest. By 1917, the income tax was beginning to look like a moderate measure. Moreover, for borrowing to continue as the centrepiece of war finance, new taxation would be necessary. In fact, by 1917, an income tax, unlike excises or tariff duties, would actually help the federal government to borrow more money. And in 1917 White needed help if Canada would be able to borrow enough of it.

"Stupendous Anxieties" in 1917: A Bad Year for Sir Thomas

White's worries about borrowing money in 1917 followed from his adventures in using the nation's credit in 1915 and 1916. At the outset of the war, it seemed that Canadian credit was excellent, founded as it was upon a record of rapid growth in the previous ten years, the potential of Canada's resource endowment, and the support and backing of Britain. To be sure, 1913 had not been a good year, and there was still a slump in 1914, but it was reasonable to expect that economic activity would soon pick up from wartime manufacturing and British demand for the products of Canadian farms. In these conditions, short-term borrowing was the obvious method of finance in 1915: revenue generated by the usual sorts of federal tax would grow along with the economy. One-, two-, and five-year loans would be easy to sell in London and New York. Government bonds were not usually marketed to Canadian lenders, but war finance would make the case for an exception. In the process of learning to sell bonds in Canada to Canadians, White and his advisers would make judgments in which perceptions would matter. Finance was not just about cold hard facts. Facts about Canadian wealth were sometimes in short supply.

In November 1915, for the first time, the dominion government nervously offered 10-year bonds to Canadian buyers through Canadian dealers. When this first domestic loan sold out at an interest rate only slightly above the usual rate, White was reassured. When he had to go back to the Canadian market less than a year later, in September 1916, however, the risk was higher. The London market was no longer open to colonial borrowers, so Canadian capital had to purchase a larger share of the war loan. And things hadn't been going well in New York. White consulted the federal government's agent, the Bank of Montreal, in such dealings. His contact was General Manager Sir Frederick Williams-Taylor. Just three years older than White, Williams-Taylor had a deeper background than White in international finance, but the two men were otherwise peers. Sir Frederick had endorsed White's initial program of taxes and, in 1915 and 1916, helped him to make difficult decisions about when and under which terms to seek war loans.[42] In August 1916, Sir Frederick warned him,

> I am afraid that your requirements are great and that you cannot finance yourself comfortably for the remainder of the calendar year without a domestic loan of at least $75,000,000. I wish you could get along with less, for $75,000,000 is a large amount for this country to absorb, and you know full well the disadvantages that would follow a public failure of the issue.[43]

The banker's judgment had to carry a lot of weight.

The risk of a bond issue's failure had already been used once to extract from Canada some costly terms for a New York loan. The pricing and terms of a bond issue were the means by which an investment bank, acting on behalf of the government, ensured that it would be able to sell a bond issue. White thought that the New York investment bank J.P. Morgan had made the terms of Canada's March 1916 loan in New York attractive to prospective buyers in ways that made the money unnecessarily expensive to Canada.[44] Williams-Taylor had recommended that White accept those terms. Soon after the terms became public, White began to hear from friends in "well-informed bond houses" that, in their view, Canada had "paid more than was reasonable." The interest rate being offered was too high, and (possibly worse) the opening price on the fifteen-year, 5 percent bonds was 94.94 cents on the dollar, discounted more than five cents below par. White was regretting having accepted the terms.[45] Williams-Taylor was offended by White's questioning his judgment. British bankers were congratulating the dominion on its loan's success, Williams-Taylor pointed out. He admitted that "financial interests in Wall Street are determined to make Canada pay more for money than their own people [Americans]," but, he added, "they will lend us money on better terms than to any other country in the world." White should realize, he continued, that American lenders, in buying up the loan, believe that "they have shown faith in and paid a great compliment to the Dominion." Argentina had had to pay considerably more interest – 7 percent – on its bonds, "and Argentina is regarded by many people, even in England, as quite as good a country as Canada."[46]

By September 1916, White was less confident of the country's position. He had been under considerable pressure not only from J.P. Morgan but also from one of Canada's largest investors, Sun Life, to allow them terms that he could not accept. Sun Life's president, T.B. Macaulay, told White that it was only his firm's "intense patriotism" that allowed him to forgo more profitable mortgage lending and instead invest in war bonds at the issue price that White expected in the September 1916 bond flotation.[47] White knew that, if he gave in to Macaulay's pleas for a discount, then the bonds already in circulation, issued at a higher price, would lose value, and the reputation of Canada as a borrower would be harmed. So White held firm, saying that he "would not feel justified in wantonly sacrificing the credit of the Dominion, upon which everything depends, by recklessly offering our securities [at] several points below prevailing prices."[48] Setting the terms of borrowing involved hard bargaining, and as White's strong language ("wanton sacrifice"!) suggests, being at the centre of these negotiations was emotionally intense. When the Canadian domestic loan sold well in September 1916, he exulted that "the Canadians are a great people."[49] If we imagined that public finance was simply based upon rational calculation, then White's emotional response would make no sense.

More than White's or Macaulay's patriotism was at work, however, in the booming Canadian market for Canadian national bonds. Rumours of future income taxation helped to sell those bonds, especially to large investors. Because the income of these bonds was designated to be free of Canadian federal income tax, and had been advertised as such since 1915, the capital value of the bonds for Canadians would increase (in open market buying and selling of bonds) as soon as an income tax came into existence. In other words, because the bond's interest income was tax free, a new income tax meant that the sale price of the bond would go up. Even the rumour of an income tax or (in Britain) an income tax rate hike could increase the market value of a bond.[50] The higher the income tax, the better the price that tax-free bonds could command in the regular bond market. Over the life of the bond, that capital value increase, parcelled out in annual amounts, combined with the tax-free interest income, made the bond more valuable. To small investors, this tax-induced benefit would mean little and even less if their taxable incomes from other sources were low. However, for large investors who had already bought many war loan bonds, the creation of an income tax would help them to make a lot more money on their investment. After yet another domestic bond issue in March 1917, any large investor in Dominion of Canada bonds would therefore be most pleased with a federal income tax. Moreover, with tax advantage in mind, the existence of an income tax meant that they would be happy to subscribe to yet more dominion bonds, perhaps even converting old prewar ones into war bonds.

Giving investors an incentive to buy Canadian war bonds would become newly important in May and June 1917 as White contemplated his loan issues for the 1917–18 fiscal year. Proposals for a Canadian income tax were about to get some powerful supporters. The United States had entered the war in April, and its Liberty Loan campaign was drawing American investment capital (and probably some Canadian investment capital) like a high-powered magnet. In the budget debates of April and May 1917, the Liberal opposition continued to hammer away (as they had since 1911) on the need for an income tax, and White persistently held that the fiscal time was not yet right.[51] But after the July 1st holiday, he began to signal to investment markets that the next war loan might be made more attractive by the impact of a new income tax. More than three weeks before White introduced his income tax bill in the House of Commons on July 25, a Toronto *Globe* story on July 2, headlined "Prospect of New

Taxation May Help New National Financing," spoke of a "hint dropped by the Finance Minister of a possible Dominion income tax at an early date." The story went on to explain how large investors in the United States had used the tax-free American Liberty Loan investments to reduce their tax bills. The journalist concluded that, even before investors knew exactly the details of a Canadian income tax, "the exemption on Dominion war bonds would be more attractive ... even than it has been in the case of the United States loan, because our war bonds bear a much higher rate of interest."[52] And sure enough, once the income tax bill was introduced in the House, but well before final features of the statute were settled, the "glut of war bonds" on the market disappeared. "Buying Generally Attributed to Preparations for Income Taxation" was the explanation offered.[53] The tax advantage would end up being so significant to large investors, Montreal financier I.W. Killam would later argue, that the tax-exempt bonds gave the more highly taxed rich a better return on their bonds than that of small investors.[54] The tax reduction was part of the return on the investment.

While the debate on the exact terms of the income tax bill continued, White got further evidence that the future of Canada's wartime borrowing now lay in Canada rather than in the United States. In July and August 1917, Canadian two-year notes (an investment product that American investors had previously snapped up) sold poorly in the New York market. In 1921, White referred to the weak sales of those notes as a "non-success."[55] White was too good a writer to deploy such a euphemism unless he just couldn't bear to say "failure." It must have been one of his worst moments on the job in 1917. And its lesson was clear: the domestic bond issue in the fall of 1917 had to succeed. To ensure its success, there had to be a tax exemption that really mattered to the big investors, and a "good stiff" income tax would do the trick.[56]

In the longer term, the tax exemption feature of the Victory Loan was actually counterproductive to public revenue. In 1918, I.W. Killam argued against allowing tax exemption on the 1918 issue. He acknowledged that tax exemption allowed the minister of finance to sell more bonds at a higher price. However, he pointed out, for every $2.50 or as much as $3.30 in price increase that White might get, he would lose $10 in future income tax revenue. In Killam's view, that future loss was too much.[57] But in 1917, especially after the "non-success" of his summer financing operation, White needed to borrow money immediately, even if it meant collecting fewer tax dollars over the lives of the ten- fifteen-, and twenty-year bonds. The cheese crisis of June 1917 had made it clear that Canada would have to provide more credit to Britain for as long as it took. Canadian farmers and manufacturers depended on British purchases to maintain employment and buy seed, supplies, and equipment. But Britain, like Canada, had been shut out of the New York market and thus was struggling to pay for its immediate needs. White turned to Canadian banks to get more credit, and, as economist C.A. Curtis pointed out, the short-term loans that the banks were "virtually forced" to make to the government had to be paid off with more and more successful Victory Loans.[58] Making the income of those loans tax free helped to sell the bonds and helped to "sell" the income tax to Canada's richest citizens.

In the end, the terms of the Income War Tax Act that passed in the House of Commons on August 17, 1917, were kind to those citizens and little celebrated by those who had called for conscription of wealth and equality of sacrifice. The Conservative Montreal *Gazette* scorned any such moral talk: the money was needed to ramp up the war effort, and an income tax would get it from those best able to spare it. Canadian wealth was not morally tainted, idle capital, deserving of confiscation, but usefully employed and honestly earned through "business enterprise and sagacity, and hard work." A small news report quietly noted that the tax was required to "maintain the credit of the Dominion." Along with other Conservative papers, the *Gazette* represented the taxation of income for war purposes as an obviously sensible, bipartisan measure, which met with almost no criticism in Parliament.[59] In Liberal circles, in contrast, the warmest praise offered was that the proposed tax was a "long step" toward equal sacrifice but overdue. White's delay had cost the war effort millions. Like Liberal papers elsewhere, *L'Avenir du Nord* of St. Jérôme, Quebec, offered that, far from hitting hardest the millionaires and war profiteers, a statute that taxed single or widowed childless men earning only $1,500 (a skilled workers' annual earnings) was not a tax on the rich.[60] Among Canadian newspapers, the most enthusiastic supporter of war income taxation had been the Liberal *Winnipeg Free Press*. Its editors and its Ottawa columnist saw in the 1917 bill little equalizing of sacrifice. The rich man's "extravagance" would scarcely be impaired. Worse, White's apparent intention to abolish in 1918 the 1916 excess profits tax on businesses (taxing those profits instead as income in the hands of shareholders) would just replace one tax with another. The *Winnipeg Free Press* also reported an unnamed women's organization's view (shared by many Liberal MPs) that the government's initially proposed $2,000 exemption for the unmarried should be lowered, particularly to reach single men still living at home.[61]

Liberal critics noticed how little sacrifice the new income tax would exact from the rich. If they had understood how much actual benefit it would confer on wealthy purchasers of government bonds, then they would have been even more outraged. White was frank about the boost that he expected his income tax to give to the sales appeal of dominion bonds, but critiques such as Killam's in 1918 would not register in the House of Commons or the major Liberal newspapers during the debate on the Income War Tax Act in 1917. As White faced the threat of evaporating demand for Canadian loans, he made it clear that these were dire days in which lives already sacrificed and dollars already spent could only be redeemed by renewed effort. With international lenders disappearing, sales of the next war loan would have to reach new buyers in the Canadian market. For this to happen, many Canadians (not all of them rich) would have to pay a federal income tax, but many more (employees and thrifty housewives, not just insurance companies) would have to become creditors of the national state, investing their savings in their nation's future.

Making Canadians in the Bond Market

One of the advantages of the shift to the Canadian market was that no New York bond dealer had to be kept "sweet."[62] In the fall of 1917, a committee of Canadian financiers, convoked by White, would manage an ambitious new kind of war bond issue, and bond dealers in Canadian communities would be modestly paid for their time spent in the routine work of a bond issue. No longer merely "war loans" marketed to big investors, the last three Canadian bond issues would be Victory Loans, marketed to "the people." Volunteer canvassers would try to make this new bond drive a kind of national movement. In doing so, they would help to build the spirit of common sacrifice that would encourage not only bond purchases but also compliance with a weakly enforced federal income tax.[63]

In the fall of 1917, with the change in the character of wartime borrowing, Canadians moved into a closer fiscal relationship with the dominion government. They had paid the indirect tariff tax, but now they were being asked to be willing contributors to a collective national project. The advertising campaigns for the newly named Victory Loan drives of 1917, 1918, and 1919 made "paying for the war" a matter of everyday talk for Canadians, rich, poor, and middling. As Sir Thomas wrote to a Toronto friend and political ally, "I fancy [the public] have really a better understanding [of the Department of Finance's responsibilities] than we give them credit for, as public matters are so keenly discussed in war time."[64] The Victory Loan drives and the new income tax that helped to make them successful engaged Canadians in a performance of interdependent citizenship, framed by participation in the bond market. The success of the bond drives involved managing and responding to public opinion, building trust, and engaging in conversations about fair contribution, a moral discourse that underpinned both taxation and bond buying. But self-interest, both narrow and broad, was always also part of the meaning of contribution.

Large investors in war loans such as the Victory Loans could readily see how their business interests were served by subscribing to the loans. Manufacturers appreciated that British purchases generated expansion in the nation's productive capacity. Banks understood that the credit they extended to the government would be covered by the revenue from the loans, and with that revenue the banks in turn could lend profitably elsewhere. Mining, logging, and cash-crop farming all benefited from the war economy. It was probably less obvious to non-economists among the general public that money given for war purposes might circulate back into their pockets via wages or other investment returns. The "Duty and Dividends" pitch of 1916 would not be the right one for a Victory Loan campaign aimed at the personal savings of the mass of Canadians.[65] The November 1917 campaign would be qualitatively different from the restrained sales efforts expended for the earlier domestic loans of 1915, 1916, and March 1917. As Sir Thomas wrote in 1921, looking back on the credit problems of the summer of 1917, "nothing short of a nation-wide movement in which appeal would be made to all members of the community to save their money and subscribe to a national loan, would at all meet the condition with which we were confronted."[66]

The earlier campaigns had addressed the general public, but without any significant advertising flair, relying instead on text-heavy ads.[67] In these ads, the headlines and the information on how to buy a war bond made the prospect of investing more accessible. But the appeal was far from compelling. The broadest form of address to the public was an intriguing postmark. The *New York Evening Post* commented on this technique, having seen it in its French-language version on a letter from Montreal: the rectangular stamp consisted of a British flag on its right side, cancelling the postage stamp, and, clearly visible on the left side, printed on the envelope, was the question "$25.00 for $21.50. How? Ask your bank or post master."[68] The emotive appeal was entirely absent and only gently present in the other ads.

In contrast, the 1917 campaign, and those that followed, would use methods designed to invoke and build a culture of contribution, based upon social networks and social perceptions. As with income taxation, some Canadians had been thinking about this aspect of war finance for years. Dr. Helen MacMurchy, one of the leaders of the Canadian suffrage movement, wrote to White in 1915 to suggest that Women's Institutes and Canadian Clubs (both women's and men's) could help to promote the purchase of war bonds. If the bonds were issued in small denominations, MacMurchy suggested, then many people would buy them as Christmas gifts. "There will be a great many Canadians who will not understand the War Loan unless it is explained to them," she noted and gently suggested that White make use of channels such as her networks to "get the matter clearly before every Canadian."[69] The idea, as prohibition movement leader G.A. Warburton wrote, was to reach the "immense sums of money in the hands of the common people."[70] In December 1915, the editor of the *Montreal Daily Mail* implored White to publish complete lists of all war bond subscribers, large and small, with amounts. The paper's managing director, a personal friend of the finance minister, offered to print the list as a news story without charge. Such lists would sell the loan by "human interest," both men argued, shaming the wealthy and stimulating emulation among smaller investors.[71] The Toronto *Globe* also urged White to make a greater effort to reach "the as yet untouched financial resources in the pocket of the wage-earner and small saver."[72] People wrote to White in 1916 to suggest specific schemes to this end: "Everyone would be able to lend money to the government, even children and especially the working class."[73] White made it clear in response to one of these correspondents that he thought "any artisan earning good wages" could buy a bond, which entailed, on the instalment purchase plan available, an outlay of $100 over six months.[74] Some Ontario employers succeeded in recruiting employees to this kind of purchase.[75]

But a provincial civil servant in Kamloops, British Columbia, wrote to suggest that the payment period be closer to a year: the staff in his office could spare ten dollars a month but not twenty dollars.[76] The "immense sums" of savings in the hands of "common people" were, household by household, not so large. Yet, with so little help available from governments in times of need, lower-income Canadians did place a high priority on saving. The idea that there were untapped funds "out there" was not imaginary. Married women's methods of economizing were the means by which rising wages and salaries were turned into savings. In the spring of 1916, the Departments of Finance and Agriculture mounted a "production and thrift" campaign, using women's magazines such as *Everywoman's World* to get across the message to housewives. The text of their large display ad emphasized the fiscal significance of household thrift:

> The larger portion of salaries and wages is spent on the home – food, fuel, light, clothing. Are any of these things being wasted? $20.00 a year saved from waste in every home in Canada will more than pay the interest on a war debt of $500,000,000 ... Tens of thousands of Canadians are daily risking their lives for us at home. Is it not our duty to be careful and economical? Canadian dollars are an important part of the war equipment. Make them tell. Have a War Savings Account. Buy a War Bond.[77]

This kind of sales pitch brought participation in war finance into the kitchens and gardens of the nation. A patriotic shopper would hear the voice of Sir Thomas White in her ear as she planned her family's meals or replaced her children's outgrown clothes.

The promotional materials of the 1917 campaign aimed to influence the decisions of daily life. Moving beyond the business pages, the bond ads of 1917 and after appeared in every section of the paper. The usual investment dealer ads continued to appear, but even they adopted the Victory Bond label.[78] The newspaper advertising took on a "movement" quality, with businesses of all sorts buying ads in local newspapers to promote the purchase of bonds.

All manner of pitches were made in these sponsored Victory Bond ads. Some were pragmatic and others high-minded, but together they produced a buzz. From humorous to melodramatic to instructive, the ads ran the gamut. The elite jewellery firm Ryrie Brothers presented a series of ads, signed by its president, that combined education and folksiness ("Tell Me Dad, What's a Coupon?") and high-quality type design. Another especially sophisticated ad was the one inserted by Sir Thomas White's old firm, National Trust. It blended the business case for buying the bonds with the higher purpose. In a few short sentences, the text explained "what it means

SELLERS-GOUGH

Canada's
Victory
Bonds

EVERY dollar you lend to Canada now will help to bring back those peaceful and profitable pursuits that Canada loves.

Buy Canada's Victory Bonds

This space donated by
The Sellers-Gough Fur
Company, Limited.

Furrier Sellers-Gough brought a sense of fun to the marketing of Victory Bonds.
Toronto *Globe*, November 14, 1917.

to finance our export trade" and concluded that the Victory Loan was about "business plus patriotism." Most of the sponsored ads were less sophisticated. Some put in a direct plug for their own businesses, while others were simply supporting the cause. A favourite line was the one offered by C.H. Horsley, "The Satisfactory Hardware Store." The ad said only that Horsley "saves you money enough to buy Victory War Bonds." Particularly inventive, but in a blatantly self-serving way, was the Calgary art shop that suggested that a framed Victory Bond would make a superior Christmas present. Many businesses simply added a Victory Loan slogan in a separate box within their usual ad. The most pragmatic advertisers offered to accept Victory Bonds in lieu of cash for purchases in their stores.[79]

Suppose YOU Were Going Over the Top

Out into night, into the roar of shell fire, through the barbed wire and the mud, into the enemy trenches —would you stop to count the cost?

No, you would go without question because it was your duty. You would not stop to ask about the safety of the undertaking. You would not stop to argue as to the amount of glory you might earn. You would not suggest that some one else be sent in your place.

You would just go, head down through hell on earth, because your country asked it.

But you are not going over the top. You are at home with your friends and your family. You are called upon by your Government simply to lend money to back up the soldiers who will go into the trenches for you in France. Your dollars will save their lives.

You will not even stop to consider that Victory Bonds are the safest investment in the world.

You will not question the interest rate of 5½ per cent.

You will not let others come forward with their money while yours lies idle.

You will act because it is your plain duty (your plain duty at a profit to yourself)—because human lives are at stake, because lending money to the Government here to-day will save human agony on the fields of France to-morrow.

You will put every dollar you have saved and every dollar you can borrow at work---at work saving lives and bringing those sons and husbands and brothers home, alive, victorious. Delay costs blood. THE BLOOD OF OUR SONS.

This Space Contributed by
W. H. Banfield & Sons, Limited,
Machinery Manufacturers, Toronto.

A Canvasser Will Call On You.

The emotional pitch of this professionally produced ad was complemented in the small print by a note that doing your duty would also pay 5.5 percent interest, a "profit to yourself." Toronto *Globe*, November 13, 1917.

Sir Thomas White is pictured here explaining that a man who shaves with a Gillette razor saves so much money by not paying barbers that he can afford to buy a Victory Bond. Win-win! *Calgary Daily Herald,* November 12, 1917.

The National Committee also ran its large and professionally designed ads in newspapers across the country. These ads either offered information or made appeals. Some emphasized that the loans were a way to back up the men on the front: "The Fighting Men Await Your Answer."[80] The 1918 and 1919 posters would present the same moral case.[81] But in 1917 the argument from economic interest was at least as important and entirely explicit. The ability of Canadian farmers to sell their wheat and Canadian factories to sell their products depended on the success of this loan. Ads such as "Why Canada Needs More Money" offered a punchy and lucid lesson in war finance: Canadians needed to lend so that farmers could be paid in cash.[82] Economic development was explicitly a reason for the Victory Loans: "Happy Will Be the Nation that Owes Its War Debts to Its Own People."[83] The poster campaign depicted in brilliant colours what prospective buyers needed to understand, even if the message in 1917 was not exactly heartwarming: "To maintain the prosperity of Canada, buy Victory Bonds. 5 1/2% interest. Tax Free." The mighty arm of the Victory Loan was scattering "prosperity" over the countryside in a poster that promised "every dollar [will be] spent in Canada."[84] War finance aligned individual interests with national interests.

News reports of the bond campaign featured stories that showed skeptical Canadians being converted to moving their savings from the bank (or from a sock in a box in a drawer) into government bonds. The *Kelowna Record*'s "Onlooker" observed that "some fine old crusted savings accounts that have slept for years" were setting out for Ottawa: "Six hundred folks in this district will hear the crisp aristocratic crackle of a bond and itch to get the scissors at work on that June 1st coupon."[85] Employers and banks offered loans to wage earners to make buying the bonds on tiny instalments feasible. The appeal to women in the Victory Loan primer acknowledged their practice of saving by small amounts and pointed out that, instead of putting their pennies in low-interest savings accounts, they could earn interest at a higher rate and have it paid out in June before they'd paid all of the bond's price. At the end of the March 1917 war loan sales, 37,000 people or institutions had purchased a bond. After the massive campaign of November 1917, Canadians had been persuaded en masse to put their savings in Victory Bonds: more than 800,000 had subscribed to the loan.[86]

The success of the Victory Loan campaigns would be recalled after the war as part of its making of "Canada" – an inclusive national community united in a common project.[87] But this campaign for collectivity encountered a divided world and sometimes inflamed those divisions. In Montreal, for example, the "French Canadian" volunteer canvassing teams in the 1917 campaign could rely on French-language newspapers such as *La Patrie* reporting the campaign launch, printing an appeal by Sir Wilfrid Laurier, and urging the practical business case for buying these solid bonds. It was hardly surprising, however, that the businesses advertising in *La Patrie*

– "the People's Paper" – saw no advantage in selling their wares by placing Victory Bond ads. With the exception of a few national advertisers, *La Patrie's* advertisers studiously ignored the whole hullabaloo. The paper's reports of the Toronto press attacking Quebec "more violently than ever" on the military registration question were hardly conducive to the warm feelings of unity that inspired Toronto's wave of sponsored ads.[88] Quebec's working class, francophone or anglophone, being stoutly protectionist, had no reason to share farmers' longing for an income tax as part of a low-tariff future. "Conscription," whether of dollars or lives, was no word to conjure up a pan-Canadian community within francophone Quebec. *La Patrie's* lukewarm support for the Victory Loan was just another marker of Quebec's distinct fiscal culture during the war years.

Quebeckers who felt targeted in a francophobic "race" war were not the only Canadians whose engagement in the national crusade was troubled. Working-class men and women could be enticed into buying bonds, but their experience could turn bad. When steelworkers, coal miners, and even female domestic servants became bondholders during the First World War, the results were sometimes tragic, or nearly so, as these patriotic workers (and others inexperienced in bond transactions) fell prey to unscrupulous securities dealers out to make a buck.[89] One pitch was to offer to trade the government bond for some other fabulous bond that would allegedly pay a higher return. Another was to offer to buy the government bond for cash right away but at less (sometimes as little as half) of its redemption value than at its future maturity date.[90] The minister of finance tried to stamp out these practices because the selling prices of the bonds would go down were such practices to spread. In a letter to the president of the Canadian Bankers' Association, White arranged for a circular to be distributed to the country's bank managers. It concluded thus: "The branch manager is authorized to say that the Minister's object [in warning inexperienced bondholders not to sell at a discount] is to protect honest holders from the wiles and deceits of these smooth-spoken promoters and salesmen of bogus securities."[91] In thus seeking to protect the market value of the bonds, White was protecting not only the war revenue but also the value of the property held by the existing bondholders. In this way, he was attempting to preserve their trust in government, which would be useful in the long term for securing tax compliance.

The ideals of community building also had a dark side, revealed in the thoughts and actions of frustrated canvassers. In selling bonds, as in assessing for taxes, it was easy to imagine people unwilling to contribute their share. Some letter writers offered White suggestions about how to exact contributions to the war effort from people who would not, could not, or (for whatever reason) did not buy war bonds. The Mennonites, for example, being pacifists, would not offer financial support to war, a lawyer wrote to White, but a bond issue designated for the Red Cross would appeal to them and to other "conscientious objectors." He noted that there were 40,000 Mennonites who had not yet "invested in Canada" and expressed the belief that they "would probably be glad to take" bonds of this sort.[92] His view of Mennonites was far more kindly than some other perceptions of "foreigners." The stereotype of recent immigrants in these letters and articles was the rootless worker who had no connection to the community. Drawing on a long-standing theme of tax assessment worries, nativist Victory Loan enthusiasts depicted foreigners as carrying with them enormous amounts of cash: "You are, of course, aware that the foreign element here today benefit largely as a result of war conditions, drawing large wages, and that the money they earn is practically all stowed away in their money-belts. The State gets no benefit from it, and the fact has given a great deal of offence to the Canadian people." These correspondents suggested taxation mechanisms, such as poll taxes, to tap this wealth if its owners would not invest in the country and the war.[93] Perhaps not surprisingly, pressure on "aliens" to contribute to both could be aggressive. One Victory Loan volunteer, leading a "party" of canvassers, wrapped himself in a British flag, entered a German Canadian's darkened house at night, and barged into the householder's bedroom. The householder shot and killed him.[94] Making a national community through the loan campaigns meant identifying free riders and framing their reluctance as causing, in part, "the burden on our own people."[95] The success of the war loans in financing the war and in building a national community must have looked much less convincing to Canadians who had been cheated or attacked in the course of the campaign.

Whether addressing the willing or the reluctant, the mostly successful public relations work of the Victory Loan campaigns did double duty. It raised money by way of prompting bond purchases, but it also sold tax compliance by highlighting "paying for the war" as a communal effort, one that brought Canadians closer to the federal government, happily or not. Like the introduction of the federal income tax, the Victory Loan campaigns invited Canadians to think of the federal government as interested in their personal spending and saving practices. Both buying bonds and paying taxes would require thrift. Economist Stephen Leacock evoked thrift as a figurative gas mask that would equip citizens to survive the toxic cloud of necessary taxation.[96] Both the implementation of the federal income tax in 1918 and the bond campaigns of 1917, 1918, and 1919 incited Canadians to scrutinize closely the taxing practices of the dominion government. On those practices would rest the security of the bonds that Canadians had purchased and the future credit of their country. In February and March 1918, as the paperwork for the Victory Loan was wrapping up and the publicity campaign for the federal income tax was getting under way, a number of citizens wrote to White to suggest solutions to the linked questions of how to tax and how to redeem the war debt. In these letters, the correspondents spoke as citizens for whom taxation was not simply an unwelcome burden but also a means of addressing a shared problem of public finance.

For these writers, the role of a federal income tax in solving that problem was not yet certain. A recurring theme in these 1918 letters was the idea of "painless" revenue methods that, like the purchase by instalment of small war bonds, entailed many, supposedly easy, payments. A common proposal was a lottery of some sort.[97] Lotteries were appealing because they seemed to be both inclusive and painless. A francophone citizen writing in English to Sir Thomas pointed this out: "Why not the government start a National lottery which would mean millions for the Country and would be welcome by the public in general, giving the same chances to the poor class as well as the rich to participate in each drawings."[98] A similar scheme was a proposal to insure the lives of all men aged thirty-five or younger, with the government paying the premium and being designated the beneficiary. All the citizen had to do was die relatively young, in this plan, for the government to benefit.[99] This insurance scheme, like the lotteries, represented a sense among those who wrote helpfully to the finance minister in early 1918 that many small acts of saving or buying could accomplish a great accumulation and in such a way that "no one would be hurt."[100] These schemes were urged because, unlike an income tax, they would keep the cost of national citizenship out of mind. In the years to come, however, the legacy of the Victory Loans would make it impossible to hide the sometimes painful price of nationhood.

$ ¢ $

The Victory Loans and the taxation debate were linked by way of evocations of the interconnectedness of Canadians. This national connectedness, far from being an uncomplicated engagement in "community," brought out inequities, real and imagined, in the contributions that Canadians were making voluntarily or through compulsion. Like conscription, which brought to light and embittered inequality in class, sectional, and racialized relationships, the enforced contribution (tax), along with the voluntary one (war savings), became a subject of debate. As in the historiography of the Great War more generally, in this story of the beginnings of Canada's twentieth-century fiscal order we can see both the emergence of a Canada-wide community and the deepening of painful divisions.[101] Neither phenomenon was simply spontaneous; both were products of efforts to shape out of human experience some useful body of public opinion. In these wartime rhetorics of community, referring to the moral standard set by the volunteer citizen soldier was inevitable. Many who called for income taxation as for war savings made the field combatant their moral justification. But it was not simply the moral pressure to put an end to the old party politics or even the more cold-blooded strategic imperatives of a coalition for conscription that moved income taxation suddenly onto the legislative agenda in July 1917, though each of these played its part. What shoved White toward that reluctant action was the need to shore up the country's credit in the bond market. In response to that need, the Canadian government would use cultural tools to build for the first time a mass domestic market for its bonds.

As both debtors (income tax payers) and creditors (bond buyers) of the national government, many Canadians from the middle class entered a more intimate fiscal relationship with this level of the state after 1917. Beyond those who actually paid federal income taxes or bought bonds, the new fiscal culture reached others through publicity campaigns. Canadian culture being what it is, these more intimate fiscal ties meant not just collective pride but also sectional and social divisions. In the next decade, the war bonds would become the subject of controversy, and so would the federal income tax. Some Canadians would fight to abolish the tax. Although the advocates of its abolition would fail, the federal income tax did not flourish. In the 1920s, Canada would once again make relatively hidden forms of consumption taxation – a sales tax added to tariff and excise taxes – the mainstay of federal revenue.

3
Canada's Conservative Tax Structure

SHORTLY BEFORE CHRISTMAS 1919, Leader of the Opposition William Lyon Mackenzie King was paying his federal income tax. In 2016 dollars, King's cheque to the receiver general was for more than $15,000. "Thank Heaven," he wrote in his diary, "I earned enough for that last year." His investment income had been substantial, it seems, because the tax bill from his parliamentary salary alone would have been about a quarter of that amount. "Never expect to pay the like again," he concluded, with noticeable relief.[1] Like many Canadians, he expected that, with the war over, the income tax rates would be reduced. In a few months, he would find that his expectation had been mistaken. The war was over, to be sure, but the work of financing it was not. (The last of the Great War debt would not be paid off until 1949.[2]) After the war, the conversation about how to pay for it continued, and so did the wartime taxes. Only with Sir Henry Drayton's May 1920 budget would a new tax system begin, and not until 1926 would there be major income tax reductions. By the end of the decade, Canada's federal income tax would shrink in importance. Consumption taxes would dominate the revenue mix. This outcome was almost exactly what Republicans in the United States fought for in the 1920s and failed to achieve.

Political struggles shaped the specific path that Canada's federal tax regime would follow, a conservative path in which the largest share of federal revenue continued to come mainly from hidden taxes on consumption. In contrast, in the more or less normal years of 1922–29, the US federal government collected most of its taxes openly, by means of direct taxation.

Income and profit taxes in the United States brought in between 55.6 percent and 63.2 percent of the total federal tax revenue. During the same period in Canada, direct taxes counted for as little as 15.5 percent of the federal tax take and rarely more than 21.0 percent. Taxes paid "painlessly," because most voters could not see them (customs, excise, and manufacturers' – as distinct from retailers' – sales taxes), made up about 80 percent of Canada's national tax revenue (see Table 1). The lesser importance of income taxation in Canada's federal revenue would still be clearly visible in the 1950s (see Table 2). One reason for this difference in the 1920s seems obvious. The United States needed income taxes more than Canada did. Prohibition in the United States meant that income taxation had to replace lost revenue from the federal excise tax on booze.[3] However, even though Canada's federal treasury continued to benefit from booze sales, it was far from floating in revenues during the 1920s. Canada had a revenue problem. Part of the solution adopted in the Conservatives' 1920 budget was a tiny federal sales tax (1 percent), which quickly rose to 6 percent in the hands of the Liberals after 1921. In Canada, the revenue problem would not, could not, be solved by a vigorous, productive federal income tax: party politics, underpinned by regional cultures and the country's fragile finances and federation, precluded that solution. Instead, Canada's interwar income tax would help only slightly with tax fairness and would have nothing to do with social justice by means of income redistribution.

Planning Postwar Taxation

In Canada, as in many other countries, the notion of national income taxation as a war measure left a legacy. Many people, even now, are attached to the idea that the federal government wickedly tricked Canadians into accepting income taxation. "They said it was going to be temporary! Typical. Humpf. Politicians!" And it's true that some of those who supported the 1917 income tax saw it specifically as a war measure. Late in 1918, after the armistice, W.C. Chisholm, a friend of the finance minister, wrote to him to recommend that White read the bits about Britain's Crimean War income tax in John Morley's *Life of William Ewart Gladstone*: "It was evidently intended to be temporary. I suppose ours is also, altho' I fear we may have it with us for some time."[4] Chisholm, like anyone who understood war finance, knew that, even as a war measure, the war income tax would be around for as long as the war debt was. Its purpose was to cover the interest owed on that debt and to build up a sinking fund to be used to redeem the bonds at their maturity dates. In contrast, the war profits tax had to be eliminated once the economy was again in peacetime mode because, as such, it was based upon a distinction between normal profits and war profits that no longer made sense after 1921.[5] The income tax was bound to be around at least until 1937, the maturity date of the longest-term war bond, the twenty-year issue sold in 1917.[6] A March 1918 Canadian Press news report referred, chillingly, to "Canada's permanent war burden" – annual debt charges and pension payments to the amount of approximately $90 million each year.[7] If those obligations were "permanent," then why not the income tax? Still, White had left the question of the future of the tax open when he had introduced it in 1917.

As a result, part of the public finance debate after 1917 and through the 1920s was whether federal income taxation should continue. Just as people were paying their first federal income taxes in June 1918, the editors of the Toronto *Globe* called for the tax to be made permanent. Pointing to the significant increases in income taxation being proposed in the United States by Treasury Secretary W.G. McAdoo, they suggested that one of White's favourite arguments against a federal income tax had now lost its force. The United States was taxing income and doing so substantially. Taking a Liberal free-trader line, the *Globe* editors argued that it was time to stop relying on the tariff for revenue, time to turn to a "more democratic system of finance" based upon income taxation.[8] Perhaps the editors didn't know that they were pushing on an open door. Back in February 1918, at the last minute before heading south on his rest cure, White left instructions with his chief income tax official, R.W. Breadner, on how to deal with the acting finance minister, income tax enthusiast and Liberal unionist A.K. McLean. White instructed Breadner to resist any attempt by McLean to make the business profits war tax more exacting, arguing that income taxation would do the necessary job of progressively taxing corporate income. In making his case, White pointed out that "the income tax is to be more sharply graded and will certainly be permanent."[9] He had resisted creating a federal income tax in earlier circumstances, and he had introduced it only as a war measure, but by February 1918 he confidently predicted what the postwar review of the system would conclude. The federal income tax was not going away.

Still, there remained the question of what kind of income tax it would be. Would it be, like the Ontario municipal income tax and the BC provincial one, set at a low and relatively "flat" rate? Would smaller incomes be exempted? At what level? Would family obligations affect the amount of tax owed? If so, which ones? What kinds of profit would be defined as income? Would different kinds of income be taxed at different rates? All of these questions brought up issues of tax fairness and broader kinds of justice. And to have an answer about the income tax required having views on a similar set of questions about a variety of indirect taxes. Those indirect taxes were more than just background. In fact, for most people, the indirect taxes were the normal ones, those about which they cared most. Whether direct taxation by the federal government would become normal, a part of Canadian tax culture, remained to be settled. As a new era in taxation emerged, all sorts of revenue ideas appeared, mingling with discussions about what kind of nation Canada would become: fully sovereign or still partly subject to Britain? More closely linked to the United States or dominated by it? Unified or lacking Quebec? Offering equal opportunity to all or centred economically on the interests of central Canadian capital? These matters of nationhood provided much of the drama of the federal elections in 1921, 1925, 1926, and 1929, and all were also questions about taxation.

The questions of what kind of nation Canada was and what kind of revenue system it could use were central to planning for the veterans of the Great War. In 1919, a bipartisan parliamentary committee heard submissions on how the national government should finance soldier resettlement. This question naturally entailed discussions of the nation's obligations, honour, and fiscal capacity. The committee was chaired by J.A. Calder of Saskatchewan, a provincial politician and former teacher, who had entered the national government for the first time in the wartime Union coalition in 1917. Although his committee's recommendation no doubt reflected the conclusions of all of its members, Calder was the sort of man who could credibly deliver its hard message, that Canada's revenues were perilously close to their maximum and even, alarmingly, possibly less than needed. The son of a young mother suddenly widowed when he was fourteen, Calder knew how the gap between need and income felt.[10]

His committee's report outlined a plan for the veterans that many found stingy, even in his home province, where Calder was well respected.[11] Liberal Unionist MP Levi Thomson, from the Qu'Appelle riding in Saskatchewan, rejected categorically the Calder committee's implication that Canada was "bankrupt, or nearly bankrupt." He did not think that the proper limits of taxation had yet been reached. For him, to meet the needs of the veterans,

Canadians should give through taxation "until the giving hurts," just as they had been urged to save through Victory Bonds until they could feel some twinge of self-denial. In Thomson's view, Canadians were "more ready to pay the taxes required than was ever previously the case in our history." He objected to increased tariff taxes only because, as was the article of faith among the organized farmers, indirect taxes generated profits for manufacturers more than they provided revenues for public purposes.[12] From the other side of the tariff debate, farm equipment manufacturer and Conservative W.F. Cockshutt also argued not only that national honour required a better program of benefits for the veterans than Calder had recommended but also that Canadians were "willing, as we must be, to submit to heavy taxation for some years to come." It was the duty of the government, Cockshutt plainly stated, to find the funds to meet what Parliament deemed the proper policy.[13]

Calder's committee had reviewed nearly every conceivable revenue option, however, and had found none that promised a rich yield. They looked most favourably on creating a new excise tax on luxuries. They couldn't bring themselves to endorse a state lottery or taxes on Sunday theatres – either from their own moral objections or from an awareness of the electoral weight wielded by sabbatarians and opponents of gambling.[14] They seriously considered "radical" ideas such as land taxation, a special tax on investment income, a tax on profiteers, and even the confiscation of capital – the capital levy. Curiously, a sales tax was not even mentioned among the suggestions that they felt obliged to address, even though, six months later, in the May 1920 budget, this tiny tax would quietly join the federal tax structure.

About the capacity of the federal income tax, the Calder committee were pessimistic for reasons that had to do with Canada's national peculiarities. Competition with the United States re-emerged as the reason why higher income tax rates were not feasible. Taxing income at the same rates and on the same rules as the United States did would produce enough to "take care of existing liabilities" – likely a reference to the war debt interest – but not enough for the veterans' pensions and gratuities. They also used comparisons to the United States and Britain to make the case that Canada could not expect to get as much revenue as these other countries from taxing income. Those countries had large urban, salary-, and wage-earning populations and deep pools of income-generating wealth; Canada was still a rural country, full of farmers and fishers, and comparatively short on plutocrats. Finally, the committee advanced a standard argument in Canada's constitutional conversation: "Many municipalities" and "at least one province" taxed income. Surely, they suggested, that would limit how much more revenue could be raised by taxing the same incomes.[15] Canada might be an honourable nation, but it could not yet tax like a wealthy, urban one.

Sir Henry Drayton and Tax Talk in 1920

In November 1919, armed with the Calder committee's advice, a new finance minister, Sir Henry Drayton, a Conservative lawyer, faced the enormous job of orchestrating reconstruction of the country's finances. It was a job in which only someone with supreme self-confidence could have felt comfortable. Drayton fit the bill. He was accustomed to managing some of the biggest and most politically difficult public administration files. After an early career in the 1890s as counsel to the City of Toronto and then to the railway committee of the Ontario legislature, he had moved on to major appointments on the Ontario Hydro Commission and the Board of Railway Commissioners. Between 1917 and August 1919, in addition to chairing the Railway Commissioners' Board, he had been the power controller under the War Measures Act. Prime Minister Robert Borden appointed him to take over as finance minister from White in August. A Conservative-Unionist MP in Kingston gave up his seat, and Drayton was elected by acclamation in October 1919.[16] He was put in play as a finance ringer.

Drayton faced a fearsome task. The available budget options in late 1919 and early 1920 were so likely to cost votes that, in February 1920, an old warrior of the Liberal Party, former Finance Minister W.S. Fielding, advised the Liberals' new leader, W.L. Mackenzie King, that the party should not force an election before Drayton's budget, precisely to avoid having to come up with a solution to the revenue problem.[17] Better to leave this job to Prime Minister Borden's already staggering Conservatives. Whatever solution they offered, higher taxes were inevitable. The country had taken on enormous debt, trade and customs revenues were still unsettled, and inflation had driven the cost of living upward. More borrowing would only fuel inflation. It was time to tax.

Drayton delivered his budget speech on May 18, 1920. In 1919, his predecessor had raised the income taxes (personal and corporate) to match US increases: Drayton added a 5 percent surtax on the tax payable. Challenging conventional wisdom, he guessed that this amount would not drive capital and immigrants from the land. He kept and indeed increased the excise and luxury taxes of the Special War Revenue Act. He told anyone who could afford to be extravagant to stop it. Thrift, not high living, was what the moment required. He added that wee 1 percent sales tax, hoping, no doubt, that it would be painless. In a two-hour-long speech, his description of the sales tax took about seventy seconds. (Some pain must have been inflicted, however, by his reading out in excruciating detail a list of items exempted from the sales tax, including, for example, every variety of butter substitute.) Drayton eased the war profits tax, but did not remove it, because conditions were not yet normal. He repealed only two taxes: the war tariff increase and, in a small concession to the junior governments, a tax on the showing of films in theatres.[18] It was a tough budget. But Drayton insisted that a nation that had done so well on the home front as well as on the battlefield had nothing to fear. He wished, almost wistfully, for the country "to again become as united and earnest as it was during the war period," for "each and all of us to sink all difference, class and sectional interests and jealousies into an effort towards re-establishing Canada as united and co-ordinated." There was little sign of that mood in the budget discussions.[19] But a finance minister can always dream.

For the next six weeks, "everyone" was talking about the budget. Parliamentarians of all stripes talked taxation. Delegations met with Drayton.[20] On income tax measures, he accepted no substantive amendments, even though he held firm on some points on which later governments would concede. For example, he rejected proposals to allow charitable donations as deductions. Drayton couldn't accept the loss of revenue that this measure (one well established in the United States) would entail, and he foresaw, impressively, that it would be vulnerable to use as a tax dodge.[21] King, leader of the opposition, privately approved of the income tax rate increases and saw nothing noteworthy in the small sales tax (whose rate his new government would promptly raise after they defeated Borden's Conservatives in 1921).[22]

On the sales and luxury taxes, Drayton affirmed the principles that had guided the budget resolutions but offered to take advice on whether the list of sales tax–free items was correct in detail and whether the price thresholds and targeted commodities of the luxury tax were right. On some points, he yielded: thanks to comments both inside and outside the House, a schoolgirl would be able to tie her hair back with a simple tax-free ribbon, but aficionados of fancy millinery would pay a new price for some of their more gorgeous trim. Baseball and lacrosse gear of an ordinary sort would escape special taxation, but athletes with a taste for finer equipment would now find it more costly. Were Canadians being pushed into buying shoddier shoes or being asked to forgo special pleasures in footwear? How expensive did a fur coat have to be in Canada before it counted as a luxury and not just a means of survival in winter? Parliamentarians talked through these humble matters of daily life. For reasons that we might well find unfathomable, Drayton insisted that jam could not be exempted from even the basic sales tax, in spite of some parliamentarians' view that it was a workingman's necessity. He held that only "rough breakfast foods" could be tax free. If Canadians wanted bejewelled wedding bands, then they would be taxed on their self-indulgence: the words *plain gold* were inserted into the Special War Revenue Act, disapproving the new fashion for nuptial excess. In short, on some questions of the sales and luxury taxes, Drayton listened to public opinion and to his parliamentary colleagues, and he offered amendments to his budget's revenue bills before they were passed into law late in June.[23]

Drayton continued during the fall months of 1920 to seek Canadians' views on taxation and to try to persuade citizens that, given demands on the public purse, this was no time for "the man who wanted to let George carry the pail and to get off just as cheaply as he could."[24] Accompanied by Senator Gideon Robertson, Drayton travelled from coast to coast conducting a Tariff Commission in which he interviewed Canadians about tax questions. Fishers, industrialists, factory workers, farm wives, and even a lawyer or two came to testify.[25] In the opinion of one academic observer, the result was a "vast mass of data relating to Canadian industry ... Much of it is *ex parte,* incomplete, unscientific and conflicting ... Little new in the way of argument was secured."[26] Farmers certainly banged a familiar drum. In every province, they came armed with the dogma of the 1910 Farmers' Platform, repeatedly proposing low tariffs, land value taxes, and graduated income taxes. Drayton grilled each of them. He scrutinized their claims about how much the tariff raised prices. Where did they get their price information? Were the commodities that they compared truly comparable? He also pressed them on how they would assess land values. Would they tell Nova Scotians to adopt Manitoba's system or inform Manitobans that their system would give way to that of Nova Scotia? And above all, repeatedly, he asked them to give him practical suggestions about sources of revenue to replace the revenues that would be lost if tariffs were lowered. Would they be willing to pay more tax on their land? More income tax?[27]

From the protectionist viewpoint, low-tariff agrarians were just another selfish interest. Here *Montreal Daily Star* cartoonist Arthur G. Racey depicts the farmer (*top right*) in the same iconographic terms – the bulging belly and bank book – that agrarian and labour newspapers used to depict eastern bankers. *A Peep into the Future: Some Prophecies for 1923,* c. 1922, McCord Museum, Paintings, Prints, and Drawings Collection, Arthur George Racey fonds, M2005.23.203. © McCord Museum.

When farmers said that they'd be happy to pay more income tax if only their farms generated higher incomes, Drayton sometimes lost his good humour. The transcriber used no exclamation marks, but when W.S. Poole, a leader of the NB farmers' organization, said that his members "have no income to pay [tax] on," it's easy to read some heated frustration in Drayton's reply: "The city man pays practically on his gross [income], while you pay on your net [after expenses] … There are lots of city laborers and workers that never have any net at the end of the year, … but they pay the tax." Drayton then fired a series of questions at Poole showing that the latter had no idea how much revenue the alternative taxes proposed in the Farmers' Platform would yield or how much any other sector of Canadian society paid. Drayton concluded by saying that he appreciated that farmers wanted tariff reductions on the necessities of life; however, if he were to cut those taxes, then he needed to know how the farmers would replace the lost revenue.[28] A protectionist cartoonist in Montreal was less polite than Drayton to farmers' special pleading, depicting them as selfish and rich.[29]

On land taxation and the tariff, the conversation between Drayton and the farm representatives was stalemated. The arguments around protective tariffs and free trade or reciprocity were tediously well worn: a few years later a pair of essays in the *Dalhousie Review* would summarize the opposing positions, each with its merits.[30] On some points, the debate had become so stereotyped that opponents could even joke together. Referring to "infant industries," the familiar term for manufacturing businesses protected by the tariff, Drayton suggested that one witness, Harriet Dick of Winnipeg, probably thought that "some of [those infants] are getting grey headed now." She agreed: "I think some of them need to shave every day."[31] These were not the infants that she had gone into child welfare and women's suffrage work to defend.[32] On other points, the farmers were at least as angry with Drayton as he was with them. In "Farmers Slam Tariff System in Hot Terms," the Toronto *Globe* quoted representatives of the United Farmers of Ontario and farm women, who blamed the tariff for rural depopulation and "race suicide." Millionaires were "robbers."[33] W.J. Orchard of the Saskatchewan Grain Grower's Association told Drayton face to face that "no man by righteous – he may by lawful – means can get $2,000,000 in a lifetime." Not himself a millionaire, Drayton might nevertheless have been a bit offended. He had among his Conservative colleagues, and likely his friends, several millionaires a few times over.[34] The policy that the farmers attacked was the National Policy designed by Sir John A.'s Conservatives to build a national market and therefore, in theory, a comity of interest among Canadians. But to the farmers, the National Policy's vision of the nation had turned into something more like an empire, with central Canada as the exploiting metropolis, draining wealth from its internal colonies, the country's other regions.

Divisions based upon tariff interests seemed to be intractable.[35] On other tax questions, though, Drayton was more flexible and his critics more able to get their way. Most strikingly, he would end up agreeing to eliminate entirely a tax that, on the face of it, had seemed to be a good idea, supported as much or more by Liberals as by Conservatives. This was a tax on luxury goods. In his May 1920 budget speech, Drayton had framed the taxing of "extravagant" spending as a means both to raise revenue and to lower the ordinary cost of living. Best of all, this was a chance for the well off to fulfill their special obligation to build capital for the nation's economic development: "On those having income more than necessary for properly maintaining themselves and families, there rests a special duty of saving whenever possible and in this manner adding to the available financial resources for development and for industrial undertakings. Extravagant buying should stop."[36]

In this heavily moralized view of taxation, the finance minister was in tune with an important mass organization, the Great War Veterans' Association, whose national convention in March 1920 drew on the vocabulary of classical antiquity to disparage luxury:

We view with alarm the increasing love of luxury which permeates all classes of our community and the riotous extravagance everywhere shown in gratifying this mania, thus courting as a nation financial disaster. Our Army fought and our men died to establish forever among us the ideals of sacrifice, unselfishness and brotherhood. We therefore protest with all our energy against the extravagance shown in dress and manner of living, against the spending of money on unnecessary social affairs and against costly public functions which are of no real value. At this time of national stress when as a nation we are faced with enormous financial responsibility, we call upon our fellow citizens for plain and economical habits of life. We summon our country to a return to Spartan simplicity.[37]

In spite of such strong support for the luxury tax, both merchants and manufacturers protested its impact. Women as managers of family budgets also challenged it. The list of luxuries in Drayton's budget speech made his rhetoric inflammatory. No one disputed (at least in public) that opera cloaks and gold dinner services were luxuries. But other items on his list were controversial. A particularly potent embarrassment was the story that the list of items taxable as luxuries classed typewriter ribbons along with the silky fripperies used to trim hats, hair, and baby clothing: all were ribbons![38] The more common issues arose around items such as ten-dollar boots and eighteen-dollar blouses. As one Saint John merchant, Robert Macaulay, explained to Drayton during the Tariff Commission hearings, "the customer doesn't object to paying $19.80 for the [shirt]waist until she is shown that $1.80 of the price is for luxury tax." Her objection, Macaulay went on to say, was to the "paternalism" implied by the tax:

We can buy cigarettes at 18 cents a package, and we all know perfectly well that that includes 7 cents tax, but we are perfectly willing to pay it. If, however, the government should say in a paternal way, "we believe it is criminal and extravagant to smoke cigarettes, and therefore we tax every packet of cigarettes 7 cents," you would resent it.[39]

The tax specialist in the National Council of Women, Halifax journalist Ella Murray, asserted that the "so called luxury tax" was not only borne by those "who indulge in extravagant, luxurious things" but also charged against purchases that were necessities to "the great middle class."[40] Drayton's argument that pinching pennies even harder would, by reducing demand, lead to lower prices failed to outweigh the offence that Murray took at the implication that middle-class housewives were "extravagant" and should cut back their spending. Macroeconomic fiscal theory was too remote from common sense to register in her analysis of the luxury tax. Her critique centred on the high cost of living and emphasized how the luxury tax and consumption taxes in general could strain household budgets. Murray's outrage at the luxury tax was widely shared. Baptist minister and economics professor W.C. Keirstead, usually a reasonable, scholarly fellow, referred to it as "the most wretched piece of legislation ever given a third reading in the Dominion House of Commons."[41] In response to this protest, within a few weeks of the finance minister's return from his cross-country taxation consultations in the fall of 1920, the federal government repealed the luxury tax.[42]

Given the different outcomes of the Tariff Commission – policy impact on the luxury tax but no movement by the Conservatives on the tariff – it is perhaps not surprising that some unsatisfied members of the Liberal Party saw in tariff reform an electoral opening. Western Liberals such as Thomas Crerar, building on the organizational strength of farmers, had formed the National Progressive Party in 1919. In the 1921 federal election, the Progressives won 65 of 251 seats in the House of Commons. In effect, the organized farmers held the balance of power in Parliament during the years when Canada's fiscal future was being negotiated. Although the Liberal Party formed the government in 1921, some Liberal MPs resented the measure of control exercised by the Progressives. One such Liberal wrote to the new Liberal prime minister to argue that "refusing to let Messrs Coote, Irvine, and Woodsworth [Progressive and Labour MPs] run the Parliament of Canada will gain respect for ourselves and will not lose us a dozen votes in Ontario ... Let the howling Radicals howl."[43] Direct taxation, and taxation of income in particular, would get parliamentary support from the Progressives, those "howling" radicals. In 1924, one of their parliamentary leaders, economist and farmer W.C. Good, told the House that "the present farmers' movement in Canada, which is represented in this House by over sixty members, is one of the most modern protests against unfair and unjust taxation; and even now, from coast to coast, an emphatic protest is being made against unjust taxation."[44] With the Progressives in the House after 1921, the income tax that they had fought for would be given a fair chance.[45] They would do their best to make urban Canada pay a proper income tax, even though, as a third party, their power was limited.

Making the Income Tax Productive

As the King Liberals prepared to govern after winning the 1921 federal election, they were urged both by Progressives and by their own membership base to save the income tax by improving its administration. Drayton had pointed out that the income tax was the hardest of all the war taxes to collect,[46] and the Progressives were surely right to suggest that the apparatus of collection was not particularly effective. Staffing had been inadequate from the start. In 1918, the first tax forms had been distributed months late. Rumours circulated. Significant accounting questions had been matters of perplexed speculation.[47] In February 1918, the "girl clerks" in the Department of Finance were still wrapping up the colossal paperwork from the 1917 Victory Loan.[48] The tax returns for 1917 had to wait. By mid-1918, some of the business profits war tax returns from 1915 and 1916 had still not been assessed and collected, and the head of the Canadian Bankers' Association pressed White to find out why.[49] Something odd seemed to be going on in the Department of Finance, where the income and business profits war tax administration had been housed, separate from the Department of Inland Revenue.[50]

Conservative MP Henry H. Stevens worried that, more than just staff shortage, there was a particular problem with Commissioner of Taxation R.W. Breadner.[51] Beginning in 1918, and continuing over the next ten years, others shared this worry. Evidence from multiple sources confirms that Breadner was vain, touchy, stubborn, secretive, controlling, obsessed with detail, probably a Conservative partisan, and apparently vindictive. In short, he epitomized the worst caricature of a despicable tax collector.[52] Without any training as an accountant, Breadner ruled on difficult questions of business finance in ways that astonished some unfortunate business income tax payers. His small taxation branch was staffed by underpaid, hand-picked men who toed his line or were forced out. Unlike all but one other civil service department, appointments to the Department of Finance were made outside the scrutiny of the Civil Service Commission.[53] The argument for this arrangement had been the need to ensure that each employee was trustworthy, whatever else his or her other qualifications, because of the abundant opportunities for embezzlement that war bonds and war taxes presented. Perhaps it is remarkable that there were only three thieves caught and one apparently related suicide documented in the department in the early 1920s.[54] Oversight of the commissioner of taxation, and indeed oversight of the financial operations of the dominion government were limited between 1918 and 1924, owing to a series of ill and temporary auditors general. One auditor general died while in office in 1919; the acting auditor general who had been serving in his stead in turn went on sick leave in 1922 and 1923, and after his resignation no appointment was made to the position until 1924. A private sector accountant, George Edwards, performed audits on the national accounts in 1921, 1922,

A Conservative paper such as the *Montreal Daily Star* blamed the lack of scrutiny of the Department of Finance on the Liberal government. The paper suspected the Liberals of using accounting tricks to understate the nation's indebtedness. *Is Canada Asleep?*, c. 1922, McCord Museum, Paintings, Prints, and Drawings Collection, Arthur George Racey fonds, M2005.23.145. © McCord Museum.

and 1925. There was no audit in 1923 or 1924.[55] In short, Breadner, like the other senior officials in Finance, had a relatively unchecked hand.

Critics were particularly frustrated by the secretiveness of Breadner's operations. Breadner insisted, in accordance with the tax statute, that taxpayers' information must be secret, in light of the sensitive business information that his office handled. However, his critics could not but remark that his respect for taxpayers' privacy was a convenient cloak for arbitrary power. They advised that there be a commission of overseers to govern the taxation branch. They also wanted some research done in the US and UK national tax offices to discover credible alternatives to the practices that Breadner defended so intransigently but explained so evasively.[56] The notion that Canada might adopt practices like those of these major world powers and creditor nations suggests an aspiration to achieve a less timid style of taxation, but the scant resources devoted to administering the new direct taxes frustrated any such ambition. Looking back in

1930, when protectionist Conservatives were again in power and Breadner's influence was again felt, Liberal leader King reproached himself for not having gotten rid of Breadner in 1922.[57] But it is understandable that King had not done so. Control of information had empowered Breadner to hold on to the jury-rigged taxation machinery that he alone seemed to be able to run.[58]

But other factors compromised the effectiveness of the federal income tax. Even with new political masters after 1921 and pressure to improve collection efforts, the new system produced discouraging results. Evasion of income tax drew much comment. One way by which observers measured the extent of evasion was to compare the productivity of the Canadian federal income tax to its equivalent in other countries. The tax in Canada generated just short of $8 million for the 1919 tax year, the president of the Canadian Council of Agriculture, a champion of the Farmers' Platform, pointed out in 1920; in per capita terms, compared with the similar economies of Australia and New Zealand, Canada's income tax collections should have been $185 million. He claimed that, if one took as a standard the per capita amount of the income tax revenue raised in the more industrialized United States or United Kingdom, it should be possible to collect between $400 and $500 million in Canada. With Canada's direct taxes generating only a tiny fraction of these amounts, something was wrong.[59] In 1923, a slightly more dispassionate observer, University of Toronto economist H.R. Kemp, drew on government documents to show that, compared with citizens of the United States, disproportionately few citizens of Canada were filing income tax returns. Moreover, the income reported in Canadian tax returns in 1919 was less than $104 per capita, whereas in the United States it was $300 per capita. Kemp acknowledged that part of this difference could be explained by genuine differences in prosperity between the two countries, the greater relative role of the subsistence economy in Canada, and an income distribution in Canada weighted more heavily to smaller, non-taxable incomes. Even taking these differences into account, however, he thought it likely that "widespread evasion" was taking place: "No country has as yet devised an evasion-proof income tax, and a sparsely-settled country where the tax has been only recently imposed can hardly be expected to lead the way."[60]

Other evidence, introduced in the House of Commons in 1923, showed that stepped-up enforcement efforts after 1921 for the 1920–23 tax years had briefly improved the productivity of the income tax, even while suggesting the extent to which it had been evaded. The dollar value of fines for tax evasion rose impressively, multiplying by as much as twenty-five times in farm-dominated Saskatchewan and by at least six times in the eastern and central provinces, with their more mixed economies.[61] In Prince Edward Island, the agricultural product of which was valued at over $30,000,000 a year, farmers had paid in 1919, in total, federal income taxes of $135.[62] These data suggest that farmers, whose income was less easily measured than wage or salary income, were disguising taxable income. Even if they were attempting to report their net incomes accurately, many of them kept such poor accounting records (if any at all) that, as one Saskatchewan accountant pointed out, the tax inspector's assessments could only be "more or less guess work."[63] It was hard to know, then, what was going on when the income tax collected from farmers nearly doubled between 1920 and 1922.[64] It seems to be certain, however, that farmers found themselves paying more income taxes than they had expected to pay.

Farmers were not the only Canadians slow to take up the role of federal income tax payers. The writs issued by the Exchequer Court of Canada to delinquent federal income tax payers during the 1920–23 wave of intensified enforcement addressed not only farmers but also well-paid, wealthy, or business-owning Canadians, including railway workers and physicians, inspectors and merchants, manufacturers and well-off widows. All were notified that they owed the crown a debt (sometimes as far back as the 1917 tax year); if they failed to pay it, then they were told that a sheriff would come and sell some of their possessions to recover the debt owed to his majesty. Some of these tax debts were for no more than a dollar or two; most were for amounts between $10 and $100.[65] Collecting these debts in a highly formal way, using a national court, made many Canadians more aware of the seriousness of a federal tax debt. Supporters of the income tax were encouraged by reports of increasing prosecutions. But the same data also indicated how much "education" was still required before this tax debt was treated seriously. It was possible to take a rather casual attitude toward an income tax debt in municipalities, where municipal income tax payers expected to negotiate their assessments and to appeal for discounts in cases of hardship. The federal income tax authorities offered no encouragement to such attitudes.[66]

The impact of greater enforcement on the productivity of the federal income tax was far from impressive. Although the totals collected annually under the federal income tax mounted dramatically in 1921 and 1922, even during the postwar recession, there was a decline of nearly equal magnitude in 1923 and 1924, years of returning prosperity and unchanged rates of tax liability. This decline tended to confirm Professor Kemp's suspicion that Canadians were not complying fully with the income tax.[67] A humour columnist, Peter McArthur, invented a new term – "the Ananias Point" – to gently mock those who spoke soberly and pseudo-scientifically of taxation having reached "the point of diminishing returns." Ananias is a biblical figure famous for lying about his money, in the same way that the Good Samaritan represents helpfulness to strangers. McArthur suggested that the Ananias Point be defined as "a point where respectable citizens will follow the example of the great typical falsifier of returns."[68]

Another difficulty in the way of making the income tax productive was shared widely across the former belligerent powers, the problem that Killam had identified in the fall of 1918: the tax-free war bonds and their tendency to "nullify the graduated income tax."[69] The farmers suggested that one way to shake loose the tax revenue kept just out of reach in Victory Bonds was to shame their owners by publicizing the names of wealthy people who paid disproportionately little tax.[70] More directly, the farmers and their allies proposed persistently throughout the 1920s that all government bonds be made taxable.[71] Income from the 1919 Victory Bonds and later Canadian bonds was, in fact, made taxable. However, investors could always buy some of the 1917 or 1918 issues if they needed to park some income-generating capital in a tax-free spot.[72] Liberal partisans continued to berate the wartime finance minister on the subject: one well-to-do Liberal wrote to finance critic W.S. Fielding in 1920 to say that "those [tax-exempt] loans should put Sir Thomas White out of public life for all time."[73]

Wealthy taxpayers became increasingly ingenious at using bonds to provide themselves with tax-free incomes, thereby shrinking the tax base and sharply reducing the progressivity of the income tax, as Killam had predicted. One abuse of the exemption was to pay out taxable corporate dividends with government bonds, thus reducing the tax liability on those dividends. (This loophole was closed by *Waterous v. Minister of National Revenue* in 1931.[74]) Not just an elite strategy, the fashion for tax avoidance by means of bondholding could also be seen in less elevated financial circles. A Toronto clothing store, Madame May ("Canada's largest high class dress exchange"), accepted tax-free bonds in payment on customers' accounts.[75] Commissioner Breadner admitted in 1920 that reaching bondholders to collect income taxes, even for coupons clipped on the taxable 1919 issue, had so far proven impossible – the coupons of bearer bonds, not registered to a particular owner, were like cash.[76] In 1923, a leading banker suggested reforms to the income tax (a lowering of the top rates) so as to prevent "capital from hiding in tax exempt securities."[77] Looking back on the interwar years, Donald Fleming, a lawyer and later finance minister, recalled how the wealthy used the tax-exempt Victory Bonds to make for themselves "a very favourable tax position."[78] The farmers were right to be worried about the tax costs of those bonds.

In taking aim at unfair tax enforcement and tax avoidance practices, the farmer politicians hoped to protect the base of the income tax. But they also thought that better enforcement would make the tax more fair and thus encourage compliance. In this, they were joined by an emerging community of tax experts – economists, lawyers, accountants, and government tax officials. Such experts expressed dismay and embarrassment at the lack of "science" in the Canadian system, compared with the American and British tax systems. They responded to and sometimes helped to feed tax protests by discussing issues and devising expert alternatives. Their views were aired in April 1923 and afterward at the annual meetings of Canada's first organization of tax experts, the Canadian Tax Conference (CTC). Founded in 1922, the CTC was a branch of a modernizing business organization called the Citizens' Research Institute of Canada (CRIC), itself an amalgamation in 1919 of several "citizen" leagues in Toronto, Winnipeg, and Calgary. Some of its members had prewar connections with the National Taxation Association in the United States and an international network of scientific government experts, the Bureau of Municipal Research. *Canadian Taxation,* CRIC's monthly information bulletin, encapsulated taxation data and ideology in pithy, four-page instalments.[79] Anyone familiar with the archives of Canadian politicians (federal, provincial, or municipal) from the interwar years will have seen at least one or two issues of *Canadian Taxation* and often many more.[80] The bulletin's sometimes crude data were often quoted by journalists and parliamentarians, occasionally with a fidelity bordering on ventriloquism. Even though CRIC's data were crude, investors as important as the Sun Life Insurance Company praised the data-gathering work on taxation that CRIC did and used its reports as bases for investment decisions.[81]

In 1922–23, the influence of the CTC-CRIC perspective was apparent in a widely circulated proposal for a reformed income tax. The proposal was first outlined in a Saskatchewan accountant's contribution to the December 1922 edition of *Canadian Taxation,* then (with more specifics) in a speech by a Toronto banker in the proceedings of the April 1923 meeting, and, soon after, in general terms, on May 18, 1923, in comments by Conservative MP (and future Minister of National Revenue) E.B. Ryckman in the House of Commons. Perhaps coincidentally, Ryckman quoted the same American investment banker as the Saskatchewan accountant had on the subject of fairness in income taxation. Instead of the 1919 income tax, which had a mix of flat rates, graduated (i.e., progressive) rates, and a surtax on high incomes, a better income tax would have a single graduated scale, with a higher basic exemption and a lower maximum rate. The basic exemption proposed was $5,000 or some agreed-upon "fair minimum cost of living."[82] Before 1926, the married exemption was $2,000, well below what these professional men were imagining as basic. (See chapter 4 for the contextualized meaning of these dollar values.) The maximum marginal rate that the Toronto banker suggested – "approximately 40% on the largest incomes" – contrasted with the current combined top rate of 70 percent. The role of this less ambitious income tax would be to complement a revenue system based otherwise entirely upon, and deriving most of its revenue from, consumption – sales taxes, excises, and tariff taxes. The income tax would serve to correct for the regressivity inherent in the main sources of revenue. At the same time, by limiting the scope of income taxation and centring the revenue system on consumption taxation, the tax reformers proposed that the main impact of taxation would be on spending rather than on earning.[83]

In this plan, "thrift" – the accumulation of capital for the purpose of investment in the nation's economic development – would be penalized only minimally, and all Canadians would contribute to meeting the country's collective obligations. The appeal of this reform was bolstered by indications of the federal income tax's declining productivity, its rates higher than any in the United States and as high as all but a few categories in the United Kingdom, and the competitive disadvantage that Canada thus allegedly suffered in attracting and keeping immigrants. These comparisons were a point of national shame, these reformers argued, suggesting a failure of management rather than any real economic difficulty. Our "governments are like children, like children crying in the night, and with no language but a cry," lamented one business commentator.[84] Compared with its mother and older brother next door, Canada seemed to the CTC-CRIC experts still to need tax tutelage. The influence of these experts was considerable: in the 1926 federal budget, the new income tax included most of the elements that they had been advising since 1922. The basic married exemption was raised to $3,000 – a solid middle-class income. The normal tax/surtax distinction was eliminated. And the progressive rate structure went up to a top rate of only 50 percent, although at $50,000 it was a mere 27 percent, and in 1928, the earliest year that we have tax statistics by income cohort, there were only 523 people who paid taxes on incomes over $50,000.[85] The immediate impact was to reduce the amount of income assessable under the act. To understand why the federal government curtailed in this way the role of income taxation in the federal tax structure in 1926, we need to appreciate that forces other than expert advice were at work. Liberal Finance Minister J.A. Robb responded to two well-armed campaigns against federal income taxation: one led by a nationwide organization of retail merchants and the other led by Quebec.

Retail Merchants against the Income Tax

Pressure from both the Progressives and the nascent Canadian community of tax experts was intended to improve the income tax and make it both more tolerable and more productive. But the arguments made by these groups could also be used to justify complete rejection of the tax. If it was too evadable, too burdensome, and too harmful to economic development, then the best solution might be to abolish it entirely. Rather than join fiscally mature nations in making income taxation the centrepiece of public finance, some thought it best to throw out the federal income tax and instead to continue the Canadian colonial tradition of financing the federal government by means of indirect consumption taxes. The campaign from that perspective to abolish the federal income tax was not successful in the end, but it must have helped to give weight to proposals for income tax reductions.

The spearhead of this campaign was the Retail Bureau of Canada (RBC). In 1925, its spokesman, E.M. Trowern, condensed its views in a passionate speech, "The Necessity of Abolishing the Income Tax." "I want to see Canada lead the world with regard to sound legislative measures," he asserted proudly. The RBC project found enthusiastic endorsement in the financial press of Montreal and Toronto. The *Montreal Herald* cheered on the RBC: "Canada would receive a wonderful advertisement throughout the world if the abolition of the Income Tax were made a national policy."

Florida attracted "desirable residents" by abolishing its inheritance tax; why couldn't Canada benefit in the same way by eliminating the income tax?[86]

That this policy option was a live one is suggested by the fact that Canada's neighbouring dominion, Newfoundland, abolished its own income tax in 1925. The speech from the throne in Newfoundland gave the same reasons that the Canadian retail merchants used:

> Income Tax returns have not been made by many, under pressure only by others, and payments of assessments have been evaded, delayed or refused in so many cases that unfairness has resulted to the honest observers of the law. It is a form of taxation unsuited to this country. It restrains the investment of capital in business, and though apparently paid by the so-called well-to-do, it is passed on to the consumer, when paid by those successful in business, while hampering severely, and sometimes destructively, those who have not prospered.[87]

Although a new government in Newfoundland reinstated the income tax in 1929, they were not able to make it a productive tax, partly because of the predominantly rural economy and partly because of ongoing evasion, including, by way of bad example, the widely known evasion by one member of the Newfoundland cabinet. By 1933, the inability of the Dominion of Newfoundland to meet its obligations to its creditors resulted in control by the imperial government.[88] Fears that Canada would have to repudiate some of its debts were circulating even before the Great Depression. That Canada had been able to preserve the income tax and make it at least somewhat effective helped to save the larger dominion from the fate of Newfoundland.[89]

The retail merchants' proposal to abolish the federal income tax was more radical than other grumblings about income taxation. That radicalism excluded the RBC's proposal from serious policy consideration. An aspiring prime minister didn't like it any more than the sitting one did. When Conservative Leader of the Opposition Arthur Meighen got a letter from a Toronto lawyer asking that the Tories include abolition of the income tax in their 1925 election platform, Meighen gave him a chilly response.[90] Although the abolition proposal was radical, the arguments made in its favour were mainstream. The RBC did not by any means invent the notion that income tax was easily evaded, nor was it the first to observe that its reliance on self-assessment constituted an incentive to be deceptive. For a bit of venerable cachet, they quoted the United Kingdom's famous Prime Minister W.E. Gladstone on the subject. Like Gladstone, the RBC claimed that to impose a tax so easily dodged was to penalize the honest and to reward the deceitful. Income taxation was therefore simply wrong: the retailers' spokesman thundered that Christians who prayed that the Lord "lead them not into temptation" should be outraged that the income tax did just that. Instead, like the CRIC reformers who accepted a small role for the income tax, the RBC pointed to consumption taxes as the proper cornerstone of public finance in Canada. Consumption taxes were fair because "you cannot dodge the tariff and you cannot dodge the sales tax."[91] In this claim, they were either naïve or less than honest: surely they knew of the smuggling, on a commercial scale, of high-value retail goods such as diamonds, silk, and of course booze. In 1924 and 1925, questions in the House and a formal protest by aggrieved Canadian manufacturers and retailers (who disliked having to compete with smugglers) finally led to a parliamentary inquiry and a royal commission in 1926.[92] Smugglers certainly dodged not only the tariff and sales taxes but also the excise duties.

While emphasizing the corrupting effects and evadability of the income tax, the retailers offered other, equally familiar reasons for rejecting income taxation as a revenue measure: income tax assessment invaded privacy, high tax rates drove capital into tax-exempt (and economically unproductive) government bonds, the legislation was complex and therefore the tax debt owed uncertain, thrift was punished, and employees were inequitably exposed to assessment, compared with the self-employed.[93] Given that none of these were new arguments, the retailers were unlikely just to have discovered it. But as tax critics, the retailers and their allies in the mid-1920s must surely have been encouraged by the resounding victory against the luxury tax a few years earlier. The arguments that had worked then were much like the ones later circulated about the income tax (corruption, injury to industry, unfairness). That the same arguments did not succeed in 1924–25 had to do with the important influence on parliamentary votes of the Progressives, squarely on the side of a more effective income tax. Like the farmers, the retailers saw themselves as advocating fair taxation rather than opposing necessary taxation. But, unlike the farmers, they lacked a party to champion their position in the House.

Quebec against the Income Tax

Meanwhile, opposition to the federal income tax was under way in another part of the polity, where different and potentially more powerful tools than moral rhetoric were being put to use. That other source of challenge to the existence of the federal income tax, and specifically the personal income tax, was distinctively Canadian insofar as it was based upon the terms of the Constitution, the British North America Act of 1867. As retired federal tax mandarin A. Kenneth Eaton wrote in 1966, "Canada, God help us, is a federation."[94] Fiscal relations in federal systems are notoriously complex. In Canada, regional variations in taxable capacity are part of what makes revenue distribution challenging within the federation; what makes the problem politically fraught is its connection to constitutional history.

For Quebec, Confederation in 1867 had returned the province to a state of relative political autonomy, freeing at least some of its fiscal sovereignty from interference from Ontario. For the old provinces of the eastern seaboard, New Brunswick and Nova Scotia, joining the Canadian provinces in 1867 was purely a loss of fiscal sovereignty, for which they were compensated in specific financial terms, by way of annual federal subsidies to provincial budgets.[95] And for the First Nations whose constitutional status was consolidated, without their consent, in the Indian Act of 1875 and negotiated through treaties at various times, quasi-constitutional law also had fiscal implications. First Nations governments were prohibited from taxing their own people, and band members were exempt from being taxed by other governments on their on-reserve properties.[96] During the 1920s, all of these internal relations of remembered conquest and compromised autonomy were expressed in opposition to the federal income tax. Although a test case originating in Quebec confirmed the federal government's constitutional right to tax income, the case also had a troubling outcome for tax culture. It made unintentional tax evaders out of most of the civil servants and provincial politicians of Quebec.

Between 1920 and 1924, Quebec mounted what has been the only serious challenge ever made to the constitutional legality of the federal income tax in Canada. In contrast to the United States, in Canada it is the senior level of government, not the junior one, that has unlimited powers of taxation. Provinces are restricted to taxation by direct means, within the province, for provincial purposes, whereas the federal government has the right to raise revenue by any means, anywhere, for any purpose (except purposes made exclusive to the province in the BNA Act). Before the First World War, only two provinces (British Columbia and Prince Edward Island) had used their direct taxation power to impose a provincial income tax. But in others, including the populous central Canadian province of Ontario, the municipalities (constitutionally, creatures of the provinces) made more or less significant use of income taxes in addition to property taxes.[97] The imposition of a federal income tax in 1917 therefore meant that incomes in major concentrations of high-income earners such as Toronto and Hamilton were now taxed for the first time by two levels of government. This "double taxation" was seen as compromising the ability of junior governments to raise revenue for projects in the areas of provincial legislative jurisdiction, such as health, welfare, and education, toward which they were being pushed by their electorates. In 1918, Premier of Quebec Lomer Gouin saw a legal opportunity to limit operations of the federal income tax and perhaps to complicate its administration so seriously as to make it unfeasible as a permanent form of federal taxation.

Gouin sought advice from Attorney General of Quebec Charles Lanctôt,[98] whose assessment of the jurisprudence and the strategic terrain was thorough – and prescient. He reviewed case law in Canada and international references from Australia and the United States on which Canadian precedents relied. He concluded that, in federal systems, there was a well-established jurisprudence that prevented one level of government from taxing the salaries of employees of another level. This was part of the doctrine of immunity of government instrumentalities: that is, immunity from interference with not only employees but also agencies, and indeed bond issues, of another level of government in a federation. "Interference" often meant taxation. The foundation of this doctrine lay in an American case of the early national period, *McCulloch v. Maryland* (1819). The doctrine rested on the principle that the power to tax was the power to destroy.[99]

That principle was clearly stated in the key precedent in Canada: the 1878 finding in *Leprohon v. City of Ottawa*. In the *Leprohon* judgment, it was a province's power to tax a federal employee that was at issue; the judge held that, "if the power [to tax a dominion official] exists at all, it can be exercised to any extent, and in the event of any Province being dissatisfied with the Dominion government it would hold in its hands a weapon which it might resort to harass the government and enforce its demands."[100]

As Lanctôt observed, *Leprohon* stood as the precedent until 1908 and had often been applied. He acknowledged that a 1908 case, *Abbott v. City of Saint John,* had qualified the doctrine. According to the judgment in *Abbott,* only in the case of a discriminatory tax, aimed specifically at the employees of another level of government, would the destructive power of taxation be unleashed. But Lanctôt thought that the logic of *Leprohon* still held: federal taxation, in his view, could compromise the autonomy of Quebec's provincial state.

Serious consideration by the Judicial Committee of the Privy Council (JCPC) in London, Lanctôt believed, would support this view if Quebec were to proceed with a test case. However, he cautiously, perhaps cynically, observed that "there might ... be reason to fear that, when the time comes, the court will take into consideration external circumstances."[101] It seems likely that the "external circumstances" that he feared might sway the judges would include the need to protect the capacity of the Canadian government to raise revenue to cover the interest that it owed to its bondholders. A decision in favour of the test case that he proposed would remove many Canadian incomes from the tax base. And, if provincial civil servants and politicians were to be exempted from federal income taxation, then that tax might come to seem so unfair that it would have to be abandoned. However, in spite of his prescient awareness of the stakes in the case and their likely weight, Lanctôt recommended going ahead.

The case was *Caron v. The King.* Joseph-Eugène Caron, a farmer, was the minister of agriculture in the Quebec Liberal government. Both Caron and his son had been charged by the federal revenue authority with failure to pay federal income taxes owed. His case was more likely to appeal to public opinion than that of a wealthier politician: without his sessional indemnity, Caron's income was too small to tax. His case became a convenient vehicle for testing the issue.[102]

More was at issue in *Caron* than simply the doctrine of instrumentalities. The case was also about the division of powers between the provinces and the federal government. In 1922, an already eminent young Liberal lawyer, who would become prime minister of Canada in 1948, Louis St. Laurent, KC, enthusiastically described to Lanctôt the argument that he had presented to the Supreme Court of Canada in *Caron.* Although the factum in the case emphasized *Leprohon,* St. Laurent was proudest of the logic by which he had shown that the federal government was acting beyond its powers in imposing any direct tax at all. Federal and provincial taxing powers, he believed he had shown, were mutually exclusive. If the provinces had the power of direct taxation, then the federal government did not.[103] The Supreme Court justices wasted no time, however, on that point. Instead, they asserted that their 1908 finding in *Abbott* bound them to find against Caron. Aware that this was a test case, they left it to Quebec to appeal to the more important constitutional court in London, the JCPC.[104] There, too, Caron (and the Quebec government) lost.

The law lords in London acknowledged that it was possible to imagine a circumstance in which the federal government's general taxing power might make it violate provincial rights. In the unlikely event that the Canadian government attempted to tax by indirect means within a province in order to provide funds for a provincial purpose (e.g., schools), it would be outside its constitutional powers. But in taxing for federal purposes (to pay interest on federal debt or to finance a national railway), it was free to use direct taxation, whether on income or on any other type of tax base.[105]

This was a serious defeat for the autonomist current in Quebec politics. Given that the case had been led and argued by Liberals, it is perhaps only slightly surprising that the main Liberal daily newspaper (*Le Soleil*) in the provincial capital dealt with the defeat simply by not reporting the story. Less partisan or more Conservative francophone newspapers in the province watched the case closely and reported the loss in *Caron*. Some noted the constitutional significance of the case, and others expressed sympathy for a farmer politician whose indemnity was meant to cover his work expenses. More commonly, though, there was a noticeable tone of satisfaction that the politician must pay his taxes as others did.[106] In one of the major Toronto anglophone newspapers, final resolution of the case didn't register at all; the *Toronto Daily Star* only published a short note on Caron's defeat at the Exchequer Court in 1921.[107] In the other big Toronto paper, the *Globe,* one brief news note announced the plan to appeal the decision of the Exchequer Court, and a slightly longer story covered the final decision in London. In Toronto, neither story made any reference to the constitutional issue.[108] So the constitutionality of a federal income tax, which had obsessed American public opinion since the 1890s, was barely noticed in Canada. The terrifying "power to destroy" in taxation, a central concept in American fiscal federalism, had no purchase in Canada. Even before *Caron,* the judge in an 1896 Nova Scotia case observed that the "crushing" effect of a provincial statute labour tax on the instrument used by the dominion government to govern (namely, a section man employed on the Intercolonial Railway) was "imperceptible."[109] The Supreme Court in *Abbott* and the imperial court in *Caron* saw no power to destroy but trusted that governments would apply revenue laws equally and without discrimination.

Although part of the attack on the income tax in the early 1920s, the *Caron* case turned out to be no real threat to the tax. The real consequence of *Caron* lay in the harm that it did to relations between Quebec politicians and the national state. The correspondence that flowed between the revenue authorities in Ottawa, including the dreadful Breadner, and various Quebec civil servants and politicians, including Quebec's new premier, L.A. Taschereau, made it clear that this case left its mark on relations between Quebec City and Ottawa. In 1922, the federal minister of finance testily urged Taschereau to cut through delays in getting the case to the Supreme Court: "While the matter is unsettled, an important part of the income tax business of our Department is paralyzed." Delays by Quebec City again prolonged the process between 1922 and 1924.[110] Then, after the case was finally decided in 1924, Caron and all of the other ministers, members of the legislature, and civil servants who had been withholding their federal taxes until the case was settled received bills for their arrears and, to their shock and dismay, for interest charges on those balances.[111]

Having been reassured that it was unnecessary to pay the taxes while the case was before the courts, and having therefore reassured friends and employees, both Lanctôt and Taschereau wrote to and phoned Breadner to protest the imposition of interest charges. Breadner, with his characteristic flair for human relations, did not answer their calls or respond to their letters. Premier Taschereau then contacted influential federal Liberals Jacques Bureau, the minister of customs and excise (and since 1924 Breadner's minister), and Minister of Justice Ernest Lapointe, urging them to intervene. But in 1925 Bureau himself was embattled on other fronts, his department caught up in a massive corruption scandal. Lapointe was threatened by the scandal too. Neither was able to do anything. Taschereau's response to Bureau was bitter and defiant: "You [federal Liberals] will do what you wish with this, but the ministers, deputies, and public servants are utterly unable to pay six or seven years of arrears with interest. All you can do now is take them to court, get a judgment against them, have their property sold, and all we can do is wish you good luck." What had started off nominally as an attempt to protect these provincial public servants from harm by the federal taxman turned out to have led them directly into it.[112]

The *Caron* case can only have embittered a generation of Quebec politicians and civil servants toward "the feds." As can be the case in taxation practice more generally, when something goes wrong in the collecting of a tax debt, taxpayers easily turn to larger frameworks to interpret the significance of their personal troubles. The choice of framework for the *Caron* victims must have been easy. To be subjected to Breadner and, in 1927, the starchily righteous new minister of national revenue would readily have been seen as an insult to the autonomy of Quebec, another sign of the need for more firmly established provincial rights and a clearer division of powers.

The Path-Setting 1926 Federal Budget

Although neither the Quebec government nor the retail merchants' campaign to end the federal income tax succeeded, such campaigns formed a political counterweight to the Progressive Party's enthusiastic support for direct taxation. In this context, the federal government's room to develop the income tax was closely constrained. There had to be an income tax, but it could not become a major source of revenue. Beginning with the 1926 budget, a series of tax-cutting budgets in the late 1920s meant that federal income tax receipts fell to the point where, as tax economist Harvey Perry later wrote, "the Dominion [came] perilously close to its former dependence on the tariff and excise duties."[113]

In the story of Canada's developing fiscal capacity, the 1920s were years of awkward adolescence rather than a confident stride into maturity. The country had great expectations, to be sure. But meeting the federal government's expenses (scarcely reducing its war debt) meant taxing income at higher rates than the United States did and imposing a sales tax, which the US federal government did not do. That said, Canada before 1926 exempted some kinds of investment income from the normal income tax (charging only the high-income surtax). In the 1926 budget, two of those distinctive features would go. At the very moment when the economy and tax revenues began to improve in 1925–26, the prime minister learned from a secret Washington informant that major cuts in the American personal income tax were coming. He wrote to his finance minister to urge him to consider doing what the Americans were doing:

> [In the coming US federal budget, the] taxes on small incomes are almost wiped out. The exemption for a single person is raised from $1000

to $1500, and for a married person from $2500 to $3500. There is also a reduction of 25% for earned income, and all incomes under $5000 are conclusively presumed to be earned incomes. The net result is that a married man with a wife and two children only pays a tax of $7.50 on an income of $5000.[114]

In the April 1926 budget, Finance Minister J.A. Robb did the best that he could to match those reductions. In so doing, he was also following the advice of the CTC-CRIC experts. He kept the sales tax, but he cut personal income tax rates and raised exemptions. He matched the new American exemption for single people, but he moved the Canadian married exemption up to $3,000, not $3,500. He didn't lower rates on earned income, as the Americans had, but he won praise from farmers for putting Canadian corporate dividend payouts on the same footing as other personal income. In effect, he got some of the same political effect by *eliminating* a kind of differentiation in tax treatment of income – not by relief of earned income but by removal of a relief for one kind of investment income.[115] In that way, he made friends for the Liberals among those who thought that income taxation could be made to reflect real ability to pay. On a more pragmatic level, he made friends among the many middle-income Canadians who had been paying personal income taxes up to that point and were now free of that obligation. As a waggish reporter in Toronto pointed out, the federal income tax changes of 1926 meant that "prolonged struggles between independent spinsters and patient [tax office] clerks were but a memory."[116] With an election on the horizon, the Liberals needed political friends, and their tax changes helped.

Early in 1927, a newly re-elected Liberal administration set out to clean house in the antiquated, ill-equipped, and in places corrupt Departments of Inland Revenue and Customs and Excise. A new minister, Waterloo businessman W.D. Euler, would promise great things of his spotless new Department of National Revenue.[117] A better-enforced income tax would be a fairer one, and better enforcement could help to pay for the reductions necessary to match American income tax reductions. But Canada's federal tax regime remained more conservative than the American one: Canada continued to tax consumption. Despite the booze revenue in Canada, the federal treasury required a sales tax (with all that it meant for lower- and middle-income earners) because opponents of the federal income tax stopped it from becoming powerfully productive. The American federal income tax provided most of the national government's tax revenue and was explicitly intended to make the rich pay for public goods. Battered by its opponents, the Canadian federal income tax became merely one means, and not the most important one, to pay for the war.

The fragility of the Canadian federation, more than Canada's strength as a sovereign dominion, shaped what was fiscally possible and what would be distinctively Canadian in the path-setting 1920s. Heavy reliance on the highly regionalized and constitutionally controversial income tax was impossible. In the end, the tax that divided Canadians the least was the federal sales tax, one hidden from the public because it was levied by manufacturers rather than at the point of retail sale. From its initial rate of 1 percent, it rose to 6 percent in 1923. A tax that did not require a strong administrative state, the hidden sales tax became essential to Canada's federal tax system because of divisions over tax policy in the 1920s.

As the Canadian government struggled with difficulties of public finance, the farmers' movement generated a powerful pressure for lowered trade taxes and increased income taxes. In the west, this movement was a kind of anti-colonial one aimed at the economic exploitation of the region by a trade and fiscal policy that had been designed, until 1917, to make the region's economy subordinate to that of the industrialized centre in an integrated mercantilist system. The income tax and business profits tax fell on central Canada's industrial provinces as disproportionately as the tariff tax fell on the agrarian west, so the debate about federal finance in the 1920s was about where the burden of taxation would fall in regional terms. Taxation was deeply divisive in federal politics.

However, unlike in the United States, taxation in Canada was divisive more in regional than in partisan ways. In the 1920s in the United States, the relative roles of income and sales taxation was a starkly partisan topic. Within the Democratic Party, a national sales tax was unthinkable. A steeply progressive (i.e., "soak the rich)" income tax was a minimum demand, driven by the power of the Democrats' farmer and labour elements. In response, business Republicans mounted a fiercely anti-tax partisan attack and made opposition to the income tax central to their party identity. Strong elements within the Democratic Party wanted to use income taxation to crush monopolistic plutocracy.[118] In Canada during the 1920s, staving off the risk of public bankruptcy and balancing regional interests dominated tax considerations. Canada's third party, the Progressives, were more likely to put plutocrats in their tax-policy sights than were the federal

Liberals. The Progressives' support for the federal income tax helped to prevent Canada from going the Newfoundland route, but their impact was sufficient only to preserve the income tax, not to make it the main source of federal revenue. The federal revenue system that emerged in Canada in the 1920s, with its heavy reliance on consumption taxes (sales, tariff, and excise), was actually similar to the conservative one advocated by the Republican Party's "anti-tax" forces in those years. In other words, defenders of income taxation won the fight in the United States and pretty much lost it in Canada. Only against the income tax abolitionists was there a minor victory in Canada. Compromised by assaults from many directions, the federal income tax in Canada would take a distant third place as a contributor to federal revenues until its large-scale reformulation during the Second World War.

4
Resistance in the Interwar Years

EXPANSION OF THE FEDERAL TAX REGIME contributed to new types of tax talk in the interwar years. The regionalizing politics of the tariff did not disappear, but income tax and sales tax politics emerged to generate new lines of citizen engagement. Party politics would have to respond to both these orientations and tariff-based alignments. In some ways, the new tax politics was more clearly class politics. But class was not always the politics of a socialist or communist imaginary, with workers on one side and owners on the other. Nor were the political configurations convoked by sales and income taxes simply the people versus the plutocrats, with the former demanding income taxes and the latter pushing consumption taxes. Tax resistance in the interwar years – whether organized protest, evasion, or reform activism – came from a variety of political locations, bringing together contingent alliances of a mixed ideological complexion. Many claims of hardship circulated, and it is tempting to characterize all of it simply as a normal tendency to "grumble" amid a "benign view of taxes."[1] But to do so would be to miss the ways in which taxation was engaging Canadians in public life. In the shifting tax regimes of the interwar years, pocketbook politics, the politics driven by the immediate worries of breadwinners and household managers, would provide the basis for cross-class taxpayer alliances. In this chapter and the two that follow, I describe how the origins of the federal regime led to further developments in Canadian tax politics and distinctive forms of political agency.

The tax-centred politics of the interwar years is a complex topic, and I can only sketch some of the means by which Canadians organized tax resistance and the impacts of that resistance on electoral politics. My emphasis here is on moments of resistance when taxpayer consciousness blurred (without erasing) the clarity of differences among class standpoints. I turn next to taxpayer politics other than class. The people of a democracy are a mixed bunch, but all of them had tax interests that inspired political action. By one measure of democracy – the ability of the governed to constrain the rulers – Canadian democracy in the interwar years was robust.[2] Tax resistance had political effects. But by another measure – empowering the government to serve the needs of all, not just some, of the people – the democratic results of tax politics were not so impressive.

Class and Family in Federal Income Tax Politics

Before I began studying tax history, I took from Canada's few experts in the field the idea that the federal personal income tax in the interwar years affected only a small number of well-off Canadians.[3] I began to be puzzled, however, when I read the House of Commons debates on the 1931 budget. Agnes McPhail, a leading figure on the agrarian left, and thus an enthusiast of the progressive income tax, objected to the proposed return in 1931 to taxing "smaller incomes": "Private individuals," she pointed out, "are carrying upon their shoulders a weight which hardly can be borne, and to add to that burden a new weight would seem to be too much."[4] She wasn't talking about "the rich." I wondered again whether I had been mistaken about the class status of income tax payers when I read J.S. Woodsworth's remarks in the same debate.[5] Woodsworth, a socialist labour MP, seemed to be defending those with relatively small incomes: he worried that the proposed income tax would load "heavier burdens upon the people of moderate means." Given his politics, it is unlikely that he was deploring the burden on the richest Canadians when he protested that "when we come to matters of taxation we find the taxes are loaded upon only a few people."[6]

I began to realize that, in the remarks by these farmer-labour champions, I was hearing something like the complaint of Nellie McClung, a reformist Liberal and women's suffrage leader, who had written in 1920 that, to salaried and professional people, the postwar taxes (income and otherwise) "will mean a further lowering of the standards of living, and they become more than ever the new poor."[7] Thinking about these comments led me to look more closely at the personal income tax exemptions to see at which income levels tax liability began, with incomes not only in dollars corrected for inflation but also contextualized within the social meanings of those income levels.(For a detailed discussion of this contextualization, see the endnotes.)[8] On the basis of this closer examination, I realized that it was only during the years between 1926 and 1930, inclusive, that the federal income tax was truly a tax only on very high incomes – those of the rich. With the 1926 budget, a full 45 percent of those who had been paying federal income taxes on incomes since 1917 – people variously described as having "moderate" or "smaller" incomes – were retroactively relieved of that tax for the 1925 tax year. In the 1931 budget, it was proposed that the relief afforded in 1926 would be withdrawn. In 1932, the change was made effective for 1931, and in the 1933 budget there was a further reduction of the exempt amounts).[9] In the 1931 budget debate, then, what disturbed Woodsworth and McPhail was the proposed reduction of basic personal exemptions in the Income War Tax Act, back to their original levels. The impact, they knew, would be to exact again a federal income tax on moderate incomes.

For the federal income tax, therefore, the normal taxpayer of 1920 or 1932 was not from the same socio-economic cohort as the taxpayer of the 1925–30 tax years. During the late 1920s, income tax payers were an exceptionally prosperous lot. But before 1925 and after 1930, the majority of federal income tax payers were earners of merely good middle-class incomes. Table 3 shows the numbers of those "moderate" salaried taxpayers removed from the obligation in the late 1920s and, with data by income cohort, how significantly the population of income tax payers grew again in 1931 when exemptions were once more dropped to allow the taxation of smaller incomes. Table 4 shows the average industrial wages of supervisory and office employees, in 2016 dollars, and compares them to the 2016 dollar values of the exemptions. Clearly, the exemptions were large enough that federal personal income taxation did not reach the masses. In the early 1920s, though, supervisory and office employees who were married and childless or whose children had reached the age of twenty-one would have come within the federal income tax net if their incomes were a mere 11 percent higher than the average in their sector. Given that the "average industrial wage" includes a wide range of sectors, and does not likely match the most common (median) industrial wage, those paid at least 11 percent more than the average would have been numerous.[10] Data from 1929 on particular middle-class occupations – McGill University engineering graduates, civil servants in Ottawa and Toronto, university professors, and collegiate institute teachers in Toronto (the best-paid senior high school teachers in the country) – show that, before 1926, those married with two children and five years of service would likely have an income tax obligation (Table 5). All of those salaried professionals who were bachelors or widowers or childless would have been federal income tax payers. After 1932, most of those Canadians were again paying a small federal tax, though higher child exemptions meant that engineering grads with children would be less likely to be taxable in the early years of their careers. And at the top end of the skilled labour class – a railway engineer, typesetter, or telegrapher, for example – those who were steadily employed and childless usually fell within the taxable group.[11]

Family situation mattered enormously in determining whether these well-paid workers and salaried professionals paid any federal income tax. The generous exemptions allowed for the support of dependent children ($300 for each child before 1926, $500 until 1932, then down to $400 thereafter) reduced or eliminated tax liabilities for many middle-class parents when their children were under eighteen (before 1926) or under twenty-one (1926 and after). Between 1925 and 1930, some Canadians dropped out of the federal taxpayer cohort when their support of some further categories of dependent relatives was recognized.[12] But those without dependent children or other dependent relatives, especially if unmarried or widowed, paid a federal income tax on even a modest income.

The odds of being in that position were higher than one might expect. Although, in the world of the drafters of the income tax statute, most Canadians married, 15 percent of men in their late forties in 1917 had never married, and that remained the common pattern until 1951. The married deduction didn't automatically produce a child deduction either. About 12–13 percent of wives of childbearing age in the 1910s ended up never having children. And, if a man counted on dependent children to spare him a tax bill, then he was likely to find that those days were over at age sixty. (For a man born in the 1860s, the median age when his last child reached twenty was 59.9, sometime during the 1920s.)[13] The income tax payers of the interwar years who paid on a modest middle-class income were often single, widowed, childless, or empty-nesters, and likely university educated, but their number also included skilled labour in the best-paid industries. They were a more varied lot than the image of a tax on the rich suggests.

The prosperous middle-class payers of income tax provided only a small portion of the personal income tax collected. But it matters politically that they existed because they greatly outnumbered those who paid taxes on high incomes. In 1933–34, taxpayers with a taxable income, after the personal exemptions, of $3,000 or less outnumbered those with incomes over $25,000 by more than 100 to 1. With the married exemption lowered to $2,000, Canadians with taxable incomes of $3,000 or less in 1933–34 totalled 68 percent of taxpayers.[14] The *Toronto Daily Star* called the impact of the lowered exemption levels on "the man and woman of *modest* salary ... staggering."[15] Taxpaying voters during the interwar years were not just a small number of the rich. Before marriage and after children left home, a Canadian became an income tax payer at a middle-class income.

The demographic profile of the pre-1926 and post-1930 income tax payer is illustrated by the evidence that I gathered from the 1920s in the Exchequer Court of Canada concerning prosecutions for failure to pay taxes owed. Most of these prosecutions were for small amounts: those accused of failure to pay were thus most likely people for whom the federal income tax was a painful charge against a moderate income. Without deduction at source to enforce saving, these income tax payers had to pay the tax on the previous year's income out of the following year's income, possibly lower. Just as with the enforcement efforts of the 1920s, so too in the 1930s, through the police court rather than through the Exchequer Court, the middle sort was overrepresented.[16] Those owing federal income tax in the 1920s were mostly men in (possibly less successful) professional practice, corner grocery store owners, travelling salesmen, merchants, and even a sprinkling of better-paid single women and men from offices or railway companies. The police court records of the 1930s income tax cases do not specify amounts owed; for precise information on which incomes were involved in tax delinquencies, then, we have to rely on the Exchequer Court cases from before 1925. For example, a Hamilton dentist was still delinquent in 1922 for a 1919 tax debt that indicated a taxable income of approximately $2,600: even with three child deductions and a Mrs. deduction, his income before those personal exemptions would have just exceeded $5,000.[17] This was a respectable income, solidly middle class, to be sure, but not great wealth. In 1923, a brakeman from Big Valley, Alberta, still owed twenty-seven dollars for the 1919 tax year (indicating that he'd had a taxable income after deductions that year of at least $2,600 and a gross income before exemptions of something like $3,600, if he was single, $4,600, if a young married man). The legal costs charged to him by the Crown in its enforcement action more than doubled his originally small tax debt.[18] From another source (not Exchequer Court information), we know that a Miss Maude McLean of the Dominion Bureau of Statistics in Ottawa was an income tax payer on her 1924 income.[19] Being a woman made her an exception among taxpayers: bachelors were more likely than spinsters to earn enough to owe taxes. About 12 percent of federal income tax payers in 1929–30 were women, according to a rough estimate made in 1931 by the Department of National Revenue.[20]

What did it mean politically that the majority of federal income tax payers had middle incomes? It meant that these taxpayers were a diverse lot with different concerns. The bottom cohort, the large number who earned (or at least were taxed after exemptions on) less than $3,000, was likely to include many salaried earners, the ones whose tax liability was easy for the tax authority to see. For these earners, the federal income tax was one among many expenses that sometimes made balancing their household budgets difficult. For them, pocketbook politics – "the high cost of living" – was the focus of tax politics. Another 22.9 percent of federal income tax payers were the broad middle class, those taxed on incomes between $3,000 and $7,000 (their incomes varied in the interwar period, but the approximate 2016 values would be from $40,000 to $100,000). In this range would fall many of the business or professional people whose personal revenues might be less visible to the state; for them, the temptations of cheating and concerns about fairness between the honest man and the chiseller were important. This cohort was preoccupied with their honour and the morality of the income tax. The remaining 9.1 percent, the fewest in number, paid most of the income tax, a fact that the tax authorities pointed out every year in graphic form. This group knew that they were perceived as those who could afford to pay more. They paid, in theory, at a higher rate; however, they also had income streams in forms that, legally or not, were hard to tax. When the tax authority took aim at these forms of income, this highest-earning cohort felt discriminated against. They also worried (then as now) about a largely imaginary, sometimes racialized, population of free riders who, they claimed, paid no taxes. My point here is simply that the political meanings of income taxation varied because the political concerns and political tools of "the income tax payer" were diverse, modified by class

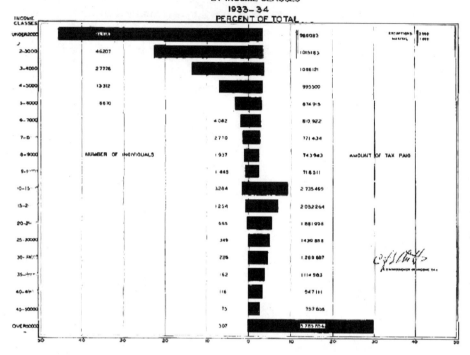

CANADA
NUMBER OF INDIVIDUAL TAXPAYERS & AMOUNT PAID
BY INCOME CLASSES
1933-34
PERCENT OF TOTAL

Every year during the 1930s, the public relations magazine of the Department of National Revenue included one of these diagrams. To the left of the centre axis, the bars represent the percentage of all taxpayers in each income class, with the smallest incomes at the top. To the right, the bars show the percentage of total tax paid by each income class. The message is clear: most of the revenue came from a small number of individuals (307 in this representation in 1935 of the receipts in 1933–34 from the 1932 tax year). Reading this one side by side with the previous years reveals much-lengthened bars to the top left and slightly shorter ones from the middle downward on the right. The longest bar to the left reaches over 45 percent. *National Revenue Review* 8, 7 (1934): 14.

(on something like a three-level, rather than a two-level, model of class) and by an array of other identities and locations.

One tool of income tax payer action, of course, was the vote. Taxpayers were a small proportion of the population, as economists and tax commissioners liked to point out. But as a percentage of urban men, an important category of voters, they were more significant in the early 1920s and again after 1932. The 1921 census data on gainfully employed males over the age of ten, minus those employed in farming, forestry, mining, fishing, and hunting, yields a balance of 1,537,369 "adult" men (in census terms). The number of income tax payers in the 1921–22 fiscal year was 290,584. On these calculations, almost twenty percent of gainfully employed urban men were federal income tax payers.[21] After the lowered exemptions of 1931–32 brought many of these taxpayers back into the taxpaying fold, a combination of intensified income tax collection and modestly improving economic conditions led to an increase in the number of federal income tax payers (300,384 in 1939, a 79.9 percent increase from the 1931 number). The increase in the number of taxpayers significantly outpaced in the same period the increase in population (which grew only 10 percent between 1931 and 1941). By 1939, there was likely a taxpayer in at least a tenth of Canadian households, most of them urban.[22]

Electorally, this group was not one to ignore, even though they were not "the people" en masse. Federal income tax payers included disproportionate numbers of well-connected and influential folk such as doctors, lawyers, small-town merchants, real estate dealers, and newspaper editors. They were mainly educated people, mostly men, likely to be active as community leaders. Their number was the greatest, so their sheer electoral weight was the heaviest in the country's more urban areas. However, in every village, town, and city across the country, they were the men and women (likely single, childless, or widowed) busy in service clubs, boards of management for churches and synagogues, chambers of commerce, councils of women, railway brotherhoods, and craft unions. Most importantly for tax politics, these people were also likely to be active in political party organizations. For example, my sample of delinquent federal income tax payers pursued by the Crown in 1922–23 included a former (and future) mayor of Vancouver, L.D. Taylor, a newspaperman (once publisher, then editor) in that city. His modest income tax debt for 1919 (not unlike the debts that had forced him to sell his newspaper in 1915) confirms that his subsequent successes in civic politics were not founded upon a substantial personal fortune.[23] His archival papers include his 1931 provincial tax return, when – as the mayor, earning $5,000 a year, and a widower – Taylor paid both provincial and federal income taxes.[24] Known as a reformer and a man of the left, he was more representative of the normal income tax payer in his social location and his resources for political power than were the handful of plutocrats whose income tax payments dominated the revenue generated by the tax.

In terms of the political impact of the income tax, Taylor's type – municipal leaders with good incomes – formed a constituency that would have had many and significant outlets in civil society for their views on taxation. They were also the sort of people who would not hesitate to write to their MP or even the finance minister if they had a complaint to make or a better idea to offer about how public finances might be managed. Whatever electoral power they had lay in their place in social networks and their role as opinion leaders.

This upper-middle-class constituency could amplify its electoral impact by speaking to the pocketbook politics that engaged lower-income groups. Those politics were expressed in letters sent to finance ministers. For example, on the eve of the pre-election budget of 1935, Finance Minister E.N. Rhodes received several suggestions from party supporters about how Conservatives could benefit politically from raising the exemptions to again relieve the lower cohort of income tax payers. In March 1935, a former assessor for the income tax branch of the Department of National Revenue, T.F. Bermingham, was invited to meet with the Department of Finance's new tax policy economist, A.K. Eaton, to present his idea for tax reform. What Bermingham had to offer turned out to be, in Eaton's view, well known: "A very large number of income taxpayers in the lower income group contributed an insignificant proportion of revenue collected." Since 1933, Bermingham had been urging the advantages from both "Revenue and Political viewpoints" of exempting those small incomes and paying for that change with a tiny increase in rates on large incomes. The electoral advantage would come, he told Rhodes, from reducing taxes on "the harassed producer" and raising them on the small number of taxpayers with incomes over $50,000 – a group numbering just over 600 whom Bermingham called "the avaricious and fortuitous." The electoral arithmetic was obvious.[25]

Another suggestion for exempting more people (and thus winning more votes) came from a man who had four children over the age of twenty, all unemployed. As his children had grown up, he had lost $2,000 worth of exemptions, and he was paying tax on much more of his income, though he was still supporting the same number of people. He suggested that there be exempt income amounts, not just for disabled children over the age of twenty, but also for unemployed ones. Finance Minister Rhodes might well have responded in person to the father, who lived in Ottawa, for there is no letter in the file. But the material for his reply surely came from a letter sent two days earlier by the commissioner of income tax, on behalf of Rhodes, to a railway union representative: exempting from tax part of the income of parents supporting their unemployed adult children was impossible simply because the state would lose too much money. The amount of income tax paid by modestly earning parents of unemployed adult children might be a small percentage of overall tax revenue, but in the dire fiscal circumstances of the 1930s, with constant deficits, both the cost and the political optics of tax exemptions were carefully calculated. Rhodes appears to have judged that capturing income tax from a middle-class constituency was important for the legitimacy of the tax, especially in the eyes of those in the higher income echelons. He was willing to attempt to convince members of the prosperous middle class, even if they had numerous family obligations, that they had an income tax responsibility, too.[26]

In that moral and practical undertaking, Rhodes faced a mighty challenge. Family exemptions were a chronic point of discussion and a source of grievance as people compared the provisions of the tax code with the realities of their family responsibilities. This was terrain where personal experiences and cultural norms rubbed up abrasively against tax policy. In the 1920s, MP Joseph Archambault, one of the Laurier Liberals, had argued that increasing the child exemption was a matter of national survival and "racial" improvement. He first argued, successfully, to have the amount of exempt income for each child raised from $200 to $300 and, then in 1923 he pressed to have it raised again to $500. He reported having had petitions signed by 15,000 fathers sent to him during the six days between March 21, 1923, when he presented his resolution to the House of Commons, and May 17, when the matter arose during debate on the budget speech. For Canada, Archambault averred, "the most desirable citizen – and I say this with due respect to those who are not such – is the Canadian-born. He is preferable to the European, the American, or even the British, because he has sprung from the soil to which he will be always attached." Permit fathers of large families to keep the income that they truly needed to raise a child (well above $500 a year, according to Archambault), and many more little Canadians would stay in Canada rather than be lured away by America's golden streets. And the French Canadian "race" would be preserved.[27]

Another emotionally charged point of contention around family exemptions was whether the married exemption belonged only to male breadwinners married to dependent wives or if it related also to the subsistence and tax obligations of a variety of responsible adults. In other words, did some relationships of support and dependency justify an "equivalent to married" level of tax exemption? Not all single people were footloose bachelors or dutiful daughters still supported in their fathers' homes, some suggested. Many others were householders with dependants. A widow or widower who supported children, an adult man or woman on whom a parent was dependent, a homeowner who employed servants in maintaining a respectable home, it was argued, all had higher subsistence costs, and by maintaining dependants and keeping up their homes they contributed to the larger social good.[28] Beginning with the 1926 tax year, as part of Finance Minister J.A. Robb's tax cuts, the federal "married" exemption had been extended to all of these groups in the form of a "householder" exemption.[29] In 1932, however, the householder exemption was abolished, and the married exemption returned to its earlier, narrower form.[30]

In response to this renewed restriction, one Ottawa civil servant wrote to Finance Minister Rhodes to complain that, after the civil servant's wife died, "I was regarded under the law as deserving no more favourable consideration or exemption than a bachelor who is not a householder. I cannot conceive how a principle of taxation can properly be defended that tends against a person owning and keeping up a home of his own."[31] A female physician from Smith Falls, Ontario, had written to Leader of the Opposition Arthur Meighen in 1924 with a somewhat more feminist version of the same complaint. She pointed out that it was being a householder, not being married, that conferred obligations. Basing tax exemptions on a sex relationship – "sex or sex conditions" – was "immoral" in her view, just as using marital status or sex as the basis for voting rights had been.[32] These worries must have been especially acute in the 1930s, when reasonably secure middle-class people (and less secure working-class people) were taking on obligations for the support of family members other than a spouse: for example, elderly parents impoverished by depleted investment income or adult children unable to get a start in life.[33] The fact that at least some municipal or provincial income taxes used householder rather than marital status as the basis for exemption underscored this issue.[34] Because the married exemption had changed and was different from government to government, the rules seemed to be arbitrary. And, depending on the family's circumstances, the 1932 restriction of exemptions in the federal income tax might have meant a sharpish pinch in the family budget at tax time. But at least as important as the dollar value of these changes was the

The four most recently raised taxes feature in the foreground in this cartoon by Manitoba's Arch Dale. There are fourteen named taxes in the gauntlet. *Winnipeg Free Press*, May 5, 1933.

"widespread irritation" that one writer, a lawyer and an MP, noted in relation to income tax regulations.[35]

Complaints about small income tax bills might seem trivial, but it was not the size of the federal income tax bill alone that was objectionable. The problem for many was that the federal income tax was one of a multitude of taxes that contributed to their household expenses. After the 1933 federal budget, this was well illustrated by an editorial cartoon in the *Winnipeg Free Press* showing the taxpayer running a gauntlet, "Ordeal by Taxes," including the federal income tax. The same cartoon, only slightly altered, signed by another cartoonist, appeared a couple of months later in a Halifax paper. This 1933 taxpayer was not the glossy municipal "citizen" seen in nineteenth-century political commentary and cartooning, fighting off the claims of spendthrift politicians or greedy workers, but a harried and threadbare "everyman," easily read as middle class or even a respectable worker.[36] The *Montreal Daily Star*'s cartoonist exploited the same theme in a cartoon on the 1932 budget in which the finance minister appears as a mischievous boy tying pots and pans to a dog's tail, each labelled with the name of a tax and several labelled "this tax," "that tax," and "the other tax." Not all Canadians were in the position of being assessed for multiple income taxes along with the many taxes introduced or increased by all levels of government during the interwar years, such as poll taxes, property taxes, household taxes, dog taxes, school taxes, meal taxes, sales taxes, special relief taxes, amusement taxes, and cheque taxes. But this multiplicity of taxes meant that tax protest was about more than just the federal income tax.

Concerns about double taxation (taxing the same income twice) were well known among the rich and in relation to corporate tax, but the cry was readily picked up in relation to personal income by organized craft workers and railway brotherhoods.[37] During the 1920s, these unions protested the taxing of their members' incomes by more than one level of government. They pointed to "inequity" in income taxation in this respect, and it was a regional rather than a class inequity. Well-paid workers in Ontario, Manitoba, British Columbia, Alberta, New Brunswick, and a few towns in Nova Scotia carried a burden that their peers elsewhere did not because in those provinces either the province or some of the cities taxed their incomes.[38] When exemption levels in the federal income tax were raised in 1926, those elite workers, along with "Mr. General Public," approved the measure.[39] In 1932, the Trades and Labour Congress of Canada, fearing (accurately) that their members were about to be brought again within the scope of federal income taxation, urged that "small salary workers' and wage earners' smaller incomes" should continue to be exempt. Although they had opposed the federal sales tax since its inception, they preferred to see it continue rather than to have those smaller incomes taxed again. And in 1932 they also preferred the sales tax to large bond issues, which, they argued, would only create further interest obligations and hence more income taxes.[40]

These unionists' criticism of tax burdens always came with the caution that tax cuts should not jeopardize necessary government spending. In both 1928 and 1932, the Trades and Labour Congress opposed the taxation of smaller incomes, but in 1932 they accepted that sales taxation was necessary if the government were to provide necessary services. Even in 1928, they cautioned against further tax cuts that "would reduce the National revenues beyond a point where provision can be made to fulfill the State's obligation to protect those who, either from old age, unemployment or sickness, find themselves unable to provide the necessities of life."[41] In contrast, the Canadian Manufacturers' Association and other critics of government extravagance urged voters to refrain from requesting services, period.[42] Voices from both left and right, however, could agree that on some matters of public spending the taxpayer was right to complain. J.S. Woodsworth, MP, presenting a labour view on the 1923 budget, aimed at a problem that animated ratepayers' associations and conservative journalists alike throughout the interwar years. The problem was the sheer quantity of government, including lieutenant governors, municipal councils, provincial legislatures, provincial senates, and government departments. Canada's population was too small to carry that much government, Woodsworth argued. "We are organized on altogether too elaborate a scale," he concluded.[43] In 1935, the *Toronto Daily Star*, at that point still sturdily a Liberal paper, illustrated the problem with a popular tax critics' trope, the heavily laden donkey. Journalist Grattan O'Leary had researched a widely reprinted four-part series in *Maclean's* in 1924 about "Ottawa's Orgy of Extravagance"; even though O'Leary was a loyal Tory, his attack on big-spending political parties included examples from Meighen's Conservatives as well as King's governing Liberals. "The cold truth," he concluded in part 3, "is that the average politician is for economy only so long as it is a cry. He will talk of retrenchment in the abstract, but he will raid the Treasury with the rapacity of Captain Kidd when it is his own riding or his own pet project that needs to be buttressed by dollars."[44] And of course, during the King years, Conservative papers such as the *Montreal Daily Star* saw waste everywhere, though particularly in spending on the government railway system.[45]

On the tax system's weight, its poor fit with varying family responsibilities, and its inequity across jurisdictions, voters across the political spectrum could agree. On spending, they agreed on the evils of waste but sometimes disagreed on what counted as waste. In the 1930s, the federal income tax was making national taxpayers not only of big business and the rich but also elements of the Canadian middle class and labour elite. They petitioned, they prepared platforms, they discussed the value of public services and the scope of the state, and they voted – as members of families,

The strapping young gardener here wields a hoe labelled "National Government" to res-
cue the "Industrial Garden" choked by weeds of selfish partisanship, debt, burdensome
taxation, extravagance in government, unemployment, and sundry other worries of the
mid-1930s. *Canada's Economic Woes,* c. 1935, McCord Museum, Paintings, Prints, and Drawings Collection, Arthur
George Racey fonds, M2005.23.179. © McCord Museum.

The Donkey: I guess I'm just plain ass, or I wouldn't be led around with an unnecessary load like this on my back

The international symbol for the taxpayer for many decades was the beast of burden, usually a donkey. Here, in Sam Hunter's rendition, the burden is an assortment of government institutions (nothing said here about social services). The reins are "political pull" attached to a "party collar." *Toronto Daily Star,* May 1, 1935, 4.

as members of organizations, and as taxpayers. In all of these ways, they were acting as citizens.

Class Variations in BC and Quebec Tax Politics

Although income tax issues could bring the less class conscious among well-paid workers together with middle-class people as worried household managers, and mix concerns about federal income tax with worries about other levels and kinds of taxation, being a Canadian taxpayer was not yet a mainly national experience. There remained regional varieties of tax culture. In the interwar years, there were still provincial differences (and indeed broadly regional patterns) in taxation practices. These differences always had some connection originally to Canada's regional variations in land, labour, and capital, but local tax traditions also had some independent effects on what people could imagine as possible or just. The western critique of the tariff as a tax is well known. But there were other distinctive local tax practices and ideas. Municipal income taxation in Ontario and New Brunswick, on the one hand, and significant provincial income taxation in British Columbia and Manitoba, on the other, put the double taxation of income on the agenda for more people in those provinces than in others during the 1920s and 1930s.[46] The nature of land markets; the scope of road, rail, or water transportation; the number of head offices; the traditions of smuggling; the different concentrations of inherited wealth – all of these and other factors shaped provincial tax regimes. Place – as political community, as economic base, and as institutional inheritance – is a big part of Canadian tax culture. Here I will illustrate this assertion with two stories of tax resistance and response: the story of the "Jones" income tax in British Columbia (part of a broader and distinctively western Canadian pattern)[47] and the sales tax revolt in Verdun, Quebec.

Calling the 1931 special revenue tax in British Columbia the Jones tax was not a term of endearment. J.W. Jones, the provincial finance minister who ushered it in, defended it stoutly and saw himself as a heroic man of principle in so doing, but he was almost alone in that view. A legion of critics inside his party as well as many opponents saw the tax as cruel or politically stupid or both. The tax was proposed in March 1931 and, with some modifications, implemented the next month as an amendment to the provincial income tax, ostensibly to raise revenue for spending on education. Jones proposed by means of this new tax to help relieve the burden on municipal property tax payers who were supporting education and other "social services" without help from "that section of the population that benefits most from Government services" – a phrase that referred mainly to wage earners and their dependants.[48] The most controversial part of the Jones tax was the wages tax, 1 percent clipped from every pay packet. Professional and business income would eventually be taxed this additional 1 percent as well, but only on annual income, after it was earned, and the doctor's or realtor's or building contractor's expenses deducted. Farmers' incomes were exempt. For wage earners, the particularly objectionable feature of the tax was that it would be collected by the employer weekly, regardless of how much the earner would end up being paid over the course of the year. So, if you earned in a single week a rate of pay that, if continued over a year, would make you taxable, then your employer would deduct some tax from your pay envelope. If your actual annual income ended up being too low to be taxable, then you could apply to get it back as a refund – but only after the province had determined that too much had indeed been collected from you.[49] The wait for a refund was especially long because there were "enormous numbers," probably tens of thousands, of refunds to be made, "many hundreds" of which resulted from disputed assessments.[50]

Charging people a tax that they did not owe (even if refunding it later) was an egregious error in judgment in a year when so many were having difficulty getting by. Men and women who had been unemployed for months, perhaps building up debts at the grocery store and with landlords, perhaps using up their small savings to help support an elderly parent or unemployed sibling, had scarce pennies or dollars taken by the Jones tax from their first small paycheque.[51] People who had nothing to spare after food, housing, heat, and medicine were being told to contribute to the needs of British Columbians on relief, the social service that Jones repeatedly emphasized when he replied to complaints. Many who wrote to protest acknowledged that they wanted to help the unemployed and admitted that they were at least temporarily better off than the jobless – but by so little and with such insecurity.[52] Casual workers and their employers were particularly incensed. Even a worker who would get only a few weeks of work would lose some income to the Jones tax.[53]

Criticism came from many different points on the class and ideological spectrum. Employers disliked both the paperwork and dealing with distressed employees. One employer urged a widowed clerk, the sole support of her mother, to write to Jones to see if he would specially exempt her from the tax. The employer had already cut her wages and now had to reduce her pay even further by deducting the tax. She believed that she really couldn't pay the sixty-nine cents a month ($11.23 in 2016 dollars) that she owed.[54] Another employer had decided that he himself would pay the monthly sixty-four cents that his one employee owed in tax. He was not against the tax but did not like to take it from his employee. What he resented most was "making out a report in duplicate every month and enclosing a cheque for 64 cents. It will cost me another 64 cents in time lost to my business."[55] Larger firms also found the labour of reporting the tax expensive.[56]

These letters and others like them got respectful replies from Jones, who defended the need for the tax and regretted that no exemption was possible. He didn't reply to the Canadian Women's Labor League letters, from the communist left, equally expressing distress and anger. Jones likely had no sympathy for the critical view of the economic system that accompanied their concerns: they wrote that his tax was an attempt "to force the poor workers to shoulder the responsibility of the crisis which is a product of decaying capitalism."[57] But those on the communist left were far from alone in their outrage. Another critic wrote from a standpoint in liberal democratic territory. He quoted the *Rubaiyyat of Omar Khayam,* referred to the Constitution and the Bible, and called the Jones tax "the most dastardly affront ever offered to a supposedly democratic people." Jones's "sanctimonious bleatings" drew his wrath.[58] The challenges to the tax came from almost every colour on the political spectrum.[59] In response to the many criticisms lobbed his way in mid-March 1931, Jones raised the exempt weekly income amount to fifteen dollars from the original twelve dollars for single earners and added an exemption of twenty-five dollars for married people, partly paying for these changes with a quarter percent increase in the province's corporation tax.[60] His deputy minister had recommended that no income at all be exempt, so public pressure had been somewhat effective.[61] But Jones continued to defend the slightly revised version of his tax for the next two years.

The tax had been designed and administered in a remarkably hamhanded way. What was Jones thinking? It was certainly not that this tax would balance the province's books. Although there was much talk in the early 1930s of the importance of balanced budgets and the need to avoid extravagance, Jones did not expect the revenue from this tax to fund all of the necessary relief spending. His 1931–32 budget included a new consolidated revenue loan of $2 million – the province was operating at a significant deficit.[62] To do so, he needed to ensure that the province could continue to borrow money. Borrowed money was the real source of unemployment relief spending (and of future development spending), and to keep the loans flowing Jones needed to protect provincial credit. To do so, he had to show lenders that the province was making the maximum tax effort. Thus, when Jones defended the special revenue tax in 1931–33, he pointed out that the immediate effect of the tax had been to change for the better the market position of provincial bonds – and thus to improve the province's ability to borrow again.[63]

Borrowing required credit, and the provincial credit, founded upon the great resource potential of British Columbia, had long been perceived, like the credit of its businesses, as somewhat risky.[64] The 1934 Treasury files contain an example, admittedly an extreme one, of a bearish view of the prospective value of British Columbia to investors. It is an excerpt from a London investment newsletter dated 1881 that disparages Canadian bonds in general (except those of Ontario) and describes British Columbia as "a barren, cold, mountain country that is not worth keeping … Fifty railroads would not galvanize it into prosperity."[65] During the 1920s, massive development projects, such as the draining of Sumas Lake, had challenged that description but had also enlarged provincial debt.[66] By 1931, fifty years after British Columbia joined Confederation, the legacy of thirty-seven years of deficit budgets had left the province with a larger debt and higher interest payments than any province other than Ontario (which included Ontario Hydro's debt). British Columbia's interest payments in 1931 were higher even than those of the much more populous province of Quebec. Even in prosperous 1927, British Columbia's debt had been 91 percent of Quebec's, and British Columbia had paid out almost as much in interest on its debt that year as had Quebec on its debt.[67]

BC finance ministers had had to continue to save in order to borrow. More completely than in other provinces, the debt in British Columbia was backed by a sinking fund, revenue reserved to pay off provincial bonds at maturity.[68] This was a point of pride, but it was also a result of international investors' caution. In 1903, the British government, under the Colonial Stock Act, had required that British Columbia make a specific series of payments to the sinking fund of its 3 percent bonds maturing in 1941. By 1931, this requirement was costing the BC government $100,000 a year.[69] As Jones observed in his 1932 budget speech, investment banks insisted that, without sinking funds, British Columbia's long-term securities could be sold only on "prohibitive terms": that is, with deep discounts from par or high interest rates. A broker at investment firm Wood Gundy told Jones privately that the sinking fund was "the only real selling fact" for BC bonds.[70]

Since 1923, the sinking fund had been maintained by money from ordinary tax receipts.[71] Tax revenue therefore did more than generate funds to make interest payments on the provincial debt; it also helped to make that debt attractive by building the sinking fund and thus removing any doubt about the safety of investing in BC bonds. Even in the hardest moments of the Depression, Finance Minister Jones continued to allocate revenues to the sinking fund to protect the province's credit and thus avoid what he called "financial chaos – political chaos."[72] Even though British Columbia's per capita rate of taxation from all sources, between thirty-four and thirty-five dollars for most of the 1920s, was by far the highest of any Canadian province (almost double that of Alberta and four times that of Prince Edward Island), in the early 1930s Jones needed to keep and extend all possible taxes in order to sell bonds and secure short-term loans from the province's bank.[73]

In this, Jones was following the bank's explicit instructions. The Bank of Commerce's general manager wrote to him in November 1931, after revenue from the new tax had begun to come in, to say that the province could not expect more credit unless it could show realistic projections of improved tax revenue.[74] British Columbia was in a far deeper fiscal hole than could be filled by the revenue from the 1 percent income tax. In spite of all the objections the Jones tax aroused, keeping it was necessary to convince the banker and prospective buyers of provincial bonds that the province had neglected no source of tax revenue. Managing the appearance of sound finances was at least as important as actually balancing the books. Initiated to reassure property tax payers, businesses, and wealthier individuals that the poor were contributing their bit, the special revenue tax was also a public relations move aimed at the province's creditors. Similar public relations efforts continued in the fall of 1932 as Jones and his allies sought to moderate the national investment dealers' association's pessimistic statements about BC finances.[75] Allies pointed out to national investment dealers that Jones had "made larger economies than any other" government and that, during the Depression, "proper taxation" and "adjustments" from the dominion government were really what was required, not more spending cuts.[76] When investment dealers cast aspersions on British Columbia's finances, Jones capped his defence by pointing to his new income tax measures: "Our recent amendment to the [provincial] Income Tax Act has increased the number of Income Tax ratepayers from 40,000 to 115,000, chiefly brought about by the 1% Tax."[77]

Note that it was the larger number of income tax payers, not the dollars of revenue, that Jones claimed as the virtuous result of taxing small incomes. Similarly, in defending his tax to the Vancouver Board of Trade, he urged that the board see it as a measure of fairness and equity to business interests, which deserved help from a "larger group of taxpayers" in carrying "the burden."[78] In a 1931 memo, his deputy minister had referred to "the purpose" of the tax as "spreading the burden over the greatest number who enjoy community benefits."[79] And in the 1932 budget speech, Jones took credit for bringing in as "contributors" people who had formerly been "free of taxes."[80] When he was challenged about the moral problems entailed in taxing the subsistence incomes of the poor, he replied that all citizens had to do their bit and "contribute their mite to the pot. All take the benefits, why not all help to bear, as they may, in the cost." Taxes were no different, he argued, than the bills that every worker and salaried man would honour when presented by the coal merchant or doctor. "All people," not just "the rich man" or the property owner, had to share the costs of social services that served everyone. It was not reasonable to expect the wealthy to continue to increase their contributions when others did not.[81]

To his supporters, these arguments were convincing because they thought that the working poor had to be taught that the benefits of public provision are never free. As a Winnipegger wrote later in the decade, to impose a progressive income tax that reached every income "from the smallest to the highest" was desirable because "fewer services will be asked for if every wage earner in the city has to bear a portion of the cost of these services."[82] Those who thought of the poor as free riders were impressed by the defence of the tax articulated by Jones.[83] They saw him as protecting the principle of "no representation without taxation."[84] This view of income tax was not that of the Progressives, of income tax as a means of moderating regressivity in the tax system through a direct tax based upon the ability to pay. Rather, the Jones tax used income tax as a means of putting a price on citizen rights, especially the rights of those who owned no taxable real property. Think of it as a "show them the price," as distinct from "soak the rich," style of income taxation.

Even among substantial property owners, however, that view struck some as mistaken. In particular, two Conservative Party insiders, both active in boards of trade, chastised Jones for the political and moral folly of the 1 percent tax. One was J.E. Sladen of the Saanich Board of Trade. Signing his letter with his Oxford University MA credentials, Sladen wrote an effective rebuttal to the claim that payers of the 1 percent tax were formerly free riders: he pointed out that the "poor man" pays his taxes indirectly when he buys matches or sugar. And, he noted, non–income tax payers paid another form of direct tax, the poll tax. Once the income that a labourer needs to live on is taxed, then "theoretically," and here Sladen drew on the tax theory of Jean-Baptiste Say, "the Government will help kill him if it collects a single cent." On moral grounds alone, Sladen thought that the Jones tax was "indefensible." But also, as a supporter of Tolmie's Conservative government, he thought that it was unwise electorally. Not only would the new income tax payers object, but also, like other employers, Sladen thought the tax unwise because it would inevitably cause friction between them and their employees. That was a lot of voters to offend.[85] The electoral theme was also emphasized by J.F. Noble, an important Conservative and Vancouver Board of Trade activist. The 1931 budget would be an "unhappy" one, Noble wrote, because of its impact on "the flapper vote": he argued that the Jones tax, as a "universal" income tax, would be felt by those who "are adversely affected for the first time, by an income tax." Even if the party's other economic and fiscal policies were impressive, he suggested, the symbolic flappers "do not grasp the exactions of Provincial finance, but are very sensitive to a personal touch."[86] Noble was right: among the many who wrote to Jones or Tolmie, the voice of the single woman was indeed heard, though not in terms that one might expect from a frivolous flapper. One woman wrote that "in reading over your income tax constitution in the evening paper I failed to notice anything about girls that have dependents [sic] [and] who are making under $25.00 per week. I have the responsibility of a married man and I make [$]85.00 per month. I pay the rent and support my mother. I think that I should be exempt."[87]

Sladen and Noble were not the only BC Conservatives to criticize the Jones tax.[88] In their public positions, however, BC businesspeople sympathetic to the Conservatives tended to call for spending cuts more than they criticized taxes on the near destitute. The highlight of the cost-cutting campaign was the report of a committee struck by the Conservative government at the instigation of its business supporters. The Kidd Report, as the committee's 1932 report was known, insisted that more taxation was impossible and that major reductions in provincial spending were necessary. Among the many items of spending that they targeted for elimination were free public education for children over fourteen and the provincial police force.[89] The Vancouver Board of Trade followed these questions closely, repeatedly meeting with and writing to Finance Minister Jones on "the need for economy" during 1932.[90] Groups such as the Taxpayers' Economy League emerged and, along with individuals writing on their own, filled the mailboxes of the premier and opposition leader with screeds against government waste, supplementing contributions on that theme from more established voices such as the Canadian Manufacturers' Association.[91] But Jones stood his ground. He made some minor modifications to the tax in 1932, but he was adamant about the need for increased revenues and not just reduced expenditures.[92]

Jones had been warned that the 1 percent tax would cost him votes, and, though elections are never decided on a single issue, the Jones tax no doubt influenced the provincial election of 1933, in which he and his party were defeated. But he had campaigned unapologetically for his increased taxes.[93] The Liberal government that succeeded the Tolmie Conservatives made much of their opposition to the tax, to the point that some voters believed that the Liberals had rescinded it. They had not done so. They had only mitigated its impact, removing the deduction at source for singletons' incomes below fifty dollars per month (and a few months later raising the exemption to sixty dollars), and provided children's exemptions for married taxpayers. For both married and single people, the tax was potentially reduced further when certain forms of savings were allowed as reductions to taxable income. The effect of these measures was to stop deductions being made from the pay packets of the poorest earners.[94] The political system had provided a channel for the expression of tax protest and had enabled the partial reversal of that conservative project of making an income tax "universal" so as to heighten resistance to public spending. The fact remained, though, that the Jones tax continued, even after defeat of the Conservatives. The Liberal government did not eliminate it. The tax kept its nickname until 1941, when it disappeared into the wartime dominion-provincial tax agreements.[95] It seems likely that the Liberals kept the tax because they, too, watched the province's credit and knew that their bankers expected maximum tax effort as a condition of credit.

The Jones tax was only the first of a series of similar changes or increases through 1932 and 1933 in provincial taxation of income, at increasingly low levels of exemption, in the western provinces. The prairie provinces, like British Columbia, faced challenges to their credit and likely similar sorts of tax protest.[96] Only further research can describe fully the responses met by those taxes on small incomes. But it is worth noting briefly that a Manitoba wages tax inspired street protests and then a constitutional challenge, *Forbes v. The Attorney General of Manitoba*.[97]

The bringer of the court challenge, James Forbes, was a modestly paid federal civil servant employed by the Department of Agriculture at an annual wage of $1,347. His lawyer argued that the Manitoba special revenue tax (1933) offended on the ground of the doctrine of instrumentalities but in the reverse order of the parties in *Caron*: the claim in *Forbes* was that the province had no right to tax the incomes of federal employees. Forbes therefore refused to pay the $20.80 he owed for the 1933 tax year.[98] While the case wound its way through the courts, from county to province to Canada and finally to Westminster, the dominion held that it could not collect the tax on behalf of the province. Thus, none of the approximately 2,700 to 3,000 federal employees in Manitoba was forced to pay it. Yet the provincial government really wanted to collect this tax from these people. An estimated $250,000 to $300,000 in tax revenue was at stake, not merely the $20.80 from Forbes. Without compulsion, how many paid the tax? According to the *Winnipeg Free Press,* of those whose tax bills depended on the outcome of the case, an estimated 200 to 300 "voluntarily paid the tax."[99] Perhaps some of that number were just being prudent, avoiding a future bill for tax arrears if the judgment finally went against Forbes. Perhaps some of them were persuaded, as Jones had argued in British Columbia, that this was a time when they should pay not just their share but also their utmost.[100] At a time when paying this tax entailed the actual handing over of cash, these 200–300 federal employees might have embraced the duty to contribute willingly, even (or especially) in hard times.

These stories from western Canada show the willingness of governments in that region to tax income, a sign of the electoral power and cultural weight of the farmers and the single tax movement. Taxing small incomes also showed how local elites sought to make lower-income people carry more of the direct tax burden, a strategy that probably also reflected the relatively small population and even smaller cohort of high-income earners compared with Ontario and Quebec. The provincial income tax introduced in Ontario in 1936 (replacing its municipal income tax) and the new municipal income taxes introduced in Quebec in 1935, in contrast, resembled the federal income tax, with its higher exemption and annual payment, and thus avoided the fury of the many smaller earners. In Verdun, Quebec, however, a sales tax generated responses like those that the Jones tax had ignited in British Columbia.

Class and Taxation in Urban Quebec

The story of the Verdun sales tax revolt resembles that of the BC Jones tax in that an unpopular tax ended up playing a part in unseating an incumbent government. But the resistance in Verdun was both more organized and more covert because of the different type of tax (sales versus income) and the constitutional culture of taxation in Quebec. In contrast to British Columbia, which taxed a wide array of its citizens in various ways, including income and per capita taxes (poll taxes), Quebec was a low-tax regime. Its two greatest sources of revenue were consumption taxes on, relatively speaking, luxury items: vehicles and liquor (see Table 6). Getting consent for more intrusive forms of direct taxation was even harder in Quebec in the 1930s than it was in British Columbia. Nonetheless, at the depth of the Depression, new taxes were ineluctable even in wealthy Quebec and in spite of the important church contributions to social services. With arrears on real estate taxes in Montreal amounting to 43 percent of the city's annual budget, the city needed to find sources of income other than property tax in order to pay out interest on its bonds. Indeed, in spite of the measures taken in 1935, the city's continuing fiscal problems would lead to its defaulting on a bond issue and a bank loan in the spring of 1940.[101] In 1935, attempting to prevent default, the Province of Quebec passed a law allowing the City of Montreal to tax retail sales and income. To prevent local "cross-border shopping" and relocation of high-income households, the legislation allowed Montreal to collect the two new taxes in eleven neighbouring municipalities and subsequently to distribute the revenue to those neighbours. Like the federal income tax, the Montreal one exempted low-wage earners, so it was the sales tax that touched working-class interests most directly.[102]

The mayor of one of those municipalities, Hervé Ferland of Verdun, spearheaded the fight, launching a protest against the sales tax in July 1935. The tax was a bread-and-butter question for Ferland. He was a merchant

– his shop was Ferland Corset – and his customers were women, buying underwear and stockings. He might well have thought that the sales tax would keep many of his customers at home mending and darning rather than visiting his shop and spending.[103] He claimed that he spoke for the workers, and, indeed, criticism of sales taxes had long been a labour position. Joining forces with him were the Foyer ouvrier ("The Workers' Home"), the Association municipale de Verdun (probably a ratepayers' association), and the Parti ouvrier du Canada (a labour party).[104] They held public meetings, circulated a petition, and encouraged merchants to pledge and to advertise that they would not collect the sales tax. Four hundred and sixty-five merchants signed the pledge. When merchants were charged with failing to collect the tax, Ferland hired a bus to take his fellow tax protesters (thirty-six of them) to the courthouse. They took a group photo, almost all of them wearing suits on what was undoubtedly a hot July day. On legal advice, Ferland argued that the tax was not only a hardship for his business and his customers but also outside the constitutional jurisdictions of the city and province. This was the first municipal sales tax in Canada. He argued that it was an indirect tax and thus, in terms of the BNA Act, a kind of tax levied legally only by the federal government.[105]

Feelings ran high during July and August 1935. Montreal's *La Patrie* reported sympathetically on the campaign. It presented Ferland in heroic terms: for example, "Mr. Ferland Will Not Be Intimidated."[106] Its news stories spelled out his constitutional arguments in some detail. It reported as harassment the visits to his shop by tax inspectors. At various stores in Verdun, tax inspectors bought things "undercover," refused to pay the tax, and then laid charges against the merchant because he or she did not force them to pay it. Even the unsympathetic Toronto *Globe* reported the arrest of a young man who had offered Ferland a rich bribe ($2,000 – over $34,000 in 2016 dollars) to cease his campaign. Two members of the labour organization raising money to finance the tax protesters' legal costs found themselves up on rather vague charges in the Recorder's Court (the equivalent of a police court). When they were able to put up bail money, the judge speculated that they were funded by Moscow. Then, on August 6, 1935, 110 cases against Verdun merchants were adjourned until the province's Supreme Court could rule on whether the Recorder's Court had jurisdiction in the constitutional matters that Ferland had raised.[107] Over September and October, a series of legal manoeuvres by Ferland managed to delay a decision. Finally, on October 25, he announced that he wouldn't continue his battle in the courts. Premier L.A. Taschereau had asked him to let it go and apparently reassured him that the legislation would be amended during the next session of the legislature. *La Patrie* published a long letter from Ferland in which he vowed to continue to criticize the tax as a citizen and mayor, even though he would now collect it as a merchant.[108] The campaign did not hurt his popularity as mayor either: he was re-elected and served until 1939.[109]

Opposing the sales tax was a good cause for a populist. The new premier, Maurice Duplessis of the Union nationale, picked up on the anti–sales tax campaign's momentum and in December 1936 supported the promise of Montreal mayoral candidate, Union nationale MLA Adhémar Raynault, to abolish the sales tax. This was a popular promise. Hervé Ferland had certainly known that: he aspired to higher political office and had linked his protest to the Action libérale nationale, briefly allied with Duplessis. In the federal election in October 1935, Ferland would run as an independent, gaining almost 17 percent of the vote when the winning Conservative candidate won just over 22 percent and the second-place CCFer won almost 19 percent. Although Ferland was not elected to Parliament, Duplessis's candidate, Raynault, won the Montreal mayoral office, defeating Camilien Houde, under whose administration the sales tax had been introduced.[110]

Telling Canadian tax history only with examples from Ontario leaves much untold. On this topic at least as much as on other aspects of Canadian history, place matters in ways that make a national narrative hard to find. In the story of the Jones tax, class rhetoric was open and heated; in the Verdun tax revolt, a rhetoric of community and a reliance on constitutional law overrode class. These observations do not unsettle our ideas of regional culture, but they do suggest that we must understand tax capacity as not merely an economic measure. Which taxes are easy to collect and which are difficult, which laws are easy to pass and which meet resistance, are matters of culture. These cultures are partly regional, not purely or simply national.

The Political Meanings of Tax Resistance in the 1930s: National Difference and Democracy

Examining regional tax resistance, however, does help us to think about national comparisons and national culture. The American municipal tax strikes in the 1930s have been depicted by historian David Beito as conservative, anti-statist struggles, revolts of beleaguered property owners defending individual rights against ever-growing, socialist, and sometimes corrupt municipal governments.[111] In contrast, Ferland's range of allies at the start of the Verdun tax strike reminds us that tax resistance can just as easily be supported by left-wing labour as by right-wing business. A closer analysis of more cities' municipal tax politics during the Depression would confirm or correct the impression from the Verdun case. For example, the largely working-class community of East York Township protested the tax burden of relief spending, not because they thought that relief was too generous, but because working-class members of the ratepayers' associations (members themselves on relief) were losing their homes to tax sales, and others, still employed, were paid such "scandalously low wages" that they had no surplus income.[112]

Among Canadian cities, Winnipeg vividly demonstrated the political varieties of tax resistance. The multi-ethnic, largely working-class North Winnipeg Taxpayers' Association planned a tax strike in April 1937 independently of the ethnically homogeneous Home and Property Owners' Association, itself considering the same action. The latter, more business-dominated group blamed their tax troubles on the unemployed, whereas the North End organization, like its socialist alderman, Jack Blumberg, urged more city jobs for people at risk of losing their homes because they could not afford to make even small payments on their tax arrears. Notably, the North Winnipeg Taxpayers' Association elected six married women to its seventeen-member board of directors in 1937, a gender composition that might have meant that household budgets (including boarding house budgets), more than business interests, were at the foreground of that organization's project.[113] The presence in cities like Winnipeg of many low-income homeowners and small businesses, and the importance for some businesses (landlords, small retailers) of working-class clientele, encouraged a cross-class protest against property tax. That said, given that so much municipal spending in the 1930s was on relief for the unemployed, a

In Toronto in 1939, journalist William Weston was a voice of the angry investor. This cartoon illustrated one of several articles that he published in *Saturday Night* magazine in 1939. William Weston, "The Tax-Paying Worm Begins to Turn," *Saturday Night,* January 21, 1939, 7.

mainly working-class constituency, the "tax uproars" of the mid-1930s tended to be led by substantial property-owning anti-statists who targeted as blameworthy the so-called extravagance of governments and the supposedly irresponsible demands of the non-property-owning public[114] (see Figure 4.5). Beito might have overlooked the variety of tax revolt ideologies as he cheered on the anti-statist tax resisters in some cities of the United States. In his central case, Chicago, he acknowledges, tax resistance went further than it did elsewhere, partly because the municipal tax authority there was exceptionally corrupt. It might be that a narrative of "Americans" on this subject misrepresents the country's homogeneity as much as a story of "Canadian" tax resistance does in Canada.

It seems likely that in the United States, as in Canada, the political hue of a tax revolt or resistance depended on matters such as timing, the particular tax in question, and the legal context of the jurisdiction. Nonetheless, there is more to say than that the United States was probably as diverse as Canada. The municipal tax resistance efforts of the 1930s in Canada were ambiguous enough in their meanings that opinion leadership by the press must surely have played a part in determining their political weight. Two of Canada's most influential newspapers took a recognizably Canadian line on the subject. While *La Patrie* was somewhat sympathetic to the Verdun strike, and Toronto's muckraking *Hush* tabloid was happy to incite revolt, the Toronto *Globe* offered no comfort to tax strikers, whether of the right or of the left. In August 1936, as rumours of a possible tax strike in York Township circulated, the *Globe*'s editorialists asserted that "the thought should not be given a start." It was "mob rule." (Shades of loyalist John Beverley Robinson!) Strikes only provided, dangerously, ammunition to those who thought that the masses were irrational and should never have been allowed to vote. Admittedly, the taxpayer "should not have to hand over one-third of his income for others to spend." But "the property owner and taxpayer is the one who should be most concerned with the preservation of law and order." The *Globe* editorialists concluded that taxpayers had "no right to go on strike. There are orderly ways of settling these problems."[115] And the influential *Winnipeg Free Press* was even less friendly to tax revolt talk by the propertied. Responding to the city's narrowly averted tax strike, the paper rebutted the claim that taxes were too heavy. Editorial writer, reporter, and former grain trader James H. Gray produced a four-part series explaining the benefits to taxpayers of the services that the city provided using taxpayers' dollars. A representative headline was "Citizens

Cross: Taxpayers May Howl but They Do Get Something for Money."[116] When President F.D. Roosevelt was chastising some American newspapers for endorsing tax evasion, two of Canada's most influential daily journals confirmed every cliché about Canada's political culture: calling for peace and order and defending good government.

More than just a few major newspaper editorials were influencing the different importance and interpretation of tax resistance in the 1930s in these two neighbouring countries. In particular, the impact of the end of prohibition late in 1932 was not paralleled in Canada. In the United States, the end of prohibition was as important in the framing of tax politics as its beginning had been. The end helped to relieve the fiscal crises of municipalities, which in both countries were foundering on the collapse of credit markets, soaring relief expenditures, and decimated property tax revenues. In the United States, but not in Canada, the repeal of prohibition provided a timely new stream of revenue to both the states and the federal government. Alcohol tax revenue meant that the states were able to increase assistance to municipalities, reducing some of the pressure on the federal government for assistance that, in Canada, continued to be fierce until war mobilization.[117] Federally, US revenues were also buoyed by the new booze dollars. Between 1933 and 1934, federal revenues grew by an astonishing 59.6 percent in the United States, and the percentage contribution of almost every tax revenue stream except the alcohol excise shrank or grew only slightly (estate and gift taxes). By 1936, the federal alcohol excise generated 13 percent of total tax collections, almost as much as personal income tax had generated in 1934 (14 percent).[118] Meanwhile, in Canada, increased tax effort and the beginning of recovery raised federal revenues between 1933 and 1934 by only 6.9 percent. It would not be until 1937 that Canada's federal tax revenues would see the kind of increase relative to 1933 that the United States enjoyed in the one year between 1933 and 1934.[119]

Rather than easing tax tensions, however, the end-of-prohibition windfall led to a new and more bitter assault on the US federal income tax. Opponents of prohibition, some of them originally supporters, had come to see it as the reason why their substantial incomes were being significantly taxed. With the repeal of prohibition, they expected income tax relief, and they got none. In contrast, in Canada, none of their wealthy peers had any expectation of tax reduction in 1932–33, so whatever the resentments of rich Canadians (and other income tax payers), their political emotions were not inflamed by dashed expectations. What quickly followed in the

United States from the disappointment of the repealers was an anti-tax campaign framed as a constitutional issue: repeal of the Sixteenth Amendment, the legal foundation of the federal income tax. Prohibition had been enabled by the Eighteenth Amendment, and its opponents had successfully orchestrated the repeal of that bit of constitutional law. If they could repeal one part, then why not another? Framing the assault on income tax as a movement of constitutional reform gave it an ideological freight and a broadly appealing coloration of high principle that the few Canadian constitutional cases on income tax never acquired. For Americans, the repeal of income tax, like the repeal of prohibition, could be made to be about liberty. In Canada, the constitutional question was only ever about federalism, and the prospect of changing the Constitution was impossibly remote. Administration and interpretation of the Constitution needed serious revision, but that was the work of lawyers and statesmen, not the stuff of a popular campaign such as had led to the end of the Eighteenth Amendment in the United States. Moreover, the Canadian Constitution was British law and thus protected from tinkering by democratically elected colonial politicians. In Canada in the 1930s, working within the current system was a virtue enforced by necessity. In the United States, the leaders of what Isaac Martin has called "rich people's movements" could rally their fellow citizens to a project of self-government through constitutional change that appeared, however deceptively, to be, thrillingly, about democracy.[120]

In Canada, the North American currents of tax resistance took an explicitly anti-democratic form, instead, one expressed in campaigns against party politics. Anti-tax protest from below could be seen as an example of how too much democracy had played a role in creating the fiscal woes of the day by allowing majority voting both for overspending and for undertaxing. For the usually powerful, it must have been worrisome that the federal government relented in the face of a vocal protest by farmers against the 1931 budget's two-cent cheque tax that applied to the small credit chits – creamery tickets – paid to them (or to their wives) by local dairies. Through a torrent of letters, and with the help of their federal MPs, a combination of farmers, local dairies, dairy associations, and local merchants won an exemption from the tax for cheques under five dollars.[121] Prime Minister Bennett and Finance Minister Rhodes seem to have recognized that, in this case at least, forcing the poor to pay was not worth the cost to Conservatives in electoral support. Such signs of voter power among the masses, and experiences such as the defeat of Finance Minister Jones in British Columbia and Mayor Houde in Montreal at the hands of angry lower-income voters and their allies alarmed the (mainly) well-to-do, who thought that electoral politics hadn't produced a good enough response to their concerns about expenditures. But there was also a critique of electoral politics from the left and in less easily categorized locations such as the Social Credit movement. Solutions such as group government appealed to the feeling in the farmers' movement that party politics was just an exercise in cynical cronyism in which the collusion of successive parties was purchased by money.[122] The labour movement in Newfoundland was so discouraged about party politics that some were willing to see responsible government suspended.[123] Neither grassroots populists nor business elites were convinced that democratic electoral politics was working.

In the 1930s, the elite version of this opposition to party politics took shape in the National Government movement, a conservative tendency that criticized party politics in fiscal terms. "Canada before Party" was their slogan. They criticized parties for being not a means to democracy but a means to serving party insiders: "A truly democratic government is one by the people, for the people, and not by [the] party, for the party." Party politics had "placed such a staggering load upon the taxpayer's shoulders that the burden is well-nigh unbearable."[124] As Don Nerbas has shown, the biggest Canadian corporate leaders (presidents of railways, steel companies, utilities companies, and banks) considered National Government favourably during the early 1930s.[125] In Montreal, the CPR's Edward Beatty was one of its advocates, and in Toronto the public face of the League for National Government, Basil B. Campbell, appears to have parlayed his political activity in this cause of the wealthy into a position with a major Toronto gold mine promoter in 1936.[126] National Government was one-party government of only the "best minds in the country, without regard to party affiliation," free to do what they thought was best and right, mainly to achieve sound national credit.[127] This plan was promoted as being what citizens really wanted, but the whole purpose of the plan was a government so constituted that it could take steps that most voters would oppose. For advocates of National Government, the problem of political partisanship was not that plutocrats controlled parties but that elections prevented "responsible men" (the biggest business leaders and financial elites) from having enough influence.

This worry was heightened by the fact that the electorate had recently been broadened. In 1933, a small-town salt factory owner in Ontario succinctly expressed the perception that democracy could lead to danger-ous change: "Under our system [of government]," he worried, "the vote of the masses and women could very readily swamp the ... intelligent class of voter."[128] In a related vein, an article in *Canadian Business* proposed remov-ing the municipal franchise from relief recipients; as their numbers mount-ed, the author feared, the unemployed could vote themselves into political office and raise relief rates.[129] This was the sort of muttering that the Toronto *Globe* editors alluded to when they spoke of those who wanted to restrict the franchise. With party politicians having to seek the votes of "the masses and women," who knew what would happen? Arguably, the defeat of fiscally conservative governments or the granting of concessions such as those made in the face of the Jones tax protest in British Columbia or the creamery ticket protest were exactly what would happen. To many elite Canadian businessmen in the 1930s, National Government was the solution to the problem of tax resistance among the masses and overspend-ing by governments. It was both a national and an international trend.[130]

At the national level in the months before the 1935 federal election, the League for National Government emerged as a well-bankrolled movement.[131] But Leader of the Opposition William Lyon Mackenzie King, confident that his Liberals would easily defeat Bennett's exhausted Conservatives, saw no benefit in adopting the league's proposed strategy. He pointed out that to unite the "capitalist" parties would leave the socialist Cooperative Commonwealth Federation (CCF), formed in 1933, as the official oppos-ition.[132] The socialists in the League for Social Reconstruction (LSR) were happy with that prospect – a contest between a party of capital and a party of the people. But they rightly pointed out in *Social Planning for Canada* that the League for National Government was not interested in electoral contests. The league's view that matters of public finance could be settled only outside electoral politics was akin, the LSR noted, to the thinking that inspired European fascisms.[133]

The tax resistance of the 1930s animated the mass electorate and threat-ened to take political aim at the tax-dodging rich. The appeal of National Government was therefore obvious to the wealthy, though it might also have appealed more broadly to those in the older non-partisan tradition in which belief in moral facts and business expertise was also strong. Its claim to put an end to patronage-driven spending spoke to a long-standing and widespread anger among progressives about the taxes of the poor – wheth-er the tariff tax or the municipal tax – lining the pockets of manufacturers, monopolists, and machine politicians.[134] Fortunately, King's Liberals presented the electorate with an acceptable alternative, and National Government missed its chance in Canadian federal politics. That this proto-fascist tendency gained the profile that it did owed much to tax resistance in the 1930s.

$ ¢ $

The tax-related pocketbook questions that appealed widely during the interwar years mattered in the politics of the 1930s. The issues of the day were not only how governments should spend their dollars but also how they should raise their revenues. And it was not only the national income tax payers' satisfaction or frustration that governments had to consider. Although those taxpayers were more numerous, less wealthy, and more electorally significant than has usually been recalled, the tax politics of the interwar years and especially in the 1930s engaged an even broader swath of the electorate because of new provincial and municipal taxes that affected both the national income tax payer and those with smaller incomes. Business conservatives wanted to ensure that all who called for public spending contributed by taxation in ways that felt like sacrifices. However, the sacrifices entailed by expanded taxation incited tax resistance and helped to defeat incumbent governments. The same pressures operated in Canada as in the United States. But in Canada's constitutional world, the radicalism of Americans' income tax repeal strategy was simply not open to a still quasi-colonial nation. Canadian tax resisters took aim, instead, at the workings of electoral democracy; in the 1935 federal election, however, voters found that party politics were still a sufficient means to register their protest.

There were broad class differences audible in the public finance discourse of the interwar years, with the organizations of big capital more likely to call for a curb on expenditure and class-conscious labour more likely to urge the state to uphold its responsibility for the vulnerable. These differences on spending were more pronounced than were the differences on taxation. Organized labour had more consistently critiqued sales taxation, but some labour organizations modified that position given the fiscal crisis of the 1930s. And the Verdun case shows that a new sales tax could trigger a cross-class resistance in which small merchants and labour elements joined forces. On income taxation, farmer and labour folk certainly advocated greater taxation of high incomes. But income taxation was a point of worry for smaller earners too. The Jones tax was an egregious case of an attempt to push the income tax burden to the lower end of income distribution, but the Jones tax was not singular. The question of who could afford to pay an income tax was an open one elsewhere in Canada during the 1930s, too, as the *Forbes* case suggests. Resistance to income taxation was part of the pocketbook politics that linked the interests of better-paid workers, spinsters and bachelors, and middle-class breadwinners. The income tax payer was a larger and more diverse electoral force than historians of the 1920s and 1930s have thought. At provincial and municipal levels, flat rate income taxes were politically a different thing than the graduated federal tax, with its higher exemptions. But even federal income tax payers included a cohort of middle-income earners whose small tax debts cut into their household budgets rather than, say, merely limiting their savings. Many organizations took positions on tax questions, and politicians had to respond to their concerns. The defeat of J.W. Jones in the Conservative rout of 1933 in British Columbia showed what happened when they did not do so.

Tax resistance is not always reasonable or far-sighted. The instances of tax resistance highlighted here might be sympathetic insofar as they were fuelled in part by the worries of people managing pennies, not millions. The notion that exacting more taxes (and especially more direct taxes) from lower-income people would help to reduce demand for public spending by making them see that nothing was free meant that, in some sense, the left could reasonably oppose what otherwise might have been seen as democratic, state-building taxes. That these taxes were aimed at maintaining public credit, while support for the unemployed was woefully weak, also makes sense of tax resistance from below. Contrary to Beito's picture of anti-statist tax resistance, the "rapacious" state imposing more taxes in Canada was not doing so, by any means, out of "socialist" state-building motives. Covering the bond interest on public debt justified these new taxes of the 1930s, as much as did providing minimal relief to the unemployed, often for reasons that were barely humanitarian, much less socialist.[135] Tax protest from lower-income people and organizations of the left was not about making common cause with anti-tax business. But defending the small household budget within a taxpayer discourse did provide support, beyond the narrow business elite, for calls for a smaller state and less "extravagant" public spending. Although the National Government movement clearly came from big business, its broader resonance was audible in the critique of the "old-line" parties that underpinned other political formations, the non-partisan or social movement politics steeped in a view of politics as a matter of right or wrong rather than a process of coordination and negotiation. In spite of the authoritarian impulses that seemed to be omnipresent in the 1930s, tax resistance in that decade ended up revealing the electorate's power to negotiate the tax bargain and limit the power of the state, for good or for ill.

5

Taxation at the Edges
of Citizenship

THE CLASS QUESTIONS THAT STRUCTURED the democratic engage-
ments that I have described so far assumed that the taxpayer was also a
voter and a full economic citizen participating in market relations without
legal or cultural constraint. But there were other Canadians – some racialized people (including status Indians[1]), the urban poor, some white women
– who negotiated taxpaying from a standpoint outside or at the margins of
the taken-for-granted power games of electoral politics and market relations. These taxpayers were not always or not quite citizens in the formal
sense with a full slate of political and civil rights. Not coincidentally, they
were also excluded in various ways from full social citizenship: economically vulnerable and collectively organized, if at all, outside the mainstream
of the larger community's political life. In the lives of these other Canadians,
income taxes were not the only ones that counted, and the relationship of
taxpaying to voting was complicated. Although "class politics is of the essence of taxation," as US Treasury official Thomas Adams asserted, one of
his eminent successors pointed out that class politics "do not adequately
illuminate" the many interests that matter in tax culture and politics.[2] To
help us understand how taxation shaped and was shaped by changes in
Canadian democracy, I consider stories about some of the Canadians who,
in the interwar years, were at the margins of citizenship but significant in
tax matters.

One of the basic rights of political citizenship in a liberal polity – the
right to vote federally, provincially, and municipally – was not yet universal

in Canada in the interwar years. So, as taxation practices changed in those years, questions arose about how or whether to tax people who could not vote. In the interwar years and early 1940s, these questions were raised around racialized categories of Canadians as they had been earlier around gendered ones.³ In the 1920 discussion of the remaining restrictions in the proposed dominion franchise, the acting attorney general affirmed that "citizenship in no country carries with it the right to vote. The right to vote is a conferred right in every case ... Citizenship of itself carries no right to the franchise."⁴ Both government and opposition members affirmed their abhorrence of having a property qualification for the federal vote.⁵ But the idea that there might be other restrictive qualifications, whether federal or at other levels, was not yet unthinkable. One of those "other qualifications" could be paying taxes.

During the interwar years, most Canadian provinces disqualified certain racialized people from voting.⁶ Packed into these disqualifications of "Indians," "persons of the Chinese race," "Japanese," people lacking "knowledge of English or French," and "Doukhobors" were ideas about what those racializing labels meant. Voting rights required whiteness of a sort whose meaning was something other than skin colour. No statutory constraint limited voting by people of African descent, for example. The deeper content of the idea of whiteness was revealed in details of the statutes. Having served in the armed forces during the Great War was sufficient to enfranchise the racially disqualified. Loyalty and contribution whitened any member of these groups for the purpose of national electoral citizenship. Doukhobors (or later anyone belonging to any pacifist sect) were excluded because their pacifism made them supposedly non-contributing and disloyal. References to "Indians" in the language of blood ("persons of Indian blood") in some of these franchise statements were accompanied in others by the language of property and legal status. In citizenship terms, marriage whitened a phenotypically Indigenous woman. As Jarvis Brownlie has shown in his case study of voluntary enfranchisement in the interwar years, having the right relation to property was a crucial element of whiteness.⁷

Citizenship, as represented by the franchise, was thus connected to a bundle of characteristics assumed to be present in some people – the most "white" – and not necessarily in racialized others. Similarly, the meaning of political citizenship for women seemed to endorse their likeness to men as rational, public beings. However, during the interwar years, the grounds for citizen entitlements remained in flux. Would some new restrictions replace property as a means of limiting citizen rights? Being a taxpayer, like being a property owner, seemed to promise access to political privileges. But that promise was often illusory or, in the case of Indigenous people, mixed in its meanings, so the impact of taxation on political culture at the margins of citizenship was different than it was at the white, male, middle-class centre. In what follows, I first discuss how taxation questions around income tax and customs duties moved to the centre of Indigenous politics, focusing a critique of oppression in ways that, as Hugh Shewell has shown, later supported new forms of broadened Indigenous political organization.[8] I then explore how other taxes, mainly municipal, expressed a civic republican (inclusion by virtue or identity or both) rather than a liberal (inclusion on universal grounds) concept of citizenship. Taxation was frequently a means of expressing racialist views of the proper citizen; in opposition to such expressions, political liberals refused discriminatory and harassing methods of taxation. In all of these processes, taxation practices forced hard questions about political rights and belonging.

Taxation of Indians' Income in the Interwar Years

The research base of this section is largely limited to correspondence files of the federal Indian administration. Further research is needed in court records and community sources. However, I found in the Indian administration records, as others have, a wide range of voices. Not only are there the voices of other state agencies (the Department of National Revenue, the Department of Justice, and the RCMP), but also there are the voices of Indigenous people as well as those of politicians, employers, lawyers, and merchants from settler society. With respect to connections among the franchise, Indian citizenship, and taxation, I found four themes. First, foundationally, was the significance of "ordinarily living on reserve" and the connection of that legal concept to the tax exemption features of the Indian Act. Second was the variety of sometimes conflicting interests and levels of knowledge within the civil service among those engaged in the discussion of whether and how Indians should be taxed and what their rights should be. Third, most commonly articulated by Indigenous correspondents, was the relationship between Indians' civil rights and their tax obligations. In its simplest form, this is the question of whether the state could expect the usual tax contributions from people who were not endowed with the usual civil rights (but who had other kinds of rights). Fourth was the question of national citizenship carried forward from the eighteenth-century Jay Treaty: how could taxation based upon a national border (as customs duties were) apply to people whose transnational status had long ago been affirmed?

To understand these aspects of tax conversation concerning Indians in the interwar years, it is important to appreciate that the tax exemption features of the Indian Act were designed with property taxation in mind. From that design emerged an unstable distinction of "on reserve" and "off reserve" that assumed great significance. As Joel Oliphant has pointed out, a tax authority could not enforce a property tax in the usual way on reserve land because to seize and sell that land was not open as a means of collecting unpaid taxes. To live "on reserve" was therefore to live on non-taxable property. In this view of the tax clauses within the Indian Act, it was the property, not the person, that held the tax-exempt status.[9] Indians living off reserve had the same municipal tax obligations as anyone else, as Indian Affairs officers regularly explained. Dog taxes, poll taxes, property taxes, or school taxes – there was nothing in Indian status that exempted from these imposts someone with that status who "ordinarily lived off reserve."[10] As a provincial tax collector told an Indigenous property owner in Hazelton, British Columbia, people who owned property in the Hazelton School District had to pay the tax whether or not they had children who would go to school there: not sending his children to the "white man's school" made him no different from the non-Canadian investor living in, say, England who owned land in Hazelton but never set foot in Canada. Both had to pay the school tax or have their land sold for tax arrears.[11]

In relation to income taxation, the Department of National Revenue maintained that on reserve/off reserve was a clear and relevant distinction. In 1925, the federal commissioner of taxation, R.W. Breadner, and the superintendent of Indian affairs, Duncan Campbell Scott, agreed that an Indian "residing, and acquiring property off the reserve, ... would appear to be liable to taxation the same as other residents of a municipality [i.e., on the assessed value of that property]." In 1931, the next federal commissioner of income taxation, C.S. Walters, pointed out that the department had used the 1925 Breadner-Scott "ruling" to administer the Income War Tax Act.[12] And indeed, throughout the 1920s, Indian Affairs had used the residence criterion, "on reserve" or "off reserve" (with no mention of property ownership), as the rule in responding to queries about any form of taxation, including income tax. Any Indian who lived off reserve paid the same taxes as any other person. Equally, any Indian living on reserve did not pay taxes. In this distinction was a republican notion that different political communities might have different membership obligations, but there was also a liberalism: an Indian off reserve was just one more market actor and property owner, an individual like any other.

However, the distinction on reserve/off reserve did not apply consistently to all aspects of Indian status. The legal prohibition on drinking was one. Some provinces' purely racial disqualification from voting was another. Being "wards" of the Crown or legal "minors" was another and most fundamental. Correspondents to the department observed that surely people in those categories didn't have citizen obligations.[13] In eastern Canada, the Royal Proclamation of 1763 and the provisions of the Jay Treaty were also offered (and contested) as evidence that "Indians" had a distinct legal status, whether on reserve or off, that implied freedom from some tax obligations.[14] As Alex Sioui, working in the aluminum plant at Arvida, put it in 1942, "I cannot enjoy Canadian citizenship, being an Indian; but I am entitle[d] to Indian privileges; meaning no Taxes."[15] Some non-Indians, including a few individuals within the sprawling Indian Affairs system, recognized the justice of Indians having at least some tax immunities when they did not enjoy full citizen rights.[16] That living on reserve or off was not consistent in legal consequences produced much confusion and reasonable resentment in the interwar and early war years among both status Indians and fair-minded non-Indigenous people, whether employers, Indian agents, or friends of Indians.

On top of the problematic foundation of the residence criterion for tax liability were laid additional difficulties. Two of them were differences in perspective among different federal departments and change over time at Indian Affairs. In the early days of the federal income tax, Indian Affairs relied on residence of the earner rather than location of the work to advise about tax liability. A significant ruling was issued in 1922 after Paul Sioui, from Indian Lorette, wrote to Indian Affairs to ask about the income tax situation of "a Seven-Island reserve Indian" whose hunting income in the past season had been $5,000. Sioui wanted to know whether the "revenue officer" could "force" that hunter to pay income tax given that the hunter was "minor according to law, is not subject to the military conscription, and is supposed to have the entire protection of the federal government." In reply, J.D. McLean, the assistant deputy and secretary of Indian Affairs, wrote that the issue was not where the "reserve Indian" did his hunting but whether he usually lived on reserve:

> If such Indian resides permanently on a reserve, the income from the sale of furs which he acquired on a temporary absence from the reserve in the hunting regions would come within the exemptions of the Indian Act and would not be taxable. If, however, such Indian habitually resides off the reserve, I should think his income derived from the hunt would be taxable.

In other words, McLean said that the hunter's income was exempt from income taxation because he lived on reserve. In this ruling, McLean had the advice of A.S. Williams, the departmental solicitor. Both McLean and Williams referred back to that 1922 ruling from time to time in later years.[17] The Department of Justice seemed to agree: as late as April 1939, Acting Deputy Minister of Justice Charles P. Plaxton issued an opinion to Indian Affairs that "Indians residing on reserves" were not liable to income taxation by either dominion or provinces "in respect of wages earned off reserve."[18]

By 1931, however, differences in interpretation were emerging among the federal departments involved. National Revenue had come to differ from Indian Affairs. The Kahnawake Kanien'kehá:ka (referred to in Indian Affairs documents as the Caughnawaga Mohawk) found this out through several cases concerning their members' salaries and expense allowances earned as steelworkers at Dominion Bridge. One of the first two cases in the 1920s concerned a man who lived off reserve, so the decisions in his case fit with the line that Indian Affairs had used consistently when asked about off reserve band members' liabilities to all manner of taxes: what mattered was where the Indian lived.[19] The income tax commissioner quoted the Breadner-Scott agreement about living off reserve as part of the foundation for his decision in that case. But in the other case, that of Joseph Cross, who did live on reserve at Kahnawake, the decision that National Revenue had made in 1929 was a more complicated one concerning the taxable status of travelling expenses and the number of dependants' exemptions.[20] Cross, a foreman and thirty-one-year employee of Dominion Bridge, had been sent an income tax assessment on his pay of approximately $4,000 a year (a good skilled labour wage). He protested, and in the end he did not have to pay. But the National Revenue authority showed that he happened to be exempt merely because the amount of his income, properly assessed, fell below the taxable threshold. It was reduced by an expense allowance adjustment and dependants' exemptions. In the Cross case, National Revenue seemed to introduce a different criterion than Indian Affairs had used. This new criterion was not where the earner lived but where he earned income. National Revenue insisted that Cross was liable for taxation on his income earned off reserve even though he lived on reserve.

That message did not get through to everyone in the Kahnawake Kanien'-kehá:ka community or, indeed, everyone in Indian Affairs. Two years later, in 1933, another Kahnawake band member, Peter Walker, got an income tax bill for the years 1927–29, years when he, too, had been employed at Dominion Bridge in Lachine. He had both lived and worked off reserve. By 1933, he was unemployed and couldn't afford to pay the tax bill for those earlier years. He had heard of the 1931 decision in Cross's case and hoped that the income tax liability that it described wouldn't apply to the income from those earlier years.[21] He wrote to Indian Affairs to ask, and they forwarded his question to National Revenue. He must have been surprised when he read the revenue authority's reply to his query. Perhaps it was not surprising that he owed those taxes – after all, everyone in the various Canadian bureaucracies had always said that living off reserve meant being liable to tax. But in the 1933 letter to Walker, the revenue authority added an aside that explicitly contradicted the long-standing emphasis of Indian Affairs on the residence of the earner rather than on the location of the earning. The income tax commissioner apparently wanted to send a message: "Furthermore, notwithstanding that an Indian may be residing on a reserve, if his income is derived from sources outside the reserve, then he is liable to taxation in respect of such income." No one in Indian Affairs had ever said such a thing. In the case of the Seven Islands hunter and J.D. McLean's 1922 memo to file, they had said exactly the opposite. The income tax commissioner went on to say something even more remarkable: "This is not a ruling that was passed in 1931 but is based on the provisions of the 1917 Income Tax Act as amended."[22]

Apparently, National Revenue had not even succeeded in communicating its position on taxing Indians' income to Acting Assistant Deputy and Secretary of Indian Affairs A.F. Mackenzie. On July 10, 1929, Mackenzie told the secretary of Dominion Bridge in response to his question about whether the company should be deducting federal income tax from Cross's pay that "our view is that if an Indian is resident upon his reservation he would be exempt from taxation as provided by the Indian Act."[23] Even more clearly, Mackenzie told a New Brunswick Indian agent on July 2, 1929, that "the income of an Indian who resides on a reserve cannot be taxed no matter from what source it is derived."[24] In April 1931, Mackenzie also told Dr. J.H. Jacobs, a Kahnawake Kanien'kehá:ka physician, that according to Indian Affairs it was the residence of the Indian earner, not whether he earned income on or off reserve, that determined whether he had an income tax liability.[25] On the West Coast, the same view appears to have been current in Indian Affairs. During the fight over the Jones tax in April 1931, BC Indian Commissioner W.E. Ditchburn argued that the residence of the Indian, not the location of his earning, determined income tax liability. He attempted to persuade Jones that only Indians living off reserve should pay the 1 percent tax on wages. The embattled BC finance minister was not persuaded. More correspondence ensued, and a public protest took place at Massett in Haida Gwaii in June. The national superintendent of Indian Affairs finally admitted in September 1931 that the department did not know, and would not really know, until a case had gone through the courts, what the income tax liability was for Indians who lived on reserve but earned income off reserve.[26]

No such court case took place during the 1930s. For National Revenue, however, the matter was clear and settled. Nonetheless, for some reason, in the spring of 1939, the Department of Justice was asked for a ruling on Indians' income tax liability. Acting Deputy Minister of Justice C.P. Plaxton proceeded to produce an opinion on Indians' income tax liability that contradicted the position articulated by National Revenue in 1929, 1931, and 1933. Plaxton wrote, "I think that in the absence of special contractual provisions as to place of payment Indians residing on reserves are not liable to be taxed on account of income tax under dominion or provincial legislation in respect of wages earned off the reserves." Depending on what "special contractual provisions" meant, this sounded like a reiteration of the residence criterion that McLean, Williams, and Mackenzie of Indian Affairs had been using in the 1920s. Andrew Paull of the Native Brotherhood of British Columbia thought so and made that case to Indian Affairs in various letters after new federal income tax obligations were introduced in June 1942.[27] But the minister of revenue, after consulting with the minister of justice, Louis St. Laurent, wrote to Paull's MP, the minister of pensions and national health, to explain why St. Laurent supported National Revenue against Paull in the reading of the Plaxton opinion. According to St. Laurent, the minister of revenue had found that "opinions of the Justice Department are not furnished to the public generally and, being opinions only, they may be followed or not, as the Departments concerned see fit. He further added that the opinion of Mr. Plaxton has not been accepted as the rule and has not been concurred in by his successors."[28] The latter point was certainly true, at least since 1940. During the war years, both National Revenue and Indian Affairs had told employers, Indian agents, representatives of Indian organizations, and various inquiring individuals that the only income exempt from income taxation was that earned by Indians on reserve who also lived on reserve. Earnings from work for employers off reserve were subject to income taxation.[29] The residence criterion had been abandoned. Now only income earned on reserve would be exempt. Indians had become nearly indistinguishable federal income tax payers.

It is understandable that, purely in administrative terms, National Revenue had good reason to reject the residence criterion. It had been difficult to apply at times: some individuals whose families lived on reserve and who returned to the reserve on weekends saw themselves as living on reserve. Neither Indian Affairs nor National Revenue had accepted that view.[30] No doubt it was easier to tell where the prospective taxpayer worked and earned than to say where he or she lived. Plaxton's opinion had attempted to clarify that question by referring to "special contractual provisions" that might establish where an income was earned. Without entirely dismissing attempts to attain administrative clarity, however, the apparently obvious explanation for the change from location of residence to location of earning was that the much lower exemptions introduced in federal income taxation in 1940–42 began to bring into income tax liability many more First Nations people than ever before. The expansion of demand for labour and, equally, the expansion of markets for the products of Indigenous fisheries now made taxing Indians a potentially more significant source of revenue. And in political terms, as the wartime defence tax and income tax began to hit hard the pocketbooks of working-class Canadians generally, the potential for racially inflected resentment among working people of settler descent was now suddenly there. To insist that status Indians earning side by side with their near neighbours also pay taxes on their small incomes was a means of responding to their neighbours' envy about a tax exemption whose scope was still being negotiated.[31]

The assertion that earning income off reserve, like owning property off reserve, conferred indistinguishable citizen obligations on status Indians seemed to be dangerous to Indigenous leaders such as Andrew Paull of the Squamish and John Tootoosis of the prairie Cree. As Hugh Shewell has explained, they linked conscription and income taxation during the Second World War as instances of Canadian state agencies misrepresenting Indigenous people's legal standing. Taxing Indians as though they were not legally distinct, like conscripting them as though they were ordinary citizens, was to act as though obligations under treaties and the Indian Act were without force. In 1943 and 1944, these concerns rallied Indigenous people's representatives for two national conferences in Ottawa. Out of these meetings grew the North American Indian Brotherhood (NAIB). During the 1950s and 1960s, NAIB would become the most important national voice for Indigenous people in Canada. Paull would carry through into peacetime the position that Indian status entailed exemption from income taxation. In the NAIB vision, the benefits of claiming citizen rights through taxpaying were not worth endorsing the implication in liberal terms that Indigenous people had the rights of individuals and nothing more.[32]

Taxes at the Border

In the interwar years, the cases involving taxation of Indians' income had been few, and, as the Indian Affairs official had acknowledged in 1931, administrative ambiguities remained unresolved. Partly, this was the result of income taxation being relatively unimportant in the mostly rural reserve communities and largely low-income demographic of both rural and urban Indigenous people. But precisely because of rurality or poverty or both, Indians in the interwar years encountered other kinds of taxation more frequently than they encountered the federal income tax, and in these taxes, too, there were problems of negotiating a fair legal regime. Probably the most fraught of these other taxes were customs duties, in particular the charging of customs duties to members of Indigenous communities on the international border.

Customs revenue was important to the federal government. As late as 1929, customs and excise duties generated 63.3 percent of federal tax receipts.[33] In 1925 and 1926, federal politics had been convulsed by revelations of massive commercial smuggling by settler Canadians and extensive corruption within the customs administration. After the department's re-organization in 1927, money flowed for customs policing. Yet local evasion of customs duties on items of personal use continued as part of normal life along Canada's long border with the United States. During the nationwide smuggling investigations of 1926, one investigator, a twenty-year veteran of customs port offices, told the senior RCMP officer that the Crown should not take legal action on "petty smuggling." The customs service depended on cooperation from the public in its efforts to police large-scale commercial smuggling, he pointed out, so customs agents normally exercised discretion in the policing of small-scale dodging to ensure a positive "public attitude" toward their work. Cracking down on normal customs evasions was "always resented"; surely, he said, it was a sign of poor judgment when "the letter of the Act has been enforced and not its spirit."[34] As reasonable as this might seem, such customary enforcement, relying on discretion, was at best confusing and at worst open to abuse.

For the Kanien'kehá:ka community of the St. Regis reserve, Akwesasne, whose territory straddles the Canada-US border at the St. Lawrence River near Cornwall, Ontario, the local customs officers' traditions were especially troublesome. As in the case of the income tax question, the civil servants of the Departments of Justice, National Revenue, and Indian Affairs were all involved in the tax questions of cross-border traffic. In the case of customs, in addition, not only the individual reserve residents were involved but also, by the 1930s, American courts and representatives of Canada's Department of External Affairs. Within and among all of these institutions and individuals were differences of opinion and power struggles. They showed up in how National Revenue handled the ordinary practices of customs enforcement. For example, it was a well-established practice that women from the St. Regis reserve made baskets and beadwork, sold them in Hogansburg, New York, and brought groceries and household goods back home without being charged customs duties. In 1911, the local subcollector had been told by head office "to be lenient with the Indians." The fact that there were 1,600 resident Indians and only two "white men" in St. Regis – the subcollector and the parish priest – was noted as a reason for leniency. It seems that racial difference mattered in enforcement: the implication seems to have been that, without racial solidarity to rely on, collectors needed to exercise caution. In 1937, after much legal commotion, a later subcollector, Edmund Caza, reported to his superiors in Ottawa that "we don't collect no duty from the Indians, but we let their groceries, supplies and personal effects in free." He claimed that this had been the practice for "many years."[35] It's easy to see here the general phenomenon of border-town customs agents preserving their authority by allowing moderate customs evasion to continue. But there was also a distinctively Indian dimension to the customs question in local cross-border economies.

The difference was that the Indigenous community had preserved in memory and in documentation the 1794 Jay Treaty rights and the reaffirmation of those rights in statute and regulation in the United States through most of the nineteenth century.[36] Among those rights was the duty-free conduct of small-scale cross-border trade. The Canadian customs authority had long maintained that those rights had expired at the outbreak of the War of 1812, but the Americans had confirmed them repeatedly in legislation until 1897. What happened then exactly was open to debate, but no one disputed that the 1897 revision of the US customs statute omitted the usual affirmation of duty-free rights in Jay Treaty terms. In 1931, as a result of requests from Akwesasne and other First Nations, Indian Affairs asked O.D. Skelton of External Affairs to talk to the United States about restoring the privileges apparently lost in 1897. Skelton first checked with formidable former commissioner of taxation, now commissioner of customs, R.W. Breadner, to see if Canada allowed duty-free imports for Indians. Breadner said no. Perhaps that stopped Skelton from going any further in asking the United States to restore privileges.[37] A few years later, seeking legal clarity, an Akwesasne woman, Mrs. P.L. (Annie) Garrow, took the problem to the US courts.

In December 1934, Garrow paid US customs agents, under protest, one dollar in customs duties on the two dozen ash baskets that she was planning to sell in Hogansburg. She based her protest upon her rights under the Jay Treaty. In March 1936, a judge of the US Court of Customs and Patent Appeals found in her favour. In his view, the repealing section of the tariff act of 1897 erased only congressional legislation, not treaties. He acknowledged that the language of treaty rights that had been reproduced in a series of tariff acts throughout the century was not reproduced in 1897 or thereafter. He held that the omission was "for some unexplained reason" and that he therefore could not say whether it was meaningful. The news of Garrow's victory quickly circulated through the Ottawa bureaucracy. The first letter, reporting the news in approving terms, came from the RCMP to the Commissioner of Customs just a few days after the court's decision. However, a US customs appeal court reversed the lower court's finding in the spring of 1937, and the US Supreme Court confirmed the decision in October that year.[38] Garrow had lost her case.

Director of Indian Affairs H.W. McGill was unhappy with the outcome. After the reversal at the customs appeal court, he had been pessimistic about Garrow's chances at the US Supreme Court. In fact, he had refused her request for funds to continue her challenge. But he advised his deputy minister that External Affairs should be brought in to work out a reciprocal customs agreement that would encourage reserves along the international boundary to trade rather than put obstacles in their way. In the next month, External Affairs consulted with National Revenue, and negotiations were launched. They ultimately failed.[39] In 1941, Canadian customs officials were still charging duty on the groceries that Akwesasne women were bringing home from a day of shopping in the United States. One Canadian customs collector in Huntingdon, Quebec, seized from "Indian ladies returning to Canada in a taxi" a humble haul of raisins, soap, mayonnaise, coffee, baking powder, and assorted small household goods (handkerchiefs, bloomers, a tablecloth) in August 1941. He wrote to the commissioner of customs to ask, "on account of the Indian question," how he should deal with these goods. The advice was that, unless the women had been out of Canada for forty-eight hours, this was a legitimate customs seizure.[40]

That an ordinary customs official himself was unsure of proper practice tells us how confusing this matter had become. Indian Affairs and External Affairs had been informed by National Revenue in 1937 that "the Canadian Government has been admitting to free entry personal household effects imported by Indians at the St. Regis reserve ... It is not proposed to disturb that situation until after the proposed negotiations [with the United States] have been concluded."[41] It is not entirely surprising, then, that in 1951 the head of the Kingston RCMP detachment reported that people on the St. Regis reserve believed that the government accepted their Jay Treaty rights. One RCMP officer, appointed to customs enforcement in St. Regis, was being "accused of 'picking on' certain Indians because others have goods purchased in the US, etc., etc. This makes hard feelings among the Indians when they feel they are being discriminated against."[42] The history of discretion in enforcement of the law had ended up making people feel vulnerable rather than accommodated.

The Kingston RCMP captain wanted a definite ruling on the question of Jay Treaty rights: the present ambiguity was making the work of his constable "useless."[43] The new (since 1943) customs commissioner, David Sim, also wanted clarity: he realized that his department could not properly administer the law because "many Indians have been acting in the bona fide belief that they were exempt by law from the payment of duties." Not surprisingly, in light of that belief, some Akwesasne residents were dubious when the Department of Justice finally ruled in 1952 that Jay Treaty rights did not entitle them to free importation of personal goods. Akwesasne resident Louis Francis, backed by at least some of his community, brought a claim against the Crown concerning the seizure of some household appliances purchased in the United States.[44] He had paid the duties under protest, like Annie Garrow, fully expecting that he would then be able to make his claim a test case for Jay Treaty rights. At both the Exchequer Court and the Supreme Court in 1954 and 1956, Canadian judges decided against him, following the interpretive canon that such rights could be enforced only if legislation embodying them had been enacted. In Canada, unlike in the United States, the customs statute had never included Jay Treaty rights.[45] In the *Francis* and *Garrow* cases, as in the *Caron* and *Forbes* cases, there were plausible legal theories on each side of the case. An ethical lawyer could have taken up this case. Each of them involved exempting what the courts would have seen as particular, legally distinct categories of Canadians (civil servants in *Caron* and *Forbes,* status Indians in *Francis* and *Garrow*) from a general citizen responsibility. The courts decided that, with respect to taxation, these were differences that could not be allowed to make a difference.

The taxation of Indigenous people is possibly the most enduring and fraught question of race and taxation in Canada. In their efforts to negotiate taxation, both First Nations individuals and communities reminded revenue officials that they lacked voting rights or were denied other citizen rights. They were not, in that sense, citizens like any other. The liberal democratic slogan "no taxation without representation" was meaningful for them as it was for the proponents of other tax resistance projects. However, even though non-voters, they had means to push back at taxes that they saw as unfair. Indigenous rights formed a well-established (if contested) basis of legal and political struggles around taxation and citizenship. Particular rights, rather than liberal equality, were foundational in those struggles.[46] On this basis, various First Nations activists petitioned and wrote letters of protest, making arguments based upon treaty rights and Indian status. In the interwar years and the early war years, neither kind of political strategy was especially successful. In relation to local customs administration in border areas, however, a discretionary lenience showed that the settler state could be accommodating. But accommodation was a mixed blessing, providing a context in which favour arbitrarily given could also arbitrarily be withdrawn.

Taxation at Other Boundaries of Political Inclusion

Because tax is always about contributing to a collectivity, tax talk and tax practice provide opportunities for marking inclusion or exclusion. While Indigenous and settler communities faced off on established lines of political belonging, there were different issues and questions for other peoples whose appearance, language, or cultural practice marked them as different from the majority. Whether in the case of immigrants not yet seen as "Canadian" or in the case of visible minorities, there were hints that taxation could pose different dangers, though commitments to liberal equality sometimes offered important protections from abusive racialized tax discourse. As Lisa Rose Mar's research in Chinese-language sources suggests, the "foreign language" press and associational records might produce more evidence of tax bargaining than I have been able to find in the English- and French-language sources on which this study relies.[47] But there is sufficient evidence in newspapers and politicians' correspondence to indicate two links between race and taxation. One is how the discussion of tax burdens sometimes took on a xenophobic tone. The other is how tax enforcement could become a tool for discriminatory harassment.

"Foreigners," "aliens," and "transients" all appeared in the assessment imaginations of white settler Canadians as likely free riders. It would be surprising if tax talk in the interwar years had been free from the anti-immigrant ideas so common then. The idea of the foreigner hiding wads of cash in a money belt had circulated during the Victory Loan campaigns of the war years, and as the first federal income tax forms were being printed, in February 1918, rumours flew in western Canada that a special tax on German Canadians or other naturalized British subjects with "enemy" homelands was being planned by the dominion government. The prime minister made a public announcement to calm fears.[48] An opinion poll in Toronto in 1918 featured the "foreign and transient population" along with doctors, lawyers, and coupon clippers among those who easily deceived tax collectors.[49] In British Columbia, there had long been a body of opinion that wanted transient labour or Chinese labour to pay a tax that would make up for their supposed freedom from property tax. In 1911, a Royal Commission on Taxation in British Columbia, headed by the province's finance minister, had resolutely squashed the idea and recommended elimination of the province's poll tax (unique in Canada at the provincial level). But the tax stayed and was in fact supplemented by a Vancouver city poll tax in 1924.[50] Supporters of the Jones tax in 1931 liked that it reached into the pockets of "aliens and young people." For the Mission Conservative Association, it did not go far enough, however, and they dreamed of following California's example of a tax on aliens. The premier thought that the value of the Jones tax was precisely that it dealt with "the Asiatic phase" of the tax question.[51]

In light of these views, the United Farmers of Alberta convention in 1929 was a beacon of tolerance. The farmers defeated by a large majority a resolution that "non-taxpaying residents" in municipal districts pay a poll tax. The rejection was partly for the usual reasons of poll taxes being hard to collect and therefore unjust to those who paid them. But two speakers also spoke about the harms to transient and recent immigrant workers of such a tax: a Mr. Snow referred to the "iniquities of our present immigration system" and called immigrants "honest workmen who have been misled."[52] Using poll taxes against immigrants might well have seemed unreasonable in the flourishing prairie west of the late 1920s.

But municipalities in eastern and central Canada were less welcoming, even in those prosperous years. Some used poll taxes as a means of keeping "outside workers" away or, at least, of raising a bit of extra revenue from them. London, Ontario, charged "aliens" a specific poll tax on top of the general poll tax, and in Quebec in 1927 the practice was becoming so common that the provincial legislature chose to pass a law prohibiting municipalities from taxing outside workers.[53] The incentives for such taxes only mounted during the Depression years. When the City of Saint John proposed a tax of five dollars on outside workers brought in to help rebuild after a fire destroyed much of the waterfront in June 1931, the mayor called the tax a measure of "moderate protection" and rejoiced that eighty-four outside workers had already paid it "cheerfully." The Carpenters and Joiners Local 919 represented protectionists of a more serious sort: they wanted the tax to be $50 per head for unskilled workers and $100 per head for skilled workers. The Board of Trade complained to Prime Minister Bennett, who threatened to stop construction entirely unless the tax was ended.[54] It is possible that, like the residency rules for poor law districts, these poll taxes were a residue of the old idea of municipalities as corporations or clubs in which citizen rights were the rights of stockholders or members rather than human rights.[55] In the protectionist 1930s, when Canadians in Windsor were paying a head tax to work in the United States, using taxes to fend off outsiders was a popular move.[56] Ideas of using taxes to control labour flows or raise funds for the municipal state were not necessarily racialized, but their consistency with xenophobic feeling is easy to see.

After the federal government abolished the Chinese head tax in 1923, there was nothing at the federal level to suggest the use of tax tools to enforce racial discrimination in immigration. In fact, during the 1930s, the Department of Finance rejected a proposal to make the income tax heavier on aliens than on permanent residents. The proposal does not survive in the finance minister's records, but we can tell by the summary in response that it consisted of denying any personal exemption, single or married, on aliens' income. The new tax specialist in the Department of Finance, Kenneth Eaton, was skeptical on both practical and moral grounds. Practically, he thought that the proposal would be costly to enforce and paltry in revenue: the target population was not likely a rich one. And other countries might retaliate. Morally, he thought, the idea seemed to express a nasty sort of anti-immigrant sentiment: "He is a foreigner. Let's heave a brick at him."[57] The old Department of Customs and Excise might have compliantly administered the anti-Chinese head tax, but Finance's new income tax expert was against that sort of thing. Although tax law can be racist, it is not inevitably so, in spite of the implication that journalist Mark Milke has recently made in using the Chinese head tax to illustrate what is dangerous about all taxation.[58]

Where taxation was dangerous, as I have emphasized above in relation to the taxation of Indians, was in giving tax collectors in local communities a degree of discretion. In the eighteenth century, Adam Smith pointed out the risks of discretion when he made "predictability" one of his four canons of good taxation. Discretionary enforcement (or relief from enforcement) made taxation ripe for racist exploitation. One example from Sydney, Nova Scotia, in 1920 suggests how that could work. According to George Creese, the high commissioner of the Universal Negro Improvement Association, an international organization active in Sydney's black community, "a system exists [in Sydney] of collecting a poll tax, everyone being required to pay $10 for police protection, good streets, etc. If the tax is not paid, the police call at the house and take the individual to jail. This practice applies only to the colored people."[59] Although poor people in general were vulnerable to having constables visit them at their homes and behave aggressively in demanding poll taxes, Creese asserted that African Nova Scotians in Sydney experienced a higher degree of harassment.[60] The abuse of tax administration for racist purposes was also evident in the 1946 Viola Desmond case, in which a black Nova Scotian businesswoman was fined for failing to pay one cent of provincial amusement tax. Her real offence had been to sit in the whites-only part of a New Glasgow, Nova Scotia, movie theatre: the one cent that she was charged with failing to pay was the difference between the tax on the ticket that she had been sold (for the "Negro" section) and the ticket for the seat that she took in the white section.[61] Finally, an opportunity for racist abuse of tax administration was also available in interwar Vancouver, where keeping the poll tax receipt on hand at all times was required by law.[62] That requirement made it easy for police to stop anyone on the street to ask to see a poll tax receipt, which made it an enforcement mechanism readily used in racist ways to intimidate certain people. Before motor vehicles provided an excuse for "driving while black" harassment, requesting a poll tax receipt would have provided a similar opportunity. Whether tax enforcement was used in this way remains a task for further research. My few examples here are only suggestive. But they draw attention to the ways in which taxation could be used rhetorically or administratively to mark belonging or exclusion. In having this capacity, tax policy is no different from other public policy: neither uniquely evil in its power nor particularly exempt from being used in larger, nasty or nice, cultural projects.

Poll Taxes and the Incomplete Process of Democratization

During the interwar years, there remained active in public memory an old world in which only property owners had full citizen rights and, even among property owners, only men. Those who disliked the new world still sought to insulate public spending from the power of a mass electorate. In cities, poll taxes and debates about their use marked this stage in the transition from elite democracy to universal, majoritarian democracy. Poll taxes were fixed per capita sums, usually not large. They were direct taxes, like the property tax or the income tax. For those who wanted to constrain the state, direct taxes were valued as a means of generating tax resistance. And tax resistance would make politicians work hard to persuade citizens as taxpayers to support the politicians' projects. In this view, the right to political voice, "representation," was purchased by contribution – paying taxes.

This link was especially important at the municipal level. In many Canadian cities, the property owners' franchise (based upon the property tax assessment roll) was supplemented by a taxpayer franchise, based not upon property ownership but upon mere residence (usually applying to unmarried men aged twenty-one to sixty) or municipal income tax paying. In Calgary, for example, there was a "special franchise tax" – a kind of minimum income tax created in 1921 – that made taxpayers out of non-property owners.[63] Like some but not all cities, Calgary thus enfranchised both male and female non-owners of property.[64] Poll taxes (whether new, as in the case of Vancouver, or old, as in the case of Saint John) could be found in some cities in every province at some time during the interwar years.[65] In Quebec City, the poll tax was the *taxe personnelle*. A poll tax was often thought of as a bachelor's tax, though it appears that only Montreal called it that.[66] Although "poll" referred to "head" (not polling districts), having paid the poll tax could serve, in lieu of paying a property tax, as a qualification for voting.[67] So, too, could the paying of a municipal income tax. In Ontario, property-less male payers of the municipal income tax (on incomes above $400) had been enfranchised as such in 1874. They were referred to as "income tax voters."[68] When Ontario's municipal income tax was replaced by a provincial one in 1936, Toronto had to scramble to figure out how not to disenfranchise citizens no longer paying a municipal tax.[69] And though Ontario enfranchised municipal income tax payers, those who paid only a poll tax didn't get the vote.[70] The diversity of legislation in this area is staggering to research but full of illuminating material. Someone should find out how it came to be in 1942, for example, that "domestic maids" were singled out by occupation to be exempt from the City of Saint John poll tax but permitted to pay it if they wished.[71] Almost certainly, the option of paying it was to give them the option of voting in the city's tax-based franchise system.[72] All of these various supplements to property taxation had a common impact on the franchise: they ensured that political citizenship had a price.

The poll tax statutes were mostly enacted in the nineteenth century, before women's suffrage victories. They were aimed at men of voting age, those deemed to have a duty to contribute, to pay the price of citizenship, even if they owned no property. Some (perhaps most) of the poll tax statutes exempted men over sixty, suggesting that the poll tax payer was almost certainly imagined as a manual labourer whose ability to earn income would decline later in life. The tax idea implied was the old one, that young men, especially single ones, were not yet properly contributing to the carrying of society's burdens, whether personally, by supporting dependent women and children in their families, or socially, by giving of their surplus to public projects.[73] Having young men pay a poll tax raised relatively insignificant amounts of revenue: the point of the tax was its symbolism. By paying it, they made themselves contributing citizens. Some cities exempted people who earned less than a minimum amount.[74] Of course, an exemption of this sort was welcome in households where every penny was precious. However, if the poll tax was an individual's only municipal tax obligation, then exemption was also disenfranchisement in city elections. Tax relief for poor people was therefore both a means of income assistance and a means of political marginalization.

This was clear in Saint John in the 1930s. As property owners' tax arrears mounted, the city considered whether to relax its requirement that only citizens bearing a receipt for paid-up taxes could vote. In 1933, bills to exempt property tax payers in Saint John and some of its neighbouring parishes from this requirement were denounced by labour leader James Whitebone as class legislation. Unless poorer people, assessed only for a poll tax, were also allowed to vote without paying, relieving others would only "place the voting power in the hands of property owners." The bills were withdrawn, presumably leaving the qualified electorate of the city to shrink, albeit without the tilt that Whitebone had protested.[75] He knew, as did other observers of Saint John tax culture, that collecting the poll tax was always difficult because poll tax payers were usually low-wage earners.[76] With employment scarce and multiple family members depending on fewer incomes, scraping together the money for even a small tax was difficult. To also lose one's vote as a result was a lesser problem than failing to make ends meet on household basics.

During the Depression, Saint John was willing to allow at least some poor people to give up their franchise.[77] The trickle of tax appeal cases in 1932 grew more than tenfold to something of a flood in 1934 and 1935.[78] The vast majority sought relief on real estate taxes and water rates; only about two dozen concerned municipal income tax, personal property tax, rental tax, or poll tax. Various kinds of relief were granted: reduced assessments on real estate, relief from interest on tax arrears, householder exemptions for single earners now supporting their parents and siblings, or sometimes just a reduction of a family man's overall tax debt if his responsibilities were heavy.[79] When unemployed men were granted tax relief, if they were carrying only income and poll tax debts (rather than real estate arrears), they were still usually required to pay their poll taxes. Single women, such as teachers and clerks, were also required to pay this price of citizenship, even if they got other tax relief.[80] Those deemed by reason of "age, sickness, infirmity, or poverty" unable to contribute to "the support of government" were freed from even poll tax debts.[81]

Notes in the minutes concerning some cases indicate, however, that men who claimed the indigency exemption were asked to confirm in writing that they were giving up their franchise in exchange.[82] Widows (even those with small rental incomes) got a different deal. They were more often relieved of all their tax arrears than were able-bodied but impoverished earners with poll tax debts, and I have found no request in my survey of the 1930s tax appeal registers in which a widow was formally required to give up her vote in exchange for tax relief.[83] Yet widows would not be allowed to vote without their tax receipts. The council seemed to assume that they, and the indigent disabled, wouldn't be voting anyway. Saint John's long-standing practice of substantially exempting some of self-supporting women's wages and widows' property from taxation – what I have called elsewhere the "chivalric" tax exemption – was part of the same marginalization of women from both citizen duties and citizen rights.[84] People who could not vote, or perhaps people who, in the minds of some municipal officials, *should not* vote, had to choose whether, on the one hand, to save for poll taxes or franchise taxes in order to claim citizen rights or, on the other, to buy the necessities of life.

Put in this light, paying one's taxes meant different things, depending on the type of tax. In the interwar years, terms such as "property tax payer" and "income voter" suggested that being a "taxpayer" was not an unmodified, egalitarian position. Being a poll tax payer or a payer of customs duties or sales taxes meant that the room for negotiation and manoeuvre within the law was small and depended largely on the discretion of others. Such differences in the meaning of "taxpayer" became more controversial, over the 1930s, as poll taxes came increasingly into disrepute. They generated little revenue, partly because they were hard to collect.[85] Making the employer ultimately responsible for workers' poll taxes, as at least some of the statutes did, was a last resort.[86] When a bailiff in the town of Grimsby,

Ontario, seized some "goods and chattels" from the local dairy to cover an employee's unpaid five-dollar poll tax, the dairy's manager turned around and sued the town for damages.[87] It was also beginning to be seen as unfair that, in many jurisdictions, unmarried women didn't pay the poll tax. Some argued that, since women now wanted equal rights, they should expect to share burdens. Others pointed out that young women earned less than young men and found many occupations closed to them; if they had little money, their fathers would end up paying their poll taxes for them.[88]

After the Second World War, the debate resumed. In 1951, a taxation commission in New Brunswick noted that rural municipalities' property owners liked to raise poll taxes, which they did not pay, in order to keep their property taxes low, a practice that the commissioner described as "particularly unfair" partly because the poorer folk who paid only poll taxes were not eligible for rural county councils.[89] Over the 1950s in Ontario, various towns and cities asked the province to change the statute so that they could get poll tax revenue from women. Small though such revenue was, some argued that every penny counted. Others heaped scorn on the tax, pointing out that in Ontario the tax carried no voting rights and that the cost of collection ate up more than half of the take. Burlington's assessor spent twelve and a half days in court on poll tax cases, and the city's net on the tax that year was $1,900. Rooming and boarding house owners disliked having to give the names of their tenants; it was even suggested in Hamilton that men's attempts to avoid the tax roster were leading to a noticeable undercounting of the city's population. In 1953, about 300 of Ontario's 927 municipalities collected poll taxes. More and more dropped them over the decade.[90] By 1963, a Canadian Press survey showed that poll taxation remained only in central and eastern Canada.[91] A turning point might have come in 1965 when the US Supreme Court struck down the use of poll taxes as voter qualifications in American elections. In 1966, New Brunswick modernized its tax regime and eliminated poll taxes.[92] Their weight in municipal balance sheets had long been insignificant, their extension to women apparently controversial, and their association with lectures on civic responsibility and harassment stigmatizing. Other tax and franchise reforms in the 1960s no doubt helped to drop poll taxes into the dumpster of history.

Paid mainly by economically and socially marginalized men, poll taxes belonged to the same world as the Jones tax, the hidden sales tax, and the customs revenue. That was a world where payers of property taxes (the "regular tax payer"[93]) and payers of progressive income taxes thought it worth their efforts to make the taxes paid by the poor either hidden or sometimes too harsh to pay. Neither kind of tax levied on the poor carried the citizen clout associated with the larger direct taxes. Just as the right relation to property was moralized and racialized in relation to on reserve Indians, so too, and relatedly, the paying of direct taxes was in general deemed the sign of a real citizen, of political belonging. The women's suffrage movement had raised the possibility that the basis of citizenship might be contributions other than taxes – motherhood, for example, or simply the capacity to engage in public reasoning. In interwar Canada, though, the residue of an older, less democratic, model of citizenship persisted in incoherent, sometimes racialized, links between political rights and taxpaying obligations. The meanings of taxation in Canadian political culture would remain unsettled through the 1950s and 1960s, until the unrestricted federal enfranchisement of Indians in 1960 and the end of the remaining municipal poll taxes in the late 1960s.[94] In the interwar years, the messy tangle of multiple tax regimes had made many injustices possible. The ones discussed here were usually invisible to white, middle-class, settler culture, but in other respects the 1930s forced into the mainstream other aspects of the chaos of Canadian taxation.

6
Honour, Confidence, and Federalism during the Depression

ALTHOUGH TAXES ARE DEBTS OWED TO THE STATE, like other debts they are a kind of deal, and like all deals the parties involved make their specific arrangements in ways that reflect the degree of trust between them. Without much trust, the deal is shored up by penalty clauses and backed up by bailiffs and courts. The taxpayer might have taxes taken before income and goods reach her hands. Poll taxes and other such taxes on the poor were simple extractions, and default could trigger a stern penalty.[1] With the Jones tax and the Manitoba wages tax, employers acted for the state, and taxpayers had no choice but to pay. When the state taxes the poor, there is little room for the pleasantries of honour. However, when the tax deal is between equals, the terms of the deal are gentler, and honour plays a role. That's why, during the interwar years, the element of coercion in federal income taxation was kept well in the background.

The credit crisis of the 1930s strained that gentlemen's agreement, however. Hard times raised the stakes in the moral game and brought into the open the power relations of public finance. Governments hungry for revenue to service debts and to back new borrowing were freshly inspired to regard citizens skeptically as tax evaders. Tax delinquencies among those able to pay began to look shameful. Deploring the cold hearts of those who could pay their taxes but did not, Senator L.A. Wilson, a millionaire, called wealthy tax dodgers "human icebergs" and urged them to "do their duty to the State, and more particularly to the poor."[2] Wilson was unusual among Canadian millionaires in his tax rhetoric. But his views on paying income tax as a matter of honouring an honest debt were part of a broader current in tax culture, one that came to the fore in the 1930s. Honour mattered in public finance, both for individuals and for governments.

The conjoined emergencies of the Depression – mass unemployment, plummeting commodity prices, and a credit crisis – made it both harder and more necessary to raise public revenue. Canada's position as a debtor nation, its governments and industries dependent on international lenders for credit, compounded those challenges. Being a debtor nation entailed a conservative fiscality. An exceptionally cautious style of taxing and borrowing, already visible during the First World War and the 1920s, was confirmed in the tax culture of the 1930s. As the challenges of survival mounted for both Canadians and their governments, so did the difficulty of borrowing and taxing. To accomplish both, revenue authorities and elected officials made personal honour and public reputation central elements of the public finance talk of Canada in the 1930s. In the process, the tax question necessarily became a constitutional question: in a federation, how did the honour of the parts (the provinces) determine the reputation of the whole? The answer depended significantly on how successfully each could tax, and that meant dealing with the Constitution.

Income Taxation and Personal Honour

Collecting a debt from someone who doesn't think they should pay it is usually more expensive than collecting it from someone who believes that they should pay it. It costs the creditor to have someone pester – or harass – the unwilling debtor. The taxman knows this and tries to keep the costs of collection low by encouraging taxpayers to step up and pay right away rather than waiting to be pursued. In 1934, the head income tax collector (C. Fraser Elliott, commissioner of income tax) proudly reported that Canadians had heard this message and that Canada's rather small corps of income tax inspectors and their staff were able to collect the taxes owed (on average) at the cost of merely 2.9 cents per dollar collected every year.[3] (In comparison, the Customs and Excise Branch averaged costs of 3.14 cents per dollar on its substantially larger annual collections between 1927 and 1930, after the big 1927 reforms.[4]) One citizen was so impressed by this point that he or she wrote free verse on the subject. Thrillingly entitled "Collecting Income Taxes," this effusion appeared in the *Quebec Chronicle-Telegraph* during the 1933 budget debates. As poetry, it plods, but it shows that Elliott's message about income tax compliance was getting public attention:

No one thought this stupendous work
Could be performed at such low cost,
But Mr. Elliott
Gave credit to Canadian tax-payers
For such results,
And appealed
To all,
To play the game,
And help Canada,
To pay her debts,
And reduce taxes,
In years to come.
Such a clarion call
Is stimulating
And makes it easier
To pay our share
Of Canada's debt
As a patriotic duty
But –
We must not forget
The low cost
Of collection.[5]

Maintaining a low cost of collection meant keeping the assessment and enforcement staff of the income tax branch to a minimum. Even in 1945, after its later Second World War growth, the enforcement unit of the national income tax service employed only four intelligence officers, whose job was to search out signs of tax fraud.[6] Their methods worked well in assessing wages and salaries: employers had to submit payroll information, and it was thus possible to spot-check individuals' reports of that kind of income. Income from property – rent and interest, for example – was harder to find. A really effective tax inspector would follow the news to note who had bought and sold income properties or who had come into an inheritance. Inevitably, though, not everything appeared in the newspapers. So the tax inspectors relied heavily on one powerful threat: going after the delinquent taxpayer's estate. Probate records, the description of a taxpayer's estate at death, would reveal the income-generating properties and other investments that the deceased had owned. It was then simple enough to see if the recently deceased had been declaring income from those assets over the years. If not, then those happy to inherit the estate would, less happily, get bills for income tax arrears.[7]

These systems were not infallible, and the tax authorities were aware that "human beings, otherwise law abiding, will always try and beat the tax collectors."[8] They thought that they were pretty good at "protecting the revenue," but some well-informed Canadians thought not. The most colourful was millionaire Member of Parliament from Vaudreuil-Soulanges, and later Senator, L.A. ("Larry") Wilson. A bilingual Quebecker of Scots and Franco-Quebec parentage, Wilson had been a deep admirer of Laurier and was a Liberal to his toes. He had made his fortune as a liquor merchant, and, if I read between the lines correctly, he liked his own products as much as he (proudly and openly) disliked prohibitionists. He delighted in his high social status, but he also liked being a man of the people: both impulses were satisfied by his benefactions to hospitals, parks, and universities. He enjoyed getting an honorary degree, but he also liked to hang out with the people in "cheap" cafés. William Lyon Mackenzie King, who depended on him for contributions to the party through the hard times of the Beauharnois scandal, called him at various times "most amusing" and "a buffoon," but, like many others, King noted especially that Wilson was "very kind."[9]

Unlike some rich populist politicians of our own time, Wilson thought that paying taxes was both a duty to the state and an expression of care for the poor. He also thought that the Department of National Revenue was incompetently allowing the rich to evade some of the taxes that they morally and legally owed. In 1933, he read into the Senate record the remarks on this subject that he had first made in the House of Commons when he was a new MP in 1926. His 1926 speech is worth quoting at length because it distills the ideal of honour that I am concerned with here, the ideal that would have kept the costs of collection low had it been not only widely endorsed but also universally followed:

> I want to impress upon the Minister of Finance that there are concealed bonds, coupons and securities hidden away in strong boxes throughout this country, not paying their honest taxes to the Government. I want to say on the floor of this House that I believe some people are concealing

their securities, bonds and coupons payable to bearer, and thus cheating this country of its just dues. These men are despicable; they should not be called Canadians, and I claim that the Minister of Finance, who has it in his power, should start the machinery to break into these strong boxes, if necessary, and make the owners of these concealed bonds pay what is due the Government ... I claim that the Minister of Finance and the Government, who are striving by every means to increase the revenue of this country, should see to it that the man who is hiding coupon bonds and trying to defraud the Government and the common people of this country who are earning their living by the sweat of their brow, should be brought before the criminal courts of this country.[10]

Wilson went on to endorse the usual method of finding bond income by investigating probate records. But he called on the government to become a bit more aggressive. He suggested that there be an announcement in the papers saying that, if tax authorities found any evidence of concealed bonds in a probate statement, then the malefactor's *whole estate* should be confiscated: "That man will then start thinking of his family and pay his honest debts. That is my advice, Mr. Minister, on that question, and I think in that way the treasury of this country would be the richer by several million dollars."[11] In a nutshell, as one newspaper reported, he called some of his fellow millionaires "rats."[12]

Wilson, as a speaker, liked to go for laughs and melodramatic shudders, and he seems not to have been much of a "team player," either for his class or for his party. He claimed that, after his 1926 speech, he had been asked ("by members and ministers on both sides of the House, by friends of the bankers and others") to restrain his remarks on the subject of tax evasion.[13] Prime Minister King muttered in his diary that "Larry" had ignored "all the proprieties."[14] But by 1933 Wilson's ideas about how to break open the strongboxes of bondholders were deemed practical. Indeed, in some circles, the measures that Wilson proposed in 1933 had become commonsensical. A conservative investment newsletter, *Financial Counsel,* said as much.[15] In November 1932 and again in March 1933, Wilson had described tax-dodging bondholders as "human icebergs" and "bloodless sharks," accusing them of failing in "their duty to the State, and more particularly to the poor."[16] The editor of *Financial Counsel* rose to the defence of the owners of government bonds, calling them "amongst the most potent influences towards the maintenance of the credit of the country." He chastised Wilson for including all "holder[s] of a bearer bond as a class that deserves ridicule and condemnation" just because "a percentage of bondholders took advantage of the negligence" of governments "to take the most obvious steps for tightening up the income tax regulations in connection with bearer coupon bonds."[17] In the view of *Financial Counsel,* this was simple discriminatory libel against a useful group. Wilson denied tarring all bondholders with the same brush, but he warned that "independent and fearless men" (clearly putting himself in the starring role) needed "able and intelligent writers," such as the editor of *Financial Counsel,* to encourage the rich to "lend a helping hand to pull unfortunates out [of] the ditch" (by paying taxes). He warned that to fail in that responsibility was to encourage "the spread of poverty and crime" and to invite "Communism and Socialism" into "peaceful Canadian homes."[18]

The remedies that *Financial Counsel* thought were obvious and that Wilson recommended also appeared in letters to Bennett and Rhodes from other Canadians. Middle-class men were as likely as the most angry workers to point to bondholders as the villains of public finance. Usually themselves the owners of some securities, they were aware of how such instruments worked and how they might be used sneakily to slough off a large measure of a personal income tax obligation. Both in a spirit of anger about their own burden, and in an endorsement of the larger ability-to-pay principle, middle-class men wrote to the finance minister to offer schemes on how to improve the collection of revenue, usually with an aim to close off avenues of evasion.[19] As one investment dealer wrote, "it is unfair to yourself, to Canada, and to the writer, to persist in following the wrong course whereby large sums can, and will, escape payment."[20] As early as 1931, MP R.C. Matthews, representing the riding of Rosedale in Toronto, home to many Bay Street financiers, wrote to Bennett to suggest plans for finding and taxing hidden bond income. That Bennett approved of such measures is strongly indicated by his appointment of Matthews as minister of national revenue in 1934.[21]

While middle-class letter writers criticized the competency of the tax apparatus from a standpoint of honest competitors and defenders of ethical investment firms, other critiques emerged during the 1930s. Socialist voices picked up and carried on the organized farmers' established critique of incompetent income tax collection. In 1935, for example, the League for Social Reconstruction quoted extensively from a *Canadian Forum* piece by economist D.C. MacGregor of the University of Toronto, rather blunt on the topic:

From the narrow fiscal viewpoint, the principal defence of Canadian public finance is this: the tax-collecting capacity of governments is less than the tax-paying capacity of the people. This is chiefly due to the incompetence of both the federal and provincial civil service, almost none of whom are properly qualified for administering finance in the post-war [First World War] world.

He was not especially impressed with the policy makers either, suggesting that

The weakness and rustic ignorance of many politicians necessarily hinders the introduction of common-sense reforms, especially in the law and administration of the income tax ... In Ontario and Quebec, where four-fifths of the taxable income exists, the moderately well-to-do are virtually untaxed.[22]

The editor of *Le Devoir* (not noticeably a socialist) agreed. Commenting on Finance Minister Rhodes's 1932 announcement of plans to take on tax evaders, Georges Pelletier asked "how will he succeed in that, when we know that, till now, the rich have hardly paid any income tax at all, while the much less well off have paid every year since 1917?"[23]

Such criticisms of the tax-assessing and -collecting competencies of the Department of National Revenue were at least somewhat warranted. The two men who headed the income tax section of the department between 1927 and 1939, Chester S. Walters and C. Fraser Elliott, were committed to a taxpayer-centred, negotiation-oriented style of collection. The statute gave the minister – the department – many opportunities to exercise discretion, and such opportunities were used. A 1931 briefing document by the department on income tax collection set out its general approach: "There are few prosecutions. The department is interested in getting the money, not in sending people to jail ... Tax evasion is so common that the tax officials do not put it down to criminality. They merely go after you to compel payment ... Even admitting that you have tried to put one over, they are lenient."[24] Commenting at a 1930 tax conference, Elliott asserted that the federal income tax was successful because tax officials had communicated to "the people" that tax inspectors were their "advocates," not their adversaries. Having been formed in the face-to-face world of municipal administration, the senior of the two, Walters, had learned to present himself as "a friend" of taxpayers, on their side, always willing to consult with them. He and Elliott had learned "the psychology of the taxpayer."[25] In avoiding both rhetorical threats and criminal prosecutions, enforcers of the federal income tax relied on persuasion more than coercion. Even when the department intensified its enforcement efforts after 1932, it relied mainly on misdemeanour charges brought in magistrate's courts rather than on criminal indictments, and the penalties that it sought were fines rather than jail terms.[26] As late as 1946, the Canadian income tax collection apparatus was judged by an American tax official to be as understaffed and ineffectual as the American Internal Revenue Service had been in 1918.[27] Whether out of necessity, from understaffing, or out of a conviction that income taxation should be a matter of honour, the approach of National Revenue made the risks of evasion low and left plenty of room for prospective taxpayers to decide how fully they would comply with the law.

Especially in the case of self-employed professionals, the income tax return must have been something like the first offer in a negotiation.[28] But for everyone assessed for the federal income tax, the temptation to understate income would have been strong. It was especially strong in occupations in which income was variable or in any occupation in a time of economic instability. When a bad year followed a good one, the tax bill for the good year came due in the middle of the bad one. Income tax was not deducted at source. Provident people were expected to save up to pay their income tax bills when they came due. In reality, some people – possibly not all of them improvident – borrowed, or tried to borrow, to pay their taxes.[29] In this situation, if you had income that you thought the tax assessors would likely not find, it would require deliberate moral choice to include it in your return and to pay the sum owed. After deduction at source was introduced in 1942, most taxpayers' range of moral choice was much reduced (though not eliminated). But before then paying an income tax bill was a moment when one's sense of right conduct, one's honour, came into play. In the absence of a large and effective revenue service, committed to the use of criminal prosecution, the dangers of being caught in misrepresenting one's income, and therefore one's tax debt, were relatively slight, and the voluntary element of compliance was high.

In this context, then, it is not surprising to see that the role of the nation's chief income tax collector was to exhort and persuade. This role seems to have come naturally to C. Fraser Elliott, the energetic and intelligent lawyer who took the helm of the federal income tax agency in 1932.

He was a veteran of the Great War, a star varsity team canoeist and single-blade paddler in his youth, and an active Rotarian. He had served in the department for five years as second-in-command to C.S. Walters.[30] Along with Walters, an accountant, also a Rotarian, and former mayor of Hamilton, Elliott had reformed the federal tax administration after its rather rickety first ten years under the controversial R.W. Breadner.[31] In public events such as a 1934 radio address, Elliott addressed income tax payers as people motivated by patriotism, business values, a sense of fairness, a regard for social status, and good moral character. In his framing, income tax to them was not "a penalty" but "simply one way in which one may discharge one's duty as a worthy citizen and serve the nation." He pointed out that collection costs for income tax revenue were low – less than three cents for each dollar collected. Why was the cost of income tax collection so low? Because, he claimed, the taxpayers of Canada had given the income tax their "loyal cooperative and patriotic support." If that were not the case, were there to arise "a general resistance movement to tax measures which would require coercive means to enforce compliance," then the cost of an income tax would be "enormously" increased.[32] So evaders not only raised costs by withholding what they owed but also increased others' burdens by requiring expensive investigations. Those whose incomes fell below the taxable level, Elliott emphasized, "should know ... of the acceptable manner in which those who do pay it are bearing it." In 1946, as he was about to retire from the taxation branch, looking back over trends in tax enforcement, Elliott deplored the effects of an emerging jurisprudence that sanctioned tax avoidance, in effect telling taxpayers that they might properly "avoid tax but not evade it." In his view, such legalism had "adversely influenced the moral tendency of the public."[33] Even in his last year as head tax collector, he insisted publicly that income taxation worked only because income tax payers were, in the vast majority, honest, intelligent, and law abiding.[34]

This sort of public rhetoric seems to be hard to reconcile with the 1931 statement from his department that tax evasion was common. But the difficulty is only apparent. If it was helpful in enforcement to assume that evasion was ordinary, it was also useful to assert that most income tax payers were cheerfully compliant. Without a considerable expansion of investigative auditing staff and a bigger team of government tax lawyers, a rhetoric of threat would be empty. Better to try to convince the public that the system was working effectively and fairly. This entailed representing the income tax payer rhetorically as an honourable citizen, doing his or her bit voluntarily. And, equally, it entailed depicting the tax authority as fair and competent.

These images were of practical use. Elliott warned the 1945–46 Senate Tax Administration Committee that "confidence is hard to attain, but it is very easily lost. I believe we [National Revenue] have the confidence of the people of Canada ... There is nothing more important in the affairs of a nation than that the people should have absolute confidence in the integrity and efficiency of those who administer the tax laws." After vividly describing critics of the department as a yapping pomeranian pestering a majestic mastiff, he concluded that "confidence, I repeat, is one of the most vitally realistic things in the administration of a law of this kind. I believe we have it. Let us not lose it."[35]

Elliott was describing a moral world of income tax administration that, by 1946, had already begun to disappear. A 1936 decision in Britain's highest court had endorsed what we now call "tax planning" or "tax avoidance": that is, arranging business affairs for no business purpose other than to reduce tax liability.[36] However, during the early 1930s, Elliott had been correct to suggest that income tax compliance was not merely a legalistic thing. There existed an idea of deliberate tax avoidance as shameful. I found it expressed in private letters, not just in public rhetoric. For example, Canadian publisher Hugh Eayrs wrote to the minister of finance in 1934 to say that he was deeply offended when he thought that he was being accused of not having complied with the law. His conscience was clear, so he was not worried about being audited – he just found it unutterably distasteful to be addressed as though he were a tax dodger.[37] Rhodes reassured him that the letter from National Revenue had merely employed a standard form of address and that no aspersion on his character was intended by its stern tone: "It may be that the character of certain letters offends the sensibilities of men like yourself, who, I am sure, have only one desire, and that is to conform both in letter and spirit to the law." Eayrs, mollified, replied that

I can quite see the point of view which you urge upon me. It is, of course, simply a question of how things should be done. The first thing one does upon receipt of a letter such as I got is to take it as a reflection on his personal integrity, and to hit the roof! However, I am now down to the floor again and cool and calm.[38]

The eminence of Eayrs made protection of his reputation unusually vital. But income tax payers from more modest circumstances also saw in allegations of tax "irregularities" comments on their characters. The manager of Saskatoon's Woolworth's store, H.H. Hunking, took offence when revenue authorities accused him in 1933 of having intended tax evasion in 1924. Back then, he had given his wife some income-bearing securities (a move that, at the time, could indeed have served to reduce his income tax bill). Writing on behalf of Hunking, the premier of Saskatchewan spoke of his status as "a highly respected citizen." The logic of such a response is that a person of Hunking's standing and moral calibre would not do such a thing. It wasn't that Hunking couldn't or wouldn't pay taxes that he properly owed; rather, he objected to the insinuation that he was avoiding a tax debt.[39]

Of course, concern about one's reputation is not inconsistent with cheating, only with being found out. This much was clear in correspondence between a Montreal financier and Deputy Minister of Finance W.C. Clark during the 1933 budget debates. The financier, V.M. Drury, wrote to say that he knew of bondholders troubled by the public shame that they would face if their past evasions were revealed:

> An Officer of one of the Trust Companies in Toronto remarked in casual conversation that a great many owners of bonds who had previously not declared their interest earnings on income tax reports, were allocating their bonds to relatives and employees, to avoid the embarrassment of an investigation into their previous interest earnings. It had been intimated to him that if it were not for the possibility of an investigation into the past, these owners of bonds would include in their 1933 Tax Reports such earnings, and were it not for the disgrace that might follow such an investigation, they would be glad to pay in the future.[40]

Clark advised Drury that, if the bondholders whom he knew would make a clean breast of past tax evasion, "I am confident that the Commissioner would handle them in such a way that they would avoid any publicity at all and probably avoid penalties, though, of course, back taxes and probably interest would have to be paid where they could be paid."[41] The results of legal proceedings by which tax evasion could be prosecuted were, in theory, public (if only in the obscure form of *Exchequer Court Reports*). So if reputation was an issue for taxpayers, then there was an incentive for the status-conscious tax evader to avoid fighting a tax case to a decision. One of the few straightforward cases of large-scale evasion of personal income tax debt that made it to the point of detailed affidavits in Exchequer Court proceedings was settled out of court in 1936 and thus was not recorded in court reports. Nor did it appear in newspapers.[42] The nature of the settlement was not recorded in the court file. The taxpayer in question was a former speaker of the Quebec Legislative Assembly and an elderly member of a family of important lawyers.[43] In choosing to settle out of court, he apparently preferred not to be remembered for his tax evasions.

Not wanting to be known for tax evasion suggests a social norm (however often violated) of honouring income tax debts. That norm was visible in R.B. Bennett's rhetorical escape route from the income tax proposals in his 1931 budget. Although the proposals would have closed a notorious loophole – the rate-reducing family and personal corporations created in 1926 – another pair of measures drew a firestorm of criticism that forced him to withdraw all of the proposed measures. The sales tax, a much-deplored charge on the pockets of the poor, had been raised from 1 percent to 4 percent, but the income taxes on the highest incomes – those between $137,000 and $1 million – had been reduced.[44] Sixty wealthy Canadians, Bennett among them, would pay less income tax under the proposed measures, critics alleged. If this charge were correct, Bennett asserted on July 16, then "I should be unworthy of standing in the place I occupy." He asked the House to approve his withdrawal of the measure from which he supposedly would have benefited. He ostentatiously bridled (possibly spuriously, some MPs thought) at the impugning of his honour. In the process, he outlined how he could avoid paying a full measure of income tax and declared that he had never used any of these standard dodges: "I have maintained no corporation; I have set up no personal or family corporation with respect to my affairs. I have paid as an individual. I have maintained no trust funds abroad where my income should accumulate and where no income tax would have to be paid on it."[45]

In this passage, he made it clear that there were means by which, with the help of a good accountant, he and others could choose how much federal income tax to pay. And, like Larry Wilson in 1926, Bennett affirmed that a wealthy man could be proud of choosing to pay a lot of income tax. He went so far as to say that he took "pleasure" in paying his income tax.[46] Perhaps he believed, as J.W. Jones had affirmed in defending the special revenue tax of British Columbia in 1931, that income tax was a bill, like any other, that a solid citizen should gladly pay: "Do you not rather set up a Government to run these affairs for you – and having done so will you say you will have no part in settling the account? My opinion of you as B.C. business men, and Kiwanians, tells me differently."[47] A decade later the same metaphor was used by tax authorities to promote the new war income taxes: in a 1941 ad for a new instalment tax payment arrangement, a businessman is shown saying that income tax is "one bill I'm glad to pay."[48] In short, this tax rhetoric equated income tax paying with the standards of character that good businessmen were expected to observe in their ordinary practices of borrowing and buying.

There is also evidence that this norm was linked to a conception of personal morality at a deeper level than simple concern for reputation. The evidence appears in the voluntary payments of "conscience money," the conventional term for money paid to the revenue authority, usually anonymously, to honour tax debts owed but previously evaded. Between 1932 and 1934, there was a modest spike in the flow of such payments.[49] Tax authorities soon discovered why. In those years, an Anglican-based religious revival called the Oxford Group was having a substantial cultural impact. Canadians were reading a new (1932) book from one of the group's leading exponents, A.J. Russell's *For Sinners Only*.[50] From March to May 1934, the Group's "Team No. 1" were touring parts of Ontario, and in 1932 they had been in Montreal.[51] Their target audience was not the "down and outers" but the "up and outers" – middle-class, even well-to-do, people who would welcome a message of religious revival that would also bring greater personal happiness and moral transformation.

Men and women who embraced the Oxford Group message were a little like new members of Alcoholics Anonymous (a movement whose origins lay partly in the Oxford Group's teachings).[52] They undertook searching moral inventories; when the findings revealed to them their moral failings, they pledged to make amends. For example, a Montreal couple reportedly said, in paying an enormous debt to the customs department, "this payment of money owing the Government was a direct result of their changed outlook on life."[53] Smaller amounts arrived in the mail at tax offices, often accompanied only by a slip of paper with the word *Oxford* on it. An unusually loquacious contributor of conscience money wrote "for the enclosed thank Heaven and the Oxford Group." The editor of *National Revenue Review* did just that, publishing a "Thanks to the Oxford Group" piece in the February 1933 issue.[54] When conscience money payments were noted in the news, as they frequently were, it was confirmed in public discourse that to pay your taxes was not simply to buckle under grudgingly to the power of the state.[55] It was also to be a good moral actor, a decent fellow. As a Toronto newspaper editor noted approvingly, "when a religious movement leads people to pay debts which they could escape paying it may be regarded as practical religion. The Oxford Group have earned this distinction."[56] Oxford Group followers understood that not to pay their taxes was a moral failing. In this, they were not eccentric but reflected the norms (however patchily practised) of the middle-class culture from which the majority of income tax payers came.

Notwithstanding its connection to the Anglican Oxford Group, this moral norm was not limited to one sect.[57] It is clear from the records and reports of conscience money payments to the National Revenue offices that the Catholic Church also took tax debt seriously. There are reports of Catholic priests in Quebec forwarding sums owed by parishioners, who preferred to remain anonymous, after assuaging their guilty consciences.[58] And commentary in *Le Devoir* on Rhodes's 1932 anti-evasion measures included an impassioned statement of one of the fundamental moral grounds for tax compliance: evasions by those able to pay are immoral because they increase the burden carried by other, often less prosperous, citizens. Speaking of technical avoidance of a small excise tax on new cars, Louis Dupire (under the pseudonym Paul Anger), wrote that

> those two dollars that you keep for yourself even though, according to the spirit of the law, they are your debt to pay, are carried by all the other taxpayers; yes, I who don't have a car and whose tax burden is so heavy that I cannot even imagine ever having one, I am called upon, like others subject to taxation, to pay my share of those 200 cents.[59]

This public text expresses as a moral norm – the shared burden – something that appears in letters as more or less well-disguised envy of evaders. Income tax payers who accepted the necessity of their role in public finance expressed something of their class position in saying that, for their own part of the income tax burden to be fair, it had to be properly shared. As Dupire pointed out, a tax evaded by one fell on the shoulders of others. In matters fiscal, the actions of each were consequential for all. When this point was emphasized, tax talk implied social interdependence. But the social connections of tax honour were not usually about compassion for the vulnerable. Sometimes they were: Larry Wilson made the connection between paying taxes and helping the poor. But a thinner version of the honourable taxpayer entailed a commitment only to fairness among notionally equal competitors, where paying the tax debt was a liability that should equally hobble all. Nonetheless, whether as fair competition or as shared responsibility, there was a moral element to the discourse of honour in taxpaying.

Honour, Tax, and National Credit

In a similar way, there was something cultural in the moral framing of public debt. In public borrowing, the equivalent to having a reputation for personal honour is a government's having the confidence of lenders.[60] This confidence can be founded in part on reasonably objective data. For example, just before the Great War, a Canadian investment dealer pioneered a method of evaluating the merits of municipal bonds by calculating the relative size of the municipality's assessed value of property per capita, its given tax rate, and the existing bonds at a given interest rate.[61] In other studies, similar efforts, admittedly experimental, were made to correlate wealth and tax capacity.[62] But less objective considerations were as important or even more so. Was a government likely to use the tools at its disposal to allow price inflation and the related depreciation of the currency? Would it use its power in the investment market in ways that might reduce returns on bond investments? In a federal system like Canada's, how much responsibility did the central government bear for the finances of the other governments? How effective was the government at raising revenue? Was the political system stable? Were public funds safe from theft and well accounted for? And behind all of these questions was the basic one: were obligations to lenders likely to be met? In other words, would the government honour the nation's debts?[63] In all of these questions were elements of judgment. There was no fixed economic law that could tell a government or its creditors exactly which arrangements for taxing, spending, and borrowing would warrant solid confidence. The 1930s would expose all of these questions to scrutiny.

Two questions in particular attracted debate about confidence during the 1930s. First, which policy measures made a government likely to default deliberately on a debt (i.e., to repudiate the debt)? Second, could governments reduce the costs of their indebtedness without repudiating the debts? Ideas about taxation and honour figured in the discussion of each question. A profoundly changed tax system and a reinterpreted Constitution would emerge as a result of the negotiations on these issues. Many Canadian historians and scholars of law and politics have written about this period and the constitutional developments that ensued. My aim here is to contribute to that literature by illustrating some of the ways that perceptions of taxation figured in the struggles with public debt, federalism, and monetary policy. These perceptions were not simply based upon objective facts of taxable capacity but also entailed moral and sociological ideas.[64] In saying this, I position myself closer to those who argue that the BNA Act was an excuse for inaction in the 1930s rather than a real barrier to a greater role for the federal government.[65] However, I take more seriously than do constitutional cynics/realists the fear of a loss of confidence, a loss of national credit, upon which both Bennett and King based their parsimonious and much-deplored policies. The Constitution might have provided legal cover for the federal government's stinginess in unemployment relief, for example, but the judgment that prime ministers had to make about what constituted a genuine risk to the Canadian government's credit was a difficult one, and the consequences that they dreaded were fearsome enough to lead to hesitation. They worried about the real risks of even more widespread hunger, economic collapse, and violence.[66] Believing as they did, in the words of sometime Finance Minister Charles Dunning, in "the inexorable laws of the market," they worried.[67]

They also knew that, on questions of credit, blue ruin talk – with its risk of undermining confidence – could be used for political advantage. The politicians who occupied the key chairs of fiscal decision making in the 1930s – Bennett, Rhodes, Dunning, and King – could remember an episode from the 1920s that illustrated how easily strong feelings could be generated around the subject of national debt and how worrisome such talk could be. In 1923, the *Montreal Daily Star* launched a campaign of fiscal panic-mongering, known (and remembered for decades) as "The Whisper of Death."[68] The title of the series of articles referred to bankers', brokers', and big businessmen's previously private, "whispered" view that the country was headed for bankruptcy. The message of the campaign was that extravagant spending, mainly on railways, by weak politicians who selfishly curried voters' favour, had led to a burden of debt that should scare international investors and Canadians alike.[69] The *Daily Star* called on "A Banker" to point out that the debt was not just from the war, which an

honourable nation should of course feel obliged to pay, but also from reck-
less splurging on railway building.[70] The paper predicted that in twenty-
five years or less (some thought ten) the country would go bankrupt. "And
what must follow bankruptcy?" asked the reporter. "Repudiation or annexation. We must crawl out or sell out!"[71]

The *Montreal Daily Star*'s spin-masters thus expertly combined threats
to national pride with threats to actual nationality: when the Toronto
Globe charged the Montreal paper with exaggerating Canada's fiscal vulnerability, compared with that of the far more indebted United Kingdom,
the *Daily Star* thundered "does the 'Globe' think [Great Britain] is in danger of being annexed by France, by Belgium – or by Ireland? If the 'Globe'
continues to fool itself and to try to fool its readers with clap-trap of this
sort, it will wake up some morning under the Stars and Stripes – and will
never have known that the avalanche was coming."[72] The Liberal finance
minister dismissed the "whisper" columns as "Tory hysteria," and the
Toronto *Globe* characterized them as "political fiction of the blood-curdling
type."[73] But, just to be certain, Liberals took to public platforms to reassure
everyone, especially holders of dominion government bonds, that the nation's credit was sound.[74]

More soberly than those who had suggested in 1923 that Canada's political sovereignty was at risk, others pointed out in the 1930s that national
debt affected national credit. To build the country's productive capacity,
Canadians needed to be able to borrow internationally the large sums necessary for this kind of economic development.[75] This basic fact of Canadian
economic life was a matter of common sense in the Canadian business
community and (mostly) among political leaders. It meant that they perceived Canada as a debtor nation. Although the definition of "a debtor
nation" was controversial among economists during the interwar years, the
common sense among managers of debt and credit in Canada, including
policy developers in the Department of Finance, was that Canada was one.
And that meant it was essential to preserve the confidence of investors,
especially skittish foreign ones.[76] A debtor nation had to be perceived as an
honourable (and cautious) one.

When existing loans (in the form of Canadian government bonds) came
up for renewal, Canadian governments needed to know that the holders of
bonds (Canadian or foreign) would agree to renew the bond contract. If
they did, then they would continue to collect interest from Canada rather

than take back the money that they had loaned to it. The effect of this situation was to bias governments in favour of covering interest on public debt before any other kind of spending. If lenders had confidence in Canada and renewed their bonds, then all sorts of public spending were possible. If this confidence disappeared, then nothing was possible.

Politicians differed in their judgment of how far the holders of government bonds could be pushed. Some (on the left) thought that the threat of default and the context of deflation gave governments both the power and the right to force creditors to take, in the place of their old bonds, new ones that paid lower rates. Others (on the right) believed that this sort of tactic represented a violation of the contract, which (however appealing in the short term) would not be forgotten when a government had to go back to the debt markets in the future.[77] The obsession with confidence was what a new young member of the Department of Finance called, in retrospect, a "debtor mentality." When that young man, future Deputy Minister of Finance Robert Bryce, joined the department in 1938, the debtor mentality was "so widespread in Canada that it reached right up through the Finance Department to the prime minister."[78] We can hear the mentality expressed by Bennett in 1933. Allow inflation, he declared, and "confidence would be gone. And, with the departure of confidence, credit also. And with credit, the country."[79]

In this respect, Bennett and Rhodes saw Canada as different from the United States. As a rich creditor nation, the United States could take risks with its currency, and it did. Governor of the Bank of Canada Graham Towers noted the difference in 1937 when discussing with the Department of Finance the terms of a major new bond issue. Part of what made dominion bonds attractive, Towers pointed out, was that, over the previous ten years, the value of the Canadian dollar had run "a very even course" compared with "shifts and disturbances noticeable in the United States" with the American dollar.[80] The Depression had deflated currencies, and there had been considerable discussion of how monetary policy might reverse this effect. Voices on the agrarian left, such as Agnes McPhail, argued for a controlled inflation to support commodity prices.[81] Premier of Ontario Mitchell Hepburn urged inflation as well.[82] Within the Department of Finance, however, Rhodes had resolutely opposed using inflationary measures. Inflation was an alternative to covering bond interest by raising taxes but not one that Finance would accept. It was committed to "sound money" and the preservation of confidence in Canadian credit.

The deputy minister explained the basis of this position in a memo written on behalf of Rhodes in 1933:

The question of inflation in this country has both sponsors and opponents, but it is well to bear in mind that Canada is a debtor country. If inflation, even to a minor degree, was started in Canada, the value of our currency in the foreign exchange markets of the world would fall ... As this is debt that has been contracted by our various governments, the resulting cost to these governments in exchange charges would mean increased taxation [in Canada], offsetting the benefits the inflationists had desired.[83]

In short, to preserve national credit (and thus to keep borrowing costs low), there could be no fooling around with the value of the currency in which interest and redemption would be paid: deliberate inflation – "printing money" – would break or at least bend the promises made to bondholders, and nothing would be gained in so doing. Rhodes and his officials also condemned inflation for the suffering that it inflicted on the poor and those on fixed incomes: "He who tampers with the currency robs labor of its bread."[84] But the Department of Finance's commitment to "sound money" was aimed primarily at keeping borrowing costs manageably low. Saying the right thing about inflation was about maintaining lenders' confidence in the country's credit. Through back channels to a leading Wall Street investment firm, in fact, Rhodes heard that, if Canada "could keep away from inflation," the country might even attract investment refugees from Roosevelt's New Deal United States![85]

The job of maintaining the nation's credit, now as then, turns many a prime minister's utterances into sales speeches on behalf of the country's bonds: any government's claim to competence has been based upon its ability to sustain confidence and therefore to borrow on the best terms possible. Political leaders are especially important as bond marketers in times of emergency, when exceptionally large sums are solicited and when international debt markets are disrupted. Not surprisingly, then, when the dominion government launched its "National Service Loan" in November 1931, the prime minister, the finance minister, and the premiers were out in full force to help with its marketing.[86] In the fall of 1931, just as in the years of the First World War Victory Loans, New York and London bond markets were closed to foreign governments' loan issues. Consequently, the 1931 loan needed to raise funds for unemployment relief was sold exclusively to Canadians. They were told that putting their savings into dominion bonds would demonstrate their loyalty, their faith and confidence in Canada, even their commitment to helping out their fellow Canadians – while still earning an excellent rate of interest.[87] "Philanthropy Plus 5 1/8" promised a prominent Montreal businessman. That was a better yield on dominion bonds than any seen since the inflationary years of 1917–19.[88]

Businessmen joined politicians to help sell bonds in the 1931 National Service Loan drive. Patriotism combined with mutual aid was the pitch. No sacrifice was required, they asserted, to participate in creating "a national unit of mutual interest."[89] Admittedly, in exchange for raising relief funds now, there would be a collective bill payable to bondholders of $7.5 million in interest over the life of the bond (five or ten years). But that interest payout, the bond marketers argued, would stay in Canada rather than leave the country. And, they pointed out, Canadians with savings to invest could be among those to collect that interest, benefiting financially in the future while helping to stimulate prosperity now.[90] If these incentives were not enough, the CPR's Sir Edward Beatty gently cautioned, there was also a threat: "If the Federal Government does not get this money in a loan," he pointed out, "its only other recourse is to taxation."[91]

In the annual bond campaigns that followed the National Service Loan of 1931, pressure mounted to force bondholders to accept lower interest rates, a measure that many regarded as partial repudiation. More than a few voters had noticed that there was direct competition between paying interest to bondholders (i.e., people who had savings to invest) and paying even a miserable pittance in relief funds to unemployed workers. Both kinds of expenditure came from the same tax revenue.[92] Consequently, as much as there were critics of the relief racket, there were those who called for bondholders to forgo at least some of their claims on the public purse.[93] In 1933, J.S. Woodsworth, leader of Canada's new farmer-labour party, the Cooperative Commonwealth Federation, would point out that the Depression had increased the purchasing power of the dollar, so that the country was paying out war bond interest in dollars worth more than those used to purchase the bonds.[94] In effect, if in 1933 you sold a fifteen-year bond that you had purchased for $100 in 1918, you'd have to spend only $82.56 of the proceeds to buy the same quantity of goods that $100 would have bought in 1918. You'd have $17.44 left for other things.[95] In addition, there were the politically unsavoury facts that (1) proceeds from selling a war bond were tax exempt as capital gains and (2) the interest earned on all but the 1919 war bonds had been specifically exempted from income taxation all along. To a corporation (or a wealthy private citizen who sheltered investment income in a personal corporation), each tax-free dollar was thus worth 12 percent more than a taxed dollar from other kinds of income.

Opposition members reminded the public of these facts through questions in the House of Commons. For example, Rhodes responded in May 1933 to a question about the dollar value of tax-free dominion bonds still circulating. The answer, that there was nearly $500 million, meant that approximately $23 million of bond income went untaxed every year. At one of the tax rates charged on a solidly middle-class income (6 percent on taxable income between $5,000 and $6,000), the resulting tax revenue forgone was $1.4 million, more income tax than was collected in total from all incomes under $4,000 in 1932.[96] Tax-exempt war bond interest continued to be deeply offensive to the many Canadians who lacked savings or, now unemployed, had used up any savings. The obligation to bondholders competed with the obligation to care for the unemployed and their families. At the least, then, the minister of finance had to try both to reduce interest rates on dominion bonds and to collect some income tax revenue on the coupon interest that the treasury was paying out.

This effort fell mainly to Edgar N. Rhodes, minister of finance between 1932 and 1935. He was assisted by the fact that other governments during those years were defaulting on their bond debts. Default could take a variety of forms, some more unilateral than others. All involved telling creditors that, if they insisted on the full payment of interest or the full price of a mature bond, they would get nothing. Convinced on that point, creditors would renew their bonds at substantially reduced rates of interest. Inflating the currency would have the same effect.[97] Canada was able to do this (sell "conversion loans") through the 1930s, turning the 5.0 percent and 5.5 percent Victory Bonds into 4.5 and 3.81 percent bonds, because the market prices of those bonds had dropped along with the prices of commodities in 1930.[98] To protect the treasury, Rhodes took away from Canadian purchasers of those conversion loans the bonds' tax-exempt features. At a time when many municipalities (and even some countries, including nearby Newfoundland) were defaulting, a modest loss (the lower interest rate and loss of tax exemption) was better than a total one.[99]

There was one other means by which a government could counteract the interest payment drain on the treasury, and that was by introducing or raising the income tax on investment income. Some investors approved of that method because, in theory at least, a tax hit to their investment income could be temporary. Income tax rates might drop over the life of a long-term bond. Once a high-interest bond was converted to a low-interest one, however, the cost was permanent: the income stream from the bond was reduced for its whole, often long, life.[100] Unlike other forms of debt reduction, there was, at least in form, no repudiation of the original bond contract when a government taxed away some of the interest that it paid to its bondholders.[101] In the 1933 budget, Rhodes tried in this way to get back some of the interest paid out to holders of dominion bonds. He found out, however, that some investors saw this as a kind of repudiation. The episode illustrates both the policy weight of preserving "confidence" and the continuing vulnerability of Canada to the empire's financial centre.

In his 1933 budget, Rhodes proposed that Canada should begin, as Britain and the United States already did, to deduct tax at source from interest payments made to non-resident bondholders and other creditors. Those British or American bondholders would be able to deduct from the income tax that they owed to their own governments any tax taken by the Canadian treasury. Foreign investors were horrified.[102] After Rhodes announced the measure in his budget speech in the House of Commons on March 21, 1933, multipage telegrams from Canada's worried high commissioner in London began to arrive daily.[103] Ten days later London Stock Exchange brokers who usually traded in Canadian securities stopped doing so. Their action was a protest against the measure. Even this small and legitimate tax on investment income was unacceptable, they asserted, because it presented "uncertainties" about investment returns.[104] They were mounting a short, sharp, capital strike, and it was effective. The next day Rhodes stood in the House of Commons to deliver a "clarification," which had the effect of reversing most of the measure. He affirmed that non-residents owed Canada *no* income tax on interest income from any Dominion of Canada bonds or those guaranteed by the dominion. Nor would there be any income tax on any interest paid on any kind of Canadian bond if the interest was paid in a currency other than Canadian dollars. Of the $7 million in tax revenue that Rhodes had predicted the tax would bring, about $4 million would now come in from the "clarified" measure. A further concession was extracted a few days later as the result of a petition to the Canadian government from London securities dealers.[105]

Even so, Canadian finance specialists remained alarmed. The manager of the Montreal branch of the Bank of Montreal, Jackson Dodds, and a leading investment dealer, Ward Pitfield, sent Rhodes or Bennett letters on the subject later in April. Each included a clipping from the *Economist* of April 8, 1933, that referred to Rhodes's tax measure as "savouring … of partial repudiation" and warned that London would not tolerate the "mulcting" of foreigners in any of the many countries around the world where British capital was in demand. Any further such moves would only impair Canada's credit in London and New York. Rhodes replied, quite rightly, that his concessions had left the British with no basis for complaint.[106] An American commentator agreed, saying at the height of the panic that the tax revenue from the proposed measure would help to reduce Canada's national deficit, which would actually improve the market for Canadian public bonds.[107] But, in the final discussion of the episode in the House of Commons, Rhodes admitted that the London dealers' strategy had been to "frighten the poor colonial" and that, undoubtedly, they had succeeded in doing so. He also made it plain that he thought their tactics panicky and despicable.[108]

One Canadian financial journalist cheered Rhodes on. Arthur J. Smith of the *Vancouver Sun* applauded his comments about the Londoners' "whipping the poor colonial into line." "Our interests, sir, are right here on this continent and hundreds of thousands of Canadians would agree with that sentiment if a Canadian leader had the intestinal fortitude to say so in public … Canada will someday have to make a decision as the then colonies did at the Boston Tea Party."[109] Taxing investment income in foreign (sometimes expatriate) hands had surely been designed as a popular measure to appeal to just such anti-imperial sentiment. That Rhodes introduced it was to his credit; that he withdrew so much of it under threat only confirmed his view that, as a debtor nation, Canada was not fully sovereign in its fiscal regime, not entirely free to tax in any way that its finance minister thought right. London finance capital had flexed its muscle.[110] The national honour, of a certain kind, had been compromised by a touch of independence and preserved by reverting to the debtor's colonial stance.

Anti-evasion, Canadian Style

Canada's taxman had been warned off by London investors, and by quietly caving in Rhodes had secured their confidence. Later in 1933 a senior British government official circulated the assurance from Rhodes that Canada would "keep faith with investors" along with detailed descriptions of the taxation measures by which Canada would do so.[111] In contrast to the attempt to reach foreign investors, other anti-evasion measures in the Rhodes budgets were more successful. His combination of raised rates, lowered exemptions, and closed loopholes successfully increased revenues from income taxation and sales taxation, even as customs revenues and the economy shrank.[112] From 1930 to 1936, the revenue from income taxation grew while the gross national product (GNP) fell: in current dollars, income tax revenue increased by 17 percent while the GNP declined by 19 percent. Increased consumption taxes (tariff, excise, and sales) still generated the majority of tax revenues, but from 1933 on the sales tax, not the customs revenue, generated the lion's share.[113] In 1936, sales tax revenue had grown 43 percent from its 1930 amount, and after 1937 it would generate annually more than income tax revenue did (see Table 7). Investors could not fault the Canadian government for an inadequate tax effort. Federal income tax collection would become more effective but in ways distinctively discreet about evasion.

Of the new enforcement measures implemented by Rhodes, the most publicly visible and widely debated was the requirement that bond houses, brokers, and law firms document the ownership of bond and other investment income. Also noticeable were the reductions in exempt income amounts on personal income (and their elimination on corporate income). Opposition members pointed out that income earners in the lowest cohort were now paying 500 percent of their previous income tax (e.g., up to fifteen dollars from three dollars). They called for graduation of the rate scale to be steeper, with much higher rates on high incomes.[114] Another measure to increase income tax revenue that triggered private protests but not, apparently, public debates was elimination of the householder "equivalent to married" exemption.[115] Widespread though such concerns were, they remained in some sense private. Even the National Council of Women, for which tax questions affecting widows and wives had drawn considerable attention, had nothing to say on the loss of the householder exemption in its sections in the 1933 and 1934 *Yearbooks* on taxation and economics.[116] Newspaper reports of criticisms of the budget's tax measures emphasized the increasing burden on the poor: the excise tax on sugar in particular triggered cries of outrage.[117]

However, the quiet, matter-of-fact presentation of the 1933 budget hid some potentially controversial income tax measures. These Rhodes referred to as "minor" amendments in areas where the "administrative provisions" of income taxation needed to be strengthened. One such measure said, for example, that expenses and allowances charged to corporate income would be limited. Another promised to "strengthen" the section in the income tax statute that dealt with undistributed profits and their use in tax evasion. In 1935 in the United States, a measure of this sort would become the focus of a vituperative attack on President F.D. Roosevelt and all of his works. Roosevelt had swathed the proposal in the glamorous, shiny rhetoric of class equalization; Rhodes clothed his in a drab apron of mere housekeeping measures. It's hard not to see some gentle misdirection in the wording of the Canadian resolution: rather than referring to undistributed profits, the budget used the section number of the statute, proposing to "clarify it" and make it "more certain and effective."[118] Who could be against that? If Rhodes had openly discussed all of the problems related to that section, about a method of corporate income tax evasion, then there might well have been a lively public discussion.

But Rhodes seems to have preferred to not arouse excited discussion on tax questions. His budget speeches were exceedingly cool in emotional tone and sparse in rhetorical flourish.[119] During the debate on his new enforcement mechanisms, however, he represented the majority of income tax payers as "honest and decent and above-board," and he refused to "cry crocodile tears" for any troubles that sterner enforcement would make for the few who have not paid "their just dues to the treasury."[120] When incontrovertible evidence of widespread evasion came to his attention, Rhodes had quieter ways of getting the money than criminal trials or dramatic tax law revisions.

The quietness of his methods presents some difficulties for historical research. One needs to notice signs such as a budget resolution that doesn't name the problem that it addresses. However, the private correspondence of Rhodes allowed me to see how he tailored his public remarks to protect confidence rather than shame taxpayers. This strategy, in contrast to the emphasis on shaming and criminal prosecution favoured by President Roosevelt in the same years,[121] had a profound effect on the constructed image of Canadian taxpayers.

One episode in 1932 illustrates this well. In this case, Rhodes dealt with a particular problem of tax evasion so quietly that no one reading newspapers or Hansard would have known that the problem existed. In April that year, writing to the premier of Ontario, Rhodes noted that "a large number of Judges, including the Chief Justice, of the Province of Quebec" had not been paying their federal income taxes. He noted that there were "a few individuals outside of the Province of Quebec, [but] in the main ... the delinquents are found there." Perhaps understandably, Rhodes preferred not to draw public attention to the uninspiring fact that certain pillars of justice were failing to do their full duty as taxpaying citizens.[122] That they were mainly Quebec judges was especially sensitive in light of the legacies of the *Caron* case. Perhaps still unconvinced of the legality of the federal government's taxing of their salaries, these judges appear not to have been moved by moral suasion.

Lacking that lever, Rhodes nonetheless found a way to extract the tax. In March 1932, he introduced a bill concerning debts due to the Crown. It covered all manner of debtors, among them judges, whose salaries were paid by the federal government. Although it made no mention of income tax, the proposed legislation would allow the minister of justice to deduct the income tax that judges owed. The chief Liberal from Quebec, Ernest Lapointe, immediately stood up and asked "will this apply to income tax?" Remarkably, Rhodes did not answer the question. The vote was taken on the motion to introduce the bill, and the House moved on to other business. Lapointe must have felt invisible. Perhaps he was out of order. But to ignore so pointed and simple a question from a senior member of the opposition suggests that Rhodes preferred not to draw attention to his move.[123] He needed to collect the money but in a quiet way.

Rhodes explicitly said so in his private correspondence. In a letter to a former colleague, the Conservative premier of Nova Scotia, he explained why he had resorted to legislated garnishing rather than to law courts. He told the premier that publicity from such trials risked having a "very bad effect upon the public mind if they knew of the defiance of law on the part of those who should be supporting it."[124] And judges weren't the only high-status Canadians who escaped prosecution because "confidence" needed to be preserved. Journalist Blair Fraser described a moment in the 1930s when a revenue official, likely Elliott, asked Prime Minister Bennett for advice on how to deal with some major evaders of the income tax. At first, Bennett said "prosecute!" However, when he saw the list of names involved, he said "we can't do it. If we prosecute these people, we'll shake public confidence in the financial leadership of Canada."[125] On the one hand, then, the income tax required for its legitimation that efforts to seek out evaders be noticeable – hence anti-evasion provisions such as those of the Rhodes budget of 1933. On the other, to preserve trust in the system among smaller-income tax payers, Rhodes and Bennett thought it best to hide news of evasions by judges and financiers. The notion of the loyal taxpayer was a revenue-generating device, and Canadian authorities deemed it a more useful one than any attempt (far from well founded anyway) to depict National Revenue as a fiercely effective collector.

Federalism and Risks to National Credit

Throughout the 1930s, Rhodes and then Liberal Minister of Finance Dunning would struggle discreetly, against resistance from many quarters, to collect more revenue. Although we can only guess at how well they succeeded in finding the hidden wealth of the rich, we know that revolts, open and covert, brewed and sometimes bubbled up.[126] Demands on governments to spend on relief, and parallel demands that governments economize in their spending of taxpayers' dollars, made the lot of finance ministers and revenue ministers, both provincial and federal, a highly pressured one. Municipal treasurers faced the same problems and were less protected by distance from the anger of their constituents. Many Canadian cities and some provinces could not sell their bonds at all, and banks dictated increasingly harsh terms or refused outright to extend credit.[127] In the United States, much of the anger about public finance was channelled by the president into an attack on tax evaders and the dishonest rich. In Canadian political life, however, the discretion of political leaders kept discussion about taxation – full of class and regional meanings as it would have been – out of the public arena. Fiscal woe ended up, instead, in constitutional debate.

When junior governments lost the confidence of lenders, they had to turn for help to the dominion. During the 1935 election, Bennett trumpeted that his government had loaned the provinces $87 million "to maintain their honor": that is, to prevent default.[128] After his government was defeated, and the Liberals under King returned to power, the new finance minister, Charles Dunning, attempted to negotiate an arrangement, a loan council, whereby the federal government could ensure that provinces taxed and spent appropriately in return for federal loans. The effort to create a loan council, as Australia had done, famously failed in Canada. Alberta held out and was duly punished by the federal government. The province defaulted on its bonds in 1937.[129] By that year, the Ontario government had already repudiated some Ontario Hydro bonds.[130] It was easy to see that Montreal was sailing toward default, and the credit of the Province of Quebec was fragile, too.[131] With the credit of the junior governments vulnerable, the credit of the federal government was also threatened. Thus, when the dominion had to go to the debt markets in 1937, to convert the 1917 Victory Loan twenty-year bonds, the prospectus for the dominion bond issue made it clear to prospective buyers that the federal government had no legal obligation to back the debt of the provinces.[132] But pointing to the legal framework of the federation was only a stopgap measure. The dominion's real obligations were based upon moral and political considerations: the Alberta default had hit small pensioners' incomes as well as corporate balance sheets. Letting more provinces default wasn't a good option. Thus, dominion loan guarantees to more compliant provinces still posed a risk to national credit. If junior governments weren't able to raise a revenue adequate to meet needs and inspire confidence among lenders, then something would have to be done. Reorganizing the federation's sharing of taxation powers was on the table. The chronic discussion of this question since the Great War needed to end.

And so, in 1937, as all Canadian historians know, King convoked a royal commission on federalism. Less well known is that it was sometimes referred to as the royal commission on taxation.[133] In the fall of 1936, one of the commission's most enthusiastic advocates had been the Canadian Chamber of Commerce (with former Minister of National Revenue R.C. Matthews as its president). Headlines made it clear that it was the fiscal dimension of federalism that was of interest to them: "Probe Requested into Tax Scheme" reported on the chamber's October 1936 resolution to ask for a royal commission "to enquire into our present system of taxation, with a view to having a more equitable distribution of the burden."[134] In December, the chamber followed up with a call for the royal commission "to examine the whole scheme of national finance, with a particular view to elimination of duplicated and overlapping Government services." Among such services was the administration of "tax assessments and collections."[135] Although federalism is more than just a tax system, it is always a tax system. The strains of the international economic crisis of the 1930s had exposed the incoherence of Canada's federalism. Its inequities were many, but none could be remedied until something was done about the constitutional interpretation of taxing powers.

Faced with junior government defaults, threats of defaults, and rumours of tax strikes, King's government undoubtedly used the Royal Commission on Dominion-Provincial Relations as a safety valve, a means to give tax protesters a channel to express their grievances. But the commission's work was useful for more than just spreading oil on the troubled tax waters. With the help of an unprecedented mustering of economics researchers, the commissioners undertook to see Canada in a fresh way, as a fiscal whole. Their reports provided the first modern history of Canada as an economy, in the sense that Timothy Mitchell has pointed out: "the economy" as an integrated system whose functioning is properly the object of scientific theory and investigation and whose characteristics are something larger than just an assemblage of particular markets.[136] The commissioners had a view of economics as an objective science, locked in a struggle with the irrational expedients and the populist pandering and patronage that they called, in a nutshell, "politics." In this, they shared a common enemy with those who campaigned for National Government, though, rather than calling for authority concentrated in a strong man, their positive project was to find a basis in authoritative social science for a systematic and coherent set of fiscal policies and constitutional powers. Time and again in the records of the proceedings, the commissioners made it clear that only witnesses with claims to a research-based view, free of anything resembling alternative ideologies or partisan commitments, would be taken seriously.[137]

In their final report, the commissioners were scathing on the subject of Canada's tax system and the politics that had built it. Canada's taxes were unfair and inconsistent with the efficient production and use of wealth because politicians made revenue policies on the basis of short-term expedience rather than on principle, and as a result the tax system was an intricate mess. Worse still, the investigation of tax incidence was so rudimentary in Canada that it was "impossible to say with confidence what weight of taxation any one taxpayer bears." Politics, with its eye to short-term "expedience," had created this situation, hiding rather than revealing the true workings of the economy. The normal methods of politics offered no solution to the unfairness of the tax system: "The ultimate consequences of taxation may be so obscure that it is quite futile to rely on the taxpayers themselves making known through their parliamentary representatives the full effects of the tax."[138]

Remarkably, but in a sense rightly, the Rowell-Sirois commissioners asserted that there was no value to tax policy makers in voters telling their MPs how voters as economic actors were harmed or helped by a particular tax policy. This was a dramatic shift in the political role of taxpayer interests, and its foundation lay in the emerging research on macroeconomics. Commonsensically now, but startlingly then, the commissioners held that taxation was not simply a burden. The "ultimate consequences" of taxation were not a direct subtraction from a wage bill or the appearance of an increased tax liability on a balance sheet. Taxation's effects could be indirect, affecting personal and business circumstances through impacts on price levels, interest rates, or money supplies. In theory, increased taxation, correctly targeted and up to an unspecified percentage of the national income, could end up improving purchasing power or increasing available credit, thus making higher taxes, however paradoxically, a net benefit to at least some voters.[139] However, the ability to see such macrolevel tax effects depended on data that most taxpayers could not access and mathematical skills that few possessed. Taxpayers, the commissioners implied, lacked the capacity to know their own interests. The economic science of the Rowell-Sirois report squared off against the ill-informed play of self-interest that, according to the commissioners, was politics.

Developments in public policy in Canada through the war years and the 1950s show that the Rowell-Sirois commissioners' view of tax politics would become the new common sense in Canadian public administration circles. Anything savouring of partisan populism got short shrift from the minister and the tax policy men in the Department of Finance until the late 1960s. In the long 1950s, the mainstream national parties usually treated tax policy questions as matters for economists. By insisting that tax questions were best answered by experts, the Rowell-Sirois Commission framed them differently than did politicians and tax resisters in the United States in the late 1930s. There the constitutional focus of tax politics was a movement to repeal the Sixteenth Amendment, the legal basis of the federal income tax.[140] The repealers had already won one constitutional victory – they had challenged the legality of prohibition and had won, through repeal of the Eighteenth Amendment. While positioning themselves during that fight as defenders of liberty, they had expected that the return of booze tax revenue would end the federal income tax. When that expectation was not met, they set out to take down the constitutional basis of federal income taxation, the Sixteenth Amendment. In this kind of campaign, as in the constitutional politics of the United States more generally, great matters of principle – liberty, privacy – were deemed necessarily to be in question, even though narrow material interests drove the campaigns.[141]

In contrast, the work of the Rowell-Sirois Commission dealt with a different kind of constitutional legal culture. First, the prospect of successfully amending the Canadian Constitution was small. Second, the taxing power of the dominion had been firmly settled in a recent test case rather than being the result of a highly contested constitutional amendment. And third, Canada's constitutional battles had not been fought primarily on large matters of principle. Canadian constitutional jurisprudence was mainly concerned with jurisdictional questions, the division of powers. The rights in question were usually the rights of governments, not those of citizens.[142] For example, Nova Scotia argued that its government could not tax income because the dominion government had "appropriated" that means of taxation in 1917. Its claim was not that fundamental human rights or property rights were violated by the dominion income tax but that the senior government had effectively taken over that part of the tax base that the province, in theory, could have exploited. Although the dominion had been rightly apologetic about adopting this measure of direct taxation, the federal income tax had nonetheless been bad constitutional manners.[143] At stake in Canadian constitutional debate were sometimes substantial matters of justice – such as the survival of religious and linguistic minorities or the capacity of the maritime provinces to develop and prosper – and from these matters sometimes arose passionate, even inflammatory, debate.[144] More often, however, jurisdictional disputes were fairly transparent legal devices by means of which politicians or business interests, or both, pursued rather grubby goals.[145]

Constitutional politics thus appeared in Canada as either profoundly divisive or irritatingly petty, more likely to destroy or degrade the nation than to galvanize it to some worthy human end. In setting themselves firmly against "politics," whether party or ideology or narrow provincial rights agitations, the Rowell-Sirois commissioners limited Canadians' engagement with certain large and dramatic questions. Instead, they framed the problems of public finance in Canada as those requiring not greater justice but better science.[146] This was a modestly conservative approach, confirming the mainstream economic liberalism of most Canadian business and political leaders. However, given how little Canadians in the 1930s could know about basic questions of national accounting and the actual scale of taxable capacity, the call of the Rowell-Sirois Commission for less politics and more research was also forward looking.[147] There really was a need for better science as a condition of greater justice.

Meanwhile, in the 1930s, there were problems with Canadian taxation that one did not need an economics degree to understand. The system wasn't fair, as every public official knew, from city treasurers, to customs collectors, to municipal magistrates, income tax inspectors, Indian agents, commissioners of income tax, and finance ministers. Hard-pressed Canadian wage and salary earners might have felt some envy of the United States if they compared the Rowell-Sirois mandate to Roosevelt's charge to the 1937 Joint Congressional Committee on Tax Evasion and Avoidance. "When our legitimate revenues are attacked," Roosevelt warned, "the whole structure of our Government is attacked. 'Clever little schemes' are not admirable when they undermine the foundations of society." He derided "certain newspapers" for claiming that tax avoidance was not unethical, he expressed "deep regret" that lawyers of "high standing" participated in tax avoidance, and he distinguished between long-term tax policy questions and immediate "glaring" problems of tax dodging. In these, he said, "the decency of American morals" was involved. The committee was directed to recommend remedies for the "evils" that their inquiry would reveal.[148]

In Canada, politicians could have made something out of the moral deficiencies of Canadian tax dodgers. They could have positioned themselves as defenders of those Canadians whose household budgets, their means of subsistence, were truly strained by property taxes, poll taxes, cheque taxes, franchise taxes, and "show them the price" income taxes. But Senator Wilson was the only one who successfully, if only momentarily, ignored "all the proprieties" and grabbed some headlines with a moral critique of tax dodgers. The CCF got little press coverage for the concerns that they expressed. With an eye to preserving confidence in "the financial system," prime ministers, finance ministers, and C. Fraser Elliott preferred to tell Canadians that income tax payers were carrying their share as honourable citizens. The newspapers reported their assertions, and the convenient image of Canadians as responsible taxpayers, unlike those rebellious Americans, was burnished.

$ ¢ $

The interwar years had seen an enormous expansion in the taxing powers and competencies of both the federal government and the provinces. The taxation apparatus was summoned into its new and more elaborate state by the costs of emergency spending (the First World War and the Depression), the costs of developing economic infrastructure (roads, railways, land developments), and the costs of human welfare (education, soldier resettlement, old age pensions, mother's allowances, blind pensions). Critics of government extravagance focused less on the emergency drivers of expenditure than on spending for development and social services. But, regardless of the origins of the debt, what drove governments to expand the tax apparatus was the risk of sovereign default and the associated risks to bond markets more generally that ran through the whole period. In a variety of ways, governments had tried to make "confidence" a matter of broad public concern, whether by enrolling citizens as bondholders or appealing to their national pride, fear of bankruptcy, and sense of honour. In all of this, taxation played its part. Critics of the tax regime, like those who called for inflation or forced loan conversions, were discouraged, but not silenced, because of Canada's vulnerability as a debtor nation.

Income taxation had spread more broadly during the interwar years, but Canada's more developed revenue system was nonetheless still reliant, by the late 1930s, on consumption taxes. Canada's income tax law and practice remained generous to foreign investors, and corporation income taxes were low enough compared with those of the United States that Prince Edward Island and (still independent) Newfoundland ranked with the Bahamas as convenient off-shore tax havens for rich Americans. (Joseph Schick, inventor of the safety razor, reportedly became a Canadian citizen in these years to avoid paying American taxes.) For at least a period in the late 1930s, Canada's keen eye for tax competition drew American tax dodgers to incorporate Canadian tax shelters.[149]

Meanwhile, finance ministers and city treasurers in every jurisdiction in the mid- to late 1930s were locked in struggles to raise adequate revenues in the face of creditors' demands, voter resistance, tax evasion or avoidance, and incipient tax revolt. The country was still full of economic potential. But it was far from unified politically. Its various regions were very different economically, and its economic and tax data were so thin that even the

Rowell-Sirois Commission had to acknowledge that, on some important questions of tax equity and efficiency, it simply could not know the answers. Canadian voters had little to draw on, other than party loyalty and immediate self-interest, in thinking about which kinds of taxation were right and necessary. In this context, pocketbook politics of fairly primitive kinds inevitably dominated tax talk.

Some members of governments found this frustrating. For example, one senior Conservative MP, Minister of Railways R.J. Manion, wrote bitterly to a friend who had complained of the extravagance supposedly entailed in a minor reversal of civil service wage cuts in the spring of 1935. In response to the friend's threat that the Conservatives would be defeated at the polls, Manion wrote that he didn't much care about what would happen in the next election: "One gets terribly fed up with doing his best and receiving merely criticism instead of gratitude."[150] Finance Minister Rhodes was also beginning to lose his temper with the Gladstonian austerity-mongers. Their clichéd remedies for a deficit – cut expenditures, don't raise taxes – finally stung him into writing a widely distributed letter in which he pointed out that firing every civil servant and cancelling all of their pensions would still leave a deficit in the federal budget. Slashing expenditures on the government railway had "almost ruined [Manion's] health," he concluded.[151] Being at the nexus of implacably conflicting pressures was no fun. Dunning, the Liberal who took the Finance reins from Rhodes later that year, was diagnosed after four years in the portfolio with "adrenal exhaustion," what we would now call a stress disorder.[152]

Ordinary Canadians' sufferings from malnutrition, exposure, and the miseries of poverty were far worse, of course, than anything suffered by financially secure politicians, and the tensions between status Indians and tax authorities were at least as bad as the conflicts between finance ministers and provincial treasurers or prime ministers and premiers. That said, the problems of raising an adequate public revenue in Canada in the interwar years were not trivial ones, and they had negative effects on both the health of finance ministers and the relations between provinces and the dominion. Over these troubled decades, governments had built some administrative capacity for taxation, and Canadians had received something of an education in public finance. Buying public bonds and paying direct taxes to the federal government were no longer the novelties that they had been in 1917. "Rustic ignorance" about public finance would be less of a problem in the years to come, though it remained a political force. As bond buyers and income tax payers, Canadians would engage more deeply in public finance conversations during and after the 1940s. As another world war began in September 1939, politicians would acquire new reasons to listen to voters as taxpayers.

7
Warfare, Welfare, and the Mass Income Tax Payer

CANADA'S WAR FINANCE POLICY during the Second World War has been a source of pride and is still widely respected by economists and historians of politics and public finance. The federal government's income tax was made modern and effective, the Canadian economy was successfully reorganized for war purposes, and, with all that, the damage to Canadians' standard of living during the war was slight. The readjustment to peacetime conditions was relatively smooth, and the nation's new fiscal capacity helped to build a more prosperous and caring society over the next thirty years. From having been a fractured and economically fragile nation in the interwar years, with an incoherent and unjust tax "system," Canada grew into a modern and well-governed country, rightly proud of the role that it had played in the Second World War. Not a small amount of the credit for these results has gone to the Department of Finance and its successful launching of a mass income tax system as part of the overall project of war finance.[1]

But in the summer of 1942, this achievement was far from guaranteed. Between the fall of 1939 and the spring of 1941, Finance Ministers J.L. Ralston and J.L. Ilsley had launched a plan that, they'd hoped, would avoid the dire consequences of White's efforts in 1914–18. Current tax dollars would pay for far more of the war's costs, and borrowing would be designed, from the beginning, to keep costs low. Income taxation and other direct taxation would reach lower incomes, but progressive rates would preserve tax fairness. A compulsory savings plan and other anti-inflation measures would prevent the destabilizing inflation of 1917–18 and avoid a crushing postwar deflation. Temporary tax agreements with the provinces would relieve constitutional problems.[2] As tax law scholar Colin Campbell has recently observed, this seemed to be the only possible program of "equitably shared financial sacrifice." Campbell presents the opposition parties' criticisms as slight and asserts their support for the fairness of the war budgets. In his account, voters don't have much of an impact, and some of them ("labour groups") object only because they don't understand Ilsley's policy.[3] However, in Campbell's work and elsewhere, the consensus on war finance policy and its objective soundness has been overstated.[4] When, in the summer of 1942, the crucial war budget was finally passed, after a month's gruelling debate, Ilsley was not triumphant but "thoroughly discouraged." In fact, he was "so damn mad he could chew the upholstery off the privy council chairs."[5] To cover the gap between spending and the wildly inaccurate estimates that his cabinet colleagues had devised, he'd been forced into borrowing from the banks, and, to cover that debt, he was compelled to impose a staggering tax burden on Canadians.

As Ilsley's anger suggests, the 1942 income tax changes were not the coolly designed capstone to a reasonable plan but a desperate strategy forced by fiscal necessity. From the day of his 1942 budget speech, and continually over the next three years, Ilsley found himself confronted with spirited and, I argue, sometimes reasonable challenges to the new income tax system. The amendments in 1943 and 1944 that Campbell and other historians have described as cleaning-up details or "minor alleviations"[6] were, I argue, actually significant: in the face of tax resistance and protest, changes in the law were meant to build consent to the new level of personal income taxation, mainly among working-class and modestly paid middle-class Canadians. A similar purpose was served by the Family Allowances Act of 1944. Seen in this context, difficulties in the early years of war finance become an intimate part of the history of the welfare state.

It was during the Second World War that the modern personal income tax was born. Although I have argued that the prewar federal income tax payers were a middle-class lot rather than merely a wealthy elite, the income tax changes of the war's early years created a huge cohort of new income tax payers – one that was not only poorer but also included more women, status Indians, and some racialized groups. These new taxpayers for war finance would push, by means of tax bargaining, toward a more democratic Canada, one in which the material circumstances of the majority of citizens had a newly direct effect on federal policy. In the first part of this chapter, I explain the particular irritants that the new income tax payers encountered, the methods of tax resistance available to them, and the problems that their tax resistance presented to federal officials attempting to secure tax compliance, war savings participation, political stability, and a sense of common purpose. In the rest of the chapter, I describe federal officials' twofold responses: persuasion and specific policy concessions. I argue that we can see in those responses the impact of the new income tax payers both on tax policy and on the conceptualizing of liberalism. Keynesian macroeconomic theory had promised a new role for the state in managing things economic, modifying liberalism in a collectivist direction. It was not economic theorists, however, but the masses of new taxpayers, pressuring the wartime government into offering both tax concessions and income security measures, who moved the government toward selling tax policy in the framework of a more social liberalism.

The new taxpayers had this kind of impact only because the Departments of Finance and National Revenue took consent – and resistance – to personal income taxation seriously.[7] Finance Minister Ilsley did not blithely ignore the voices of small income tax payers. He was tired and angry in August 1942, exhausted to the point of breakdown on the eve of his great 1943 budget speech, and cracking at the seams in the summer of 1944 (as a distinguished visitor to Ottawa, J.M. Keynes, noticed) in part because he was worried about tax resistance.[8] Criticisms of his tax plans in the House of Commons represented serious opposition – on shop floors, in boardrooms, and in neighbourhoods.[9] If all that Ilsley had cared about was reelection, then this opposition would have been worrying enough, but opposition to his tax proposals mattered because it put in jeopardy the success of the Victory Loan campaigns and the solidity of the wage and price ceilings – the whole anti-inflation "stabilization" project.

Ilsley and the others charged with war finance – Graham Towers of the Bank of Canada, Clifford Clark of Finance, and their less famous collaborators, Revenue Minister Colin Gibson and Commissioner of Income Tax C. Fraser Elliott – carried on their shoulders the burden of preventing a postwar crash or wartime inflation that would lead to privation and conflict, especially but not solely between classes. Their intellectual confidence was considerable, but there is good evidence that the voices of their opponents and their worried supporters reached through that confidence and had effects not only on their moods but also on their policy choices. Deeply democratic in their responses to opposition, these government men did not dismiss policy criticism as "hostility" but took it as useful information that required a thoughtful response.[10] As complaints of tax-related hardship proliferated in 1942 and 1943, fiscal policy makers began to see that making a connection between taxes on small incomes and the development of a newly social state would be necessary if they were to persuade working-class Canadians to be compliant taxpayers and voluntary savers.

The New Taxpayers' Burden

By 1941, the number of Canadians who paid personal income tax at the start of the war (approximately 300,000) had more than doubled (see Table 8). Many of these new income tax payers were in a separate category, not paying the standard prewar personal income tax (PIT) but paying a new tax on income, the national defence tax (NDT), introduced in the 1940 budget. The NDT was different from the PIT in four ways. First, unlike the PIT, the NDT was charged at a flat rate: 3 percent or 2 percent (with single individuals paying the higher rate and married persons the lower rate). In 1941, those initial low rates were raised to 7 percent and 5 percent, respectively. Second, under the NDT, an individual did not pay at all if he or she earned less than the exempt amount ($600 or $1,200 in 1940, depending on marital status), but as soon as earnings exceeded that threshold the specified tax rate applied to the individual's total income. Third, instead of the PIT's generous exemptions for dependent children, the NDT provided tax credits: each of a taxpayer's children was worth eight dollars against the NDT bill. So, for example, a modestly paid wage earner supporting a wife and three children on $1,300 a year would owe two dollars in NDT rather than the twenty-six dollars (2 percent of $1,300) that he would owe if married and childless. Finally, wage and salary earners had the NDT deducted by their employers from their pay packets, rather than being expected to save to pay an annual tax bill or quarterly instalments. Through the NDT, hundreds of thousands of Canadians became income tax payers in small ways on their small incomes. In addition, some of the new taxpayers acquired a liability under the PIT, which, after the 1940 budget, was assessable on income over $750 (for a single individual) or $1,500 (for a married person).

Some of these new taxpayers were actually returning to the ranks. After all, it was only between 1925 and 1930 that the best-paid wage earners had been exempt from federal income taxation. The NDT reached much lower incomes, though at low rates. It triggered a spate of inquiries from employers of Indigenous people, often low-waged workers in rural industries, about whether "Indians" were exempt from the taxation.[11] Single female wage earners in general, usually less well paid than male labourers, were now undoubtedly a larger proportion of income tax payers, too, though tax statistics were not yet broken down by sex. The impact on lower-income cohorts was felt more in Nova Scotia, where there had been no income taxation, than in British Columbia, where income taxation on relatively low incomes had long been in place. In Montreal, where income had been untaxed before 1935, the addition of a provincial income tax (using the federal exemptions and rates) and the NDT, both in 1940, suddenly created a new population of income tax payers.[12] Provincial differences in income taxation became glaringly obvious. In 1941, a posting in Montreal meant that, even on modest military salaries, an officer paid three income taxes (federal, provincial, and municipal), whereas in Halifax there was only the federal one to pay.[13] When Ralston and Ilsley spoke of avoiding "arbitrary and unfair" income taxation in 1940 and 1941, it was remedying the grounds for these complaints that they had in mind.[14]

The changes in 1940 and 1941 foreshadowed the really massive increase in the number of income tax payers that followed from the 1942 budget. The PIT exemption was lowered, making PIT and NDT exempt amounts the same: $660 for a single individual and $1,200 for a married person (with a dependent spouse). The old PIT was now called "the graduated tax," and the new NDT would be known as "the normal tax." Earnings above $660 or $1,200 were now liable to the graduated tax as well as the normal tax on the earner's whole income. Put simply, for the 1942 tax year, income earners, large and small, would make one tax payment calculated upon two different bases: (1) the amount earned in a year above an exempt amount (used to calculate the graduated tax) and (2) the whole amount earned in a year (used to calculate the normal tax). And now, for the graduated tax, instead of exempting from taxation $400 (as in 1939) of income for each child, taxpayers would get, for each child, a credit of $108 against income tax owed.[15] Although the new rules seemed to be complicated, there was at least one major simplification: the various municipal and provincial income taxes were all gone. Between February 1941 and early 1942, the federal government had negotiated, somewhat aggressively, "wartime taxation suspension" agreements with the provinces, ending for the duration of the conflict the crazy quilt of municipal and provincial income taxes, old and new.[16] Given that many of those other taxes had distinctive definitions of incomes, exemptions, rates, and forms, the personal income tax payer of 1942 might have been grateful to have fewer forms and rules to deal with.[17] That benefit was not immediately noticed, however. Instead, Ilsley told his cabinet colleagues, "the budget was full of trouble. The small man is complaining bitterly for the first time."[18]

Tax Troubles and Resistance

The banner headline for the first budget story in the *Globe and Mail* highlighted taxation as coercion: in big type, the headline announced that "Forced Saving Starts Sept. 1."[19] Under the new budget measures, not only would smaller incomes be taxed more heavily than before, but also both the graduated tax and the normal tax would now be collected at each pay period by employers. Some of what was taken was actually savings and would be returned, with 2 percent interest, after the war. But the dollars were deducted from the pay packet without any clear distinction between the savings (which would return) and the taxes (which would not). Employers weren't required to supply a pay slip that recorded deductions, though some did.[20] Ilsley promised that government certificates for the amounts saved would be issued to employees; however, the amount of savings would be calculated only after the taxpayer had filed a return and paid the tax and after the tax authority had assessed the return, made a refund, or required further payment – only then would the amount of savings be determined and officially receipted. The first certificates of refundable tax amounts would not be issued until December 1943. That process left lots of time for people to worry. And the savings cut into pay packets just as the taxes did.

The compulsory savings portion of the newly deducted-at-source personal income taxes affected rich, poor, and corporations (on whose income there was also a savings deduction). But several other new features of income taxation were felt particularly by small earners.[21] Of these features, the most painful was the result of a measure intended to protect smaller incomes. As noted, $660 were supposed to be exempt from a single person's income tax (and $1,200 from a married person's income tax). However, the amount of the normal tax and the graduated tax liabilities combined could leave a taxpayer with less than $660 (or $1,200). The tax designers had anticipated this notch problem and specified that the payment of taxes would not be allowed to reduce anyone's income below one of those two thresholds. That was a good idea. But it had an unfortunate, even perverse, consequence, creating a new notch problem. Once the taxes kicked in, because the normal tax took 7 percent of total income starting at $660 or $1,200, and then the 30 percent graduated tax rate was applied to the first $500 above the exemption, some lower-income taxpayers with no dependants (likely those middle-aged with grown children or no children) were being taxed on 100 percent of their income over the $660 or $1,200 threshold, up to gross incomes of $733 or $1,362. In other words, on the first $73 or $162 over the exemption amounts, these people paid a 100 percent marginal tax rate.[22] That $162 over a year meant that a married man without children would see disappear from his pay every week an amount that would feed him and his wife for about five days.[23]

Not surprisingly, then, tax complaints from lower-income men and women soon flooded into the Department of Finance. In the weeks following the June 1942 budget speech, Ilsley and his staff received hundreds of letters from Canadians anxious about how they were going to balance their personal budgets.[24] The minister and his staff read and replied to all of those letters, usually within a few days.[25] Material from them provided some of the content for speeches and other public relations efforts aimed at the new income tax payers. It was imperative that Ilsley convince Canadians that these taxes, causing so many of them sleepless nights, were both essential and fair. He knew that people could avoid income taxation even when the tax was deducted at source.[26]

Two mechanisms of tax avoidance that wage earners were quick to adopt following the 1942 budget were limiting their hours of work ("absenteeism") and refusing overtime. One employer complained, for example, that "some of the girls have figured out that if they work fifty weeks at $13.00 a week they will not have to pay any taxes ... The result of this is that they work four or five days a week."[27] A shipyard worker in Port Arthur wrote to suggest that overtime work be tax free and paid in war savings certificates. He believed that "a great many of the workers here take time off, to avoid paying taxes."[28] Finance officials also learned about organized labour's views by means of labour press surveys – monthly digests of themes in labour newspapers and magazines – compiled by the Wartime Information Board (WIB).[29] In the spring of 1943, the Department of Finance was seriously considering advice from a payroll systems specialist about how to disguise the fact that working overtime immediately increased tax deductions.[30] A group of civil servants convened by the WIB's John Grierson in 1943 to address problems of "industrial morale" were told that "many workers felt that deductions were so considerable on the sixth or seventh day of work that it was not worth their while to work more than five or six days a week."[31] J.L. Cohen, the labour member of the National War Labour Board, reported that "the problem of income tax deductions had been touched on in virtually every submission before the National War Labour Board during the course of its public inquiry" and urged those concerned about industrial morale not to brush aside labour's concerns.[32]

The most pressing of these concerns came from families in which a married woman was earning more than $660. In the early days of the debate on the 1942 budget, Ilsley heard from women such as Violet Flaherty:

> I am a woman of 48 & working in a munition factory with hundreds of others, and I am in a position to get the reaction of the workers as they come & go. The reaction to this latest tax is that all married women or at least 90 p[e]r c[ent] of them are ready to stay home by the 1st of September [when the 1942 tax rates and deductions at source would come into effect]. I will state my own position[.] I have 5 children, my husband is a rubber worker. Last year we started to buy our own house. So this year I had the opportunity to help him out by going to work at the "Sunshine" plant, 6 miles from home. I make 25 [cents per] hour, 8 hours [per] day. Now as I understand, the government will take 7 of every 15 dollars I earn yet I must pay a girl to look after the children, [and I must] come home from work to wash the linen, iron it & cook the meals. Do you think that we married women will continue to work under the terms the government will enforce[?] It won't pay us to go out at all. By the time we pay car fare & the girl[']s wages, we won't have anything left. So I, and I can safely say hundreds more will *not* work under the terms set by the government for September 1st 1942. (Being among the women I know their reaction better than most people.)[33]

By the time that Mrs. Flaherty put the case to Ilsley so clearly, he had already heard that married women were thinking of giving up on war work in response to his tax measures. While her letter was on its way to Ottawa, the government had made a change to meet her criticism. Ilsley replied to her that he had already amended the statute with cases such as hers in mind: she would be taxed as single, but her husband would keep the married man's level of personal exemption.[34] As a result, the married couple's total exemption would be $1,860, a bit more than the $1,500 that had been exempt from the graduated income tax in 1941. This was a fairly small concession, and it alleviated financial pressures in working-class families only slightly. A year later, as a letter from a married woman who had returned to her prewar job in telegraphy explained, the costs and inconveniences associated with having both partners work meant that some patriotism was still required for a married woman to take up war work.[35] Nonetheless, the government had responded to the protests of married women who worked by amending the 1942 budget proposals before the new tax legislation was enacted.

Other distinctively situated groups would also threaten to withdraw their work in protest over their new tax liabilities. The Indian superintendent in Brantford, Major E.P. Randle, pointed out that, reasonably in his view, the Six Nations people might well give up war work if their new incomes were taxed: "Some of them will do this as a matter of principle because they consider taxing them is an injustice and unfair. Others feel that after the tax is off and their daily expenses paid there is not enough left to make the long hours and the worry of commuting [by 'inferior or difficult means of transportation'] worth while."[36] These workers would not have been alone in withdrawing their labour. At the Arvida, Quebec, aluminum plant, some workers did so temporarily: tax protest played a part in the strike there in the summer of 1941.[37] And, in British Columbia in 1942–44, Chinese Canadian workers in the shipyards and sawmills went on strike to protest how new tax regulations imposed exceptional costs on men supporting wives and children back in China. Taxed as single men, on wages that reflected the racism of the local labour market, these workers couldn't always document their family support obligations in ways that met Ottawa's standards. At first, they struck on their own; then, as tax issues became more central for organized labour, the Chinese Canadian workers' tax protest won the support of the shipyard unions and the woodworkers' union.[38] Here the attempt to bring lower-income Canadians into the role of income tax payers created new sorts of conflicts and alliances, making it a challenge for Finance and Revenue to secure cooperation from taxpayers and prompting new uses for existing organizations.

Beyond the worry about resistance among hourly wage earners, Ilsley had to convince the slightly better off that a heavier income tax burden was fair and necessary. Whereas the poorest could only threaten to withdraw their labour, others had at their disposal a different means of tax protest: they could threaten not to buy war savings certificates or Victory Bonds or, worse, to cash and spend those that they had bought.[39] In commenting on the new tax burdens, voices from this cohort claimed that the personal income tax took up anything that they had to spare. "They ask us to buy bonds, but with paying tax and other expenses how can we?" inquired the wife of an air force mechanic.[40] A single woman earning a decent clerical salary (for a woman) of $1,907.36 per annum explained to Ilsley exactly what she spent her income on and asked him how she could pay the new income tax: "What am I to do, drop this Insurance for my old age? Let my home people starve or go on relief? Subscribe nothing to the War Effort?"[41] Another correspondent was incredulous that the government expected both income tax and war savings from him. This opinion was shared by Leader of the Opposition R.B. Hanson, who had raised in the House of Commons the case of a clergyman who "receives in cash $1,500 out of which you intend to take $105 leaving him with the princely sum of $27 per week with which to feed, clothe, educate, pay for medical and dental care etc. etc. etc. and then apparently buy some war saving certificates and bonds with the balance."[42]

Threats to the purchase of war savings products mattered because the revenue that those products generated was nearly as important as tax revenue (and more important than direct taxation) in financing war expenditure. Looking back on 1942–43 in his March 1943 budget speech, Ilsley celebrated the relatively equal contributions to the federal budget of tax revenues (of all kinds) and borrowing: 52 percent tax to 48 percent borrowing. He also noted how much the contribution of direct taxation had grown, now constituting two-thirds of total tax revenues. That amounted to direct tax revenues of approximately $1.4 billion compared with over $2.4 billion to be raised by borrowing.[43] Quite apart from its value as a source of revenue, personal income taxation mattered because it might threaten the new income tax payers' willingness to lend to government.

The success of the borrowing program depended importantly on participation by small buyers. To be sure, the vast majority of the Victory Loan issue was purchased by financial institutions, big businesses, and possessors of substantial fortunes. The last group were enthusiastic bond buyers, not only because they could afford to be, but also because, as a Kincardine hosiery manufacturer told *Globe and Mail* readers, "the

"WHAT – ANOTHER VICTORY LOAN?"

"Mister – the Casualty lists
come out every day!"

"YOU SHOULD SEE MY INCOME TAX!"

"There's a lad in hospital
who'll never see again!"

"WE'RE DOING MORE THAN OUR SHARE NOW!"

"There's no share when
you give your life!"

BELIEVE US: THE MOST IMPORTANT BOND
YOU CAN BUY IS THE ONE YOU CAN'T AFFORD

This Message Prepared and the Space Donated by **ᵀᴴᴱT. EATON C⁰.**ʟɪᴍɪᴛᴇᴅ Get Ready to Buy Bonds in Canada's Sixth Victory Loan Campaign

Resentment of the burden of income taxes threatened the success of the war savings campaigns. The volunteer leaders of the War Finance Committee could rely on prominent businesses, such as the T. Eaton Company, themselves major holders of war loan bonds, for support through sponsored ads in countering the combination of tax resentment and resistance to the 1944 bond sales drive. *Globe and Mail*, April 18, 1944.

Government has to raise a certain amount of money, and ... if it is not produced by a loan it will be extracted by less pleasant means."[44] The bankers who ran the National War Finance Committee (NWFC) persistently urged wage earners to purchase war savings products in order to reassure the big institutional buyers. As George Spinney, Bank of Montreal president and NWFC head, pointed out to a group of bankers in 1942, it was in the interest of banks, as large holders of government of Canada bonds, that many Canadian voters should also own such bonds:

> It is sometimes difficult to get the public at large to realize that any development which might harm the investment portfolio of banks and insurance companies is against their own interests. It is less difficult, however, to convince a man that his own interests are imperilled if some move is on foot [sic] which might affect the worth of a War Savings Certificate or Bond which he has in his own bureau drawer or safety deposit box.[45]

If the government was going to be committed to a program of market support that would shore up the price of bonds, then the optics of protecting the small investor would be helpful.[46] Ilsley pointed out that it was the government's "deliberate policy" to ensure that Canadian bonds were widely held: he estimated that 60 percent of income earners would also be recipients of bond interest after the war.[47] He didn't want payouts of interest to bondholders to be seen in the future, as they had been in the past, as draining earnings from the pockets of modest earners into the coffers of the rich.[48] As a First World War veteran, A.W. Frazer, put it, if tax revenues went largely to service a vast national debt held by the wealthy, then the government would be just the same old "gang of bond collectors."[49]

The relationship between war savings and tax policy was also noted by CCF MPs. From the outset of the war, the leader of the CCF, M.J. Coldwell, had called for the conscription of wealth through the taxation of capital gains, such as profits on the sale of stocks. In demanding this change in tax policy, the CCF drew attention to the real difference between taxing income and taxing wealth: income taxation bore down heavily on small incomes while leaving untouched vast capital assets that produced real differences in economic power. When the NDT was introduced, Coldwell distinguished it as a wage tax, rather than an income tax, and called for the taxation of capital gains along with a further tax on capital in the form of a dominion succession duty.[50] In their tax thinking, socialists (by no means politically marginal in 1942–43 in Canada) had begun to take into account the potential revenue that could be reached by taxing investments, especially war loan bonds on which the wealthy had earned tax-free income.[51]

In 1941, Coldwell made this point by sending Ilsley a letter from a veteran and Saskatchewan farmer, William Casey Teneycke, whose views, Coldwell said, exemplified those expressed in many other letters that he had received. A "plain hardboiled Canadian" who wanted nothing to do with "any of the isms," Teneycke asserted that "the common producer class" was "taxed for everything we have or can get while the monied class buy war bonds for our children of future generations to pay ... Why do you not tax the rich the same as you do us for all they got?" After calling for conscription more generally, he concluded that "if you took all their money by taxation there would be no war debt after the war as you would have all the money already." That money could then be "justly divided among the people who won the war and not as after the last war be in the control of a few bloated millionaires and their useless offspring."[52] This was far from a sophisticated technical statement of how to tax capital, but the general drift was clear. In the Department of Finance, Robert Bryce tried to devise more subtle ways of conscripting wealth by minimizing the returns offered by Victory Loans to big capital. His proposals were no more successful than was Coldwell's advocacy of capital gains taxation.[53] But it is worth noting the full range of ideas about war finance that critics expressed and the continuing impact of dissatisfaction with the methods initiated during the First World War.

The anti-capitalist currents of the interwar years had made bankers aware of the risk to capital posed by the power of the mass electorate: the February 1942 victory of a CCF candidate over a wealthy Conservative alarmed investors. Although the CCF's motion to require interest-free war loans had been defeated in the House of Commons in February 1942, the party's popularity (especially in the western provinces) was a matter of lively speculation.[54] Staving off a socialist threat and thus preserving political stability was closely connected to the viability of the war loan program. In September 1943, George Spinney (still the head of the NWFC) found out that worry about the popularity of the CCF extended to New York, where fears of growing support for the party threatened Victory Bond sales. The first question that Spinney heard from his banking friends there was "what about the threat of the C.C.F. Party?" As the fifth Victory Loan campaign approached, New York bankers' remarks served to "impress upon [his] mind afresh" the importance of "confidence." Writing to Clifford Clark, Spinney warned that "a good many people throughout Canada" were "fidgety and perplexed" about inflation and "worried over the infiltration of C.C.F. theories."[55] He and Clark discussed asking Coldwell to make a public statement that would quiet alarm by affirming the party's commitment to honouring public debt (which included not reducing the return to investors by taxing their capital gains). Clark worried that Coldwell could do more harm than good to the market for Canadian bonds if he refused or elaborately hedged his support.[56] Coldwell ended up making an almost perfectly anodyne statement about the complete safety of investing in war bonds. Only the initiated would have suspected a reference to capital gains taxation in his comment that "disagreeing with the government's war finance methods" wasn't a reason to boycott the Victory Loan campaign.[57]

One other challenge to the success of the new income tax (and the Victory Loan campaigns) was more subtle than organized protest or complaints from individual letter writers, and its impact on tax rhetoric and even tax policy is harder to assess. That challenge was the force of rumour. Stories about tax evasion brought the fairness of income taxation into question, and rumours about savings certificates or bonds discouraged voluntary savings. Most commonly, there were rumours that other taxpayers were getting away with evasion. Some of these rumours were expressions of the usual general suspicion that the corporations and the rich were getting off lightly. Others alleged, more specifically,

the hiding of sales and income by small storekeepers; the renting of three or four rooms in home after home to bring in as much as $20 weekly with never a thought of declaring that income; an instance of "another source of extra income" of $50 a week that was never likely to be traced and therefore "forgotten to be declared," and so on.[58]

There were also rumours that the government might make it illegal to cash bonds and savings certificates or that all income tax would be refunded after the war.[59] And, finally, there was resentful talk of income tax money being wasted through incompetent or partisan spending. Listed as rumours number 210 and 239 by the WIB's "Rumour Clinic," these stories of waste were apparently common.[60] They showed up in questions raised by union leaders in Montreal too: union members had told their leaders that "things were not being done as economically as possible" in the plants where they worked.[61] Such rumours filled in gaps in knowledge and gave expression to fear, anger, and mistrust. Mutterings of this sort could help people to feel justified in tax evasion or reduce their willingness to invest in war savings, putting self-interest before social interest. The Finance and Victory Loan people attempted to allay mistrust and calm feelings by feeding stories to the press and by supplying answers for use by the WIB's Rumour Clinic. In this material, they emphasized collective responsibility and the social value of the work of government employees.[62]

Responses to Resistance

Finance and Revenue tried in other ways to overcome the new resistance among taxpayers. To support war finance, they carefully cultivated the sense of community that many Canadians recall from the war years. As I've shown, there were two main responses to resistance. One was the revision Ilsley made to the 1942 budget, a revision designed to fend off a tax-driven withdrawal of labour – that of married women employed in war-related jobs. The other was the initiative taken by Finance officials in supplying responses to the fiscal rumour mill. But there were also other rhetorical and educational responses, particularly a campaign of persuasion carried out in responding to citizens' letters and crafting public relations materials. That tax rhetoric would shape the terms in which family allowances were introduced in 1944. In fact, I argue, the government's strategy was designed not only to legitimize personal income taxation beyond the period of war finance but also to secure tax compliance from the new income tax payers during the war. As we'll see, tax relief amendments of 1943 and 1944 served these purposes while also protecting the overall financial system and the federal government's ability to borrow.

This process of democratic response was imperfect; not all sectors of the public were equally successful in having their professed needs met. But both Finance and Revenue made serious attempts to engage citizens in intelligent discussions of war finance and to respond in ways that balanced the collective project of war finance with the needs of individuals or particular groups. These were self-consciously democratic leaders, confident that all groups of the public were intelligent and reachable by appeals to justice and the common good. They were liberals whose idea of the common good rested on mutual interest, more than on mutual responsibility, but in its own way that was a form of social liberalism.

Educating Taxpayers

The respect that fiscal policy makers showed the public extended even to those whom they believed to be in the grip of socialist or social credit error or obsessed by waste and bloated public expenditure. For example, Finance wasn't willing to accept the CCF and Social Credit view that no interest should be paid on Victory Bonds, but it did provide no-interest bonds as an option for Canadians who thought that they shouldn't be paid for money loaned to the war effort.[63] Another sign of Finance's democratic commitment at this time was that Clifford Clark required his staff to respond to letters from Canadians who proposed unorthodox fiscal or monetary schemes. This work was sometimes burdensome.[64] But in maintaining a civilized tone and by supplying evidence, argument, and reading suggestions, the patient efforts of Harvey Perry, Robert Bryce, Kenneth Eaton, W.C. Ronson, and others to explain and justify, to one Canadian at a time, the federal government's war financing policy must impress anyone who reads these files.

For example, it might have seemed to these Finance officials that Oliver Wright of Glansworth, Ontario, was simply a cranky old Gladstonian when he wrote that, "wherever high taxes are discussed, this matter of unnecessary employees comes up, and if something is not done to rectify it, you are going to have difficulty in making collections."[65] No one in Finance knew who Wright was; in fact, staff had to make a special effort to find his return address. However, Ilsley had Assistant Deputy Minister Ronson compose a reply. Ronson wrote a 1,000-word, information-packed response to Wright. He apologized to the department's typist for its length: "My only excuse for so long a letter is the importance I attach to a complaint of this nature."[66] This was the work of a man convinced of the merits of government policy and possessed of the belief that the citizen-taxpayer could be persuaded by reason and evidence to share his conviction. In the same way, the exchange of letters between First World War veteran A.W. Frazer and Bryce impresses. Frazer was impassioned and somewhat CCF leaning. He and Bryce disagreed on some basic points. But each made his case and acknowledged the merits of some aspects of the other's perspective.[67]

Finance officials were capable of dismissing writers whom they knew to be doctrinaire, such as the authors of Toronto's *The Printed Word* and Horace Brittain of the Citizen' Research Institute of Canada, on the right, or committed opponents of capitalism, on the left.[68] But even to these people replies from Finance noted their differences rather than simply ignoring the grounds of disagreement.[69] Ilsley and his staff took seriously the democratic work of explaining and justifying policy to citizens who chose to participate in open debate.

Finance, Revenue, and the NWFC also worked with the WIB to craft a public relations campaign that would encourage tax compliance and voluntary saving. Themes for this campaign were generated in part through an interdepartmental committee on industrial morale. ("Industrial morale" was the bloodless term for the problem of "intolerable strain and worry" among people who earned less than $3,000 per year that WIB correspondents had reported in their summary of responses to the 1943 budget.)[70] Convened in March 1943 by John Grierson of the WIB, this committee considered how to address this problem and others: wildcat strikes, refusal of overtime, demand for collective bargaining rights, and frustrated expectations of respect (discussed in the hearings of the National War Labour Board between April and June 1943). The labour conflicts of 1941–42 form an essential part of the background to the tax rhetoric and policy of 1943–44.[71]

Bryce told Clark that he hoped the committee on industrial morale would be useful to Finance in helping to put across "certain ideas with regard to taxation, and possibly with regard to borrowing, as well."[72] Bryce or Eaton attended the committee's meetings between March and July, telling the group that Finance had "a considerable amount of data from letters received" on the subjects of compulsory saving and tax on overtime pay and that the department was "seriously concerned with the relationship of income tax deductions to absenteeism and industrial morale."[73] In May, the WIB's labour liaison, David Petegorsky, followed up by asking Bryce to let him know which industrial morale objectives Finance wanted to see addressed. Bryce made it clear that both rational argument and emotional persuasion were necessary if "the working man and his wife," in his view "the bulk of Canadian citizens," were to help make war finance work. The department, he wrote,

> was interested to see that our major financial and economic policies, the reasons for them and the effects of them, are properly understood by

the working man and his wife. In particular we are interested in their understanding of the taxes that affect him, the need for saving, and the whole price and wage stabilization program. We want labour to understand our tax measures and to be convinced that they are necessary and equitable, so that they will cause the least possible dissatisfaction and loss of productive effort. We very much need the cooperation of workers and their families in our savings program. Furthermore, and perhaps more difficult than all the others, we would like to see labour sufficiently well convinced of the need for avoiding inflation that they would refrain from pressing for higher wage rates which would mean higher prices.

We believe that an understanding of the real issues will help to promote these ends.

We don't believe that understanding or acquiescence [alone] is enough; we believe there is need for some emotional drive, particularly on such things as savings campaigns, where more is needed than mere acceptance of measures. In other words, I think it is true to say that the Finance Department would like to see an effort made to arouse some mass support and mass feeling behind the economic measures that have been devised to make it possible to fight the war without inflation. This, I realize, will take some real salesmanship.[74]

In short, Bryce believed that most Canadians could be persuaded to share his belief in the government's tax policy and act enthusiastically on it. Petegorsky later sent him recent US poll data showing that most Americans did not actually believe that "higher taxes" for "everyone" could help to keep prices stable: 57 percent thought that there was no connection between prices and taxation, and 19 percent thought that higher taxes would raise prices.[75] If the same level of incomprehension prevailed in Canada, as it likely did, then there was indeed work to be done.

From June on, the WIB, Finance, and Revenue developed educational and promotional material aimed directly at workers, both unionized and non-unionized, to combat tax protest and to persuade wage earners that demands for increased pay were inflationary and therefore self-defeating. Revenue's contribution to this campaign included a fourteen-page, pay-packet-sized pamphlet. It was produced and circulated in 1943 sometime between June, when the tidal wave of new income tax returns (over 2 million) hit the crowded desks in Revenue, and December, when the department began to issue refundable tax certificates.[76] The front cover of the

Revenue pamphlet showed a puzzled worker, a middle-aged man in over-alls, bombarded by questions such as "is too much deducted?" and "is overtime worthwhile?" The back cover gave the gist of the pamphlet's message: "False rumours" about the unfairness of the income tax were "based on misunderstandings and half truths." In particular, the "refundable portion ... *will be repaid to you with interest*," despite what workers might have heard to the contrary. Inside the text-heavy pamphlet was more detail on why the income tax was fair (the rich and businesses pay more), the advantages of payroll deduction (no tax debt to hang over the worker's head), and why certificates for refundable amounts were slow to appear (for faster results, Revenue would have to hire and then fire an army of temporary workers). Overdeductions were possible, though unlikely, but they would be refunded. And overtime always resulted in more income for the worker. Detailed calculations were provided for the arithmetically inclined to peruse. In December, display ads making these points in cartoon form were circulated to company newsletters and personnel managers. In what might have been a first, the joy of a tax refund cheque was illustrated. And, in a further emotional appeal, there was the rhetoric of solidarity in the fight against Hitler.[77]

As well as the information campaign aimed at the new income tax payers, the anti-inflation campaign targeted both wage earners and consumers. Before 1943, anti-inflation themes appeared mainly in the advertising of insurance companies, banks, and investment dealers.[78] "Sound money" was a perennial concern of these large investors in public bonds. The government's advertising campaign around inflation ramped up, however, following the labour activism of 1941–43. Aside from the occasional notice concerning particular price controls,[79] the first of the Finance-driven anti-inflation ads, a sternly official one, appeared in December 1943. Over the course of 1944, government of Canada ads offered an education in economics in cartoon form, presenting images of workers and warriors together as heroes, images of interconnectedness, and a message of individual responsibility.[80] Although wage and price controls were central to this campaign, at least three of the anti-inflation ads included increased taxation among the list of measures employed to control inflation.[81] As organized labour fought during 1943 and 1944 to raise the wages of the poorest workers to something like a subsistence level, union officials had to answer these messages from the government of Canada: it had become harder to argue that perhaps a little inflation wouldn't be so bad.[82]

In December 1943, the Wartime Information Board provided employee publications with ads designed to reassure employees that the personal income tax was fair to them. The ads were supplied in an ad mat format, allowing publishers to select images that best addressed the concerns of their readers. Ad mats mailed out January 4, 1944, LAC, Finance fonds, RG 19, vol. 4030, file 129-W3.

Among the bulwarks against the scourge of inflation in this educational ad, third in a series from the government of Canada, two are tax related: "Excess profits are taxed away," and "individual incomes are taxed more heavily." *Globe and Mail,* April 14, 1944.

Ilsley's 1943 Speech to the Trades and Labour Congress of Canada

In addition to speaking to wage earners and consumers generally, Ilsley made a special effort to recruit the assistance of organized labour in fighting the tax protest elements of the industrial morale problem. His emblematic effort was a speech at the September 1943 annual meeting of the Trades and Labour Congress.[83] This speech, later reprinted by the National Liberal Federation, with an approving foreword from the *Toronto Daily Star*, was also supplied by Finance officials in the fall of 1943 when they answered letters complaining about taxation of the cost-of-living bonus. In the speech, Ilsley attempted to address every argument and rumour that had been raised in letters to his department from working-class Canadians. He acknowledged that some thought that inflation was an "invented ... bogey."[84] He showed that he understood doubts about forced savings amounts. He repeated the concerns about tax falling on incomes already too low, tax on overtime, and tax on cost-of-living bonuses. Some of his answers to these concerns spoke effectively to labour's concerns about tax fairness, whereas others would have been less convincing. He was certainly on common ground with his labour audience when he defended the principle of progressivity and pointed out that it underlay the taxation of overtime earnings. However, in some of the other ways in which he framed his messages of social solidarity and a positive role for the state, his views would not have made sense to at least the socialist members of his audience: it was not socialism but social liberalism that he was selling.

A key element of Ilsley's argument was that taxing "even the lower brackets" was necessary in order to get "even half as much in taxes as this war is costing us."[85] This assertion makes sense only on a rather curious understanding of "the lower brackets." Ilsley seems to have defined the term in the same way that the *Globe and Mail* editors in 1946 defined "the small income group": those who earned "$5,000 a year or less"[86] Although these were "lower" incomes, literally, in relation to "upper" incomes, those between $3,000 and $5,000 were good middle-class incomes. Even the best-paid unionized industrial workers among those whom Ilsley was addressing in 1943 rarely earned above $4,000, and the average wage of an hourly paid male worker in Canada in 1943 was $1,726.[87] And, in assessing the necessity of income tax contributions from the lower brackets, it's worth noting that personal income taxation in total, across all income levels, contributed only 23 percent of all tax revenue in 1943.[88] Exactly how much the lower brackets contributed during 1943 we don't know in precise terms: the taxation statistics for that year reported tax for broad occupational groups rather than by income classes. The first wartime income tax statistics reported by income brackets were the 1945 estimated statistics published in the 1946 *Canada Year Book*.[89] They give some broad orders of magnitude about the scale of income tax assessments, and they show how little need there was in war budgets for the many small and painful payments by low-income earners.

As many in Ilsley's labour audience would have been aware, from their experiences during the Depression, taxing the poor served symbolic rather than balance sheet purposes. Those purposes had been imported into the federal tax system along with other features of special provincial income taxes, such as those introduced in British Columbia and Manitoba in the 1930s.[90] The BC and Manitoba taxes had broad bases, charging small flat rates on all incomes. Unlike the graduated taxes aimed at higher-income earners – "soak the rich" taxes – these new provincial income taxes had been "show them the price" taxes. That is, they had been intended to make lower-income earners tax conscious so that they would understand their obligation to help finance activities of the state, especially activities such as unemployment relief likely to benefit them or their families directly.[91] In arguing that every cent of low-income workers' taxes was essential, Ilsley also drew on an older, elite vocabulary of tax fairness according to which, in fairness to those who paid income taxes at higher, progressive rates, the working poor had to carry a burden whose weight they would feel.

As a result of adopting this perspective, Ilsley, like other finance ministers before him, overstated the need for the nickels and dimes of income tax tribute from less-well-paid workers. In 1945, the 425,000 Canadians (17.9 percent of all personal income tax payers) assessed on incomes under $1,000 contributed as a group just 2.79 percent of total individual income tax revenues. At a total of $19,032,000, those tax payments amounted to just eighty-six cents a week. But a single person could eat for almost three days on that amount. When Ilsley argued that the tiny contributions from the smallest taxable wages were necessary to finance the war, he was asking for considerable scrimping in return for a trivial tax contribution – 1.42 percent of the total federal tax revenue (direct and indirect taxation together), based upon the 1945 tax statistics that I have used here.[92] The rhetoric of the responsibility of the small earner was thus more about preventing the poor from being free riders and making them see themselves as conscious taxpayers than it was about buying bombers and feeding troops.[93] The same rhetoric would be summoned up again in 1946 and later to make the case that the social security state required the multitude of low-income Canadians to continue to pay income taxes. Reading the same 1945 tax incidence figures that I drew on above, the *Globe and Mail's* editorial writers in 1946 concluded that the data left "no doubt as to who will pay the cost of social security. It will be the small wage earner."[94] This was "show them the price" tax talk. When labour leaders charged that the wartime income taxes were too heavy on lower incomes, they did not misunderstand tax policy; rather, they recognized an old, familiar, elite discourse of tax fairness and challenged its morality.

That elite view of tax fairness emphasized that all should contribute to the public goods that tax dollars bought. It was liberal in its emphasis on the individual but social in its acknowledgment of those common goods. Oliver Wendell Holmes famously said that, in paying our taxes, the good that we buy is civilization. During the war, his assertion seemed to be literally true: at stake was the preservation of a democratic society. As a benefit argument for income taxation (if you benefit, then you should pay), that notion of fairness could work both for and against a positive role for the state. On the one hand, taxes were simply the tools of a democratic people's common purpose. On the other, by taxing low incomes beyond what wage earners could bear, those who opposed a more active state could deliver an anti-statist lesson of tax consciousness – don't expect much from the state because it will cost you – along with the rhetoric of social solidarity.

The other message of social liberalism in Ilsley's 1943 Trades and Labour Congress speech was his emphasis on individual Canadians' role as income tax payers in maintaining price stability. In making his pitch to labour to accept his income tax measures in the name of fighting inflation, Ilsley urged them to consider the "financial and business economy," a system in which their individual choices about working overtime would have systemic effects. It was not only a sense of togetherness or mutual responsibility but also an impersonal system – the economy – that bound all together in a web of choices and consequences.[95] "Stabilization," a condition of that system, was eminently a *social* good created collaboratively by the choices of governments and individual citizens.

In addition to associating the new income taxes with paying for the war and inflation prevention, Ilsley invoked social goods in the form of social security. He argued that the "financial capacity" that the nation had developed during the war must be applied to "the improvement of the Canadian standard of living."[96] Financial capacity meant borrowing methods as well as taxing methods, of course. Indeed, the two were always intertwined. Like the mass income tax, widespread sales of dominion bonds to small investors would continue, as Canada Savings Bonds, after the war. But Ilsley's 1943 use of the term "financial capacity" in his speech to some of Canada's most influential labour leaders also referred to tax capacity, in particular to the income tax that members of the labour movement were being asked to pay. In a year when income tax protest was one of a cluster of sore points in labour relations, it made sense that Ilsley would say that, after the war, the income tax designed for war finance would be put to use for those social security purposes that the labour movement had long advocated. It was not only good politics to do so but also a sign of the emerging social liberalism: justifications for the stabilization policy, war finance methods, and social security measures were all shot through with a social liberal vocabulary of "togetherness" – an ideal of connectedness in which individuals' self-interested actions were linked by macroeconomic mechanisms to social goods.

The Budget Speeches of 1943 and 1944

Ilsley's budget speeches were substantial statements of this social liberalism. Having read floods of letters and having answered torrents of questions about the new mass income tax of 1942, Ilsley made one of his most memorable defences of the citizenship of contribution in his budget speech of March 2, 1943: "Taxes and loans are not exactions from the people by a government. They are weapons which the people through their elected representatives and the free methods of democracy have fashioned for their own use and their common purpose."[97] He also gave a fine short lesson on which kinds of borrowing are inflationary and which kinds are not. He defended the 1942 tax measures, showing that Canadians were paying larger percentages of their personal incomes in income taxes than were Americans or Brits. Ilsley insisted that wage and price controls would continue along with restrictions on corporate profits. He maintained that the democratic methods of war finance were those that inhibited inflation, and he stood by those methods on principle. And he appealed for help, especially in support of the Victory Loan campaigns. It was not until 1944, however, that his budget speech brought together social spending, tax relief, and the good of the economy in a discussion of measures aimed at low-income taxpayers.

The rhetoric of that speech was shaped by Prime Minister King. Three days before the budget was to be presented, King had Ilsley read out the budget speech in cabinet. King had been thinking hard about how to play up the links among inflation prevention, social security, and working-class tax protest. Without wanting to absolve King of all his faults, I read his advice to Ilsley on how to present the 1944 budget speech as showing not mere vote counting but an appreciation of the connections among household budgets, public budgets, and stabilization.[98] King urged that the budget speech show that the government knew that the taxation of personal incomes was causing "real hardship." He wanted Ilsley to emphasize that the government had chosen a means of tax relief that would not only put money in the hands of "persons of low income" (social support) but also prevent "men [from] quitting their work because of additional earnings which bring them into higher [tax] brackets" (response to tax protest). He also urged an emphasis on the government's effective "battle against inflation" and its decision to bring in a system of family allowances. All of this would show that "there was real relief in taxation though without yielding any principles."[99]

Ilsley's speech on June 26, 1944, did all of these things. Ilsley even managed to respond to the Victory Loan campaigners' worries that ending the compulsory savings part of the personal income tax would make their job harder. The elimination of compulsory savings (the refundable tax) was the budget's core measure of tax relief, and Ilsley defended this relief explicitly as a means to prevent absenteeism and "special difficulty and hardship."[100] His other recommendations, he explained, "were thoroughly in keeping with the greater emphasis that we shall be placing on family welfare after the war. With the introduction of family allowances we are taking a great stride forward in improving the position of those with low incomes and family responsibilities."[101] None of these tax measures had a single cause; all of them were presented within a framework that linked macroeconomics, greater income security of poorer families, and tax relief in response to tax protest.

In this framework, none of the three elements can be discounted. They were all of a piece. Here a perspective that includes tax policy makes the connections clear. For example, I both agree and disagree with historian Raymond Blake, who suggests that some scholars have overemphasized the part played by wage control in creation of the family allowance.[102] He bases this position on a dichotomy between humanitarian social security projects and "cold-blooded" macroeconomics, a binary opposition that social worker and prominent federal civil servant George Davidson used in the 1940s. If we accept this dichotomy, however, then we miss seeing the moment in 1942, as most earners were becoming income tax payers, when the tax system began to appear as a tax-transfer system, linking taxation and income assistance. When Robert Bryce made the case for family allowances to W.A. Mackintosh in January 1943, when Bank of Canada Governor Graham Towers made the case to the Canadian Manufacturers' Association in June 1943, when Clifford Clark made the case to cabinet in January 1944, and when King made the case in the House of Commons that July, each man pointed out the tax dimension of the family allowance program. The program was not as costly or unprecedented as it might seem, they emphasized, because there was already, in effect, "spending" on child welfare in the form of tax provisions – tax-exempt income before the war and deductions from tax payable during the war.[103]

At first, in 1945–46, minimizing the cost of this substitution of direct payments for tax reductions was achieved through a family allowance repayment tax, carefully arranged to avoid making the family allowances themselves taxable. Both explaining and administering this tax treatment of family allowance income were difficult. In the 1946 budget, Ilsley found a simpler way to achieve the same result. He returned to the familiar prewar system, in which the amount of a family's taxable income would be decreased by a certain amount per child. But parents whose children aged sixteen and older were now too old to "earn" a family allowance cheque would get a bigger reduction of taxable income (a reduction of taxable income of $300 per child) than would parents of "family allowance children" ($100 per child). The after-tax situations of the two families would end up being similar. It was a mix of tax expenditure and direct expenditure that served lower-income families better than did the prewar system, in which most were not income tax payers and got nothing from the state to help them with their parental responsibilities. In the new 1946 arrangement, many ended up getting on balance more from family allowance payments than they paid in income taxes. In the 1947 budget, Finance Minister Douglas Abbott pointed to an income level of $2,500 as the highest level where a married parent of two children would benefit in this way. Those who argued that this method of delivering income assistance for children continued a past practice were right that even before the war the federal government had been "spending" money on the support of children through forgone revenue. In the new system, some of that spending would be reduced and replaced by direct payments that would benefit not just the middle-class income tax payer but also those too poor to pay income tax.[104] Tax fairness and social welfare were thus tightly tied together in a policy that had the additional welfare effect of preserving the price ceiling.

Tax measures had both macroeconomic and welfare effects. Stabilization measures not only protected capital but also meant, for low-income people, a measure of protection from the dangers both of inflation in the prices of necessities and of job cuts driven by deflation. There are reasons to distinguish among methods of delivering social assistance, but in 1942–45, when these tax and welfare measures were being designed and first delivered, the tax dimension of the story indicates that personal income tax relief, inflation control, and social spending had common origins – the new ideology of social security. In this sense, Blake is right to point to the force of social security discourse that surrounded birth of the family allowance.[105] But for King and Ilsley, social security included stabilization. An unstable dollar threatened both poor and rich. The Liberals' tax program connected social security and stabilization policy, and their response to lower-income Canadians' tax resistance became an occasion to explain those connections.

Negotiated Concessions, 1942–44

Although the rhetorical reorientation and signs of respect for workers as "the bulk of Canadian citizens" were important, the impact of public opinion also appears concretely in the actual changes made to tax law and administration in 1942, 1943, and 1944. The "minor alleviations" of those budgets were not trivial. As measures taken in response to lower-income Canadians' expressions of distress, they should be seen in the same frame as collective bargaining law and the family allowance, as part of wartime democracy's slow working toward recognition that the material conditions of the majority of Canadians had to have more of an impact on public policy. Or, to put it differently, personal income tax, along with, more obviously, conscription and wage and price controls, made the national state so much more intimately involved in daily life that a responsiveness to popular opinion was newly important as a means of legitimating state power. On an array of tax matters, from those affecting the poor to those affecting taxpayers in "special" circumstances, Finance and Revenue listened to concerns raised by taxpayers and took steps to address those concerns. Most of these steps were related to variations in family obligations and the relationship between saving and taxation. In this respect, it is easy to see how modifications of personal income taxation would come to be connected to child welfare and old age security dimensions of the nascent welfare state.

As we have seen, the first modification to the mass-based personal income tax was the concession granted in response to the immediate threat of married women's refusal to work. The other protest-inspired change in July 1942 was also family related. In class terms, protesters were mostly wealthy or at least middle class, but the concession was limited by Ilsley's concern to avoid undermining the progressivity of income taxation (its claim to class fairness). The protesters were divorced men who paid part of their incomes to their former wives as alimony. The alimony payers tended to be relatively well off because lower-income couples settled the terms of separation in family court rather than paying the higher costs of a parliamentary divorce. The complaint of divorced men was that the tax law forced them to pay income tax on the money that the courts required them to give to their ex-wives, as though the alimony were part of the ex-husband's income. Ilsley agreed with the protesters that divorced wives should pay tax on the alimony that they received. For the women, this was alarming and sometimes disastrous: their settlements had not been designed to cover income tax obligations. For the men, this was helpful: the tax authority would permit alimony payers to subtract from their tax bills the amounts of income tax now paid by their ex-wives. The women mostly paid at a lower tax rate, so the men would still pay more taxes than they would have had the full alimony amounts been subtracted from their gross incomes. For Ilsley, however, that richer exemption would have been contrary to the spirit of taxing on ability to pay and the legitimating class fairness of that spirit.[106]

During the summer and fall of 1942, income tax payers, mostly the new ones, continued to tell Ilsley about the problems that they faced as a result of the new tax measures. In the March 1943 budget, Finance responded to some of these complaints, making a few significant changes. The nasty notch problem with the 100 percent tax rate was partially remedied. In the income ranges in which there was a risk of 100 percent marginal tax rates, there would be new regulations to limit the rate to 66 percent, of which half would be refundable savings. In two other measures, Finance responded to complaints that were both class and region based. Both were about savings that could reduce the refundable tax. After March 1943, Ilsley conceded, payments on dominion government annuities – mainly held by people with modest incomes – would be allowed for that purpose. The other concession concerning savings was that payments on mortgage principal for a home "owned" by a taxpayer's wife would be allowed as a reduction of the refundable tax. Home-owning families of all classes often kept the family home in the wife's name for a municipal tax reduction. They hadn't liked it when federal taxation counteracted that benefit. But Quebeckers had particularly disliked not being able to claim payments made from a husband's income to a wife's asset, because Quebec's marital property regime left them unable to shift ownership back to the husband to secure the federal tax break.[107] In the March 1943 budget, Ilsley gave in on these points even while continuing, as I suggested above, to hold a hard line.

Changes to the means of collecting income tax required only administrative care, not new budget measures. Concerns about overdeductions, especially for workers with highly variable earnings, continued to be vocally expressed throughout 1943 and became the basis for special accommodations later that year. In his speech in September to the Trades and Labour Congress, Ilsley mentioned these accommodations as being worked out with coal miners and invited unionists to write to Revenue Minister Gibson with suggestions and comments.[108] Then, in November, Commissioner of Income Tax C.F. Elliott convened a meeting of labour organizations, employer organizations, and government departments to see if a consensus about deductions and refunds could be developed. In his account of this meeting (perhaps inevitably a bit self-congratulatory), everyone spoke their piece in a roundtable, he prepared an agenda based upon that discussion, and the solutions that he developed were approved by the meeting. Details of the solutions are vague in his report, but it is clear that the problem of overdeductions for seasonal workers and others with highly variable earnings was named and at least partly addressed through a genuine consultation.[109]

A concession concerning the means of collection also had to be worked out for the Indigenous fishing fleet in coastal British Columbia. Enjoying higher wartime prices and demands for their catch, Nuu-Chah-Nulth, Tsmishian, and other Indigenous fishers were alarmed to learn that income taxes would be deducted from their pay amounts. Most of them would have no tax liability at year end and would be refunded what had been deducted. But in the meantime they felt short-changed of a long-awaited improvement in their earnings. As one Musqueam member wrote, "I am fishing and they are taking taxes of[f] my fish. And I'm suppose[d] to be free not to pay taxes. And I'm old 78 years. I can't do any work, that all I do is fishing." Organized by Andrew Paull of the Native Brotherhood of British Columbia, they threatened not to fish, in an echo of the 1931 protest in Massett about the Jones tax. In response, the Department of Fisheries made completion of income tax paperwork for deduction of income tax by fish-processing firms a condition of getting a fishing licence.[110] Complicating the situation was that, though the coastal fishers were being taxed as small businesses, few of them had the bookkeeping experience to ensure that they were not being overtaxed. In the end, the federal tax collector prevailed, with some cooperation from Fisheries and Indian Affairs. To get the fishery going, licences were to be issued on the understanding that Indian agents would help Indigenous fishers with the paperwork. In Bella Coola, and likely in other rural areas, the Indian agent completed hundreds of tax returns in order to ensure that members of his agency would get the refunds that they were owed. Revenue accepted that these were special circumstances and allowed an extension of two months to the tax-filing deadline. The work of Indian agents ensured that these fishing communities had substantial deducted amounts refunded to them, as much as $60,000 in one district in 1944.[111] As one MP had predicted, the cost of assessing and refunding income taxes from these low-income fishers meant that taxing their incomes was not producing any net revenue.[112] The legitimacy of the tax itself would remain an unsettled question along the coast. Having to administer a mass income tax with deduction at source meant that the revenue minister had to think more carefully about the household cash flow of low-income Canadians. Protests such as those of the coal miners and BC Indigenous fishers meant that a cavalier attitude toward the impacts of pay deductions threatened to have political costs.

In the June 1944 budget, the main material concession was elimination of the refundable part of the personal income tax. Ilsley acknowledged that, even with the capping at 66 percent of the tax imposed on lower incomes, the effective rate was still high. He also admitted that refundable tax certificates couldn't be provided quickly. And though he refused to state publicly what he had vigorously argued in cabinet, that income taxation was motivating absenteeism and refusal of overtime, he acknowledged that morale might have been adversely affected.[113] So, while insisting that war savings were more important than ever, he terminated the savings portion of the personal income tax. This measure would cost the war chest between $110 and $115 million, amounts that would have to be made up by voluntary contributions. As a bit of face saving, Ilsley argued that the campaigns for voluntary savings were now more effective than they had been in the summer of 1942, so the argument for compulsory savings was less compelling. Moreover – and this was the message that lower-income Canadians had succeeded in communicating – he appreciated that voluntary savings provided some flexibility in personal budgets.[114] The tide of letters that had landed on the Finance desks in 1942–43 had made vividly clear that, even with careful budgeting, the wartime income tax had left people on modest incomes without anything to spare and often with less than they needed to eat and pay their bills.

Members of the other parties in the House of Commons had called, and would continue to call, for higher exempt amounts for both the normal tax and the graduated tax.[115] As King had urged, Ilsley rejected this strategy: higher exemptions overall would produce relief for the rich as well as the poor, unlike the targeted relief measures that the government was proposing. And, in a theme that echoed the September 1943 Trades and Labour Congress speech, and that would be repeated by others in postwar tax planning, Ilsley reiterated that the contributions of the many small taxpayers were an essential part of the revenue.[116] The forms of tax relief that he offered were therefore aimed at cases of "special hardship" that had emerged in the first two years of the "pay-as-you-earn" regime. Several of these cases dealt with medical expenses or expenses of people with disabilities. The majority had something to do with family. One measure frequently requested since 1917 was that an income earner who supported in-laws could have tax relief by means of an exemption or credit equivalent to that for children. That measure was introduced in the 1944 budget.[117]

Another of the family measures was that any children dependent on the taxpayer, regardless of biological relationship, could be claimed for tax purposes. That concession removed the glaring injustice of an unmarried mother being unable to claim a tax credit for her "illegitimate child" unless she legally adopted the child. Earlier protests over the disqualification of "illegitimate" children in British Columbia had emphasized the expense of adopting even if there were two parents; this issue only worsened the irritation in BC coastal communities where the ordinary practice of common-law marriages among Indigenous people meant that tax inspectors did not recognize many children when calculating taxes owed in common-law households.[118] Ilsley also introduced a measure that would provide relief for elderly couples for whom the wife's small investment income risked creating a tax bill that the couple couldn't afford. This measure helped people who had been able to save – by definition those who'd had middle-class or better incomes during their earning years. But the letters that Ilsley had received from such couples made it clear that at least some of the beneficiaries of this provision would be low-income taxpayers. The beneficiaries of the other family measure were in a different category: in 1944, alimony payers got the more generous exemption that they had demanded in 1942 – complete elimination of any tax liability on the amounts paid to ex-wives.[119] Still, overall, these "special hardship" measures were aimed at making the new income tax less punishing for the poor by easing the conflict between taxes and demands of family support on a breadwinner's income.

Some problems remained. The CCF's Stanley Knowles pointed out two of them. While approving of the measures that Ilsley had introduced, Knowles noted that parents of student nurses (unlike parents of university students) were not allowed to claim their children as dependants. He also pointed out that the travel expenses for sleeping car porters (an African Canadian occupation in mid-century Canada) were not allowed as deductions from incomes as were the expenses of other railway workers (organized in different unions). Exactly how these differences in treatment were justified is not clear – likely policy makers' class and race blinkers explained them. As Knowles observed, equity demanded that these groups be offered comparable exemptions.[120] Two other demands remained unaddressed, each the subject of substantial political protest since 1942. Both, again, had to do with the sharing of income in families. One was the taxation of annuities – a savings mechanism frequently used by male breadwinners to provide for their widows. The other had to do with transfers within family businesses. Ilsley explained how the remedies that he had heard proposed by members of the House would provide easily exploited tax loopholes for the wealthy, so he proposed that the questions receive further study. Perhaps reasonable reliefs could be provided in ways that would not end up destroying the progressivity of the income tax system.[121]

But the tax relief that Ilsley's budget had provided meant immediately reduced deductions at source for many of the new income tax payers, and politically this was useful to the Liberals. As Prime Minister King had speculated, compared with other measures, the ones that they offered in 1944 meant that "a much larger number of people will be helped in a way that will give them more money at once, albeit their own money, and that in relieving burdens on those of the lower class and making for a better feeling over a larger number, the yielding up of income [tax] may prove to be a preferable course."[122] In justifying his approach, King had impressed on Clifford Clark that holding on to every legitimate cent of tax revenue risked giving the CCF victory in the next election, and if that happened then "the whole financial position," including the work of the Victory Loan people, would be seriously harmed.[123] Here King's worry about the CCF threat was not merely mindless vote counting: King thought "it was necessary to emphasise this [threat to the financial system from the CCF] strongly."[124] Tax policy that was too hard on lower-income Canadians put too much at risk. Forgoing some income tax revenue from small incomes was necessary in order to protect Canada's ability to borrow and to protect Canadians' investments in government bonds, both of which King deemed would be in danger if the mass of voters were to turn sharply leftward.

$ ¢ $

Wars create a sense of community but not without some help. Whether enlisting, or grocery shopping, or taxpaying, Canadians did not easily let go of their prewar differences and grievances. In organizing war finance, Ilsley, Towers, Gibson, and their officials had to deal with legacies of bitterness and conflict that fed suspicion and tax resistance. First World War veterans had reason to believe that bondholders' rights to interest payments had been put ahead of their needs for unemployment relief. The Victory Loan campaigners were selling bonds to a public no longer so innocent about the risks and rewards that awaited the small investor compared with those available to big capital. Nor were all segments of the public now easily convinced that Canada's shortage of high-income earners was a "stubborn fact" that justified taxing lower and lower incomes.[125] People on the left had started to think about broadening the income tax base in another way – by redefining taxable income to include income previously sheltered as capital gains.

In response to these and other threats to capital, the Liberals marketed government bonds to small investors in order to make as many Canadians as possible, in their own interest, into supporters of protections to investment capital. In addition, they vastly broadened the income tax base by taxing smaller incomes rather than targeting capital. They also actively sold "sound money" policies, using public education to engage broad participation in making those policies work. All of these steps were justified by a commitment to preserving and protecting the "financial and business system." And all required mass consent and participation. Spirited attempts by the Department of Finance to enlist Canadians in the government's war finance policy, to listen to criticism, and to respond with reasoned argument show how the need to win taxpayers' consent contributed to a democratic style of public administration and a more social form of liberalism. The Finance rhetoric established links among public borrowing, currency stability, social security, and taxation that, though Keynesian in complexion, were conceived in support of the immediate projects of selling bonds, collecting taxes, preventing labour strife, and disarming the CCF. In this rhetoric, the new income tax payers were told that they were interconnected in multiple ways, whether caring and mutual ones or impersonal systems operating in markets for credit and consumer goods. This was a social liberalism that also relied importantly on recognizing the self-interest of individuals as a necessary consideration in designing public policy.

This powerful but potentially unstable mix of appeals was addressed to people who, collectively, had come into a position of real power. The labour of the new income tax payers, their tax compliance, and their savings were all essential to the war effort. The labour movement harnessed some of that power for the project of collective bargaining, but the impact of the new taxpayers' power was also delivered in less organized and less class-specific ways, such as individuals' letters, references to those letters in the House by MPs, and reporting of those references in newspapers. To make the war finance scheme work, Ilsley (and sometimes Clark) had to bring the voice of the ordinary tax grumbler and not just the well-soaked rich into the cabinet chamber.

In doing so, they shifted the income tax payer from the elite position that he (or less often she) had occupied in federal income taxation before the war. Paying direct taxes to the federal government was now a feature of daily, working-class life; for many more Canadians, the categories of citizen and income tax payer now increasingly overlapped. The legacy of war finance was a more socially active state, but the new income tax payers of that new state were addressed in a quasi-collectivist discourse that blended social responsibility and individual self-interest. Complaints about the burden of income taxes on household budgets were present at the birth of the new taxpayer, and individualist pocketbook politics would continue to play a part in postwar citizen engagement. For better or for worse, the new taxpayer would become a new breed of citizen – socially minded, to be sure, but always also tax conscious.

8
New Publics and the Taxman in the 1950s

THE MASS INCOME TAX HAD BEEN·SOLD during the Second World War as something that would finance social security and fight inflation. In the tax reform projects that lay ahead in the 1950s and 1960s, both projects would continue to feature in different ways across the political spectrum. On the right, the symbolic value of taxpaying by the poor and near poor continued to be cited. Because consent to higher taxes among lower-income earners rested on the social security state, those hostile to that state would try to persuade working-class people that they were being "bribed with their own money" and that they should prefer to keep it and save for their security.[1] At the political centre, all acknowledged that, in the new world of macroeconomics, income taxation was more than just a source of revenue. It also served as a means of managing spending and saving in ways supposed to ensure general prosperity and a stable currency. In justifying taxes, finance ministers would regularly now draw on that macroeconomic language.[2] Inflation had irreversibly moved into the mainstream of tax talk, even though the precise role of taxation in producing large systemic effects on prices remained to be specified and effectively deployed.[3] Organized labour drew on economics expertise to challenge some theories of inflation and disputed the right's assertion that workers wanted "something for nothing." In a nutshell, the Canadian Labour Congress asserted, "Workers [Are] Willing to Pay Fair Share."[4] Tax talk remained varied and vigorous after 1945,[5] but income taxation had displaced the tariff from the centre of debate.

Wartime consent to personal income taxation had to be remade on a new basis. Federal finance required a substantial income tax revenue, regardless of social security spending. The federal debt had risen from the prewar level of 43 percent of GNP to 100 percent of GNP. Reducing that debt and meeting ongoing interest obligations, along with other reconstruction expenses, would mean that income tax cuts would be less than hoped for. To be sure, in Canada, sales taxation would again quietly ease the revenue-generation responsibility of federal income tax payers.[6] But mass income tax would continue. Its overstretched administrative apparatus and its rickety statute would have to be reformed, however. In 1945 and 1946, a Senate committee interviewed both Canada's head tax collector and a slightly odd selection of interested organizations in order to prepare recommendations for improvements in income taxation procedures.[7] A new statute was passed in 1948, the first federal income tax statute not to have the word *war* in the title. Income taxation was now firmly established as an important contributor to federal revenue. And being a federal income tax payer was now an ordinary part of adult citizenship.

Not surprisingly, one of the earliest effects of the broadening of the national taxpayer public was that the range of voices in tax talk diversified. In the twenty years after 1945 – the long 1950s – we can find the early days of the tax conversation that would become the heated tax reform debate of Canada's short 1960s (1965–75). In this chapter, I introduce the new or newly situated tax publics of the postwar period and the assiduous efforts of the Department of National Revenue to teach them income tax compliance. Then, by describing some of the tax advice available for free or a fee from non-government sources, I explore the new moral world of income tax in the long 1950s. From that world emerged debates about the taxation of capital gains. That topic focused the conflict over whether income taxation, as supposedly the fairest of taxes, really reflected differences in ability to pay. In the chapters that follow, I further develop the other distinctive issues of the postwar period: taxpaying grievances among the poor, worries about "bureaucracy," entanglements of tax and constitutional questions, and the macroeconomic role of income taxation. Like other historians of the welfare state, I argue that the 1950s were no paradise of consensus and prosperity and that the work of building a more democratic Canada, with governments responsive to all the people, took place in a changing moral world, amid the long shadows of the class and constitutional conflicts of the 1930s.[8]

New Publics in the Relations of Extraction

Most electorally significant of the new tax publics were the numerous low-income payers of income tax. At the beginning of the period, it briefly seemed as though the population of personal income tax payers would revert to something like its small prewar number. In his 1949 budget, to widespread approval, Finance Minister Douglas Abbott raised the levels of exempt income to match prewar levels. The tax on individuals' incomes was perhaps the "fairest and best tax we have," he noted in his first budget speech, but Canadians "just don't like it, or at least we don't like too much of it."[9] The single exemption for 1949 was set at $1,000 and the married exemption at $2,000. The impact of these changes (and other minor adjustments) was to reduce by 96.6 percent the number of Canadians paying income tax on incomes (after basic exemptions) under $1,000.[10] Even those with slightly larger taxable incomes were much fewer, down by 27 percent in the 1949 calendar year statistics from the 1948 number. Overall, the total decline in the number of personal income tax payers between 1948 and 1949 was just over 17 percent. Not as dramatic as the 1926 reductions, the changes were nevertheless intended to be important as a means of relieving tax burdens on lower-income earners.[11]

In spite of reduced exemption levels, however, relief was largely illusory. Low-income earners were still paying income taxes. In 1949, $1,000 had the equivalent in buying power of only $628 in 1939. And over the 1950s inflation would continue to erode the value of the exemptions, which would remain unchanged until 1971.[12] Combined with the impact of rising wages (often inflation driven) and a progressive rate structure (15 percent on the first $1,000, 17 percent on the second $1,000, 19 percent on the third $1,000, and so on), the lowered exemptions in 1949 did not reduce overall personal income tax revenues, and overall taxpayer numbers continued to rise. The moment in 1949 when the number of Canadian income tax payers rose to 3 million (exceeding the wartime number and well up from 300,000 before the war) was noted in newspaper headlines.[13] By 1959, the $1,000 exemption would have only half of the purchasing power that it had had in 1939. Over the same period, *average* wages in current dollars rose over 300 percent (from about $1,200 a year to $3,810 a year).[14] But those numerous Canadians whose incomes were less than the average, but still taxable, would increasingly feel a pinch. More than ever, toward the end of the long 1950s, the majority of personal income tax payers were paying small amounts out of stretched budgets, much as had been the case during the unprecedented war tax days of 1942–45. This new majority would have an impact on tax talk.

Among the growing population of vote-wielding, wage-earning income tax payers, another newly numerous public constituency for tax questions was composed of income tax–paying farmers. In 1942, the last year when the category "agrarians" had been used for classifying federal taxpayers by occupation, 21,158 had filed returns and been assessed.[15] After 1942, the classification "primary producers" was used, bundling in with "agrarians" the "natural resources" category (much smaller) that had contained fishers and trappers. In 1948, before the reliefs offered to lower incomes in 1949, the primary producer category had grown to 72,700; in 1949, poorer farmers, fishers, and trappers were no longer in the mix, and the number of personal income tax–paying "primary producers" dropped to 56,150.[16] Farmers were the object of some suspicion by urban commentators on tax questions. Their enthusiasm for the income tax had long been seen as a kind of rural tax dodge because farm income was that left over after the farmer's costs (including subsistence) were deducted, whereas wage and salary earners were assessed on all that they earned. The suspicion of farmers as tax dodgers continued after 1945, as noted in a June 1952 article in *Saturday Night* on the "Mystery of Farmer's Income Tax." Its author, political commentator Michael Barkaway, speculated about why so little income tax was paid by many of the country's wealthier farmers.[17] A week after his piece appeared the Federation of Agriculture explained why they thought that his comments were mistaken. But they also acknowledged that, when local tax inspectors provided help in completing forms, there had been "a great increase in the numbers of farmers filing income tax returns."[18] A suspicious mind might infer that more than formphobia had prevented farmers from doing that paperwork and that something other than gratitude for clerical assistance had motivated more of them to make returns under tax inspectors' watchful eyes.

Finally, another group who had been new among income tax payers when exemptions dropped during the war were those living on small annuities and inheritors of small estates, such as widows of small-town doctors or well-paid tradesmen. The low levels of income tax exemptions partly explains the increased presence of these groups, but also a 1938 amendment to the Income War Tax Act had made widows liable to income taxes on some kinds of income-generating legacies. In addition, the Dominion Succession Act of 1942 continued in peacetime the novelty of both the federal government and the provincial governments imposing inheritance taxes based upon wealth and not just income. The appreciation of house values since the 1930s made it more likely that a deceased working man's estate might be valuable enough to attract this form of taxation. An agitation in 1944 drew the attention of women's organizations to the taxation of widows' incomes and the property rights held by wives in their husbands' estates. Breadwinner/housewife marriage, if it rested on the housewife's forgoing the development of a marketable skill, relied for its fairness on a husband who provided something – an annuity or life insurance or a house – for his widow. In the long 1950s, concerns about the tax treatment of widows mobilized tax activism by women's organizations.[19]

In addition to such new or newly active tax publics, the existing "normal" federal income tax payer, the urban man with a relatively high income, encountered new tax experiences during the long 1950s. In particular, this taxpayer faced higher marginal rates than those during the interwar years. The highest marginal rate of personal income tax was dropped only to 84 percent in the tax reduction budget of 1949: before the war, it had been 66 percent.[20] One response to the higher rates came from an economics research organization, funded by the owners of some of Canada's largest industrial and financial firms, the Canadian Committee on Industrial Reconstruction.[21] Donations from these chief executives paid for the production and dissemination of *The Burden of Taxation: Pre-War and Post-War* to make the case that extravagant spending (in particular on social security) and cheap money (with its risk of inflation) should make Canadians worried about the scale of the federal government's taxation and possible increases in debt and debt charges. Although full of data and sonorous with the tone of objective expertise, *The Burden of Taxation* was also frank in its expressions of political ideas. In its closing paragraphs, "a larger burden of taxation" was presented as a threat to economic freedom and "true" social security.[22] Such principles might have been meaningful to high-income earners. For many, as tax law historian Richard Pound has noted, higher rates – "the size of shovel being put into their stores" – were taken as reason enough, without further justification, to adopt a more active practice of tax avoidance.[23] But the political ideas of *The Burden of Taxation* offered a higher purpose, if one seemed to be necessary.

With tax avoidance thus motivated, the elite income tax payer found himself offered a new legal environment for reporting income. The 1948 Income Tax Act provided some of the certainty and clarity required for effective tax avoidance. Changes such as the removal of ministerial discretion from many clauses of the act and the publication of some of the department's key accounting tools allowed the precise calculation of the impact of avoidance strategies. And if taxpayer and tax collector disagreed on an assessment, then the new Tax Appeal Board of Canada provided an inexpensive, quick, and expert arbiter of the disagreement.[24]

A consequence of these changes was the formation of another new tax public: a significantly expanded cohort of tax advisers, people who earned their living helping businesses and the well-to-do manage their tax affairs. In the interwar years, tax specialists in accounting firms had assisted auditors who sought their specialized knowledge of clients' tax issues. This backroom role shifted as the prospects of new tax avoidance methods appeared as business opportunities for accounting firms. Retired accountants interviewed in 2014 for Deloitte's retirees' newsletter recalled that only after the Second World War was "the volume of tax work ... sufficient to support full time tax professionals." One man remembered having been asked in the mid-1950s by the partner in charge of the Toronto office to look into clients' files to see if there were any "little 'gems' – tax opportunities that had been missed by the auditors." "That was the way most tax people were operating at that time," he recalled. They were building a new specialty by marketing tax avoidance strategies to their clients.[25]

The new tax regime also brought business opportunities in law. Richard Pound documents the founding and flourishing of a boutique tax law firm that took the same kind of entrepreneurial role as did Deloitte's accountants. As Pound pointed out in his address at Stikeman Elliott's fiftieth anniversary, the small firm built its business by beating the bushes, explaining to prospective clients how the money spent on tax lawyers would leave them richer.[26] With the new statute and new Tax Appeal Board, the opportunities flowed in, and the number of tax cases surged, growing by the late 1960s to at least five times their number in the late 1940s.[27] At their most idealistic, the keen new tax practitioners brought to their contest with revenue authorities a view that they were helping to make the practice of government more competent and more respectful of citizens' rights by revealing weaknesses in the statute and its administration.[28] The enticing prospect of tax-related business opportunities could be made even more appealing by the notion (overemphasized, perhaps, but not fictional) that the tax authority might sometimes exceed its proper limit. As the administrative apparatus grew, tax professionals and their clients could characterize their challenges to Revenue in terms of ideas about the dangers of bureaucracy that had been circulating since the 1920s, in works such as Lord Chief Justice Gordon Hewart's *The New Despotism.*[29]

Finally, the new tax publics of the postwar period included economists. Public finance had been neither a prestigious nor a large area of economics research before the war.[30] Reservations expressed by the Rowell-Sirois commissioners on the state of Canadian economics research on tax had been well warranted. As Duncan McDowall has shown, before 1939 Canadian economists lacked access to a system of national accounts, and without such data claims about the economic impacts of taxes remained microeconomic or ideological.[31] Even the federal government's taxation statistics had been thin before the war. Economist Oskar Morgenstern's 1950 observation that, because of taxpayer deception, "income tax returns ... have only a vague resemblance to the actual, underlying income patterns" seems likely to have been true during Canada's interwar years, when enforcement capacity was so limited.[32] In 1945, a new series, *Taxation Statistics,* provided more thorough and probably more reliable data.[33] In 1946, Winnipeg grain trade economist D.A. MacGibbon wrote, bluntly, that "the income tax should be carefully integrated to the whole economic life of the country. This requires study."[34] In 1951, a brief history called *Taxation in Canada* would provide some of the basic tools for that study, and in 1955 would follow a two-volume history of Canadian taxation by the same author, economist and wartime member of the Department of Finance J. Harvey Perry.[35] For the first time, Canadians could know the basic facts of their tax history. Over the 1950s, the number of academic economists in Canada grew, and, as part of the flourishing interest in macroeconomics, taxation began to be an area of research interest.[36] In the amassing of economic wisdom in 1957 that was the report of the Royal Commission on Canada's Economic Prospects, "the tax structure" figured alongside wages and social security as a link that "transmitt[ed] dynamic impulses" through the "complex and sophisticated mechanism" that was "the economy."[37] In this framing, tax was not merely a burden on economic activity but also one economic force among others, with multiple possible effects.

Another innovation of the long 1950s was the Canadian Tax Foundation (CTF). Founded in 1945 as a joint effort of the Dominion Association of Chartered Accountants and the Canadian Bar Association, the CTF brought together tax practitioners, civil servants, and economists to share data, discuss problems, and consider policy. As a representative of the new tax professionals, it would occupy a central place in Canadian tax politics. Its membership was more ideologically mixed and professionally diverse than that of the Citizens' Research Institute of Canada had been. In the interwar years, CRIC had relentlessly opposed the proliferation of taxes and the extravagance of governments, with a special focus on the problems of municipalities. Representatives of insurance companies, municipalities, and provinces figured prominently in its conferences. During the 1950s, the more diverse membership of the CTF fostered significant debates, as did its periodical, the *Canadian Tax Journal*. Neil Brooks's description of the first ten years of the journal suggests that some points of tax debate were already stalemated. But, as Brooks also points out, CTF staff played a considerable role in making tax matters comprehensible in a calm, even-handed way to the serious lay reader. Gwyneth MacGregor, editor of the *Canadian Tax Journal*, produced many booklets on tax law whose clarity and wit made them a great asset to me, as they must have to journalists and business-people when the booklets began to appear in the late 1950s.[38]

These institutional resources were complemented by expanding activities in civil society. There were no exact equivalents to the numerous Constitution-focused, self-consciously anti-statist, anti–income tax organizations that flourished in the United States during the 1950s and 1960s. There was no Liberty Belles for women, no Committee for Constitutional Government, or anything like the American Taxpayers Association. As striking as they were, with their bold claims for the abolition of federal income taxation, they were phenomena of the McCarthy and Goldwater moments, grassroots movements that failed to gain a solid foothold in the national Republican Party.[39] In Canada, in contrast, comparable ideas – tax as theft, constitutional challenges to the federal government's right to tax income – found a home in the party system, in Social Credit in Quebec and the west and in the Union nationale in Quebec. The language of high principle made tax critique flashy in the United States compared with the shabbier grinding of self-interested axes. But that grinding was present in both countries, as were tax-focused organizations.

In Canada, a variety of particular interests organized not to abolish the income tax but to limit some of its impacts. Most strikingly named, the Income Taxpayers' Association was in reality narrowly focused. It concerned itself mainly with challenging the tax privileges of cooperatives, an enormously sore point in the western Canadian grain trade. Succeeded in 1962 by the Equitable Income Tax Foundation, this element continued to be outraged by cooperatives' tax advantages. It claimed a membership of 70,000 and would help to oppose tax reform in 1967.[40] Canadian middle-class women produced a tax-oriented splinter group from the National Council of Women. Its purpose was also hidden by a generic name, and even its membership numbers were undocumented. But the Canadian Committee on the Status of Women conducted a campaign about widows' and wives' income tax concerns during the 1950s. By the 1960s, the other national women's groups, advancing similar issues, reabsorbed this line of tax critique.[41] Similarly, the Canadian Labour Congress developed views on tax structure in labour terms, critiquing income tax evasion, sales taxes, and exemption levels. The Chamber of Commerce also initiated Operation Freedom, with its echoes of the John Birch Society's campaigns. If one is looking to find in Canada's long 1950s "a nation of serfs,"[42] complaisantly accepting high taxes, then one is looking in vain. Each of these organizations claimed a principled base for tax resistance.

In the 1950s, as in the 1920s, tax protest's constitutionalism in Canada took on the coloration of a Quebec issue, with a tint of regionalism. New in the 1950s, however, was that advocates of an activist federal welfare state proposed centralization of taxing powers as an essential measure of social justice, via social security and full employment.[43] These policy actors put high stakes on the table, but the stakes were not about some proper maximum marginal tax rate – the Americans' constitutional cause, which had persisted through the war into the 1950s.[44] The Canadian cause appeared to be about the division of taxing powers, putting the very nature of the federation in play. The unfinished business of the 1930s remained to be addressed. But there was also a heightened Quebec autonomism, fuelled by the wartime conscription crises. That autonomism hid within its folds a defence of the considerable wealth domiciled in English Quebec. More than the rights of provinces or founding nations was at stake. The division of powers had some dollar signs attached, as I will explain in Chapter 9. In this chapter, I explore how questions of personal morality, honour, responsibility, prudence, and competence figured in the Canadian tax culture that emerged among the new tax publics of the postwar period.

New Methods in the Relations of Extraction

The new demographics, organizations, and institutions of Canada's relations of extraction made the long 1950s a distinct period in public finance.

Methods of tax collection changed, and with them emerged new images of and ideas about tax avoidance and evasion. In these ideas, tax law would occupy an important place. Avoidance is legal; evasion is not. When the law changes, so do the specific referents of these terms. The Income War Tax Act of 1917 had built into it some vagueness about which sorts of business practices would fall on the wrong side of the line between planning and dodging. The new Income Tax Act of 1948 was meant to clear up some of these points of ambiguity.[45] In his history of the Stikeman Elliott law firm, Pound describes the shift in legal culture that the new statute marked. His account relies significantly on the memories of Heward Stikeman, a key witness of that change, not only because he launched a tax law firm but also because he had worked in the Department of National Revenue under C. Fraser Elliott between 1939 and 1945. Stikeman had a lot of affection and respect for Elliott, not only his former boss but also the father of his business partner. In Stikeman's recollection, Elliott senior represented the legal regime that was passing.[46]

The old statute had allowed the minister of national revenue considerable discretion to judge on technical questions that determined tax liability – often on the then crucial question of whether a particular transaction was motivated by legitimate business purposes or by an intent to evade taxes. In effect, it was not the minister but the commissioners of income tax – Breadner, Walters, and then Elliott – who had the power to make those judgments, and if the taxpayer disagreed he or she had recourse to the Exchequer Court and the Privy Council in London. Elliott and his predecessors saw their power of discretion as enabling them sometimes to spare a taxpayer or to snare one. Elliott told the Senate committee that replacing discretion with specific statutory rules risked doing taxpayers more harm than good – rigidity could play either way.[47] Discretion has many risks, of course. Occasionally, businesspeople seeking some favourable discretion offered bribes to highly placed Revenue officials. But, according to Stikeman, Elliott effectively fended off such temptations and courageously faced down politically motivated pressures on behalf of particular wealthy and connected taxpayers, even when those pressures were backed by Prime Minister Bennett or King.[48]

In addition to the risks posed to particular taxpayers, Elliott thought that introducing greater legal precision would carry a cost to the general tax culture. He pointed out that, when judges endorsed as legal business arrangements that allowed taxpayers to avoid tax debts that the state, in a moral sense, intended them to pay, the courts "influenced adversely the moral tendency of the public."[49] Such tax-avoiding shifts, at the boundary of legality, had become well known during the war. After the war, in 1949, Quebec Independent Liberal MP Wilfrid Lacroix listed off in the House of Commons five such methods of tax avoidance that, in his view, allowed "companies and big-business men to avoid a large part of the income tax," leaving "the wage-earner" to carry "practically alone" the burden of the income tax during and since the war.[50] Lacroix and others were no longer willing to participate in the strategy of silence to maintain confidence in the income tax system. Elliott, however, never stopped praising the honest Canadian taxpayer: "I do believe there is something inherent in our people to see that taxes must be paid, and to pay them."[51] But his day and his approach to enforcement were over. In 1946, he was appointed to an ambassadorship in sunny, temperate Santiago, Chile.[52] The department that he left behind would shift the emphasis in its enforcement strategies. In the department's postwar communications, a note of threat and an invitation to prudent legalism emerged in the foreground, largely replacing Elliott's invocations of the responsible, honourable, thoroughly middle-class taxpayer.

The change in the department's mode of address and related enforcement methods was easily observed. Its influence on Canadians' own attitudes is more difficult to pin down to a specific period. But there is evidence to suggest that, during the long 1950s, changes in tax law that affected mainly the wealthy were echoed in the general culture, in magazines and newspapers, in opinion polls, in letters to editors, and in letters to politicians. Some elements of the general culture were hospitable to a narrowly prudential view of tax obligations. Cultural historians of the 1950s note a questioning of moral absolutes and a certain endorsement of selfishness.[53] The newly broad cohort of citizen-taxpayers was ready to take up a narrowly self-serving view of income tax compliance. The editors of the influential Liberal *Winnipeg Free Press* noted the presence of "a pretty general and systematic attempt to beat the income tax by every possible legal means" in response to a perception that postwar income taxes were "excessive."[54] However persistent (and it did persist) the moral residue of the interwar image of the income tax payer, there was also a reimagining of the income tax, not as guaranteeing a fair sharing with consumption taxes of the tax burden, but as itself a burden whose distribution was wrong and thus legitimately avoided.

Key in the ongoing reimagination of income taxation were discussions about the morality of tax avoidance and the relation of avoidance to evasion. According to an after-dinner speaker at the new Canadian Tax Foundation in 1948, "when all are stealing, none is a thief," and "otherwise law-abiding people" will "evade taxation."[55] Historians cannot help but note that what counts as ethically sound is often just what is ethically current. Even now many non-experts confuse avoidance and evasion when they talk about tax compliance. Partly, this comes from ignorance of the law, but partly we aren't always certain how far we can go with legal avoidance without encountering moral issues. Tax avoidance is so settled a practice in our daily lives that even those of us with simple tax returns understand that we can qualify for tax reductions and hence refunds if we do simple things such as keep charitable receipts or less simple things such as put savings into RRSPs. By these means, we can legally reduce our tax obligations. We could choose to pay more by giving to causes not registered as charities or by saving our money in non-registered investments. But why pay more than we owe? Few hesitate to protect every last cent from the taxman even if their household budgets are not pinched. Tax avoidance of that "just doing the paperwork" sort is a normal part of taxpayer life. Even some tax evasion methods are normal. Doing a bit of work without writing up an invoice; paying your nanny in cash; declaring most, but not all, of your tip income – in such practices we participate in tax evasion. "Normal" evasion, like legal avoidance, if not mere carelessness, is about survival, prosperity, protest, or greed. It is hard to measure, but it is not the subject of collective revulsion when small amounts and poor people are involved.[56] It is only when larger amounts are involved and the well fed evade and avoid that some of us sometimes see immorality. In the creation of a new peacetime tax system, the Canadian federal tax collector had to counter normal tax dodging underpinned by attitudes that would, if not checked, raise the cost of collection.

In September 1947, as discussion of Canada's proposed new Income Tax Act proceeded, a Gallup poll provided a snapshot of Canadians' attitudes toward income tax evasion. The poll asked respondents to rank six "crimes" according to their "seriousness." Canadians ranked them as follows, with unusual unanimity across age, sex, income, and occupational group:

Cruelty to children
Drunken driving
Burglary
Cruelty to animals
Black market offences
Avoiding income tax

Note that the poll question lists "avoiding" – not a criminal act – instead of "evading" – the criminal act. In asking about crimes but referring to avoiding tax, the poll's designers suggested that the distinction was not yet widely grasped. Questioned in this way, those polled agreed, predictably, that avoiding income tax was less serious even than the other property-related offences. And it was *definitely* less serious than harms to children and animals.[57] The poll seems to have been designed to foreground popular tolerance of income tax evasion by comparing it with personal kinds of violence. Readers must have wondered whether avoiding income tax even belonged on the same list as cruelty to children. Yet it is suggestive that the pollsters found it plausible to link these activities (with the exception of burglary) as the things that an ordinary man of sadly ordinary bad character might routinely do. Change burglary to pilfering at work, and it would be easy to imagine the guy who might commit all of these crimes: a boozer who cuffs his kids, kicks his dog, short-changes the boss, drives drunk, and fudges his tax return. This was an ugly mirror image of the masculine respectability associated with the interwar income tax payer. At the same time, in the ranking of income tax avoidance at the bottom of the list, there is also a hint that dodging income tax was losing some of its moral taint, as Elliott had suggested it might, in a legalistic tax culture.

With this kind of thinking in the air, Canada's income tax authority had to do some explaining and persuading. Part of what was needed was a new public relations strategy for the federal tax collector. Late in 1947, the Department of National Revenue hired a new director of public information, amid joking remarks about the miraculous powers required of the man who would have to "sell" the income tax. Whoever it was, he did not build upon Ilsley's legacy: rather than paeans to the potential of the postwar state, the PR campaign launched in 1948 promoted guilt and fear and a promise that strenuous and even-handed enforcement would make the system fair. Tax cheaters, whether rich or poor, would be caught and appropriately punished. Dramatic penalties for big evaders, including jail sentences, would help to educate even "evaders in the low income brackets ... of the seriousness of their offense."[58] Rumours of tax dodging had been rife during the war. The new PR line of National Revenue was that those derelictions would be found out and that a new day of dauntingly efficient tax collection would commence.

A feature story in *Maclean's* helped to publicize the new regime. In "Who Are the Income-Tax Dodgers?" senior political journalist Blair Fraser reported that, after the war, in federal tax offices across the country, the number of assessors, the people who checked over tax returns, had risen from 398 in 1939, to 1,200 by 1947, and almost to 2,000 in 1948. In addition, newspaper stories covered the expanded and more effective revenue agency's powers. The Intelligence Branch, the officers in the field who sought out signs of tax fraud, had been a mere four badly paid men in 1945. By 1948, the branch had grown to fifty, and the hiring of a further 110 officers had been authorized, with better pay to attract the right sort. "Canada's largest collection agency" was being built.[59]

With new staff on deck, a wave of prosecutions ensued, many of them for offences committed during wartime. In Winnipeg, a first-page banner headline proclaimed in 1950 that a successful investigation and prosecution meant "Two Tax-Dodgers Fined $144,500." The judge who convicted the two wholesale merchants for falsifying income tax and excess profits tax returns during the war was quoted as saying "you were obstructing the war effort instead of helping. You didn't play fair with anyone."[60] A Montreal millionaire dry goods merchant grabbed the front page in the *Toronto Star* for his $100,000 fine for similar wartime offences.[61] In many of the stories on such prosecutions, judges (and even one defendant's lawyer) were quoted on the theme of tax evasion and treason, underscoring the links between taxpaying and "duty to ... community and country."[62]

During the late 1940s and early 1950s, National Revenue delivered on its 1947 promise that, for the first time in Canada's history, big income tax evasions would be punished with jail time.[63] And wage-earning evaders learned that, if they owed income tax debts from some other sources of past income, collecting it would be a simple matter for the taxman. The new PR program at the department made it known that the tax authority could take directly some or most or all of a wage in payment of a tax debt. In its late 1940s press releases, the department suggested that, by 1951, whether by prosecutions or by confessions of tax delinquents frightened into coming clean by news of punishments meted out to other fraudsters, it would have collected all that Canadians owed in income tax arrears to their country's coffers. The government expected to reduce tax collection staff after 1951, with an eye to shrinking the civil service.[64] By September 1952, Revenue Minister J.J. McCann, working from Fraser Elliott's old script, cheerfully reported that Canadians were paying their income taxes and that, as a result, the cost of collection was lower than ever before: "There are few crooks," he was quoted as saying; "they have found that tax evasion doesn't pay."[65] But the president of the Royal Bank of Canada told his annual shareholders' meeting in 1951 that "income tax evasion [is] now all too apparent."[66] Who to believe?

Over the 1950s, crackdowns by National Revenue were periodically publicized.[67] Some aimed at investment dealings, others at real estate transactions. One theme was taxpayers claiming that they had honestly believed that some of their income was non-taxable capital gain. Another was that the income in question was not income but non-taxable payment by the employer for work-required expenses. As the Department of National Revenue pursued such cases, they encountered the assertion that a lack of clarity in the statute or an incorrect judgment by a tax inspector was making evasion cases out of avoidance practices.[68] It's easy to see how such assertions could be self-serving twaddle. As one local magistrate observed, in finding for National Revenue against a tax dodger, these were "intelligent people who ought to know better."[69] But the practices of the revenue authority sometimes did its reputation no good. For example, in the name of cleaning up dodgy expense account practices in 1956, it went after Canadian construction workers. Construction firms had long been able to pay for their employees' travel to job sites and daily expenses while away from home without the employees' having to pay taxes on the value of those expenses. This was not actually permitted by the statute, but it was an established practice, confirmed in 1942 and 1946 National Revenue rulings. As the revenue authority studied the problem of people being paid in non-taxable forms, it discovered this violation of the law. On July 10, 1956, a bulletin from National Revenue instructed employers to start deducting from employees' pay income tax payments that reflected living allowances as income. Questions were vigorously raised by both the CCF and the official opposition in the House of Commons. After the Liberals were ousted in a federal election later that year, reversing the measure was one of the first steps of Diefenbaker's new finance minister.[70]

While the tax authority developed its ability to catch evaders, it also trained Canadians to be tax avoiders. Being an income tax payer entailed keeping records, and, for professionals, farmers, and businesspeople more than for wage earners, being an adult meant tax planning – making choices with tax consequences in mind. To an unprecedented extent, the idea of adult economic competence was coming to include a host of small considerations and regular practices based upon the income tax code. The revenue authority was training Canadians to adopt new habits in their daily lives. The tax authority promoted the bookkeeping required for tax compliance by holding up for taxpayers the possibility that they might be paying more tax than necessary: as a National Revenue ad asked farmers in 1948, "Are You Getting the Tax Deductions You Are Entitled To?"[71] National Revenue fully developed the image of the law-abiding, tax-minimizing income tax payer in literature aimed at prairie farmers, the community in which the income tax had once promised salvation from the tariff. A 1948 guide to income tax was produced especially for them.[72]

Most of the questions and answers in the prairie farmers' tax guide indicated that the PR experts in the income tax division saw farm resistance to income taxpaying as converging in its logic with small-business concerns. Farm income, like business income, was the calculated difference between the farm revenue and the expense entailed in earning it. So farm income was greater or lesser depending on what counted as legitimately deductible expenses. The guide pointed out that, contrary to what might have seemed to be common sense on the farm, the farm family's food and clothing were not properly deductible charges against farm income. Here farmers were on the same ground as small businesses or professional practices, in which payment for family members' labour was not deemed a proper business expense. Farmers also shared with small businesses and professionals concerns about the costs of compliance: that is, the time and effort spent keeping accounts of the farm's transactions and then reporting the results of those accounts on an income tax form that seemed to be unduly complex. "Are you not expecting a lot from a farmer, who often comes in from the fields just ready to drop, that he should turn bookkeeper?" the PR man imagined farmers wanting to know. It's hard to imagine that the guide's answer was perceived as uncontroversially sensible: to paraphrase, the guide advised that keeping farm accounts is not that much work, it'll make your farm more profitable, and it'll be no burden if you make it a daily habit. Being advised by the government to form a new habit is rarely popular. But it exemplifies what Foucauldians point out is the requirement of a modern government: that individuals remake themselves in order for the administration of public policy to work.[73] An appetite for working the tax code to one's advantage was inculcated as part of being a modern farmer.

But even wage earners were offered and took their own minuscule loopholes as good, tax-avoiding citizens. The "mass production" methods of income tax enforcement after 1942 offered to lower- and middle-income earners opportunities for small evasions and avoidances. In 1957, for example, the introduction by the Liberals of a standard $100 tax deduction without receipts, for expenditures on any combination of charitable contributions, medical costs, and union dues, acknowledged that scrutiny of such minor details of compliance was simply not worthwhile. Almost certainly, many claimed that deduction without having expended $100.[74] Although brought up to be a good citizen, I recall using that deduction in my first tax returns of the 1970s. This was normal behaviour.

The tax authority's enthusiasm for every taxpayer deploying every exemption, allowance, and deduction was affirmed in a 1951 *Maclean's* article by George Neville titled "How to Save Money on Your Income Tax."[75] "The income tax gatherer," Neville wrote, "doesn't want you to pay a cent more than the law says you have to. However, it's your job, not his, to make sure you don't pay too much." The search for the little guy's loophole was part of the cheese-paring postwar tax culture. Neville told sympathetic tales of poor fellows who paid a few bucks too much because they didn't understand their rights. One such right was a tax reduction device, a "loophole," that Neville pointed out: a man who wasn't actually married could be "married for tax purposes" (i.e., qualify for the married exemption). Moreover, that exemption lasted all year, even if the dependant upon whom the exemption was based died in the first month of the year. The article enthusiastically catalogued this and other "dodges" that readers could use to save something on their tax bills.

Neville also provided a few cautionary tales of what could happen if, out of carelessness, one did not follow the legalities to the letter. The reader's blood was meant to run cold at the sad story of a Cape Breton grocer who began proper bookkeeping in 1948 only to discover that he'd made a profit every year since 1936 and owed $1,100 in back taxes ($12,341 in 2016 dollars). Not keeping honest business accounts was a classic tax evasion device, but in Neville's framing this story was of an innocent mistake by a fellow from the backwoods who just didn't know better. Rural traders, some of whom were barely literate, might well have been perplexed by the notion of keeping records, much less planning tax avoidance, as part of their daily work.[76] But the message of Neville's article and much of the newspaper-level tax advice was that the taxpayer had to pay attention to ensure that he was playing his part and serving his own interests. The message was "be competent or be a chump." And competence consisted of knowing the law and knowing how to use it to one's advantage. Tax talk of the sort that Neville offered was aimed at the "smart manager" rather than the "moral citizen." That the examples in his narrative were all of adult men rather than women would only have underscored the association of taxpaying with the normative economic actor.

Being good at tax avoidance was not entirely about economic rationality, however. For comfortable middle-class folk, the amounts saved by a careful searching out of all possible angles of avoidance were not likely large. Pointing out this phenomenon, newspaper editor John McKay mildly mocked the victim of "taxitis" – a disease that drove ordinarily reasonable men to waste hours in nearly fruitless struggle over tax filing. He described a sufferer who "followed each [paper] trail with excited little grunts, like a dog after a rabbit." Finally, McKay wrote, the taxitis victim "stood up triumphantly, waving his form ... His research had cut his net tax by $3.73, he said ... We were tempted to point out he had spent four hours on it, which was a rather poor rate of return but we forbade ... To a T-phobia or taxitis victim, such arguments are incomprehensible."[77] But with the finance minister saying that Canadians don't like taxes, and tax compliance being sold as competent avoidance, taxphobia was becoming an acceptable, somewhat social disease. There were still reserves of taxpayer honour; another bit of newspaper humour points to it: "When it comes to paying income taxes, some people think filing means chiselling."[78] Using the tools correctly was the common concern.

Marketing and Morality in Tax Advice

While the Department of National Revenue was training Canadians to think of themselves as law-abiding tax avoiders, alert to the distinction between avoidance and evasion, other providers of tax advice found in the new mass income tax an opportunity for service and profit. Tax advice proliferated. Newspaper ads, small and large, advertised inexpensive help with tax returns.[79] Among the services provided by newspapers themselves was free tax advice. In the *Toronto Daily Star,* a weekly "Your Income Tax" column by John Plowman began sometime in the 1940s. The column was still running in the 1960s under the name "Doc Tax." Jointly with the Institute of Chartered Accountants, the *Star* hosted an annual Income Tax Forum in March, and it published a major feature story on the advice given at that event. In addition, the "Questions and Answers" column on the *Star's* editorial page frequently attracted income tax questions. New immigrants turned to Dorothy Lash of the *Star* both for advice and to air their views on how they saw the tax bargain offered in Canada. Magazines such as *Maclean's*, *Saturday Night*, and *Canadian Homes and Gardens* joined in too.[80] Entries in the Canadian Periodical Index show the *Financial Post* as the main source of tax journalism, but these other sources indicate that the conversation about competent tax filing was not confined to a business audience and that providing tax advice was one way to sell newspapers.[81]

Like the business audience, these other audiences wanted advice on how to avoid taxes. Their questions explored the border between avoidance and evasion and hinted at the means of tax evasion used by private citizens who couldn't afford costly tax practitioners' services. One recent immigrant to Canada, writing to Lash in 1960, wanted to know if he really had to declare as income the seventy-two dollars a month paid to him by the tenants of his three-room flat. From his point of view, he thought that one in every four houses in Toronto had some kind of mortgage-helper flat and that few of these small landlords declared this income. His Canadian-born wife was urging him to come clean to the tax authorities, and he wanted to know if she was right: "I know a lot of people who rent out flats for years, but never pay income tax on it. If I do report it, I will make a laughing stock of myself." Urging him never to be ashamed of being laughed at for being honest, Lash said that he did, in fact, need to declare the rental income and that there was a campaign under way to find such tax evasions, so it would be prudent as well as righteous to follow his wife's advice.[82] To housewives fell the responsibility for documenting many tax-deductible expenses, so the home rental income was partly women's business. Good housekeeping entailed knowing which receipts – heating bills, repair bills, or, for other deductions, receipts from doctors, nurses, and pharmacists – might be useful.[83]

There was undoubtedly also informal advice among friends in which the scrupulous distinctions between avoidance and evasion might have played no part. In how many kitchens and beer parlours did one labourer point out to another that the taxman would never know about cash earned on a second job? In the days before the social insurance number, this was a convenient fact of life. Perhaps not surprisingly, the age of the mass income tax saw a new use of the word *moonlighting* – the practice of working two jobs. Rates of moonlighting were of increasing concern in the late 1950s and sporadically through the 1960s. Although a 1958 Canadian Gallup poll found that only 6 percent of the overall sample (combining both men and women over age twenty-one), and as much as 9 percent in the younger age cohorts, worked a second job for extra income, most of them were in relatively low-income groups. The effectiveness of moonlighting for tax evasion was marked by the fact that those with two jobs worked in basic labour, skilled trades, or "outside sales" – all areas where payment in cash would make it relatively safe not to report income.[84] By 1964, a Montreal electrician told Prime Minister Lester Pearson, the perception was that the occurrence of moonlighting was significant. He referred to a 1964 report on income tax that said "175,000 [Canadians were] working at two jobs and 125,000 of them not making any income tax return."[85] Pearson's correspondent was distressed by this evidence of bad citizenship, but apparently many were not.

For big businesses and wealthy taxpayers, tax avoidance exploited more significant vulnerabilities in the law or its administration, and how-to advice was a marketable service. Much of this sort of tax avoidance remained hidden behind the formidable barriers of accounting language. For example, "End Surplus Stripping!" is hard to imagine as a political rallying cry. Few outside fairly rarefied business circles would appreciate the advantages of converting corporate income into sellable capital assets without that income passing through the tax collector's hands. But since 1926 the Department of National Revenue had been tracking down and trying, with only limited success, to prevent various forms of surplus stripping.[86] Both National Revenue and Finance continued to be aware of the problem, and in 1960, Finance Minister Donald Fleming promised that his department would "undertake a comprehensive study" of it.[87] In 1963, Finance Minister Walter Gordon, himself an expert practitioner of the method while in private practice in the 1950s, tried to close that loophole but had limited success.[88] Those who claimed that the department in general was incompetent during the 1950s had in mind National Revenue's prolonged failure to eradicate surplus stripping, among other worries, such as the "twelve ways of successfully avoiding taxes" that a retired departmental employee reportedly listed at a CTF conference in 1961.[89]

Among these twelve ways must have been the tax-targeted use of business expenses. Specialized advisers would certainly have been helpful in navigating this controversial and often-amended aspect of income tax law. The scope of allowable business deductions had been broadened in the Income Tax Act of 1948.[90] One of those deductions, expense allowances, enabled companies to enrich an employee's compensation package without increasing his or her tax bill. In addition, professionals in private practice could deduct a wide range of living expenses. Changes in 1957 made the deductible expense regulations less subject to abuse by requiring that expenditures made against non-taxable allowances be itemized and reported.[91] However, even after that reform, "expense account living" continued to symbolize the class-configured unfairness of the new income tax. Reducing taxable income by means of living expenses "encourages luxury spending out of all proportion to the needs of the business," the CTF's Gywneth MacGregor charged: "It encourages tax cheating."[92] She asked why business entertainment expenses were deductible from income when the tradesman's tools, the musician's bass fiddle, the journalist's research expenses – expenses incurred to earn their own, more modest incomes – were not.[93] If workers had to live away from their homes in order to earn incomes, or if they needed to purchase tools to work, it was argued in various forums, then they were in no different a position than were the business owners able to claim expenses incurred in order to produce incomes.[94] This was a matter both of equity and of real need in some working-class households, and examples from UK and US income tax law showed that Canada's rules in this matter were unusually restrictive.[95] When the law on deductible expenses was both open to interpretation and exceptionally restrictive, calls for reform brought a moral language into the tax talk of the 1950s.

The old middle-class propriety in tax talk could be seen in the criticism of tax avoidance through non-taxable business expenses. In a 1959 article, recent University of Toronto graduate, Young Liberal, and future lawyer David Greenspan argued that the tax regulations only encouraged spiritual and moral emasculation. The expense account–living, martini-swilling salesman who could eat steak while entertaining clients could only afford a hamburger budget for his wife and family. "This double standard [of living] ... creates a garbled sense of personal values that is often destructive morally." If a businessman tries to drive and dress in his daily life up to the standard of the hospitality and status that he shows to clients, then he ends up failing as a breadwinner: pressured in spending more from his real earnings than he earns, "he must finance himself either by going into debt or by sending his wife out to work. In either case, he and his family suffer." Even the wealthy top executive faced a risk to his manhood from the expense account's subtle effects: he became something like the aristocrats of old but without the confidence and security of old money or money earned. Such executives, Greenspan claimed, became "a society of kept men," like the blonde with a mink coat bestowed by her sugar daddy. Greenspan's outrage would have struck that chord in middle-class culture that held luxury to be a bit effeminate. Businesses defending their entertainment expenses, in response, described them as simple necessities. For example, the Exchequer Court found in favour of Royal Trust, against National Revenue, when Royal Trust argued that paying its executives' dues at the posh St. James Club was a properly deductible business expense. It was the fact that the food at the club was not particularly good that persuaded the judge that its choice as a venue for negotiating deals had nothing to do with frivolous pleasure.[96]

Moral questions were raised not just around class justice. Businesspeople also brought an intra-class moral perspective to the question of legal tax reduction. Some regarded exploiting technical vulnerabilities in the tax statute as just part of a game, one in which victory could win (or save) them a lot of money. But others, especially finance professionals, were offended by legal avoidance strategies that seemed to be ethically dubious.[97] Frederick Field, a former president of the Institute of Chartered Accountants of British Columbia, brought to the attention of the income tax division's chief technical officer a tax reduction scheme involving holding companies. Field followed up with a letter to the deputy minister of finance, concluding that "anything you do toward making sure that all citizens pay the same taxes will be much appreciated."[98] And the president of the Royal Bank saw "vigorous reduction of income tax evasion now all too apparent outside the fixed wage and salary group" as required both by "equity" and as a means to keep income tax rates low.[99] Another businessman reported anonymously a particular piece of "income tax cleverness" and begged the tax authority to prevent its use. He pointed out that, if the government allowed some businesses to get away with tax evasion, "then only a fool would invest in any business endeavour, pioneer through all the grim years, and then pay taxes on all drawings from the company."[100] Perhaps these were minority voices. But, like the businessmen who had launched the smuggling inquiry in 1926, and those who had fought for more effective tracking of bond income in the 1930s, such men had an interest in fairer competition.[101] Conceivably, some also thought that exploiting vulnerabilities in the tax law was dishonest and irresponsible. The Crown sometimes expressed that view. In 1961, Crown Prosecutor C.L. Dubin chided a tax-evading realtor: "Unfortunately, Mr. Youngblut had a double standard of honour ... He was apparently fair with those he was doing business with, but not when it came to making his income tax returns."[102]

Deeper kinds of fairness aside, the legalistic positioning of the income tax payer in the 1950s and 1960s led to much tax conversation about what was fair and unfair in the distribution of tax avoidance opportunities for income tax payers. This discussion was framed around the emerging role of tax exemptions and deductions as a system of rewards and incentives for particular kinds of business practice or, indeed, personal behaviour. In other words, there was more involved in the moral language of tax talk than just fairness, honour, and paying your share. Using the tax code to one's advantage was not only about stepping carefully near the line between avoidance and evasion. Tax advantages were put into the law in part for social and economic purposes. To benefit from such advantages was really to act in accordance with some larger collective purpose.[103] If the case for a tax exemption was not simply self-interested special pleading designed to shift more of a joint burden onto the shoulders of others, then it had to be shown to deliver some general benefit. Justification for each exemption or credit thus reached beyond the fiscal register into economic or moral terms or both. Although such proposals were no doubt self-interested, they were also often proposed or justified in broader moral terms.

Take, for example, the deductibility of mortgage interest from taxable income. As many Canadians knew, especially those in border towns, US homeowners were able to deduct from their taxable incomes the amounts of interest that they paid annually on their mortgage loans. Buying a home was purchasing a capital asset, and the interest paid was a cost of that borrowing. This subsidy to home owning was justified, persuasively to some Canadians, with an analogy to a business that could treat such costs as deductible expenses.[104] In the prairie west, this analogy seemed to be especially persuasive because mortgage interest on farmers' family homes was factored into the farm's business accounts.[105] If farmers, then why not city dwellers? Canadians who wrote to the Department of Finance and party strategists on the subject of mortgage interest argued that this issue would win huge numbers of votes for their party.[106] Individual interest was thus enlarged to include partisan interest. But in addition there emerged in their letters larger justifications. One was a moralized picture of home owning – not a new theme but one newly deployed in a macroeconomic way. Proposers of the mortgage interest deduction claimed that homeowners resist the call of the agitator; they are responsible managers of property. The interest deduction not only is fair (on the analogy to business) but also rewards macroeconomically beneficent, inflation-fighting saving and, of course, family responsibility and financial stability.[107] Unions argued in class justice terms that home ownership could be possible for working-class people only with some tax help of this sort.[108] In these kinds of arguments for an exemption, macroeconomic and "macromoral" – social regulation – logics marked the expansion of the income tax from a mechanism of tax fairness to a device for broad economic and social management.

Not Taxing Capital Gains

Students of tariff history will recall the promises of national vigour and competitive virtue that ritually accompanied calls for lowered tariffs. Finding a kind of macroeconomic morality in tax policy was not new to the 1950s. But the systemic conception of "the economy" that accompanied the new econometric and forecasting ambitions of scientific Keynesian economics made of each income tax exemption, credit, and allowance a lever for broad effects. At the centre of the moralized macroeconomic turn of the 1950s were the arguments made for and against taxing capital gains. This long-standing differentiator of Canadian and American income taxation was defended in terms like the nineteenth century's "infant industries" defence of the protective tariff. The fact that capital gains were not taxed, supporters of the status quo persistently proposed, encouraged domestic savings, brought foreign capital to Canada, and enabled the development of Canadian resources, for the good of all. An American journalist, sum-marizing Canada's appeal as a place for investment, described a cornucopia of tax advantages available to the American investor, with the absence of a capital gains tax as the centrepiece.[109] Those who thought that Canada should start taxing capital gains, like the low-tariff crowd of the 1870s on, saw in the status quo (like the protective tariff) a tax-shifting mechanism that landed the burden of collective finance on the shoulders of those least able to pay.

These issues came up as rumours of imminent capital gains taxation circulated in the early 1950s.[110] When increases in sales taxation were pro-posed in the 1951 Korean War budget, CCF and some Social Credit MPs pushed to see the revenue from income taxation expanded instead by the taxation of capital gains as income. James Sinclair, the finance minister's parliamentary secretary, offered what in his view were the decisive argu-ments against the proposal. The "general good" elements in the argument had to do with that perpetual Canadian fiscal refrain, the need for foreign capital. If Canada's natural resources were to be made economically useful, then Canada's tax regime had to be attractive to foreign investors. Sinclair also argued that the capital gains exemption helped to steer capital toward productive uses. If the high returns of riskier investments (returns that compensated for other risky investments that failed) were taxed away, then investment would flow into safe but unproductive places, such as government bonds. He also pointed out, without giving details, that US tax administrators found the capital gains tax a source of "certain problems" – that is, a means of tax reduction – because in the United States capital gains were taxed at a lower rate than other kinds of income. In the same vein, he mentioned that allowing capital losses would be required, again without spelling out that devising "paper" capital losses was well established in the United States as a means of tax avoidance.[111]

The CCF, the Social Credit, and some dissident Liberals went after all of these arguments. One CCF MP from British Columbia, H.W. Herridge, pointed out the similarities of capital gains to the unearned booty of gambling and real estate speculation and asked whether tax law should encourage that kind of thing. Surely this was not real economic development. Saskatchewan's Ross Thatcher wondered if the exemption of capital gains might be replaced with a lower rate that would continue, but more modestly, to encourage investment. In 1952, when M.J. Coldwell of the CCF raised the question again, Sinclair suggested that, since all of the arguments had been aired the previous year, there was no point in going at it again. With a nod to the moral weight of Henry George and the evil of the unearned increment, Sinclair echoed the "young country" point that J.A. Calder's committee had made in 1919: in Canada, unlike in Britain, there were no large pools of dead capital merely growing from compound interest without producing economic good. In Canada, venture capital was socially useful and deserved its exemption from taxation. The CCF and Social Credit members remained unconvinced and continued to associate capital gains with what Lethbridge MP John Blackmore called "exploitation and speculation."[112] And oil company shares that produced only modest incomes from dividend payments continued to sell like hotcakes because their capital values were soaring. Even federal government bonds were sometimes marketed in a similar way – issued with low interest rates, but at a deep discount and a guarantee of redemption at par, these bonds offered prospective purchasers substantial capital gains. For most taxpayers, the gains from selling those oil stocks or government bonds wouldn't be taxed.[113]

By 1956, worries about tax avoidance through exempt capital gains meant that personal income taxation seemed to the parliamentary left and organized labour to be a fair tax only in theory. The CCF referred to personal income tax along with sales tax as a "burden" on "the lower income groups."[114] They argued that taxing capital gains as income would allow the federal government to relieve the burden on those groups by either reducing sales tax rates or raising the amount of personal income exempt from taxation. But they faced solid opposition to the taxing of capital gains. In 1949, Diefenbaker's future finance minister, Donald Fleming, had claimed to detect a hidden element of capital gains taxation in the new income tax statute and warned against allowing any room to that "vicious principle." The following year Fleming had asked in the House of Commons whether it was on the instructions of the government that National Revenue officials were taxing capital gains, and the Liberal revenue minister had plainly asserted that no one was taxing capital gains.[115] The debate between Liberals and Conservatives then, and later in the 1950s, was whether the tax authority was improperly taxing as income what in reality were capital gains.[116] In commenting on a 1950 case in which a capital gain was taxed as income, the *Globe and Mail* editors reached for almost an American level of tax outrage: "The very essence of tyranny is the levying, at the whim of officials, of taxes not clearly specified or intended by the law. Our national Government, *as is its wont,* is seizing with enthusiasm an opportunity to employ the tyrannical method."[117] In 1966, Fleming would refer to socialists' "old cherished idea of a capital levy" to dismiss reform proposals to tax capital gains.[118] The mainstream parties were united in opposing the taxation of capital gains.

According to the *Labour Gazette,* the monthly magazine of the Department of Labour, only Quebec's francophone Catholic unions made taxing "capital assets" part of their annual legislation proposals.[119] But the *Labour Gazette's* summaries are incomplete: a news story in the *Toronto Star* in 1950 reported that the Canadian Congress of Labour (CCL) "urged that a capital gains tax be instituted." The CCL's point was that differentiation of capital gains from income was a means of tax "evasion."[120] Within the broader labour movement, according to Eugene Forsey, the research director of the CCL's post-1956 successor, the Canadian Labour Congress (CLC), many activists believed that improvements in social security programs could be "financed quite easily by a capital gains tax or an excess profits tax." Forsey told National Revenue authorities that he himself knew that such was not the case, but he invited tax officials to meet with people in local unions to try to teach the taxation "facts of life" and to give labour people a chance to test their ideas on a departmental official.[121] When in 1960 the CLC called for a reformed "tax structure," its position was less closely tied to a specific income tax reform, but it still made a case for larger income tax obligations for those better able to pay.

From 1942 on, Canadian critics of the income tax system had raised the prospect of capital gains taxation. A non-issue in the interwar years, capital gains taxation began to crop up during the 1950s in public debates. It worried investors then because the uncertain definition of capital gains meant that their tax avoidance strategies were vulnerable to challenges by National Revenue. The left and labour cheered on the tax authority, whose attempts to uncover income masquerading as capital gains were part of routine enforcement work and an effort to preserve the progressivity of income taxation. But the real solution, critics from the left argued, was simply to include capital gains in income, thus eliminating all of the procedural problems and temptations that its exclusion entailed. Other incentives to Canadian resource development would have to be found.

$ ¢ $

The 1950s saw a concerted attempt to make most adult Canadians think of themselves as income tax payers, ready to fulfill their record-keeping, receipt-collecting responsibilities. In a more individualistic discourse than that of wartime sacrifice, National Revenue's public relations urged farmers, and all taxpayers implicitly, to see their role not as contributors to particular social projects but as equally situated citizens with clear and limited legal obligations:

> You have to look at it that everyone in Canada is subject to this law, that Parliament has tried to be sure it is a fair law and that the Government employs the best men it can get to try to see not only that everyone pays his just share but also that no one pays more than the law requires. Tell them the facts honestly and completely and you will find them fair and decent as a rule. Fairness and decency create fairness and decency.[122]

From this view, being an income tax payer entailed no particular commitment to social equality. The citizen-taxpayer is simply a fair dealer. There is a social element in that identity, to be sure, but nothing of sacrifice for others. Progressive rate taxation of income, with its idea of equalizing sacrifice, faced some resistance in the postwar world of tax morality. The widespread use of surplus stripping and related use of strategies based upon capital gains not being "income" suggests that, on a practical level, wealthier Canadians were challenging the ability-to-pay model of tax fairness. The legalistic discourse of loopholes, whether large or small, suggests that liberal ideals of equality were now more about a universal right to avoid paying taxes than about a shared commitment to equality of sacrifice. But the fair-dealing standard preserved in the new world of mass income taxation a widespread contempt for chisellers, cheats, and taxphobes. Legal tax avoidance came under fire in moral terms, and reports of unsuccessful avoidance, punished as evasion, heightened awareness that income taxation might be failing to achieve tax fairness goals. At the same time, ideas about income tax as a lever of macroeconomic management or an incentive for desired behaviour were beginning to generate a kind of tax talk, however controversial, that during the 1960s would link income taxation to social equality and not just tax fairness. Between 1960 and 1964, in the tax reform language of the labour movement, "redistribution of national income" would appear where "redistributing the national tax burden" had been.[123] That shift depended on a rethinking of the role of the state, and on that question Canadians in the long 1950s did not cheerfully agree. But a conversation had at least begun: citizens troubled by taxes were drawn into debates about what governments could, should, and should not do. In the process, they were helping to build a democratic culture.

9
Poverty, Bureaucracy, and Taxes

THE 1950S ARE FAMOUS FOR ELVIS and tail fins on cars, but if you are interested in politics and how democracy works they are striking for another reason. It was a new golden age of scientific public administration, a time when economics and other social sciences came into their own as technologies of government. Buoyed up on a tide of newly rigorous data, modern economic development theory rose to influence. Polling data put the "science" into political science.[1] At the beginning of the period, most of the provinces were led by premiers who didn't care for the modern modes of public administration. Old ideas about government still had influence. But even those provincial strongmen were modernizers in some ways, dazzled by hydro power and excited by ideas about state-led economic development.[2] While public administration practice was changing, so were expectations about political democracy. The norms of participation had decisively shifted from the old world of property qualifications, racial exclusion, and elite rule. Reality did not yet meet expectations.[3] But notions of equality and social rights, a state for everyone and not just property owners, motivated new forms of political rhetoric and citizen engagement.[4] This broader sense of the democratic state was connected to taxpaying through concerns of the poor, through anxieties about bureaucracy, and through aspects of daily life in which culture and constitutional questions came together in distinctively Canadian ways. In all of these connections, Canadians were participating in a larger transnational reconfiguring of politics and democracy that would take dramatic forms in the 1960s but was thoroughly rooted in the 1950s.

Part of that reconfiguration happened as the property qualification for voters took its final steps off the political stage. With it departed that old, narrow sense of municipal citizen-taxpayer. Political participation was no longer the privilege of a minority, and popular mobilizations supplemented the casting of ballots. The most well known of these postwar mobilizations were the mass, and now professionalized, labour movement and civil rights/human rights activism. With roots stretching back to the interwar years, these movements took on new tactics in the 1950s and 1960s and helped to build the welfare state at all levels of government. There were also in Canada's Cold War years modern forms of conservative activism intertwined with vestigial Victorianism. Canada didn't escape entirely the trends that produced the Poujadists in France, the John Birch Society in the United States, or the People's League for the Defence of Freedom in the United Kingdom.[5] All of these groups drew on anti-statist ideas. The ideas were old, but their advocates adopted modern methods. They also targeted people's newly multiplying dealings with government agents: data collectors, unemployment insurance clerks, tax inspectors, recreation directors, and subsidy dispensers. Not all of these dealings ran smoothly, and frustrations fed anti-statist currents. Although supporters of new social services were numerous, across class lines, there were also worried sceptics (and not only in the back rooms of big businesses).

There were real advances in social provision during the years of the Cold War, but every development in that direction met with both enthusiastic support and vigorous resistance. As a result, for example, the federal government launched an important new social program in 1952, a universal old age pension, but funded it in such a way as to make its precise tax cost as visible as possible.[6] And there was active debate about the nature and scale of need for better income assistance and better social services.[7] In retrospect, historians have confirmed that poverty was a daily reality for many Canadians, even though it was only "rediscovered" in the 1960s. The income distribution in the mid-1950s was "scarcely one of generalized affluence."[8] In particular, rural Canada, from small-town business to farming and fishing, faced massive restructuring and dislocation. One response to poverty and business trouble was to call for lower taxes to alleviate the cost of living and the burden on small business. Another response was to question the effectiveness of Canadian federalism as a mechanism for distributing both wealth and tax burdens. In this context, people's experiences of administrative difficulties, economic hardships, and tax obligations could combine into a particularly toxic mix.

However, unlike the anti-tax movements that flourished in the United States in the 1950s, Canadians angry about taxes and government had no convenient single target like the Sixteenth Amendment on which to focus "freedom" talk, and in effect they still had no power to amend their Constitution.[9] Canadian tax protest was different, but it existed. Problems of taxpayers' "civil rights," framed as a critique of arbitrary state power, engaged Canadians across a variety of social and ideological positions and helped to mobilize populist politics. Anti-statism and struggles with poverty were as much a part of the long 1950s as the now more familiar stories of affluence and innovation in building a welfare state and a more scientific federal public service. Much was accomplished in making the Canadian state modern and socially useful in the long 1950s, but the transition to new relations of extraction generated frictions. Although the Cold War in Canada was not the all-organizing framework that it might have been in the United States, something of that larger geopolitics lent meaning and emotion to tax talk in Canada too. Debates about taxation were closely linked to discussions of the proper aspirations of a democratic society.

Taxes as a Burden on the Poor

It can be hard to imagine how the small amounts of federal income tax owed by low-income Canadians in the long 1950s were a burden. After all, wage earners had taxes deducted from their pay. But even in this sensible system individuals could get into trouble. For example, in August 1963, Fred Baxter, from a prosperous southern Ontario city, wrote to Prime Minister Lester Pearson just to let him know what "your people" were "up against."[10] At age fifty-nine, Baxter was out of work after forty-three years on the job at the same plant where he'd started work at sixteen, in about 1920. His unemployment benefits had run out, and the youngest of his eleven kids, now sixteen years old, had left school for a job washing dishes to help support his parents. "Down right shame," wrote Baxter. The Baxters had fallen behind on their mortgage payments and had lost their home. Baxter had finally managed to get a job that "brings in a few dollars a week, enough to live on." But he owed some income taxes, and he found that his wages were being garnished to pay that debt. He asked how Pearson thought he'd be able to pay his bills. "I am fed up with this [w]hole thing, all I ask is a job, and I'll pay my way, and no one will even know we're here. But God, in heaven, there is coming a day for final judgement." His letter was typical of wage or salary earners who faced income tax debts,[11] but less commonly, Pearson's assistant, Mary E. Macdonald, was actually able to do something for Baxter. She forwarded the letter to Revenue Minister J.J. Garland, whose office then got a report from the tax office near where Baxter lived. They discovered that his job was temporary. This meant that the legal conditions that triggered the garnishing were not met, and it was possible to delay his paying his tax debt until he was again fully employed.[12]

Baxter had had a run of bad luck, to be sure. He found himself in a place where tax obligations threatened his subsistence needs. His case represents what, from a working-class perspective, was the central policy question about personal income taxation in the 1950s. In the prewar income tax, and indeed in the eighteenth-century and nineteenth-century theory of income taxation, the "personal exemptions" prevented income tax from being taken from the income needed by a household for the necessities of life. Income tax was supposed to fall on any surplus, just as other kinds of taxes were to target only luxury spending or accumulated wealth.[13] As early as 1902, however, British tax authority Sir Roger Giffen articulated what he thought was common sense among tax experts, that it was impossible to determine at what income level subsistence needs were met.[14] Following this general line in 1942, J.L. Ilsley had taken "some members" to task in the budget debate for their belief that "the difference between the tax which the single man pays and the tax the married man pays is the amount which the married man's wife and children are supposed to live on." "No such theory was ever promulgated," he said.[15] In 1944, a publicly minded accountant and future finance minister, Walter Gordon, acknowledged that differences in the ratio of dependants to earners in a household could mean that income tax might mean little to one family but "bring real hardship" to another family in which one earner supported many dependants, not all of whom represented tax deductions. Nonetheless, he asserted that "the income tax system does not and cannot make sufficient allowance for people in different circumstances." Finance Minister Douglas Abbott would use the same arguments to defend against further raising of the basic personal exemption after 1949.[16]

However, in spite of tax experts' skepticism about tying income tax law to estimations of families' subsistence needs, popular discussions of taxation took exactly that connection to be crucial to tax fairness. Throughout the 1950s, Canada's three main labour centres called for personal exemptions to be raised to match subsistence costs: the Canadian Congress of Labour regularly called for levels of $1,500 for single people and $3,000 for married people. This position crossed ideological lines: both the communist United Electrical Workers (UE) and the anti-communist International Union of Electrical, Radio, and Machine Workers (IUE) lobbied the federal government to have the married exemption raised to $3,000.[17] The Toronto-area International Woodworkers called for a single person's exemption of $2,000 in 1957; however, if the *Labour Gazette* reports are representative, then most individual unions, labour centres, and provincial labour federations took the same line ($1,500 and $3,000) as the CCL and later CLC.[18] By the time of the March–April budget debate in 1957, MPs from every party would call for higher personal exemptions, usually $3,000 for married people and $1,500 or $2,000 for "bachelors," mostly noting that inflation had eroded the value of the exemptions set in 1949 dollars.[19] This had become a commonsensical position.

Not only possibly pandering politicians but also some men in business pointed out that increased personal exemptions would come closer to exempting from taxation the amounts of income necessary for families' minimum expenses. Frustrated by the Liberals' March 1956 budget, insurance agent J. Chevalier of Montreal wrote that

> it is impossible for a Canadian mother, especially without family allowances being doubled as requested by the Social Crediters, to feed, clothe and house her children with a deduction of only $150.00 per child. The father of a Canadian family cannot pay the ever-increasing and excessive federal, provincial and municipal taxes with a deduction of only $2,000 per year. What would you do, Mr. Minister, if instead of $27,000 your salary was $2,000? You would certainly resign.[20]

Along the same lines, chartered accountant S.A. Morrison wrote to Progressive Conservative Finance Minister Donald Fleming in 1958 that the tax system needed a major overhaul, not least because there was no genuinely tax-exempt income for basic subsistence spending. After itemizing a variety of consumption taxes, Morrison went on to suggest that the whole of indirect taxation (sales taxes, excise taxes, and so on) be eliminated and that there be a true exemption of personal income up to an amount that "a family of two can reasonably exist today on ... for necessities with no luxury." In his view, that amount was $3,800.[21] Although Morrison was clearly a political supporter and perhaps a friend (addressing and being addressed by the minister on a first-name basis), Fleming replied to him curtly that his proposals would be "exceedingly costly to the treasury." Like Walter Gordon in 1944, and like other finance ministers in the interim, Fleming saw the elimination of many small tax accounts by raising personal exemptions as unreasonably expensive. The personal income tax would continue to cut into the flesh of subsistence spending, even though perhaps not to the bone of a family budget. As one wife and mother wrote to Fleming, "the income tax leveled at the poor man is cruel ... I am worried beyond words because we can't meet our expenses, through no fault of ours. These taxes must be cut."[22]

Whether in opposition or in power, leading politicians heard from their constituents about the little man's tax problems. In 1950, as the federal income tax collectors were finishing off their postwar enforcement blitz, one Saskatchewan farmer wrote to his MP, John Diefenbaker, seeking reassurance in the face of that threat:

> I am an ex-service man just trying to make a go. Married and one child. We had a very light crop last year and it is taking all we have to try and get one small crop in this spring. If they should take court action this is what I would like to know. I have a tractor V.L.A. [Veteran's Land Act] and land bought through V.L.A. Also a ½ ton truck [and] a few other items. Could they seize my truck to pay off this debt of $76.52? If so, what would be the best thing for me to do? I definitely haven't the money to pay them.[23]

Mindful of how disabling such pressures could be, friends of the "little man" wrote with policy suggestions to their MPs. In the late 1940s, C.L. Burton, a leading Toronto businessman (and in the interwar years a good friend to the King Liberals), spoke out in favour of raising the amount of the single person's exempt income, on the ground that "there is nothing more discouraging to Canadians, in particular young men and women, than to find they have lost a big share of their weekly earnings through high taxation." He recommended that $3,000 (double the existing exemption) be allowed tax free to the single person.[24] A less eminent constituent from Whalley, British Columbia, writing to Diefenbaker in 1955, claimed that "a lot of people are getting pretty well fed up with this income tax on small incomes." He, too, emphasized the plight of the young, saying that the income tax made it "hard on young men getting started." He approved of Diefenbaker "trying to tell the Ottawa Gov where they are hard on the small wage earner."[25] In 1957, a young married woman in Halifax said that she was angry and disappointed that the basic personal exemptions had not been raised in the 1957 budget; as a result, she argued, she and her husband would still find it difficult to save toward home ownership.[26] In 1965, the theme was still being raised. A St. John's man asked Pearson "do you think it is fair and reasonable for a young man trying to raise a family of two boys and a girl to have to pay out over $200.00 for Income Tax when he is only making $4600.00?" By this point, Canada had developed a poverty line of $3,000 a year.[27] But the married exemption was still $2,000. Even with three child exemptions on top of the basic one, that St. John's family budget was pinched.

Like younger people, older people also pointed to their time in life as the basis for their tax complaints. Many of those who wrote to Diefenbaker, King, and Fleming about taxpaying and poverty tended to be roughly the same age as the politicians, in their sixties or older. The tax protests of the elderly had a specific historical freight. Fred Baxter's concern about his son having to quit school to work, for instance, reflected a new sense of what was owed to children – a longer period of dependency than Baxter himself had enjoyed. And, at the same time, seniors, now somewhat supported by a means-tested public pension in retiring at sixty-five, noted that they were paying taxes to provide social services – the family allowance and, after 1957, hospital care, to name two major federal programs – that had not been available to them during the years of "tough sledding." Some had borrowed to pay for higher education for their children. Taxes became another of those burdens, from year to year, as Thelma Skerry of Hudson, Quebec, pointed out, that they struggled to carry, along with insurance, heat, electricity, and medications.[28]

They saw themselves as having asked for nothing from the state and having accomplished a great deal in raising their families. They wrote to their politicians now to point out how much of a difference a few dollars of relief would make to those who, like Skerry and her husband, were "not paupers" but still constantly anxious about making ends meet. One older man wrote of seeing in the grocery store as he was shopping "elderly people on the same errand counting their money carefully and looking wistfully at food they would like to buy, then turn away and buy cuttings such as better off people buy for their dogs and cats." As Annie Mae Kavan put it, "what a pity when small amounts, very small amounts, mean so much to so many." For her, these were "the proletariat," "as necessary" to the nation as "the great ones." Their contribution, hearkening back to the ancient Roman meaning of proletariat, had been to raise children for the state. Now they had little patience for big-spending governments and even less for well-paid politicians. For them, thrift was the moral foundation of their survival. Even if they didn't have to eat cat food to survive, their resentment of "extravagant" spending and therefore any "unnecessary" tax burden was visceral.[29] Older people could remember the prewar years, when the exemptions spared most earners from income taxation. But for young and old alike, the idea of a basic personal exemption that spared at least subsistence-level earnings was a central demand.[30]

In addition to requests for higher personal exemptions, other exemptions drew political support from middle-aged voters and across the low-middle-income dividing line. Medical expenses were a particularly lively area of taxpayer complaint. In 1942, when the tax on income began to cut deeply into smaller household budgets, a medical expenses allowance had been introduced. It was aimed at helping people who faced unusually large medical costs. The idea was that, ordinarily, such things as doctor's bills, drugs, eyeglasses, obstetrical care, and surgery could be covered by after-tax income, by savings, or by insurance. In the unusual circumstances of wartime taxation, however, the tax policy makers understood that those who had no savings or insurance plans might well find their after-tax incomes inadequate to pay for exceptional expenses. At the launch of the medical exemption, the assumption of some medical spending as "ordinary" showed up in the limit of deductible dollars to those in excess of 5 percent of income (reduced to 3 percent in 1953). There was also a cap on the amount that could be claimed. A short list of drugs claimable under this provision included ones deemed unusually expensive, such as a diabetic's insulin.[31]

Over the 1950s, the pressure to enrich this medical exemption was more or less constant.[32] In 1957 alone, according to Revenue Minister George Nowlan, twenty specific drugs (from cancer treatments, to sedatives, to new antibiotics) were proposed for exemption. Drugs for diabetics were particularly perplexing: insulin was deductible, but other drug therapies that replaced insulin were not. Some citizens advised Nowlan and, in Finance, Fleming that all prescription drugs should be deductible.[33] That was certainly the position of Canada's central labour organization, the Canadian Labour Congress. It, and particular unions, called for some or all of medical, dental, hospital, and optical expenses to be deductible from taxable income. In taking this position, the labour movement was well within the mainstream of political culture. The Canadian Home and School Association also passed a resolution at its annual meeting of 1958 calling for "all medical expenses, including all expenses for the eyes and all dental care," to be tax deductible.[34] These broad policy interventions drew on organizations' knowledge of personal cases, but individuals also wrote to tell their government about heartbreaking personal struggles. A small-town newspaper editor's child had survived with cystic fibrosis longer than anyone had expected, but the father now bore a heavy financial burden in buying the drugs that would keep his daughter alive.[35] MPs found in such troubles opportunities to do case work and wrote to both Revenue and Finance on behalf of constituents.[36] Canadians with chronic or otherwise expensive illnesses had advocates in the new or expanded disease charities of the 1950s, representing multiple sclerosis, cancer, and arthritis/rheumatism. Letters from such groups filled ministers' mailboxes. More self-interestedly, so did letters from the professional organizations of pharmacists and optometrists.[37] The list of approved drugs and other medical expenses remained short, but in 1960, as a tax reduction measure, Finance Minister Fleming increased the dollar amounts that could be claimed.[38]

Although expanding the medical expenses deduction appealed to anyone who had been hit with exceptional expenses, demands for other deductions had a more specific class tinge. Calls for deducting from taxable income the costs of workmen's tools or commuters' cars or students' tuition continued to deluge Finance and Revenue in the late 1950s and early 1960s.[39] These calls were sometimes expressed in terms of relieving hardship. For example, a Montrealer working in construction in Black Lake, Ontario, wrote on behalf of his workmates. They all had wives and children living in Montreal and were finding it hard "to feed our families and keep things going." The problem, as they saw it, was that the weekly allowance for their living expenses in Ontario was subject to federal and provincial income taxes and, "to add insult to injury," a 5 percent Ontario hospital tax.[40] After some travelling workers gained exemptions, others asked for the same, now on the ground of fairness and not simply need.[41] Tax experts knew, as Kenneth Eaton advised his new finance minister, Donald Fleming, that income tax administration of millions of accounts "cannot ... proceed

on the basis of minute inquiries into a multiplicity of personal circumstances of individuals."[42] However, on matters of the boundary between
subsistence and taxable surplus, missives to Finance show that Canadian
wage earners really wanted to tell their government both the particulars of
their household budgets and their sense of what was fair taxation. One
polite woman might represent this impulse: she wrote a four-page, richly
biographical letter, acknowledging that "rules are rules, and the law is the
law." But she just wanted "to use the privilege of the wonderful democratic
country of ours to render my feelings on the personal situation between
myself and the income tax department."[43]

In the various campaigns for increased exemptions, much was symbolic,
(e.g., tax fairness) rather than material (e.g., real remedies for working-
class poverty). The 1957 debate about medical exemptions brought out this
contrast. A Torontonian named Michael Wright, in a letter to the editor of
the *Globe and Mail*, made the case against using deductions from taxable
income as a means to help low-income taxpayers. He agreed that a $100
medical bill, though only 3 percent of the income of a "$3,000 a year family
man," would present a crisis for that "beleaguered family." But allowing all
of that $100 to be deducted from the breadwinner's taxable income in his
April tax return would produce a refund of only $13.50. Better to preserve
tax revenue and spend it on direct assistance to low-income families, to
cover their actual medical costs, Wright argued, than to dish out minuscule tax refunds in the name of tax fairness.[44]

Wright was responding to a *Globe and Mail* editorial that, perhaps un-
expectedly, sided with CCF MP Stanley Knowles in arguing that the 3 percent floor for medical expenses was unjust. The editors claimed that
allowing all medical expenses as deductions against income would return
to "the people in the low income brackets," more than to any other class,
the money from the taxes not collected.[45] But that claim only reproduced
in a new form the newspaper's 1946 defence of "show them the price" income taxation. Just as the many small tax payments collected from working people had made them the largest contributors (as a class) of tax
revenue for social security spending, so too would making many tiny refunds lead to a large dollar amount sent out to small taxpayers (as a class).
Not so much as individuals. But the benefit of a large collective refund to
people in need of affordable health care would be much less than the benefit to them of a comparable amount spent directly on public, accessible
medical services. Even people opposed to "state medicine" could, and did,

make the case that their particular medical deductions were required by fairness.[46] In advocating tax refunds, the *Globe and Mail* was not arguing for better social programs. Making more tax refunds was not about better provision for medical need.

Making the income tax system more "fair" – in an Anatole France sort of way, with rich and poor equally eligible for medical expense refunds – was no more than a way for the *Globe and Mail* to justify the continuing taxation of small incomes as the price that the poor and the near poor must pay for national citizenship. This is not to dismiss tax fairness as unimportant. By the late 1950s, the personal income tax was bearing with disproportionate weight on the subsistence cores of small family budgets. High-flying avoidance was rumoured to be rife. There was some kind of problem of fairness. But in the discourse of tax fairness, small exemptions bred more small exemptions. They mattered only for their symbolic value. Raising the personal exemption would have done more for real need, but only if the lost revenue had been made up by almost imperceptibly heavier taxes on higher incomes.

The Diefenbaker Progressive Conservatives (PCs) were well aware of the symbolic value of small exemptions. Diefenbaker had been calling for tax cuts "to keep the tax collectors poor" and to "give the Canadian people a break" since at least 1951.[47] In government after June 1957, the PCs offered tax reductions on various fronts, including those aimed specifically at lower-income breadwinners. The exempt amount for dependent children was raised in the 1957 budget, and in the 1959 budget taxable incomes under $3,000 were spared the 2 percent rate increase that Fleming applied otherwise to the personal income tax. In response, there was outrage from some and appreciation from others, along predictable income lines.[48] However much some well-to-do Progressive Conservatives were offended by concessions to low-income taxpayers, Fleming liked to tell a story of the PCs as reducers of income taxation for the less well off. In his April 1962 budget speech, facing the likelihood of an election, he used this story to position his besieged party. He declared that four and a half years of Tory government had left "six out of seven individual income-tax payers in Canada ... better off under the present tax rates." He emphasized the tax reliefs afforded to "persons of lower and medium incomes."[49] Tax reduction was part of the Tory populist appeal.

In 1960, a friendly critic of the Tories, a prosperous Toronto businessman named Abram Merkur, wrote to Diefenbaker to challenge the Tories'

1960 line on tax cuts. In a letter marked as "Seen by Diefenbaker," Merkur pointed out the problem of Canada's unjust income distribution. Citing a recent Toronto newspaper story, he pointed out that 70 percent of Canadians earned less than seventy dollars per week, whereas 10 percent earned more than $10,000 per year, and a mere 20 percent "control our entire wealth." In a gesture to geopolitics, he hinted that such was the kind of inequality that had led to the recent Cuban Revolution. He argued that he would happily pay "an extra tax of 5 to 10% on [his] corporation's annual earnings" if that money would go to protect the unemployment insurance fund (in deficit in 1960). It was, in his view, the role of government "to employ the unemployed when private enterprise fails." Tax money spent in that way would be a "valuable safeguard to my estate." He argued that it was possible to honour an election promise of no tax increases to "the 70%." But "you must fail in that promise to the 30% with vested interests – to the corporations, they must pay higher taxes." He urged Diefenbaker to "rise above" the pressures of the "well-to-do group" who would use their considerable influence to oppose an extra corporation tax. In closing, Merkur referred in Cold War terms to the dangers of the "hostile world" – missiles, atomic power, and automation. "It calls for realistic appraisals," he concluded.[50] This sense that income inequality was a pressing problem and that social unrest called for fortified social spending was perhaps an unusually broad view of the interests of business in 1960. But in just a few years the extensive sociological research of John Porter would confirm Merkur's claims about income inequality, and the Royal Commission on Taxation would assert that there was a role for income tax reform in mitigating the economic vulnerability of the poor.[51]

Over the long 1950s, the meaning of the mass income tax both shifted the nature of tax talk and preserved it. To accept that paying the federal income tax was the lot of a married person earning over $3,000 a year was to affirm the prewar norm. But it was also to accept a shift in the class incidence of the tax: in the 1950s, many working-class earners made that much and accepted the small payroll deductions entailed by taxing incomes above that level, seeing themselves as contributors to the family allowance, the old age pension, and after 1957 unemployment assistance and hospital insurance. The well-paid worker in mid-life would pay his share. It remained a point of controversy, however, whether incomes between $1,000 and $3,000 (fifty-eight dollars per week or under for a full year) left room for wage earners to contribute to collective provision. As a result, the level of personal exemptions became central to popular criticisms of the personal income tax. In response, the Diefenbaker PCs tried to show that, between 1957 and 1962, they had relieved the small-income taxpayer. But they did not raise the basic personal exemptions. They understood, as many did not, that higher basic exemptions would not only relieve the poor but also move well-paid people into lower tax brackets all the way up the income scale.[52] Those calling for higher personal exemptions were not thinking of the cost to public revenue of those reliefs for the well-to-do but only of how to make the personal income tax once again a means of shifting some of the overall tax burden off small and middle incomes. The symbolic meaning of the unchanging personal exemption as an affliction to the poor only gained weight. In the 1960s, as the rate of inflation accelerated, revising that exemption level would come to be not simply a matter of tax fairness but also a banner issue for those who believed that tax reform could help to remedy income inequality.

Taxpaying and the Growing Administrative State

Arguments about the role of the state in the long 1950s found a focus in Canadians' experience of paying taxes. For many, the personal income tax was the newest form of direct taxation, so it drew attention. From a wide variety of social and economic positions, Canadian taxpayers protested aspects of income tax reporting requirements, payment methods, assessment rules, and collection procedures. Communications from the federal tax authorities triggered various expressions of outrage, some understandable, others almost comically self-serving. Whereas concerns about hardship such as I have described above earned the interest of politicians in part because of the connections of those concerns to larger social justice projects on the political left, procedural complaints got their political purchase elsewhere, mainly from the liberal centre or the right of the political spectrum. A defence of "freedom" and suspicion of an expanding state magnified particular grievances. Although some of the procedural complaints had a cringe-inducing note of hysteria, others (notably about problems of administrative justice entailed in creating a modern mass income tax system) were genuine. Diefenbaker, Pearson, and especially Diefenbaker's first minister of revenue, George Nowlan, were sensitive to the risks of procedural unfairness and worries about costs of compliance in the mass income tax. They knew that there could be electoral consequences when such complaints were not handled carefully.[53] Bringing the federal income tax collector into the mass of Canadian households opened up conversations that were not always friendly.

During the long 1950s, there was a cat-and-mouse game of litigation and legislation between big taxpayers and the revenue authority, as sketched by Richard Pound. Less well known is the evolving relationship between tax administrators and the many small taxpayers – businesses, professionals, farmers, and employees – during those years. Making the mechanisms of tax administration smooth and effective on such a large scale was no trivial challenge. There were, broadly, three sources of friction. First was that Canadians were being asked to do new, or newly difficult, kinds of form filling and record keeping. Second was that on the receiving end of the forms that taxpayers filed was a vastly altered agency of government, a revenue authority that had to investigate more widely, enforce more effectively, and communicate more skillfully to a whole new audience. Third was that social, economic, and political change meant that tax policy, as embodied both in legislation and in administration, did not always keep up with the socio-economic world in which taxes, income and otherwise, were assessed and collected. There is room for a book-length study of these matters for this period. I will explore just a few topics that speak to small taxpayers' experiences of the new relations of extraction, the tax collector's attempts to secure compliance at reasonable costs of collection, and three areas of cultural and institutional change – family, francophone Quebec, and (relatedly) federalism – that especially troubled the process of personal income taxation. From the grubby materials of receipt collecting and rate calculating, Canadians made up some magnificent ideological stories, sometimes plausible, sometimes not, about what taxation meant for justice, the role of the state, and the state of freedom in their nation. Along with the experiences of hardship discussed above, these stories laid the foundation for tax reform politics in the 1960s.

Anyone who has stayed up late at night doing administrative paperwork, blearily struggling to make sense of rules and regulations, will recognize the mood expressed by the owner of a small electrical service and supplies business who wrote in 1964 to Prime Minister Pearson. The "stationery" that he used was one of his company's invoice forms:

Dear Sir, I sit here – a small businessman in the middle of the night still doing books. I'm also listening to the radio and the news of L.B.

Johnson's American tax cuts. I'm tired of breaking my back to pay taxes. Why must we have eight dollar exit lights in schools and [electrical] panels priced beyond all reason? Why must we have board rooms and banquets for board members who live fifty times as simply at home? Why? Because it's my tax money that's being spent and nobody cares but me. So I'm quitting breaking my back. Soon you can get your taxes from somebody else. I'm through.[54]

This letter communicates well how the owners of small businesses might experience the costs of tax compliance physically as an aching back, sore eyes, sleeplessness, and a tension-twisted gut. Tax compliance was extra work, harder if the person thought that it was paying for public spending that she or he didn't endorse. Larger businesses complained, too, of compliance costs, and the Canadian Tax Foundation conducted a study of the dollar costs of keeping appropriate records, preparing financial statements, knowing the necessary elements of law and accounting (or hiring those who did), filing returns, and if necessary making appeals against errors.[55] But the labours and risks of tax compliance were particularly and viscerally resented by small businesses.

In 1965, the owner of a small-town furniture-manufacturing firm in southwestern Ontario wrote so eloquently of these problems that his letter was specially directed by PMO staff to Pearson to read. Edwin Barnett's screed was triggered by a new requirement that the cheque remitting his employee's income tax payments be certified. Barnett was not alone in his outrage at this regulation. Small businesses sometimes live close to the edges of their bank balances, managing cash flow by coordinating payments to suppliers and collections from customers without much room for manoeuvre if cheques are to clear. In such circumstances, to certify a cheque means that the tax payment to the government comes out of the bank account maybe two weeks, maybe a month, sooner than it would were the cheque cashed only after wending its way through the mail and bureaucracy. In tight times, having that money to use for the business for those extra weeks would make a difference, perhaps in making payroll or maybe in repairing a broken lathe. Noting that government demands came with peremptorily expressed hard deadlines, unlike his other bills, Barnett wrote that

no one cares a hang whether or not our business goes on or not, just so long as a certain demand is met and *complied to herewith* ... A small town business such as ours just has neither the facilities nor the financial backing [i.e., credit] necessary to see that the government always comes first at the expense of our suppliers and others who must wait until the department receives its pound of flesh.

An apparently small thing, then, such as the requirement that tax remittances be made by certified cheque, as though paid in cash, could be experienced as a final, intolerable stressor, added to the other duties of running a business in a modern regulatory state. Barnett called the certified cheque regulation "just another encroachment on his freedom and on his rights as an ordinary citizen."[56] This was the sort of experience described by Timothy Mitchell: "the economy" as a transpersonal force came crashing into daily life via the imposition of cash transactions instead of credit ones.[57] In some places, the federal income tax was the mechanism of this intrusion.

Although Barnett also complained about the cost to his company in clerical time and his own time, the theme of his complaint, repeated by others, was resentment of "dictatorial" power exercised from above, in contrast to the feeble power that he could exercise at the polls. In the same vein, an engineer in Toronto described the clerical duties that he performed for his consulting firm as including the licking and affixing of unemployment insurance stamps. Totting up the hours that he spent in tax and social insurance record keeping, he concluded that the Canadian government owed him $500 in wages as a clerical worker. Otherwise, he was doing that work without pay (not even getting meals, which "slaves" usually get, he pointed out). Surely working for free was not something that those "socialists" (in Ottawa) would condone. All of this extravagant rhetoric was triggered by a demand from the tax authority for the correction of a five-dollar error and for nineteen dollars in interest on an earlier underpayment. The issue for this small business owner was not so much financial hardship as the unilateral imposition on him of tedious administrative labour – he being, one imagines, someone used to considerable autonomy.[58] Sometimes the tone of a letter from the tax authority inflamed this kind of sensitivity, and the results were intemperate allegations about reds and creeping socialism, dire threats of secession, and exaggerated fears of confiscation.[59]

The accusation of cruel bureaucracy was not simply the cry of small business or independent professional men and women. There were all sorts of ways in which the mechanisms of assessment and collection could trouble employees or others paying only small personal income taxes. For example, some pensioners were caught by surprise when, for the 1963 tax year, individuals not paying their tax liabilities at source by means of payroll deductions were required, for the first time, to pay quarterly, in instalments, rather than annually. The Hamilton United Electrical union local went to bat for one such pensioner who was going to be charged interest for having failed to pay quarterly even though he'd had his return approved by the local tax office as he'd done every year previously. Echoing the businessmen who referred to "dictatorial" behaviour of the income tax authorities, the officer of this left-wing union deplored the "imperious demand" that they had made of the pensioner. Perhaps for the UE emperors were worse than dictators. Another pensioner refused to pay the $1.10 interest charged to her for the same reason, noting that $1.10 would provide her with "food supply for three or four days." Alluding to the tax rebel whose attempted arrest launched the seventeenth-century English Civil War, she concluded that "if you want a Canadian 'John Hampden' – then here I am!" And one sad letter came from an elderly single woman, a retired nurse, whose mobility was so limited and social isolation so extreme that, for her, getting out of the house in the winter to go to the tax office to pay a quarterly instalment or even to mail the instalment payment was an insurmountable difficulty.[60]

Concerns about the taxpayer's rights and abuses of the tax collector's power flourished in the long 1950s. Although the income tax statute conferred privacy rights and rights to appeal, there was nothing in place like Canada's 1985 Declaration of Taxpayer Rights or today's Taxpayer Bill of Rights, which have educated the public about procedures and service standards in tax administration, an area that in the 1950s was still a work in progress or, to shift metaphors, a political football.[61] Ever since the war, the Progressive Conservatives had called for not only reduced taxes but also more polite and efficient service from National Revenue. In the build-up to the 1957 federal election, the *Toronto Daily Star* gave a banner headline to a Tory MP's claim "Citizens Abused by 'Little' Income Tax Officials." That MP, H.O. White of London, Ontario, and its rural environs, compared the income tax collectors to "Gestapo agents." In his private member's bill, he sought to limit to one year rather than four the period when National Revenue could reassess the returns of small- and middle-income taxpayers (those with less than $10,000 taxable income). His motion was defeated ninety-two to fifty-five, but the CCF and Social Credit had voted with him and the Tories against the Liberal majority.[62] While the 1957 election was on, the taxpayer rights issue got some play. *Globe and Mail* business columnist Fraser Robertson deplored investigatory practices that allowed officials to "come into a man's house and count his suits and his shoes" and tell him, in relation to the role of capital gains in his accounts, "that the advice of his lawyer and his accountant, carefully followed, [has] turned him into a crook." Robertson spoke to readers who wouldn't have found his rhetoric pitched too high. He even concluded that, "for the poorer man, submission in fear is the only alternative to probable ruin."[63]

After the electoral dust of 1957 had settled, the Canadian Tax Foundation's Gwyneth McGregor tried to calm things down, reminding taxpayers that, in fact, they had a plausible recourse should they disagree with National Revenue. She explained the history and procedures of the Tax Appeal Board of Canada created by the Income Tax Act of 1948.[64] The *Globe and Mail*'s editors took a dimmer view, finding the next day a menace worth deploring in public remarks by former National Revenue lawyer Pat Thorsteinsson. Thorsteinsson said that evaders "are caught sooner or later – even to the probating of estates." Incongruously large estates left by taxpayers whose lifetime declared incomes could not explain their wealth had long been a target of revenue authorities, municipal as well as federal. But the *Globe and Mail* now worried that this "efficiency" was "uncomfortable." A letter to the editor echoed its concerns and called on the Progressive Conservatives to rein in the tax department's "Little Caesars." McGregor continued to interpret the tax authority to its public, defending its honour if occasionally questioning its competence.[65] Once in office, Diefenbaker's revenue minister, George Nowlan, impressed on his staff that communications with taxpayers had to be more respectful. Nonetheless, he sometimes found himself called to account in the House of Commons or cabinet for "regrettable" mistakes when an "excess of zeal" led a tax collection employee into error or at least into unmannerly behaviour. When the tax returns began to be processed by computer in 1960, annoyances multiplied.[66]

No doubt some of these concerns were oversensitive posturing. But it's not difficult to understand the concern of one of Prime Minister Pearson's correspondents in 1966. A Vancouver engineer of Chinese descent wrote to object that a copy of his tax return held in the Vancouver office had been stamped with the word *Oriental*.[67] The archive offers no hint of why that had been done; however, given the history of nativist suspicions in British Columbia about tax evasion among Chinese Canadians, this man no doubt guessed that there was what we would now call racial profiling at work in the tax office. In the Department of Finance archives, there is a host of complaint letters on many topics from private individuals, lawyers, accountants, firms, and private organizations.[68] Among the usual dross of special pleading are some nuggets, such as the one from the Chinese Canadian engineer, that reveal the social relationships of taxation. Whether ensuring a right to competent service, a right to be given consistent rulings, or a right to accessible means of appeal, National Revenue had its work cut out for it during the long 1950s, not only in achieving a good standard of performance, but also in persuading a mass public that it was doing so.

Horrified expostulations about "bureaucratic tyranny" in the tax office and "democracy imperilled" by tax administration can sound like Cold War paranoia. But worries about the dangers of an expanding central state had their roots in a philosophically respectable concern about the unchecked power of the sorts of "ministerial discretion" that had been emerging in administrative practice since the 1920s. As Doug Owram has shown, the idea that civil servants' recourse to objective research might trump politicians' and businessmen's instincts set up a conflict, visible in Canada, for example, over formation of the central bank.[69] We should be happy that the economists won the battle in the 1930s for control of the central bank. But worries about the tyranny of experts, such as those expressed in Hewart's *The New Despotism,* were not trivial. They arose from important liberal values of broader application. The notion that unelected technical experts needed to be accountable was reasonable. The creation of independent ways to appeal "ministerial" – administrative – decisions was proper. Although new appeal procedures provided the big taxpayer with new means to game the system, at least smaller tax problems could now be less expensively addressed, too, and that made income taxation more responsive. It is worth recalling that creation of appeal boards for social assistance recipients also flowed from a similar, albeit broader, critique of the imbalance of power between civil servants and citizens.[70] Worry about that imbalance was reasonable, even though in some tax discourse the issue was raised in Cold War terms that equated tax-funded social welfare with the Stalinist gulag as a threat to "freedom."[71]

In spite of such worries, bureaucratic modernization was a success with some taxpayers. In 1951, a change in administrative routine made compliance easier and even inviting for the many payers of small income tax amounts. The innovation was having employers deduct at source 100 percent of tax owed, paycheque by paycheque, on their payrolls. This spared about two-thirds of personal income tax payers the unpleasant task of forking over actual cash with their tax returns. Before 1951, only 95 percent of personal income tax was deducted at source, and many citizens whose taxes were mainly covered by payroll deductions still had to pay some small amounts when they filed. The result of the 1951 change? In the spring of 1952, for the first time, Canadian payers of personal income tax filed their returns with the anticipation of receiving, in a few weeks, a tax refund. They had followed enthusiastically the advice circulated in the taxation division's PR campaign in February 1952: "File Early! Get Your Refund Faster!" If they'd had a child or been married late in the year, the refund would be a tidy sum. Donating to charities meant a larger refund too. Only those who'd overpaid because they'd been unemployed for part of the year or who'd had heavy medical expenses bought their refund at an unpleasant price.[72]

The editors of the *Globe and Mail* were livid about the new deduction protocol. They pointed out that Finance Minister Douglas Abbott knew perfectly well that the sums being collected were in excess of what would actually be owed at year end. As a result, the editors asserted, the collections were, strictly, "illegal," "contrary to the principle underlying our constitution," and "stupid." Many rural newspapers also published an apparently syndicated editorial critical of the change, pointing out that the money overpaid would not be refunded with interest earned. The *Winnipeg Tribune* was opposed, too, and praised the old system, in which people had "a small tax balance to pay at the end of the year." They worried that, without that individual experience of contribution, taxpayers would forget that "government was spending a great deal of money."[73] Deduction at source on the new method threatened income taxation's "show them the price" function.

Taking the *Globe and Mail*'s line, the Tories continued to call tax refunds "overpayments." In 1955, PC MP Waldo Monteith repeated the point raised by the rural newspapers in 1951, that issuing refund cheques must require more civil servant labour and therefore raise collection costs. Revenue Minister J.J. McCann's reply (not for the first time) was that the 100 percent deduction lowered the number of wage earners who owed debts to the Crown. The fewer of those debts owed, the fewer the cases that would ultimately have to be collected by garnishment of wages. That method of collection imposed an unpleasant collection chore on the employer and often a hardship on the taxpayer. It was better to expend a bit of civil servant labour to avoid unnecessary garnishees. Making the government the source of a refund cheque was more soothing to the citizen-state relationship than making many wage and salary earners into debtors (as many as 412,000 in 1953). The deducting of 100 percent of taxes owed imposed a kind of enforced savings, but the refund, initially at least, was so reliably returned that income taxation became for many small taxpayers a useful part of personal budgeting.[74]

When refunds came late, taxpayers' reliance on this method of saving was revealed. The Jonquière local of the Brotherhood of Railroad Trainmen pointed out that a late refund could mean that some members would have to take out loans "to take care of their normal needs." One man trying to get work was waiting for his refund so that he could get licence plates for his car. He wrote bitterly to say that he had already lost one chance at a job because the refund had taken too long to arrive. A testy tone was not uncommon in the mid-1960s. "We are trying to farm here," wrote a Lowbanks, Ontario, farming couple, "and we can't afford to wait for our money any longer than you can." One calm and articulate Winnipeg man, feeling the lack of the $300 refund that he and his wife were expecting, was nostalgic in 1966 about the quicker refunds of the early 1950s, when cheques were produced locally rather than at "your Tax Centre" in Ottawa.[75]

Another method by which National Revenue tried to mitigate the pain of tax compliance was the reviewing of tax returns by staff at local tax offices. This helped urban Canadians better than rural ones, however, and with expansion of the tax service the quality of training was allegedly not uniform.[76] Mistaken advice from the tax office could lead to inconveniences or worse. The taxpayer's sense of indignation at the rigidity of bureaucracy mounted, naturally enough, when his or her tax troubles came from tax employees' incorrect advice. One taxpayer, having had his return checked over by a government staffer, was understandably testy when sent a demand for a tiny amount of interest owing on payments that he was supposed to have made by instalments:

> I know there is no excuse for not knowing the law, but when a citizen is not corrected or is allowed to continue making the same mistake for years and then is suddenly served notice that for his mistake he will be penalized with no rebuttal, Canada is showing signs of going down hill fast ... $5.10 means nothing to either party. It is simply a case of whether the Government is honest or dishonest.

Given that many of the staff at the tax offices must have been newly hired during these years of expansion, and given that in the early 1960s computerized systems were being introduced, the probability of mistakes by tax office staff must have been higher than in the more stable years (in terms of staffing and technology) of the 1930s.[77] The existence of a court of appeal – the Tax Appeal Board (TAB) – might have made the tax authority more accountable for errors. Between 1950 and 1955, there were about 400 TAB cases a year – both large and small.[78] Whether well used or not, the TAB was part of the case made to the new mass taxpayer that the tax collector would be "fair and decent."[79]

The long 1950s saw many efforts to remake Canadian institutional life on a better and more modern basis. The "normal" world of the 1950s was a new normal. Suspicions about "bureaucracy" raised in the interwar years were still present, reanimated by the description in Cold War terms of a too-powerful state as totalitarian. Canadians could reach for high-flown vocabulary when they were unhappy with how revenue officials dealt with them. Sometimes, perhaps usually, this rhetoric was disproportionate. But revenue officials believed that administering an income tax could not accommodate all the varieties of taxpayer life. Minor administrative wounds that government officials inflicted, perhaps a bit carelessly, helped to persuade some Canadians that, instead of just random human error, there was something wrong with the growing administrative state. An anti-statist vocabulary developed largely to protect big property interests was available for anyone to adopt. Not everyone did. However, some specifically Canadian legal and cultural conditions shaped how much and where anti-statist critiques of bureaucracy caught on. Three areas in particular were rife with worries about the administrative state.

Law, Culture, and Canadian Distinctiveness

1. Family

Tax law both shapes and reflects views about families. Consider the removal in 1947 of the 1942 tax incentive for married women to earn income. That removal is generally taken as evidence of a larger campaign to get married women back into the home. But whether their paid work was socially useful was actually a matter of debate. As veterans sometimes struggled to regain their place in working life, a family's basic needs might depend on a married woman keeping her good job. Even a conservative parliamentarian could see the value of married women's market labour. Toronto PC MP Douglas Ross – not a noted feminist – voiced in the House of Commons the idea that the demand for married women's labour in "women's jobs" was still strong: the labour supply of single women would not provide enough nurses and schoolteachers and laundry workers. Ross claimed to know of married nurses quitting work because, without sufficient tax incentives, "it was not worth their while to continue working." He argued that married women served their families as mothers by earning wages after their children were of school age. Why increase married men's tax burdens if they had working wives whose wages were useful to the families and whose occupations met clear market needs?[80] But Finance Minister Abbott was determined to simplify the income tax act and avoid needless tax expenditures. He refused to continue the "incentive" to persuade a "special group" to work.[81] Tax law did not simply reflect consensus: in this case, it took sides for the sake of preserving revenue.

But the facts of family life meant that working wives would not go away. With cancellation of the wartime incentive to married women's paid work, dual-income families (if not able to manage with unpaid help) were paying for childcare from smaller pools of tax-exempt income. From this shift sprang a prolonged campaign about the deductibility of childcare expenses, one not yet fully settled. One of the earliest cases taken to the new Tax Appeal Board dealt with this point of intersection between a woman's social role, family relations, and income taxation. Tax law scholar Rebecca Johnson has described the case, launched in 1950. The appeal came from a married woman, an optometrist, who wished to claim a nanny's wages as an expense against her professional income, a claim that National Revenue had rejected. The TAB decision on her appeal was saturated with an older view of women's place in life. Justice Fordham described childcare as though it entailed hiring a servant – in his view, this was a luxury expense, one that allowed wives to busy themselves with volunteer work, amateur painting, or other personal pursuits. If, instead of engaging in such leisure activities during the hours freed from child care, a wife chose to practise her profession, then that was similarly a personal choice that the tax system had no obligation to subsidize.[82]

That the optometrist's case wasn't successful in 1950 didn't stop female professionals from continuing to make the case that their expenses for caregivers should be recognized in tax law. The Business and Professional Women (BPW) included a recommendation to this effect in their 1963 submission to the Carter Commission. Indeed, they enlarged the scope of the claim from childcare expenses to include expenses for care of the elderly, the ill, and dependant disabled members of their families. Responding to the by then familiar line that an income tax system couldn't possibly take into account such complexities of personal life, the BPW asserted that "ease or difficulty of administration should not be allowed to justify the continuing existence of unfair tax measures." The world was changing, they pointed out. More women, especially married women, were working. The income tax bureaucracy would have to accommodate them.[83]

For wage-earning married men, as distinct from professionals or others with business incomes, the tax problems created by a working wife involved fewer dollars. However, as one of Prime Minister Pearson's correspondents explained in 1963, losing the substantial married exemption when his wife's earnings made him "single" in the eyes of the tax law meant the difference between debt and no debt. In 1963, George Francis of Niagara-on-the-Lake explained that he had earned only $2,510 in 1962, on which he had paid $51.68 in income tax as a married man with a $2,000 exemption. But in that year his wife, to help out the family finances, had taken a part-time job. Even though Francis was a bona fide married man, he pointed out, his wife's income meant that he had lost his married exemption, and when the tax department had pointed this out it had reassessed the amount of tax that he owed for 1962. He now owed an additional $78.50. He had received what he called "a threatening note" from the tax office to that effect. He knew that he had to pay the amount owing, but he wrote to Pearson to point out how hard it would be for him to do so. He didn't own a car, he noted, so it wasn't clear to him where in his household spending he could start to "make sacrifices."[84] How could he clear even this small debt? This was not a case for the Tax Appeal Board. It was just a sign that the postwar income tax was not yet working right for lower-income Canadians.

At the other end of the income scale, the sharing of income in families meant something quite different, not a threat to survival but a means to accumulate wealth by reducing effective tax rates. And in this respect the wealthy were in a different situation in Canada from the wealthy in the United States. As tax authorities had long known, allocating income-generating property (rental units, stocks) to a wife or children was a way for well-to-do men to reduce the income attributed to them by the tax authority while still exercising control over the income-generating property and still benefiting from that income. In effect, the male head of the family split off some of his income so that each part (the part held by family members and the part still in his hands) would be taxed at a lower rate. Such manoeuvres are called income splitting. Before the war, in Canada as in the United States, tax policy treated familial income splitting as tax evasion. Well-to-do taxpayers, with some help from women's organizations, fought back, arguing that income splitting was a legitimate method of tax avoidance.

In the United States, however, defenders of income splitting had on their side not only the tax-dodging wealthy and women's rights groups but also constitutional defenders of states' rights. Eight US states had civil law–based marital property laws – "community property" – that gave wives more default property rights than they had in common law states. The same kind of distinctive property law governed marriages in Quebec. During the 1940s, with income splitting in mind, six states actually converted their whole marital property regimes from the common law to the community property regime. Another nine considered the change.[85] After the war, the pressure of the property regime conversions and the postwar demand for tax reductions were finally decisive, and in 1948 the US Treasury lost its battle against marital income splitting (and lost considerable revenue from personal income tax as a result). In Canada, the Department of Finance held out more successfully. But the pressure was on, both from tax practitioners in support of wealthy clients and from some Canadian women's groups.[86]

For a few months in late 1957, there was a moment of alarm in Finance and cabinet when a TAB ruling made it look like marital income splitting might succeed in Quebec.[87] An English-speaking businessman, Frank Sura, from an upper-middle-class Montreal enclave, the Town of Mount Royal, had argued that he should benefit from the lower income tax obligation that would result if his considerable income was split between him and his wife. Over the next four years, both the Exchequer Court and the Supreme Court would reverse the TAB decision. They found that the community property regime gave wives no real "power of ownership" of the incomes from marital properties or their husbands' earnings. The women's groups' arguments about housewives properly having claims on assets that their labour helped to create found no purchase with the courts. Protecting revenue (or perhaps avoiding a constitutional issue) was the priority of the higher courts. They decided that Quebec's property regime would not provide a way for wealthy Quebec men to dodge some of their income tax obligations.[88]

There were other recourses for the wealthy who wanted not to pay the highest marginal rates, however. The Department of Finance was aware that personal corporations, entities that held investments, "were being used to split income within members of a taxpayer's family." In the June 1961 budget speech, Finance Minister Fleming proposed "a comprehensive overhaul of the definition of a personal corporation and the rules for taxing shareholders of such corporations."[89] However, budget resolutions designed to put this overhaul into effect were withdrawn – "over the weekend" according to the Liberal finance critic – after a "storm of criticism" that did not reach the floor of the House of Commons. It likely took place in Fleming's office or over the phone. The *Ottawa Citizen* gave the unexplained hoisting of personal corporations reform equal front-page billing with the government's attempt to depose the governor of the Bank of Canada, but the financial pages of the *Globe and Mail* were quiet on the subject.[90] The proposed overhaul, along with the whole question of how income tax should fall within families, would be folded into the work of the Royal Commission on Taxation launched in 1963. It was indeed a complex matter. Where family, tax administration, and income tax law intersected, there was a thick intermingling of social values, subsistence needs, professional-grade tax avoidance, and a bit of constitutional interest, touching on Quebec's jurisdiction in property rights and its different family law. In the long 1950s, rhetoric about the rights of women and the meaning of family was deployed for political advantage, but the impact of income splitting for women's career options and work incentives (later raised by feminists) barely registered. Finance Ministers Harris and Fleming resisted income splitting, insofar as they could, in order to protect the personal income tax revenue from erosion.

2. Francophone Quebec

Francophone Quebec brought another complex mix of beliefs and worries to the supposedly simple matter of paying a personal income tax. Most fundamental was simply the language of communication. From Quebec came objections about taxpayers getting correspondence in the wrong language or with the French in smaller type. The latter objection was raised by a prominent senior member of the Union nationale in Quebec, Hormisdas Langlais. He described the impression conveyed by such typography in a printed receipt from the tax authority as "being treated as an inferior race, like the negroes in the United States."[91] His status and influence were clearly reflected in the quick and emollient response addressed to him, first by Pearson's private secretary and not long after by Pearson himself.[92] By the 1960s, the chronically inflamed relationship between Ottawa and Quebec on income tax questions meant that even an ordinary taxpayer thought to use Quebec nationalist language to add force to a complaint about frustrating assessment procedures. "Such things are forcing us to hope for a Québec independent," wrote one man from Donnacona in an English footnote addressed to Pearson at the end of a copy of a French letter to the local tax office.[93] Another, annoyed at a slow refund cheque from Ottawa, pointed out that the Quebec tax authority had acknowledged his return and sent his refund a month after he had filed it. Now, five months later, he was still waiting for any communication from the "Central Government." Were civil servants in Ottawa under special instructions to keep Quebeckers waiting? He told the representative of the "Central Government" that this sort of treatment was not "making us appreciate the system we live in, to say the least."[94]

One issue linked a narrative of francophone Quebec's distinctiveness, the frustration with bureaucracy, and a certain anti-statism. That issue was charitable donations. The deduction for charitable donations had become a favourite method of tax dodging for "the little guy." The National Revenue office began to target this practice of evasion in the early years of the Diefenbaker government, and continued to do so, with the Liberal minister's blessing, as late as (and perhaps later than) 1965. Awareness of the abuses was widespread. A federal government report in 1960 alleged that $17,000,000 of revenue had been lost in Montreal alone because of fraudulent donation receipts and that claims for charitable donations in Quebec City were four times those in the comparably sized city of Windsor, Ontario. This was clearly identified as a Quebec-centred problem.[95] Publisher of Quebec City's *Le Soleil* newspaper, Oscar Gilbert, wrote in 1961 to advise Diefenbaker that eliminating the charitable donation deduction would save a lot of money for other purposes (e.g., raising the level of exempt income) because the donation deduction had become "a source of abuse and criticism everywhere."[96]

A concentration of correspondence in the Pearson papers suggests that in 1964 and 1965 this method of evasion continued to be used and policed in small-town Quebec. Charitable donation receipts were being issued worth many times more than the actual amounts received by some parishes. One parish near Rouyn issued "church receipts" for five times its revenue from donations. This was sensitive territory: to challenge donation receipts issued by a church is to call into question an institution that stands for moral rigour. A senior official in the Quebec provincial tax administration suggested that Catholic Quebeckers just might be giving more to their churches: they were constantly being asked to contribute not only to their congregations' expenses but also to foreign missions, hospitals, and universities. The tax office solution to the problem of disproportionate church receipts was not to reject them entirely but to reduce their values to estimated reasonable sums. Not surprisingly, to some taxpayers, this seemed to be odd: either the receipt was valid, or it was not, several observed. The procedure, possibly intended to be generous, ended up seeming, as one of Pearson's correspondents put it, arbitrary and dictatorial.[97]

As we have seen, accusing the tax collector of dictatorial power came easily to Canadians facing even minor tax troubles with the federal income tax. In Quebec, Premier Maurice Duplessis himself reached for that vocabulary in all of his confrontations with Ottawa. He staked out this rhetorical territory in the 1945 and 1946 federal-provincial conferences. There the federal government proposed that the provinces should forgo the three most productive direct taxes: personal income tax, corporate tax, and succession duty. The provinces would keep resource-related taxes (royalties, fees, and some resource profit taxes) and minor imposts such as amusement taxes. In return, the provinces would be ensured adequate revenues through per capita grants, adjusted to track growth in the economy. And the federal government, with its enlarged revenues, would provide new social spending, some of which would relieve the provinces of expenditures. The proposed old age pension program, for example, would be all federal rather than federal-provincial on the 1927 cost-sharing model. The broader objective was to put in the hands of the federal government the levers of taxation and spending that would allow it to manage the economy in a modern, macroeconomic way.[98]

The proposals reignited debates of the interwar years about the proper role of the dominion government in confederation. Prime Minister King recognized that the program that his government proposed would entail a shifting of taxing power and legislative responsibility to the dominion from the provinces and challenge ideas of provincial rights that had often been a Liberal Party cause. The premiers of Ontario and Quebec saw in the proposals a political opening.[99] Premier Duplessis put the matter bluntly in 1946. The federal government's proposals were a centralization of the federation, and centralization was a sign of totalitarianism, the kind that had recently wrought such havoc in Europe. He held up the sovereignty of the states in the United States as a model of democracy. If the provinces were to be able to do their work (including in Quebec, importantly, the work of preserving the French Canadian people), then they needed the power to tax their citizens. "The power to tax," Duplessis insisted, "is the power to govern."[100]

On that point, he was surely right. Without the capacity to raise revenue, a government lacks the "sinews of power," the means to make policy effectual.[101] But more was at stake in the early 1950s than simply both Quebec and Canada having sufficient revenue to accomplish clearly established purposes. The role of government itself was changing and contested. The objectives of Duplessis in government were not those of the Ottawa centralizers. He stood for a limited state, robust and privately funded social institutions, and a welcoming, low-tax environment for business. The Quebec Chamber of Commerce supported not only his stand on the constitutional organization of taxation but also his view of government. In a brief on taxation submitted by the chamber to Duplessis in 1952, they echoed his own words: "We believe, Mr. Prime Minister, that the time has come to counteract this centralizing propaganda by a somewhat similar propaganda in favour of the decentralizing point of view, the only truly democratic one." It called for a royal commission in Quebec on constitutional matters to provide a challenge to the continuing prestige of the report of the Rowell-Sirois Commission. As the report of the Quebec commission – the Tremblay Commission – would later emphasize, the chamber claimed that centralization meant that extravagant provincial governments elsewhere in the country, spending on social services and infrastructure beyond their fiscal capacities, were being subsidized by taxes collected in Quebec. Prime Minister St. Laurent insisted that it was right that surplus federal tax revenue be used to help in the provision of public goods in provinces with smaller, weaker economies than those of Quebec and Ontario. Duplessis and his supporters in the Chamber of Commerce thought that income taxes collected in Quebec should go to meeting needs in Quebec.[102]

3. Federalism

The struggle over how to share taxing powers was intimately linked to the future of the welfare state in Canada. In the first decade after the war, at stake was the kind of country that Canada would become. Those who wanted to build a welfare state saw the constitutional position of Duplessis, his florid opposition to centralization, as both bad constitutional law and a barrier to the urgent matter of building a more effective state.

For example, McGill University law professor F.R. Scott challenged Duplessis's conception of provinces' rights in a 1947 paper. He began by observing with alarm that reversing wartime centralization, returning to "constitutional 'normalcy' ... , may be extremely serious." Since Confederation, Canada's economy had changed in ways that created nationwide social and economic problems that no province on its own, acting within its constitutional powers, could address. More, not less, federal "jurisdiction and control" would be needed: Duplessisist decentralization could only mean a return to the ineffective fiscal practices and hobbled policy responses of the 1930s. Scott argued for a "reasonable adaptation" of the division of powers based upon the facts of our constitutional history. Canada was not "federal" but "quasi-federal," without the strong version of states' rights (provincial autonomy) that defined (and troubled) the United States.[103]

For Scott, making this point was no mere scholarly score. At stake was the capacity to build a welfare state – to use the government to manage the macroeconomic levers of the national economy and to provide, through more programs like the recently introduced unemployment insurance, the kind of social security that had been promised to the new federal income tax payers in 1944. Although Scott's presentation was made in an academic paper, the most senior Ottawa centralizer, Deputy Minister of Finance W.C. Clark, felt just as strongly. The 1945 proposals designed in the Department of Finance and the Bank of Canada were to "provide the machinery which will permit [the federal government] to fulfill the functions of a central government in this modern age." If the provinces could block the innovations, "then Confederation is a failure, and Canada cannot be a nation."[104]

The positions in this constitutional conflict were clearly drawn. To call for innovation in the division of powers was to stand for social security and modern macroeconomic management. In contrast, insisting on preserving provinces' rights, resisting the centralization of economic planning and taxation, was a stand against expanding the role of government. In the hands of Duplessis, a hold-fast style of constitutional argument also meant that he could stand as a defender of the religion, language, laws, and culture of the *canadien* people. Premiers who stood with him, temporarily at least, were also reluctant builders of the welfare state – Manning of Alberta, Macdonald of Nova Scotia, and Drew of Ontario.[105] In contrast, the mainstream labour movement, both Québécois and Canadian, slammed Duplessis's ideas as echoed in the Tremblay Commission report. Labour charged that social security programs would collapse in the strict division of powers that the report sought to preserve: "Social progress would be set back half a century."[106] These debates about jurisdiction were not merely selfish wrangles among little men who each wanted a bigger throne. It was easy, to be sure, to find autocrats, wafflers, and demagogues among them. But the stakes were real and serious.

In all of this, the details of income tax proposals carried real political weight. Duplessis made a major play in 1954 when his government introduced the first province-wide personal income tax.[107] The bill presented in February by the provincial treasurer, law professor, and former minister in R.B. Bennett's cabinet, Onésime Gagnon, began by making, in effect, a declaration of constitutional war: its preamble declared that the provinces' right to direct taxation (e.g., income taxation) had legal priority over that of the federal government. The bill immediately made that constitutional position politically salient by imposing double taxation on some Quebeckers' incomes. The Quebec income tax had higher exemptions than did the Canadian one: there was no income tax liability on income under $1,500 earned by single people and under $3,000 earned by married people (figures that would have been familiar to critics of the federal income tax elsewhere in Canada). As a result, of the 600,000 Canadian income tax payers in Quebec, only 300,000 would now also be Quebec income tax payers. The mass base – the small earners, the modest farm incomes – was untouched by the new provincial tax; its impact hit only the upper middle class and the wealthiest urbanites. However, the new Quebec tax would be lighter on those higher income earners than was the Canadian one: for example, a married earner taxed on $8,000 of a $10,000 income by Canada would be taxed on only $7,000 by Quebec. The rates were set so that, if the federal government would allow Quebeckers to deduct their provincial tax payments as a credit of 15 percent against their federal income tax bills, then the double taxation of those well-to-do urban Quebeckers in effect disappeared. But would the feds allow that large a credit? In their arrangements with the other provinces, they allowed only a 5 percent credit.

Duplessis's new tax bill thus cleverly batted the double taxation ball into the federal government's court.[108]

The ensuing negotiations forced a clarification of principles that ultimately led to the complex fiscal federalism of the post-1956 equalization system. In launching talks with Duplessis, St. Laurent articulated three conditions for any fiscal arrangement, whether with Quebec or otherwise. The constitutional rights of both levels of government had to be respected, all arrangements had to be available to any province, and the revenue left to the federal government had to be sufficient to meet its "national obligations." On October 5, 1954, a much-hyped one-on-one meeting of Prime Minister St. Laurent and Premier Duplessis was said to have resulted in a special "deal" for Quebec.[109] Duplessis agreed to amend his provincial tax bill to remove the provocative preamble, thus respecting Ottawa's rights. In return, St. Laurent offered not the ability for those paying the Quebec income tax to deduct 15 percent from their cheques to the federal receiver general but a 10 percent reduction of their federal tax bills for all payers of Canadian income tax in Quebec. The 10 percent plan dealt with the difference in the personal exemptions between the Quebec tax and the Canadian tax. It gave all 600,000 Quebec payers of Canadian income tax a break rather than just the top 300,000. And it avoided giving too generous a credit to those at higher incomes. The differences in exemptions meant that those taxpayers had smaller taxable incomes for the Quebec tax than they did for the Canadian tax. A temporary measure, this arrangement would be available to all provinces when they renewed their tax agreements in 1957. Many of these details were lost in the news coverage, either misunderstood or misrepresented. The well-to-do, getting 10 percent off rather than 15 percent, were portrayed as still losing 5 percent, while the report of the Tremblay Commission asserted that the arrangement "did nothing to settle the problem of fiscal relations" between Quebec and Canada.[110] But both taxes allowed each government to appear sensitive to the smaller income earner.

The tedious tangle between the province of Quebec and the federal government in Ottawa on whether the federal income tax improperly invaded the province's jurisdiction might have seemed to many a matter beyond their ken. In April 1946, a Gallup survey showed that between 9 percent and 22 percent of Canadians had no opinion on which level of government should be taxing income. Among those with opinions, different categories of respondent had widely different views. The variation was across income classes (as the poll reported): the wealthiest favoured giving exclusive power to tax income to the dominion (62 percent), whereas only 37 percent of the lower-income group did. Whether the opinion varied by province the poll did not report.[111] The cheering crowds that greeted the foe of centralization, Duplessis, in April 1946 at the Quebec City train station and his successive electoral victories suggest that, in Quebec, the percentage results for that poll might have been different by province.[112] However, for Duplessis's critics in Quebec, his use of provincial rights language came to seem sterile, an excuse for inaction. When some of these critics came to power as the provincial government, they would develop over the 1960s a new, less narrowly fiscal, constitutional reform language.[113] The fight for fairer taxation that mobilized so many outside Quebec in the late 1960s would be a secondary issue inside Quebec in the grip of the question about "separatism."

However, throughout the postwar period, reforming fiscal federalism and making modern state capacity were conjoined projects.[114] Proposals for better tax sharing were part of a vision in which there was a positive role for governments, both federal and provincial, in economic development and social security. An equalization formula, legislated in 1956, provided a new way to recognize the differences in taxable capacity among Canadian regions, providing transfers that reflected the different yields of major types of tax. Supplemented in 1958 by adjustment grants to the Atlantic provinces, the equalization system integrated tax fairness with a social objective: regional equity in public services. Fiscal federalism was especially important to Canada's newest province, Newfoundland. A passionate defender of its people, Premier Joey Smallwood drew on a historical narrative of difference to argue not for keeping more of the province's revenue but for having the province's limited tax receipts supplemented by exceptional federal grants. Newfoundland and Labrador in time would become a province like the others, for fiscal purposes, but for that to happen, he argued, it needed special support for economic modernization.

It was hard to reconcile Smallwood's case with the three conditions that St. Laurent had articulated in the Quebec fight. Short-term supplementation of the province's budget was consistent with the rights of the province as established in the 1949 deal, but Smallwood's vision of long-term support over a generation or more was harder to fit into the box of all provinces being treated alike. And there was some dispute about the actual fiscal needs of the province: some, both in Newfoundland and in Ottawa, thought that the Smallwood government had spent unwisely and too much. But, as Raymond Blake has shown, Smallwood had powerful cultural materials to work with in mustering electoral support. In 1959, when Diefenbaker set hard limits to future federal support for Newfoundland, angry crowds cheered Smallwood's claim that "the rest of Canada [was] ready to rise up in rebellion against Mr. Diefenbaker's betrayal of Newfoundland." In the next two federal elections, Newfoundland went Liberal.[115]

Continuing in daily life, however, below the level of elite accommodation and militant constitutional reform, was a pressing practical problem derived from fiscal federalism – municipal taxation. Municipal taxes soared during the long 1950s. At the beginning of the period, Canada's towns, cities, and rural municipalities were facing the legacy of twenty years of limited budgets. Roads, sidewalks, schools, sewers, and housing all needed investment. Prosperity and, in the major centres, growing populations meant rising expectations for and expanding needs of public transit, recreation services, and facilities for the mushrooming school-age population. Expanding municipal revenue sources to meet these needs wasn't easy. On the one hand, claiming from the provinces larger contributions to the cities' costs was appealing, but the provinces themselves were engaged with the federal government in struggles for more money. On the other, rising property values helped to increase the cities' major tax revenue source. But in relation to costs and mounting expectations, that affluence bump was not enough. The municipalities were still under fiscal stress. The rate of property tax, the main source of revenue, was not easily hiked. As one experienced city administrator observed, "theoretically, it is always possible to raise property tax rates. Practical economics and practical politics do not support the theory. In practice, as we know, tax rates can be raised, but not too drastically or too often."[116]

Among the considerations that militated against raising rates was that doing so would increase the burden on lower-income homeowners. In Toronto during the 1950s, property taxes assessed and outstanding (arrears) amounted to between 5 percent and 6.25 percent of the total amount levied. According to city treasury officials, these arrears could be blamed on two categories of taxpayer: those who could pay but didn't because they could use the money for business purposes and profit even after paying the 6 percent penalty to the city and those who simply couldn't make ends meet. In one such case in 1960, a Toronto couple were about to lose their home over tax arrears of $49.10. The city had been sending bailiffs to try to collect the debt but was also trying to find a job for the couple's nineteen-year-old son so that the family could pay off the debt.[117] Both of these reasons for non-payment held true in New Brunswick as well. A 1951 royal commission there observed that property tax payers postponed paying "indefinitely" and would use the money for their own purposes until the municipality went after them. This suited local collectors fine since they were paid extra to collect overdue accounts. Still, even in New Brunswick, attempts were sometimes made to sell the homes of poor families for taxes. In one case, in which the tax bill was a substantial $600, the mother and children had tied the constable who delivered the notice to a chair.[118] Tax arrears were far less of a problem in the 1950s than they had been in the 1930s, but some homeowners still found the municipal taxes fearful. By the 1960s, a number of provinces had taken steps to relieve the tax burdens of smaller property owners.[119]

For middle-income earners, the municipal property taxes were not so much a threat to their subsistence as just part of the problem of "higher taxes."[120] Faced with such worries, each level of government could point to the other. In 1967, federal Finance Minister Mitchell Sharp called the municipal property tax "undoubtedly the most unpopular and troublesome of taxes" and "higher in proportion to income [in Canada] than in any other advanced countries." If Canada's tax system was to become more fair, then something would have to be done about that regressive tax.[121] In 1964, in an address on "high levels of taxation," Finance Minister Walter Gordon was careful to note that the "biggest increase" in public expenditure over the 1951–61 decade was by provinces and municipalities. He noted that the fiscal needs of those governments were great and that their responsibilities were important, but cooperative federalism didn't mean that he would write a blank cheque. The needs and priorities of each level of government had to be assessed fairly.[122] Some homeowners saw the interaction among federal and municipal taxes differently. Letters from citizen-taxpayers frequently suggested that municipal taxes should be deductible from income, as they reportedly were in the federal income tax in the United States. But even when such a suggestion came via the prime minister, as it did once from Diefenbaker, the Department of Finance rejected it. Not only would it mean significant revenue loss, but also it would inequitably favour homeowners versus renters.[123] It was also a raid on the federal treasury. With municipal tax deductibility, cities could raise property taxes secure in the knowledge that their citizens would just pass along the costs via their federal income tax returns. As a back-door rebalancing of fiscal federalism, deducting municipal property taxes was a non-starter.

On the left in the federalism debates of the 1950s, the idea that "provincial rights" should prevent improvements in social security looked like legalistic excuse making. Among the Business and Professional Women (BPW), the notion that administrative difficulty prohibited deducting their particular business expenses appeared as merely bureaucratic stonewalling. In francophone Quebec, the "central government" was readily demonized as being insensitive to the rights of Quebeckers. And, for wealthy Canadians seeking income splitting or municipal property tax deductions, the arguments offered by Finance would have seemed arbitrary. If these policies were possible in the United States, then why not in Canada? In all of these quarters, tensions with the tax authority took on the coloration of larger causes. Development of the payroll deductions system was a success for the newly expanded peacetime income tax system, but during the long 1950s frustrations with the process of taxpaying were understandably common. The temptations of anti-statist language were real and present.

$ ¢ $

Canadian constitutional conversations in the long 1950s were shot through with hopes and fears about state-led economic development, social welfare, and national unity through nationwide standards. This was a debate not about the black-letter law of the BNA Act, though some claimed that it was, but about visions of Canada's future. The many new federal income tax payers might not have cared in 1946 about which government taxed income, but after 1954 some influential Quebeckers certainly did, in English-speaking Quebec as much as in autonomist French-speaking Quebec. They would find allies in their opposition to centralization among Canadian Tories elsewhere who were critical of unelected experts and a too-active state. In contrast, the newly expanded labour movement recognized in enhanced federal social programs an effort to use the revenue-raising power of the federal income tax to fund not only warfare – and the Korean War certainly contributed to the income tax bill – but also welfare. Considering the hostility of some premiers to the new status of the labour movement, centralization of the confederation mainly offered hope, not fear, to unionists. The only problem with income taxation from a labour perspective was that, even after the

1948 reforms, the impact of inflation and the non-taxation of capital gains meant that the poor paid more income tax than they could afford and that the rich paid less than the progressive rates seemed to suggest that they should. As the rates of explicitly regressive taxes rose over the decade – the federal sales tax, municipal property taxes, various provincial health taxes – the household budgets of lower-paid wage and salary earners, small businesses, small farmers, fishers, loggers, and pensioners were noticeably pressured by "the taxes." Struggles over the division of taxing powers seemed to be technical and obscure. But the impact on underfunded local governments and the long delay in sorting out how to accomplish equalization had real consequences in Canadians' daily lives.

Attempts to reorganize fiscal federalism were just one part of the larger project of organizing income taxation on a national scale in peacetime. The "mass production" methods of income tax assessment and collection included a new, more accessible appeal board and payroll deductions that produced refunds, not garnishees. Local tax offices checked over income tax returns, and PR programs promised fairness and threatened vigilant enforcement. Small exemptions alleviated some pressures on small incomes. Other reliefs, proposed or provided (income splitting and deductions for municipal taxes, mortgage interest, and charitable donations), were supposed to appeal to all but promised more to the wealthier. Perhaps most importantly for politics, exemption policy provided opportunities to parliamentary critics. Before 1957, the CCF, Social Credit, and Tories allied in Parliament against the Liberals on measures such as the medical exemption floor, and after the Diefenbaker victory the Tories tried to position themselves as tax cutters, particularly concerned to relieve the vote-rich smaller income group. The Duplessis income tax also claimed the mantle of a tax on those best able to pay. There was a populist element in these positions, with vote-catching tax cuts rather than the building of social services at the centre of their appeal.

Tax reduction for small- and middle-income groups was one way to try to improve fairness of the tax system. The other was to make collection effective and polite. These objectives were not always easy to combine. This was, after all, debt collection. Investigation was inevitably intrusive. The statute permitted serious and non-negotiable penalties, which made income tax collection considerably less a gentlemanly, *entre nous,* matter than it had been in the interwar years. The taxpayer population was diverse, and the bureaucracy was large and growing. The voice of the tax collector sometimes appeared in the wrong language in Quebec. The relationship between taxpayer and state was full of potential for friction. Some tax measures required National Revenue to know about personal matters such as divorce settlements and family businesses. Some found that intrusive. However, in letters to the prime minister and MPs, many lower-income taxpayers were eager to share personal details of illness and struggle and the price of food to explain how hard it was for them to carry their share of the federal income tax. These writers trusted that, if they told these politicians what their lives were like, the men of the state would respond as human beings with compassion. Recognition seems to have been more important than personal privacy to these letter writers. In telling their stories to the state, they were asserting their place in democracy more fully than by speaking to a polling company or by voting.

The new federal income tax regime of the long 1950s brought many more Canadians, as individuals and as families, into closer relations with the federal government. An older view of the income tax payer as a voluntary contributor, a man of honour doing his share to help pay his nation's debts, was challenged by an emerging view of the income tax payer as the battered and hapless victim of a dictatorial, imperious, perhaps socialist, and certainly bureaucratic state. Where once farmers and workers had championed the federal income taxes (both personal and corporate) as soak-the-rich instruments of tax fairness, these low- to middle-income Canadians, now taxpayers themselves, sometimes experienced, along with small businesses, a style of address by the state that chafed, irritated, or worried them. They were constantly reminded that the welfare state had a price. Even those who expressed their awareness that the new welfare state provided value to lower-income people nonetheless had to develop a fairly sophisticated form of trust in government, the confident belief that dollars taken from their paycheques would ultimately return in the form of equivalently valuable public services. Given the generational dynamics of a welfare state that seemed initially to benefit breadwinners with young children more than the elderly, seniors were particularly likely to doubt the merits of the welfare state exchange. There were many ideological perspectives from which tax troubles could be made into something more than just the normal inconveniences of daily life. The cohort of new income tax payers, or newly positioned ones, during the long 1950s had a number of historically contingent reasons to be angry about tax. In the 1960s, efforts to make Canada more democratic would be among the channels into which this anger flowed.

10
Reform and Populism
in the 1960s

By NOW, I HOPE TO HAVE PERSUADED the reader that taxation has been more than a matter of economics, obscure accounting gambits, and high politics. Beyond advancing that general proposition, I have also tried to show how tax has been woven throughout what some scholars call "social politics," the practices in which social relations of power intersect with the government and the state. Here, in the concluding episode of this series of stories, I want to show that, during the short 1960s, tax talk featured in a new phase of Canadian democracy, one in which the promise of democracy, that all people would be heard and well served by the state, seemed to be on the verge of fulfillment.

Cold War idealism about democracy in the long 1950s had fostered both ideas and organizational methods that emphasized citizen participation, in both policy making and service delivery, as a means by which free people made government legitimate. The varieties of citizen participation were diverse: community leagues in Edmonton, voluntary planning in Nova Scotia, social development and planning councils in many cities, many kinds of cooperatives, and, in most parts of the country, grassroots-friendly rural community development programs, such as the Bureau d'aménagement de l'est du Québec.[1] Nationally as well as internationally, intellectuals in many fields were puzzling over the social basis of political legitimacy. Worries about the risks of apathy, the appeal of extremism, and the viability (if any) of consensus troubled the theorists of liberalism.[2] In 1971, coming out of the 1960s, philosopher John Rawls's landmark work of political philosophy, *A*

Theory of Justice, captured something essential about these liberal worries, something that links them especially well to tax reform. As Rawls asked, when participants in a policy process hold to fundamentally incompatible moral standpoints and apparently irreconcilable competing interests, how can people committed to just public policy come to an agreement?[3]

My analysis of the role of public opinion in tax reform in Canada in the 1960s will speak to two elements of his answer, as Rawls presented it in his later summary work, *Justice as Fairness.* In particular, I want to suggest that tax talk speaks to the role of "non-controversial social science" in justice and to the problem of how non-rational commitments can be integrated into liberal political conversation.[4] The struggles for tax reform in the 1960s in Canada (as in the United States) strikingly illustrate the problems influencing even the most apparently abstract political philosophy of the day. If liberal justice requires that citizens and their elected representatives reason together, as Rawls held, then the egalitarian inclusiveness proclaimed during and since the Second World War required some new efforts to deal with the new facts of political life. Not only had tax publics proliferated, but also the "public" was changing in many areas of politics. Political parties and government departments faced constituencies that included not only the old economic sectors but also well-organized people of colour, Indigenous people, professional groups, and increasingly people organized around a multiplicity of statuses and identities (pensioners, women, people with disabilities, gay men and lesbians, youth, and more). In this new phase of Canadian tax conversation, the influence of authoritative social science and the power of emotionally charged populisms were clearly evident. If the public was to participate, then politicians would have to confront the reality of new publics and new challenges of bringing together authoritative knowledge and potentially uncivil emotions.

Always important, public opinion on tax questions figured exceptionally in events that marked an important moment in the development of democracy in Canada. Beginning in 1963, a process of tax reform at the federal level unfolded, culminating in the budget of 1971, in which the left's long-sought goal of capital gains taxation was partly realized. A million low-income Canadians ceased entirely to be federal income tax payers, and 4.7 million (about 58 percent of income tax payers) had their personal income tax bills lightened. A substantial number of middle-class income tax payers would see a small increase (less than 1 percent). Higher-income earners, about 1.3 million, would pay at least 1 percent more, but the top marginal rate would be lowered from 82.4 percent to 61.1 percent.[5] In the first part of this chapter, I argue that the centrepiece of the process that led to the 1971 budget, the Royal Commission on Taxation (Carter Commission), had its origins not only on Bay Street but also in conservative populism. In the second part, I sketch the tax reform process from the 1967 Carter Commission report to the presentation of tax reform proposals in 1969, the Benson White Paper, that would launch an unprecedented exercise in public budget consultations. I suggest that the modernist current in the tax reform process, the attempt to make economic science prevail over political expedience, was on a collision course with conservative populism. In the very period when federal welfare state building was in its golden age, 1963–72, it was troubled and inhibited by long-simmering fear and anger about taxes among the voting public on both the right and the left and in various other political positions. Through letters sent to federal politicians during the peak of the debate in 1969–70, I trace a variety of the tax-related emotions stirred up during the White Paper consultations. To complement the view that the White Paper debates were simply a sorry victory for the forces of narrow self-interest and ignorant unreason, I suggest that they also offer a useful lesson about the inevitable role of emotion in deliberative democracy.

Populism Ready to Pounce

In the interwar years, conservatives such as the National Government enthusiasts worried that populism threatened sound government. The small minority of university-educated Canadians spoke knowingly of "demagogues" in disparaging politicians such as William Aberhart of Alberta or Camilien Houde of Montreal, who positioned themselves as voices of the people against the vested interests. The Manichean simplicities and bitter emotions of these populists were easily dismissed as the tools of cynical manipulation. But the celebrations of mass democracy launched during the Second World War and prolonged during the Cold War gave public opinion a new weight and the desires of the masses a new cachet. The progress of the labour movement in negotiating a new order of industrial democracy gave birth to the idea of the responsible union leader as a partner in a stable accommodation between the business elite and the working people. The broadening of both political and social rights brought women and racialized groups increasingly into public life.

These changes meant that the problems of taxation without representation were fading in fact and in memory. Perhaps not coincidentally,[6] engagement with electoral politics was building – the federal elections of 1958, 1962, and 1963 were the only ones in Canadian history in which more than 79 percent of eligible Canadians voted.[7] At the same time, however, a wave of dissatisfaction with the accomplishments of liberal inclusion was about to break. A new left in the labour movement, a new feminism in the women's movement, and new "red" and "black" nationalisms among racialized groups would take on more challenging goals. They all drew some of their energy from the emotional well that fed populist politics – alienation, anger, and skepticism about elite authority. So did conservative populism. The difference lay in the positive meanings that conservative populism's adherents and leaders assigned to the past. Populisms of all sorts would find political fuel in tax questions during the 1960s. A lower-income voter from Charlottetown, writing to Finance Minister George Nowlan in 1962, urged him to deal with poverty by lowering personal income tax rates: "These are issues that interest the average people, not this nonsense over nuclear arms or whether we sell wheat to China." He went on to underscore what he believed was the power of the mass electorate: "These large corporations are necessary but they don't elect governments." If the Diefenbaker government were to do something "concrete and benefitting to the people, I am sure they would show their appreciation on election day."[8] There was electoral power to be harnessed both in cutting taxes and in challenging the practices of tax administration, and that power was not only gained from addressing the needs of big business.

At the constituency level, in retail politics, an individual MP could make political lemonade out of tax lemons. One impact of a larger and poorer population of income tax payers was that more constituents had tax troubles, and those problems were of more varied kinds. If the constituency correspondence files of future Prime Ministers Lester (Mike) Pearson and John Diefenbaker are like those of other MPs, then much of their constituency casework was helping out on tax questions.[9]

Diefenbaker's constituency correspondence illustrates most clearly how an ambitious political up-and-comer could respond to such tax complaints in ways that would catch and keep votes. His formula was perfect (if slightly despicable). Diefenbaker would express sympathy for the taxpayer's trouble and outrage at how the taxpayer had been treated, and he would promise to take up the issue with the governing party's minister of revenue.

But in either his first letter to the constituent or in a subsequent one, he would point out how inflexible said minister and his officials were and thus attribute to the failings of the governing party and their public servants his own inability to accomplish anything material for the constituent.[10] This routine was certainly strategic, though it's easy to see how affecting were some of his constituents' tax problems. One woman, suffering from life-threatening heart problems, told Diefenbaker, by then prime minister, that she was worried nearly to death about the cost of her medication and the tax on it, and she hoped that the cost of heart medications, like diabetes ones, might be made a deductible expense. On his private secretary's sympathetic draft reply, which included an expression of the prime minister's regret at not replying personally, Diefenbaker wrote that "one page is hardly enough."[11] To have the proper impact, to be read as truly concerned, he wanted this voting taxpayer to get a generous measure of response. This was a judgment about the emotions of retail politics. Tone mattered. Even when his party was in power and a complaint about the behaviour of revenue officials came to his ear, he dressed down the department in cabinet for its "arbitrary and unnecessarily severe methods."[12] Defending the taxpayer against National Revenue worked for him as part of his populist style.

The Algoma constituency files of Pearson also show that he intervened to help individuals with tax problems, but in a considerably more careful way, offering more neutral promises to inquire and never, as far as I have found, feeding the view that local tax offices were tyrannical or unreasonable.[13] Nonetheless, as prime minister, Pearson was quickly responsive to complaints of procedural wrong more than to complaints of hardship. For example, a complaint from a small-town physician, received on November 28, 1963, was resolved and a letter of apology sent by the revenue minister, at Pearson's request, in under two weeks.[14] But even though there were differences of style between these two politicians' responses to constituents' tax troubles, it's easy to see that helping out with income tax troubles informed politicians about where the points of friction were in the raising of revenue and gave them a chance to act as the caring and responsive face of the state.

In Quebec, Social Credit MPs (the Ralliement des Créditistes) did this kind of constituency work around income tax with a different twist. Within the larger context of Quebec-Ottawa tax politics, the Créditistes could channel anger about bureaucracy in a way that combined hostility to centralized federalism with a wider and deeper objection to the state and the federal income tax as an expression of both the mysteries of modern economics and the expertise-based state. Social Credit as a national political force in the early 1960s also had, of course, a western Canadian face, but the francophone Quebec variant was especially successful in the spring 1962 election, winning twenty-six of the seventy-five Quebec seats and thus providing all but four of the thirty Social Credit/Créditiste MPs who went to Ottawa in the fall of 1962. If we see them in the context of the picture that I have drawn of the new relations of extraction and their frictions, the Créditistes appear less like ignorant political deviants and more like the voice of one part, maybe even a substantial one, of the Canadian electorate. In calling for an end to the federal income tax, they expressed a view that had been common thirty-five years before. And their call resonated with the more common demand in the long 1950s to raise the exemption level. Remarkably, the Créditistes called for the exemption level to be raised to $5,000 a year.[15] Add the dependent child exemptions and, in effect, this was a proposal to end the mass-based income tax: the vast majority of married breadwinners with two children (each worth a further $250 deduction) had an income before taxes of less than $5,500 a year.[16]

The Créditistes' view was that of a largely working-class and rural population, and their complaints resembled those from other parts of rural and working-class Canada. For example, one of Créditiste MP Guy Marcoux's Montmorency county constituents wrote to the revenue minister, cc'd to Marcoux, to complain about the inability of working men to deduct employment expenses from their taxable incomes, an issue that had been raised across the country.[17] As Marcoux, though himself an educated man, said, "the traditional parties give you the feeling that they live on a high sphere of their own – that they are talking down to the people, whereas in our case we spring from the people, talk their language, live with them and understand them."[18] In relation to tax politics, it's worth noting that, according to Maurice Pinard's study of the experiential roots of Créditiste ideology, income tax grievances corresponded even more strongly than did economic status to membership in the party.[19] That the Créditistes were a populist formation is well known. My point here is that the tax issues that many Canadians thought about and worried about in the long 1950s were threaded through their policies. The success of the Créditistes gave voice to that part of Canadian tax culture that saw taxes as one of the burdens carried not by the economic engines of production but by consuming households. Whether by miners' wives in Sullivan Mines, Quebec, or by an Acadian potato farmer with twenty-three children, the Créditistes were seen as defenders against a tax state that did not understand the sacrifices and virtues of the self-reliant poor.[20]

They were not alone in their concerns. More urban and educated Canadians shared a similarly moralized hostility to the personal income tax, with an anti-statist inflection. One of these was A. Kenneth Eaton, a former assistant deputy minister of finance. I have seen no clearer description of anti–welfare state views and anti–graduated income taxation than the one that he provided in his *Essays in Taxation,* published in 1966, just after his death.[21] The son of a Nova Scotia farm family, Eaton had served nearly five years in the First World War and had twice been wounded in action. Later he earned a PhD in economics at Harvard University, and in 1934 he had been hired as a tax expert for the Department of Finance. He had served as the department's chief tax expert through the period of complex policy making that followed, until he retired in May 1958, when he was sixty-three.[22] His voice in the department's internal correspondence had an ironic, humorous toughness. In his essays, this tone reveals unmistakably that this was a man fed up with hypocrisy. The family allowance policy was particularly a focus of his contempt. It was nothing more, to him, than a means of buying votes from the majority with money collected primarily from a minority.[23]

Eaton accepted that the state had an obligation to help the needy: for instance, allowances for "disabled persons" and "blind persons" seemed to him to be "good and proper legislation" about which "no one should complain."[24] And he thought that a reasonable rich man should agree that he could pay more in taxes than could most, and, if paying the same percentage of his income, and therefore more dollars, he willingly would. But Eaton also did some electoral math and argued that, once his hypothetical rich man agreed to that deal, he was "on the skids" toward progressive rates, under which he would be paying "a whole lot more." For "the majority," there was no reason to restrain public spending because, on balance, even if they paid some income tax, they always got "something for nothing." The family allowances, universal old age pensions after seventy, and hospital insurance were all driven by "pure political expediency" rather than noble ideals, in his view.[25] The universal programs infuriated Eaton. For him, making the masses tax conscious had not made them skeptical of public spending. Instead, becoming "taxpayers" had produced in more voters a sense of righteous entitlement: "Who today in the midst of this collectivist indoctrination fed down from the national government can really blame anybody for deciding that the smart thing to do is to collect as much as possible? After all[,] he can say that he is paying the taxes."[26]

Eaton had played a unique role in developing Canada's federal tax system, but he wasn't its biggest fan. In his hostility to the welfare state and his skepticism about the morality and justice of progressive income taxation, he was a voice of his generation. A survivor of world wars and the Depression, an ironist rather than an idealist, Eaton spoke for those of his generation who believed that a man's struggle to survive and provide was a means of improving his character and founding self-respect rather than, for many, an unfair and likely unwinnable fight against implacable, impersonal forces. (Whether he had views on women as citizens is unclear.) Eaton represented those who saw only moral hazard – the promise of something for nothing – in universal suffrage and a progressive-rate income tax.[27] Those who know Canadian social work history will recognize that Eaton was to tax reform what Charlotte Whitton was to the modern welfare state: on the losing side of public policy debates but not an isolated eccentric. Like Whitton, Eaton had been a modernizer in his day, but he would be seen as a traditionalist by the next generation. He died at age seventy in 1965, so he didn't speak in the debate on tax reform about to break open. However, in the conservative populist mobilization that emerged in 1969–71, voices like his would be loud and clear.

A conservative populist mobilization was already present well before 1969. It was launched by Canada's Chamber of Commerce in the months before the June 18, 1962, federal election. Beginning in February 1962, the chamber mounted a challenge to high taxes and the welfare state called Operation Freedom. Organized by leaders of big business, the chamber drew much of their authority from a broad base of local organizations. Speaking to that base, Operation Freedom used a distinctively grassroots kind of participatory tactic: the publicity listed seventeen things that individuals could do in their hometowns and daily lives, among them writing letters to politicians and newspapers. In this, they were possibly following the approach of the John Birch Society, known for this method of mobilizing its members.[28] The chamber's theme was the contest between free enterprise and socialism. Prime Minister Diefenbaker had declared this contest to be the issue on which the 1962 federal election would be fought. Needless to say, the chamber was on the side of free enterprise, along with Social Credit and the Tories.[29] They wanted to fight "the apathy and indifference of Canadians with respect to freedom."[30] The threat to free enterprise, according to Operation Freedom, lay in the provision of "too much security" to "individuals."[31] As one supporter put it, Operation Freedom was needed to counteract the "statist propaganda" that led to reliance on "more and more social welfare" and failure to understand that "welfare means higher taxation." Another enthusiast for the cause argued that "communist cells, newspapers and agents ... are working harder than ever to turn Canada into a Soviet dependency."[32]

Most likely they were worried about the recent alliance of the CCF and CLC to form the New Democratic Party (NDP). The thoroughly anticommunist NDP was not pleased at being red-baited. Prominent New Democrats and the leader of the Canadian Labour Congress charged the Chamber of Commerce with McCarthyism and Birchism. The chamber responded by pointing out, not all that reassuringly, that they had warned enthusiastic chamber members to leave to the RCMP the arresting of communists.[33] They urged the real need for their work by alleging that a Communist Party pamphlet called *The Road to Socialism* had "found its way into the hands of many of our school children." The chamber's pamphlets (*The Fallacies of Socialism*) and films (*The Story of Creative Capital*) were, in their view, essential countermeasures, to be deployed in the school system. Criticism from the parliamentary left and the labour movement did not deter the chamber. Their "Freedom Seminars" continued in February and March. However, in April, the Toronto Board of Trade, one of the chamber's biggest members, called Operation Freedom suitable only for "small towns" and "too naïve for larger communities" and its populist methods "objectionable."[34] Operation Freedom was sent back to the drawing board. The Toronto board shared the chamber's aim, its president said, but negative "publicity" had "exposed the organization to criticism."[35] Perhaps the Toronto board thought that the chamber was hurting the cause of free enterprise in the 1962 election more than helping it, if allegations of neo-fascism against the chamber were giving the NDP a cause.[36]

Although Operation Freedom was pulled from any role in the 1962 election campaign, it's not hard to see why the Chamber of Commerce might have expected, and in fact did receive, support for anti–welfare state rhetoric from Canadians unhappy with rising taxes and the increasing scope of social provision. For many lower-income Canadians, however, the chamber's claims that Canada's patchy welfare state was already providing "too much security" and that the threat of communism was a pressing danger would have been hard to believe. But Diefenbaker had heard in the chamber's campaign, in his constituents' letters, and in Social Credit rhetoric enough to think that tax reform could speak powerfully both to business and to struggling lower-income taxpayers, albeit in different ways.

Tax reform became "the main plank" in the 1962 Diefenbaker platform, and in presenting its merits he alluded to hardships and injustices suffered at the hands of the tax state by both poor (rural and otherwise) and rich (different hardships, different injustices).[37] His platform-launching speech promised a Royal Commission on Taxation that would "examine anomalies in the existing laws, consider inequitable tax burdens, close loopholes that now existed and ease hardships now caused by some tax laws."[38] Canadians who loathed rich tax dodgers and thought that exemptions were too low could have heard that message as aimed at them. Tax practitioners and their clients who worried that capital gains were not reliably protected would also have heard an appealing promise. Accounts that have depicted Diefenbaker as pushed by a Bay Street businessman into launching tax reform suggest something more hidden and with a narrower appeal than the actual use to which the PCs put tax reform promises in the 1962 election.[39]

The PCs won that election, albeit with a minority. Facing a challenge from the Créditistes on their right flank, they made heavy use of populist pitches aimed at fear and suspicion of elites. They presented themselves as decentralizers, lightening the Ottawa yoke by returning some control over income taxation to the provinces. They talked about "shadowy" economic advisers whose arcane ideas secretly shaped Liberal policies. And they appealed directly to those who saw Liberals as income tax–crazed spenders. Diefenbaker and Fleming repeatedly threatened that the Liberals' spending plans would raise "personal income taxes" by 30–40 percent, or 50 percent, or even 60 percent.[40] In all of these moves, the PCs were responding to the presence of the Social Credit on the right, making an appeal to an anti-statist element in the electorate. After the election shouting had stopped, the Social Credit/Créditiste Party had gained nine seats and held the balance of power in the House of Commons. It must have seemed to the PCs that their legislative support would likely come from the Socreds/Créditistes, in common cause against threats to free enterprise. But they proved to be unreliable allies: less than a year later, in the winter of 1963, the Socreds and Créditistes voted with the Liberals to defeat Diefenbaker's PCs.

Modernism Meets Populism

The royal commission on which Diefenbaker had placed so much weight in 1962 began its work in 1963 and produced a major challenge to the normal ways of doing tax policy business. The story of the Carter Commission is well known in tax law circles and, perhaps to a lesser extent, among political scientists and economists. There is even a dramatic popular treatment of it by journalist Linda McQuaig. It's not that difficult to imagine casting a Hollywood movie about its modernist hope and political tragedy. Its chair, prominent and public-spirited accountant Kenneth Carter, would play a man ready to make his mark but doomed, by reason of his optimism and integrity (tragic virtues rather than tragic flaws), to an Icarus-like fall. J. Harvey Perry, an economist and a former member of the Department of Finance plucked from a plum job in the Canadian Bankers' Association, would appear as Carter's right-hand man, and like Carter he would face a deep struggle with old loyalties (not least to the Department of Finance) as he formed new convictions. In 1974, Perry went on to help organize the Canadian Foundation for Economic Education, inspired, one can only imagine, by what he had learned about Canadians' low level of economic literacy during and after the Carter Commission hearings.

If movies were better at managing complexity, then there could be a third lead. Jack Stewart, the commission's counsel, was also forced to resolve challenges to the common sense of his home community – the tax law practitioners of corporate Toronto. The movie would provide opportunities for many small but juicy roles: the dissenters (Nova Scotia trust company lawyer Donald Grant and the Quebec representative, tax accountant Émile Beauvais); the farmer, Charles Walls (whose sector had once championed taxation of income); and the silent representative of women's organizations, "housewife" and accountant Eleanor Milne (what *was* she thinking as she sat quietly during the commission hearings?). Knowing Hollywood, the Best Supporting Actor Oscar would have gone to the actor who played the brilliant, idealistic, and perhaps politically naive young research director, economist Douglas Hartle, who championed the commission's final goal – to replace a doddering tax system shaped by political tactics, expedience, and two decades of litigation with one that made economic and administrative sense.[41] The nub of the plot would be the modernist men of economic science in white hats, cleaning up the fiscal chaos caused by the black-hatted politicians and tax practitioners.

The commission's mandate was broad. The commissioners were to investigate the incidence and effects of taxation (excepting the tariff), not just on individuals, but also on every aspect of the economy, including Canadian ownership. They were to aim at devising ways to achieve "greater clarity, simplicity and effectiveness" in the administration of Canadian taxation. They were not to investigate provincial and municipal taxation in detail, but in considering the "distribution of [tax] burdens" they were to take into account the "jurisdiction and practices" of these other governments.[42] In their final report, the politics of federalism was relegated to a very un-Canadian minor role.[43] From their work came a blueprint for tax reform. It was highly consistent internally, based upon expert scientific economics research, and informed by the best of modern tax theory. The solutions that they devised to apparently intractable problems such as surplus stripping, family-based tax avoidance, and abuse of the small business tax rate were driven by the right principles – fairness, such that tax obligation would clearly match the economic position of the taxpayer, and neutrality, such that no particular kind of economic activity would be privileged or discouraged. Key measures in light of these principles would be to eliminate elaborate differentiations among kinds of income and remove the usefulness of the family as a tax dodge. The hope was that the particular reforms that followed from these principles would simplify and make less uncertain the processes of paying and collecting taxes. The reforms would allow top rates to be lowered because previously exempt forms of income, most importantly capital gains, would be taxed but at not so high a rate on top incomes. At the same time, the reformed system would lighten the burden on the poor in a variety of ways, including a larger personal exemption.[44]

What actually happened once the Carter report was released for discussion in February 1967 was that some of the special interests to which he had referred – notably mining firms – effectively managed to use the threat of a capital strike to halt changes that would have cost them money.[45] And, from a variety of corners, people rose to defend their investment strategies by objecting to the proposed taxation of capital gains. Small businesses also objected loudly to the proposed end to their lower corporate tax rate, which unfortunately had also been used as a tax dodge by larger businesses (pretending to be a cluster of smaller ones). In the commission's report, the two dissenting commissioners sketched some of the lines of critique. Both emphasized that the proposed methods for taxing capital gains would tax them more heavily than either the United States or the United Kingdom did.[46] A year after the report was tabled in the House of Commons, Carter told the Law School at the University of Chicago that he was still hopeful for tax reform in spite of "noisy and strong" opposition from "special interests." He believed that his committee's recommendations fit with the new majority Liberal government's commitment to a "Just Society."[47] The new Liberal government was led by a university professor, Pierre Trudeau, someone who disliked the old prejudices of Canadian politics and wanted to see public institutions meet new social scientific standards of effectiveness.[48] But one senior Liberal, unhappy with the flood of critical comment to which the Carter report had exposed his party, grumped that he'd never seen why a public process such as a royal commission was necessary. Surely, he muttered to a friend, taxation was "the one subject on which Governments and Parliaments should make up their own minds."[49] But more public consultation, rather than less, was to come.

  During 1968 and 1969, Department of Finance officials developed a new package of tax reform proposals, designed, like the Carter recommendations, to broaden the base of taxable income, provide relief to lower incomes, achieve greater tax neutrality, and close loopholes. In November 1969, they launched the new proposals in a ninety-six-page booklet, the red and white of its cover referencing the still-new Canadian maple leaf flag.[50] The package was summarized in five lucid pages, but there was lots of room for discussion. Would the proposed method for treating capital gains as taxable income produce a tax obligation where there was no "real" income? Would removing the special lower rate for small businesses be adequately replaced by other kinds of support? Would the raised amounts of exempt personal income really meet the needs of the lower-income cohorts for relief, without adding intolerably to the obligations of the larger lower-middle class? Were there industries that depended on tax-exempt larger expense accounts to recruit talent or to find a market for their services? Did the proposed change in tax treatment of oil and mining enterprises threaten the viability of a regionally important sector?[51] Over the next twenty months, until his tax reform budget of June 1971, but with particular intensity in the nine months after the White Paper's launch, Finance Minister Edgar J. ("Ben") Benson engaged all comers on these and other questions concerning the proposals in a debate that he and the prime minister would call an exercise in participatory democracy.[52]

This framing of public consultation as participatory democracy was a particularly 1960s thing to do. The novelty was not that a government was seeking public comment on tax policy. In 1918, Sir Thomas White had sought and received advice from the public on how to pay for the war. The Tariff Commission of 1920 had sought and received public comment, well informed or not, on how to change the tariff. The Rowell-Sirois Commission had heard from a host of civil society organizations in its attempt to revise the fiscal structure of federalism. During the Second World War, J.L. Ilsley had received lots of letters from the public, and he and Department of Finance staff had engaged in a dialogue with many of those writers. But the attempt by Benson and his department to engage the public in tax policy conversation in 1969 took place in a different context. By the 1960s, the fact of universal suffrage was firmly established. In addition, public opinion was now knowable in a more inclusive way, or so it seemed, through polling data. And the ideals of democratic government had been confirmed in wartime and developed in peacetime in ways that gave community life a more genuinely democratic character than it had had before the 1930s. The emergence of a mass labour movement is the most well known of these developments, but democratic culture at the community level had flourished in the 1950s. A foundation for the popular mobilizations of the 1960s had already been laid. When Benson called for citizen participation in November 1969, he was speaking to a nation whose people expected to be heard.

The other important change in the context of his attempt at fostering citizen engagement was the greater importance of social science, particularly macroeconomics, in tax talk. The intervenors in the 1920s Tariff Commission testified based upon their partial (in both senses) experience of business conditions or household budgets rather than as researchers. The Rowell-Sirois Commission, in contrast, employed trained researchers and affirmed a preference for objective economics as the basis for tax policy. The commissioners disparaged normal tax policy as having been too much determined by "politics" (both ideology and partisan manoeuvring). But they could only express a hope for research-based tax law: their pioneering production of research on the Canadian economy provided the foundation for a new kind of fiscal policy, but they lacked modern data. By the 1960s, Canada had developed a system of national accounts and a body of economic data (though still less developed than that available for the

United Kingdom and United States) that gave economics a central place in tax conversations.[53] With both social science and the ideal of the people's voice emerging as prestigious policy languages, the 1960s brought a new dynamic to politics and policy.[54] In the work of the Carter Commission and subsequent political mobilizations, we see modern social science and the people's voice, that icon of populism, speeding toward each other on a crash course.

The populist response to the White Paper equalled the fury of the Progressive farmers on the protective tariff, the Depression-era municipal tax resisters, and the disaffected letter writers of the 1950s. It also borrowed from their themes – rural against urban, poor against rich, anti-statists against state builders, provincial rights defenders against centralizers, and more. There were community meetings, television debates, ad hoc committees of the House and Senate, and of course floods of letters. At the end of it all, the tax reform measures in the budget of June 1971 seemed to be anticlimatically small: one pithy summary offered in 1972 was that the tax reform process had "aimed for the Moon and landed somewhere near the United States."[55]

Political scientists, economists, journalists, working and retired politicians, and tax law specialists have all written accounts of this process. All agree that, between Mitchell Sharp's tabling of the Carter report in the House on February 24, 1967, and the delivery by his successor, Ben Benson, of a landmark budget in 1971, tax reform had gone from a sleekly modern, coherent package to a rather muddled shadow of its former self, usually described as "watered down." Some have regarded this as more or less the inevitable result of proposals insensitive to political and social contexts and ill suited to secure a broad consensus.[56] Many have considered this a loss, having seen in the Carter blueprint the possibility not only of a remedy for glaring grievances, such as high tax rates and widespread avoidance by those supposed to pay them, but also the promise of more Canadian control and Canadian ownership in economic life and a better-supported welfare state.[57] In 1967, the *Toronto Telegram* had said that "no measure made law in the last decade of the welfare state in Canada will bring true social democracy closer than implementation of all the basic recommendations of the Carter Royal Commission on Taxation."[58] For those who most regret the loss, blame typically attaches to some equivalent of business or capital or special interests and the tax professionals who worked for them.[59] The NDP made good electoral use of this analysis in the 1972 federal election, in which they convinced quite a few voters that opponents of the Carter recommendations and the White Paper proposals were worse leeches on the public purse ("corporate welfare bums") than any unemployed worker or single mother.[60]

In this account, though much is incontrovertible fact, we do not see what a longer historical view can tell us about the significance of that process. Over the period since 1920, there had been a slow incorporation into tax negotiations of the voices of a diverse mass electorate. Over the same period, there was also the development of social science, with the increasing prestige of economics and, with it, more data gathering and analysis of statistical descriptions of debt, production, interest, money supply, and employment – the whole apparatus of national accounting.[61] Both phenomena – the mass electorate and the emergence of the economy as the object of science – are part of what is broadly understood as social modernity. One element of modernity was a confidence in the power of science to yield such solid truth about the social world that political life could be cleansed of violent clashes of ideology. For instance, when Trudeau wrote about a federalism that would be "functional" and rise above the old cultural divisions, he was applying this kind of modernist mindset to Canadian constitutionalism.[62] Understandable as a response to the hatreds of the interwar years, and admirable in its humanism, this perspective was itself an ideology. Trudeau's antipathy to Québécois nationalism was typical of this ideology in his disparaging of particular social identities as parochial and prone to extremism.

But parochial identities could not be wished away. The mass electorate opened up possibilities for both left-wing and right-wing populisms, antimodernist phenomena that could be either a resource to political elites or a challenge to their control of politics. On questions of public finance, electoral pressures from widely popular, supposedly commonsense currents in the 1920s and 1930s had helped to drive support for graduated income taxation and opposition to sales taxation. Those populist forces had helped the King Liberals during the 1920s. During the 1930s, the Social Credit movement, the CCF, and the National Government people had given voice to a populist style of anti-politician talk and had tried (with some success at the provincial level) to take control of governments away from the usual political classes, describing them as a self-interested minority. During the war, the federal government had attempted to persuade the mass electorate to join the men of the state in the move to macroeconomics, with some success. By means of public service advertising and ministerial speeches, the Department of Finance urged Canadians to see their personal choices as tightly linked to macroeconomic phenomena. Yet, at the end of the 1960s, there was still a big gap between the tax vocabulary of economists, senior civil servants, and cabinet ministers, on the one hand, and that of most of the voting public, on the other. When Finance Minister Benson invited the public to step up as citizens and weigh in on the tax reform proposals of 1969 – proposals calculated to benefit, on balance, the majority of taxpayers – he was a bit taken aback by the volume of fear and anger that he heard in response. In the transition from the Carter Commission's smooth modernism to the Rube Goldberg contraption of the 1971 budget, the White Paper consultations showed how demanding the labours of participatory democracy would be for the politicians who faced the conflict between social scientific planning and populist currents of mass democracy.

The Voice of the People

The source through which I have explored that exercise in participatory democracy is the ocean of letters that deluged the minister of finance and his colleagues after publication of the White Paper. Some observers outside the government at the time discounted these letters as hysterical. Political scientist Leslie Macdonald relied on a few such comments to dismiss most opposition to the White Paper proposals as coming from ill-informed people misled by anti-reform experts.[63] Seen in a longer historical context, however, the contents of those letters must be taken more seriously as a reliable source of public opinion, both against and for the White Paper proposals. And, like tax opinion in general, as I have shown in this context, the framing of interest and identity was varied and more interesting than just a simple assertion of narrow self-interest.

Letters from the public had long played a role in tax policy making. This was still the case in the 1950s and 1960s, as Finance Minister Fleming explained in his memoirs. Within Finance, he recalled, files were kept on "Budget Proposals from the Public."[64] A selection of the letters contained in these files was assembled every year in a large binder (called "The Black Book") circulated among officials from Finance and National Revenue, and, as budget preparation meetings began in February for budgets to be delivered in April or May, these letters provided part of the material for the deliberations.[65] Having read many of those letters, I can testify that the special pleading and predictable, often extreme rhetoric in them can be tiresome. It is unlikely that anyone in Finance ever got a new idea solely from these letters. Finance Minister Mitchell Sharp described them as a mixture of "interest, amusement, and boredom."[66] However, as a mirror of public opinion or, more precisely, of the beliefs and values of multiple publics, this big black book of budget proposals was at least as useful as poll results and, in one way, more so. The letter writers were not passive respondents to preframed questions but people describing public finance problems in their own terms. This was therefore a richer, thicker source of information about public opinion than any poll could provide. When former finance ministers (and former tax officials, in the case of Ken Eaton) mentioned the role of these letters in speeches about the budget process, they told Canadians that there was a mechanism by which their voices were heard. The inflexibility and secrecy of the parliamentary budget procedures in Canada made the writing of letters to finance ministers a particularly meaningful avenue of influence.

Compared with letters written to prewar finance ministers, those written about the White Paper to Finance alone between November 1969 and September 1970 are remarkable for their sheer number. There were 15,194 of them.[67] In addition, Sharp's papers include thousands of letters. The archival papers of House Finance Committee Chair and chair of the July 1970 hearings Alastair Gillespie also contain abundant letters. Some of them were cries of rage, others effusions of gratitude, and many full of fascinating details about household budgets and life stories.[68] By April 1970, the finance ministry had to staff a special correspondence unit to catch up with the backlog of unanswered mail. All of the letters sent to Finance received replies, many of them substantial (albeit often composed from a bank of standard paragraphs).[69] In addition, the ministry was deluged by coupons clipped from newspaper ads. Even these coupons were individually acknowledged, and the substance of the campaign from which they sprang was addressed in a letter supplied to MPs to distribute in their constituencies.[70] The anti–White Paper campaign aimed at the mass electorate was taken seriously, and television and magazine responses to counter that campaign were quickly deployed. It is true that relatively few private citizens and, especially, few supporters of the Benson reforms addressed the parliamentary committees' meetings during July 1970, which prompted accusations of an elite-biased process, then and later. But their absence from the committee sessions does not mean that they were silent or ignored. The Liberals sought the views of the public, and the public responded.[71] The letters that individual citizens sent to politicians, and the associated avalanche of coupons, amounted to a roar of public opinion.

The content of that roar would have been entirely recognizable to Benson and others who had been engaged in constituency politics during the 1940s, 1950s, and early 1960s. After November 1969, when Benson first called on national television for people to tell him what they thought about the White Paper proposals, a great array of voices spoke up from across a wide spectrum of social positions and from ideologies that included both non-socialist collectivisms and individualists among the working class. Important voices within the Liberal Party, such as MPs Barnett Danson and Robert Kaplan, worked with Benson's staff to try to address a complicated public whose concerns were not just about the pocketbook. Other loyalties and anxieties also factored into views on tax reform.[72] In calculating political cost, the tax reformers had a more complicated political task ahead of them than simply mediating between two positions, "left" and "right" or "the people" and "big business."

Of course, that straightforward left populist framing of the issue did appear in the letters and in the currents of organization inspired by the Carter Commission. In 1967 and 1968, organized labour had been active in attempts to support implementation of the Carter recommendations. While the CLC provided carefully thought-out, nuanced support in its detailed response to the commission report, the slogan disseminated to members was "if you are an ordinary wage or salary earner then the Carter Report is for you!"[73] When, by December 1967, CLC leaders had come to the conclusion that Finance Minister Sharp had decided to reject the Carter approach, they organized a letter-writing campaign to point out that Sharp was choosing the special business interests over the people.[74] For the CLC's Citizenship Month topic of 1968 (in February, as was usual), they chose taxation as the theme, continuing the effort to defend the hope that they had seen in the Carter Commission that taxation would no longer be driving lower-income earners into poverty while the well-to-do escaped paying the nominally high rates. During the peak of the White Paper debate, the topic of Citizenship Month was not taxation again but social policy. However, workers' taxpayer identity was featured. The briefing materials pointed out that the Trudeau government had introduced a 2 percent "social development" surtax on income capped at a tax payment of $120, so that it fell disproportionately on incomes under $6,000 ($41,387 in 2016). They also pointed out that social programs were not "free stuff," as Trudeau had allegedly said, but benefits for which workers as taxpayers had already paid. The CLC leaders objected to having a new income tax burden land disproportionately on the lower end of the income scale.[75] In the period leading up to and after the White Paper, the main Canadian labour centre had presented a clear class analysis of tax reform, and it had a populist tinge – good guys and bad guys and simple choices.

That voice appeared in the White Paper letters, though not noticeably from unionists. "The rich" appear in these letters mainly as enjoyers of loopholes and of high living on expense accounts.[76] One woman noted that her factory worker husband and she had barely enough to live on while salesmen and farmers sometimes had two cars.[77] Another noted that he had voted for the "just society" and that the combination of raising the personal exemptions and taxing capital gains was a sign that the Liberals were delivering on their promise. He expected that big business would put up a fight, but he believed that the proposed measures would help those with incomes under $6,000, "most Canadians."[78] One keen Liberal pointed out that even the NDP voters he had talked with liked the combination of higher exemptions and taxation of capital gains.[79] As protest against the White Paper got louder in February 1970, one correspondent urged Benson to see protest as a sign that he was doing the right thing, cutting into the incomes of the rich and raising up the resources of the poor.[80] The narrative of a battle joined against a privileged, morally suspect elite was part of the language in which people supported the White Paper. The outrage was proper: federal taxation had been implicated in the hardships of the poor. But the elements of sometimes vitriolic anger, envy, and simply drawn sides were the hallmarks of a populist politics.

Whereas some of the class-focused letters blended proper anger at unfairness with elements of personally felt envy, another voice that used a loose vocabulary of class was animated by unselfish compassion. These letters provided a refreshing note of real generosity. They came from people like Agnes Roulston of East York, who listed off as virtues of the White Paper taxing capital gains, closing expense account loopholes, raising exemptions, and encouraging Canadian industry and investment. Her own income tax obligation would go up, she said, but if her higher taxes meant reduced poverty then those taxes would be well justified.[81] Mr. and Mrs. Dieter Raatz noted that his pay increase the next year would be "swallowed up" by their increased taxes, but they found that to be just when capital gains were to be taxed.[82] One housewife pointed out that her husband's taxes would increase a bit but exclaimed that Benson's White Paper was "the greatest thing in taxes yet!"[83] It is often said that no one likes to pay taxes, but these supporters of tax reform were pretty enthusiastic about the value in help for the poor that their extra tax payments promised. Their letters give few hints about what had led these individuals in particular to regard their higher tax bills with moral satisfaction. But a palpable relief was recognizable in their belief that, finally, the burdens of the tax system on the poor were going to be lifted. The emotions that they expressed were more morally appealing than fear and anger, but their letters were simple and not deeply reasoned. These writers weren't speaking as experts. Yet the emotional generosity of their responses marks them off from the natural audience of populist politics, in which fear and anger predominate.

Most often the letters to Benson, Sharp, and Gillespie emphasized their authors' narrow personal interests. The focus was usually Benson's attempt to remove some of the tax privileges for corporate and capital gains income. But even among the self-interestedly angry opponents of the White Paper proposals, interestingly, there were ideas and emotions that went beyond special pleading and Cold War hysteria about creeping socialism (though both were present). Dislike of the personal income tax was often presented as part of a worry about the cost of living. Present in the long 1950s, that worry had only intensified. Gallup polls in 1966 and 1967 positioned high taxes along with inflation as among the top five problems facing Canada or among the main criticisms of the federal government. In the summer of 1967, a Gallup poll that puckishly asked an open-ended question about the "worst things about living in Canada" found that the high cost of living, inflation, high taxes, and government extravagance, bundled together in positions one and two, got 30 percent of the "votes." The festering "national unity" question trailed far behind at 6 percent.[84] Pocketbook politics was foundational to tax talk.

But blended intimately with pocketbook terms were also worries and beliefs not simply about the discomforts of a tight household budget. Some of the populist tax critique came from places that we might not recognize today as locations of a particular tax standpoint. For example, the Canadian Protestant League's (CPL) representations to the Carter Commission called for an end to the tax exemptions enjoyed by Catholic clergy. This problem of tax fairness now seems to be a quaint relic of nineteenth-century sectarianism. But ultra-Protestantism was not yet dead or politically inert in the mid-1960s. Since 1957, the CPL had been helping to fuel the attack on charitable deduction fraud in Quebec, and its representative to the Carter Commission in 1963 had been the mayor of Toronto eight years previously and in 1969 was still successful in metropolitan Toronto politics. The thousands of city people who voted for him knew that they were voting for a militant ultra-Protestant. As political identities, Protestantism and Catholicism were important to older Canadians, and there existed specifically Protestant positions on some matters of income taxation.[85]

As Benson would have appreciated much more clearly than the Carter Commission, such positions were part of tax policy's political terrain. With such forces in play, the range of political effects of particular tax reforms was beyond what any abstract counting of the dollar consequences could predict. What Finance Minister Sir Thomas White had said of the tariff in the 1910s was also true of the income tax – that it was "a jungle and that no one could tell when he threw a stone into its recesses what animal he might rouse up."[86] Religion was only one of those strange animals – there were many other tax reform standpoints that combined personal identities and tax interests with great intensity. A brisk and bloodless summary of some of these standpoints was produced by tax policy director F.I. Irwin for his colleague J.R. Brown during the heat of the White Paper debate. That list included artists, amputees, the mentally ill and their families, students, people living in the North, foster parents, First Nations, female professionals, firefighters, and parents of young children.[87] In tax politics, these were not simply people with economic interests or politically charged personal identities. Both were compelling, but interests and identities, when combined inseperably, were an intensely emotional mix, ripe for populist politics.

Exemplifying this mix were small business owners, who offered frequent objections to the White Paper. They had an obvious material interest in opposing the White Paper's proposed removal of the lower tax rate for the first $35,000 of corporate income. Many believed, perhaps too pessimistically, that the taxation of capital gains and the loss of the preferential rate would "sound the death knell of most small businesses."[88] However, some of their letters revealed commitments more heartfelt and sympathetic than simple special pleading for a narrow self-interest. For example, Betty L. Frantz created and circulated a petition in a letter in which she argued that the impact of the reformed tax system would be not only "economic" but also "sociological." "Be big or get out!" is how she described the social change that she feared. Small corner drugstores, local dress shops, and independent service stations were among the businesses whose owners signed her petition, she wrote. Without the protections that the Canadian tax system provided to them, they feared that only big businesses, "monopolies" as she put it, would survive.[89] Both in her tactics and in her views on tax systems, there was a strain of collectivism, one reminiscent of the Progressive era. Annie Thompson, a widow supporting her six children with "modest" investments in real estate, was worried about how she would manage if some of her income from those properties went to higher taxes. She was proud of how she had achieved "independence" through the exercise of her "brains and energy" and saw, in the threat to her income, a lack of respect for the effort that she had made.[90] She was a proud individualist, to be sure, but at a time when individualism wasn't readily claimed by women her letter doesn't read simply as a defence of privilege. Family duty also imparted emotional force to the arguments of many of the men who wrote from a small business position. One man, clearly feeling stressed by having taken big risks in borrowing to expand his business and having had to spend his disposable income on insurance premiums to protect his seven children and wife, worried that his father's legacy to him, the trucking business, would not be passed on to his sons.[91] His concern about taxes cutting into his business's success undoubtedly reflected a desire for success and security, but he and others who wrote that they were "frightened, angry, and frustrated" also expressed their feelings as fathers.[92] Letters such as these from small business owners made it clear to tax reformers that small business ownership was not just an economic interest but also a personal identity "as sacrosanct as motherhood" – or fatherhood – for some Canadians in the late 1960s.[93]

Probably the most powerful of the non-business communities engaged in tax reform questions was the elderly. They brought to the critique of the capital gains tax, or to the small tax increases on lower-middle-class incomes, a generational experience that took their special pleading to a more morally appealing and emotionally touching level. This was the group that we might think of as "the twentieth-century generation" – those born within a few years of 1900 and thus in their late sixties or early seventies during this debate. These Canadians had a powerful generational identity, cited again and again in their letters to politicians. Here was the litany: "We lived through two world wars, the great depression, and now ... galloping inflation."[94] Some prided themselves on having saved in spite of these obstacles, whereas others argued that their historical bad luck entitled them to public support. Even those who had come through it all with some savings of their own were aware that inflation was an impersonal force that put them in a position similar to that of less provident pensioners. The latter depended on a public pension whose value had been steadily shrinking in relation to prices, and the thrifty savers were seeing their comfortable living decline into a subsistence one.[95]

Some pensioners took this socio-economic insight in a left-wing direction, organizing as Pensioners Concerned and extending their movement in support of all low-income taxpayers.[96] Others found in their generation's narrative a reason to reiterate the pre-Keynesian bywords of their youth – that Canada could do with fewer provincial governments, that politicians were too richly paid, that government printing costs were excessive, and that bureaucracies had expanded beyond reason.[97] This anti-statism was a variant of liberalism. But this was not simply an individualist ideology. Indeed, as Mill argued in *Principles of Political Economy*, keeping the state small was a condition of a successfully self-organized civil society – a society that could oversee the always-suspect state.[98] Members of the twentieth-century generation were the sons and daughters of Victorians, and through the power of organized numbers they mobilized as pensioners from 1969 to 71.[99] Through them, the "limited state" language of Mill, Gladstone, and "Clear Grit" George Brown was powerful in the White Paper debates.

That ancient ideology came into conflict with the economics that underpinned the White Paper and for many letter writers complicated the problem of knowing their own interests clearly and confidently. Even economics, supposedly objective, could arouse anxiety. Ministers of finance told the public not to worry about the expanding state. They pointed to the long trend of prosperity since the war and argued that the expansion of social programs, along with other public spending, had contributed to everyone's good fortune. Moreover, countercyclical management of demand and its accompanying public debt were producing price stability.[100] Unfortunately for public confidence, not all economists agreed. As recently as 1961, in the Coyne affair, differences about how to manage the economy had led to a highly public and political spat in which a group of academic economists asserted publicly that James Coyne, governor of the Bank of Canada, was incompetent. They disagreed deeply with his view that "sound money" – fighting inflation – was a top priority. Reading the press about Coyne and monetary policy might well have left non-experts worried about whether inflation was a serious problem or how it might be addressed.[101] Like Coyne's critics, both the Carter commissioners and the White Paper authors "took a cavalier attitude" about inflation.[102] But in 1967 one of the Carter report's academic fans, Harvard University economist Richard Musgrave, wrote that he felt "uneasiness" about "the Report's lack of concern for distinguishing inflationary from real capital gains."[103] There were mixed messages.

When it came to the role of inflation, many of the letter writers shared Musgrave's concern. As the inflation rate began to rise in 1967, these concerns grew and were difficult to allay. Although the relationship between inflation and capital gains taxation was an immediate concern only to people with substantial savings and fairly valuable houses, such property owners found allies among working-class families for whom the destructive impact of inflation had been a painful reality for many years. As one autoworker wrote to Finance Minister Fleming in 1957, "inflation is a plague to all of us. It corrodes the value of our dollar and makes it hard to save to buy anything."[104] For less-well-paid workers, the concern was not the erosion of a savable surplus but the taxing of subsistence-level income.[105] While suffering from the impact of inflation, they'd had to listen to successive finance ministers, from Harris in the early 1950s through to Sharp and Benson in the mid-1960s, speak of tax increases as a means of reducing inflation.[106] The notion that taxation might improve "the economy" yet make it harder to make ends meet in a particular household was hard to digest.

A case in point was made in 1955 by Harvey Perry concerning anti-inflationary taxes on major appliances and cars during the Korean War years. These commodity taxes were introduced to "mop up excess purchasing power." As Perry observed,

> this of course is an expression which all economists can understand, but the unfortunate truth is that economists represent a tiny segment of the buying public. Not one housewife in a thousand would admit to having "excess purchasing power." And not one in ten thousand could be persuaded that there is the remotest connection between the defence effort and her purchase of a needed washing machine or stove which the Government has permitted to be manufactured and put on sale. Least of all can she understand why a government running a very substantial

surplus feels it necessary to levy a stiff tax that puts some essential article beyond her reach.[107]

Perry wondered whether the use of taxation for macroeconomic purposes could be successful if the general public did not understand the relevant economic theory. He suspected not.[108] He was probably right to think that lectures in economics did not reach many voters.

Although it was good macroeconomic theory, the power of taxation to curb inflation was observable only in large data sets assembled and interpreted by economists. For voters and letter writers, to understand how inflation was relevant to their self-interest as taxpayers meant relying on experience. For many Canadians who lived on modest incomes, it was irritating to be told that higher taxes would reduce prices when they had seen no lowering or even stabilizing of their grocery bills to compensate for their increasing tax obligations. As the clerk of Kingston township wrote to his MP, Benson, in November 1967, "I am sure you do not need us to tell you that one of the top contributors to the high cost of living is high taxes at all levels, Federal, Provincial, and Municipal." He acknowledged that raising taxes was supposed to inhibit inflation but insisted that there must be some other way. "Regardless of what the experts tell Mr. Sharp, taxpayers cannot afford any more taxes."[109] To expect that people struggling to make ends meet would trust the wisdom of inflation-fighting policies that cost them even a few dollars was to expect them to place a considerable level of trust in the authority of macroeconomics. Furthermore, that authority was openly contested within the world of public finance and macroeconomics. Upset voters implored Benson not to implement policies that went against the advice of "recognized experts."[110] That there were competing experts only further compromised lower-income voters' trust in the tax policy world that had allowed inflation to produce "bracket creep" and taxation of the poor. Now they were being asked to accept that the rising values of their houses would be protected from the proposed capital gains tax. But with the mechanism of the protection being a cap, a specific dollar value on the house sale, opponents of the Benson reforms could easily persuade even middle-class people that one day, in an inflation-ballooned real estate market, that cap wouldn't protect them from big tax bills on the capital gains realized from selling their houses.[111] Uncertainty about inflation combined with the intense importance of houses as personal property made many enemies of the proposed taxation of capital gains.

Interests are not simply rational calculations: the pocketbook motive gives heat and force to tax talk, but other fuels are mixed in and make flames of varied colours. Family, independence, ideas of the state, class compassion, consumption envy, fear and pride of home ownership, and sectarian suspicions are just some of the aspects of the "self" in self-interest visible in the great tax debate of 1970. Not all of these emotions are morally appealing. But many of them are useful to democracy. The notion of the ideal political citizen as merely a reasoner, floating Vulcan-like on an objective plane above identity, has been valuably critiqued by historian William Katerberg in an essay on nativism. He points to the ideal of the dispassionate citizen, contrasted to nativist particularity, as existing only in abstraction. He shows that the real liberal democratic citizen made in twentiethth-century Canada and the United States had to be trained and inculcated with pride in the Greco-Roman classics, loyalty to the Christian (usually Protestant) tradition, and a proper, never extreme, level of emotional expressiveness in public life. The organizations designed to train immigrants from non-Anglo-Protestant cultures to be properly Canadian demonstrated the parochialism of this particular and supposedly universal set of values and demeanours. While not exonerating nativism of its violent forms, Katerberg draws our attention to the social good served by passionate commitments to particular cultures and identities and the loss to democracy in failing to consider what is honourable in any such commitment.[112] In response to Rawls's conception of the means toward justice, political philosophers have developed this point extensively. An inclusive democracy, in which people can be effectively involved in decision making that matters to them, must integrate passions of many kinds in constructive ways. In her discussion of this literature, philosopher Cheryl Hall concludes that "deliberation requires both thinking carefully and caring thoughtfully."[113]

The passions of selfishness, greed, and envy have nothing to recommend them. But neither the businessperson's creative ambition nor the outraged suffering of the poor must be reduced to these morally lesser forms. When some aspect of a tax system needlessly impedes a productive business vision, the passion for the business enterprise rightly makes its agents angry with that aspect of the system. When someone struggles against heavy odds just to pay for groceries, why would that person or compassionate friends not be properly outraged at others who carelessly enjoy comfort or consume in great luxury? Anger at politicians' craftiness and tax collectors' callousness is often, though not always, right. Prime Minister King's crabwise ways were related to the skills of a good broker, and when a finance minister is rigid, as Ilsley had to be, we recognize that the reason might be integrity. There have been many reasons to fear the taxman and to be angry at the state. The anger might be reasonable or not. But it almost always provides a spur to action. And when that anger is about taxation, the best result is when it brings citizens as taxpayers to the table of public debate, as it did in 1970. Better that people fulminate loudly about taxes and make themselves heard than that they pour their anger into quiet avoidance and evasion.

I have described the emotions of populism as bitter ones, fear and anger and envy. These emotions were mobilized against tax reform in the period between 1967 and 1971 by a Toronto business school teacher, John Bulloch Jr., and a London, Ontario, insurance broker, Colin M. Brown. Bulloch's Canadian Council for Tax Fairness became the Canadian Federation of Independent Business, and Brown's initiative laid the foundation of the National Citizens' Coalition. The two men saw the proposed reforms as threatening their businesses and confiscating rightly earned wealth in the name of the Trudeau Liberals' projects of welfare state building. Their supporters often seem to have been motivated primarily by fear for their savings, their homes, their family heirlooms, their business ventures. But "the people" of this conservative populism were also moved by passions – not ignoble ones – for family legacy, independent achievement, and accountable government. On the left, the NDP channelled the outrage of Canadians who saw wealth earned by exploitation, wealth in large measure being drained away to the United States, while special interests defended a regressive and leaky tax system. Altruistic objectives dominated in left-wing tax critiques, but these were also the years of serious anti-capitalist radicalism whose intense anger, whether one thinks it proper or not, was unmistakable and coloured with connections to a fervent and sometimes furious nationalism. The left wing of the NDP, the Waffle, organized as a party within a party, called for "extensive public control over investment and nationalization of the commanding heights of the economy, such as the essential resources industries, finance and credit, and industries strategic to planning our economy." A progressive tax structure and a better welfare state would not be enough.[114] These disagreements were real and serious, not so much about the details of whether a particular tax reform would actually usher in armageddon or utopia. But Canadians had to talk, and talk seriously, about what their state should do and how it should be financed. Tax talk at its best asks us those big questions. Such talk was not new in Canada in the 1960s, but tax reform brought out deeply felt competing positions, and that was proper.

The debate about taxes engaged citizens broadly. "Citizens" were no longer just those property owners who negotiated their municipal assessments and the well-off who generously chose to pay the somewhat avoidable personal income tax. Taxpayers and citizens had become largely overlapping groups. As citizens in a welfare state, the new taxpayers sought benefits different from the older benefits of railways, postal systems, courts, and police forces, which had been designed to support property and production. There was now a kind of citizen wage, as James Snell has called the old age pension of 1952.[115] The middle-class and rich taxpayers of the interwar years had expected that governments would provide services to the productive economy and had worried about the impact of tax on production and saving. The mass taxpayers expected services that would support their ability to consume to at least a minimum standard, but they also worried about the impacts of taxes on their ability to consume and save. All sorts saw or imagined that others were free riders, getting more than they contributed. The public debates of 1969–70 exposed the full variety of such worries and resentments.

Populism – demagoguery –: understands that people will be motivated to participate in politics if their emotions are aroused. The danger is that, as with the nativist and racist forms of populism, the emotions enlisted can be solely self-regarding and ill informed. Tax represents a particular problem in this respect because it engages self-interest so powerfully. And becoming well informed about tax is sometimes difficult. The economic science has some areas of real controversy, and the technical dimensions in law and accounting of tax reform are genuinely complex. The Canada Revenue Agency does not publish tax compliance studies, and economists who study the underground economy acknowledge that their methods are imperfect.[116] It is difficult to develop reasonable views on who is dodging taxes and by how much when the data are so incomplete. We have better data with which to discuss the mechanisms of prosperity now than did Canadians in 1970, when GDP data series were only thirty years long. But even now it's difficult for citizens to be genuinely well informed about tax compliance and evasion and their consequences. Where there are such gaps in social science, political talk is easily disfigured by ideologically driven overstatement and all its accompanying panic mongering and hatred fomenting. Even though I have argued that the letters to the Department of Finance in 1969–70 were not merely hysterical, we should also notice that the strong emotions that they expressed made building a consensus harder for the Liberals. The participatory democracy exercise had brought out fully and publicly the complex and intensely felt array of viewpoints on tax reform.

The 1971 revision of income taxation made gestures to all of those viewpoints and made the tax law famously more complex. There were bald concessions to noisy objections – the capital gains people received from selling their homes (their "primary residences"), no matter how luxuriously beyond basic housing, would not be taxed as income. As for other kinds of capital gains, only 50 percent of them would be taxed as income. The poorest of the income tax payers would be let off the hook, but at $2,850 the married exemption was still less valuable than it had been in 1949 – to be worth as much in 1971, the exemption would have had to be $3,421. But the limits of Benson's achievement on that point were mitigated somewhat by exemptions for workers' tools and travel and childcare expenses, increased exemptions for the elderly and people with certain disabilities, and deductions of more kinds of medical expenses.[117]

The tax law became more complex after 1971, and that has made it full of difficulty. Politics, too, have become more complex.[118] Among the reasons for that change are the continuing and since 1970 more open conversations about tax questions, such as introduction of the GST. "Taxpayer" can be a harmful identity, simplifying the complex policy realm into higher or lower taxes. And the dangerous emotional comforts of ideological simplification are always present. Complexity has its hazards, but it's the proper condition of democratic politics. To be a taxpayer, or even the blended citizen-taxpayer, is to be a creature of self-interest, certainly, but both self and interests are shaped by a variety of commitments and motivations, none of them simply springing naturally from the facts of our physiology. Taxation is a cultural phenomenon. In a healthy democracy, an episode like the White Paper debates is valuable because, in taxpayer complaints, what is being said is always, in some sense, about more than money.

11
Self-Interest, Community, and the Evolution of the Citizen-Taxpayer

OVER CANADA'S SHORT TWENTIETH CENTURY, income taxation in Canada changed. Before the federal income tax, it existed as an unpopular form of direct taxation, used in cities or provinces where easier-to-collect taxes were not sufficient to pay for public works and the interest on public debts. But when emergencies struck – whether wars or economic slumps – governments at all levels brought in not only new income taxes but also other new taxes, ones that have been less often foregrounded in our national history. Poll taxes were used to force the poor and propertyless to share the burden of municipal services, cheque taxes collected many pennies for general revenue, and the tax exemptions of "Indians" were made fewer and smaller. Some income taxes (wage taxes) were designed to extract many small sums from the poor, while progressive-rate income taxes were promoted as simple justice or protested as a form of unfairly targeted plunder. The customs taxation and international borrowing that had financed federal spending at the outset of the First World War were replaced by much more domestic borrowing and direct taxation. As tax consciousness grew around federal income taxation, some economists advised politicians to use the tax system in increasingly complex ways as a means of governing – using incentives and disincentives to direct the consumption and business choices of citizens. The old method of using the tariff to manage markets or using excise taxes to tax luxuries (and perhaps to keep the poor sober) became the notion that taxation, and especially income taxation, could be used to generate desirable behaviour. By the 1950s, more

Canadians were being asked to think of themselves as taxpayers, both ful-filling precisely their legal obligations and responding rationally to tax-related incentives and opportunities.

In 1914, the identities of "taxpayer" and "citizen" were closely connected for well-to-do Canadians at the municipal level, but the identities were less often evoked as a pair in national tax talk, from which the engaged liberal citizen of direct tax regimes was absent.[1] The Great War brought taxpayer and citizen identities more closely together at the national level. The war justified new taxes and engaged the federal government in affirmations of citizen responsibility and interconnectedness. Like the use of worries about typhoid to justify municipal sewage improvements, this was a benefit argu-ment for taxation. It worked not by urging altruism but by explaining how interests (including credit conditions) connected Canadians in the polit-ical nation as surely as members of local communities were connected by sewage disposal and water supply. Although "the economy" as a trans-personal entity moved to political centre stage only during the Second World War, the taxation debates of the First World War and the related discussions of lending and saving made taxation a public question in terms that soon went beyond the tired tariff issue. In the Second World War, war finance decisively made fiscal politics part of social politics in a liberal mode on a national scale. The family allowance program blended taxation and transfers to citizen-beneficiaries and thus linked the social and the fiscal. Tax affected business conditions and unemployment in ways that made the success of an enterprise or the security of a family appear as a social matter rather than simply a sign of individuals' intelligence or morality.

In time, benefit would become primarily an anti-tax argument, bran-dished by those wishing to slough off responsibility for services that they themselves did not use. But tax arguments can be deployed for multiple, and sometimes conflicting, projects. Reasoning from benefit was central to justifying the first federal income tax, and finance ministers relied on bene-fit arguments to retain that tax, to promote it, and to expand its reach into a mass base. The other justification for the federal income tax, of course, was that its progressive rate structure and basic exemptions reflected tax-payers' ability to pay. In this respect, progressivity legitimated contribution across the income spectrum, supposedly showing small contributors that their sacrifices in personal consumption were matched by the greater con-tributions of the better-off. There was also an economic logic to progres-sive income taxation: by falling on surplus (variously and controversially defined), an income tax was less likely to harm productive capital or impair effective demand – if rightly arranged. And progressive taxation appealed to morality, glimpsed occasionally through the clouds of tax resistance. To be a taxpayer in response to an ability-to-pay argument was not merely to respond grudgingly and to become a voice for retrenchment and small government. It was also to recognize that being able to pay the income tax was a mark of status and that to pay willingly was a sign of good character. Citizenship of a generous sort was compatible with the identity of income tax payer.

However, a closer connection between taxpayer and citizen identities at all levels of government made for frictions. My purpose in describing so much tax protest, tax evasion, and in general tax resistance has not been to celebrate tax resisters as heroes (or, god forbid, "patriots," an identity claimed by American tax resisters).[2] Rather, I have wanted to make two points. One is that Canadians are not some species apart from the normal run of human beings, deferentially happy to pay our taxes. Some of us are some of the time. But more commonly, like most people in the rest of the world, we are inclined to think that we or our socio-economic group pay more taxes than others do and that there must be some way, other than digging into our particular pockets, for governments to pay for what we want them to do. And again, like citizens of other countries, many of us have long looked askance at wasteful or corrupt spending by governments. Whether any particular form of spending is wasteful, of course, is a matter of debate. When we get sufficiently angry about the impact of tax on our personal projects (whether feeding our children or meeting the payroll), we have been known to engage in intemperate rhetoric about "the cruel taxes" and their unfairness, sometimes their "iniquity" even. This point is perhaps obvious, but I take a kind of perverse Canadian pride in showing that we are not, actually, always "nicer" than Americans. Being angry and saying so are virtues of independent people. Only the colonized are always (and then only publicly) nice. But being angry does not entail being un-reasonable: some tax anger is reasonable, some is not.

The other point of my cataloguing of tax resistance has been to show its location in various political communities and projects. As Nicolas Delalande and Romain Huret have argued, tax resistance is not always right wing or never left wing and not always anti-statist. Anti-statists resist tax, but not all tax resistance is anti-statist.[3] Tax resisters' ideas of "fairness" have been creatively diverse. In the 1920s, opponents of the tariff tax were internationalist, grassroots, and suspicious of a particular political alliance between manufacturing capital and the Conservative Party. Opposition to income taxation had been Progressive (left wing or technocratic or both) when the target was the municipal income tax but was small business based without being anti-statist in the 1920s. A Conservative financier like Izaac Walton Killam could support the federal income tax that would hit high incomes hard when it looked to him during the First World War as if taxing income was a good alternative to massive government borrowing that would distort bond markets. But during the 1930s central Canadian investment community leaders pressured British Columbia (and likely Manitoba) into imposing a regressive provincial income tax to help finance relief spending and debt charges. In Canada, as in the United States, support for the sales tax came from those who thought that a "hidden" tax would incite less resistance than would income tax. Opposition to the sales tax among women's organizations, organized labour, and the parliamentary left pointed out that such a tax, like Drayton's doomed "luxury tax," became part of the rising cost of living and visible in this effect. The policy choice between income tax and sales tax was almost purely – but not quite – a class opposition. Much depended on the design of the income taxes. Middle-class salary earners joined wage earners in protesting income taxes that farmers and independent professionals could more easily evade. Most consistently, what really differentiated working-class organizations and business ones were different ideas about the relationship of tax methods to social spending. Becoming federal income tax payers in the 1950s only confirmed labour's view that, as taxpayers, working men and women deserved services from the state.

The cleanly class character of tax critique, evasion, and avoidance is muddied when a broad range of taxes is taken into account and when rural people, racialized people, and women are included among the political actors whom historians investigate. Indigenous people's opposition to various kinds of taxation clearly shows that a tax's legitimacy derives from the taxpayer's membership in a political community. Members of First Nations found it objectionable to be asked to pay taxes to a state of which they weren't citizens and with which they didn't seek to join. In making this association, the Mohawk, Haida, Squamish, and others understood the settler polity's conventions well. Voting and taxpaying were, in fact, linked. But "Indian" tax resistance, like the income tax protests of Chinese Canadians in British Columbia and the various expressions of distress in response to the taxation of low incomes in the 1930s municipally, and in the 1940s and after federally, also marked a sense that income taxation was making the many sacrifice more than the few for the funding of governments. Like poll taxes and sales taxes, a poorly enforced income tax, no matter its stated rate structure, could be regressive. Sometimes, as in the cases of the creamery tax, the luxury tax, the capital gains tax on homes, and most dramatically the compulsory savings portion of the Second World War income tax, tax protesters were successful in having a tax measure reversed or altered. Even the inclusion of 50 percent of capital gains in taxable income in 1971, though part of a larger defeat for progressive tax reform, belongs in this list of effective efforts at tax resistance by democratic means for tax fairness ends. Like most of these protest-driven changes, it benefited people in a variety of class positions.

Some modes of tax resistance were class specific. A fairly quiet but effective resistance was the working-class habit of not paying poll taxes. Voting and tax strikes were also tools that ordinary people could and did use. The threat of non-participation in the Victory Bond campaigns was important and, in a way, a women's method of protest given the role of housewives in creating savings through thrift. The protest techniques of wealthier Canadians were harder to see than the number of poll taxes not paid and harder for governments to catch and correct. During the 1930s, associations of property owners were open tax critics, as were particular industry associations and, later, the Income Taxpayers' Association. In the early 1960s, there were tax protest elements in Operation Freedom, the anti–welfare state campaign of the Canadian Chamber of Commerce. Tax evasion and avoidance were less visible when they involved accounting manoeuvres such as surplus stripping.

Finally, some tax resistance was constitutional but not in the same way that it was in the United States. Although the legality of the federal income tax was quickly established, the propriety of Canada's presence in that tax field was debated throughout the interwar years. In both Quebec and Newfoundland, the fiscal organization of Confederation remained a live question through the 1950s. At stake in this tax question, as in many others, was much more than particular individuals' tax bills. The possibility that a more centralized federation would be a better macroeconomic manager and a better provider of social security made the debate about taxing powers a debate about the role of the state. A defence of provincial rights was more than just politicians playing turf wars. Insurance companies in

Montreal, oilmen in the west, and many small manufacturing firms in Ontario all encountered the tax system in different ways, and those influential sectors inevitably swayed their provincial governments.

Although political and fiscal purposes are sometimes distinguishable and sometimes blended, in constitutional debates they are always interconnected. For Canadian voters, the limited scope of action in constitutional amendment during the mid-twentieth century made for frustrating policy stalemates and helped to produce a pattern of chronic buck passing, inimical to democratic accountability. The "traditional Canadian practice in tax matters" was not an absence of discussion, as Bucovetsky and Bird alleged in 1971. There were many public discussions of tax policy over the period studied here. Rather, by the 1950s, the past that Bucovetsky and Bird knew personally, national tax talk in Canada was submerged in constitutional questions. Innovatively, the tax reform debate of 1967–71 temporarily distanced tax equity and efficiency from the provincial rights conversation and thus brought a wider variety of public opinion more closely to bear on specific pocketbook, social, and economic tax questions. After the repatriation of the Constitution in 1982, a range of other tax questions has opened up, among them new "Indian" tax cases.[4]

Having spent so much of this book explaining and exploring tax resistance, I want to remind readers here that some Canadians have been willing taxpayers. They have heard and agreed with finance ministers and city treasurers who have said that, when the community calls for a contribution to the costs of collective life, it's no time to say "let George carry the pail." One of the sparks for my research on taxation was my discovery, during research for an earlier project, of Halifax club women resolving to ask that propertyless housewives be charged the city's household tax so that they could have the vote as taxpayers.[5] During this project, I found other taxpayers who possibly seemed to be motivated by a sense of social duty or personal morality or both. Remember the unambiguously moral, conscience-cleaning members of the Oxford Group. Recall the civil servants who paid the Manitoba wage tax before it was legally required. Perhaps we can also count Canada's eleventh prime minister, R.B. Bennett, among honourable taxpayers: he knew perfectly well which tax avoidance methods he could use to hide his millions, and he claimed proudly, if he can be believed, not to have used them. Think of the Canadians who made no-interest loans to the government during the Second World War: though not strictly taxpayers, they contributed some of their wealth for the public good. In this tradition of willing contributors also belong the supporters of the Benson White Paper who were happy to see their taxes increase in order that the burden on the poor be lessened.

Perhaps no one likes paying taxes. But some of us do like to feel that we are honest and honourable, that we are full citizens, and that we have done our share in paying for what we need as a community. Although we always pay under threat of legal penalty, tax systems that rely wholly on taxpayer prudence to secure compliance can be neither productive nor cost effective. Effective enforcement includes appeals to more social motives, and the evidence that I have found of their specific role in these odd circumstances counterbalances to some degree the more easily found evidence of tax resistance, avoidance, and evasion. Citizenship involves making claims on the state for services. It involves judging the means of funding those services, and at its best it entails thinking about those services not merely as personal benefits but also as the connective tissue of collective life. Both in noisy protest against unjust taxation and in quiet compliance with legitimate imposts, from a variety of social positions and moral emotions, Canadians as taxpayers have also acted as citizens.

National Difference and Democracy

When I began this project, I was reluctant to focus on a comparison of taxation in Canada and the United States. Canadians are connected by common national laws, foreign policy, and trade policy, but there are equally important ways in which laws in Canada's provincial and municipal jurisdictions sprang from and teach different social realities. These differences are compounded by provincial and regional differences in economic assets and immigration and Indigenous histories. Each province and territory, moreover, has its own story of how it came to be part of Canada. Canadian political culture is not homogeneous. This is true of the United States as well even though its narrative of national culture might be more entrenched than that of Canada. How reasonably can one compare "average" this or that between two such complex entities? Yet it was clear, when I presented parts of this work as I was writing it, that historians and other audiences wanted to know how Canada compared with the United States in terms of tax culture.

So, with skepticism about narratives of national culture in mind, as I researched in Canadian archives, I also read American tax history to see how familiar or strange it seemed. The comparisons that I found are threaded through this book and summarized here. At the national level, in the period before the Second World War, there are some striking differences. Canada appeared as a low-tax country, providing a tax refuge for rich Americans. With a regime that blended indirect taxes and income taxes in a regressive balance, the Canadian tax system weighed more heavily on the consumer than did the American one. Canada extracted national revenue disproportionately from the less well-off in a nearly invisible and therefore supposedly painless way. And Americans' enforcement of the income tax was more energetic, targeted at criminally convicting tax dodgers. However, during the Second World War, tax administration in Canada began to look more like that in the United States as both moved to a mass base for the personal income tax and managed collection of it by means of an impersonal style of administration. In the postwar years, Canadians made envious comparisons to the means of income tax reduction available south of the border, means such as marital income splitting and deductions for both mortgage interest and municipal taxes. The prospect of taxing capital gains, as the United States did, began to look inviting to those who wanted to put an end to certain kinds of tax avoidance strategies in Canada. Canada's mining and petroleum industries in the postwar years were built on the basis of the tax advantages that they offered to American investors. Tax resisters in Canada couldn't adopt the constitutional methods used by the more extreme opponents of the income tax in the United States, but the Canadian Chamber of Commerce in the early 1960s represented the presence in Canada of the Goldwater Republican style of anti-statism. Canada's tax reform efforts in the 1960s, contemporaneous with US federal tax reforms, won admiration for their conceptual thoroughness and clarity, even if the result in the 1971 budget was only to bring the Canadian tax structure closer to the American one. Given the economic interconnections between Canada and the United States, increasing markedly in the 1940s on, and the partly overlapping legal and cultural traditions of the two countries, it is remarkable how much difference there is in these two histories.

Underpinning some of the differences is the constitutional law of the two federalisms. Sovereignty is divided in both countries, but in matters fiscal the American states have a better constitutional poker hand than do the Canadian provinces. The states' rights tradition in the United States, born of the battle over slavery, contrasts with Canada's division of powers, a compromise born of the commitment of francophone Quebeckers to

cultural survival, Ontario's desire to contain the threat of "French domina-
tion," and both Canadas' desperate need to escape from the fiscal crisis
of the 1850s.[6] Also, a history of more frequent constitutional amendment
made the American constitution a prime field of combat. Income taxation
was only one of several battles fought on that terrain. In contrast, Canada's
tax conversations have been, like federal-provincial negotiations on other
social issues (divorce, income assistance, education), prolonged and often
stalemated by constitutional debate. For the period discussed here, making
change by a constitutional route was a bit like renovating a bathroom in a
one-bathroom house using a crew of unreliable tradespeople – seemingly
endless and damnably inconvenient. Canadian tax reformers were conservative about constitutional change because it was exceptionally difficult,
not because Canadians are intrinsically conservative.

In addition to how sovereignty is divided in the Canadian federation
compared with the American one, another foundation for the tax history
differences was the difference in fiscal sovereignty. Frustrating though the
debtor state mentality was to the Department of Finance's newest recruit
in 1938, Robert Bryce, Canada, compared with the United States, was indeed in a less autonomous position in public finance. The nearly invisible
leading strings of the Colonial Stock Act were one sign of Canada's incomplete sovereignty at the beginning of the period. Another was the brief
suspension of trade in Canadian bonds on the London market in 1933,
which clearly told Canada's finance minister that certain taxation measures
wouldn't be tolerated by London money. National sovereignty in law is not
exactly the same as full autonomy. In the 1960s, tax reformers attempted to
remove some of the tax incentives that brought American capital so abun-
dantly into Canada, and again the threat of a capital strike set a limit on
the legislative risks that the Canadian government could safely take.
Canada's ability to master its own fiscal destiny has been limited by its relations to two great world powers: its modern mother country and its next-
door neighbour. Canadian governments have stepped carefully around tax
conflict with these inescapable allies.

The third substrate of Canada's different tax culture was the nation's
relative poverty. Perhaps as important was its lack of knowledge about its
wealth and poverty. In the United States, the taxation of capital gains in the
national income tax meant that wealth statistics were produced. In contrast, in Canada the revenue minister in the 1930s was genuinely unable
to answer a parliamentarian's question about the taxation of wealth. The

Canadian government did not collect these data. Unlike the United States (and Britain), Canada had neither a central bank (until 1937) nor a national statistics bureau (before 1918). During the 1920s, Canada's new statistics bureau worked up some rough estimates of aggregate production by sector, but the internal distribution of income and wealth remained opaque. In 1933, as Duncan McDowall reports, the dominion statistician was still unable to supply data on "total realized income by type" – wages, business profits, and dividends.[7] Canada did not even know, before the tax enforcement reforms of 1933, who held the majority of its tax-free war bond issues. As economist H.R. Kemp remarked in 1923, it was known in general terms that Canadians depended more on subsistence production than did Americans and that Canada's pools of great wealth were smaller and fewer than those of the United States and United Kingdom. But "general terms" do not settle taxable capacity questions, as the prolonged debates between Ottawa and the maritime provinces showed. Canada was possibly poorer, and definitely more data poor, in ways that made its income tax a less effective fiscal instrument than the American one was before 1945.

For these and other reasons – the vast size of the country, the limits on the local franchise, and the racial exclusions at the federal level – it's hard to see Canada's political culture as democratic in the majoritarian sense before the Second World War. Elites representing their province, their region, or their people worked out compromises on matters of public policy largely related to business interests. The National Government movement of the 1930s represents a moment of fearful reaction among business elites to the possibility of mass democracy. Limits such as these on Canadian democracy are the basis for a fourth explanation of Canada-US difference. There was no need in Canada for the American practice of rousing the electorate in support of "rich people's movements," aptly named by historical sociologist Isaac Martin.[8] The wealthy of Canada were already well protected. Not until the mobilization against the Carter Commission recommendations in 1967–69 and the White Paper debate in 1969–70 do we see an attempt to build a populist anti-tax-reform movement that transcended business (the Chamber of Commerce) or regional culture (the Créditistes). I suspect that a March 1969 presentation by tax lawyer and active Liberal W.A. Macdonald to the Toronto and District Labour Council might have been the first time that this Labour Council had been favoured with a presentation by a high-profile tax lawyer.[9] Whether through his rational efforts or the more inflammatory methods of John Bulloch and

Colin Brown, the tax-reform period of the short 1960s shows Canadian elites seeking support of the mass electorate for a revolt against expert-devised and government-supported public policy. That effort echoed American tax revolt organizations of the 1930s–50s that Martin has described.

What does this history say about Canadian democracy? Neither tragedy nor triumph is an adequate interpretation of what the White Paper moment meant in relation to the rest of the history that I have told here. Canada's record as a democracy in the twentieth century is decidedly mixed. Looking at it through tax history, I have been disappointed more than once but also impressed more than once by the political actions of individuals or organizations, politicians or private citizens. "The people" haven't always been admirable, nor have the "leaders" or "experts" (suspiciously general categories), though public pressure, research expertise, and seasoned judgment have been useful from time to time. Sadly, I have often thought how clumsy Canadian political institutions were, how little equipped to make Canadians known to each other and to make decisions that served all parts and peoples of the country fairly. I include among "political institutions" the newspapers and magazines that I read. None of them represented all that well the country beyond their regions, and their editorial positions were mostly predictable voices of partisan or sectoral interests. Letters from individual Canadians were often no narrower than newspaper editorials in the information and perspectives that they provided. Similarly, private individuals sometimes showed a broad, generous, well-informed grasp of public finance issues. What came the closest to showing me Canadian tax questions in the round and deliberative democracy in progress were the proceedings and results of royal commissions, an institution from Canada's British parliamentary tradition. Commission research was nevertheless the product of situated choices, and the processes of recruiting intervenors did not always work to welcome a full range of relevant voices.

Considering this mixed record of democratic evolution, the early Trudeau-era efforts to try more broadly inclusive practices of consultation – participatory democracy – were surely warranted. Like the Royal Commission on the Status of Women that reported in 1970, the Carter Commission animated and relaunched a continuing conversation in a difficult policy area. As people on the left typically say, and rightly so, the struggle continues. In response to the report of the Commission on the Status of Women, feminists organized the National Action Committee on the Status of Women. In response to the report of the Carter Commission, economists launched the Canadian Foundation for Economic Education, trying to include both labour and business. Advocates of Carter-style tax reform produced a new periodical, scholarly works, and popular journalism.[10] Those who sought tax reform in other directions have similarly worked to develop a Canadian corpus of tax expertise.[11] All of this is part of the good work of democracy, the building of informed engagement. Whatever one's political position on any given topic, the job of a democratic citizen is to listen, observe, learn, collaborate, talk, organize, persuade, and seek the power to advance worthy projects. A liberal democracy benefits from open conflict when that conflict means educational campaigns, vigorous elections, soaring oratory, sharply investigative journalism, and passionate but peaceful public demonstrations. Tax questions have produced much of that kind of conflict.

Tax is inevitably a realm of conflict. Its value as a subject of politics is precisely that it exposes our conflicting interests and imposes an accommodation, though never a final one. In tax talk, we tend to see free riders everywhere, imagined differently from various ideological standpoints. A politics worth admiring would show, as I have tried to do in this history, that the existence of free riders is sometimes invented or their numbers inflated. People can assume too glibly that we know others' projects or circumstances and the resources that they need. A politics that values tax conflict as a way to understand our varied interests would encourage us to be skeptical about predictable free-rider claims and curious about challenges to ideologically stagnant tax talk. It would be informed by good data, essential for that classic test of a policy's fairness: imagining yourself as the one who might feel the policy's worst consequences.[12] In this way and others, not only data but also a generous imagination are essential to good citizenship. Here, in raising images of a society's various different parts and standpoints, politicians can play an essential role in fostering good citizenship. In tax as in other policy areas, politicians do useful work when they speak wisely and in a well-informed way to our imaginations. In this, they share the role of other social professions, such as educators, social workers, clergy, and journalists. That role is to make "society" – an imagined community – visible and comprehensible, in all the variety and interconnectedness of its constituent parts. Good tax talk can show us our connections as well as our divisions.

As tax history illustrates, the collective life that politicians and others show us, if they show it to us accurately, is not simply a warm and cozy community. Interests often conflict. But a way of living together among these conflicts, a *modus vivendi,* can be fair and be understood to be fair. The condition of arriving at a decent modus vivendi is that we participate in policy making as an arena of honourable conflict, in which all interests are seen and understood in their own terms and all holders of particular interests try, unceasingly, to see and understand the interests and emotions of others.[13] In this arena, politicians can do useful work by performing ritual combat that brings conflict into the open in a careful way. But they can also build the modus vivendi by interpreting citizens of this always deeply fragmented country to each other, creating the framework for well-informed give and take. If in either role politicians speak to us openly and honestly and passionately about taxation, and if we listen carefully to them and talk respectfully among ourselves, then tax has much to teach us about our common life. And the better we know our common life, the more competent we will be as citizen-taxpayers.

Acknowledgments

My greatest intellectual debt is to Elsbeth Heaman. Her recent book, *Tax, Order, and Good Government: A New Political History of Canada, 1867– 1917*, is this book's fraternal twin. I hope people will read the two books together and enjoy talking about the ways in which they connect as much as she and I did as we were researching and writing.

Along with Elsbeth Heaman, three other excellent historians – Jerry Bannister, Bruce Curtis, and Jeffrey McNairn – joined me in 2007 in a research group on the cultural history of taxation. They involved graduate students in the project and shared their work at conferences and in articles. And there will be more to come. I have benefitted so much from our conversations, and not only because they helped me connect my twentieth-century tax history to its past.

. Because tax studies have a daunting technical side, I have been grateful for advice, editorial comments, and encouragement from tax law scholars. There is a stereotype of tax lawyers as soulless servants of big money, but as scholars and teachers, they come in many political varieties. I have met none that fit the stereotype. Several have been particularly generous in checking my work and encouraging me to make a contribution to their scholarly world. In particular, I thank Kim Brooks, Neil Brooks, Colin Campbell, Allison Christians, Tim Edgar, Richard Krever, and Lisa Philipps (whose support I recognized only after she was revealed as one of the anonymous readers selected by the publisher). Other law profs, not tax specialists, have helped too. Philip Girard sent me off to look at the legal history literature early in my research, and Jim Phillips joined him in encouraging me to see my work as part of the law and society historiography. Dalhousie law librarian David Michels helped me navigate legal history sources.

For reading parts of the manuscript, for asking questions, for passing along useful references and primary source materials, for showing up at or arranging talks, for making connections between tax and other topics, I am grateful to many other historians too. I apologize in advance if I have left anyone out, but I think all listed here will remember a moment when they helped me with this project: Blake Brown, Penny Bryden, Greg Donaghy, Chris Dummitt, Magda Fahrni, Don Fyson, Janet Guildford, Tina Loo, Lynne Marks, Ian McKay, Gordon McOuat, Brad Miller, Suzanne Morton, Martin Petitclerc, Jarrett Rudy, and David Tough. Some of them will remember many conversations! In that category belong architectural historian Peter Coffman and his spouse, Diane Laundy. Long after my grant money was spent, Peter and Diane supported my research in the national archives by giving me a home away from home in Ottawa.

Some of the best critical comment on the work in progress came from the weekly research seminar of the Dalhousie History department. My colleagues and our graduate students were the first to say to me, "Who knew tax could be so interesting?" That sentiment was echoed most recently by novelist and retired journalist C.S. Reardon, who read a complete draft of the manuscript in its penultimate stage. She identified a few not-so-interesting bits, and I edited accordingly. Another journalist, Kelly Toughill, helped me turn some of the material into forms suitable for newspapers. Having her voice in my head influenced my writing.

I want also to acknowledge a special debt to Holger Nehring, who introduced me to Romain Huret and Nicolas Delalande. The international conference that they organized in 2010 was an essential catalyst for my thinking in this book.

Then there were the people who did some of the research. The five whose work I have constantly relied upon were Orion Endicott Kerestezi, Stacey Barker, Alex Tremblay, Will Langford, and Wallace MacLean. Their labour was funded by the Social Sciences and Humanities Research Council of Canada. Three others – Colin Grittner, Don Nerbas, and Andrew Bateman – helped me fill important research gaps quickly.

I would like to acknowledge here the help I have had from librarians, archivists, and circulation staff at many archives and libraries, all of which struggle to preserve and make available important materials of our history. A special thanks to the archivist at Library and Archives Canada for believing me when I said that the records of the Exchequer Court of Canada had to exist and helping me find them in the Court Services Administration.

Preparing the manuscript, especially the lengthy and complex documentation, was a long slog, and I would not have made the final deadline without the help of Jan Sutherland on Chapter 7. She claims to like fixing footnote formatting. The editors at UBC Press – Darcy Cullen and Lesley Erickson – were encouraging, professional, and great communicators. I appreciated their help so much. The readers that they found to do the work of assessing the manuscript gave good advice. Copy editor Dallas Harrison saved me from several omissions and errors and polished the footnotes to a high gloss.

In spite of this long list of debts, I did most of the research and all of the thinking and writing myself, and I take all the responsibility for any errors or omissions and deficiencies of style.

In this place where authors often acknowledge the support of a spouse, I want to thank the Halifax friends who have not only encouraged me in this project but also cared for me as a human being over these past ten years. Sunday night dinners with Janet, monthly meetings with members of my book club, dinners with Andrée, theatre with Shao Pin, hikes with Lynette, and drinks in the garden with Sue and Jan – people such as these, but also many wonderful others, in Halifax and elsewhere, create the life-world that makes work meaningful.

$ ¢ $

Funding for this project came from the Social Sciences and Humanities Research Council of Canada and the University of King's College.

I would like to thank the *Canadian Tax Journal* for permission to include in Chapter 7 material from Shirley Tillotson, "Warfare State, Welfare State, and the Selling of the Personal Income Tax, 1942–45," *Canadian Tax Journal* 63, 1 (2015): 1–38

Earlier versions of some paragraphs in Chapters 3, 5, and 6 were previously published in Shirley Tillotson, "Relations of Extraction: Taxation and Women's Citizenship in the Maritimes, 1914–1955," *Acadiensis* 39, 1 (2010): 27–57.

Earlier versions of some paragraphs in Chapter 9 were previously published in Shirley Tillotson, "The Family as Tax Dodge: Partnership, Individuality, and Gender in the Personal Income Tax Act, 1942 to 1970," *Canadian Historical Review* 90, 3 (2009): 391–425

An earlier version of part of Chapter 10 was previously published in Shirley Tillotson, "The Politics of Carter-Era Tax Reform: A Revisionist Account," in *The Quest for Tax Reform Continues: The Royal Commission on Taxation Fifty Years Later,* ed. Kim Brooks (Toronto: Carswell, 2013), 31–52.

Appendix: Tables

Average annual income and profit taxes in relation to average annual tax receipts, 1910–29, Canada and the United States

Canada, periods	Period average annual income and profit tax receipts, 000$	Period average annual receipts, all taxes, 000$	Period average income and profit as percentage of total tax receipts
1910–16	0	107.2	0
1917–21	45.5	253.5	18
1922–25	73.0	322.7	23
1926–29	55.6	359.1	15
United States, periods			
1910–16	56.3	654.4	9
1917–21	2,637.1	3906.8	68
1922–25	1,839.5	3308.5	56
1926–29	2,180.8	3450.7	63

Sources: J. Harvey Perry, *Taxes, Tariffs, and Subsidies: A History of Canadian Fiscal Development*, 2 vols (Toronto: University of Toronto Press, 1955), Table 6, 2: 624–27; Paul Studenski and Herman E. Krooss, *Financial History of the United States: Fiscal, Monetary, Banking, and Tariff, Including Financial Administration and State and Local Finance*, 2nd ed. (New York: McGraw-Hill, 1963), Table 46, 314. The periods used in this table are those used by Studenski and Krooss.

TABLE 2

Federal tax receipts by type in billions of dollars, by percent of total tax receipts, and subdivided by direct and indirect types

	Canada 1954	US 1954	Canada 1961	US 1961	Canada 1954	US 1954	Canada 1961	US 1961
Individual income tax	1.47[1]	32.4	2.36[2]	46.1	33.8%	44.3%	34.5%	47.1%
Corporate income tax	1.06	21.5	1.22	21.8	24.4%	29.4%	17.8%	22.3%
Employment taxes	0.16[3]	5.4	0.27[4]	12.5	3.7%	7.4%	3.9%	12.8%
Estate and gift taxes	0.04	0.9	0.85	1.9	0.9%	1.2%	12.4%	1.9%
Manufacturer sales tax	0.57	0	0.75	0	13.1%	0.0%	10.9%	0.0%
Customs	0.4	0.6	0.52	1	9.2%	0.8%	7.6%	1.0%
Miscellaneous	0.15	2.3	0.25	4.1	3.4%	3.1%	3.6%	4.2%
Excises	0.5	10	0.63	10.5	11.5%	13.7%	9.2%	10.7%
Total	4.35	73.1	6.85	97.9	100.0%	100.0%	100.0%	100.0%

	Canada 1954	US 1954	Canada 1961	US 1961
Direct	62.8%	82.4%	68.6%	84.1%
Indirect	37.2%	17.6%	31.4%	15.9%

1 Includes Old Age Security tax.
2 Includes Old Age Security tax.
3 Unemployment Insurance contributions.
4 Unemployment Insurance contributions.

Sources: W. Irwin Gillespie, Tax, Borrow, and Spend: Financing Federal Spending in Canada, 1867–1990 (Ottawa: Carleton University Press, 1991), Table C2, 286; Paul Studenski and Herman E. Krooss, Financial History of the United States: Fiscal, Monetary, Banking, and Tariff, Including Financial Administration and State and Local Finance, 2nd ed. (New York: McGraw-Hill, 1963). 538.

TABLE 3
Number and percent of small to moderate income tax payers subtracted or added from/to the federal rolls, selected years

	Total				
1924	209,539				
1925	116,029				
% change (+ or −)	−45%				

	Total	Under $2K	$2K–3K	$3K–4K	$4K–5K
1930	133,621	37,002	19,595	21,160	16,555
1932	203,957	93,316	46,207	27,778	13,312
% change (+ or −)	44%	61%	58%	24%	−20%

Source: J. Harvey Perry, *Taxes, Tariffs, and Subsidies: A History of Canadian Fiscal Development*, 2 vols. (Toronto: University of Toronto Press, 1955), Table 38, 2: 696, and Table 40, 2: 698–99.

TABLE 4
Amount of income exempt from personal income tax, 1919–39, various taxpayer categories, adjusted for inflation/deflation to 2016 dollars

Tax Year	Single 1918–24 and 1932–39 $1,000	Single 1931 $1,200	Single 1925–31 $1,500	Married 1918–24 and 1932–39 $2,000	Married 1931 $2,400	Married 1925–31 $3,000	1918–24 and 1932–39, married with two children 2016 $	Amount	Dependant Exemption	Supervisory and office employees 2016 $	Supervisory and office employees current $
1919	$12,588			$25,176			$30,212	$2,400	$200	$18,845	$1,497
1920	$11,464			$22,928			$27,514	$2,400	$200	$20,750	$1,810
1921	$13,659			$27,318			$32,783	$2,400	$200	$25,325	$1,854
1922	$13,956			$27,912			$36,286	$2,600	$300	$25,345	$1,816
1923	$13,956			$27,912			$36,286	$2,600	$300	$25,917	$1,857
1924	$14,109			$28,218			$42,329	$3,000	$500	$26,301	$1,864
1925			$20,709			$41,418	$55,226	$4,000	$500	$25,845	$1,872
1926			$20,934			$41,868	$55,826	$4,000	$500	$26,378	$1,890
1927			$21,164			$42,328	$56,440	$4,000	$500	$27,232	$1,930
1928			$20,934			$41,868	$56,440	$4,000	$500	$27,020	$1,936
1929			$20,489			$40,978	$54,638	$4,000	$500	$26,991	$1,976
1930			$21,886			$43,772	$58,363	$4,000	$500	$29,299	$2,008
1931		$19,503			$39,006		$55,260	$3,400	$500	$30,621	$1,884
1932	$17,589			$35,178			$49,249	$2,800	$500	$30,587	$1,739

Tax Year	Single $1,000 (1918–24 and 1932–39)	Single $1,200 (1931)	Single $1,500 (1925–31)	Married $2,000 (1918–24 and 1932–39)	Married $2,400 (1931)	Married $3,000 (1925–31)	married with two children 2016 $ (1918–24 and 1932–39)	Amount	Dependant Exemption	Supervisory and office employees 2016 $	current $
1933	$18,084			$36,168			$50,637	$2,800	$400	$29,080	$1,608
1934	$17,833			$35,666			$49,933	$2,800	$400	$28,801	$1,615
1935	$17,351			$34,702			$48,584	$2,800	$400	$28,422	$1,638
1936	$17,120			$34,240			$47,936	$2,800	$400	$28,402	$1,659
1937	$16,461			$32,922			$46,092	$2,800	$400	$27,853	$1,692
1938	$16,894			$33,788			$47,305	$2,800	$400	$29,059	$1,720
1939	$16,461			$32,922			$46,092	$2,800	$400	$28,742	$1,746

Note: To contextualize the data on average industrial wage, consider that in the October 2016 data, the industrial aggregate average earnings in annual terms (weekly data multiplied by 52) are $49,602, but that aggregate hides a wide variation among industrial sectors. The lowest is $19,174 in accommodation and food services, and the highest is $108,409 in mining, petroleum, and so on. The aggregate includes twenty sectors, and in the top ten, the average annual earnings are higher than $57,000, indicating that the distribution is skewed.

Sources: Statistics Canada, "Series E41-48. Annual Earnings in Manufacturing Industries, Production, and Other Workers, by Sex, Canada, 1905, 1910, and 1917 to 1975," http://www.statcan.gc.ca; "Earnings, Average Weekly, by Industry, Monthly, Canada," September and October 2016, http://www.statcan.gc.ca/tables-tableaux/sum-som/l01/cst01/labor93a-eng.htm; Bank of Canada Inflation Calculator, http://www.bankofcanada.ca/rates/related/inflation-calculator/; J. Harvey Perry, *Taxes, Tariffs, and Subsidies: A History of Canadian Fiscal Development*, 2 vols. (Toronto: University of Toronto Press, 1955), 2: 593–606.

TABLE 5

Sample salary ranges for mostly male middle-class salaried employees, 1929

Civil service and public institutions,
non-administrator ranks

Engineer – Ottawa national	$3,120–$4,920
Engineer – Ontario provincial	$2,700–$4,000
Engineer – Toronto municipal	$4,300–$6,000
Assistant engineer – Ottawa national	$1,800–$3,300
Assistant engineer – Ontario provincial	$2,100–$3,300
Assistant engineer – Toronto municipal	$1,800–$4,000
University professor – eastern Canada	$2,500–$7,000
University professor – western Canada	$2,400–$5,000
Toronto Collegiate Institute teachers, first-year to thirtieth-year employee	$2,400–$4,575

Private sector engineers,
non-administrator ranks

Engineer	$3,500–$6,200
Junior and assistant engineer	$2,000–$3,700

Civil service and public institutions,
administrators

Administrator rank civil service engineers and deans (any discipline)	$4,500–$7,500
Private sector, administrator rank engineers	$6,500–$12,000

Median earned incomes of McGill University engineering graduates at certain intervals after graduation	*At graduation*	*5 years*	*10 years*	*15 years*	*20 years*
Government employees	$1,000	$1,800	$2,300	$3,000	$3,300
Teachers	$900	$1,800	$3,000	$3,000	$4,500
All graduates	$900	$2,100	$3,500	$4,800	$6,000
Average salary (weighted five-year intervals) of Toronto Collegiate Institute teachers		$2,511	$3,006	$3,244	$3,381

Sources: Canada, Royal Commission on Technical and Professional Services, *Report of the Royal Commission on Technical and Professional Services* (Ottawa: King's Printer, 1930), 50–56; for the ranking of Ontario urban collegiate institute teachers, see the 1936 Annual Survey of Education in Canada data cited in H. Carl Goldenberg, *Municipal Finance in Canada: A Study for the Royal Commission on Dominion-Provincial Relations* (Ottawa: King's Printer, 1939), 54.

TABLE 6

Quebec and BC 1932 revenues by major revenue sources (000$)

	Succession duties and probate fees	Quebec corporation tax/ BC corporation and personal income tax	Motor vehicle revenues	Natural resources revenues	Property taxes	Liquor revenues	Total
BC	$501	$5,524	$3,734	$3,221	$1,975	$3,422	$18,377
% of total	3%	30%	20%	18%	11%	19%	
Quebec	$3,799	$3,488	$10,382	$3,552	$0	$6,152	$27,373
% of total	14%	13%	38%	13%	0%	22%	

Per capita distribution of revenues from major provincial taxes from 1932

BC population	694,263
BC per capita total tax*	$24.47
Quebec population	2,874,255
Quebec per capita total tax	$9.52

* At the provincial level, British Columbia also collected a poll tax, an amusement tax, and a racetrack tax. The revenues from these taxes were small enough to affect only trivially the calculations in these tables.

Sources: J. Harvey Perry, *Taxes, Tariffs, and Subsidies: A History of Canadian Fiscal Development*, 2 vols. (Toronto: University of Toronto Press, 1955). Table 15, 2: 646–47; Table 20, 2: 664–65; Statistics Canada, *Canada Year Book, 1932, 91*, and *Canada Yearbook Historical Collection*, http://www65.statcan.gc.ca.

TABLE 7

Income tax (IT) receipts, sales tax (ST) receipts, and gross national product (GNP) (000$) annual changes, 1930 to 1939

	IT revenue	IT change	ST revenue	ST change	GNP $ value	Real GNP growth
1930	$69.0		$44.1		$5,720.0	
1931[1]	$71.1	3%	$20.1	−119%	$4,693.0	−13%
1932	$61.3	−16%	$41.7	52%	$3,814.0	−10%
1933[2]	$62.1	1%	$56.8	27%	$3,492.0	−7%
1934	$61.4	−1%	$61.4	7%	$3,969.0	12%
1935[3]	$66.6	8%	$72.4	15%	$4,301.0	8%
1936	$82.7	19%	$77.6	7%	$4,634.0	4%
1937	$102.4	19%	$112.8	31%	$5,241.0	10%
1938	$120.3	15%	$138.1	18%	$5,272.0	1%
1939[4]	$142.0	15%	$122.1	−13%	$5,621.0	7%

1 IT, ST, and GNP all in current not constant dollars.
2 GNP decline 1930–36 of −38%.
3 IT growth 1930–1936 of 49%.
4 Gross revenue from ST = or > IT 1934–39.

Sources: J. Harvey Perry, *Taxes, Tariffs, and Subsidies: A History of Canadian Fiscal Development*, 2 vols. (Toronto: University of Toronto Press, 1955), Table 6, 2: 626–27; W. Irwin Gillespie, *Tax, Borrow, and Spend: Financing Federal Spending in Canada, 1867–1990* (Ottawa: Carleton University Press, 1991), Table C-1, 283.

TABLE 8

Comparison of changes in number of personal income tax payers as a percentage of the labour force, by gender, 1941–51 (estimated) and 1964 (actual) [1]

Year	Personal income tax payers (PITP)[2] Male (M)	Female (F)	Total (T)	Labour force (LF)[3] M	F	T	PITP (M, F, or T) / LF (M, F, or T) M/M	T/M	F/F
1941			871,484	3,594,079				<24.2%	
1943			2,163,354	>3,594,079				<60.2%	
1951			2,777,950	4,130,802				<67.2%	
	M	F	T	M	F	T	M/M	T/T	F/F
1964	3,774,343	1,526,876	5,301,219	5,273,700	2,458,700	7,732,400	71.6%	68.4%	62%

1 1964 was the first year in which the Department of National Revenue reported numbers of personal income tax payers (PITP) by sex, so only the 1964 ratios are exact. I justify using male labour force figures as the denominator for the 1941, 1943, and 1951 estimated fractions on the grounds that women's labour force participation patterns and rates of pay made them less likely than men to be income taxpayers in those years. One estimate of the proportion of women in the population of interwar income tax payers was 12 percent in 1929-30. The sex-specific statistics for 1964 allow us some measure of the difference between the breakdown by sex of the labour force and the breakdown by sex of PITP. By 1964, men were 62.2 percent of the total labour force, but they were 71.2 per cent of the total PITP. By 1964, women's labour force participation had risen and inflation had begun its work of imposing an income tax liability on an increasing number of low-paid workers. Still, women remained a smaller percentage of PITP (28.9 percent) than they were of the total labour force (31.8 percent). If the percentage of PITP who were male and the percentage of the labour force who were male corresponded in 1951 as they did in 1964, then knowing that 76 per cent of the labour force was male in 1951, we can estimate that men were approxmately 87.36 per cent of the PITP in 1951. On those assumptions, male PITP in 1951 would be 2,426,817, and thus 58.7 per cent of the male labour force. Actual PITP as a percentage of the labour for 1951 could thus be as much as 9 per cent lower than the estimates reported in the table, and similarly lower for 1943 and 1941. The estimate of women income tax payers is from data in Department of National Revenue, "Income tax brief," undated, circa 1931, QUA, Dexter fonds, coll. 2142, box 20, file 199. For sex ratios of the Canadian labour force in 1931, 1941, and 1951, see Alison Prentice, et al. Canadian Women: A History (Toronto: Harcourt Brace Jovanovich, 1988), 422.

2 For 1941, 1943, and 1951, the numbers of personal income tax payers are from Perry, vol. 2, 698 (taxation years 1951, 1943, and 1951). For the 1964 year, the number of personal income tax payers is from Department of National Revenue, Taxation Division, 1966 Taxation Statistics, Part One – Individuals, Analyzing 1964 T1 Individual Income Tax Returns (Ottawa: Queen's Printer, 1966), 92 (1964 line).

3 For 1941, the labour force figures are the number of gainfully employed men (including men in Active Service), ages 15 to 69, in Census of Canada 1941, vol. 7, at 12-13. For 1943, the labour force number was in reality probably larger, so the 1943 percentage is therefore slightly low. For 1951, the labour force figure is the figure given for total labour force, male, 14 years and over, in Census of Canada 1951, vol 5, page 1-1. The 1964 labour force figures are from Sylvia Ostry, Unemployment in Canada (Ottawa: Dominion Bureau of Statistics, 1968), 39.

Notes

Chapter 1: Talking Tax

1 Quoted in Kenneth LeM. Carter, "Canadian Tax Reform and Henry Simons," *Journal of Law and Economics* 11, 2 (1968): 241.

2 Ibid.

3 The primate research subjects are more often rhesus monkeys, but neither Cole Porter nor I would like the sound of this more accurate term. See, for example, "Animals Pay Taxes, Too," in "Social Studies," *Globe and Mail*, April 21, 2009, L6.

4 Paul Fox and Donald Creighton, *A Long View of Canadian History* (Toronto: CBC Publications Branch, 1959), 3–6; excerpted in Michael S. Cross, ed., *The Frontier Thesis and the Canadas: The Debate on the Impact of the Canadian Environment* (Toronto: Copp Clark Publishing, 1970), 42.

5 Mark Milke, *A Nation of Serfs? How Canada's Political Culture Corrupts Canadian Values* (Mississauga, ON: J. Wiley and Sons, 2006), Chapter 3.

6 See, for example, Barry Ferguson and Robert Wardhaugh, "'Impossible Conditions of Inequality': John W. Dafoe, the Rowell-Sirois Royal Commission, and the Interpretation of Canadian Federalism," *Canadian Historical Review* 84, 4 (2003): 551–83; E.R. Forbes, *The Maritimes Rights Movement: 1919–1927: A Study in Canadian Regionalism* (Montreal: McGill-Queen's University Press, 1979); Penny Bryden, *"A Justifiable Obsession": Conservative Ontario's Relations with Ottawa, 1943–1985* (Toronto: University of Toronto Press, 2013); and Jean Claude Racine and François Rocher, "Duplessis vu d'Ottawa," in *Duplessis et son époque*, ed. Xavier Gélinas and Lucia Ferretti (Quebec: Septentrion, 2010), 263–84.

7 J. Harvey Perry, *Taxes, Tariffs, and Subsidies: A History of Canadian Fiscal Development*, 2 vols. (Toronto: University of Toronto Press, 1955); J. Harvey Perry, *A Fiscal History of Canada: The Postwar Years* (Toronto: Canadian Tax Foundation, 1989); W. Irwin Gillespie, *Tax, Borrow, and Spend: Financing Federal Spending in Canada, 1867–1990* (Ottawa: Carleton University Press, 1991); David W. Slater and R.B. Bryce, *War, Finance, and Reconstruction: The Role of Canada's Department of Finance 1939–1946* ([Ottawa: Department of Finance,] 1995); R.B. Bryce, *Maturing in Hard Times: Canada's Department of Finance through the Great Depression* (Kingston, ON: McGill-Queen's University Press, 1986); R.B. Bryce and

Matthew J. Bellamy, eds., *Canada and the Cost of World War II: The International Operations of Canada's Department of Finance, 1939–1947* (Montreal: McGill-Queen's University Press, 2005); Dave McIntosh, *The Collectors: A History of Canadian Customs and Excise* (Toronto: NC Press, 1985); Richard Krever, "The Origin of Federal Income Taxation in Canada," *Canadian Taxation* 3, 4 (1981): 170–88; David Tough, "The Rich ... Should Give to Such an Extent that It Will Hurt': 'Conscription of Wealth' and Political Modernism in the Parliamentary Debate on the 1917 Income War Tax," *Canadian Historical Review* 93, 3 (2012): 382–407; Bob Russell, "The Politics of Labour-Force Reproduction: Funding Canada's Social Wage, 1917–1946," *Studies in Political Economy* 13 (1984): 43–73; Robert Gardner, "Tax Reform and Class Interests: The Fate of Progressive Reform, 1967–72," *Canadian Taxation* 3 (1981): 245–57; Leslie Macdonald, "Taxing Comprehensive Income: Power and Participation in Canadian Politics, 1962–72" (PhD diss., Carleton University, Department of Political Science, 1985); Neil Brooks, ed., *The Quest for Tax Reform: The Royal Commission on Taxation Twenty Years Later* (Toronto: Carswell, 1988); Geoffrey Hale, *The Politics of Taxation in Canada* (Peterborough, ON: Broadview Press, 2002). Elsbeth Heaman and I have begun to add historians' voices to this conversation; see Shirley Tillotson, "The Family as Tax Dodge: Partnership, Individuality, and Gender in the Personal Income Tax Act, 1942 to 1970," *Canadian Historical Review* 90, 3 (2009): 391–425; Shirley Tillotson, "Relations of Extraction: Taxation and Women's Citizenship in the Maritimes, 1914–1955," *Acadiensis* 39, 1 (2010): 27–57; Shirley Tillotson, "The Politics of Carter-Era Tax Reform: A Revisionist Account," in *The Quest for Tax Reform Continues: The Royal Commission on Taxation Fifty Years Later*, ed. Kim Brooks (Toronto: Carswell, 2013), 31–52; Shirley Tillotson, "Warfare State, Welfare State, and the Selling of the Personal Income Tax, 1942–45," *Canadian Tax Journal* 63, 1 (2015): 1–38; Elsbeth Heaman, "The Politics of Fairness: Income Tax in Canada before 1917," in *The Quest for Tax Reform Continues: The Royal Commission on Taxation Fifty Years Later*, ed. Kim Brooks (Toronto: Carswell, 2013), 15–30; and Elsbeth Heaman, "'The Whites Are Wild about It': Taxation and Racialization in Mid-Victorian British Columbia," *Journal of Policy History* 25, 3 (2013): 354–84.

8 Some examples from this range include K.W. Taylor, "Draft, Memorandum to the Minister: Re Memorandum of January 16, 1962," submitted by Ken Carter of McDonald, Currie and Company on "Tax Incentives for Increases in Export Sales," LAC, Finance fonds, RG 19, vol. 4237, file 5025–03–1 part 2 1960–62; "Wilf" (W.H. Hall) to "Walter" (Minister of Finance Walter Gordon), August 7, 1964, LAC, Finance fonds, RG 19, vol. 4237, file 5025–03–1 part 4 1964; and Agnes Anderson to Minister of Finance, March 26, 1964, LAC, Finance fonds, RG 19, vol. 4237, file 5025–03–1 part 4 1964.

9 A. Kenneth Eaton, *Essays in Taxation* (Toronto: Canadian Tax Foundation, 1966), 20.

10 One of the rare comments saying that "in our opinion there is no point in further correspondence" with a particular citizen known for intemperate and unreasonable complaints can be found in R.N. Handy (Executive Assistant to the Minister of National Revenue) to Mary E. Macdonald (Executive Assistant to the Prime Minister), June 20, 1963, LAC, Pearson fonds, MG 26-N3, vol. 331, file 335 AE01.91 Dumont. An instance of concern about being a crank can be found in Lars Larson to Lester B. Pearson, October 23, 1967, LAC, Pearson fonds, MG 26-N3, vol. 54, file 252.211-M.

11 For discussions on and use of such letters as evidence, see Sheila Fitzpatrick, "Supplicants and Citizens: Public Letter-Writing in Soviet Russia in the 1930s," *Slavic Review* 55, 1 (1996): 78–105; Lara Campbell, "'We Who Have Wallowed in the Mud of Flanders': First World War Veterans, Unemployment, and the Development of Social Welfare in Canada, 1929–1939," *Journal of the Canadian Historical Association* 11, 1 (2000): 125–49; and Joan Sangster, "Invoking Experience as Evidence," *Canadian Historical Review* 92, 1 (2011): 135–61.

12 Vivien A. Schmidt, "Taking Ideas and Discourse Seriously: Explaining Change through Discursive Institutionalism as the Fourth New Institutionalism," *European Political Science Review* 2, 1 (2010): 1–25.

13 Monteith Douglas, "Taxable Capacity and British and Canadian Experience," in *The Limits of Taxable Capacity*, ed. Dan Throop Smith et al. (Princeton, NJ: Tax Institute, 1953), 30.

14 Martin Daunton, "How to Pay for the War: State, Society, and Taxation in Britain, 1917–24," *English Historical Review* 111, 443 (1996): 882.

15 The author of Canada's main reference works on tax history avoids this focus, and his books are rather list-like as a result; see J. Harvey Perry, *Taxes, Tariffs, and Subsidies: A History of Canadian Fiscal Development*, 2 vols. (Toronto: University of Toronto Press, 1955); and J. Harvey Perry, *A Fiscal History of Canada: The Postwar Years* (Toronto: Canadian Tax Foundation, 1989). The British historian whose approach is similar to mine makes taxation of income his focus but sets it in a well-developed context of other taxes; see Martin Daunton, *Just Taxes: The Politics of Taxation in Britain, 1914–1979* (New York: Cambridge University Press, 2002). The emphasis on income taxation is more noticeable in the more developed tax literature on US federal taxation; see Randolph E. Paul, *Taxation in the United States* (Boston: Little, Brown, 1954); W. Elliot Brownlee, *Federal Taxation in America: A Short History* (New York: Cambridge University Press, 1996); Carolyn C. Jones, "Class Tax to Mass Tax: The Role of Propaganda in the Expansion of the Income Tax during World War II," *Buffalo Law Review* 37, 3 (1988–89): 685–737; Julian E. Zelizer, *Taxing America: Wilbur D. Mills, Congress, and the State, 1945–1975* (New York: Cambridge University Press, 2000); and Molly C. Michelmore, *Tax and Spend: The Welfare State, Tax Politics, and the Limits of American Liberalism* (Philadelphia: University of Pennsylvania Press, 2012).

16 W. Elliot Brownlee, "Tax Regimes, National Crisis, and State-Building," in *Funding the Modern American State, 1941–1995: The Rise and Fall of the Era of Easy Finance*, ed. W. Elliot Brownlee (New York: Cambridge University Press, 1996), 96–97; Neil Brooks, "Taxation and Citizenship," *Labour/Le Travail* 48 (2001): 354–55. Daunton, *Just Taxes*, provides a more developed narrative about the different British history; Britain is not a federal system and had a well-established income tax at the beginning of the twentieth century, but his narrative also notes the turn to Thatcherism as a departure from an earlier, and more harmonious, tax culture.

17 Timothy Lewis, *In the Long Run We're All Dead: The Canadian Turn to Fiscal Restraint* (Vancouver: UBC Press, 2003).

18 Robert Nozick, *Anarchy, State, and Utopia* (New York: Basic Books, 1974); James M. Buchanan, "Can Democracy Promote the General Welfare?," in *The Welfare State*, ed. Ellen Frankel Paul, Fred D. Miller Jr., and Jeffrey Paul (New York: Cambridge University Press, 1997), 168–71. Lest we think that this position is held only in the United States, note the work of eminent Canadian philosopher Jan Narveson, for example "On Economic Rent: Michael Jordan, the Reichmann Brothers, and Jim Smith, Day-Laborer: Whom Do We Get to Tax, and Why?," *Reason Papers* 25 (2000): 29–53.

19 The leading exponent of a national culture scale of comparison between Canada and the United States summarizes his position and some of the criticism that it attracts in Seymour Martin Lipset, "The Values of Canadians and Americans: A Reply," *Social Forces* 69, 1 (1990): 267–72.

20 Michael A. Livingston, "Law, Culture, and Anthropology: On the Hopes and Limits of Comparative Tax," *Canadian Journal of Law and Jurisprudence* 18, 1 (2005): 119–34; Ann Mumford, *Taxing Culture* (Aldershot, UK: Ashgate, 2002). Regarding statute labour on roads in the prairie region, see "Municipal District of Pine Lake," *Red Deer News*, March 12, 1924, 7. On statute labour and poll taxes more generally, see Chapter 5.

21 Jeremy Webber, *Reimagining Canada: Language, Culture, Community, and the Canadian Constitution* (Montreal: McGill-Queen's University Press, 1994); Roderick A. Macdonald and Robert Wolfe, "Canada's Third National Policy: The Epiphenomenal or the Real Constitution?," *University of Toronto Law Journal* 59, 4 (2009): 469–523.

22 "A Nova Scotia 'Blast,'" editorial, Toronto *Globe*, April 25, 1931, 4.

23 Minutes, September 15, 1921, Papers of the Halifax Local Council of Women, vol. 535, Nova Scotia Archives (hereafter NSA).

24 Margaret Levi, *Of Rule and Revenue* (Berkeley: University of California Press, 1988); Deborah A. Brautigam, Odd-Helge Fjelstad, and Mick Moore, eds., *Taxation and State-Building in Developing Countries: Capacity and Consent* (New York: Cambridge University Press, 2008), Introduction and Chapter 2. Max Herb raises the question of whether, once states have representative institutions, taxation has a further impact on democratic structures. I argue here that it does by generating civil society organization and activism. See Max Herb, "Taxation and Representation," *Studies in Comparative International Development* 38, 30 (2003): 3–31.

25 Edmund Pries, "Taxpayers vs. Citizens," *Toronto Star*, September 15, 2011.

26 E.A. Heaman, *Tax, Order, and Good Government: A New Political History of Canada, 1867–1917* (Montreal: McGill-Queen's University Press, 2017).

Chapter 2: We, the Taxpayers

1 Sir Thomas White, *The Story of Canada's War Finance* (Montreal: privately printed, 1921), 58, 60.

2 "Sir Thomas to Rest," Toronto *Globe*, January 28, 1918, 5; Hector Charlesworth, ed., s.v. "White, the Rt. Hon. Sir William Thomas," *A Cyclopaedia of Canadian Biography: Brief Biographies of Persons Distinguished in the Professional, Military, and Political Life, and the Commerce and Industry of Canada in the Twentieth Century* (Toronto: Hunter-Rose Company, 1919), 15, https://archive.org/details/cyclopdiaofcanoocharuoft.

3 W. Irwin Gillespie, *Tax, Borrow, and Spend: Federal Financing in Canada, 1867–1990* (Ottawa: Carleton University Press, 1991), 92–93; J. Harvey Perry, *Taxes, Tariffs, and Subsidies: A History of Canadian Fiscal Development*, 2 vols. (Toronto: University of Toronto Press, 1955), 1: 156; Richard Krever, "The Origin of Federal Income Taxation in Canada," *Canadian Taxation* 3, 4 (1981): 170–88; David Tough, "'The Rich ... Should Give to Such an Extent that It Will Hurt': 'Conscription of Wealth' and Political Modernism in the Parliamentary Debate on the 1917 Income War Tax," *Canadian Historical Review* 93, 3 (2012): 382–407.

4 Prewar discussions of income taxation have had little serious scholarly attention. Innovative works such as Krever's and Tough's noted above and the old standard by Perry, *Taxes, Tariffs, and Subsidies*, cover some general themes. What is new in what follows is based in part upon my own archival research but owes much to conversations with my colleague Elsbeth Heaman.

5 Frederick Williams-Taylor to Thomas White, February 12, 1915, and H.A. Stewart, KC (Belleville), to Thomas White, February 13, 1915, Library and Archives Canada (hereafter LAC), Sir William Thomas White fonds (hereafter White fonds), MG 27 II D 18, vol. 20, file 84.

6 Canada, House of Commons, *Debates*, February 11, 1915, 85.

7 Elsbeth Heaman, "The Politics of Fairness: Income Tax in Canada before 1917," in *The Quest for Tax Reform Continues: The Royal Commission on Taxation Fifty Years Later*, ed. Kim Brooks (Toronto: Carswell, 2014), 15–16.

8 Charlesworth, "White, the Rt. Hon. Sir William Thomas," 13.

9 Heaman, "The Politics of Fairness," 16–27.

10 White, *Story,* 30; F.H. Brown, J.D. Gibson, and A.F.W. Plumptre, *War Finance in Canada* (Toronto: Ryerson Press, 1940), 10, 33.

11 J.J. Deutsch, "War Finance and the Canadian Economy, 1914–1920," *Canadian Journal of Economics and Political Science* 6, 4 (1940): 531.

12 A capsule history of the origin and purpose of the Colonial Stock Act can be found in Deborah Brautigam, "Contingent Capacity: Export Taxation and State-Building in Mauritius," in *Taxation and State Building in Developing Countries: Capacity and Consent,* ed. Deborah A. Brautigam, Odd-Helge Fjelstad, and Mick Moore (New York: Cambridge University Press, 2008), 149–50. Regarding its application in Canada into the 1930s, see R.B. Bryce, *Maturing in Hard Times: Canada's Department of Finance through the Great Depression* (Kingston: McGill-Queen's University Press, 1986), 259n10; W.P.M.K.[ennedy], "Colonial Stock Act of 1934," *University of Toronto Law Journal* 1, 2 (1936): 348–50; A. Berriefield Keith, *The Sovereignty of the British Dominions* (London: Macmillan, 1929), 219–20; and Canada, House of Commons, *Debates,* May 26 and 30, 1930, 2719 and 2726.

13 Canadian methods of describing debt in the national accounts were regarded somewhat skeptically by American authorities and opposition critics. See J.A. Maxwell, "The Distinction between Ordinary and Capital Expenditure in Canada," *National Tax Association Bulletin* 19, 5 (1934): 146–48; Raymond Tatlovich, "Revisiting Post-Confederation Fiscal Policy: Liberal Dissent from Conservative Deficits," *Journal of Canadian Studies* 47, 2 (2013): 204–5; and Robert Freeman Smith, "Latin America, the United States, and the European Powers, 1830–1930," in *The Cambridge History of Latin America, Vol. 4, c. 1870–1930,* ed. Leslie Bethell (Cambridge, UK: Cambridge University Press, 1986), 101–2.

14 W.E. Rundle to Thomas White, December 1, 1915, LAC, White fonds, MG 27 II D 18, vol. 3, file 12(b).

15 Tatlovich, "Revisiting Post-Confederation Fiscal Policy," 180–214.

16 Deutsch, "War Finance," 527; C.A. Curtis, "The Canadian Banks and War Finance," *Contributions to Canadian Economics* 3 (1931): 9.

17 White, *Story,* 11.

18 Brown, Gibson, and Plumptre, *War Finance in Canada,* 10, 33.

19 John Lewis, "Canada at War," in *Canada in the Great World War: An Authentic Account of the Military History of Canada from the Earliest Days to the Close of the War of the Nations, by Various Authorities,* vol. II, *Days of Preparation* (Toronto: United Publishers of Canada, 1918), 35–37. Regarding Lewis's political affiliation, see "Occupations of Senators," http://www.lop.parl.gc.ca/ParlInfo. The W.L. Mackenzie King Diaries contain several specific references to Lewis's occupation and role as editor of political literature for the federal Liberals, beginning in January 1920: diary entries for December 15, 1919; January 7, 1920; and January 22, 1920, LAC, Diaries of William Lyon Mackenzie King (hereafter King Diaries), MG 26 J 13, http://www.collectionscanada.gc.ca/databases/king/index-e.html.

20 Canada, House of Commons, *Debates,* August 20, 1914, 41; August 21, 1914, 71–72.

21 Canada, House of Commons, *Debates,* August 21, 1914, 73.

22 O.D. Skelton, *Federal Finance,* Bulletin No. 16 of the Departments of History and Political and Economic Science (Kingston, ON: Queen's University, 1915). Skelton's influence in the remaking of Canadian Liberalism and the role of tax ideas like those of the Farmers' Platform in his thought are put in context in Barry Ferguson, *Remaking Liberalism: The Intellectual Legacy of Adam Shortt, O.D. Skelton, W.C. Clark, and W.A. Mackintosh, 1890–1925* (Montreal: McGill-Queen's University Press, 1993), Chapter 7, and in Terry Crowley, *Marriage of Minds: Isabel and Oscar Skelton Reinventing Canada* (Toronto: University of Toronto Press, 2003), 52–54. See E.A. Heaman, *Tax, Order, and Good Government: A New Political History of Canada 1867–1917* (Montreal: McGill-Queen's University Press, 2017),

for a thoroughly developed account of thinking about income taxation in late-nineteenth-century and early-twentieth-century Canada.

23 Frederick Williams-Taylor to Thomas White, August 10, 1914, LAC, White fonds, MG 27 II D 18, vol. 2, file 10(a).

24 Izaac Walton Killam, *The Case Against Tax-Exempt Bonds: Open Letters to the Right Honourable Sir Robert Borden, P.C., G.C.M.G., Prime Minister of Canada, and to the Honourable Sir Thomas White, K.C.M.G., Minister of Finance* (Montreal: privately printed, 1918), 11.

25 Martin Daunton, *Just Taxes: The Politics of Taxation in Britain, 1914–1979* (New York: Cambridge University Press, 2002), 49–50; R.J.Q. Adams, *Bonar Law* (London: John Murray, 1999), 253–55.

26 James Marran, "Why Change the Name Socialist," letter to the editor, Toronto *Globe*, September 2, 1916, 15.

27 "End War Debt in Thirty Years," Toronto *Globe*, January 18, 1917, 3.

28 See, for example, the platform of the independent farmer-labour candidate in Lethbridge, presented as reflecting the conscription of wealth position of the "labor party of Canada" and "the farmers of Alberta." It called for tax on income and tax on corporate profit. Its wealth taxes were a progressive rate tax on inheritance and a tax on undeveloped, privately owned land. Its call for public ownership of utilities would have entailed expropriation rather than taxation of wealth. None of these taxes was a capital levy, even though they called their platform conscription of wealth. See "Mr. Pack's Position," letter to the editor, *Lethbridge Daily Herald*, November 21, 1917, 9. My attention was drawn to this representative example by Robert Rutherford, *Hometown Horizons: Local Responses to Canada's Great War* (Vancouver: UBC Press, 2004), 173.

29 The Toronto *Globe* story on White's statement called it "somewhat cryptic" because White referred only to a "certain uneasiness" among the public. In fact, it was not "the public" in general to which he referred but those Canadians "whose savings constitute a vital factor in the business and industrial life of the Dominion," whose uneasiness he sought to allay. As important as small investors were, the phrasing suggests that he had in mind larger owners of capital. His later acknowledgment in *The Story of War Finance* that there had been the risk of a banking crisis suggests that the idea of a capital levy was well enough known to fuel rumours and incite a small panic. And at least one Liberal, E.M. Macdonald, a lawyer representing Pictou, Nova Scotia, had urged the taxation of "accumulated wealth" during the spring 1917 budget debate. See House of Commons, *Debates*, July 10, 1917, 3187; May 15, 1917, 1441; "Legitimate Savings Will Not Be Taken" Toronto *Globe*, July 11, 1917, 5; "Savings of People Will Not Be Taxed," *Calgary Daily Herald*, July 10, 1917, 1; and White, *Story*, 53.

30 "Shall Canada Be Ruled by Quebec, Asks Michael Clark," *Calgary Daily Herald*, December 1, 1917, 7.

31 James Alexander Calder, "Suggested Forms of Taxation," in item 8, "Confiscation of Capital," in *Soldier's Civil Re-Establishment: Fourth and Final Report of the Special Committee in Bill No. 10, An Act to Amend the Department of Soldier's Civil Re-Establishment Act* (Ottawa: King's Printer, 1919), 47–48; "Committee Sifts Vital Resolutions. One to Come before Convention Calls for a Tax on Capital," *Toronto Daily Star*, August 6, 1919, 9; "Committee Against Any New Tax Plans," *Toronto Daily Star*, November 5, 1919, 4; Canada, House of Commons, *Debates*, May 19, 1920, 252.

32 Elsbeth Heaman, "The Politics of Fairness: Income Tax in Canada before 1917," in *The Quest for Tax Reform Continues: The Royal Commission on Taxation Fifty Years Later*, ed. Kim Brooks (Toronto: Carswell, 2014), 15–30.

33 Perry, *Taxes, Tariffs, and Subsidies*, 1: 124–36; Martin Daunton, *Trusting Leviathan: The Politics of Taxation in Britain, 1799–1914* (New York: Cambridge University Press, 2001), 237–44; Daunton, *Just Taxes*, 157, 349.

34 The single tax program of the league was set out in "Circular Letter from the Canadian League for the Taxation of Land Values, 1917," doc. 2453, LAC, W.C. Good fonds, MG 27 III C1, vol. 4, file "Correspondence 1917."

35 "Urge Dominion-Wide Tax on Land Values," Toronto *Globe*, August 21, 1916, 4. In addition to Drury, Dunning, and Crerar, the MPs and provincial members, current or future, included Nelly McClung, Michael Clark, Arthur Roebuck, Fred Dixon, Thomas M[a]cNutt, Senator [?] Gilmour, J.G. Tur[r]iff, W.C. Good, and Henry Wise Wood.

36 On the Southams' business history, see Minko Sotiron, *From Politics to Profit: The Commercialization of Canadian Daily Newspapers, 1890–1920* (Montreal: McGill-Queen's University Press, 1997), 88–92.

37 W.M. and H.S. Southam to Sir Robert Borden, October 30, 1918, LAC, White fonds, MG 27 II D 18, vol. 7, file 24.

38 F.H. Gisborne (Parliamentary Counsel) to Thomas White, October 31, 1918, and F.H. Gisborne, "Land Tax Memorandum," October 31, 1918, LAC, White fonds, MG 27 II D 18, vol. 7, file 24. Gisborne's letter refers to a tabulation of provincial land tax data that appears, from internal evidence, to be the undated documents 2747–2756 in LAC, White fonds, MG 27 II D 18, vol. 5, file 17(a).

39 See, for example, House of Commons, *Debates*, March 9, 1917, 792.

40 Desmond Morton, *Fight or Pay: Soldiers' Families in the Great War* (Vancouver: UBC Press, 2004), 130, 186–87, 195–97, 199–200, 202–3. Ames made much of this explicit in 1918 in "Toronto Must Look Ahead," Toronto *Globe*, March 18, 1918, 6. In 1917, the City of Saint John actually borrowed money in order to cover its Patriotic Fund contribution; see *Reports and Accounts of the Corporation of the City of Saint John for Year Ending December 31st* (hereafter *Saint John Reports*), 1915, 357, and *Saint John Reports*, 1917, 281–82. Held at the Saint John Common Clerk's Office when I consulted them in 2007, these documents are now located in the Saint John Free Public Library.

41 Shirley Tillotson, *Contributing Citizens: Modern Charitable Fundraising and the Making of the Welfare State* (Vancouver: UBC Press, 2008).

42 Hector Charlesworth, ed., s.v. "Williams-Taylor, Sir Frederick," in *A Cyclopaedia of Canadian Biography: Brief Biographies of Persons Distinguished in the Professional, Military, and Political Life, and the Commerce and Industry of Canada in the Twentieth Century* (Toronto: Hunter-Rose Company, 1919), 200, https://archive.org/details/cyclopdiaofcanoocharuoft; Frederick Williams-Taylor to Thomas White, August 10, 1914, and August 14, 1914, LAC, White fonds, MG 27 II D 18, vol. 2, file 10(a); Thomas White to Frederick Williams-Taylor, January 7, 1915, LAC, White fonds, MG 27 II D 18, vol. 3, file 11(a).

43 Frederick Williams-Taylor to Thomas White, August 23, 1916, LAC, White fonds, MG 27 II D 18, vol. 4, file 14(a).

44 White's annoyance can be read between the lines in White, *Story*, 21, 31. It is explicit in his correspondence with Williams-Taylor in April and May 1916, LAC, White fonds, MG 27 II D 18, vol. 3, file 13.

45 Thomas White to Frederick Williams-Taylor, April 12, 1916, LAC, White fonds, MG 27 II D 18, vol. 3, file 13. For the 94.94 issue price, see "Government Bond Issue Announced," Toronto *Globe*, March 24, 1916, 10.

46 Frederick Williams-Taylor to Thomas White, April 11, 22, and 26, 1916, LAC, White fonds, MG 27 II D 18, vol. 3, file 13.

47 T.B. Macaulay to Thomas White, August 25, 1916, LAC, White fonds, MG 27 II D 18, vol. 4, file 14(a).

48 Thomas White to T.B. Macaulay, August 26, 1916, LAC, White fonds, MG 27 II D 18, vol. 4, file 14(a).

49 Thomas White to W.E. Rundle (National Trust Company), September 26, 1916, and Thomas White to A.E. Ames (A.E. Ames and Company), September 25, 1916, LAC, White fonds, MG 27 II D 18, vol. 4, file 14(b).

50 "Income Tax Increase Helped British Bonds," Toronto *Globe*, July 30, 1917, 10.

51 See, for example, his saying that income tax might be appropriate "if the war goes on for another year or two." Canada, House of Commons, *Debates*, May 15, 1917, 1441.

52 "Prospect of New Taxation May Help New National Financing," Toronto *Globe*, July 2, 1917, 12.

53 "War Loans Are Still Firm Spot in Market," Toronto *Globe*, August 1, 1917, 12.

54 Killam, *The Case Against Tax-Exempt Bonds*, 9.

55 White, *Story*, 56.

56 The call for a "good stiff" income tax is in Canada, House of Commons, *Debates*, August 21, 1914, 72.

57 Killam's exact words were "any additional price that may be realized for such tax exempt securities cannot offset more than, at most, a quarter or a third of the direct loss arising from this method of finance." Killam, *The Case Against Tax-Exempt Bonds*, 8.

58 Curtis, "Canadian Banks," 21.

59 The first version of the bill was reported to the Senate from the House on August 15. The final version, slightly amended by the Senate, was passed more quietly on September 15. Canada, House of Commons, *Journals*, 567–68, 662–63. "Gov'ts Income Tax Proposals Are Announced," Montreal *Gazette*, July 26, 1917, 1; "The Income Tax," Montreal *Gazette*, July 26, 1917, 8; "Sir Thos. White's Speech," Montreal *Gazette*, July 26, 1917, 1; "About the Income Tax," *Western Globe* (Lacombe, AB), August 8, 1917, 6; "Wealth Conscription Bill Introduced," *Charlottetown Guardian*, July 26, 1917, 1; "Imposing Tax on Incomes to Meet War Expenses," *Daily Colonist* (Victoria), July 26, 1917, 1; "Conscripting Wealth," editorial, and "Province Makes No Objection to Tax," *Daily Colonist* (Victoria), July 26, 1917, 7.

60 "Income Tax Is Introduced by Sir Thomas White," Toronto *Globe*, July 26, 1917, 1 and 5; "The Federal Income Tax," editorial, Toronto *Globe*, July 26, 1917, 6; "Income Tax Resolution Is Passed by House," *Winnipeg Free Press*, July 26, 1917, 1 and 4; H.E.M.C., "The Day at the Capital," *Winnipeg Free Press*, July 26, 1917, 9, and July 27, 1917, 9; "L'Impôt sur le revenu," *L'Avenir du Nord* (St. Jérôme, QC), August 10, 1917, 1. Part of the *Avenir's* critique was based upon data from the *Toronto Daily Star*.

61 "The Day at the Capital," *Winnipeg Free Press*, August 3, 1918, 9; "A Staring, Glaring Anomaly," *Winnipeg Free Press*, August 9, 1917, 9; "Income Tax Will Antagonize Many," *Winnipeg Free Press*, July 27, 1917, 5.

62 "It is essential that we should keep our credit 'sweet' in our only available market, New York," was the phrase used by Frederick Williams-Taylor to Thomas White, August 25, 1916, LAC, White fonds, MG 27 II D 18, vol. 4, file 14(a).

63 Even Finance Minister Sir Henry Drayton acknowledged in his May 1920 budget speech that collections on the income tax had been fraught with difficulty; see Canada, House of Commons, *Debates*, May 18, 1920, 2488.

64 Thomas White to R. Home Smith, December 13, 1916, LAC, White fonds, MG 27 II D 18, vol. 20, file 84.

65 "Duty and Dividends!," Wood Gundy display ad, Toronto *Globe*, September 16, 1916, 15.

66 White, *Story*, 60–61.

67 For examples of ads illustrating the "war loan" usage and examples of the Department of Finance ad/prospectus, see *Toronto Daily Star*, November 22, 1915, 15, and Toronto *Globe*, September 5, 1916, 10; September 12, 1916, 13; March 8, 1917, 13; March 23, 1917, 11.

68 My translation. "The Markets. War Bond Advertising," Toronto *Globe*, March 7, 1917, 12.

69 Helen MacMurchy to Thomas White, November 11, 1915, LAC, White fonds, MG 27 II D 18, vol. 3, file 12(b).

70 G.A. Warburton (Citizens Committee of One Hundred, a non-partisan Ontario prohibi-tion organization) to Thomas White, March 17, 1916, LAC, White fonds, MG 27 II D 18, vol. 3, file 13.

71 Brenton A. McNab (Vice-President and Editor of *Montreal Daily Mail*) to Thomas White, December 1, 1915; M.E. Nichols (President and Managing Director of *Montreal Daily Mail*) to Thomas White, December 2, 1915; Thomas White to Robert Borden, December 11, 1915, LAC, White fonds, MG 27 II D 18, vol. 3, file 12(b). In the end, it seems, privacy turned out to be the better politics. No comprehensive list was published.

72 "The Loan Subscribed from Within," editorial, Toronto *Globe*, September 23, 1916, 6.

73 H.V.F. Jones (bank president) to Thomas White, August 10, 1916, LAC, White fonds, MG 27 II D 18, vol. 4, file 14(a); R.B. McElheran (clergyman) to Thomas White, September 1, 1916, LAC, White fonds, MG 27 II D 18, vol. 4, file 14(b); Albert Villemaire to Thomas White, January 14, 1918, LAC, White fonds, MG 27 II D 18, vol. 5, file 17(a). The quotation is my translation from Villemaire's letter.

74 Thomas White to R.B. McElheran (clergyman), September 6, 1916, LAC, White fonds, MG 27 II D 18, vol. 4, file 14(b).

75 "The War Loan," Toronto *Globe*, November 23, 1915, 12; "Oversubscription of Loan Is Conceded," Toronto *Globe*, September 21, 1916, 12; "To Divert Munitions Wages to War Bonds," Toronto *Globe*, September 20, 1916, 15; W.S. Davis (notary public and financial broker) to Thomas White, December 1, 1915, LAC, White fonds, MG 27 II D 18, vol. 3, file 12(b).

76 C.H. Dunbar (District Registrar of Land Registry Office) to Thomas White, August 7, 1916, LAC, White fonds, MG 27 II D 18, vol. 4, file 14(a).

77 "Production and Thrift," display ad, *Everywoman's World* 5, 5 (1916): 27.

78 See, for example, an Imperial Bank ad, Toronto *Globe*, November 13, 1917, 6.

79 "For Victory," National Trust ad, Toronto *Globe*, November 12, 1917, 17; "What Will It Be? A Dollar Bill or Kaiser Bill?," Elias Rogers Company (coal merchants) ad, Toronto *Globe*, November 23, 1917, 12; "I'll Buy a Victory Bond Bye and Bye," Hamilton B. Wills (stock-broker) ad, Toronto *Globe*, November 13, 1917, 16; "Tell Me Dad, What's a Coupon?," Ryrie Brothers ad, Toronto *Globe*, November 13, 1917, 9; "Buy a Victory Bond by Following the Gillette Banking System," Gillette Safety Razor ad (one of the few by a national advertiser, this one appeared in both English and French, in Calgary and Montreal), *Calgary Daily Herald*, November 12, 1917, 7, and Montreal *La Patrie*, November 12, 1917, 9; "Serious Business," Calgary Brewing Malting Company ad, *Calgary Daily Herald*, November 10, 1917, 24; "Have It Framed," Art Shop ad, *Calgary Daily Herald*, November 12, 1917, 9; "Stoves and Ranges," Rogers Hardware Company ad, *Charlottetown Guardian*, November 13, 1917, 4; "Buy Victory Loans to the Very Limit of Your Ability," R.T. Holman (depart-ment store) ad, *Charlottetown Guardian*, November 13, 1917, 5; C.H. Horsley Hardware ad, *Youngstown* [AB] *Plaindealer*, November 8, 1917, n.p.; "Vente de la 'victoire,'" George Waller department store ad, Montreal *La Patrie*, November 29, 1917, 9.

80 "The Fighting Men Await Your Answer," Victory Loan Committee/Department of Finance ad, *Kelowna Record*, November 29, 1917, 1; "400,000 ... Alignez-vous!," Victory Loan Committee/Department of Finance ad, Montreal *La Patrie*, November 29, 1917, 11; "400,000 ... Fall In!," *Charlottetown Guardian*, November 29, 1917, 7. The 400,000 re-ferred, according to the ad's text, to the number of "enlisted men who have offered their lives for Canada." It appears that, in contrast to the ads, the posters in the 1917 cam-paign made less use of this theme. Support for the troops, however, was an important theme in the 1918 and 1919 posters; see "Doing My Bit. Four Years. Do Yours, Buy Victory

Bonds," poster, 1918, 9750046–008; "Back Him Up. Buy Victory Bonds," poster, 1918, 19920108–016; "C'mon. Let's Finish the Job," poster, 1918 or 1919, 19720121–129, Canadian War Museum, George Metcalf Archival Collection.

81 "Doing My Bit," poster, 1918, 19750046–008; "C'mon! Let's Finish the Job," poster, 1918 or 1919, 19720121–129, online exhibition, *Canada and the First World War*, Canadian War Museum, http://www.warmuseum.ca/cwm/exhibitions.

82 "Why Canada Needs More Money," *Youngstown* [AB] *Plaindealer*, November 1, 1917, 1.

83 "Happy Will Be the Nation that Owes Its War Debts to Its Own People," Victory Loan Committee/Department of Finance ad, Toronto *Globe*, November 23, 1917, 4.

84 The posters in the Archives of Ontario collection can be dated more precisely than their accession information suggests. Posters that use the term "Victory Loan" or "Victory Bonds" were from 1917, 1918, or 1919. If they show an interest rate of 5.5 percent, then they cannot have been used to promote the 1915 or 1916 war loans, sold at 5 percent. The statistic offered on one of the posters ("1 in 187 of the population of Canada bought our last loan") was used only in the 1917 campaign. "To Maintain the Prosperity of Canada," 1917–19, C 233-2-0-1-2; "Canada's Weak Spot," C 233-2-0-1-298; "Every Dollar Spent in Canada," C 233-2-0-1-15, Archives of Ontario, War Poster Collection; http://www.archives.gov.on.ca/en/explore/online/posters/bonds.aspx and http://www.archives.gov.on.ca/en/explore/online/posters/gallery.aspx.

85 "Notes by an Onlooker," editorial, *Kelowna Record*, November 29, 1917, 2.

86 "37,000 Subscribers to Third War Loan," Toronto *Globe*, March 31, 1918, 20; "Canada's War Loans, Including Victory Bonds," A.E. Ames display ad, Toronto *Globe*, January 23, 1918, 10.

87 See, for example, "Community Chest Campaign Today," clipping, May 1925, Nova Scotia Archives, MG 20, Halifax-Dartmouth United Way fonds, vol. 1717, United Way scrapbook, 1925–40.

88 The absence of commercial advertisers supporting the Victory Loan campaigns is based upon reading the Montreal *La Patrie*'s ads for November 12, 13, and 29, 1917 (the same dates reviewed in the Toronto *Globe*, Peel's Prairie Provinces database, the *Calgary Daily Herald*, and the *Charlottetown Guardian*). The news and editorial support for the campaign is from the Montreal *La Patrie*, November 12, 1917, 1 and 3, and November 29, 1917, 4. On the same page as the editorial, "L'emprunt de victoire," in the section titled "La liberté de parole," the editors reported the anti-Quebec content of the Toronto press (the quoted passage is my translation).

89 White's private secretary to G.H. Wood, February 8, 1918, LAC, White fonds, MG 27 II D 18, vol. 5, file 18; Victory Loan Special Committee circular to bond dealers, October 8, 1918, vol. 5, file 18; Canadian Bankers' Association circular to bank managers, February 4, 1919, vol. 5, file 9(a); W.E. Errett (printer) to Thomas White, March 25, 1919, vol. 5, file 19(a); Thomas White to J.C. Douglas (MP for the Cape Breton riding in which Glace Bay is located), June 28, 1919 (includes a reference to coverage in the press of inexperienced owners of Victory Bonds being cheated as well as a report on coal miners being fleeced), vol. 5, file 19(a); Kenneth Molson (Molson and Robin) to Edgar Smith (Montreal Stock Exchange), copied by Smith to Thomas White, March 3, 1919, vol. 5, file 19(a).

90 S.J. Williams (clothing manufacturer) to Thomas White, September 21, 1918 (encloses clipping entitled "Selling Victory Bonds below Par"), LAC, White fonds, MG 27 II D 18, vol. 5, file 18; H.T. Ross (Canadian Bankers' Association) to Thomas White, February 15, 1919, LAC, White fonds, MG 27 II D 18, vol. 5, file 9(a).

91 Canadian Bankers' Association circular to bank managers, February 4, 1919, LAC, White fonds, MG 27 II D 18, vol. 5, file 9(a).

92 Frank Baalim (barrister) to Thomas White, March 17, 1918, LAC, White fonds, MG 27 II D 18, vol. 5, file 17(a); telegrams from W.H. Malkin (Victory Loan campaign chair for

British Columbia) to Thomas White, November 12–17, 1919 (regarding a similar issue concerning Doukhobors, endorses "strong steps" by Ottawa to tell them "the absolute necessity of subscribing at least fifty thousand. Anything less will not satisfy public opinion in British Columbia"), LAC, Finance fonds, RG 19, series E5, vol. 4009; "Victory Loan Near $65,000," *Youngstown* [AB] *Plaindealer,* November 22, 1917, 1.

93 Ontario MPP, signature illegible, to Thomas White, April 29, 1918 (reporting discussions with the mayor of Sudbury), LAC, White fonds, MG 27 II D 18, vol. 5, file 17(a); M.J. Galvin (North Bay) to Thomas White, July 3, 1918, vol. 5, file 17(b); M.B. (or W.B.?) Perry (The Pas) to Thomas White, September 14, 1918 (a variation in which "the foreign element" have no income but are rich in farm commodities), vol. 5, file 18; Mrs. J.D. (Mina) Lamont to Thomas White, September 26, 1918 (a variation in which "aliens" enjoy hidden mortgage wealth), vol. 5, file 18. A long-standing debate about fairness in taxation had identified cash as one of the invisible forms of property, impossible for assessors to measure by normal methods. For a summary of and an intervention in this debate, see F.H. Bell, *Principles of Civic Taxation* (Halifax: privately printed, 1899).

94 "Victory Loan Canvasser Shot," Toronto *Globe,* November 15, 1918, 5.

95 (Miss) H.E. Halliday to Thomas White, April 29, 1918, LAC, White fonds, MG 27 II D 18, vol. 5, file 17(a).

96 Leacock proposed this metaphor in an essay circulated, by March 1917, in a quarter of a million copies, as a pamphlet from the federal government's National Service Board. It was reprinted and in circulation before June 4, 1917, in a collection of essays. Stephen Leacock, "Our National Organization for the War," in *The New Era in Canada,* ed. J.O. Miller (Toronto: J.M. Dent and Sons, 1917), 419, 421; "National Service Literature," *Empress Express,* March 5, 1917, 1; "The New Era in Canada," Toronto *Globe,* June 4, 1917, 4.

97 M.A. Miller to Thomas White, July 8, 1918 (re the Cuban lottery), LAC, White fonds, MG 27 II D 18, vol. 5, file 17(b); A. Beliveau to Thomas White, May 11, 1918, vol. 5, file 17(b); Canada, House of Commons, Special Committee on Soldiers' Civil Re-Establishment, *Soldiers' Civil Re-Establishment: Proceedings of the Special Committee to Whom Was Referred Bill No. 10, An Act to Amend the Department of Soldiers' Civil Re-Establishment Act, Together with Certain Orders in Council Relating to the Work of the Said Department etc., etc. Comprising the Reports and Proceedings of the Committee, the Evidence Taken* (Ottawa: King's Printer, 1919), 45.

98 A. Beliveau to Thomas White, May 11, 1918, LAC, White fonds, MG 27 II D 18, vol. 5, file 17(b).

99 George C. Baber (1st Canadian Expeditionary Force veteran and insurance broker) to Robert Borden, April 26, 1918, LAC, White fonds, MG 27 II D 18, vol. 5, file 17(a).

100 Phrases such as "this would hardly be felt" and "no one would be hurt" mark many of the revenue schemes sent to White. See, for example, H.M. Robinson (Secretary-Treasurer, Canadian Hackney Horse Society) to Thomas White, August 27, 1919, LAC, White fonds, MG 27 II D 18, vol. 5, file 18; M.B. (or W.B.?) Perry (The Pas) to Thomas White, September 14, 1918, LAC, White fonds, MG 27 II D 18, vol. 5, file 18; L. Lefcovitz (commercial agent) to Thomas White, October 23, 1918, vol. 5, file 18; W. Mann (coal merchant) to Thomas White, December 3, 1918, LAC, White fonds, MG 27 II D 18, vol. 5, file 18.

101 Mark Osborne Humphries, "Between Commemoration and History: The Historiography of the Canadian Corps and Military Overseas," *Canadian Historical Review* 95, 3 (2014): 384–97; Amy Shaw, "Expanding the Narrative: A First World War with Women, Children, and Grief," *Canadian Historical Review* 95, 3 (2014): 398–406; Mourad Djebabla, "Historiographie francophone de la Première Guerre Mondiale: Écrire la Grande Guerre de 1914–1918 en français au Canada et au Québec," *Canadian Historical Review* 95, 3 (2014): 407–16.

Chapter 3: Canada's Conservative Tax Structure

1 Diary entry, December 15, 1919, 356, LAC, King Diaries, MG 26 J 13, http://www.collectionscanada.gc.ca/databases/king/index-e.html. The figure of $15,000 is derived from the Bank of Canada's inflation calculator: the amount of King's income tax payment in 1919 dollars was "over $1200."

2 Austin Winch, "Ottawa Plan May Lift Cost of Borrowing," *Toronto Daily Star*, July 17, 1958, 20. Winch reported that the Victory Bonds of the First World War were converted in a 1934 financing operation, and the bonds issued in 1934 were paid off in fifteen years. I infer from this that they were paid off in 1949.

3 Paul Studenski and Herman E. Krooss, *Financial History of the United States: Fiscal, Monetary, Banking, and Tariff, Including Financial Administration and State and Local Finance*, 2nd ed. (New York: McGraw-Hill, 1963), 309. Anticipations of the need for income taxation appeared regularly in prohibition literature; see "Shall Canada Have an Income Tax?," *Saint John Daily Telegraph*, April 20, 1894, 1; F.S. Spence, comp., *The Facts of the Case: A Summary of the Most Important Evidence and Argument Presented in the Report of the Royal Commission on the Liquor Traffic, Compiled under the Direction of the Dominion Alliance for the Total Suppression of the Liquor Traffic* (1896; facsimile ed., Toronto: Coles Publishing, 1973), 285–87.

4 W.C. Chisholm to Thomas White, December 29, 1918, LAC, White fonds, MG 27 II D 18, vol. 5, file 18.

5 The Business War Profits Tax Act expired at the end of 1920 and was not renewed in the 1921 revenue bills. Revenue from this tax continued to come in through the decade. J. Harvey Perry, *Taxes, Tariffs, and Subsidies: A History of Canadian Fiscal Development*, 2 vols. (Toronto: University of Toronto Press, 1955), 1: 198–99; Canada, House of Commons, *Debates*, May 9, 1921, 3120.

6 Although some argued in favour of Canada issuing permanent bonds, ones that would never be called back or cancelled, as Britain did, this view seems to have been unusual. Thomas White to Lindsay Crawford (editor of *Toronto Statesman*), October 28, 1918, LAC, White fonds, MG 27 II D 18, vol. 5, file 18.

7 "Main Estimates Two Million Less," Toronto *Globe*, March 23, 1918, 14.

8 "Canadian and American Taxation," Toronto *Globe*, June 10, 1918, 4.

9 Memorandum from the Minister (Thomas White) for R.W. Breadner, February 5, 1918, LAC, White fonds, MG 27 II D 18, vol. 7, file 24.

10 Gordon Barnhart, "Calder, John Alexander (1868–1956)," in *Encyclopedia of Saskatchewan*, http://esask.uregina.ca/entry/calder_james_alexander_1868-1956.html.

11 "Union Government Is Evading Duty towards Veterans," Saskatoon *Phoenix*, November 3, 1919, 1; "Hand Outs to Vets Opposed by Winnipeg MP," Saskatoon *Phoenix*, November 6, 1919, 1; "Union Government Will 'Kick In' If Gratuity Scheme Thrown Out," Saskatoon *Phoenix*, November 7, 1919, 1.

12 Canada, House of Commons, *Debates*, November 6, 1919, 1825–26.

13 Ibid., 1821–23.

14 Canadians writing to offer advice to the finance minister often recommended lotteries. See, for example, Hector MacKenzie and Ernest A. Browne to Thomas White, December 2, 1918, LAC, White fonds, MG 27 II D 18, vol. 5, file 17(A); A. Beliveau to Thomas White, May 11, 1918, and M.A. Miller to Thomas White, July 8, 1918, LAC, White fonds, MG 27 II D 18, vol. 5, file 17(b). On the moral objections to lotteries as a means of public finance, see Suzanne Morton, *At Odds: Gambling and Canadians, 1919–1969* (Toronto: University of Toronto Press, 2003), Chapter 1.

15 Canada, House of Commons, Special Committee on Soldiers' Civil Re-Establishment, *Soldiers' Civil Re-Establishment: Proceedings of the Special Committee to Whom Was Referred Bill No. 10, An Act to Amend the Department of Soldiers' Civil Re-Establishment Act, Together with Certain Orders in Council Relating to the Work of the Said Department etc., etc. Comprising the Reports and Proceedings of the Committee, the Evidence Taken* (Ottawa: King's Printer, 1919), 43–48.

16 "Drayton, Sir Henry," in *Canadian Parliamentary Guide,* 1921 (Ottawa: A.L. Normandin, 1921) and in *Canadian Who's Who,* 1936–37 (Toronto: Trans-Canada Press, 1936); "Drayton, the Hon. Sir Henry Lumley, P.C., K.C., K.B.," and "NICKLE, William Folger," Parlinfo, House of Commons, Members of the House of Commons, Parliamentarian File, http://www.parl.gc.ca/ParlInfo/; "Sir Henry Drayton Likely Minister of Finance," Toronto *Globe,* August 1, 1919, 2; "Drayton in the Cabinet," Toronto *Globe,* August 4, 1919, 5.

17 Diary entry, February 4, 1920, 37, LAC, King Diaries, MG 26 J 13, http://www.collectionscanada.gc.ca/databases/king/index-e.html.

18 Canada, House of Commons, *Debates,* May 18, 1920, 2487, 2492–95; diary entry, May 18, 1920, 163–64, LAC, King Diaries, MG 26 J 13, http://www.collectionscanada.gc.ca/databases/king/index-e.html.

19 Canada, House of Commons, *Debates,* May 18, 1920, 2476, 2490–92; June 9, 1920, 3316.

20 J. Castell Hopkins, *Canadian Annual Review of Public Affairs* (hereafter *CAR*), *1920* (Toronto: Canadian Review Company, 1921), 52–55; Canada, House of Commons, *Debates,* June 9, 1920, 3329.

21 Canada, House of Commons, *Debates,* June 8, 1920, 3244–46, and June 9, 1920, 3311–13; "More Luxury Tax Changes Made by Parliament: All Items Keenly Debated," *Toronto World,* June 16, 1920, 1; "Numerous Amendments to Luxury Taxes Adopted by Ottawa House: Taxes in Budget Still in Force," *Edmonton Bulletin,* June 16, 1920, 1.

22 Diary entry, May 18, 1920, 163–64, LAC, King Diaries, MG 26 J 13, http://www.collectionscanada.gc.ca/databases/king/index-e.html.

23 Canada, House of Commons, *Debates,* June 9, 1920, 3316–35; June 18, 1920, 3795–97; June 26, 1920, 4288–91.

24 Closing remarks at Saint John by Henry Drayton, November 9, 1920, LAC, Records of the Tariff Commission of 1920 (hereafter Tariff Commission), RG 36-8, vol. 7, file 15.

25 This list of occupations of intervenors is not exhaustive but is meant to give some idea of the range of Canadians who participated in the process. The list here is based upon intervenors who appear in the following files: LAC, Tariff Commission, RG 36-8, vol. 4, file 2; vol. 5, file 7; vol. 5, file 14; vol. 7, files 15 and 17.

26 W.C. Clark, "Tariff Commission," *Queen's Quarterly* 28 (1921): 302.

27 For examples of Drayton's cross-examination of farmers and farm women, see T.W. Caldwell, MP (United Farmers of New Brunswick), November 9, 1920, LAC, Tariff Commission, RG 36-8, vol. 7, file 15, 115–25; testimony of N.P. Lambert, September 14, 1920, LAC, Tariff Commission, RG 36-8, vol. 4, file 1, 57–62; testimony of J.B. Musselman and W.J. Orchard (Saskatchewan Grain Grower's Association), October 11, 1920, LAC, Tariff Commission, RG 36-8, vol. 5, file 8, 1257–61; testimony of August Trudel (Central Agricultural Society), November 11, 1920, LAC, Tariff Commission, RG 36-8, vol. 7, file 17, 2378–81; and testimony of Mabel Finch (Women's Section, Canadian Council of Agriculture), October 13, 1920, LAC, Tariff Commission, RG 36-8, vol. 5, file 7, 1317–49.

28 Testimony of W.S. Poole (Vice-President, United Farmers of New Brunswick), November 9, 1920, LAC, Tariff Commission, RG 36-8, vol. 7, file 15, 53–70.

29 For a similarly blunt protectionist viewpoint, see the coverage in a Montreal scandal and temperance tabloid, "The 'Rob' Budget," *Axe,* May 23, 1924, 2.

30 A.B. Balcom, "Why All Tariffs Are an Evil," *Dalhousie Review* 4 (1925): 476–84; J.R. Shaw, "Why Tariffs Should Be High," *Dalhousie Review* 4 (1925): 485–93.

31 Testimony of Mrs. John Dick, Winnipeg, October 14, 1920, LAC, Tariff Commission, RG 36-8, vol. 6, file 10, 1647–48.

32 On her political life, see Linda McDowell, "Some Women Candidates for the Manitoba Legislature," *MHS Transactions*, series 3, 32 (1975–76), http://www.mhs.mb.ca/docs/transactions/.

33 "Farmers Slam Tariff System in Hot Terms," Toronto *Globe*, December 4, 1920, 3.

34 Testimony of J.B. Musselman and W.J. Orchard (Saskatchewan Grain Grower's Association), October 11, 1920, LAC, Tariff Commission, RG 36-8, vol. 5, file 8, 1258; "Conservatives Name New Head," *St. Petersburg* [Florida] *Independent*, October 13, 1927, 12.

35 Clark, "Tariff Commission," 301–4.

36 Canada, House of Commons, *Debates*, May 18, 1920, 2486; emphasis added.

37 "Declaration of Principles," in "Resolutions Adopted at Annual Dominion Convention of the Great War Veterans' Association of Canada, Held in Montreal," March 22, 1920, Nova Scotia Archives, W.S. Fielding Papers, MG 2, vol. 527, file 106.

38 Testimony in Halifax, November 8, 1920, and in Saint John, November 9, 1920, LAC, Tariff Commission, RG 36-8, vol. 7, file 15; testimony of J.D. Palmer, November 15–16, 1920, LAC, Tariff Commission, RG 36-8, vol. 7, file 19, 2714–16; Canada, House of Commons, *Debates*, May 18, 1920, 2486; "To Make Sure They Tax Everything: Some Protection Given Consumer," Toronto *Globe*, May 21, 1920, 1; "Ribbons for Typewriters Liable to Tax," Toronto *Globe*, May 26, 1920, 4; "Brefs commentaires," Montreal *La Patrie*, May 26, 1920, 4.

39 Testimony of Robert Macaulay, November 9, 1920, LAC, Tariff Commission, RG 36-8, vol. 7, file 15, 75, 82–83.

40 Ella Murray, "Taxation," *Yearbook of the National Council of Women of Canada* (1920), 120–21.

41 W.C. Keirstead, "Intercollegiate Debate: The Luxury Taxes," c. 1921, University of New Brunswick Archives and Special Collections, Wilfred Currier Keirstead fonds, UA RG 63, series 6, subseries 3, item 35, 12. Also see testimony of W.G. DeWolfe, Robert Macaulay, and F.A. Dykeman, November 9, 1920, LAC, Tariff Commission, RG 36-8, vol. 7, file 15, 72–88, 111–14; testimony of E.A. Sa[u]nders and H.S. Colwell, November 8, 1920, LAC, Tariff Commission, RG 36-8, vol. 6, file 14, 2033–42; testimony of Walter M. Lea, November 4, 1920, LAC, Tariff Commission, RG 36-8, vol. 6, file 12, 1859–60; "More Luxury Tax Changes Made by Parliament: All Items Keenly Debated," *Toronto World*, June 16, 1920, 1; "Numerous Amendments to Luxury Taxes Adopted by Ottawa House: Taxes in Budget Still in Force," *Edmonton Bulletin*, June 16, 1920, 1; "Luxury Tax Abolished Effect[ive] Today: Sales Tax Holds," *Edmonton Bulletin*, December 20, 1920, 1; and "Many Objections to Luxury Tax," *London Free Press*, December 6, 1920, 1. Because there is no archive of Drayton papers, it's not possible to see the full scope of letters on this topic, but producers and retailers of luxury goods wrote to Liberal budget critic W.S. Fielding. See, for example, evidence of a letter-writing campaign from merchant tailors, M.F. Flemming to W.S. Fielding, June 16, 1920, NSA, Fielding Papers, MG 2, vol. 527, file 106.

42 Perry, *Taxes, Tariffs, and Subsidies*, 1: 197–98, 207–8; *CAR 1920*, 56.

43 G.N. Gordon, MP, to W.L.M. King (hereafter WLMK), April 21, 1923, LAC, William Lyon Mackenzie King fonds (hereafter King fonds), MG 26-J, reel M2252, doc. 73222.

44 Canada, House of Commons, *Debates*, May 22, 1924, 1891.

45 A federal tax on land was also an important part of the platform, but though Good was a keen advocate Progressive Party leader Robert Forke was not, nor was the farmers' chief

economist ally, Oscar Skelton. In his *Production and Taxation in Canada,* Good featured the land tax, not the income tax, as his preferred alternative to the tariff, and he advocated it tirelessly (some thought tiresomely) in Parliament. When he retired from electoral politics to lead the Cooperative Union of Canada in 1926, the land tax lost its last serious advocate in Parliament, thereafter being the ideal only of a still enthusiastic social movement. W.C. Good, *Production and Taxation in Canada* (Toronto: J.M. Dent and Sons, 1919), 112; "Biography/Administrative History," William Charles Good fonds, MG 27 III C1, http://www.collectionscanada.ca.

46   Canada, House of Commons, *Debates,* June 11, 1920, 3449.

47   "Income Tax Form Ready This Week," Toronto *Globe,* February 12, 1918, 10; "Many Questions for Income Tax," Toronto *Globe,* February 19, 1918, 10; "Premier Reassures Those of Alien Birth," Toronto *Globe,* February 21, 1918, 5; "The Income War Tax Act," Department of Finance display ad showing a completed sample income tax return, Toronto *Globe,* March 18, 1918, 7; "The New Income Tax," Toronto *Globe,* March 23, 1918, 18.

48   "Federal Income Tax Regulations, Publicity Campaign to Begin Next Week," Toronto *Globe,* February 16, 1918, 16.

49   Frederick Williams-Taylor (Bank of Montreal) to Thomas White, June 7, 1918; Thomas White to R.W. Breadner, July 17, 1918; and E.L. Pease (Canadian Bankers' Association) to Thomas White, July 19, 1918, LAC, White fonds, MG 27 II D 18, vol. 7, file 24.

50   This institutional arrangement signalled the temporary character of the federal direct taxes. Until 1927, the revenue function of the dominion government was carried out within two ministries, Inland Revenue and Customs; they were combined in 1918, renamed Customs and Excise in 1921, and reorganized as National Revenue in 1927. The outside (customs port) service of Customs and Excise was revealed to be widely corrupt in 1925–27. The income tax administration was initially located in the Department of Finance and later transferred to Customs and Excise in 1924. Income taxation then became part of the new Department of National Revenue.

51   H.H. Stevens to Thomas White, February 7, 1918, LAC, White fonds, MG 27 II D 18, vol. 7, file 24.

52   Andrew Haydon to WLMK, "Memorandum Regarding the Taxation Branch of the Department of Finance of Canada," February 13, 1922, LAC, King fonds, MG 26-J, reel C2245, docs. 61111–14. An illustration of Breadner's vindictiveness and secretiveness can be found in a conflict described in "Memorandum from Jack Mitchell (Private Secretary to the Minister of the Interior) to Arthur Meighen (Prime Minister)," April 24, 1919, LAC, Arthur Meighen fonds, MG 26-I, vol. 9, doc. 5196, and the following documents, 5197 to 5228, circulated over the next two weeks among Mitchell (a taxpayer and Manitoba Conservative), the minister of finance, and Breadner himself. A detailed account of problems in Breadner's office was supplied to King by a member of the Liberal caucus in the summer of 1923; see G.N. Gordon, MP, to WLMK, "Confidential Memo," July 5, 1923, LAC, King fonds, MG 26-J, vol. 86, doc. 73229; diary entry, March 8, 1930, 116, LAC, King Diaries, MG 26 J 13, http://www.collectionscanada.gc.ca/databases/king/index-e.html; Memoirs of Robert Watson Sellar, 87–89, LAC, Robert Watson Sellar fonds, MG 31 E 5, vol. 3, file 1.

53   Andrew Haydon (National Liberal Federation) to WLMK, "Memorandum Regarding the Taxation Branch of the Department of Finance of Canada," February 13, 1922, LAC, King fonds, MG 26-J, docs. 63111–12; Proceedings of the Special Parliamentary Committee on the Civil Service of Canada, Appendix No. 5, *Journals of the House of Commons,* January–June session 1923 (Ottawa: King's Printer, 1923), 182, 748–68; WLMK to G.N. Gordon, MP, with "Memorandum re Taxation Branch, Dept. of Finance, under Business Profits War Tax Act and Income War Tax Act," July 5, 1923, LAC, King fonds, MG 26-J, reel C2252, docs. 73228–29.

54 R.B. Bryce, *Maturing in Hard Times: Canada's Department of Finance through the Great Depression* (Kingston, ON: McGill-Queen's University Press, 1986), 29–31, refers to only two defalcations, but in fact there were three, one of them discovered in 1921, another in 1922, and a third in 1929 (under way since at least 1922); see "Artz and Woman Alone Implicated," Toronto *Globe*, December 16, 1921, 9; "Mutilated Bills Alleged Stolen," Toronto *Globe*, July 18, 1922, 3; "Government's Bond Declared Deposited in Hyndman's Bank," Toronto *Globe*, September 20, 1929, 1; and "Hyndman Guilty of Bond Thefts," Toronto *Globe*, January 24, 1930, 1. Later in the decade, people were still discussing connections between the suicide and the Artz embezzlement, though the nature of those connections is unclear; see "Takes His Life in Depression," Toronto *Globe*, December 12, 1921, 5; J.R. Forsyth (former staff member, Department of Finance) to WLMK, December 30, 1929, LAC, King fonds, MG 26-J, reel C2309, doc. 137574. The events of 1917–22 were reviewed, and their shadow over the Department of Finance was discussed in the *Special Investigation into Defalcations and Irregularities in the Department of Finance, Conducted by Walter Duncan, Special Investigating Officer for the Department of Finance, Report of Walter Duncan, Respectfully Submitted to Honourable Charles A. Dunning, Minister of Finance*, 1930, 16–17, 31–35, Queen's University Archives, A.Arch. 2121, box 38, file 319.

55 A.J. Richardson, "Building the Canadian Chartered Accountancy Profession: A Biography of George Edwards FCA CBE LLD, 1861–1947," *Accounting Historians Journal* 27, 2 (2000): 107–9; "Figures Cannot Lie," editorial, *Halifax Herald*, October 19, 1925, 6; "Le budget de 1924–1925 est clair court et substantiel," *Le Soleil* (Quebec), April 25, 1924, 17.

56 Andrew Haydon (National Liberal Federation) to WLMK, "Memorandum Regarding the Taxation Branch of the Department of Finance of Canada," February 13, 1922, LAC, King fonds, MG 26-J, docs. 63111–14.

57 Diary entry, September 20, 1930, 465, LAC, King Diaries, MG 26 J 13.

58 Memoirs of Robert Watson Sellar, LAC, Robert Watson Sellar fonds, MG 31 E 5, vol. 3, file 1, 89.

59 Testimony of E.P. Lambert, September 14, 1920, LAC, Tariff Commission, RG 36-8, vol. 4, file 1, 61; Special Committee on Soldiers' Civil Re-Establishment, *Soldiers' Civil Re-Establishment*, 44.

60 Canadian Tax Conference, *Proceedings, Held under the Auspices of the Citizens' Research Institute of Canada* (Toronto: Citizens' Research Institute of Canada, 1923), 13–14.

61 Canada, House of Commons, *Debates*, April 25, 1923, 2180.

62 Remarks by Henry Drayton, November 4, 1920, LAC, Tariff Commission, RG 36-8, vol. 6, file 12, 1839.

63 "First Contributed Article for the Canadian Tax Conference of the CRIC by G.C. Rooke, FCA, B.ACC, Regina, Saskatchewan. Being a Discussion of Federal Taxation, with a Special Reference to a Proposed 'Turnover Tax' in Conjunction with a 'Super Income Tax,'" *Canadian Taxation*, December 4, 1922, n. pag.

64 [E.M. Trowern], "A Vigorous and Aggressive Campaign Has Been Undertaken by the Retail Trade Bureau of Canada to Have the Dominion Income Tax in Canada Abolished," *Retail Trade Review*, series 1, 2 (1925): 7.

65 These observations are based upon my review of 1,636 income tax cases ("Information re Claim: Payment of Taxes and Penalties Alleged Due under Income War Tax Act 1917 and Amendments Thereof"), all but a handful being for personal income tax, recorded in three registers of the Exchequer Court of Canada, vol. 58 for 1920, vol. 79 for 1921–22, and vol. 80 for 1922–23. For vol. 80, I examined all 109 dockets in which the subject of the information laid did not pay and was further subject to a writ of *fieri facias* ("seizure and sale of goods") in payment of the tax debt. I attempted to find an occupation for each of these 109 people if none was given on the docket and succeeded in doing so for 75 of

the 109. There remains great potential for research in these documents to explore occupational and regional patterns, and change over time, in failure to pay and enforcement. Note that docket registers are held by LAC, but the actual dockets are held by the Courts Administration Service of the Government of Canada and must be requested separately through that agency.

66 Regarding taxpayer education, see "Think Hydro Ought to Pay Business Tax," Toronto *Globe*, June 5, 1920, 2, and testimony of E.P. Lambert (Canadian Council on Agriculture), September 14, 1920, LAC, Tariff Commission, RG 36-8, vol. 4, file 1, 59. Regarding difficulties in collecting 100 percent of municipal taxes owed, see George Hurst (Income Tax Assessment Branch, City of Toronto), "Administration of a Municipal Income Tax," in Canadian Tax Conference, *Proceedings* (1924), 32–36, and New Brunswick, Department of Provincial Secretary-Treasurer, *Report of the Royal Commission on the Rates and Taxes Act* (Fredericton: Royal Commission on the Rates and Taxes Act, 1951), 60. I describe one dimension of the practice of partial payment on the ground of indigency in the City of Saint John in "Relations of Extraction: Taxation and Women's Citizenship in the Maritimes, 1914–1955," *Acadiensis* 39, 1 (2010): 27–57. In the early decades of the century, some tax authorities thought that municipal income tax was so easily evadable that it "is almost [regarded] as voluntary ... and is considered pretty much in the same light as donations to the neighbourhood church or Sunday school." Quoted in F.H. Bell, *Principles of Civic Taxation* (Saint John: Sun Printing Company, 1899 [?]), 13. A similar attitude was reported about municipal income tax in the London, Ontario, area in 1920, along with the hope that federal income taxation would improve the reliability of income tax assessment; see "Less than Thousand Citizens Are Paying the Income Tax Here," *London Free Press*, December 4, 1920, 1.

67 The amounts given by Trowern were, in 1920, in round figures, $20 million; in 1921, $46 million; in 1922, $78 million; in 1923, $60 million; in 1924, $54 million. Trowern, "A Vigorous and Aggressive Campaign," 6. Perry, a more objective observer, confirmed these data in his *Taxes, Tariffs, and Subsidies*, 1: 210.

68 Peter McArthur, "The Ananias Point," Toronto *Globe*, January 5, 1924, 4; for the Bible story of Ananias, see Acts 4: 32–37 and 5: 1–11.

69 Izaac Walton Killam, *The Case against Tax-Exempt Bonds: Open Letters to the Right Honourable Sir Robert Borden, P.C., G.C.M.G., Prime Minister of Canada, and to the Honourable Sir Thomas White, K.C.M.G., Minister of Finance* (Montreal: privately printed, 1918), 9.

70 "An Income Tax Guide Will Soon Be Working," *Toronto Daily Star*, May 8, 1920, 2.

71 The same question was the subject of discussion and debate, but little effective action, in the United States during the interwar years; see Robert H. Tucker, "Some Aspects of Intergovernmental Tax Exemption," *Southern Economic Journal* 6, 3 (1940): 277–90.

72 Defending the tax-free bonds in 1920, Drayton pointed this out, suggesting that these tax shelters were not just for a favoured few. But the exemption mattered little to the poor owner of a single fifty-dollar bond. Canada, House of Commons, *Debates*, June 11, 1920, 3447–48.

73 William Mitchell to W.S. Fielding, May 22, 1920, NSA, MG 2, Fielding Papers, vol. 527, file 106. Continuing partisan comment on this question can be seen in Canada, House of Commons, *Debates*, March 18, 1924, 418; April 14, 1924, 1345; and April 24, 1924, 1456.

74 *Waterous v. Minister of National Revenue*, [1931] Ex. C.R. 108; "Important Judgment in Income Tax Case," *National Revenue Review* 4, 8 (1931): 14.

75 Madame May regularly advertised in the classified ad section of the *Toronto Daily Star* during the 1920s with variations on the phrase "Victory Bonds taken at full market value for any of our goods"; see, for example, January 20, 1922, 30, and February 14, 1921, 12.

76 "Net Tightens about Income Tax Dodgers," Toronto *Globe*, May 8, 1920, 1.

77 D.A. Cameron (Canadian Bank of Commerce), "Federal Taxation, Having Regard to War Expenditures," in Canadian Tax Conference, *Proceedings* (1923), 82.

78 Donald Fleming (Minister of Finance) to J.G. Diefenbaker, October 28, 1959, LAC, Records of the Department of Finance, RG 19, vol. 4165, file T-3.

79 The origins of the Canadian Tax Conference are described in in Canadian Tax Conference, *Proceedings* (1923), 36–37.

80 Shirley Tillotson, *Contributing Citizens: Modern Charitable Fundraising and the Making of the Welfare State* (Vancouver: UBC Press, 2008), 26–27, 250–51n13, 251n14. Since documenting in *Contributing Citizens* the ubiquity of the CRIC publications in various fonds, I have found more examples in the Mitchell Hepburn fonds at the Archives of Ontario and, at LAC, the federal Department of Finance fonds and the Arthur Meighen fonds.

81 W.L. McKinnon, "The Function of Statistics in the Control of Public Expenditure," in Canadian Tax Conference, *Proceedings* (1931), 75–81.

82 Rooke, "First Contributed Article," n.p.; Cameron, "Federal Taxation," 75–85; Canada, House of Commons, *Debates,* May 18, 1923, 2913–16.

83 Cameron, "Federal Taxation," 80; Rooke, "First Contributed Article," n. pag.

84 S.R. Parsons, discussion of Cameron, "Federal Taxation," 85.

85 Canada, House of Commons, *Debates,* April 15, 1926, 2457; Perry, *Taxes, Tariffs, and Subsidies,* 2: 696. Assessments and revenues rebounded in 1927–28 because reorganization of the tax administration meant more vigorous enforcement.

86 Trowern, "A Vigorous and Aggressive Campaign," 7, 14–15.

87 Newfoundland, *Journal of the House of Assembly,* February 18, 1925, 15.

88 Newfoundland, *Journal of the Legislative Council,* May 25, 1929, 77; Newfoundland Royal Commission 1933, *Report* (London: His Majesty's Stationery, 1934), paragraphs 161–63; S.J.R. Noel, *The Politics of Newfoundland* (Toronto: University of Toronto Press, 1971), 198.

89 For one example, see "The Whisper of Death," *Montreal Daily Star,* July 12, 1923, 1.

90 G.W. Morley to Arthur Meighen, September 2, 1925, and Arthur Meighen to G.W. Morley, September 5, 1925, LAC, Arthur Meighen Papers, MG 26-I, reel C3441, docs. 37998–99 and 38002. The editorialists of the *Toronto Daily Star* commented disapprovingly on the "agitation on foot to abolish the income tax levy"; see "The Federal Income Tax," *Toronto Daily Star,* December 6, 1923, 6.

91 Trowern, "A Vigorous and Aggressive Campaign," 12.

92 Lita-Rose Betcherman, "The Customs Scandal of 1926," *Beaver* 81, 2 (2001): 14.

93 Trowern, "A Vigorous and Aggressive Campaign," 3–5, 8, 10–11.

94 A. Kenneth Eaton, *Essays in Taxation* (Toronto: Canadian Tax Foundation, 1966), 5.

95 Perry, *Taxes, Tariffs, and Subsidies,* 1: 40–48.

96 Richard H. Bartlett, *Indians and Taxation in Canada* (Saskatoon: University of Saskatchewan, Native Law Centre, 1992).

97 Perry, *Taxes, Tariffs, and Subsidies,* 1: 46, 75, 80–85, 133–35.

98 G. Lanctôt to L. Gouin, March 11, 1918, Bibliothèque et archives nationales du Québec (BANQ), Ministère de la Justice, E17, series "Jurisprudence du Conseil Privé de Londres: Documents judiciaires" (hereafter Privy Council Jurisprudence documents), 1960-01-036, box 2090, file 1703/41.

99 A thorough discussion of the cases to which Lanctôt referred can be found in James A. Doyle, "The Immunity of Government Instrumentalities in Canada, Australia, and the United States: A Comparative Study," *Nebraska Law Bulletin* 18 (1939): 157–80. See in addition A.L. Powell, "Constitutional Law: Federal Instrumentality – *McCulloch v. Maryland* in Canada and Australia," *Michigan Law Review* 31, 6 (1933): 797–803.

100 *Leprohon v. City of Ottawa,* [1878] 2 Ont. App. Rep. 548, quoted in Doyle, "Immunity of Government Instrumentalities," 161.

101 My translation. G. Lanctôt, opinion on the applicability of the Income War Tax Act to the ministers, members, and civil servants and officials of the Government of Quebec, March 11, 1918, BANQ, Privy Council Jurisprudence documents, 1960-01-036, box 2090, file 1703/41.

102 J.E. Caron to L.A. Taschereau, April 29, 1920, and L.A. Taschereau to J.E. Caron, May 1, 1920, BANQ, Privy Council Jurisprudence documents, 1960-01-036, box 2137, file 1911/41; G. Lanctôt to E.G. Bayly (Deputy Attorney General of Ontario), April 13, 1921, BANQ, Privy Council Jurisprudence documents, 1960-01-036, box 2090, file 1703/41.

103 L. St. Laurent to G. Lanctôt, May 22, 1922, and "Factum of the Appellant," January 17, 1921, BANQ, Privy Council Jurisprudence documents, 1960-01-036, box 2137, file 1911/41.

104 *Caron v. The King*, [1922] 64 S.C.R. 255.

105 *Caron v. The King*, [1924] U.K.P.C. 66.

106 My research assistant, Alex Tremblay, surveyed the microfilm holdings at Laval University for *Le Devoir* (Montreal), *Le Droit* (Ottawa), *L'Événement* (Quebec), *Le Nouvelliste* (Trois Rivières), *La Patrie* (Montreal), *La Presse* (Montreal), *Le Soleil* (Quebec), and *La Tribune* (Sherbrooke) for the four publication dates following the court judgment: for the Exchequer Court judgment, June 27–July 1, 1921; for the Supreme Court of Canada judgment, May 17–22, 1922; and for the Privy Council judgment, June 1–6, 1924. Canadian Press covered the Exchequer Court decision and the Privy Council one but apparently not the Supreme Court one. All of the newspapers except *Le Soleil* reported the Exchequer Court decision. Only *La Presse*, *Le Devoir*, and *Le Droit* covered the 1922 judgment. In contrast, all but three (*La Patrie*, *Le Soleil*, and *La Tribune*) covered the Privy Council's judgment in 1924. For an example of the satisfied tone in reporting that politicians' sessional indemnities were taxable as income, see "L'indemnité parlementaire imposable," *La Patrie*, June 28, 1921, 2. For an example of sympathy for Caron, see "Égaux devant la taxe," *L'Événement*, August 2, 1924, 1. Perhaps not surprisingly, the constitutional dimension of the case was emphasized consistently mainly by *Le Devoir*, though *La Presse* also noted it; see "M. Caron a perdu au Conseil privé: Le traitement d'un ministre est taxable en vertu de la loi de l'impôt sur le revenu," *Le Devoir*, August 2, 1924, 3, and "L'indemnité de nos ministres et députés est sujette à l'impôt," *La Presse*, June 28, 1921, 9.

107 "M.P.P.s Must Pay Tax," *Toronto Daily Star*, June 28, 1921, 5.

108 "Hon. J.E. Caron to Appeal," Toronto *Globe*, June 30, 1921, 3; "Provincial Minister to Pay Federal Tax," Toronto *Globe*, August 2, 1924, 5.

109 A.L. Powell, "*McCulloch v. Maryland* in Canada," 799.

110 W.S. Fielding to L.A. Taschereau, February 1, 1922, and E.L. Newcombe to L.A. Taschereau, May 26, 1923, BANQ, Privy Council Jurisprudence documents, 1960-01-036, box 2137, file 1911/41.

111 R.W. Breadner to G. Lanctôt, July 26, 1925; L.A. Taschereau to J. Bureau, July 31, 1925; and L.A. Taschereau to E. Lapointe (federal Minister of Justice), August 13, 1925, BANQ, Privy Council Jurisprudence documents, 1960-01-036, box 2137, file 1911/41.

112 My translation. The understanding regarding non-payment while the case was before the courts that Taschereau believed to have been established, and the arrangement for instalment payment of arrears and waiving of interest, were the subjects of a memorandum to Breadner (probably written by Lanctôt) "covering briefly the subject which was discussed at the conference that you [probably Breadner] had with him [Taschereau] and others in Quebec a few weeks ago," written at the request of L.A. Taschereau, April 14, 1925; L.A. Taschereau to J. Bureau, July 31, 1925; L.A. Taschereau to J. Bureau, August 13, 1925; L.A. Taschereau to E. Lapointe (federal Minister of Justice), August 13, 1925, BANQ, Privy Council Jurisprudence documents, 1960-01-036, box 2137, file 1911/41. Whether the federal tax authority ever risked the political cost of prosecuting so many influential Quebeckers

will require additional research in the Quebec court records. But no prosecutions took place before 1927. L.A. Taschereau to W.D. Euler, copied to WLMK, October 10, 1927, LAC, King fonds, vol. 178, doc. 127445. With the help of research assistant Alex Tremblay, I ascertained that there were no such prosecutions in the Recorder's Court records for Quebec City, nor were there any in the Exchequer Court dockets, 1927–32. I leave it for another researcher to investigate whether prosecutions on these cases proceeded either through the Court of King's Bench or the provincial Supreme Court or both.

113 Perry, *Taxes, Tariffs, and Subsidies,* 1: 210.
114 WLMK to J.A. Robb (Finance Minister), February 22, 1926, LAC, King fonds, MG 26-J, reel C2292, doc. 116611.
115 Perry, *Taxes, Tariffs, and Subsidies,* 1: 214–15. In addition to the sections quoted by Perry, see the commentary on this measure, ranging from enthusiastic support for the removal of an injustice to strident criticism of its impact on investment choices. See Canada, House of Commons, *Debates,* April 22, 1926, 2713–14; April 30, 1926, 2981; and May 3, 1926, 3046–47. The differentiation of rates between earned and unearned income had been introduced in the United States in the Revenue Act of 1924 (favouring earned income). W. Elliot Brownlee, *Federal Taxation in America: A Short History* (Cambridge: Cambridge University Press, 1996), 61.
116 "No Rush Mars Income Tax Day as Citizens Enjoy New Budget," Toronto *Globe,* May 1, 1926, 15.
117 "Law Will Be Enforced, Taxes Due to Be Paid, Is Euler Declaration," Toronto *Globe,* May 31, 1927, 1–2.
118 Randolph E. Paul, *Taxation in the United States* (Boston: Little, Brown, 1954) 110–22; Brownlee, *Federal Taxation in America,* 51–54.

Chapter 4: Resistance in the Interwar Years

1 Alex Himmelfarb and Jordan Himmelfarb, "Introduction," in *Tax Is Not a Four Letter Word: A Different Take on Taxes in Canada,* ed. Alex Himmelfarb and Jordan Himmelfarb (Waterloo: Wilfrid Laurier University Press, 2013), 1–2.
2 In taking this to be a necessary element of democracy, I follow the criteria set out in Charles Tilly, "Processes and Mechanisms of Democratization," *Sociological Theory* 18, 1 (2000): 1–16.
3 W. Irwin Gillespie, *Tax, Borrow, and Spend: Financing Federal Spending in Canada, 1867–1990* (Ottawa: Carleton University Press, 1991), 117, 162. Perry was more cautious than Gillespie and estimated "perhaps 5 percent of the working population." J. Harvey Perry, *Taxes, Tariffs, and Subsidies: A History of Canadian Fiscal Development,* 2 vols. (Toronto: University of Toronto Press, 1955), 2: 360.
4 Canada, House of Commons, *Debates,* June 15, 1931, 2640.
5 Shirley Tillotson, "A New Taxpayer for a New State: Charitable Fundraising and the Origins of the Welfare State," in *Social Fabric or Patchwork Quilt: The Development of Social Welfare in Canada,* ed. Raymond B. Blake and Jeffrey Keshen (Peterborough, ON: Broadview Press, 2006), 153–76.
6 Canada, House of Commons, *Debates,* June 9, 1931, 2455, 2457–58, 2460.
7 J. Castell Hopkins, *Canadian Annual Review of Public Affairs, 1920* (Toronto: Canadian Review Company, 1921), 52–53.
8 I began by using the price index numbers in the Bank of Canada's inflation calculator (based upon Statistics Canada's Consumer Price Index historical data). It adjusts nominal dollar values to correct for historical price inflation and deflation. I have summarized the data in Table 4. But the numbers that result from that adjustment suggest to

twenty-first-century readers that personal income tax fell on lower-income individuals and families: to us now, an exemption of only $11,464 to $14,109 for a single person or $22,928 to $28,218 (Table 4) for a family breadwinner sounds like a mass income tax, and the interwar income tax was not that. Colin Campbell has devised one way to further contextualize the dollar values of the personal exemptions by describing the exemption levels as ratios of the average annual earnings for manufacturing and office employees to the basic exemptions of single and married people. He then applies the same ratio, using today's average industrial wage data as the basis for the ratio, and concludes, in his discussion of the meaning of the exemption in 1939, that the equivalent exemption today for a married taxpayer with a dependent spouse and two children would be $108,000. See Colin Campbell, "J.L. Ilsley and the Transformation of the Canadian Tax System: 1939–1943," *Canadian Tax Journal* 61, 3 (2013): 640–41n22. This is a useful correction to the simple inflation adjustment method, but the results that it provides cannot make sense of the qualitative data that I have found in court records, newspapers, Hansard, and archival fonds. Were the basic personal exemptions that high, evidence of the impacts of the personal income tax on family budgets and the difficulties in paying it that I found in those sources would be inexplicable. Further contextualization is necessary to explain why, for example, reasonable people asserted that the tax was too burdensome on "smaller incomes" or why railway workers' unions protested the burden of the tax on their members. My further contextualization includes (1) information on salary scales rather than averages, (2) earnings described in life stage terms, and (3) specific middle-class and elite labour occupations (engineers, civil servants, collegiate institute teachers, railway engineers, typesetters, and telegraphers). The information on specific occupations better describes the meanings of exemption levels for income tax incidence because, when broad sectoral categories are used, the average is skewed low by the large basic labour and clerk populations in "manufacturing" and "office" categories.

9 Perry, *Taxes, Tariffs, and Subsidies*, 1: 219, 260; 2: 602–3. The income tax measures of the 1931 budget were withdrawn because of public criticism of the disproportionate benefits afforded to "millionaires."

10 Calculated with data from the 1922 line in Table 4.

11 "Wages and Hours of Labour in Canada, 1901–1920," *Labour Gazette*, special supplement, 21, 3 (1921): 464, 469; *Labour Gazette* 17, 2 (1917): 168.

12 Perry, *Taxes, Tariffs, and Subsidies*, 1: 219.

13 Ellen M. Gee, "Historical Change in the Family Life Course of Men and Women," in *Aging in Canada: Social Perspectives*, 2nd ed., ed. Victor W. Marshall (Markham: Fitzhenry and Whiteside, 1987), 271, 273, 278. For women of that age cohort, the median was 56.2.

14 Perry, *Taxes, Tariffs, and Subsidies*, 2: 698. Calculations are based upon the figures of taxpayers for 1931 that Perry reports on the 1932–33 line of his table.

15 "Exemptions Less[,] Levy Doubled on Small Wage," *Toronto Daily Star*, March 22, 1933, 1; emphasis added.

16 After 1927, Revenue was reorganized, and its pursuit of income tax debts shifted from the Exchequer Court to magistrate's or police courts. Only forty-five personal and corporation income tax cases appear in the Exchequer Court docket files for the years 1928–32 (1928: 18, 1929: 8, 1930: 6, 1931: 3, 1932: 10) and a vanishing number over the remainder of the 1930s (during the early years of C.F. Elliott's tenure as commissioner of income tax and Edgar N. Rhodes's years as minister of finance). To find a comparable data series, I turned to a sample police court fonds. The City of Vancouver fonds, Police Department series 182 and 185, court calendars, provided me with a complete data series for 1928–49 of cases comparable to those that travelled through the Exchequer Court in the early years of the Income War Tax Act. Instead of particular debts, however, these cases were prosecuted as failure to file a return, and those found guilty paid a fine of twenty-five dollars (in 1937, that fine

would have been the equivalent of $412 in 2016 dollars). Over those years, 217 cases (186 individuals and 31 limited companies) were prosecuted, as few as two in some years, more frequently eighteen or nineteen, and in 1928, 1937, and 1948 from thirty-two to thirty-nine in each year. City of Vancouver Archives (hereafter CVA), City of Vancouver fonds, series 182, calendar 39-C-7, and series 185, calendars 38-A-1, 38-A-3, 38-A-4, 38-A-10, and 38-B-1.

17 "Information re Claim: Payment of Taxes and Penalties Alleged Due under Income War Tax Act 1917 and Amendments Thereof," November 18, 1922, Court Services Administration, Exchequer Court of Canada, vol. 80, docket 5124. Note that the indexes to the Exchequer Court dockets are located in LAC, series R14188-2-8-E, Exchequer Court of Canada fonds.

18 "Information re Claim: Payment of Taxes and Penalties Alleged Due under Income War Tax Act 1917 and Amendments Thereof," February 24, 1923, Court Services Administration, Exchequer Court of Canada, vol. 80, docket 5167.

19 Miss Maude I. McLean (Dominion Bureau of Statistics) to E.L. Newcombe (Deputy Minister of Justice), April 24, 1925, LAC, Department of Justice fonds, RG 13, vol. 297, file 1925–797.

20 Department of National Revenue, "Income Tax Brief," c. 1931, Queen's University Archives, Grant Dexter fonds, collection 2142, box 20, file 199. This document estimates that, of 142,154 income tax payers in 1929–30, approximately 20,000 were women (12 percent).

21 Perry, *Taxes, Tariffs, and Subsidies*, 2: 696; Statistics Canada, *Canada Year Book 1929*, 137, 140, calculated from Tables 47 and 49, Canada Yearbook Historical Collection, http://www65.statcan.gc.ca.

22 Perry, *Taxes, Tariffs, and Subsidies*, 2: 602–7, 698 (1932–33 line for 1931 taxation year, 1940–41 line for 1939 taxation year); *Census of Canada* (1931), vol. 7, 277 (men aged twenty–sixty-nine). For overall population growth, 1931–41, see Statistics Canada, *Canada Year Book 1942*, 85, Canada Yearbook Historical Collection, http://www65.statcan.gc.ca.

23 "Information re Claim: Payment of Taxes and Penalties Alleged Due under Income War Tax Act 1917 and Amendments Thereof," May 26, 1922, Court Services Administration, Exchequer Court of Canada, docket 5046. Note that the indexes to the dockets are located in LAC, series R14188-2-8-E, Exchequer Court of Canada fonds. John Mackie, "The Mayors of Vancouver," *Vancouver Sun*, November 30, 2002, B4; Daniel Francis, *LD: Mayor Louis Taylor and the Rise of Vancouver* (Vancouver: Arsenal Pulp Press, 2004), 116, 205–6.

24 The 1931 provincial income tax return and receipts for his instalment payments of his 1931 dominion income tax (dated July, August, September, November, and December 1932), CVA, L.D. Taylor family fonds, AM 1477, L.D. Taylor sousfonds 1, series 3, box 950-C-3, file 2.

25 Confidential memo from A.K. Eaton to J.R. McGregor (private secretary to E.N. Rhodes), January 28, 1935, doc. 75060-61; Thomas F. Bermingham to E.N. Rhodes, March 4, 1935, doc. 75056; Thomas F. Bermingham to E.N. Rhodes, March 16, 1935, NSA, Rhodes fonds, MG 2, vol. 1196, doc. 75054.

26 J. Wilson to E.N. Rhodes, March 18, 1935, NSA, Rhodes fonds, MG 2, vol. 1196, doc. 75076; C.F. Elliott to W.L. Best (Secretary-Treasurer, Dominion Joint Legislative Committee, Railway Transportation Brotherhoods), March 16, 1935, NSA, Rhodes fonds, MG 2, vol. 1196, doc. 75078.

27 Canada, House of Commons, *Debates*, March 21, 1923, 1383–85; May 17, 1923, 2880.

28 A.G. Griffin to J.L. Ilsley, July 22, 1942; Dr. John Dearness, "Taxation Troubles," 1944, LAC, Finance fonds, RG 19, vol. 452, file 111-14E, 4–5.

29 An Act to Amend the Income War Tax Act, 1917, SC, 1926, 16–17 George V, c. 10, s. 1; Income War Tax Act, 1917, c. 28, s. 5, RSC, 1927. This change took effect for the 1926 tax year, but administration of the new "householder" exemption was made more rigorous for the 1927 tax year. Compare Form T-1 1926 with Form T-1 1927; the latter includes a detailed description of the new tax category of "householder" and "dependent relatives" – father or mother, grandfather or grandmother, sister or daughter of any age and ability, and son or brother if

under twenty-one or incapable of earning a living owing to mental or physical disability. Dominion of Canada Income Tax Return of Income for the Year Ended 31st December 1926 and for 1927, LAC, Revenue fonds, RG 16, vol. 1006, file T-1 1926 and file T-1 1927.

30 This change took place late enough in the usual annual cycle of tax administration that tax return forms for 1932 had to be modified by means of a "REVISED EXEMPTIONS" stamp giving the lower personal exemptions and stating "Householder Exemption Abolished." Dominion of Canada Income Tax Return of Income for the Year Ended 31st December 1932, LAC, Revenue fonds, RG 16, vol. 1006, file T-1 and T-1A 1932.

31 J. Phillip Bill to E.N. Rhodes, March 30, 1933, NSA, Rhodes fonds, MG 2, vol. 1132, doc. 55795.

32 Agnes D. Craine, MD, to Arthur Meighen, April 17, 1924, LAC, Arthur Meighen fonds, MG 26-I, series 3, vol. 134, doc. 80878.

33 Names of correspondents in the Treasury Department General Correspondence fonds (GR 1773) have been replaced with X or Y: (Miss) X (supports sister and elderly mother) to J.W. Jones, April 15, 1931, British Columbia Archives (hereafter BCA), Treasury Department General Correspondence series (hereafter Treasury Correspondence), GR 1773, box 47, file 8; Miss X (supports sister) to J.W. Jones, August 17, 1931; Mrs. X (supports mother) to J.W. Jones, August 21, 1931; Mr. X on behalf of his employee Mr. Y (supports mother) to J.W. Jones, May 9, 1931, BCA, Treasury Correspondence, GR 1773, box 47, file 9. Case 92 (accountant supporting his father and aunt), Case 72 (drugstore clerk supporting his sister), Case 78 (male hotel owner supporting four children in their twenties, none of them earning an income), July 1935; Case 621 (supported his aunt through her final illness and burial), March 1935; Case 41 (unemployed, living with his daughter), Case 47 (foreman, supporting his mother, mother-in-law, brother-in-law and family), June 1935, Public Archives of New Brunswick, Saint John County Council fonds, RS 156, series C, file C2(e)2, Board of Revision ledger for 1935–36.

34 Assessment Act, *Revised Statutes of Ontario*, 1927, c. 238, s. 4 (22); Income Tax Act, *Statutes of Manitoba*, Consolidated Amendments, 1924, c. 91, s. 4(a).

35 G.N. Gordon, MP, to Lomer Gouin, MP, September 30, 1922, LAC, Department of Justice fonds, RG 13, vol. 272, doc. 1922–1832.

36 "Ordeal by Taxes," editorial cartoon, *Winnipeg Free Press*, May 5, 1933, 13; "57 Varieties," editorial cartoon, *Halifax Chronicle*, July 15, 1933, 6; *Montreal Daily Star*, editorial cartoon, April 7, 1932, 12.

37 Perry, *Taxes, Tariffs, and Subsidies*, 1: 220–22, 232, 323. Brian J. Arnold summarizes the case law of the late 1920s and early 1930s on the non-deductibility in the income war tax of income tax paid in other jurisdictions. See Brian J. Arnold, "The Canadian International Tax System: Review and Reform," *Canadian Tax Journal* 43, 5 (1995): 1794n3.

38 Perry, *Taxes, Tariffs, and Subsidies*, 1: 260.

39 "Mr. General Public Receives Some Balm in Budget Changes," Toronto *Globe*, April 16, 1926, 7; "Labor Approves Tax Reductions – Moore, However, Would Have Abolished Sales Tax," *Montreal Daily Star*, April 16, 1926, 16.

40 "Memorandums Presented to the Dominion Government, Monday, January 9th, 1928 ... Along with a Summary of the Legislative Programme of the Trades and Labor Congress of Canada," LAC, Finance fonds, RG 19, vol. 525, file 129-45; "Legislative Programme of Trades and Labor Congress Submitted to the Dominion Government," *Labour Gazette* 32, 2 (1932): 181.

41 Ibid.

42 "Public Economies, Reduced Taxation, Demanded by C.M.A.," Toronto *Globe*, June 9, 1932, 3; "Public Economy Needed," editorial, Toronto *Globe*, January 22, 1932, 4. Calls for reduced expenditure were usually more general, emphasizing cuts to controllable expenditures rather than focusing on the citizen's duty to refrain from asking for services.

See, for example, "Income Taxation in Canada," *Canadian Taxation*, September 23, 1932, 4; "Report of the Committee Appointed by the Government to Investigate the Finances of British Columbia," July 12, 1932, 27–28, 68–76, 161, BCA, Jones fonds, MS 23, box 4, file 1; Citizens' Research Institute of Canada, *Special Study of Taxation and Public Expenditure in Canada: Report to Donors* (Toronto: Citizens' Research Institute of Canada, 1937).

43 Canada, House of Commons, *Debates*, May 14, 1923, 2719.

44 Grattan O'Leary, "Ottawa's Orgy of Extravagance," reprint from *Maclean's*, beginning January 15, 1924, LAC, W.C. Good fonds, MG 27 III C1, vol. 24, file Taxes 1923–1938 Clippings. The reprint includes a date for only the first of the series of four.

45 The *Montreal Daily Star*'s senior cartoonist, Arthur George Racey, found many ways to illustrate and critique government extravagance during the interwar years. See, for example, the following cartoons from the collection of his work at the McCord Museum: *The Tax Burden*, M2005.23.22; *The Red Liner and Its Jolly Crew*, M2005.23.135; *And They Grow Heavier All the Time*, M2005.23.87; and *Canada's Economic Woes*, M2005.23.179.

46 Perry, *Taxes, Tariffs, and Subsidies*, 1: 260–64.

47 Ibid.

48 J.W. Jones, budget address, March 4, 1931, 41–42, BCA, Jones fonds, MS 23, box 4, 3.

49 The minister of finance routinely had to explain the process to confused taxpayers. See, for example, Minister of Finance to Mr. X (New Westminster), April 27, 1934, BCA, Treasury Correspondence, GR 1773, box 55, file 7.

50 The general description of "enormous numbers" and "many hundreds" of small assessments being disputed comes from a letter by the provincial commissioner of income tax in 1933. Delays occasioned by the large number of small refunds continued to be a political problem for the Liberal government that took office on November 15, 1933. Although exact refund numbers in the early years of the tax are not available, evidence from 1937 confirms that there were approximately 111,000 refunds issued for the 1936 tax year in Vancouver and Victoria alone. C.B. Peterson (Commissioner of Income Tax), "Memorandum to the Honourable [John Hart], the Minister of Finance," November 21, 1933; Minister of Finance to Commissioner of Income Tax, July 18, 1934, with attached letters of complaint about slow refunds; Street Railway Employees Union to Minister of Finance, October 11, 1934, BCA, Treasury Correspondence, GR 1773, box 55, file 10; Commissioner of Income Tax to Minister of Finance, c. late May 1937, and Reverend X to Provincial Treasurer, August 11, 1937, BCA, Treasury Correspondence, GR 1773, box 6, file 2.

51 Miss X (a "born Conservative") to J.W. Jones, April 15, 1931, BCA, Treasury Correspondence, GR 1773, box 47, file 8; Secretary and Chairman of a company union in the BC Interior to J.W. Jones, March 13, 1931; Miss X (recently employed as a nursery governess) to J.W. Jones, August 17, 1931; Mr. X (aged fifty-nine) to J.W. Jones, March 25, 1931; Mrs. X (newsstand clerk) to J.W. Jones, August 21, 1931, BCA, Treasury Correspondence, GR 1773, box 47, file 9; Mrs. X (a widow) to J.W. Jones, March 27, 1931, BCA, Treasury Correspondence, GR 1773, box 4, file 9.

52 J.W. Jones to Mr. X (in Sandon), June 12, 1931; Mr. X to J.W. Jones (in Sandon), June 18, 1931; J.W. Jones to Mr. X ("robbing the poor"), April 30, 1931; J.W. Jones to Miss X (twenty-one cents of tax per week), April 15, 1931; Mr. X (aged fifty-nine) to J.W. Jones, March 25, 1931, BCA, Treasury Correspondence, GR 1773, box 47, file 9; Recording Secretary, Brotherhood of Railway Carmen of America, Lodge 58, to J.W. Jones, March 13, 1931, and President and Secretary, British Columbia Projectionists' Society to J.W. Jones, March 10, 1931, BCA, Treasury Correspondence, GR 1773, box 47, file 8.

53 Mr. X (in Sandon) to J.W. Jones, June 7, 1931, BCA, Treasury Correspondence, GR 1773, box 47, file 9; Mr. X (working on a boat) to J.W. Jones, date-stamped October 7, 1931, BCA,

Treasury Correspondence, GR 1773, box 47, file 8; Mr. X (general manager of a power company) to J.W. Jones, May 22, 1931, BCA, Treasury Correspondence, GR 1773, box 47, file 9; W.C.D. Crombie (Manager, BC Shipping Federation) to Provincial Assessor Courthouse, Vancouver, attention C.R. Brown, April 3, 1934, CVA, BC Shipping Federation fonds, AM 279, series 1, box 521-A-1, folder 3.

54 Mrs. X (newsstand clerk) to J.W. Jones, August 21, 1931, BCA, Treasury Correspondence, GR 1773, box 47, file 9.

55 Mr. X to J.W. Jones, n.d., March 1931, BCA, Treasury Correspondence, GR 1773, box 47, file 9.

56 Mr. X (Sidney, BC, business manager) to J.W. Jones, December 7, 1931, BCA, Treasury Correspondence, GR 1773, box 4, file 9.

57 Canadian Women's Labor League (two different branches) to J.W. Jones, June 2 and 8, 1932, BCA, Treasury Correspondence, GR 1773, box 47, file 9.

58 Oswald Hassell to Premier S.F. Tolmie, March 10, 1931, BCA, GR 441, Premiers' fonds, box 300, file F-9-D.

59 Much more correspondence from March 1931 can be found in file F-9-D of Premier S.F. Tolmie's papers. Organizations alone, aside from individuals, represented a wide range of criticism, temperate and intemperate, constructive and hostile, left, right, and middle of the road. Critical letters came from Vancouver's left-wing labour council (the All Canadian Congress of Labour affiliates), the City of Nanaimo, the mine workers of Fernie, the Mission Conservative Association, the Vancouver Federated Ratepayers, and even the Ku Klux Klan. See BCA, Premiers' fonds, GR 441, box 300, file F-9-D.

60 J.W. Jones, budget address, March 4, 1931, 43, BCA, Jones fonds, MS 23, box 4, file 3.

61 E.D. Johnson (Deputy Minister of Finance), "Memorandum to the Honourable the Minister of Finance, re: New Tax Exemptions," March 11, 1931, BCA, Treasury Correspondence, GR 1773, box 47, file 8.

62 J.W. Jones, budget address, March 4, 1931, 43, BCA, Jones fonds, MS 23, box 4, file 3.

63 J.W. Jones, speech to the Kiwanis Club, April 16, 1931, BCA, Jones fonds, MS 23, box 6, file 2.

64 "The Place of Loans in Public Finance," c. 1932, BCA, Jones fonds, MS 23, box 4, file 1. In private financing, D.G. Paterson argued, forms of risk reduction such as investing through family networks emerged in the patterns of foreign investment in BC resource industries. See D.G. Paterson, "European Financial Capital and British Columbia: An Essay on the Role of the Regional Entrepreneur," in *British Columbia: Historical Readings*, ed. W. Peter Ward and Robert A.J. McDonald (Vancouver: Douglas and McIntyre, 1981), 330–33.

65 "Extract from Editorial, from 'London Truth.' 1881. The Canadian Dominion Bubble," BCA, Treasury Correspondence, GR 1773, box 55, file 6.

66 Untitled account of debts incurred by the Oliver government on supposedly revenue-generating, self-supporting development projects in an undated speech, around the 1933 election; first line is "the Honourable the Leader of the Opposition has repeatedly indulged in criticism of the fiscal policy of the present Government," BCA, Jones fonds, MS 23, box 4, file 2, 76–79.

67 British Columbia's debt and interest compared with Quebec's in millions of dollars:

Year	BC interest	BC debt	Quebec interest	Quebec debt
1927	$3.68	$75.5	$3.83	$79.2
1931	$5.06	$95.9	$3.28	$84.3

Sources: *British Columbia in the Canadian Confederation: A Submission Presented to the Royal Commission on Dominion Provincial Relations by the Government of the Province of British Columbia* (Victoria: King's Printer, 1938), 178; *Canada Year Book*, 1929, 819; *Canada Year Book*, 1933, 859, 161.

68 British Columbia, *British Columbia in the Canadian Confederation,* 194; J.W. Jones, budget address, 1931, 18, BCA, Jones fonds, MS 23, box 4, file 3. Thanks to Patricia Roy for pointing out this claim in the province's submission to the Rowell-Sirois Commission.

69 J.W. Jones, budget address, 1931, 18, BCA, Jones fonds, MS 23, box 4, file 3.

70 J.W. Jones, budget address, 1932, 15–16, BCA, Jones fonds, MS 23, box 4, file 3; A.H. Williamson of Wood Gundy to J.W. Jones, December 29, 1932, BCA, Jones fonds, MS 23, box 2, file 1.

71 *Canada Year Book,* 1929, Table 24, 822n4.

72 E.D. Johnson, "Memorandum to the Honourable the Minister of Finance," November 16, 1931, BCA, Jones fonds, MS 23, box 4, file 2; J.W. Jones to A.H. Williamson (Wood Gundy), December 23, 1932, BCA, Jones fonds, MS 23, box 2, file 1; J.W. Jones to P.B. Fowler, March 8, 1933, BCA, Jones fonds, MS 23, box 2, file 1, 78–80. The authorship of this letter is mistakenly attributed in the finding aid to the "deputy minister" rather than to Jones, but the internal evidence makes it clear that Jones wrote the letter. For example, the letter includes the sentence "I have carried on my task as Minister of Finance under the utmost difficulty."

73 *Canada Year Book,* 1929, Table 25, 823. In 1927, for example, per capita "ordinary receipts" in British Columbia were $35.23, whereas in other provinces comparable rates were in the teens, and in Prince Edward Island it was $9.65 per capita.

74 S.H. Logan (General Manager, Canadian Bank of Commerce, Toronto), to J.W. Jones, November 12, 1931, BCA, Jones fonds, MS 23, box 1, file 3.

75 Handwritten note from A.M. Brown to J.W. Jones, October 18, 1932, accompanied by "Copy of Wire" from Toronto, October 17, 1932, BCA, Jones fonds, MS 23, box 1, file 5. The wire was from "Kingsmill" to Stanley Burke of Pembertson and Son, Vancouver.

76 A.M. Brown, telegram to Colonel Weir (McLeod Young Weir and Company, Toronto), October 22, 1932, BCA, Jones fonds, MS 23, box 1, file 5.

77 J.W. Jones to A.H. Williamson (Wood Gundy), December 23, 1932, BCA, Jones fonds, MS 23, box 2, file 1.

78 Council Minutes, Regular Meeting, April 2, 1931, CVA, Vancouver Board of Trade fonds, vol. 10.

79 E.D. Johnson (Deputy Minister of Finance), "Memorandum to the Honourable the Minister of Finance, re: New Tax Exemptions," March 11, 1931, BCA, Treasury Correspondence, GR 1773, box 47, file 8.

80 J.W. Jones, budget address, March 16, 1932, 25–26, BCA, Jones fonds, MS 23, box 4, file 3.

81 J.W. Jones, "Random Thoughts on Taxation," n.d., addressing the Kiwanis Club, 208, and "Provincial Finances and Taxation," April 16, 1931, 149, BCA, Jones fonds, MS 23, box 6, file 2.

82 This particularly succinct statement is from Manitoba, not British Columbia, but variations of it were common. I.M.T., "Tax on Income Should Replace Property Tax," letter to the editor, *Winnipeg Free Press,* July 3, 1937, 21.

83 R.S. Lake to J.W. Jones, November 5, 1933, BCA, Jones fonds, MS 23, box 2, file 3.

84 An important national voice in public finance who articulated this concern and used this phrase was H.E. Manning, KC, *Local Taxation and Municipal Finance* (Halifax: Dalhousie University Bulletins on Public Affairs, 1938), 12. He might well have read the phrase in quotations from the head of the leading American opponent to federal income taxation, the American Taxpayers League, quoted in Romain D. Huret, *American Tax Resisters* (Cambridge, MA: Harvard University Press, 2014), 140. It can also be found earlier in Canadian tax talk; see the reference to "no participation without contribution" in "Discussion of 'Income Taxation,'" in Canadian Tax Conference, *Proceedings, Held under the Auspices of the Citizens' Research Institute of Canada* (Toronto: Citizens' Research Institute of Canada, 1923), 97.

85 J.E. Sladen to Premier Tolmie, March 13, 1931, BCA, Premiers' fonds, GR 441, box 300, file F-9-D. For Say's tax economics, see Evelyn L. Forget, *Social Economics of Jean-Baptiste Say: Markets and Virtue* (London: Routledge, 1999).

86 J.F. Noble to S.F. Tolmie, March 11, 1931, BCA, Premiers' fonds, GR 441, box 300, file F-9-D.

87 Miss X to Dear Sir, April 14, 1931, BCA, Treasury Correspondence, GR 1773, box 47, file 9.

88 Secretary, Mission Conservative Association, to S.F. Tolmie (Premier), March 20, 1931, BCA, Premiers' fonds, GR 441, box 300, file F-9-D; Mr. X (aged fifty-nine) to J.W. Jones, March 25, 1931, BCA, Treasury Correspondence, GR 1773, box 47, file 9.

89 "Report of the Committee Appointed by the Government to Investigate the Finances of British Columbia," July 12, 1932, 27–28, 68–76, 161, BCA, Jones fonds, MS 23, box 4, file 1.

90 See, for example, Council Minutes, Regular Meeting, January 7, 1932, February 18, 1932, and March 3, 1932, CVA, Vancouver Board of Trade, vol. 11. I thank Todd McCallum for sharing his notes on the Vancouver Board of Trade minutes during the early 1930s.

91 Platform of the Taxpayers' Economy League, May 7, 1932; A.S. Tod to Duff Pattullo, January 5, 1932, and January 21, 1932, BCA, Thomas Dufferin Pattullo fonds, MS 3, vol. 47, file 18; open letter of Harold Brown, representing the Canadian Manufacturers' Association and the Vancouver Board of Trade, February 23, 1932, BCA, Thomas Dufferin Pattullo fonds, MS 3, vol. 47, file 22; Mrs. X to J.W. Jones, October 24, 1932, BCA, Treasury Correspondence, GR 1773, box 47, file 9.

92 In this, he was echoing exactly the line that federal Finance Minister E.N. Rhodes took in a general letter to editors of Canadian newspapers, that cutting expenditures couldn't possibly meet the spending needs of the government: "If the Government were in a position to shut up shop and dismiss every Civil Servant and stop payment of their superannuation, we would still have a deficit of $26,000,000." E.N. Rhodes to Dear Mr. ..., March 30, 1933, with a cover letter from W.C. Ronson (private secretary to Rhodes) to R.J. Manion, April 11, 1933, LAC, R.J. Manion fonds, MG 27 III B 7, vol. 84, file 84-2.

93 Financial statement for the 1933 campaign, 10, BCA, Jones fonds, MS 23, box 6, file 3.

94 Mr. X (thought tax had been rescinded) to Minister of Finance, August 3, 1934, and Secretary of Minister of Finance to Mr. X, August 6, 1934, BCA, Treasury Correspondence, GR 1773, box 55, file 10; "Explanatory Notes re Income Tax Act Amendments" re s. 7, 1934, BCA, Treasury Correspondence, GR 1773, box 55, file 10. Somewhat oddly, the figure of sixty dollars appears on provincial income tax circular I.T. 6–2 – 20 M-434-7076 for employers, April 16, 1934, CVA, BC Shipping Federation fonds, AM 279, series 1, box 521-A-1, folder 3.

95 The protection afforded to the least well paid still made casual or intermittent labour vulnerable. Even one month's earnings in excess of fifty dollars resulted in deductions that could be refunded. "Explanatory Notes re Income Tax Act Amendments" re s. 7, 1934, BCA, Treasury Correspondence, GR 1773, box 55, file 10. The continuing impact through the 1930s is evident in the payrolls of the BC Shipping Federation, a large employer of casual labour. In the late 1930s, some employees still called the 1 percent tax the Jones tax. See, for example, letters to the BC Shipping Federation clerk dated February 3, 1936; January 12 and 20, 1937; February 5, 1937; January 6, 1941; and March 5, 1941, CVA, BC Shipping Federation, AM 279, series 1, box 521-A-1, folders 2 and 3.

96 On relief taxes, see Perry, *Taxes, Tariffs, and Subsidies*, 2: 602–3; on credit problems of the western provinces, see Robert L. Ascah, *Politics and Public Debt: The Dominion, the Banks, and Alberta's Social Credit* (Edmonton: University of Alberta Press, 2000), 56–66.

97 "Wage Tax Must Remain, Says Bracken," *Winnipeg Free Press*, May 8, 1933, 1; "Repeal of Wage Tax Sought by Council of O.B.U.," *Winnipeg Free Press*, March 4, 1935, 1; *Forbes v. The Attorney General of Manitoba*, Privy Council Appeal No. 92 of 1936, December 17, 1936.

98 "Ottawa Judgment Holds Wage Tax Legal; Appeal to Privy Council Looms," *Winnipeg Free Press,* January 16, 1936, 3; "May Appeal," Toronto *Globe,* January 16, 1936, 9.

99 "Final Ruling on Wage Tax Is Confirmed," *Winnipeg Free Press,* December 18, 1936, 3.

100 J.W. Jones, budget address, 1932, 37, BCA, Jones fonds, MS 23, box 4, file 3.

101 "Face Deficit for Montreal," Toronto *Globe,* May 1, 1940, 5; "Do Not Worry, Creditors Told," Toronto *Globe,* May 16, 1940, 9; Terry Copp, "Montreal's Municipal Government and the Crisis of the 1930s," in *The Usable Urban Past,* ed. G.A. Stelter and Alan Artibise (Toronto: Macmillan, 1979), 112–29.

102 Jean-Pierre Collin, "Les stratégies fiscales municipales et la gestion de l'agglomération urbaine: Le cas de la Ville de Montréal entre 1910 et 1965," *Urban History Review* 23, 1 (1994): 24; Jean-Pierre Collin, "City Management and the Emerging Welfare State: Evolution of City Budgets and Civic Responsibilities in Montreal, 1931–1951," *Journal of Policy History* 9, 3 (1997): 343–49; Perry, *Taxes, Tariffs, and Subsidies,* 1: 263.

103 Another merchant in a working-class district told the Montreal *Gazette* in 1936 that, in the first ten months that the tax was in effect, he had lost "$300 in profits ... because of customers walking out and refusing to pay the tax." Allegedly, "many of his former clientele have boycotted the store because he insist[ed] on collecting the tax." Quoted in "Hard to Collect," Toronto *Globe,* April 7, 1936, 4.

104 "Verdun refuse de payer la taxe de vente," "Ferland exemple," and "Le maire Ferland," Montreal *La Patrie,* July 10, 1935, 1, 3, and 38.

105 "Le maire Ferland," Montreal *La Patrie,* July 10, 1935, 38; "465 actions intentées à Verdun," Montreal *La Patrie,* July 12, 1935, 1; "La cause Ferland remise au 1er août," Montreal *La Patrie,* July 23, 1935, 2; "M. Houde invité du maire Ferland," Montreal *La Patrie,* August 6, 1935, 4; "Les causes de taxe de vente ajournées," Montreal *La Patrie,* August 6, 1935, 6.

106 My translation. "M. Houde est prêt à prendre 200 actions contre M. Ferland" and "M. Ferland ne se laisse pas intimider," Montreal *La Patrie,* July 11, 1935, 1, 3; "La grève fiscale," front-page banner, Montreal *La Patrie,* July 13, 1935, 1. The paper also reported on a later court decision that called the sales tax tyrannical, meddlesome, and unworthy of inclusion in the province's laws. "La taxe de vente tyrannique, selon le juge A. Forest," Montreal *La Patrie,* October 26, 1935, 36.

107 "465 actions intentées à Verdun," front-page banner, Montreal *La Patrie,* July 12, 1935, 1; "Des inspecteurs de la ville mal reçus par M. Ferland," Montreal *La Patrie,* July 12, 1935, 3; "Ferland exige une cour ouverte," Montreal *La Patrie,* July 15, 1935, 3, 4; "Ferland se plaint des procédés de nos inspecteurs," Montreal *La Patrie,* July 26, 1935, 3, 30; "Tax Spotters Censured," Toronto *Globe,* July 27, 1935, 2; "La taxe de vente ne pècherait pas contre la loi provinciale," Montreal *La Patrie,* August 5, 1935, 5; "Les causes de taxe de vente ajournées," Montreal *La Patrie,* August 6, 1935, 6; "Charged with Bribery," Toronto *Globe,* August 6, 1935, 14.

108 "M. H. Ferland cesse sa lutte contre Montréal," Montreal *La Patrie,* October 15, 1935, 9.

109 "Verdun's Mayors and Other Political Personalities," http://www.ville.montreal.qc.ca.

110 "Déclaration de M. Hervé Ferland," Montreal *La Patrie,* October 15, 1935, 14; "Contestation de l'élection à Verdun?," Montreal *La Patrie,* evening ed., October 23, 1935, 2; "History of Federal Ridings since 1867: General Elections," http://www.parlinfo.gc.ca; "[Camilien Houde] Predicts End of Tory Party," Toronto *Globe,* September 1, 1936, 3; "Union nationale Wins," editorial, Toronto *Globe,* December 17, 1936, 6; "Montreal Balances the Budget," *Globe and Mail,* February 23, 1937, 6; "Verbal Brickbats Fly in Montreal Campaign," *Globe and Mail,* December 6, 1938, 3. In the end, Raynault did not abolish the sales tax; see Conrad Black, *Duplessis* (Toronto: McClelland and Stewart, 1977), 163–64.

111 David Beito, *Taxpayers in Revolt: Tax Resistance during the Great Depression* (Chapel Hill, NC: University of North Carolina Press, 1989).

112 Patricia V. Schulz, *The East York Workers' Association: A Response to the Great Depression* (Toronto: New Hogtown Press, 1979); Maude (Mrs. F.O.) Drury (Secretary, Central Council of Ratepayers, East York Township) to H.R.L. Henry (private secretary to W.L.M. King, Ottawa), 30 March 30, 1936, and Arthur William to Charles A. Dunning (Minister of Finance), April 9, 1936, LAC, Finance fonds, RG 19, vol. 2669, file 2.

113 On Blumberg's position on relief and municipal employment and his socialist politics, see "Huge Arrears," *Winnipeg Free Press*, June 1, 1937, 1, 9, and "Ward Three Aldermen," *Winnipeg Free Press*, November 16, 1937, 2. "North-End Body Asks Change in Seniority Rule at City Hall," *Winnipeg Free Press*, February 1, 1935, 19; "400 City Ratepayers Organize to Launch Tax Strike," *Winnipeg Free Press*, April 5, 1937, 1; "New Unit Approved for Hydro," *Winnipeg Free Press*, April 7, 1937, 1; "Give City Till June to Cut Tax: Homeowners Body Plans Referendum on Strike Proposal," *Winnipeg Free Press*, April 9, 1937, 2; "Plans for Tax Strike Left in Abeyance," *Winnipeg Free Press*, April 12, 1937, 12; "Gives Tax Strike Soft Answer," *Winnipeg Free Press*, April 26, 1937, 13; E.D. Honeyman, Alderman, to Norman Rogers, Minister of Labour, May 27, 1931, with enclosures "Tax Reduction Ballot," *Civic News*, May 31, 1937, and copy of E.D. Honeyman (Chairman, Finance Committee) to Premier John Bracken (Manitoba), May 22, 1937, LAC, Finance fonds, RG 19, vol. 2669, file 2; "The Dissatisfaction of Property Owners," letter to the editor, *Winnipeg Free Press*, May 30, 1937, 25; "Taxpayers' Strike Mooted at Meeting," *Winnipeg Free Press*, February 26, 1937, 1; "Taxpayers' Strike Threat Fails to Halt Civic Wage Boost Drive," *Winnipeg Free Press*, June 22, 1937, 1, 4. On the gender composition of the North End organization, see "Taxpayers of North Re-Elect J. Stepnuk," *Winnipeg Free Press*, December 18, 1937, 6.

114 "The Taxpayer Rebels," *Hush Magazine*, March 30, 1935, 3; "Clean Up at North Bay," *Hush Magazine*, January 15, 1931, 9; "Stop This Relief Racket," *Civic News*, May 31, 1937, 6; Herbert H. Smith (City Clerk, St. Catharines) to Minister of Finance (Ottawa), October 28, 1936, with St. Catharines City Council Motion 329, and F. Saunders to Charles A. Dunning (Minister of Finance), January 3, 1938, LAC, Finance fonds, RG 19, vol. 2669, file 2; "Lower Taxation: Ratepayers to Continue to Fight," *Vancouver Sun*, November 11, 1933, 28; reprint by the Associated Property Owners of Vancouver of William Weston, "The Tax-Paying Worm Begins to Turn," *Saturday Night*, January 21, 1939, 7. Beginning in May 1938, a weekly series of front-page editorials entitled "How Far Can Taxation Go?" featured questions about municipal property taxation and "extravagance"; see, for example, "How Far Can Taxation Go?," *Globe and Mail*, May 21, 1938, 1.

115 "If the Taxpayers Struck," editorial, Toronto *Globe*, August 6, 1936, 4.

116 "Citizens Cross: Taxpayers May Howl but They Do Get Something for Money," *Winnipeg Free Press*, July 5, 1937, 9; "Value Received: Analysis of Tax Bill Reveals Home Owner Well Protected," *Winnipeg Free Press*, July 6, 1937, 8; "Valuable Assets: Taxpayer Gets More for Money Paid City than Anything Else," *Winnipeg Free Press*, July 7, 1937, 7; "Roar for Cut: Services Furnished by City Cost Home-Owners $2 Weekly," *Winnipeg Free Press*, July 8, 1937, 8. All articles were by Gray.

117 Paul Studenski and Herman E. Krooss, *Financial History of the United States* (New York: McGraw-Hill, 1963), 432–33; James Struthers, *No Fault of Their Own: Unemployment and the Canadian Welfare State, 1914–1941* (Toronto: University of Toronto Press, 1983), 151–64, 168–74, 192–96; Ascah, *Politics and Public Debt*, Chapter 3.

118 Mark Leff, *The Limits of Symbolic Reform* (New York: Cambridge University Press, 1984), 12, 33.

119 Perry, *Taxes, Tariffs, and Subsidies*, 2: 626–27, calculated from the total tax revenue column in Table 6 (Appendix).

120 Isaac W. Martin, *Rich People's Movements: Grassroots Campaigns to Untax the One Percent* (Oxford: Oxford University Press, 2013), 69–72; Huret, *American Tax Resisters*, 143.

121 Canada, House of Commons, *Debates,* June 1, 1931, 2175, and July 1, 1931, 3269–75. Regarding letters, see Armand Lavergne to Bennett, June 8, 1931, doc. 464793; D.W. Beaubien, MP, to Bennett, June 16, 1931, doc. 464797; J.W. Carlyle to Dr. J.D. Stanley, MP, July 6, 1931, doc. 464827; W.L. McQuarrie (Provincial Secretary, Retail Merchants' Association), Saskatchewan, to Bennett, July 10, 1931, doc. 464834; and Bennett to F.J. Reynolds (Alberta Dairymen's Association), July 28, 1931, doc. 464850, LAC, Bennett fonds, MG 26-K, reel M1422. See also "Regarding Stamp Tax," *National Revenue Review* 6, 9 (1933): 7. That this issue was of particular interest to farm women was likely the case, but confirmation would require research in the papers of the United Farm Women of Alberta, present at the 1931 United Farmers of Alberta Convention that passed a motion protesting the cheque tax. See "Forward Policy Called for by Westaskiwin U.F.A. Convention," *Wetaskiwin Times,* July 23, 1931, 4.

122 David H. Laycock, *Populism and Democratic Thought in the Canadian Prairies, 1910–1945* (Toronto: University of Toronto Press, 1990).

123 James Overton, "Economic Crisis and the End of Democracy: Politics in Newfoundland during the Great Depression," *Labour/Le travail* 26 (1990): 95–96.

124 Basil B. Campbell, "National Government Canada's Need Today," Address No. 2, Toronto, before the Gyro Club on May 1, 1935, and before the Progress Club on May 3, 1935. See also Basil B. Campbell, "National Government Canada's Need Today," Address No. 1, Toronto, on March 14, 1935, to a Group of Toronto and Ontario Businessmen. Issued from the League for National Government, Temporary Organizing Headquarters, 54 Wellington Street West, Toronto. The league's recruitment flyer was "Canadians – Do You Know?"

125 Don Nerbas, *Dominion of Capital: The Politics of Big Business and the Crisis of the Canadian Bourgeoisie, 1914–1947* (Toronto: University of Toronto Press, 2013), 138–39.

126 Press coverage characterized the 1935 League for National Government organizers as Toronto businessmen; see "Toronto Business Men Plan Big Campaign for National Government," *Winnipeg Free Press,* April 6, 1935, 1. The man named as the league's founder, and its chief orator, was Basil B. Campbell. His future employer, Rupert Bain, built for himself a palatial home, Graydon Hall, the same year that he hired Campbell. The firm was apparently doing well. H.R. Bain appointment advertisement, Toronto *Globe,* June 25, 1936, 12; http://www.graydonhall.com.

127 "Bennett Reported Planning National Govt. for Canada," *Winnipeg Free Press,* September 4, 1935, 3, 7.

128 C. Wurlete to E.N. Rhodes, December 4, 1933, LAC, Finance fonds, RG 19, vol. 3386, series E2(d), file 0747-1 Inflation.

129 Quoted in "Relief and the Franchise," editorial, Toronto *Globe,* May 15, 1936, 4.

130 In addition to the creation of a national (i.e., non-party) government in Britain in 1931, Canada's League for National Government held up as models Australia (presumably referring to its United Australia Party, founded in 1931) and South Africa (likely referring to the United Party of 1934). In British Columbia, one-party ("union" but definitely not labour) government was discussed, and Newfoundland went beyond discussion and actually elected a "United Newfoundland" party. "League for National Government Answers: Canada before Party," advertisement, Toronto *Globe,* October 12, 1935, 5; Robert Groves, "Business Government: Party Politics and the British Columbia Business Community, 1928–1933" (MA thesis, University of British Columbia, 1976), 53, quoted in George M. Abbott, "Duff Pattullo and the Coalition Controversy of 1941," *BC Studies* 102 (1994): 36; Overton, "Economic Crisis and the End of Democracy," 90–91, 97, 106. Another National Government organization was launched later in the 1930s; see Pierre Berton, *The Great Depression, 1929–1939* (Toronto: McClelland and Stewart, 1990), 480–82.

131 Campbell, "National Government Canada's Need Today," Address No. 2, 8; "Canadians – Do You Know?" (League recruiting pamphlet, n.d.).

132 Nerbas, *Dominion of Capital*, 139.

133 League for Social Reconstruction, Research Committee, *Social Planning for Canada* (Toronto: T. Nelson, 1935), 484–87.

134 In 1935, the League for Social Reconstruction noted the resemblance between the anti-party line of the Progressive Party and that of the National Government movement; see ibid., 466. Two classic Canadian statements that emphasize unfair taxation resulting from the corruption of parties by monopolists and manufacturers are W.C. Good, *Production and Taxation in Canada, from the Farmers' Standpoint* (Toronto: J.M. Dent, 1919), 37–44, and W. Frank Hatheway, *Poorhouse and Palace: A Plea for a Better Distribution of Wealth* (Saint John: n.p., 1900).

135 Statements claiming that the unemployed would become violent if their needs were not met can be found in Marjorie Bradford (social worker) to J.H.T. Falk (charitable fundraiser), October 18, 1934, LAC, Canadian Council on Social Development fonds, MG 28 I 10, vol. 13, file 59; former Prime Minister Robert Borden to Finance Minister E.N. Rhodes, January 30, 1935, NSA, Rhodes fonds, MG 2, vol. 1185, file 12, doc. 71753; and James Tighe (union leader), quoted in Carol Ferguson, "Responses to the Unemployment Problem in Saint John, New Brunswick, 1929–1933" (MA thesis, University of New Brunswick, 1986), 116. For the profit motive of the relief industry, see Todd McCallum, *Hobohemia and the Crucifixion Machine: Rival Images of a New World in 1930s Vancouver* (Edmonton: Athabasca University Press, 2014).

Chapter 5: Taxation at the Edges of Citizenship

1 In Canadian law, the term "Indians" differentiates them from other Canadians, including from some others of Indigenous descent, in relation to the state. In what follows, I use it in that sense without quotation marks, and otherwise I use different terms – "First Nations," "Indigenous," particular proper names – as appropriate. In terms of tax law and election law, however, the general legal term is usually relevant. It is the legal meaning of "Indian" that framed the tax problems and politics between and among Canadian government agencies, the Haudenosaunee, Squamish, Haida, Mi'kmaq, Anishnaabe, and other Indigenous peoples.

2 Louis Eisenstein, *The Ideologies of Taxation* (New York: Ronald Press, 1961), 4–5, 8–11.

3 Hilary Frances, "'Pay the Piper, Call the Tune!' The Women's Tax Resistance League," in *The Women's Suffrage Movement: New Feminist Perspectives,* ed. Maroula Joannou and June Purvis (Manchester: Manchester University Press, 1998), 65–76; Ellen DuBois, *Feminism and Suffrage: The Emergence of an Independent Women's Movement in America, 1848–1869* (Ithaca, NY: Cornell University Press, 1999), 49, 50, 123n53, 179, 193; Emily J. Heard, "Gendered Notions of Citizenship and Service in Interwar Halifax" (MA thesis, Dalhousie University, 2001), 73; Nancy M. Forestell, ed., with Maureen Moynagh, Women's Christian Temperance Union, Hantsport, Nova Scotia, "Petition for the Enfranchisement of Women (1878)," in *Documenting First Wave Feminisms, Vol. 2: Canada – National and Transnational Contexts* (Toronto: University of Toronto Press, 2014), 119; Gwendolyn Davies, "The Literary 'New Woman' and Social Activism in Maritime Literature, 1880–1920," in *Separate Spheres: Women's Worlds in the 19th-Century Maritimes,* ed. Janet Guildford and Suzanne Morton (Fredericton, NB: Acadiensis Press, 1994), 240, 243; Shirley Tillotson, *Contributing Citizens: Modern Charitable Fundraising and the Making of the Welfare State* (Vancouver: UBC Press, 2008), 34.

4 Canada, House of Commons, *Debates*, April 29, 1920, 1821.

5 However, there was also support on both benches for exclusion from the franchise of people who are "practically wards of the government" – Indians and those completely dependent on public charity. Debate was simply on whether the wording of the bill was too vague and would risk disenfranchising men temporarily living in hospitals, sanatoriums, or old people's homes that were partly government subsidized. Canada, House of Commons, *Debates,* April 29, 1920, 1815–16, 1818–20.

6 This paragraph is based upon Elections Canada, *A History of the Vote in Canada* (Ottawa: Minister of Public Works and Government Services Canada, 1997), 80–81, and Wendy Moss and Elaine Garner-O'Toole, Law and Government Division of the Library of Parliament, *Aboriginal People: History of Discriminatory Laws,* BP-175E (Ottawa: Library of Parliament, 1991). The term "racialized" here distinguishes my point from the statements made in *A History of the Vote in Canada* that only British Columbia "discriminated against large numbers of potential voters" and that Saskatchewan disenfranchised a "much smaller" number of residents of "Chinese origin." I include as racialized people those referred to as "of Indian blood" in provincial franchise statutes in Manitoba, Quebec, Alberta, and British Columbia and the federal franchise statute. By the 1950s, most provinces had restricted the racial language to describe the "Indian" who could not vote in legal terms, not simply racial terms, as "ordinarily resident on an Indian reservation" or "entitled to receive an annuity or other benefit under any treaty with the Crown." *Statutes of Alberta 1956,* c. 15, s. 2(n).

7 Robin Jarvis Brownlie, "'A Better Citizen Than Lots of White Men': First Nations Enfranchisement – An Ontario Case Study, 1918–1940," *Canadian Historical Review* 87, 1 (2006): 29–52.

8 Hugh Shewell, "Jules Sioui and Indian Political Radicalism in Canada, 1943–44," *Journal of Canadian Studies* 32, 3 (1999): 211–42.

9 Indian Act, R.S.C. 1985, c. I-5, s. 87 (in earlier versions of the act, the tax provision was s. 105). Joel Oliphant, "Taxation and Treaty Rights: *Benoit v. Canada*'s Historical Context and Impact," *Manitoba Law Journal* 29, 3 (2002–3): 365. Other scholars have analyzed how applications of the statute's original provisions have been recently interpreted, suggesting that extrapolations made to deal with different kinds of property in the modern context might be discriminatory or at least inconsistent with standard practices of legal interpretation. See Martha O'Brien, "Income Tax, Investment Income, and the Indian Act: Getting Back on Track," *Canadian Tax Journal* 50, 5 (2002): 1570–96; Constance MacIntosh, "From Judging Culture to Taxing 'Indians': Tracing the Legal Discourse of the 'Indian Mode of Life,'" *Osgoode Hall Law Journal* 47, 3 (2009): 399–437.

10 See, for example, J.D. McLean (Assistant Superintendent and Secretary) to Thomas Toney ("Indian"), November 24, 1924, LAC, Department of Indian Affairs and Northern Development fonds (hereafter Indian Affairs fonds), RG 10, vol. 6821, file 492-20-1; Martin Sherry (Jordan Station) to "Indian Department," January 29, 1917, re "only indian being charged dog tax," and November 18, 1917; J.H. Topping (Secretary-Treasurer, Escoumains) to Jos. F.-X. Bossé (Indian Agent), November 18, 1917; "Memo, the Secretary, Ottawa, 15 March 1922"; J.D. McLean to O.R. Perron (School Section 1, Temagami), July 22, 1922; Lajoie and Lajoie (Avocats, Trois-Rivières) to Duncan C. Scott (Deputy Superintendent), July 22, 1922; J.D. McLean (Acting Deputy Superintendent) to Lajoie and Lajoie, July 29, 1922, LAC, Indian Affairs fonds, RG 10, vol. 6822, file 493-1-7, part 1.

11 James E. Kirby (Acting Provincial Collector) to Charles Martin ("Indian," Hazelton, BC), October 15, 1923, and Charles Martin to "the Indian Affairs, Ottawa," January 10, 1924, LAC, Indian Affairs fonds, RG 10, vol. 6822, file 493-1-7, part 1.

12 Scott's 1925 letter to Breadner was quoted in C.S. Walters (Commissioner of Income Tax) to A.F. MacKenzie (Secretary, Indian Affairs), November 4, 1931, LAC, Indian Affairs fonds, RG 10, vol. 6822, file 493-1-7, part 1.

13 R.W. Hines (Pubnico, NS) to "Indian Agent, Ottawa," August 3, 1933, LAC, Indian Affairs fonds, RG 10, vol. 6821, file 492-20-1; J.A. Mathieu (President, J.A. Mathieu Limited, Rainy Lake, ON) to H.W. McGill (Director of Indian Affairs), July 11, 1940, and Georges Picard (grocer) to Dominion Bureau of Statistics, April 6, 1943, LAC, Indian Affairs fonds, RG 10, vol. 6821, file 493-1-6, part 1; Dave Chisholm (Indian Agent, Armdale, NS) to "Secy, Dept Indian Affairs, Ottawa," August 17, 1925; Maurice Bastien (Indian Agent, Jeune Lorette), July 9, 1928; Frank Claus to Indian Affairs, September 21, 1931; Joseph M. Lavalley to "Indian Agent, Ottawa," April 7, 1932 and February 12, 1929; Peter Williams (Caughnawaga) to A.F. McKenzie (Indian Affairs), October 27, 1931; "Refuses to Pay Taxes," clipping, Montreal *Gazette*, February 14, 1931; Andrew Paull to Duncan C. Scott (Deputy Superintendent General), May 8, 1931, LAC, Indian Affairs fonds, RG 10, vol. 6822, file 493-1-7, part 1.

14 Eugene A. Sioui (Huron Indian, Indian Lorette) to Governor General Lord Byng of Vimy, January 21, 1924, and Louis Bananish to Department of Indian Affairs, August 13, 1925, LAC, Indian Affairs fonds, RG 10, vol. 6822, file 493-1-7, part 1; Chief Thunderwater (Tehotiokwawakon) of the Council of the Tribes to Indian Affairs, March 17, 1915, and J.D. McLean (Indian Affairs) to Chief Thunderwater, March 24, 1915, with a copy of a February 9, 1911, letter, J.D. McLean to George E. Baxter (Indian Agent, Andover, NB); A.G. Chisholm (barrister and solicitor, London, ON) to Commissioner of Customs, March 27, 1918; copy of Assistant Commissioner of Customs and Excise to Collector of Customs (Cornwall, ON), July 6, 1921, LAC, Department of Revenue fonds, RG 16, vol. 789, file A7613. Having been deployed in objections to customs duties, some of the same treaty arguments were made later in relation to income taxation. See Petition of North American Indians to the Minister of National Revenue (Income Tax Department), July 14, 1942, and Petition of Frank MacDonald Jacobs of Caughnawaga, for exemption, February 17, 1943, LAC, Indian Affairs fonds, RG 10, vol. 6821, file 493-1-16, part 1.

15 Alex Sioui to Mines and Resources Department, Indian Affairs Branch, December 15, 1942, LAC, Indian Affairs fonds, RG 10, vol. 6821, file 493-1-6, part 1.

16 See Jos. F.-X. Bossé (Indian Agent) to Secretary, Department of Indian Affairs, and C.C. Perry (Assistant Indian Commissioner, BC) to Duncan C. Scott (Deputy Superintendent General), May 27, 1931, LAC, Indian Affairs fonds, RG 10, vol. 6822, file 493-1-7, part 1. In the early 1940s, a Montreal law firm, Boyer, Coderre, and Therrien, advised the Kahnawake community that they had no legal liability to income taxation or conscription. C.F. Elliott (Commissioner of Income Tax) to T.R.L. MacInnes (Indian Affairs), January 26, 1943, LAC, Indian Affairs fonds, RG 10, vol. 6821, file 493-1-6, part 1.

17 Paul Sioui to Superintendent General, date-stamped November 15, 1922, and J.D. McLean (Assistant Deputy and Secretary) to Paul Sioui, November 20, 1922, LAC, Indian Affairs fonds, RG 10, vol. 6822, file 493-1-7, part 1. The contents of the McLean letter were also filed as "Memo. Ottawa, 20th November 1922," and later referred to, by date, as policy in a letter to another member of the same community, J.D. McLean to Eugene A. Sioui, January 31, 1924. In 1927, the departmental solicitor, A.F. Mackenzie, referred to that memo and described himself as having written it in association with an inquiry from a Toronto resident (and Hiawatha reserve member) about the city's right to tax Indians, letter dated June 14, 1926, and date-stamped January 17, 1927; H.J. Anderson to "Sir," June 14, 1926, LAC, Indian Affairs fonds, RG 10, vol. 6822, file 493-1-7, part 1.

18 A copy of the Plaxton opinion had found its way into the hands of Native Brotherhood of British Columbia leader Andrew Paull by April 1942, and he wanted to know why Indian Affairs was contradicting Plaxton; "Re: Liability of Indians to Pay Dominion Income Tax," April 26, 1939, copy, LAC, Indian Affairs fonds, RG 10, vol. 6821, file 493-1-6, part 1. Paull also reproduced the Plaxton opinion in "Appendix AD, Grand Council North American

Indian Brotherhood, the Indians of Canada, Contravention of Certain Rights, by Andrew Paull, President," in Canada, Parliament, Special Joint Committee of the Senate and the House of Commons Appointed to Continue and Complete the Examination and Consideration of the Indian Act, *Minutes of Proceedings and Evidence* (Ottawa: King's Printer, 1947–48), 835.

19 C.S. Walters to A.F. Mackenzie, November 4, 1931, LAC, Indian Affairs fonds, RG 10, vol. 6822, file 493-1-7, part 1.

20 Concerning Cross's living on reserve, see Secretary, Dominion Bridge Company, to Department of Indian Affairs, July 6, 1929, LAC, Indian Affairs fonds, RG 10, vol. 6822, file 493-1-7, part 1.

21 Peter Walker to Department of Indian Affairs, January 24, 1933, LAC, Indian Affairs fonds, RG 10, vol. 6822, file 493-1-7, part 1.

22 C.F. Elliott (Commissioner of Income Tax) to Peter Walker, January 28, 1933, LAC, Indian Affairs fonds, RG 10, vol. 6822, file 493-1-7, part 1. The file copy of this letter is a carbon copy with no signature; I assume that it was signed by Elliott, then the commissioner, but the typist's notation gave the initials FHL to indicate the letter's civil servant author. That was F. Harold Lewis, the officer in charge of administration for National Revenue. See *National Revenue Review* 1, 1 (1927): 4.

23 Secretary, Dominion Bridge Company, to Department of Indian Affairs, July 6, 1929, LAC, Indian Affairs fonds, RG 10, vol. 6822, file 493-1-7, part 1; A.F. Mackenzie to Secretary, Dominion Bridge Company, July 10, 1929, LAC, Indian Affairs fonds, RG 10, vol. 6822, file 493-1-7, part 1.

24 A.F. Mackenzie to D. Art. Richard, July 2, 1929, LAC, Indian Affairs fonds, RG 10, vol. 6822, file 493-1-7, part 1.

25 A.F. Mackenzie to Dr. J.H. Jacobs, April 11, 1931, LAC, Indian Affairs fonds, RG 10, vol. 6822, file 493-1-7, part 1.

26 W.E. Ditchburn to J.W. Jones, April 13, 1931; J.W. Jones to W.E. Ditchburn, April 28, 1931; C.C. Perry (Assistant Indian Commissioner, BC) to Duncan C. Scott, May 27, 1931; Duncan C. Scott to F.J.C. Ball (Vancouver Indian Agent), September 22, 1931, LAC, Indian Affairs fonds, RG 10, vol. 6822, file 493-1-7, part 1.

27 Andrew Paull to D.M. MacKay (Indian Commissioner for BC), April 8, 1942; Minutes of the Convention of the Native Brotherhood of British Columbia, November 24, 1942; Colin Gibson (Minister of National Revenue) to Andrew Paull, November 25, 1942, LAC, Indian Affairs fonds, RG 10, vol. 6821, file 493-1-6, part 1.

28 Colin Gibson to Ian Mackenzie, MP, February 17, 1943, LAC, Indian Affairs fonds, RG 10, vol. 6821, file 493-1-6, part 1.

29 For an example of the standard letter sent in response to inquiries at that time, see T.R.L. MacInnes (Secretary, Indian Affairs) to J.F. Walker (Indian Agent), July 24, 1940, LAC, Indian Affairs fonds, RG 10, vol. 6821, file 493-1-6, part 1.

30 See, for example, T. Fraser to Department of Indian Affairs, December 2, 1929, and A.F. Mackenzie to T. Fraser, December 5, 1929, LAC, Indian Affairs fonds, RG 10, vol. 6822, file 493-1-7, part 1.

31 "Non-Franchised Indian" James Jamieson to "Dear Sir," April 6, 1942, LAC, Indian Affairs fonds, RG 10, vol. 6821, file 493-1-6, part 1.

32 Shewell, "Jules Sioui and Indian Political Radicalism," 222–24, 226, 230; Andrew Paull, President, Grand Council North American Indian Brotherhood, "Indians of Canada: Contravention of Certain Rights," Appendix AD, in Canada, Special Joint Committee of the Senate and the House of Commons Appointed to Continue and Complete the Examination and Consideration of the Indian Act, *Minutes of Proceedings and Evidence* (Ottawa: The Committee, 1947–48), 835–36.

33 Calculated from the 1929 line in Table 6, J. Harvey Perry, *Taxes, Tariffs, and Subsidies: A History of Canadian Fiscal Development*, 2 vols. (Toronto: University of Toronto Press, 1955), 1: 626–27.

34 Another investigator also expressed regret at the enforcement of absurdly inconvenient customs regulations, such as those that required a farmer to travel twenty miles out of his way to declare a few groceries. Because the farmer would flout those regulations, he was then more ready to dodge customs duties on more significant imports. H.U. Green to A.J. Cawdron (Director of Criminal Investigation, RCMP, for Customs and Excise), November 19, 1926, and J.W. Allan to A.J. Cawdron, November 10, 1926, LAC, Revenue fonds, RG 16, vol. 789, file 128256.

35 The Ottawa commissioner of customs did not approve of the local customs, as some St. Regis residents found when they appealed to him. Commissioner of Customs to H.A. Lemieux (Inspector of Customs, Montreal), March 7, 1911; Inspector of Customs at Montreal to Commissioner of Customs, March 24, 1911; Commissioner of Customs to Mitchell C. Jacobs and John Jacobs, March 30, 1911; Collector of Customs at Cornwall (no addressee), date-stamped April 11, 1911; Edmund Caza, quoted in "Memorandum by P.L.Y. General Executive Assistant of Customs Division to H.D. Scully" (Commissioner of Customs), June 1, 1937, LAC, Revenue fonds, RG 16, vol. 789, file A7613.

36 Bryan Nickels, "Native American Free Passage Rights under the 1794 Jay Treaty: Survival under United States Statutory Law and Canadian Common Law," *Boston College International and Comparative Law Review* 24, 2 (2001): 327–30.

37 J.D. McLean to George E. Baxter, Indian Agent, February 9, 1911; Commissioner of Customs to Customs Collector at Cornwall, April 6, 1911; Commissioner of Customs to Mitchell C. Jacobs, April 6, 1911; Tehotiokwawakon (Chief of the Council of the Tribes) to J.D. McLean, Indian Affairs, March 17, 1915; O.D. Skelton to R.W. Breadner, January 19, 1931; R.W. Breadner to O.D. Skelton, January 22, 1931, LAC, Revenue fonds, RG 16, vol. 789, file A7613.

38 *Garrow v. The United States*, US Treasury Decisions 69, 12 (March 19, 1936): 24–27; M.H. Vernon (RCMP Criminal Investigation Branch) to H.D. Scully (Commissioner of Customs), March 19, 1936; "Jay Treaty Still Holds for Indians," undated clipping attached to Chief Nicholas Plain to Ross W. Gray, MP, March 16, 1963; H.D. Scully to Ross W. Gray, March 23, 1936; "Mrs. Garrow Loses Case in U.S. Court," undated clipping attached to E.W. Bavin (RCMP Criminal Investigation Branch) to H.D. Scully, October 11, 1937, LAC, Revenue fonds, RG 16, vol. 789, file A7613.

39 Harold W. McGill, Director, memorandum to the Deputy Minister re: Imposition of duty on Indian merchandise entering the United States, April 2, 1937, LAC, Revenue fonds, RG 16, vol. 789, file A7613.

40 Collector at Port of Huntingdon, Quebec, to H.D. Scully, August 9, 1941 and L.H. Taylor to Collector at Port of Huntingdon, Quebec, August 15, 1941, LAC, Revenue fonds, RG 16, vol. 789, file A7613.

41 H.D. Scully to J.E. Read (Acting Under Secretary of State for External Affairs), 15 November 1937, LAC, Revenue fonds, RG 16, vol. 789, file A7613.

42 R.W. Duff (Section NCO, Kingston Detachment) to Officer I/C "A" Division CIB, re Enforcement of the Customs Act, St. Regis Detachment, October 24, 1951, LAC, Revenue fonds, RG 16, vol. 789, file A7613.

43 Ibid.

44 David Sim (Commissioner of Customs) to F.P. Varcoe (Deputy Minister of Justice), July 25, 1951; David Sim to F.P. Varcoe, December 7, 1951; David Sim to Laval Fortier (Deputy Minister of Citizenship and Immigration), December 7, 1951; F.P. Varcoe to David Sim, January 29, 1952, LAC, Revenue fonds, RG 16, vol. 789, file A7613.

45 *Francis v. The Queen*, [1956] S.C.R. 618–31; Dan Lewerenz, "Historical Context and the Survival of the Jay Treaty Free Passage Right: A Response to Marcia Yablon-Zug," *Arizona Journal of International and Comparative Law* 27, 1 (2010): 218–21; Nickels, "Native American Free Passage Rights under the 1794 Jay Treaty," 327–30.

46 E.A. Heaman, "Rights Talk and the Liberal Order," in *Liberalism and Hegemony: Debating the Canadian Liberal Revolution*, ed. Jean-François Constant and Michel Ducharme (Toronto: University of Toronto Press, 2009), 147–75.

47 Lisa Rose Mar, "Beyond Being Others: Chinese Canadians as National History," *BC Studies* 156 (2007–8): 13–34.

48 "Premier Reassures Those of Alien Birth," Toronto *Globe*, February 21, 1918, 5.

49 "The Assessment Question and 'Public Opinion' in Toronto," Bulletin No. 70, November 16, 1918, City of Toronto Archives (hereafter CTA), Toronto Bureau of Municipal Research fonds 1003, series 973, subseries 1, file 81–90.

50 British Columbia, Royal Commission on Taxation, *Synopsis of Report and Full Report of Royal Commission on Taxation, 1911* (Victoria: King's Printer, 1912), 16–19; duplicate of the first poll tax receipt issued by the City of Vancouver, January 22, 1925, and "City of Vancouver Poll-Tax" poster or display ad, n.d., CVA, Major Matthews fonds, AM54, series S23, subseries 2, fiche 3702, file Poll Tax, Vancouver; Accounting Department, "City of Vancouver, Statement of Poll Tax Receipts for the Years 1925–1937 (Inclusive)," January 20, 1938, CVA, City of Vancouver fonds (hereafter COV), City Treasurer records, s428, box 95-A-4, file 2, Poll Tax 1937–40. Thanks to Elsbeth Heaman for the reference to the 1911 royal commission. She discusses aspects of the nineteenth-century history of race politics and culture in BC taxation in Elsbeth Heaman, "'The Whites Are Wild about It': Taxation and Racialization in Mid-Victorian British Columbia," *Journal of Policy History* 25, 3 (2013): 354–84.

51 S.F. Tolmie to J.W. Jones, March 13, 1931, BCA, Premiers' fonds, GR 441, box 300, file F-9-D; Mr. Macdonald to J.W. Jones, May 5, 1931; Mr. Robinson to Your Honour, March 8, 1931; Mission Conservative Association to S.F. Tolmie, March 20, 1931, BCA, Treasury Correspondence, GR 1773, box 47, file 9. In conformity with the research agreement under which I accessed these records, personal identifiers of private individuals who wrote to the government have been altered or removed.

52 "Reject Poll Tax Idea," *U.F.A.*, February 15, 1929, 44.

53 In 1918, London City Council voted to require "alien laborers" to pay "a fee of $10 per year for working in London in addition to the poll tax." The title of the Quebec statute was An Act to Prohibit the Levying of Taxes on Persons outside of a Municipality Who Work Therein." "London Appointments," Toronto *Globe*, February 19, 1918; *Labour Gazette* 27, 5 (1927): 506.

54 Carol Ferguson, "Responses to the Unemployment Problem in Saint John, New Brunswick, 1929–1933" (MA thesis, University of New Brunswick, 1986), 99–104. See also continuing discussion of attempts to "build a tax fence" around Saint John in New Brunswick, Legislative Assembly, *Synoptic Report of the Proceedings of the Legislative Assembly of the Province of New Brunswick, Committee Proceedings* (Saint John: Legislative Assembly of New Brunswick, 1933), March 29, 17.

55 William J. Novak, "The Legal Transformation of Citizenship in Nineteenth Century America," in *The Democratic Experiment: New Directions in American Political History*, ed. Meg Jacobs, William J. Novak, and Julian E. Zelizer (Princeton, NJ: Princeton University Press, 2003), 85–119, especially 97–105; Tillotson, *Contributing Citizens*, 31. A valuable discussion of analogous particular corporate rights can be found in Heaman, "Rights Talk and the Liberal Order Framework." The editors of *Eastern Labor News* critiqued the common-sense assumption that property ownership was what conferred membership in the

municipal political community, with both property's obligations (tax liability) and rights (the franchise). "Human rights," they averred, were not recognized in that system. "Over Half Moncton's Voting Population Disfranchised," *Eastern Labor News*, February 5, 1910, 4.

56 "Census of Americans for Head-Tax Levy Suggested at Border," Toronto *Globe*, February 10, 1931, 1.

57 "Memorandum on Resolution to Exclude Aliens from Income Tax Exemptions," 1935, NSA, Rhodes fonds, MG 2, vol. 1196, doc. 75090.

58 Mark Milke, *A Nation of Serfs? How Canada's Political Culture Corrupts Canadian Values* (Mississauga, ON: J. Wiley and Sons, 2006), Chapter 3.

59 Quoted in Carla Marano, "'Rising Strongly and Rapidly': The Universal Negro Improvement Association in Canada, 1919–1940," *Canadian Historical Review* 91, 2 (2010): 250–51.

60 A Saint John union leader, J.E. Tighe of the Longshoremen's Union, in a debate on the City of Saint John Amendment Act in 1915, described such visits from city constables. See New Brunswick, Legislative Assembly, *Synoptic Report, Committee Proceedings*, 1915, 7–8.

61 Constance Backhouse, *Colour-Coded: A Legal History of Racism in Canada, 1900–1950* (Toronto: University of Toronto Press, 1999), 226–32.

62 Duplicate of the first poll tax receipt issued by the City of Vancouver, January 22, 1925, and poster or display ad titled "City of Vancouver Poll Tax," explaining the individual's responsibility under the poll tax, CVA, J.S. Matthews fonds, AM 54, fiche 3702, "Poll Tax."

63 The tax was called a "service tax" in the Calgary city charter; a review of Canadian municipal taxation in Toronto in 1923 referred to it as a "special franchise tax." *Statutes of Alberta*, 1921, An Act to Amend the Ordinances and Acts Constituting the Charter of the City of Calgary, c. 70, s. 7; *Ordinances and Statutes Comprising the Charter of the City of Calgary*, 1945, s. 5, s. 42-A; *Report of the Committee on Taxation of the City of Toronto re: Single Tax* (Toronto: City of Toronto, 1923), 10.

64 *Statutes of Alberta*, 1921, An Act to Amend the Ordinances and Acts Constituting the Charter of the City of Calgary, c. 70, s. 7.

65 H. Carl Goldenberg, *Municipal Finance in Canada: A Study Prepared for the Royal Commission on Dominion-Provincial Relations* (Ottawa: King's Printer, 1939), 84; *Statutes of New Brunswick*, 1882, c. 59, s. 25; By-Law 1685, A By-Law to Impose a Poll-Tax on Male Persons Residing within the Limits of the City of Vancouver, December 22, 1924, CVA, COV, City By-Laws, series 36, file By-Law No. 1685; duplicate of the first poll tax receipt issued by the City of Vancouver, January 22, 1925, CVA, J.S. Matthews fonds, AM 54, fiche 3702, "Poll Tax." The City of Toronto did not impose a poll tax, but many other Ontario municipalities did, including Hamilton, London, and Oshawa, under the province's Statute Labour Act.

66 The Ontario statute, the Statute Labour Act, RSO, 1927, c. 239, s. 2; RSO, 1937, c. 274, contained no reference to marital status in its description of who could be charged a poll tax, but most men would be exempt by reason of paying a greater sum in other taxes. A 1959 commentator on the poll tax characterized those who paid it as "lodgers, adult sons at home, internes [sic] in hospitals, and so on": that is, men who were neither property owners nor tenants; see "Abolish This Tax," *Toronto Daily Star*, January 21, 1959, 6. My knowledge of the Quebec City *taxe personnelle* is based upon a report by my research assistant, Alex Tremblay, who examined the "registre des executions sur avis pour non-paiement de taxes personnelles" for the period 1915–32 in the Quebec City Archives. Further investigation into municipal records would provide the by-law and legislative history of this tax. I thank Sonya Roy, a doctoral student in history at McGill University, for drawing my attention to the use of the term "bachelor's tax" in Montreal. An example of one reaction to that tax can be found in "The Bachelor's Tax," letter to the editor, Montreal *Gazette*,

August 10, 1918, 15. The Ontario poll tax did not limit its liability to unmarried men; however, the terms of the relevant statutes – the Voters' Lists Act, the Municipal Institutions Act, and the Statute Labour Act, RSO, 1937, c. 7, s. 6; c. 266, ss. 56, 57, 60; and c. 274, s. 2 – together made it likely that the usual payers were urban bachelors. A bit of filler copy in 1934 underscored this point; see "Saskatoon Bachelors Are Being Soaked $3 a Piece as a Poll Tax. Well, Bachelordom Is Cheap at the Price, Isn't It?," *Toronto Daily Star,* November 26, 1934, 4.

67 See, for example, the discussion of the poll tax as meeting the civic franchise qualification in lieu of an income tax on incomes under $1,000 in New Brunswick, Legislative Assembly, *Synoptic Report, Committee Proceedings,* 1915, 6–8. For the Maritime provinces, I have documented in detail the links between different forms of taxpaying and their differentiation by sex and marital status over the period 1910–72. The elimination of taxpayer elements in franchise law of the cities and other municipal jurisdictions of the Maritime provinces began in 1953 and was completed only in 1972. Shirley Tillotson, "Relations of Extraction: Taxation and Women's Citizenship in the Maritimes, 1914–1955," *Acadiensis* 39, 1 (2010): 43. For a discussion of the distinction between the taxpayer franchise and the property franchise in the United States, see Alexander Keyssar, *The Right to Vote: The Contested History of Democracy in the United States* (New York: Basic Books, 2000).

68 Roman Wasyl Franko, "Towards Liberal Democracy in Ontario, 1868–1888" (PhD diss., Queen's University, 1992), 212–40, quoted in Todd Stubbs, "'A Stake in the Country': Wage-Earning Men and the Income Franchise Debate in Ontario, 1866–1874," paper presented at Transformation: State, Nation, and Citizenship in a New Environment, York University, October 15, 2011; "6,000 Voters Lose Ballots," Toronto *Globe,* December 20, 1935, 13.

69 "6,000 Voters Lose Ballots," Toronto *Globe,* December 20, 1935, 13; "White Receipts Qualify Voters," *Globe and Mail,* November 25, 1936, 2. In the 1950s, discussion of possibly eliminating the poll tax emphasized that it did not confer municipal voting rights; see, for example, "Abolish This Tax," editorial comment, *Toronto Daily Star,* January 21, 1959, 6.

70 Voters' Lists Act, Municipal Institutions Act, and Statute Labour Act, RSO, 1937, c. 7, s. 6; c. 266, ss. 56, 57, 60; and c. 274, s. 2. Requests that poll tax payers be given the right to vote occasionally appeared in Ontario in the 1950s. For example, the Oshawa and District Labor Council made that request of Oshawa City Council; see "Ask Vote for Those Who Pay Poll Tax," *Toronto Daily Star,* February 8, 1955, 10.

71 *Statutes of New Brunswick,* 1942, City of Saint John Assessment Act, c. 80, s. 41.

72 The Ontario Municipal Taxation Act, RSO, 1927, c. 238, s. 7(1), allowed low-income earners to vote if they were willing to pay a tax on income that fell below the general exemption level. They could request that their incomes be assessed, pay the taxes, and thus get their names on the municipal voters list. In 1941, a New Brunswick municipal official worried that the wartime tax agreements might eliminate the poll tax; if that happened, then some people would not be assessed for a tax and therefore disappear from the voters list; see W.A.R. (County Secretary) to George L. Walker (New Brunswick Commissioner of Municipal Affairs), November 27, 1941, Public Archives of New Brunswick (hereafter PANB), Saint John County fonds, RS 156, series C, file C6.

73 Kathryn V. Snyder, *Bachelors, Manhood, and the Novel, 1850 to 1925* (Cambridge, UK: Cambridge University Press, 1999), 21–22; Patrizia Albanese, *Mothers of the Nation: Women, Families, and Nationalism in Twentieth-Century Europe* (Toronto: University of Toronto Press, 2006), 54.

74 See, for example, Halifax City Charter, 1914, s. 400.

75 New Brunswick, Legislative Assembly, *Synoptic Report, Committee Proceedings,* 1933, March 15, 1933, 13; March 17, 1933, 15; March 22, 1933, 16.

76 "New Taxation Scheme for City of Saint John," *Saint John Daily Sun,* November 6, 1906, 8; "Chamberlain's Report," in *Reports and Accounts of the Corporation of the City of Saint John, for Year Ending December 31st, 1911* (Saint John: City of Saint John, 1912), 35. The Saint John experience was not unique. In 1934, BC municipal politicians described all such "minimum taxes" as "difficult and costly to collect, and fundamentally unsound as [they ignore] 'ability-to-pay.'" See "Brief Presented by the Union of British Columbia Municipalities to the Honourable Members of the School Finance Commission and the School Finance Survey Committees," August 1934, BCA, Treasury Correspondence, GR 1773, box 55, file 7. Some of the many difficulties in collecting poll taxes were summarized in Harvey Walker, "The Poll Tax in the United States," *Bulletin of the National Tax Association* 9, 3 (1923): 69–70.

77 My observations in this paragraph about patterns in these cases are based upon comparing August cases of tax appeals made to the Saint John County and City Board of Revision in 1932, 1933, 1934, and 1935 and examining in detail the 125 cases involving women as taxpayers or representatives of taxpayers in relation to the 139 cases involving men as taxpayers or representatives of taxpayers in August 1935. PANB, Saint John County Council fonds, RS 156, series C, file C2(e)2, Board of Revision ledgers for 1931–34 and 1935–36.

78 The annual tax due date varied somewhat, but either August or September was the first month following the due date, and tax appeals were the highest in those months. In 1932, there were no appeals in August and twenty-nine in September. In 1934, there were 434 cases across those two months, and in 1935 there were 469.

79 See, for example, case 149 (reduced valuation that reduces property tax debt from $225 to $209), case 212 (interest struck off tax arrears that were mainly water rates), case 110 (single female schoolteacher is allowed the householder exemption – equivalent to the married exemption –on her municipal income tax), and case 156 (married man, railway clerk, wife and seven children, reduction of tax arrears from just over sixty-six dollars to twenty dollars, mostly municipal income tax over three years, some payments having been made already on account), PANB, Saint John County Council fonds, RS 156, series C, file C2(e)2, Board of Revision ledger for 1935–36.

80 Cases 123, 144, 147, 158, 285, 287, 305, and 306, PANB, Saint John County Council fonds, RS 156, series C, file C2(e)2, Board of Revision ledger for 1935–36.

81 Cases 168, 210, 214, 218, 220, 221, 238, 239, 279, 288, 311, 312, 314, 377, and 378. Statutory indigency for the purpose of tax was different from municipal relief. The quoted phrases here defined in the 1918 statute for the first time what had always been allowed, an exemption for indigency; see *Statutes of New Brunswick,* Saint John Assessment Act, 1918, c. 73, s. 7, ss. 7. Relief recipients were not always exempted from tax responsibilities, and a few had some tax held back from their relief payments; see cases 211 and 360, PANB, Saint John County Council fonds, RS 156, series C, file C2(e)2, Board of Revision ledger for 1935–36.

82 Case of A.B.W., minutes of October 28, 1932, PANB, Saint John County Council fonds, RS 156, series C, file C2(e)2, Board of Revision ledger for 1931–34, 28; case of J.E.C., minutes of July 10, 1940, PANB, Saint John County Council fonds, RS 156, series C, file C2(e)2, Board of Revision ledger for 1940, n. pag. No such explicit requests were recorded in the August 1935 cases; perhaps such niceties fell away under the exceptional pressure of the board's work.

83 Both the number of poll tax cases and the number of clearly identified widows were small: seventeen poll tax cases (of which only five were relieved of the debt) and thirteen widows (of which nine were relieved of their various tax debts, two got extensions or partial relief, and two had their appeals dismissed). One of the five poll tax payers relieved was one of the thirteen widows. In Ontario, the *Toronto Daily Star* protested the aggressive enforcement against that province's men-only poll tax, editorializing against the imprisonment by one town of six unemployed young men who pleaded inability to pay as their reason for defaulting on the poll tax; see "A Queer Sort of Case," *Toronto Daily Star,* May 23, 1931, 6.

84 Tillotson, "Relations of Extraction," 45–47. In this essay, I phrased my conclusion concerning widows and taxation in Saint John somewhat differently, saying that, by relieving some women of their taxes, the council was treating their votes as "dispensable." On further reflection, I have realized that, in *not* requiring widowed real estate tax payers to relinquish their vote formally, the council could have been allowing them to continue voting. However, it seems more likely that, because women's suffrage was so new in 1935, the council might have assumed that these women (often older) were not likely to vote. The overall implication of both interpretations is the same: these women were not seen as voters.

85 For example, a son living with his parents could avoid the tax by having himself assessed as a joint owner of the family home; see "Want Single Women to Pay Poll Tax Same as the Men," *Toronto Daily Star,* August 30, 1934, 12. That enforcement wasn't always thorough and persistent is suggested by a resolution passed in Acton, Ontario, by the council that "the poll tax must be enforced"; see "Enforce Poll Tax," *Toronto Daily Star,* December 22, 1934, 14. A bit of editorial page filler reported that Hanover, Ontario, had collected its poll tax for 1933 from "only about a dozen young men"; see *Toronto Daily Star,* October 14, 1933, 4. Enforcement was not just a problem in Ontario. The records of the Vancouver treasurer include a file on the poll tax, 1937–40, that shows how much effort was involved in getting refractory employers to play their role in enforcing the tax. See, for example, the case of a construction firm that pretended to have lost the poll tax receipt forms. The city official reported "an attitude of inattention and non-co-operation" at the firm and remarked that one of its "prominent employees has dodged payment of Poll-Tax for the past three years." Withholding money owed by the city to the firm and launching an investigation by "City Detectives" were recommended; see T.J. Corley (Poll Tax Collector) to Hugh Christie (Acting Collector of Taxes), September 7, 1937, CVA, COV, City Treasurer records, s428, box 95-A-4, file 2 "Poll Tax" 1937–40. Vancouver ended its city poll tax in 1948. See also "Poll Tax Lagging," *Winnipeg Evening Tribune,* December 23, 1939, 3.

86 Statute Labour Act, RSO, 1927, c. 239, s. 2; RSO, 1937, c. 274; "City of Vancouver Poll-Tax," poster or display ad, n.d., CVA, Major Matthews fonds, AM54, series S23, subseries 2, fiche 3702, file "Poll Tax, Vancouver"; By-Law No. 2009: A By-Law to Impose a Poll-Tax on Male Persons Residing within the Limits of the City of Vancouver, July 8, 1929, CVA, COV, City By-Laws, s36, file "By-Law 2009"; "Demand for Payment of 1937 Poll Tax to Employers of Labour," January 2, 1937, CVA, COV, City Treasurer records, s428, box 95-A-4, file 2 "Poll Tax" 1937–40.

87 "Pays Tax, Sues Town," *Toronto Daily Star,* November 8, 1934, 51.

88 New Brunswick, Legislative Assembly, "Appendix – Report of the Proceedings of Committees," in *Synoptic Report, Committee Proceedings,* 1936, 8; "Would Tax Spinsters," *Toronto Daily Star,* January 25, 1933, 28; "Want Single Women to Pay Poll Tax Same as the Men," *Toronto Daily Star,* August 30, 1934, 12. One BC woman wrote to her provincial finance minister that "it seems hardly fair to compel young men to pay this tax and allow young women to go free, especially when they are active competitors of men in nearly every position"; see Miss X to J.W. Jones, January 19, 1932, BCA, Treasury Correspondence, GR 1773, box 47, file 13.

89 New Brunswick, Department of Provincial Secretary-Treasurer, *Report of the Royal Commission on the Rates and Taxes Act* (Fredericton: Royal Commission on the Rates and Taxes Act, 1951), 56.

90 "Poll Tax for Women," letter to the editor, *Toronto Daily Star,* October 15, 1952, 6; "Condemns Poll Tax," letter to the editor, *Toronto Daily Star,* October 20, 1952, 6; "Stratford Includes Women in Poll Tax," *Toronto Daily Star,* February 27, 1953, 11; "Windsor Favors Tax for Women," *Toronto Daily Star,* March 13, 1953, 5; "Suburban Round-Up," *Toronto Daily Star,* June 24, 1958, 8; "Suggests Poll Tax for Women," *Toronto Daily Star,* January 13,

1959, 10; Lotta Dempsey, "New Tax for Single Girls?," column, *Toronto Daily Star*, May 14, 1960, 59; "Panel Asks Revision of Municipal Laws," *Globe and Mail*, June 27, 1962, 13; "Asks Vote for Those Who Pay Poll Tax," *Toronto Daily Star*, February 8, 1955, 10; "Metro Must Grow," letter to the editor, *Toronto Daily Star*, January 22, 1957, 6; "Would Drop Poll Tax," *Toronto Daily Star*, October 11, 1958, 4; "London Ends Poll Tax," *Toronto Daily Star*, November 18, 1958, 29; "Won't Pay, Chose Jail," *Toronto Daily Star*, January 9, 1948, 7; "Vote to Abolish Burlington's $10 Poll Tax," *Toronto Daily Star*, March 18, 1958, 8; "Wants Poll Tax Eliminated," *Toronto Daily Star*, September 12, 1962, 28; "100,000 Should Pay $25 Poll Tax – Nash," *Toronto Daily Star*, September 15, 1962, 49; "Abolish This Tax," editorial, *Toronto Daily Star*, January 21, 1959, 6; "Not Fair," letter to the editor, *Toronto Daily Star*, June 8, 1961, 6; "88 Summoned [to Court]," *Toronto Daily Star*, August 11, 1961, 4; "A Poll Tax? No Thanks," editorial, *Toronto Daily Star*, April 2, 1963, 6.

91 "This Bite Hurts Only East," *Toronto Daily Star*, January 16, 1963, 11.

92 "U.S. Kills Anti-Negro Poll Tax," *Toronto Daily Star*, April 28, 1965, 66; "Robichaud Ups Sales Levy, Takes Slice of Property Tax," *Toronto Daily Star*, February 22, 1966, 4.

93 "Metro Must Grow," letter to the editor, *Toronto Daily Star*, January 22, 1957, 6.

94 Halifax eliminated its municipal poll tax in 1971. *Statutes of Nova Scotia*, Halifax City Charter Amendment Act, 1971, c. 78, s. 1. This might have been Canada's last municipal poll tax. Further research in the Nova Scotia and PEI assessment statutes and other city charters would be needed to confirm this.

Chapter 6: Honour, Confidence, and Federalism

1 In some jurisdictions, a fine, the sale of personal goods, or jail time (if the first two weren't options) was actually used as an enforcement mechanism for small personal taxes; see W.A.R. (municipal official, Saint John) to Ernest Payne, August 16, 1933, PANB, RS 156, series C, file C 4(c)8. More commonly, conviction in a magistrate's court meant a fine or labour in lieu of the tax; see "Depends on How Good the Begging Is," *Toronto Daily Star*, May 21, 1931, 25.

2 Canada, Senate, *Debates*, March 7, 1933, 307.

3 "Regarding Income Tax," *National Revenue Review* 7, 9 (1934): 5.

4 "Low Cost of Collection," *National Revenue Review* 4, 1 (1930): 3.

5 F.C., "Collecting Income Taxes," clipping enclosed with C.F. Elliott to Miss A.E. Millar (private secretary to the Prime Minister), May 2, 1933, University of New Brunswick, Harriet Irving Library, R.B. Bennett fonds, reel 372.

6 Blair Fraser, "Who Are the Income-Tax Dodgers?," *Maclean's*, March 15, 1948, 65.

7 "Income Tax Brief," 1930, 4–5, Queen's University Archives (hereafter QUA), Grant Dexter fonds, collection 2142, box 20, file 199; "Guarding Income Tax Revenue," *National Revenue Review* 6, 3 (1932): 17.

8 "Income Tax Brief," 1930, 4, QUA, Grant Dexter fonds, collection 2142, box 20, file 199.

9 Canada, House of Commons, *Debates*, May 18, 1926, 3538–39; diary entries for May 18, 1926; January 26, 1929; June 3, 1930; January 20, 1932; April 26, 1933; and May 10, 1933, LAC, King Diaries, http://www.collectionscanada.gc.ca/databases/king/index-e.html; Canada, Senate, *Debates*, March 6, 1934, 114–16; "Importante funérailles du Sénateur L.A. Wilson," Montreal *La Patrie*, March 6, 1934, 2.

10 Canada, House of Commons, *Debates*, May 18, 1926, 3543.

11 Ibid.

12 "Commons Now Ready to Consider Budget in Committee Stage," Toronto *Globe*, May 20, 1926, 1.

13 "Senator May Resign Seat to Protest Tax Evasion," *Toronto Daily Star*, November 13, 1933, 17, 19.

14 Diary entry, May 18, 1926, LAC, King Diaries, http://www.collectionscanada.gc.ca/databases/king/index-e.html.

15 That Finance Minister Rhodes followed *Financial Counsel* is evident in the presence of several issues in his papers during this period. See, for example, the issue of March 29, 1933, in NSA, Rhodes fonds, MG 2, vol. 1144, file Folder 4-2T02 Taxation, and the editorial clipped from the issue of May 12, 1933, in NSA, Rhodes fonds, MG 2, vol. 1132, file 10 Income Tax. In the latter case, *Financial Counsel*'s editorial echoed the position of Rhodes in the House of Commons (Canada, House of Commons, *Debates*, May 5, 1933, 4623–24) when he defended reduced personal exemptions.

16 Canada, Senate, *Debates*, March 7, 1933, 307; November 16, 1932, 143.

17 The passages from the *Financial Counsel* newsletter quoted here were read by Wilson into the Senate debates on March 28, 1933, 353.

18 Ibid.

19 See in NSA, Rhodes fonds, MG 2, G. Stroyan to E.N. Rhodes, January 7, 1932, vol. 1110, doc. 48252; R.H. Baker to E.N. Rhodes, February 18, 1932, vol. 1110, doc. 48381; A.J. Russell Snow to E.N. Rhodes, January 18, 1935, and February 4, 1935, vol. 1196, docs. 75112 and 75106; David Mills to E.N. Rhodes, February 1, 1933, and May 6, 1933, vol. 1132, docs. 55766 and 55764; and, referring to tax-dodging investors as "unpatriotic," Frederick O. Mills to E.N. Rhodes, February 20, 1933, vol. 1132, doc. 55506. Also see R.C. Matthews to R.B. Bennett, October 28, 1932, LAC, Bennett fonds, MG 26-K, reel M-1423, doc. 466005. Even as Senator Wilson was raising his moral critique, earners of undeclared bearer bond income were seeking advice from investment dealers on how to "escape the consequences of their acts"; see "Ottawa Ruling Hits Many Bondholders," *Toronto Daily Star*, March 29, 1933, 1.

20 David Mills to E.N. Rhodes, May 6, 1933, NSA, Rhodes fonds, MG 2, vol. 1132, doc. 55764.

21 R.C. Matthews to R.B. Bennett, October 28, 1932, LAC, Bennett fonds, MG 26-K, reel M-1423, doc. 466005; "Matthews, Robert Charles," http://www.parl.gc.ca/.

22 League for Social Reconstruction, *Social Planning for Canada* (1935; reprinted, Toronto: University of Toronto Press, 1975), 342–43.

23 My translation. Georges Pelletier, "Le premier budget de M. Rhodes: Il n'est facile ni pour lui ni pour nous," *Le Devoir*, April 7, 1932, 1.

24 "Income Tax Brief," 1930, 5–6, QUA, Grant Dexter fonds, collection 2142, box 20, file 199.

25 Remarks by C.F. Elliott in discussion period on C.S. Walters et al., "Income Assessment for Taxation Purposes," in Canadian Tax Conference, *Proceedings, Held under the Auspices of the Citizens' Research Institute of Canada* (Toronto: Citizens' Research Institute of Canada, 1930), 98.

26 The research underpinning my claim here began with a reading of the Income War Tax Act sections concerning penalties and continued through newspaper keyword searches, the *National Revenue Review*, Department of Justice dockets, records of the Department of Finance (senior officials' correspondence), records of the Department of National Revenue, papers of prime ministers and finance ministers (White, Fielding, Dunning, Bennett, and Rhodes; Drayton and Robb left no papers), dockets and docket registers of the Exchequer Court of Canada, and an examination, with the help of research assistants, of surviving police court registers from the interwar years in Vancouver, Hamilton, Halifax, St. Thomas (ON), and Charlevoix County (Quebec City). I found no evidence of criminal indictments. A modest fine for failure to file a return, writs of *fieri facias*, and the occasional writ of extent in rare cases in which large sums risked being distributed to other creditors before the Crown were the common methods. The only evidence that I found of prosecution in a police court for filing a false return was the case of Willard S. Jeffrey, fined $700

and costs in March 1932; see "Made False Return," *National Revenue Review* 5, 7 (1932): 7. On the basis of what I did not find in these varied sources, I believe the department's own statement about its reluctance to use criminal proceedings. "Income Tax Brief," 1930, 5–6, QUA, Grant Dexter fonds, collection 2142, box 20, file 199.

27 Canada, Parliament, Senate, Special Committee on the Income War Tax Act and the Excess Profits Tax Act, 1940, *Proceedings* [Senate Tax Administration Committee, *Proceedings*], 1946 session (Ottawa: E. Cloutier, Printer to the King, 1945–46), 189.

28 The department's approach to professional men was to assess them for higher incomes than they reported and, if they claimed not to have kept thorough account books for their practices, to warn them to start doing so or risk more severe treatment the next time; see "Income Tax Brief," 1930, 5–6, QUA, Grant Dexter fonds, collection 2142, box 20, file 199. When health insurance planners in British Columbia in the 1930s used physicians' income tax data as a guide for compensation rates under the plan, they were told by the doctors "my dear fellow, a doctor's income tax return is not an accurate guide to a doctor's income." Fraser, "Who Are the Income-Tax Dodgers?," 8.

29 Testimony of J.T. Edwards in "Proceedings, 1933, Royal Commission on Banking and Currency," Vol. 2, Robert Brydie, official reporter, unpublished, 621; Canada, House of Commons, *Debates*, June 15, 1931, 2640.

30 "New Commissioner of Income Tax Appointed," *National Revenue Review* 5, 12 (1932): 12.

31 My account of Elliott's way of managing tax administration is informed by remarks that Elliott made in public settings in 1931, 1934, 1945, and 1946. It is also informed by the recollections of an admiring junior, Heward Stikeman, who was hired by Elliott as a National Revenue lawyer in the late 1930s and worked with him for a number of years. Richard D. Pound, *Stikeman Elliott: The First Fifty Years* (Montreal: McGill-Queen's University Press, 2002), 8–15.

32 "Regarding Income Tax," summary of the principal points of a radio address by C. Fraser Elliott on "The Relationship of the Individual to Revenue Laws and the Income War Tax Act in Particular," *National Revenue Review* 7, 9 (1934): 5.

33 Quoted in Pound, *Stikeman Elliott*, 13.

34 Senate Tax Administration Committee, *Proceedings*, 1945 session, 44, 53.

35 Ibid., 18.

36 *Inland Revenue Commissioners v. Westminster (Duke)*, [1936] AC 1.

37 Hugh Eayrs to E.N. Rhodes, December 4, 1934, NSA, MG 2, vol. 1164, doc. 65964.

38 E.N. Rhodes to Hugh Eayrs, December 5, 1934, NSA, MG 2, vol. 1164, doc. 65963; Hugh Eayrs to E.N. Rhodes, December 7, 1934, NSA, MG 2, vol. 1164, doc. 65962.

39 Premier J.T.M. Anderson to E.N. Rhodes, August 25, 1933, enclosing A.M. (Estey, Moxon, Schmitt and McDonald) to C. Fraser Elliott, August 5, 1933, NSA, Rhodes fonds, MG 2, vol. 1132, doc. 55732.

40 V.M. Drury to W.C. Clark, April 10, 1933, LAC, Finance fonds, RG 19, vol. 3989, file Income Tax T-1-1.

41 W.C. Clark to V.M. Drury, April 11, 1933, LAC, Finance fonds, RG 19, vol. 3989, file Income Tax T-1-1.

42 *Hon. Henri B. Rainville v. MNR*, December 16, 1936, Court Services Administration, Exchequer Court of Canada, docket 17348; *Canada Law Reports: Exchequer Court of Canada*, 1936–38. Because the proceedings of the Exchequer Court were not public, no reporter would have been able to see a case settled like this one was.

43 "Hon. H.B. Rainville Dies at Age of 85," Montreal *Gazette*, August 7, 1937, 9.

44 Canada, House of Commons, *Debates*, June 1, 1931, 2174, 2176–79; July 16, 1931, 3855–57; April 6, 1932, 1767; January 31, 1933, 1672; "Slashing Criticism of Bennett Budget Planned at Ottawa," Toronto *Globe*, June 4, 1931, 2; "Bennett Drops Personal Income Tax Revisions."

His Motive Doubted, His Honour Impugned, He Says, Near Tears," Toronto *Globe,* July 17, 1931, 1–2; "L'impôt sur le revenu," *Le Devoir,* June 4, 1931, 1; "Budget de vie chère," *Le Soleil,* June 3, 1931, 4; "Price Rise Certain, Middleman Suffers from New Sales Tax," Toronto *Globe,* June 6, 1931, 1. In the 1932 budget, the abolition of family corporations was again proposed and finally enacted in 1933 (Act to Amend the Income War Tax Act). "Regarding Filing Income Tax Returns," *National Revenue Review* 6, 6 (1933): 4. The mechanism by which the personal corporations provisions of 1926 had been used to reduce or avoid income taxation was described by Rhodes during the second reading of the 1933 amending statute; see Canada, House of Commons, *Debates,* January 31, 1933, 1672. A summary of legislative attempts during the 1930s to prevent tax avoidance through the use of family corporations can be found in Canada, Royal Commission on the Taxation of Annuities and Family Corporations, *Report of Royal Commission on the Taxation of Annuities and Family Corporations* (Ottawa: King's Printer, 1945), 54–60.

45 Canada, House of Commons, *Debates,* July 16, 1931, 3855–59.

46 Ibid., 3855.

47 J.W. Jones, "Random Thoughts on Taxation," 1931, BCA, Jones fonds, MS 23, box 6, file 2.

48 "New Instalment Plan of Paying Income Tax without Interest," Department of National Revenue display ad, *Globe and Mail,* January 10, 1941, 9.

49 A digital search in the Proquest Historical Newspapers *Toronto Star* database on the phrase "conscience money" shows 1934 as the year with the highest number of results per year in the 1930s (nine). A closer examination of the paper reveals thirteen occurrences of the phrase, eight of them in April and May 1934. I have tracked the totals of conscience money listed under "Casual Revenue" in the "Details of Revenue and Expenditure" for the Departments of Finance and National Revenue in *Report of the Auditor General for the Year Ended 1931* and annually to 1937. The annual total amounts vary considerably: the 1933 amount was the highest ($15,152.66) and the 1931 amount the lowest ($536.42). Most fell between $1,000 and $4,000. The sizes of common individual payments can be inferred from the reports on conscience money that were a regular feature in the *National Revenue Review.* The following list gives dollar values referred to from December 1931 to December 1935: $10, 5, 3 (1931): 7; $120, 5, 5 (1932): 16; $396.73, 5, 10 (1932): 5; $100, 5, 12 (1932): 4; $12,200, 6, 3 (1932): 6; $100, 6, 4 (1933): 3; $605, $700, $300, and $50, all in 6, 8 (1933): 3; $40, $8, $30, $30, and $100, all in 6, 9 (1933): 3; $11.71, 6, 10 (1933): 4; $10 and $25, 6, 11 (1933): 3; $19.89, 7, 1 (1933): 3; $35, 7, 7 (1934): 3; $5,400, "among the largest single amount of conscience money of which the Department has record" and a story titled "The Great and the Small" – fifteen conscience money payments during the past fiscal year ranging from 1¢ cent to $31, 7, 8 (1934): 4; $19.01 and $15, 7, 11 (1934): 3; $10, 8, 3 (1934): 6; $14, 8, 5 (1935): 3; $14.37, 8, 7 (1936): 5; $6.21, 8, 12 (1935): 3.

50 "Credit Oxford Group with Teacher Refund: Read Book Then Decided to Return $30 to Board of Education," *Toronto Daily Star,* December 16, 1932, 7.

51 "Oxford Group Evangelists Speak at Toronto Churches," *Toronto Daily Star,* March 19, 1934, 7; "Converted by Oxford Group, Remits Conscience Money," Toronto *Globe,* April 13, 1934, 7. Their earlier presence in Montreal was referred to in "Record Payment of Conscience Money," *National Revenue Review* 6, 3 (1932): 6, and in "Conscience Wort[h] $100," *Toronto Daily Star,* April 10, 1933, 3. It is possible, of course, that both the *Toronto Daily Star* editors and the editor of the *National Revenue Review* were trying to foster a climate of moral support for tax compliance, in concert with the federal government's anti-evasion measures in the 1933 budget.

52 Ernest Kurtz, *Not-God: A History of Alcoholics Anonymous* (Center City, MN: Hazelden Educational Services, 1979), 9–10, Chapter 2.

53 "Record Payment of Conscience Money," *National Revenue Review* 6, 3 (1932): 6.

54 "Conscience Wort[h] $700," *Toronto Daily Star,* April 10, 1933, 3; "Thanks to the Oxford Group," *National Revenue Review* 6, 5 (1933): 16; "Converted by Oxford Group, Remits Conscience Money," Toronto *Globe,* April 13, 1934, 7; "Conscience Money Sent by Student," Toronto *Globe,* May 1, 1934, 10; note beginning "'Changed' by the Oxford Group ... ," *Toronto Daily Star,* April 24, 1934, 6; note beginning "Another consignment of conscience money ... ," *Toronto Daily Star,* July 16, 1934, 6; "'Oxford' Sends $500 in Conscience Money," *Toronto Daily Star,* September 28, 1936, 1; note beginning "When a religious movement leads people to pay debts ... ," *Toronto Daily Star,* October 20, 1936, 4.

55 I learned about the receipting practice from the two files of conscience money correspondence that remain in the records of the Department of Finance: LAC, Finance fonds, RG 19, vol. 3718, files Conscience Money 1954–56 and 1957–59. Newspaper references to conscience money sometimes noted that the source of information was a request from the government to acknowledge receipt; see, for example, "A Toronto Conscience Eased," *Toronto Daily Star,* April 21, 1934, 1, and "$10 Due 'the People' Now Where It Belongs," Toronto *Globe,* July 27, 1935, 11.

56 "Notes and Comment," *Toronto Daily Star,* October 20, 1936, 4.

57 It would be worthwhile to investigate a variety of religious communities' views on taxation.

58 "Conscience Money Paid at Montreal," Toronto *Globe,* May 2, 1934, 1.

59 My translation. Paul Anger, "Lettre à un contribuable," *Le Devoir,* April 7, 1932, 1. My research assistant, Alex Tremblay, drew my attention to the fact that "Paul Anger" was a pseudonym used by long-time *Le Devoir* journalist Louis Dupire.

60 By using the language of "Canada's good name," the *Globe and Mail's* financial editor, Wellington Jeffers, shows the discursive use of this association; see "Business Men of Canada Ask Ottawa to Disallow Alberta Acts on Broad, National Grounds," *Globe and Mail,* May 19, 1938, 24.

61 W.L. McKinnon, "The Function of Statistics in the Control of Public Expenditure," in Canadian Tax Conference, *Proceedings* (1931), 75–81.

62 See, for example, Wilfred Currier Keirstead, "The Case of New Brunswick for an Increase in the Federal Subsidy" (1926), Harriet Irving Library, Special Collections, University of New Brunswick, W.C. Keirstead Papers, series 4, box 6, item 40. The skeptical reply from the Department of Finance is "Memorandum for Honourable Mr. Robb," November 7, 1927, LAC, Finance fonds, RG 19, vol. 2670, file 1927.

63 "Some Debts that Are No More," *Toronto Daily Star,* June 25, 1934, 4.

64 See, for example, the assertion by the president of the Chamber of Commerce that "our economic life should be based on the encouragement of thrift and industry ... Daily our taxes increase, but even so, this fact does not prevent our leaving an unfair burden to posterity." Quoted in "Higher Debt Is Deplored," *Globe and Mail,* October 30, 1937, 17. What's "encouragement"? What kind and degree of "thrift and industry"? What's "an unfair burden"?

65 James Struthers, *No Fault of Their Own: Unemployment and the Canadian Welfare State, 1914–1941* (Toronto: University of Toronto Press, 1983), 184–87, 209–10. A vivid if less intellectually coherent expression of this view in the 1930s was that of Dr. Lyle Telford, the CCF leader in British Columbia, quoted as saying that "the only law really constitutional was the law of nature. If the B.N.A. Act did not permit a normal reasonable life for the people then it should be declared unconstitutional." In "Higher Tax on Incomes," *Victoria Daily Times,* April 13, 1937, 5. A mason from Edmonton also expressed the view that, if "the B.N.A. Acts [sic] ... or anything stands in the way of Canada's Democrative [sic] progress, they must be brushed aside." Sidney Parsons to Premier and Cabinet, March 4, 1939, LAC, Finance fonds, RG 19, vol. 2669, file 2. Probably the leading exponent of the view that the BNA Act was used as an excuse for inaction was the CCF's J.S. Woodsworth, who, more temperately,

called during the 1935 federal election campaign for amendment of the Constitution; see "Says C.C.F. to Cut Private as Well as Public Debts," *Toronto Daily Star*, October 1, 1935, 2.

66 Robert Borden to E.N. Rhodes, January 30, 1935, NSA, Rhodes fonds, MG 2, vol. 1185, file 12, doc. 71753; R.C. Berkinshaw and Horace L. Brittain, "There Will Be Another Year," *Canadian Taxation*, March 28, 1935, 1–2.

67 Charles Dunning to J.A. Cross, December 27, 1932, QUA, Dunning fonds, box 10, file 85; E.N. Rhodes to Rodolphe Lemieux, April 4, 1933, NSA, Rhodes fonds, MG 2, vol. 1144, doc. 59863. See also R.B. Bennett, quoted in Robert Ascah, *Politics and Public Debt: The Dominion, the Banks, and Alberta's Social Credit* (Edmonton: University of Alberta Press, 1999), 40–41.

68 "Current Opinion," *Berkeley Daily Gazette*, October 13, 1923, 3; "Witness Suicide of Reparations," Montreal *Gazette*, November 5, 1923, 8; Leslie Roberts, *We Must Be Free* (Toronto: Macmillan Company of Canada, 1939), 215–16. In 1945, the campaign was invoked in the Saskatoon *Star-Phoenix* as a marker of the 1920s, along with flappers and Tutankhamen's tomb; see "The Crossword Puzzle Man," Saskatoon *Star-Phoenix*, January 24, 1945, 9.

69 "The Whisper of Death: Will Canada Be a War Casualty?," *Montreal Daily Star*, August 22, 1923, 1.

70 "The Whisper of Death: Startling Increases in Debt, Not Counting War Costs," *Montreal Daily Star*, August 24, 1923, 1.

71 "The Whisper of Death," *Montreal Daily Star*, July 12, 1923, 1. Fear of annexation was also present in "The Whisper of Death: Will Canada Be a War Casualty?," *Montreal Daily Star*, August 22, 1923, 1, and "The Whisper of Death: What Must We Do to Be Saved?," *Montreal Daily Star*, August 30, 1923, 1.

72 "The Whisper of Death: No Corporation or Speculator Should Bar Settlers from the Best Western Lands," *Montreal Daily Star*, August 7, 1923, 1.

73 "Giving Us the Creeps," editorial, Toronto *Globe*, July 27, 1923, 4.

74 "Position Sound, Outlook Bright. Firm Confidence in Canada's Future Expressed by Hon. T.A. Low," Toronto *Globe*, September 4, 1923, 8; "Pessimists Scored by Deputy Speaker. George N. Gordon, K.C., M.P. Says 'Whisper of Death' Is Choked by Prosperity," Toronto *Globe*, February 26, 1924, 3; "Says Government to Meet Obligation Regarding Viaduct" (report of a meeting of the Toronto Mackenzie King Liberal Club, planning to counter Tory blue ruin talk), Toronto *Globe*, May 8, 1924, 14.

75 The *Toronto Daily Star* reiterated the axiom of investors that "Canada still requires money of foreign source for ... financing of new development"; see "Market Sidelights," *Toronto Daily Star*, March 22, 1933, 15; Canada, Royal Commission on Dominion-Provincial Relations, *A Report of the Royal Commission on Dominion-Provincial Relations*, Vol. 2 (Ottawa: King's Printer, 1940), 128–29; and Stewart Bates, *Financial History of Canadian Governments: A Study Prepared for the Royal Commission on Dominion-Provincial Relations* (Ottawa: n.p., 1939), 87–88.

76 For expressions of this view, see Canada, House of Commons, *Debates*, April 6, 1932, 1749; Canada, Senate, *Debates*, May 15, 1933, 518; and "Resolution Adopted by the Montreal Board of Trade at a Special General Meeting Held Tuesday, 20th April, 1933," LAC, Bennett fonds, MG 26-K, reel M1424. On the controversy, see Paul T. Dickens, "Criteria for Determining the Creditor-Debtor Position of a Country," *Journal of Political Economy* 47, 6 (1939): 846–56.

77 Berkinshaw and Brittain, "There Will Be Another Year"; "Says CCF to Cut Private as Well as Public Debts," *Toronto Daily Star*, October 1, 1935, 1.

78 R.B. Bryce, *Maturing in Hard Times: Canada's Department of Finance through the Great Depression* (Kingston, ON: McGill-Queen's University Press, 1986), 130, 146.

79 "Inflation Fallacy Fine Non-PartizanSpeech by Bennett," *Charlottetown Guardian*, March 4, 1933, 5.

80 G.F.T. [Graham F. Towers], "Confidential. Memorandum re Discussions on 1937 Autumn Loan," October 28, 1937, 2, LAC, Finance fonds, RG 19, vol. 3978, file F-1-7.

81 See, for example, "United Farmers 'Join Up' with 'C.C.F.' Movement," Toronto *Globe*, December 2, 1931, 1.

82 John T. Saywell, *Just Call Me Mitch: The Life of Mitchell F. Hepburn* (Toronto: University of Toronto Press, 1991), 177.

83 Report to E.N. Rhodes on a financial plan proposed by E.R. Sloan and supported by E.J. Gott, MP, August 16, 1933, NSA, Rhodes fonds, MG 2, vol. 1132, doc. 55635.

84 E.N. Rhodes to Hervé Lafleur, December 19, 1932, LAC, Finance fonds, RG 19, vol. 3386, file 04747-17 Inflation.

85 W.C. Clark to E.N. Rhodes, May 3, 1933, NSA, Rhodes fonds, MG 2, vol. 1144, file 4-2 To2 Taxation, doc. 59801.

86 "Loan Subscriptions Near $100,000,000 Mark," Toronto *Globe*, November 26, 1931, 1, 2; "Radio Tonight," Department of Finance display ad, Toronto *Globe*, November 25, 1931, 15. W.C. Clark, a Queen's University economist and soon to be deputy minister of finance, also contributed to the campaign with a speech stressing Canada's robust financial system; see "U.S.A. Is Amateurish as World's Lender, Economist Thinks," Toronto *Globe*, November 24, 1931, 5.

87 "Canada – The Best Investment for Canadians," Wood, Gundy and Company display ad, November 24, 1931, Toronto *Globe*, 6; A.E. Ames, "The Loan – A Question of Quality," Toronto *Globe*, November 27, 1931, 4; "Let Your Dollars Serve Canada ... with Profit to Yourself," Department of Finance display ad, Toronto *Globe*, November 27, 1931, 5; "A Chance to Serve Canada ... with Advantage to Yourself," Department of Finance display ad, Toronto *Globe*, November 30, 1931, 13.

88 "More than $100,000,000 Subscribed to Loan," Toronto *Globe*, November 28, 1931, 1; "A Dominion of Canada Bond to Yield over 5%," Dominion Securities display ad, Toronto *Globe*, November 27, 1931, 7.

89 "Faith and Confidence," Department of Finance display ad, Toronto *Globe*, November 25, 1931, 5.

90 "A Whole-Hearted Response," editorial, Toronto *Globe*, December 1, 1931, 4; "Small Investors Swell Service Loan Total," Toronto *Globe*, November 27, 1931, 1.

91 "More than $100,000,000 Subscribed to Loan," Toronto *Globe*, November 28, 1931, 1.

92 "Councillors Face Big Fine Unless $100,000 Relief Paid," *Toronto Daily Star*, April 16, 1935, 29.

93 Ascah, *Politics and Public Debt*, 39–40.

94 "Says CCF to Cut Private as Well as Public Debts," *Toronto Daily Star*, October 1, 1935, 1.

95 Figures calculated using the Bank of Canada inflation calculator at http://www.bankof canada.ca/rates/related/inflation-calculator/.

96 1932 T.1A Individual Income Tax return for non-farmers, schedule of rates, 4, LAC, Department of Revenue fonds, RG 16, vol. 1006, file T.1 T.1A 1932; "Number of Individual Taxpayers and Amount Paid by Income Classes," *National Revenue Review* 6, 6 (1933): 14; Canada, House of Commons, *Debates*, May 10, 1933, 4788.

97 F.B. Housser (Financial Editor), "Will Canada Go through Australia's Experience?," *Toronto Daily Star*, February 13, 1935, 17. Housser points out that the sequel to this austerity episode was a secession movement in Western Australia. Ascah points out that Canada was seen in the New York market as economically similar to Australia and that Comptroller of the Treasury Watson Sellar successfully suppressed statistical reports on the Canadian economy and public debt in order to manage Canada's "reputation" in New York; see Ascah, *Politics*

and Public Debt, 33–36. Housser's fears about the saleability of Canadian bonds worsened in September when rumours circulated that holders of Canadian bonds would face a de facto forced conversion of them; see F.B. Housser, "Debt Conversion in Canada," *Toronto Daily Star,* September 23, 1935, 13. Rhodes offered reassurances in his 1933 budget speech; see Canada, House of Commons, *Debates,* March 21, 1933, 3620.

98 "A Billion in Bonds Offered to Holders in Refunding Plan," Toronto *Globe,* May 5, 1931, 1; "Convert Your War Bonds," editorial, Toronto *Globe,* May 11, 1931, 4; "Over $35,000,000 Subscribed for Loan in Day," Toronto *Globe,* October 2, 1934, 1, 3.

99 Ascah, *Politics and Public Debt,* 34, 36; Great Britain, Newfoundland Royal Commission, *Report* (London: King's Printer, 1933), 51–52; C.H. Huestis, "Some Debts that Are No More," *Toronto Daily Star,* June 25, 1934, 4.

100 A Toronto banker told Rhodes that "various financial executives" whom he knew were in favour of a new tax on investment income, and he directed Rhodes to a piece on this subject that he had published in the January 6, 1934, issue of *Saturday Night.* A.J. O'Donohoe (Canadian Bank of Commerce, Toronto) to E.N. Rhodes, January 6, 1934, NSA, Rhodes fonds, MG 2, vol. 1144, file 4-2To2 Taxation, doc. 59747; E.N. Rhodes to A.J. O'Donohoe, January 17, 1934, NSA, Rhodes fonds, MG 2, vol. 1144, file 4-2To2 Taxation, doc. 59744.

101 "Toronto Economists Favour Conversion of Bond Debt," *Toronto Daily Star,* December 4, 1935, 3.

102 Canada, House of Commons, *Debates,* March 21, 1933, 3225. For the reactions of foreign investors, see in NSA, Rhodes fonds, MG 2, vol. 1144, file 4-2To2 Taxation, [signature illegible], Senator, regarding views of J.H. Gundy and telegram from Lord Queenborough, to E.N. Rhodes, March 30, 1933, doc. 59875, and Rodolphe Lemieux to E.N. Rhodes, April 3, 1933, doc. 59863. It seems likely that some of the "non-residents" were actually Canadians whose money was housed in British brokers' accounts; see William Marchington, "Exemptions from Federal Bond Tax Extended ... Ottawa Fears Evasion by Canadian Holders, through Transfer of Securities to the U.S.," Toronto *Globe,* April 1, 1933, 1.

103 Telegram, Personal, Ferguson (High Commissioner) to Bennett, March 27, 1933; Telegram, Confidential, Ferguson to Bennett, March 30, 1933; Telegram, Immediate, Personal and Confidential, Ferguson to Bennett, March 31, 1933, doc. 466256, and Telegram, Immediate, Personal and Confidential, Ferguson to Bennett, March 31, 1933, doc. 466258, LAC, Bennett fonds, MG 26-K, reel M-1424.

104 "Tax Discrimination in Canada," undated clipping from the *Economist,* attached to Jackson Dodds (Bank of Montreal) to E.N. Rhodes, April 20, 1933, NSA, Rhodes fonds, MG 2, vol. 1144, file 4-2To2 Taxation, docs. 59814 and 59813.

105 William Marchington, "Exemptions from Federal Bond Tax Extended ... Trading Suspended on London Market," Toronto *Globe,* April 1, 1933, 1; E. George Smith, "Rhodes' Statement," Toronto *Globe,* April 1, 1933, 1–2; "Tax Discrimination in Canada," clipping from the *Economist,* April 8, 1933, enclosed in Ward C. Pitfield to R.B. Bennett, April 24, 1933, LAC, Bennett fonds, MG 26-K, reel M-1424, doc. 466304.

106 Jackson Dodds (Bank of Montreal) to E.N. Rhodes, April 20, 1933, with clipping "Tax Discrimination in Canada" attached from the *Economist,* and E.N. Rhodes to Jackson Dodds, April 24, 1933, NSA, Rhodes fonds, MG 2, vol. 1144, file 4-2To2 Taxation, docs. 59814 and 59813; Ward C. Pitfield to R.B. Bennett, April 24, 1933, LAC, Bennett fonds, MG 26-K, reel M-1424, doc. 466304.

107 Dr. Max Winkler, "New York Writer Thinks Credit of Canadians to Stand Up under Levy on Bonds," clipping from the *Evening Telegram,* March 31, 1933, NSA, Rhodes fonds, MG 2, vol. 1144, file 4-2To2 Taxation, doc. 59870.

108 Canada, House of Commons, *Debates,* May 5, 1933, 4640.

109 Arthur J. Smith (Financial Editor of the *Vancouver Sun*) to E.N. Rhodes, May 9, 1933, NSA, Rhodes fonds, MG 2, vol. 1144, file 4-2To2 Taxation, doc. 59788.

110 The legal framework restricted Canada's ability to legislate on matters related to debt. Note that periodically renewed Colonial Stock Acts continued to operate, with the power of imperial disallowance, after that power was otherwise eliminated by the Statute of Westminster in 1931.

111 United Kingdom, Department of Overseas Trade, *Economic Conditions in Canada 1932– 33, Report by F.W. Field, CMG, His Majesty's Senior Trade Commissioner in Canada and Newfoundland* (London: His Majesty's Stationery Office, 1933), 16, NSA, Rhodes fonds, MG 2, vol. 1132, file 2Foo Miscellaneous, doc. 55490.

112 His budgets closed more loopholes than anyone listening only to the budget speeches would know. In Bill 11, Rhodes abolished the family corporations provision that allowed wealthy families to treat their investment as corporation income rather than personal income, to get the corporation income tax's lower rate, and he enacted a measure designed to prevent company shareholders from taking their dividends as return of capital (and thus not taxed as income (House of Commons, *Debates,* on November 3, 1932, 795, and March 27, 1933, 3455). The former was mentioned in the House, but the latter was not. His 1933 anti-evasion measures included not only those mentioned in the speech (abuse of personal exemptions for extended family and hiding of bond income) but also "other measures of a minor character" to "strengthen administrative provisions" – these measures included removing a broad, easily abused exemption for householders, restricting the amounts of payments to relatives that could be treated as business expenses, and "clarifying" corporate tax provisions in s. 13 (March 21, 1933, 3224–25, 3239). The 1934 budget also included a "minor amendment," not described in the speech, designed to prevent tax avoidance by transferring investments to minor children, and in 1935 a further gift tax measure was introduced (April 18, 1934, 2291, 2293–94, and March 22, 1935, 1986). The 1935 measure was described by William Marchington as a "Blow at Rich," Toronto *Globe,* March 23, 1935, 1–2. Rhodes repeatedly defended increased taxation, and his supporters praised him for raising the personal income tax and for closing loopholes. See, for example, in NSA, Rhodes fonds, MG 2, vol. 1132, file 10 Income Tax, E.N. Rhodes to the General Manager of Ontario Paper Company, via George H. Pettit, MP, March 21, 1933, doc. 55801, and J.L. Bowman, KC, MP, to E.N. Rhodes, February 23, 1933, doc. 55805; also see Arthur R. Ford (*London Free Press*) to E.N. Rhodes, April 11, 1933, NSA, Rhodes fonds, MG 2, vol. 1132, file 1 Miscellaneous, doc. 55498.

113 W. Irwin Gillespie, *Tax, Borrow, and Spend: Financing Federal Spending in Canada, 1867–1990* (Ottawa: Carleton University Press, 1991), 280; J. Harvey Perry, *Taxes, Tariffs, and Subsidies: A History of Canadian Fiscal Development,* 2 vols. (Toronto: University of Toronto Press, 1955), 2: 626–27.

114 Canada, House of Commons, *Debates,* May 5, 1933, 4626, 4629–31.

115 Ibid., March 21, 1933, 3224–25, 3239.

116 The Economics and Taxation Committee presented no report in 1931, 1932, and 1933, but the committee revived under Lottie O'Doyle's leadership in 1934 and submitted regular reports from 1935 on. Reports from the 1920s that included references to widows and wives are National Council of Women, *Yearbook* (1922), 53; *Yearbook* (1923), 77–78; and *Yearbook* (1926), 73.

117 This assessment is based mainly upon a survey by my research assistant, Alex Tremblay, of the coverage of the 1933 budget speech in three Quebec newspapers (*Montreal Daily Star, La Patrie,* and *Le Soleil*). Clarence Hogue, "Un impôt exorbitant: L'impôt sur le sucre est, en fait, un impôt de 50 pour cent – Quels sont ceux qui ont été renseignés d'avance afin de pouvoir s'approvisionner?," *Le Devoir,* March 22, 1933, 6; "Le budget de la détresse," editorial, *Le Soleil,* March 22, 1933, 4; "La taxe sur le sucre est vivement critiquée," *Le Soleil,* March 23, 1933, 3; W.F. Grey, "Getting It in the Neck," letter to the editor, *Montreal Daily Star,* March 24, 1933, 10; "Need for Higher Taxes Admitted in Interviews," *Montreal*

Daily Star, March 22, 1933, 3. See also "Rich Man's Budget, Says Woodsworth," Toronto *Globe,* March 27, 1933, 4; "Sugar Profiteering Denounced in House and Remedy Sought," Toronto *Globe,* March 28, 1933, 1; "No Confidence Move Is Liberal Answer to Rhodes Budget," Toronto *Globe,* March 25, 1933, 2; "Suggests Impost on Tax Free Bonds," *Medicine Hat News,* May 4, 1933, 7; and "Magrath U.F.W.A. to Protest Federal Govt. Tax on Sugar," *Lethbridge Herald,* April 5, 1933, 3.

118 Canada, House of Commons, *Debates,* March 21, 1933, 3229, 3239; *Revised Statutes of Canada,* 1927, Income War Tax Act, 1927, c. 92, s. 13, "Undistributed Profits of Corporation." The American story related to undistributed profits taxation in the Revenue Act of 1936 is discussed in Mark Leff, *The Limits of Symbolic Reform* (New York: Cambridge University Press, 1984), 207–9.

119 E.N. Rhodes, budget speeches, 1932, 1933, 1934, and 1935, http://www.parl.gc.ca/.

120 Canada, House of Commons, *Debates,* January 31, 1933, 1679. In contrast, Bennett engaged in bold rhetorical image making around taxpaying: "As I go about the country, afterwards receiving letters... I find that many of them, instead of asking to be relieved from this taxation, take this view: 'Well, we think it is pretty hard, but we are glad to do our part.'" Canada, House of Commons, *Debates,* July 1, 1931, 3269.

121 Leff, *Limits of Symbolic Reform,* 175–76, 185–90, 196–201; W. Elliott Brownlee, *Federal Taxation in America: A Short History* (New York: Cambridge University Press, 2004), 96–97. Romain Huret argues that one cause of the wave of anti-tax activism was a defensive response to the Roosevelt treasury's "relentless attacks against tax evaders and selfish businessmen." Romain D. Huret, *American Tax Resisters* (Cambridge, MA: Harvard University Press, 2014), 153–54.

122 E.N. Rhodes to G.S. Henry, Premier of Ontario, April 1, 1932, and E.N. Rhodes to G.S. Harrington, Premier of Nova Scotia, March 30, 1932, NSA, Rhodes fonds, MG 2, vol. 1110, docs. 48198 and 48367.

123 Canada, House of Commons, *Debates,* Bill 25, March 2, 1932, 717–18.

124 E.N. Rhodes to G.S. Harrington (Premier of Nova Scotia), March 30, 1932, NSA, Rhodes fonds, MG 2, vol. 1110, doc. 48367.

125 Fraser, "Who Are the Income-Tax Dodgers?," 63.

126 Looking back on the 1930s at the beginning of the Second World War, journalist William Weston described the decade as a period of relentless attack on the investor and warned of resentment that had arisen among the wealthy; see William Weston, "The Case of the Investor versus the People," *Saturday Night,* November 25, 1939, 11. The more visible revolts were the sort discussed above in Chapter 5.

127 S.H. Logan, General Manager, Canadian Bank of Commerce, to J.W. Jones, Provincial Treasurer, November 12, 1931, BCA, Jones fonds, MS 23, box 1, file 3; J.W. Jones to R.B. Bennett, February 3, 1932, BCA, Jones fonds, MS 23, box 2, file 1; unsigned letter identifiable by content as being from J.W. Jones to P.B. Fowler, Branch Manager, Victoria, Canadian Bank of Commerce, March 8, 1933, BCA, Jones fonds, MS 23, box 2, file 1; H.H. Stevens, MP, to F.J. Burd, April 5, 1933, NSA, Rhodes fonds, MG 2, vol. 1144, doc. 59854. Rhodes more generally defended particular tax measures because the revenue that they generated enabled the dominion to raise money by borrowing; see E.N. Rhodes to Rodolphe Lemieux, April 3, 1933, and E.N. Rhodes to A.W. Robb, April 5, 1933, NSA, Rhodes fonds, MG 2, vol. 1144, docs. 59863 and 59849.

128 "Get Married Bennett Tells Girl Quizzing about Relief," *Toronto Daily Star,* September 25, 1935, 5.

129 Ascah, *Politics and Public Debt,* Chapter 4; diary entries, April 25, 1936; January 6, 1937; and January 8, 1937, LAC, King Diaries, MG 26 J 13, http://www.collectionscanada.gc.ca/databases/king/index-e.html. Rhodes referred to the Australian loan council as a model in his 1935 budget speech; see Canada, House of Commons, *Debates,* March 22, 1935, 1965.

130 Saywell, *Just Call Me Mitch,* 204–5, 213. Bennett put a figure of $700,000 on the cost to the federal government of Hepburn's move; see "Get Married Bennett Tells Girl Quizzing about Relief," *Toronto Daily Star,* September 25, 1935, 5. News of Ontario's decision reached Australia; see "Canada. Political Sensation. Ontario Repudiation," *Townsville Daily Bulletin* [Queensland], April 4, 1935, 5.

131 Ascah, *Politics and Public Debt,* 80. Montreal *Gazette* cartoonist John Collins drew an editorial cartoon, c. 1938, that shows "Montreal's Credit" as a baby at risk of dying in a burning building. McCord Museum, John Collins fonds, image M465.199.4094.4. Also see Wellington Jeffers, "Quebec Vote Sets Quebec's Financial Prestige on Climb Back to High Place Its Great Resources and New Government Program Amply Justify," *Globe and Mail,* February 10, 1940, 16.

132 "Prospectus, $85,000,000 Government of the Dominion of Canada Bonds," January 21, 1937, 13–14, LAC, Finance fonds, RG 19, vol. 3978, file F-1-7.

133 "Taxation System Inquiry," *Ottawa Citizen,* February 19, 1937, 24; reference to a motion from Hamilton City Council to request that the prime minister include municipal taxation in the terms of the "Royal Commission on Taxation," *National Council of Women Yearbook* (1937), 64, 65; "Now or Never Low Declares: Treasurer Sees Tax Inquiry as Last Hope for Alberta," *Globe and Mail,* June 12, 1937, 1; "Outside Experts Desirable," editorial, *Globe and Mail,* June 19, 1937, 6; Canada, House of Commons, *Debates,* May 5, 1933, 4624.

134 "Probe Requested into Tax Scheme," *Globe and Mail,* October 9, 1937, 9.

135 "National Finance Probe Is Asked," *Globe and Mail,* December 9, 1936, 7.

136 Timothy Mitchell, "Economists and the Economy in the Twentieth Century," in *The Politics of Method in the Human Sciences: Positivism and Its Epistemological Others,* ed. George Steinmetz (Durham, NC: Duke University Press, 2005), 126–41.

137 Jessica Squires, "Creating Hegemony: Consensus by Exclusion in the Rowell-Sirois Commission," *Studies in Political Economy* 81, 1 (2008): 159–90.

138 Canada, Royal Commission on Dominion-Provincial Relations, *A Report of the Royal Commission on Dominion-Provincial Relations* (hereafter *Report*), 2 vols. (Ottawa: King's Printer, 1941), 1: 210–15; 2: 154.

139 Ibid., 2: 150.

140 Isaac W. Martin, *Rich People's Movements: Grassroots Campaigns to Untax the One Percent* (Oxford: Oxford University Press, 2013), Chapter 3.

141 In addition to Martin's account of the repealers' constitutional rhetoric in *Rich People's Movements,* see Huret's description of the mobilization of concerns about privacy in *American Tax Resisters,* 147–52.

142 Michael Behiels, "Canada and the Implementation of International Instruments of Human Rights: A Federalist Conundrum, 1919–1982," in *Framing Canadian Federalism: Essays in Honour of John T. Saywell,* ed. Dimitry Anastakis and P.E. Bryden (Montreal: McGill-Queen's University Press, 2009), 151–84.

143 *Submission by the Government of the Province of Nova Scotia to the Royal Commission on Dominion-Provincial Relations* (n.p.: n.p., 1938), 121–23, 109.

144 The schools questions of the late nineteenth century exemplify the passions engaged in Canadian constitutionalism. See, for example, Paul Crunican, *Priests and Politicians: Manitoba Schools and the Election of 1896* (Toronto: University of Toronto Press, 1974). The Maritime Rights movement had an apparently more pragmatic, economic purpose, but the passions that it unleashed were fully on display in William Rand (Secretary, Nova Scotia Party), "A Blast from Nova Scotia," letter to the editor, Toronto *Globe,* April 24, 1931, 4. More soberly but still more than merely pragmatically, W.C. Keirstead, an economist at the University of New Brunswick, argued that the claim for equalization grants was based not upon legal right but upon something like the obligations owed to a family member. The province was part of an "organic" nation, not a party to a contract; see W.C. Keirstead

to W.P. Jones, April 18, 1938, especially 7 and 11–12, University of New Brunswick, Harriet Irving Library, University Archives, W.C. Keirstead fonds, RG 63, series 6, item 18.

145 Garth Stevenson, *Ex Uno Plures: Federal-Provincial Relations in Canada, 1867–1896* (Montreal: McGill-Queen's University Press, 1993), Chapter 9; note especially his observation that many disallowance petitions were solely on "economic self-interest of the petitioners" (249).

146 Canada, Royal Commission on Dominion-Provincial Relations, *Report*, 2: 153–54; W.C. Keirstead to W.P. Jones, April 18, 1938, 2–3, University of New Brunswick, Harriet Irving Library, University Archives, W.C. Keirstead fonds, RG 63, series 6, item 18.

147 Duncan McDowall, *The Sum of the Satisfactions: Canada in the Age of National Accounting* (Montreal: McGill-Queen's University Press, 2008), 31–40.

148 President F.D. Roosevelt, "Speech to Congress," June 1, 1937, and "Joint Resolution to Create a Joint Congressional Committee on Tax Evasion and Avoidance," both reprinted in United States, Congress, Joint Committee on Tax Evasion and Avoidance, *Tax Evasion and Avoidance: Hearings before the Joint Committee on Tax Evasion and Avoidance*, Seventy-Fifth Congress, First Session (Washington, DC: US Government Printing Office, 1937), 7–8.

149 United States, Congress, Joint Committee on Tax Evasion and Avoidance, *Tax Evasion and Avoidance*, 54, 60–63; "Becomes Canadian to Dodge U.S. Taxes," *Toronto Daily Star,* June 18, 1937, 1–2; "Canada-U.S. Plan to Stop Tax Evasion," *Toronto Daily Star,* Auust 10, 1937, 7.

150 R.J. Manion to E.S. Rutledge, May 20, 1935, LAC, R.J. Manion fonds, MG 27 III B 7, vol. 12, file 12-22.

151 E.N. Rhodes to Dear Mr........., March 30, 1933, LAC, R.J. Manion fonds, MG 27 III B 7, vol. 84, file 84-2 1934–41. The letter from Rhodes was sent out to twenty newspapers by James R. MacGregor of the *Halifax Chronicle* on April 8, 1933, NSA, Rhodes fonds, MG 2, vol. 1144, file 4-2T02 Taxation, docs. 59825–45; "James R. MacGregor Dies at 74," *Ottawa Journal,* January 12, 1965, 32.

152 Typescript copy of letter written by hand, Charles A. Dunning to Mr. [W.L.M.] King, August 30, 1938, QUA, Dunning fonds, collection 1212, box 11, file 94. My speculation about Dunning's diagnosis is based upon the endocrinologist Todd B. Nippoldt's response to "is there such a thing as adrenal fatigue?" under "Addison's disease" at http://www.mayoclinic.org/diseases-conditions/.

Chapter 7: Warfare, Welfare, and the Mass Income Tax Payer

1 See David W. Slater and Robert B. Bryce, *War, Finance, and Reconstruction: The Role of Canada's Department of Finance, 1939–1946* (Ottawa: D.W. Slater, 1995), 273–79; J. Harvey Perry, *Taxes, Tariffs, and Subsidies: A History of Canadian Fiscal Development*, 2 vols. (Toronto: University of Toronto Press, 1955), 2: Chapter 21; Colin Campbell, "J.L. Ilsley and the Transformation of the Canadian Tax System: 1939–1943," *Canadian Tax Journal* 61, 3 (2013): 633; Douglas H. Fullerton, *Graham Towers and His Times: A Biography* (Toronto: McClelland and Stewart, 1986), Chapters 9 and 10; and Robert Wardhaugh, *Behind the Scenes: The Life and Work of William Clifford Clark* (Toronto: University of Toronto Press, 2010), Conclusion.

2 Canada, House of Commons, *Debates,* September 12, 1939, 137–44; June 24, 1940, 1011–12; 1023–26, 1030–31; April 29, 1941, 2334–36, 2345–48.

3 Campbell, "J.L. Ilsley and Transformation," 635, 661, 664–67.

4 This is a matter of judgment and interpretation, of course, but I find evidence of a too broadly drawn consensus in Slater's internalist account (see, e.g., his description of the

building of consensus within the tax team in Finance in *War, Finance, and Reconstruction,* 74) and in Campbell's summary of war finance ("equitably shared financial sacrifice could be done no other way" in "J.L. Ilsley and Transformation," 635). Perry acknowledges that there were criticisms of the war finance program, saying that "for many people" it was "the most oppressive aspect of the war." But he leaves the summary assessment of the program to Finance Minister Ilsley – not the most objective of interpreters – with a long quotation from his October 1945 budget speech; see Perry, *Taxes, Tariffs, and Subsidies,* 2: 337, 338–40.

5 Memorandum, Grant Dexter to G.V. Ferguson, August 2, 1942, 4, QUA, Grant Dexter fonds, collection 2142, box 3, file 23.

6 With respect to the 1943 budget measures, see Slater, *War, Finance, and Reconstruction,* 68; with respect to the 1944 budget measures, see Perry, *Taxes, Tariffs, and Subsidies,* 2: 337. Campbell makes no mention of the few but important measures included in the 1943 budget that provided tax relief to low-income earners; see Campbell, "J.L. Ilsley and Transformation," 663–64.

7 Here, I state only slightly more emphatically what Perry wrote in the 1950s in *Taxes, Tariffs, and Subsidies,* 2: 333–34.

8 For evidence of Ilsley's anger, stress, and fatigue, see memorandum, Grant Dexter to G.V. Ferguson, August 2, 1942, QUA, Grant Dexter fonds, collection 2142, box 3, file 23, 4; diary entry, February 5, 1943, LAC, King Diaries, MG 26 J 13, http://www.collectionscanada. gc.ca/databases/king/index-e.html; Wardhaugh, *Behind the Scenes,* 277–78; and J.M. Keynes, quoted in ibid., 261.

9 Campbell understates the scope and political weight of the opposition to Ilsley's tax measures in 1941–43. His evidence for public satisfaction is one letter from 1941 and an observation from war historian C.P. Stacey's book on wartime policy; see Campbell, "J.L. Ilsley and Transformation," 664.

10 See, for example, R.B. Bryce to David Rogers, January 12, 1943, LAC, Finance fonds, RG 19, vol. 4030, file 129W-3.

11 J.A. Matthieu (employer) to H.W. McGill (Director of Indian Affairs), July 11, 1940; E.P. Randle (Indian Agent) to Secretary, Indian Affairs Branch, July 24, 1940; D.M. MacKay (Indian Commissioner for British Columbia) to Secretary, Indian Affairs Branch, July 15, 1940, LAC, Indian Affairs fonds, RG 10, vol. 6821, file 493-1-6, part 1.

12 Perry, *Taxes, Tariffs, and Subsidies,* 2: 604, 608. For a discussion of the administrative issues posed by these taxes, see C. Fraser Elliott to J.L. Ilsley, June 3, 1940, LAC, Finance fonds, RG 19, E1(c), vol. 2679, file I-02.

13 A "feeling of unfairness" on this point was reported by H.G. Norman (Financial Adviser, British Commonweath Air Training Plan) to A.K. Eaton, March 10, 1941, LAC, Finance fonds, RG 19, vol. 3543, file Taxation.

14 Canada, House of Commons, *Debates,* June 24, 1940, 1024; April 29, 1941, 2344.

15 Perry, *Taxes, Tariffs, and Subsidies,* 2: 361. The figure of $108 is the total of a $28 credit against the normal tax and an $80 credit against the graduated tax.

16 Slater, *War, Finance, and Reconstruction,* 47–49; Wardhaugh, *Behind the Scenes,* 192–93; Campbell, "J.L. Ilsley and Transformation," 652–55, 658–59.

17 Reference to this multiplicity as a chronic irritant since the 1920s can be found in Perry, *Taxes, Tariffs, and Subsidies,* 2: 302.

18 Memorandum, Grant Dexter to G.V. Ferguson, July 19, 1942, 2, QUA, Grant Dexter fonds, collection 2142, box 3, file 23.

19 "Forced Saving Starts Sept. 1," *Globe and Mail,* June 24, 1942, 1. For an example of continuing criticism in late August, see "Ilsley Denies Budget Harsh as It Seemed," *Globe and Mail,* August 27, 1942, 2.

20 David Petegorsky, "Report of Discussions with Government Officials and Personnel Managers in Toronto, Washington, and New York on Problems of Industrial Morale," c. 1943, LAC, Finance fonds, RG 19, vol. 4030, file 129W-3. A commercial traveller, commenting on the compulsory savings feature, which he liked, noted that some employees feared that the employer might lose tax remittance records (e.g., in a fire) and thus in effect lose their savings; see A.M. Farr to J.L. Ilsley, June 30, 1944, LAC, Finance fonds, RG 19, vol. 452, file 111–14E.

21 For MPs' comments on these issues, see Canada, House of Commons, *Debates*, July 31, 1942, 5090–92; July 16, 1942, 4312–13; and July 17, 1942, 4328–29.

22 Perry, *Taxes, Tariffs, and Subsidies*, 2: 361–62. In a graduated income tax, the total amount of income tax that you pay can be stated as a percentage of your total earnings; for example, you pay 22 percent of your income in income tax. But that 22 percent is actually made up of several "marginal rates" – say 14 percent on the first $20,000, 21 percent on the next $20,000, and 26 percent on the amount above $40,000. In that case, your marginal rate on each dollar reported above $40,000 is 26 percent.

23 Someone earning $1,362 in a fifty-two-week year took home $26.19 a week, and the taxes in 1942 took $3.11 of that amount. The number of days over which that dollar amount would stretch (between 4.33 and 5.18 days at thirty or thirty-six cents per day) was calculated from the Health League of Canada's figure of thirty cents per person per day quoted in the *Globe and Mail*'s "Homemaker Kitchen Library" column. The columnist's own estimate was that thirty-six cents per person was the best she could manage for her own family, so the Health League might have exaggerated slightly how far one could stretch thirty cents; see "Dear Neighbors," *Globe and Mail*, June 8, 1942, 10.

24 The records of the Department of Finance contain several volumes of letters (roughly a metre's worth) written by members of the public to either Prime Minister King or Finance Minister Ilsley on income tax questions between 1940 and 1943. These files are organized alphabetically. Choosing files at random, my research assistant and I read and took notes on approximately 200 letters, specifically all of those from correspondents whose last names began with D, E, F, G, I, J, K, L, or M, plus a small series of letters on the income tax treatment of cost-of-living allowances. LAC, Finance fonds, RG 19, vol. 452, files 111–14A-0–1 to 5, 111–14M, and 111–14E; vol. 453, file 111–134M; and vol. 449, file 111–14–827. Some aspects of the labelling of the files suggest that, extensive though they are, this set of files was sampled by the accessioning archivists rather than preserved in their entirety. These letters came from a wide range of Canadians from all over the country, including a church-mouse-poor parson in Saint John; a single female barrister in Regina; a sickly pensioner in White Rock; a young woman in a rural Quebec factory; and, in what looked like a furious, drunken scrawl, a Toronto worker barely surviving on a small wage and supporting his dependent father. Whether these letters expressed the full range of opinions among Canadians is unknowable, but they are the letters that officials in the Department of Finance (and sometimes the minister) saw. It was not a scientifically selected sample, but it was still, in some sense, the voice of the people. That the letters were taken into consideration is suggested by the fact that their essential points were summarized for Ilsley by Robert Bryce in a list compiled in late August or early September 1942; see "Questions Most Commonly Asked about the Income Tax in Correspondence," c. August 29, 1942, LAC, Finance fonds, RG 19, vol. 3543, file Taxation. And, on more than one occasion, Ilsley referred to the letters that he had received as a source of his knowledge about people's concerns. See, for example, J.L. Ilsley, *Sharing the Cost of War: An Address before the Trades and Labour Congress of Canada at Quebec City, September 1, 1943* (Ottawa: National Liberal Federation, n.d.), 13, and "Income Tax Increases Are Defended by Ilsley," *Toronto Daily Star*, July 18, 1942, 9.

25 Replies in 1942 and 1943 were commonly dated as little as two to four days after the date of the writer's letter. Most went out over Ilsley's signature; some, but not all, were initialled as having been composed by senior staff (assistants to the deputy minister) such as "AKE" (A. Kenneth Eaton), "JHP" (J. Harvey Perry), or "RBB" (Robert B. Bryce). Ilsley's private secretary, Miss A.W. Wickwire, also wrote some of the replies.

26 Wage earners' strategies for avoiding tax featured in debates about taxation in the House of Commons; see, for example, Canada, House of Commons, *Debates,* July 11, 1944, 4723. In 1948, journalist Blair Fraser commented that not reporting tips and earning income through two different jobs were common ways of hiding income, methods frequently used during the war. These sorts of dodges seem to have been common knowledge; see Blair Fraser, "Who Are the Income-Tax Dodgers?," *Maclean's,* March 15, 1948, 7.

27 "A propos the need for glamorizing the refundable portion," quoting employer S.E. Nixon to J.D. Wood, National War Finance Committee, May 7, 1943, LAC, Finance fonds, RG 19, E(3)b, vol. 3543, file Taxation.

28 James Duncan to J.L. Ilsley, April 16, 1943, LAC, Finance fonds, RG 19, vol. 452, file 111–14E.

29 Labour press survey, August 15–September 15, 1943, LAC, Finance fonds, RG 19, vol. 4028, file Labour Press Surveys.

30 R.B.B. (Bryce), "Memorandum for the Minister re: Proposal of Mr. Maddock and Mr. Bartram," February 5, 1943, LAC, Finance fonds, RG 19, vol. 3543, file Taxation.

31 Minutes of a Meeting of the Committee on Industrial Morale, June 11, 1943, LAC, Finance fonds, RG 19, vol. 4030, file 129W-3. See also R.B. Bryce on the same theme, Minutes of a Special Meeting on Problems of Industrial Morale, March 30, 1943, LAC, Finance fonds, RG 19, vol. 4030, file 129W-3.

32 Minutes of a Meeting of the Committee on Industrial Morale, June 11, 1943, LAC, Finance fonds, RG 19, vol. 4030, file 129W-3.

33 Violet Flaherty to J.L. Ilsley, July 14, 1942, LAC, Finance fonds, RG 19, vol. 452, file 111–14E.

34 J.L. Ilsley to Violet Flaherty, July 17, 1942, LAC, Finance fonds, RG 19, vol. 452, file 111–14E.

35 Margaret G. Gillespie to J.L. Ilsley, April 30, 1943, LAC, Finance fonds, RG 19, vol. 452, file 111–14E. In a similar vein, see Gladys Ell to J.L. Ilsley, July 23, 1942, LAC, Finance fonds, RG 19, vol. 452, file 111–14E.

36 Major E.P. Randle to Secretary, Indian Affairs Branch, September 22, 1942, LAC, Indian Affairs fonds, RG 10, vol. 6821, file 493-1-6, part 1.

37 *Canadian Tribune,* September 6, 1941; *Labour Gazette* 41, 8 (1941): 943–45, and *Labour Gazette* 41, 9 (1941): 104, as cited in Bob Russell, "The Politics of Labour Force Reproduction: Funding Canada's Social Wage, 1917–1946," *Studies in Political Economy* 14 (1984): 61.

38 Lisa Rose Mar, "Beyond Being Others: Chinese Canadians as National History," *BC Studies* 156 (2007–8): 27–32.

39 For an example of the threat to sell, see Annie Horncastle to Minister of Finance, December 10, 1941, LAC, Finance fonds, RG 19, vol. 3404, file 7001–7050.

40 Mrs. Rexford Duckworth to J.L. Ilsley, March 15, 1943, LAC, Finance fonds, RG 19, vol. 452, file 111–14E.

41 Miss W.E. Drummond to J.L. Ilsley, July 15, 1942, LAC, Finance fonds, RG 19, vol. 452, file 111–14E.

42 Viv. H. Graham to J.L. Ilsley, July 21, 1942, LAC, Finance fonds, RG 19, vol. 452, file 111–14E. The quoted passage is Graham's paraphrase of Hanson's remarks as reported in the *Montreal Herald.* Hanson's actual remarks can be found in Canada, House of Commons, *Debates,* July 20, 1942, 4442.

43 Canada, House of Commons, *Debates,* March 2, 1943, 840–42.

44 "'Circle-Bar' Fourth Column," advertisement, *Globe and Mail,* May 1, 1944, 12. See also President Roosevelt's observation that, "the more bonds we buy, the less our burden of taxation," quoted in "This 'Victory Loan' Is Canada's Affair," *Financial Counsel* [investor newsletter], February 7, 1942, LAC, Finance fonds, RG 19, vol. 2706, file 500-7.

45 A.W. Rogers to General Manager, Bank of Nova Scotia, December 12, 1941, confidential enclosure entitled "The National War Finance Committee and the Chartered Banks," dated December 9, 1941, as quoted in Robert L. Ascah, *Politics and Public Debt: The Dominion, the Banks, and Alberta's Social Credit* (Edmonton: University of Alberta Press, 1999), 105.

46 Ascah, *Politics and Public Debt,* 105.

47 Canada, House of Commons, *Debates,* June 26, 1944, 4172.

48 This worry is expressed in R.B. Bryce, "Notes on 1942–43 Financing and the Conscription of Capital," April 1, 1942, LAC, Finance fonds, RG 19, vol. 3978, file F-1-15.

49 A.W. Frazer to J.L. Ilsley, October 30, 1942, LAC, Finance fonds, RG 19, vol. 2704, file 500–1.

50 Canada, House of Commons, *Debates,* September 9, 1939, 55; June 28, 1940, 1230.

51 Richard Toye, "Keynes, the Labour Movement, and 'How to Pay for the War,'" *Twentieth Century British History* 10, 3 (1999): 277.

52 M.J. Coldwell to J.L. Ilsley, June 9, 1941, with an enclosure from William Casey Teneycke, LAC, Finance fonds, RG 19, vol. 2704, file 500–2.

53 Bryce, "Notes on 1942–43 Financing and the Conscription of Capital." My assertion that the measures that Bryce proposed in this memorandum were not taken up is based upon my reading of the wartime budget speeches and Ascah's brief discussion of this document in *Politics and Public Debt,* 111. However, a close examination of the work of the Victory Loan committee would be necessary to determine whether the subtle methods of rationing access to Victory Loan subscriptions might have been accomplished quietly.

54 "Surprise Motion Follows Rejection of Coldwell Plan," *Globe and Mail,* February 19, 1942, 1, 2. Raymond Blake summarizes the literature emphasizing the CCF political threat as key in prompting King's move to develop a social security program; Blake also disputes that view. He is right to emphasize the social security move as somewhat autonomous from partisan considerations, but I suggest that the CCF threat was more than just an electoral worry. Raymond B. Blake, *From Rights to Needs: A History of Family Allowances in Canada, 1929–92* (Vancouver: UBC Press, 2009), 73–74, 297n79.

55 George Spinney to Clifford Clark, September 24, 1943, LAC, Finance fonds, RG 19, vol. 3978, file F-1-11-6.

56 Clifford Clark to George Spinney, September 28, 1943, LAC, Finance fonds, RG 19, vol. 3978, file F-1-11-6.

57 "Coldwell Asks Full Support for New Loan," *Globe and Mail,* October 12, 1943, 13.

58 A. Edington to W.C. Clark, July 7, 1942, LAC, Finance fonds, RG 19, vol. 4030, file 129W-2. These and other rumours were implied in the questions summarized by R.B. Bryce, "Questions about Income Tax, the Budget, and War Saving Raised during Tour of the Minister of Finance through Ontario [sic], August 24–29, 1942," LAC, Finance fonds, RG 19, vol. 453, file Taxation.

59 Illegible signature, memorandum to Dr. Clark re attached letter regarding Victory Loan, March 30, 1943, David Petegorsky to R.B. Bryce, October 13, 1943, LAC, Finance fonds, RG 19, vol. 4030, file 129W-2.

60 "C" (likely W.C. Clark) to R.B.B. (Bryce), April 14, 1943, and memorandum from W.C. Clark to Reg Hardy (Ottawa Press Gallery), April 21, 1943, LAC, Finance fonds, RG 19, vol. 4030, file 129W-2. The Rumour Clinic sent its materials, rebutting rumours, to thirty newspapers each week.

61 R.B. Bryce, "List of Questions Raised at Trade Union Meeting in Montreal, August 21, 1942," August 22, 1942, 2–3, LAC, Finance fonds, RG 19, vol. 3543, file Taxation.

62 See, for example, the memorandum from W.C. Clark to Reg Hardy (Ottawa Press Gallery), April 21, 1943, LAC, Finance fonds, RG 19, vol. 4030, file 129W-2.

63 Slater, *War, Finance, and Reconstruction*, 81, Table 7.1; J.L. Ilsley to John F. Macdonald, December 30, 1940, LAC, Finance fonds, RG 19, vol. 2704, file 500-2.

64 Robert B. Bryce, *Maturing in Hard Times: Canada's Department of Finance through the Great Depression* (Kingston, ON: McGill-Queen's University Press, 1986), 228.

65 Oliver Wright to J.L. Ilsley, January 20, 1941, LAC, Finance fonds, RG 19, vol. 3543, file Taxation.

66 W.C.R. (Ronson) to Miss Wickwire, undated transmittal note (likely February 2, 1941). The letter went out over Ilsley's signature to Oliver Wright, February 3, 1941, LAC, Finance fonds, RG 19, vol. 3543, file Taxation.

67 A.W. Frazer to J.L. Ilsley, October 30, 1942; J.L. Ilsley ("RBB") to A.W. Frazer, November 2, 1942; A.W. Frazer to J.L. Ilsley, November 25, 1942; J.L. Ilsley ("Mr. Bryce") to A.W. Frazer, December 2, 1942; A.W. Frazer to Ilsley, December 11, 1942, LAC, Finance fonds, vol. 2704, file 500-1.

68 R.B. Bryce to Davidson Dunton, February 24, 1944, LAC, Finance fonds, RG 19, vol. 4030, file 129W-3; memorandum to Dr. Clark from R.B.B. (Bryce), pencil notation by A.K.E. (Eaton), October 27, 1942, LAC, Finance fonds, RG 19, vol. 3543, file Taxation.

69 See, for example, J.L. Ilsley ("WCC") to Phineas Pfunder Onderdonck, September 14, 1943, LAC, Finance fonds, RG 19, vol. 3402, file 6301-6400.

70 "Public Reaction to the 1943 Budget," report of WIB correspondents' communications "two or three days" after the March 2 budget, LAC, Finance fonds, RG 19, vol. 4030, file 129W-6.

71 That context is described in Canadian labour history surveys such as Bryan D. Palmer, *Working-Class Experience: Rethinking the History of Canadian Labour, 1800–1991*, 2nd ed. (Toronto: McClelland and Stewart, 1992). An important monograph on one significant strike is Laurel Sefton MacDowell, *"Remember Kirkland Lake": The History and Effects of the Kirkland Lake Gold Miners' Strike, 1941–42* (Toronto: University of Toronto Press, 1983). During the National War Labour Board hearings in the spring, labour executive Aaron Mosher noted organized labour's frustrated aspirations to be represented on wartime administrative bodies. Without giving labour a seat at the table, he pointed out, the government could not expect to get workers' "whole-hearted support of the war effort." Canada, National War Labour Board, *Proceedings*, Report No. 1–13 (Ottawa: King's Printer, 1943), 131.

72 R.B.B. (Bryce) to W.C. Clark, March 30, 1943, LAC, Finance fonds, RG 19, vol. 4030, file 129W-3.

73 Minutes of Meeting of the Committee on Industrial Morale, May 13, 1943, LAC, Finance fonds, RG 19, vol. 4030, file 129W-3.

74 R.B. Bryce to David Petegorsky, May 26, 1943, LAC, Finance fonds, RG 19, vol. 4030, file 129W-3.

75 David Petegorsky to R.B. Bryce, July 22, 1943, LAC, Finance fonds, RG 19, vol. 4030, file 129W-6.

76 "Answers to Your Questions about Income Tax Deductions," c. 1943, City of Toronto Archives, fonds 200, series 361, subseries 1, file 42. The likely date of this document was determined from statements within it and information about when the certificates began to be issued.

77 LAC, Finance fonds, RG 19, vol. 4030, file 129W-3. The date of the production of these ad mats is indicated in R.B. Bryce to Davidson Dunton, February 24, 1944, LAC, Finance fonds, RG 19, vol. 4030, file 129W-3.

78 See, for example, "Protection ... of the People ... by the People," advertisement (sponsored by life insurance companies operating in Canada), *Globe and Mail*, May 29, 1942,

7; "Price Ceiling Combats Inflation," advertisement (Bank of Nova Scotia), *Globe and Mail*, February 5, 1942, 2; and "Canada Enters 1943," advertisement (Wood, Gundy and Company), *Globe and Mail*, January 7, 1943, 32.

79 For example, "Effective Now, Prices of Tea, Coffee, and Oranges Are Reduced by Law," advertisement (Wartime Prices and Trade Board), *Globe and Mail*, December 7, 1942, 9.

80 "Economics in Laymen's Language," advertisement, *Globe and Mail*, May 3, 1944, 7; "We Can Do Better," advertisement, *Crag and Canyon* [Banff], April 14, 1944, 1; "One Man's Income Is Another Man's Out Go," advertisement, *Globe and Mail*, June 27, 1944, 9; "Into One Pocket – Sure! But OUT of the Other," advertisement, *Crag and Canyon* [Banff], October 6, 1944, 3; "The Road Back – Without Price Control," advertisement, *Globe and Mail*, November 16, 1944, 17.

81 "The Story of Inflation," *Globe and Mail*, April 14, 1944, 7; "Economics in Layman's Language," *Globe and Mail*, May 3, 1944, 7; "The A,B,C's of De In flation," *Globe and Mail*, June 12, 1944, 10.

82 Rationing, price control, and taxing the income of better-paid workers comprised the package of measures that Aaron Mosher of the Canadian Labour Congress offered as the way to prevent inflation. National War Labour Board, *Proceedings*, 130–31.

83 Ilsley, *Sharing the Cost of War*.

84 Ibid., 5.

85 Ibid., 11–12.

86 "Who Pays the Piper!," *Globe and Mail*, May 29, 1946, 6.

87 For salaried men in manufacturing, $2,680 was the average annual income in 1946, the first year of available data; see Statistics Canada, Series E60–68, average annual, weekly, and hourly earnings, male and female wage earners, manufacturing industries, Canada, 1934–69; and Series E69–77, average annual, weekly, and hourly earnings, male and female salaried employees, manufacturing industries, Canada, 1946–69, http://www.statcan.gc.ca.

88 Perry, *Taxes, Tariffs, and Subsidies*, 2: 626–27.

89 Dominion Bureau of Statistics, *Canada Year Book, 1943–44* (Ottawa: King's Printer, 1944), 824–25, 858–60; Dominion Bureau of Statistics, *Canada Year Book, 1946* (Ottawa: King's Printer, 1946), 935–36.

90 Perry, *Taxes, Tariffs, and Subsidies*, 2: 360.

91 In the 1939 Senate debate on the Special War Revenue Act, former prime minister Arthur Meighen argued for a dramatic lowering of income tax exemptions "so that the whole population, or nearly the whole of it, will be tax conscious." Canada, Senate, *Debates*, September 12, 1939, 37.

92 Perry, *Taxes, Tariffs, and Subsidies*, 2: 626–27; *Canada Year Book, 1946*, Table 5, "Individual Income Tax Estimates, Taxation Year, 1945," 934–35. For the expense of daily eating, see note 23.

93 The connection of a particular small-wage tax to tax consciousness is mentioned in Robert Edmund Groves, "Business Government: Party Politics and the British Columbia Business Community, 1928–33" (MA thesis, University of British Columbia, 1976), 101.

94 "Who Pays the Piper!," *Globe and Mail*, May 29, 1946, 6.

95 Timothy Mitchell, "Economists and the Economy in the Twentieth Century," in *The Politics of Method in the Human Sciences: Positivism and Its Epistemological Others*, ed. George Steinmetz (Durham, NC: Duke University Press, 2005), 126–41.

96 Ilsley, *Sharing the Cost of War*, 15.

97 Canada, House of Commons, *Debates*, March 2, 1943, 840.

98 King's point was not to change any of the agreed-upon measures but to ensure that the rhetoric was right. The decisions had been made in cabinet ten days earlier; see diary entry, June 13, 1944, LAC, King Diaries, MG 26 J 13, http://www.collectionscanada.gc.ca/databases/king/index-e.html.

99 Diary entry, June 23, 1944, LAC, King Diaries, MG 26 J 13, http://www.collectionscanada. gc.ca/databases/king/index-e.html.

100 Canada, House of Commons, *Debates*, June 26, 1944, 4177.

101 Ibid., 4174–78.

102 Blake, *From Rights to Needs*, 42.

103 Ibid., 63–64, 73, 82, 91–92; Canada, House of Commons, *Debates*, July 25, 1944, 5329; Perry, *Taxes, Tariffs, and Subsidies*, 2: 396.

104 Blake, *From Rights to Needs*, 135–38. The terms "deduction," "exemption," "allowance," and "credit" are easily confused in describing this subject. The budget speeches are clarifying, as is Perry; see Canada, House of Commons, *Debates*, October 12, 1945, 1000; June 26, 1946, 2914–16; April 29, 1947, 2557; and Perry, *Taxes, Tariffs, and Subsidies*, 2: 396.

105 Blake, *From Rights to Needs*, Chapter 2.

106 The following is a sample of coverage of the protest in the Toronto press: "Alimony Payers Urge Ex-Wife Pay Income Tax," *Globe and Mail*, July 3, 1942, 5; "Group of Alimony Receivers Discuss Sliding Scale," *Globe and Mail*, July 28, 1942, 9; "Alimony Payers Join Hands to Ask Ottawa for Relief," *Toronto Daily Star*, July 6, 1942, 3. Organizers among the ex-wives tried, unsuccessfully, to prevent this shifting of the tax burden, asking "why should we and the children suffer because the men's taxes have gone up?": "Ex-Wives Gang Up, Ask Ottawa to Keep Ex-Hubbies Paying Off," *Toronto Daily Star*, July 10, 1942, 4.

107 Canada, House of Commons, *Debates*, March 2, 1943, 856–57.

108 Ilsley, *Sharing the Cost of War*, 12.

109 Canada, Parliament, Senate, Special Committee on the Income War Tax Act and the Excess Profits Tax Act, 1940, *Proceedings*, 1945 session, vol. 1 (Ottawa: King's Printer, 1945), 47–48.

110 A.O. Daunt (Indian Agent) to Secretary, Indian Affairs, December 1, 1942; T.R.L. MacInnes to Ernest Bertrand, Minister of Fisheries, January 15, 1943; quoted in H.W. McGill (Director, Indian Affairs) to F.J.C. Ball, Indian Agency, February 24, 1943; Andrew Paull and Daniel W. Assu to Ernest Bertrand, January 4, 1943; T.A. Crerar (Minister of Mines and Resources) to Ernest Bertrand; T.R.L. MacInnes (Secretary, Indian Affairs Branch) to D.M. MacKay (BC Indian Commissioner), January 28, 1943; clipping, "Indians from B.C. on Warpath in Ottawa," *Vancouver Sun*, June 23, 1943, LAC, Indian Affairs fonds, RG 10, vol. 6821, file 493-6-1, part 1.

111 J.A. Motherwell, Chief Supervisor of Fisheries, to D.B. Finn, Deputy Minister of Fisheries, February 22, 1943; D.M. MacKay, BC Indian Superintendent, to Indian Affairs Branch, August 6, 1943, LAC, Indian Affairs fonds, RG 10, vol. 6821, file 493-1-6, part 1; Deputy Minister (Mines and Resources) to Deputy Minister (Taxation, C.F. Elliott), National Revenue, April 29, 1944; M.S. Todd, Indian Agent, "Report on Kwawkewlth Indian Agency for the Month of Februrary, 1944"; Frederick J.C. Ball, Indian Agent, to Harold W. McGill, Director, Indian Affairs Branch, February 23, 1944; C.F. Elliott, Deputy Minister (Taxation), to Dr. Charles Camsell, Deputy Minister, Department of Mines and Resources, May 8, 1944; Earl Anfield, Indian Agent, to D.M. MacKay, BC Indian Commissioner, July 11, 1944, LAC, Indian Affairs fonds, RG 10, vol. 6821, file 493-1-6, part 2. Elliott had refused the initial request for an extension in 1943, arguing that to extend the deadline on the ground that some Indigenous fishers were illiterate would require that the same extension be made to all "persons and groups of persons who are illiterate"; see C.F. Elliott to Acting Director of Indian Affairs, August 19, 1943, LAC, Indian Affairs fonds, RG 10, vol. 6821, file 493-1-6, part 1.

112 As reported by D.M. MacKay, BC Indian Commissioner, to Indian Affairs Branch, July 20, 1944, LAC, Indian Affairs fonds, RG 10, vol. 6821, file 493-1-6, part 2.

113 Regarding Ilsley's remarks in cabinet, see diary entry, June 13, 1944, LAC, King Diaries, MG 26 J 13, http://www.collectionscanada.gc.ca/databases/king/index-e.html. Regarding Ilsley on the same point in the House, see Canada, House of Commons, *Debates*, June 26, 1944, 4177.

114 Canada, House of Commons, *Debates,* June 26, 1944, 4177.

115 Ibid., 4531–32.

116 Canada, House of Commons, *Debates,* June 27, 1946, 2915; Walter L. Gordon, "Post-War Taxation," reproduced from the *Canadian Chartered Accountant,* December 1944, LAC, Finance fonds, RG 19, vol. 212, file 164-P; "Who Pays the Piper!," *Globe and Mail,* May 29, 1946, 6.

117 Canada, House of Commons, *Debates,* June 26, 1944, 4187.

118 Canada, House of Commons, *Debates,* April 20, 1943, 2368; James Coleman for D.M. MacKay (BC Indian Commissioner) to Indian Affairs Branch, January 11, 1944, and enclosure, F. Earl Anfield, Indian Agent, to D.M. MacKay (BC Indian Commissioner), January 6, 1944, LAC, Indian Affairs fonds, RG 10, vol. 6821, file 493-1-6, part 2.

119 Canada, House of Commons, *Debates,* June 26, 1944, 4177–78.

120 Ibid., 4781.

121 Ibid., 4179.

122 Diary entry, June 13, 1944, LAC, King Diaries, MG 26 J 13, http://www.collectionscanada. gc.ca/databases/king/index-e.html.

123 Ibid., June 23, 1944. King's key sentence is "they would deal with the financial situation in a way which would make all efforts at saving etc. pretty much at naught." "Make ... pretty much at naught" in this context certainly indicates something harmful: "render pretty much futile" might be a more recognizable idiom.

124 Ibid.

125 Canada, House of Commons, *Debates,* June 24, 1940, 1024.

Chapter 8: New Publics and the Taxman in the 1950s

1 Gordon Chown, MP, to Donald Fleming (Minister of Finance), May 20, 1959, LAC, Finance fonds, RG 19, vol. 4164, file T3 – General; Edward G. Byrne, QC, to Michael Pitfield (Secretary to the Royal Commission on Taxation), June 25, 1963, brief to the Carter Commission, Submission 116; "Taxes – and Social Security," *Halifax Herald,* April 10, 1951, 6; Ambrose Hills (pseudonym of Walter A. Dales), "Of Many Things. Election Opportunities," syndicated column published, for example, in *Kingsville Reporter,* May 10, 1962, 5; "Ce que l'avenir reserver pour Jean," attachment to Gilbert E. Jackson to Charles A. Dunning, September 8, 1952, QUA, Dunning fonds, A.Arch. 2121, box 18, file 170; Wellington Jeffers, "Real Hero of Second Half of Twentieth Century Will Be Johnny Canuck, Now Just 21 Years Old," *Globe and Mail,* July 11, 1952, 18.

2 J. Harvey Perry, *Taxes, Tariffs, and Subsidies: A History of Canadian Fiscal Development,* 2 vols. (Toronto: University of Toronto Press, 1955), 2: 381–94.

3 D.C. MacGregor, "The Problem of Price Levels in Canada," *Canadian Journal of Economics and Political Science* 13, 2 (1947): 157–96.

4 "The Congress Memorandum, Submitted to the Dominion Government by the Canadian Labour Congress, on January 28, 1960," *Canadian Labour* 5, 2 (1960): 26, 48; Russell Bell, "Unemployment and Inflationary Pressures," *Canadian Labour* 4, 4 (1959): 25–29.

5 Issues included sales taxes, soft drink taxes, road taxes, poll taxes, and property taxes, along with income taxes and tariffs. The following sources sample the broader discussion: Hadley Cantril, *Public Opinion 1935–46* (Princeton, NJ: Princeton University Press, 1951), 846; "Budget Surplus Prevents Balancing Family Budget," *Manitoba Ensign,* November 27, 1948, 10–11; R.W. Gladstone, MP, to J.L. Ilsley, March 15, 1945, LAC, King fonds, C-9874, 342604; Senator John J. Bench to W.L.M. King, April 11, 1945, LAC, King fonds, C-9871, 329540-1; Mrs. G.D. Finlayson to W.L.M. King, January 8, 1947, LAC, King fonds, C-9874, doc. 384226; Stuart Armour, *The Burden of Taxation: Pre-War and Post-War*

(Toronto: n.p., 1945); Bernice R. Martin, President, Dartmouth Baptist Young People's Union, to W.L. Mackenzie King, May 23, 1946, LAC, Finance fonds, RG 19, vol. 3712, file "D"; Ray Atkinson, BoysWork Secretary, YMCA, Calgary, to W.L. Mackenzie King, May 7, 1946, LAC, Finance fonds, RG 19, vol. 3717, file "Y"; J.E. Lattimer, *Taxation in Prince Edward Island: A Report* (Charlottetown: Department of Reconstruction, 1945); H.C. Goldenberg, Royal Commission on Municipal-Provincial Relations in British Columbia, *Report of the Commissioner* (Victoria: King's Printer, 1947); Province of Saskatchewan, *Report of the Committee on Provincial-Municipal Relations* (Regina: King's Printer, 1950); New Brunswick, Department of Provincial Secretary-Treasurer, *Report of the Royal Commission on the Rates and Taxes Act* (Fredericton: Royal Commission on the Rates and Taxes Act, 1951); submissions of the Association of Ontario Mayors and Reeves to the Provincial-Municipal Committee for the adjustment of the municipal position and tax structure, January 18, 1952; John F. Due, "The Role of Sales and Excise Taxation in the Over-All Tax Structure," *Journal of Finance* 11, 2 (1956): 209–10; Canada, Sales Tax Committee, *Report of the Sales Tax Committee* (Ottawa: Department of Finance, 1956).

6 See Table 2 in the Appendix. See also W. Irwin Gillespie, *Tax, Borrow, and Spend: Financing Federal Spending in Canada, 1867–1990* (Ottawa: Carleton University Press, 1991), 158–60.

7 As well as the Canadian Manufacturers' Association and the Dominion Chartered Accountants' Association, they interviewed an organization focused on eliminating the income tax benefits enjoyed by producers' cooperatives (the deceptively named Income Taxpayers' Association). Curiously, but perhaps predictably, they interviewed Canada's two more conservative labour centrals (the Trades and Labour Congress and the Canadian Federation of Labour) and not the Canadian Congress of Labour, affiliated with the more left-wing American labour central, the Congress of Industrial Organizations; Canada, Senate, Special Committee on the Income War Tax Act and the Excess Profits Tax Act, 1940, *Proceedings*, 1945 session, vol. 1 (Ottawa: King's Printer, 1945).

8 James Struthers, "Shadows from the Thirties: The Federal Government and Unemployment Assistance, 1941–1956," in *The Canadian Welfare State: Evolution and Transition*, ed. Jacqueline S. Ismael (Edmonton: University of Alberta Press, 1987), 9–26; Ann Porter, *Gendered Stats: Women, Unemployment Insurance, and the Political Economy of the Welfare State in Canada, 1945–1997* (Toronto: University of Toronto Press, 2003), Chapters 2 and 3; James Struthers, *The Limits of Affluence: Welfare in Ontario, 1920–1970* (Toronto: University of Toronto Press, 1994), Chapters 5 and 6; Penny Bryden, *Planners and Politicians: Liberal Politics and Social Policy, 1957–1968* (Montreal: McGill-Queen's University Press, 1997), Chapters 1 and 2.

9 Canada, House of Commons, *Debates*, March 22, 1949, 1795.

10 Perry, *Taxes, Tariffs, and Subsidies*, 2: 594, Table 36.

11 Calculated from *Canada Year Book*, 1951, 995–96, and 1952–53, 1044.

12 Canada, House of Commons, *Debates*, June 18, 1971, 6894.

13 "Evasion Chances Poor, 3,000,000 Are Warned as Tax Deadline Near[s]," *Toronto Daily Star*, April 17, 1949, 19.

14 Statistics Canada, Series E49–59, average weekly wages and salaries, industrial composite, by province, 1939–75.

15 *Canada Year Book*, 1947, 1002. Statistics for "1942–43" offered in graphic form in the 1945 year book give a much lower number. I have taken the 1947 data to be more reliable since they were explicitly prepared for the purposes of research.

16 *Canada Year Book*, 1951, 995, for the 1948 data and 1952–53, 1043, for the 1949 data.

17 Michael Barkaway, "Mystery of Farmer's Income Tax," *Saturday Night*, June 1, 1952, 13. See also "Farm Income Tax," reprinted from *Calgary Albertan*, *Crossfield* [AB] *Chronicle*, March 16, 1953, 4.

18 "Farmers and Income Tax," *Toronto Daily Star,* June 10, 1952, 6.
19 Shirley Tillotson, "The Family as Tax Dodge: Partnership, Individuality, and Gender in the Personal Income Tax Act, 1942 to 1970," *Canadian Historical Review* 90, 3 (2009): 403–5; Wellington Jeffers, "Finance at Large," *Globe and Mail,* March 31, 1944, 16; Perry, *Taxes, Tariffs, and Subsidies,* 2: 401; Justice (pseudonym), "An Unjust Law," letter to the editor, the *Call* [Calgary] 1, 5 (1945): 3.
20 The prewar top rate combined a regular rate of 56 percent on income over $500,000 and a 10 percent surtax on income over $200,000. Canada, House of Commons, *Debates,* March 21, 1933, 3241, and March 22, 1935, 1985–86; Perry, *Taxes, Tariffs, and Subsidies,* 2: 399.
21 Founded in 1943, and renamed the Canadian Council for Economic Studies in 1947, the organization channelled free-market, anti-welfare state, and anti-communist ideas through civil society opinion leaders such as newspaper and magazine editors, university presidents and professors, clergy, and the Chamber of Commerce. Its public voice was economist Gilbert E. Jackson. The organization was dissolved in 1956, with some of its resources channelled into other private business policy organizations. Don Nerbas, *Dominion of Capital: The Politics of Big Business and the Crisis of the Canadian Bourgeoisie, 1914–1947* (Toronto: University of Toronto Press, 2013), 183–86, 198–201.
22 Armour, *The Burden of Taxation,* 22.
23 Richard Pound, *Chief Justice W.R. Jackett: By the Law of the Land* (Montreal: McGill-Queen's University Press), 69.
24 Perry, *Taxes, Tariffs, and Subsidies,* 2: 416–21.
25 Hugh Miller, "From the Back Room to the Front Line," *Au courant* 1 (2014): 8.
26 Richard W. Pound, *Stikeman Elliott: The First Fifty Years* (Montreal: McGill-Queen's University Press, 2002), 459–60.
27 Leslie Macdonald suggests that the growth in tax litigation cases might serve as a rough index for the growth of "tax professionals." He compares five-year periods. Looking at his numbers for 1945–49, and those for 1965–69, including Tax Appeal Board cases, the increase was more than tenfold. Counting only the difference in the numbers in court cases in the same two periods, the increase was fivefold. See Leslie Macdonald, "Taxing Comprehensive Income: Power and Participation in Canadian Politics, 1962–72" (PhD diss., Carleton University, 1985), 72–73.
28 H. Heward Stikeman and Robert Couzin, "Surplus Stripping," *Canadian Tax Journal* 43, 5 (1995): 1860; Pound, *Stikeman Elliott,* 376.
29 I thank Blake Brown for pointing out the popularity of Hewart's 1929 book in Canadian legal circles in the 1930s. I have also found that *The New Despotism* was enthusiastically endorsed by a past and future Liberal finance minister in C.A. Dunning to D.C. Coleman (Vice-President, Canadian Pacific Railway), November 16, 1932, QUA, Dunning fonds, A.Arch. 2121, box 10, file 85.
30 A. Kenneth Eaton, *Essays in Taxation* (Toronto: Canadian Tax Foundation, 1966), 3.
31 Duncan McDowall, *The Sum of the Satisfactions: Canada in the Age of National Accounting* (Montreal: McGill-Queen's University Press, 2008), 17–52.
32 Oskar Morgenstern, *On the Accuracy of Economic Observations,* 2nd ed. (Princeton, NJ: Princeton University Press, 1963), 18–19.
33 Sociologist John Porter argued that these statistics understated the sizes of higher-income groups, but, assuming that "special methods of compensation" were available to only a "small proportion of income earners," "the profile of class derived from tax statistics, although imperfect, is not likely to be very far wrong." John Porter, *The Vertical Mosaic: An Analysis of Social Class and Power in Canada* (Toronto: University of Toronto Press, 1965), 105.
34 D.A. MacGibbon, "The Administration of the Income War Tax Act," *Canadian Journal of Economics and Political Science* 12, 1 (1946): 76.

35 The novelty of Perry's first book was celebrated in the "Finance at Large" column by Wellington Jeffers in the *Globe and Mail,* October 23, 1951, 18. The indispensable two-volume work is *Taxes, Tariffs, and Subsidies.*

36 An early call for more research on the tax-income level, calmer and more aware of the limits of his data, can be found in D.C. MacGregor, "The Problem of Price Level in Canada," *Canadian Journal of Economics and Political Science* 13, 2 (1947): 157–96, especially 163 and Appendix Part II. Robin Neill and Gilles Paquet, "L'économie hérétique: Canadian Economics before 1967," *Canadian Journal of Economics* 26, 1 (1993): 3–13, survey the development of the discipline. McDowall, *The Sum of the Satisfactions,* 75–164, describes the building of national accounts capacity and technique from the 1940s to the mid-1960s.

37 Royal Commission on Canada's Economic Prospects, *Final Report* (Ottawa: Queen's Printer, 1958), 95.

38 Neil Brooks, "*Canadian Tax Journal:* The First Decade – 1953–1962," *Canadian Tax Journal* 50, 1 (2002): 262–67.

39 Romain D. Huret, *American Tax Resisters* (Cambridge, MA: Harvard University Press, 2014), 191–207.

40 "What's Wrong with Canada's Tax Policy?," Bulletin No. 2 (Winnipeg: Income Tax Payers' Association, 1944), 15, http://www.wartimecanada.ca; "Why Should a $500,000,000 Business Escape Income Tax?," display ad, *Globe and Mail,* May 27, 1946, 4; "Attack on Co-Ops Alleged," *Winnipeg Free Press,* December 6, 1962, 53; "Lumber Men Rap Tax Act," *Winnipeg Free Press,* February 1, 1963, 11; "Equitable Income Tax Foundation," appointment ad, *Globe and Mail,* January 17, 1967, B10; I.H. Asper, *The Carter Commission Report on Taxation: An Objective View* (Winnipeg: Equitable Income Tax Foundation, 1967).

41 Tillotson, "The Family as Tax Dodge," 405–7.

42 Mark Milke, *A Nation of Serfs? How Canada's Political Culture Corrupts Canadian Values* (Mississauga, ON: J. Wiley and Sons, 2006).

43 F.R. Scott, "The Special Nature of Canadian Federalism," *Canadian Journal of Economics and Political Science* 13, 1 (1947): 13–25.

44 Isaac William Martin, *Rich People's Movements: Grassroots Campaigns to Untax the One Percent* (New York: Oxford University Press, 2013), Chapters 4 and 5.

45 Pound, *Stikeman Elliott,* 14–15.

46 Ibid., 5–15.

47 Canada, Parliament, Senate, Special Committee on the Income War Tax Act and the Excess Profits Tax Act, 1940, *Proceedings,* 1946 session, vol. 2 (Ottawa: E. Cloutier, Printer to the King, 1945–46), April 3, 1946, 93; May 7, 1946, 31.

48 Pound, *Stikeman Elliott,* 11–12, 14.

49 Ibid., 13. Both Elliott and Walters saw income tax compliance as entailing moral character. Remarks by C.F. Elliott in discussion period on C.S. Walters et al., "Income Assessment for Taxation Purposes," in Canadian Tax Conference, *Proceedings, Held under the Auspices of the Citizens' Research Institute of Canada* (Toronto: Citizens' Research Institute of Canada, 1930), 98. C.S. Walters, Commissioner of Income Tax, to R.B. Bennett, "Memorandum for the Right Honorable the Minister of Finance. Re 1931 Amendments to the Income War Tax Act," May 29, 1931, NSA, Rhodes fonds, MG 2, vol. 1110, doc. 48399.

50 Canada, House of Commons, *Debates,* February 25, 1949, 2. Lacroix's sense of justice would not necessarily be ours today. Lacroix brought to the House of Commons in 1939 a Saint-Jean Baptiste Society petition bearing 127,000 signatures opposing immigration and especially Jewish immigration. He was also active in attacking the Labour Progressive Party. In all of these positions, however, including the income tax ones, he seems to have represented a body of opinion among his constituents in Quebec-Montmorency, and he was re-elected repeatedly from 1935 on until his defeat by a Conservative in 1958. "Lacroix

Tries New Plan to Outlaw Reds, LPP," *Globe and Mail,* January 28, 1949, 12; "Canada Will Not Adopt Open Door to Refugees, Premier King Intimates," *Globe and Mail,* January 31, 1939, 1; s.v. "Wilfrid Lacroix," http://www.parl.gc.ca.

51 Senate, Special Committee on the Income War Tax Act and the Excess Profits Tax Act, *Proceedings,* November 15, 1945, 53.

52 Pound, *Stikeman Elliott,* 15.

53 Psychoanalytic theory, anthropologically inspired moral relativism, logical positivism, and existentialism all offered educated people in the 1950s the intellectual resources with which to question the Victorian philosophical idealism and moral realism of the interwar years. See, for example, Anna Freud's description of altruism as a defence mechanism in *The Ego and the Mechanisms of Defense* (New York: International Universities Press, 1946), Chapter 10. I thank Greg Donaghy for pointing to this larger cultural context of "smart" (cynical) attitudes in the 1950s and Richmond Campbell for pointing to the shifts in scholarly philosophy. L.B. Kuffert describes attempts by cultural critics in Canada in the 1950s to defend moral idealism against perceived materialism and moral emptiness; see L.B. Kuffert, *A Great Duty: Canadian Responses to Modern Life and Mass Culture, 1939–1967* (Montreal: McGill-Queen's University Press, 2003), Chapters 3 and 4.

54 "Evasion of Taxes," *Winnipeg Free Press,* February 11, 1947, 11.

55 "'If All Stealing, None a Thief,' Said Feeling of Many Tax-Dodgers," *Toronto Daily Star,* November 23, 1948, 25.

56 For a survey of methods for measuring tax evasion and a critique of their effectiveness, see Joel Slemroad and Caroline Weber, "Evidence of the Invisible: Toward a Credibility Revolution in the Empirical Analysis of Tax Evasion and the Informal Economy," *International Tax and Public Finance* 19, 1 (2012): 25–53.

57 "Agree Cruelty to Children Worse than Tax Gyp, Theft," *Toronto Daily Star,* September 6, 1947, 5.

58 "Revenue Department Seeks Miracle Man to 'Sell' Income Tax to Canadians," *Ottawa Journal,* October 14, 1947, 16; Robert Taylor, "High-Bracket Tax Dodgers Promised Jail," *Toronto Daily Star,* March 19, 1947, 1.

59 Blair Fraser, "Who Are the Income-Tax Dodgers?," *Maclean's,* March 15, 1948, 7–8, 63–65.; "Income Tax Evaders Pay $326,000 in Fines [for] $1,676,000 Back Taxes," *Toronto Daily Star,* February 3, 1948, 13; "Don't Woo 'Spies' but Some Get Pay – Income Tax Office," *Toronto Daily Star,* December 21, 1948, 10; "Evasion Chances Poor 3,000,000 Are Warned as Tax Deadline Near[s]," *Toronto Daily Star,* April 17, 1949, 19; "Many 'Tricks' Used to Evade Income Tax but None Foolproof," *Toronto Daily Star,* April 3, 1950, 19; "Income Tax Collector Tough, Some Take All Delinquent's Salary," *Toronto Daily Star,* December 13, 1950, 29; "Even 'Crooks' Paying Their Income Taxes, Few Evaders – McCann," *Toronto Daily Star,* September 26, 1952, 21.

60 "Two Tax-Dodgers Fined $144,500," *Winnipeg Free Press,* March 18, 1950, 1.

61 "Tax Evader Is Fined $100,000," *Toronto Daily Star,* April 22, 1949, 1.

62 "Evaded Income Tax[,] Couple Fined $5,050," *Toronto Daily Star,* October 25, 1947, 1; "To Pay $8,000 Taxes Plus Fine of $1,000," *Toronto Daily Star,* October 14, 1948, 3; "$24,575 Tax Evasion Brothers Are Guilty," *Toronto Daily Star,* June 26, 1948, 23; "45 Complaints Filed Against Textile Man in Tax Evasion Charge," *Toronto Daily Star,* February 11, 1949, 25; "Evaded $86,114 in Taxes, Admits Guilt on 11 Counts," *Toronto Daily Star,* March 4, 1948, 27; "22 Months Jail or $5,801, Tax Dodger's Choice," *Toronto Daily Star,* January 20, 1949, 3; "Fine 4 Soo Men $44,800 Total on Income Tax," *Toronto Daily Star,* March 6, 1953, 29. As late as 1957, prosecutions of wartime offences continued. A Vancouver magistrate trying an evasion case in 1957 pointed out that, because the offences stretched back into the war years, they "were in the nature of treason" and warranted a jail term with no alternative of a fine;

see "Doctor Hid $60,000 like Treason – Cadi," *Toronto Daily Star,* November 26, 1957, 1; "Evaded Income Tax[,] B.C. Doctor Jailed," *Toronto Daily Star,* December 3, 1957, 12.

63 "Store Operator Must Serve His Jail Term," *Toronto Daily Star,* June 28, 1947, 11; "Heart Trouble Cuts Jail Term to a Day," *Toronto Daily Star,* August 4, 1948, 10; "Must Pay $138,000 and Serve 6 Months," *Toronto Daily Star,* October 28, 1950, 27.

64 "Evasion Chances Poor 3,000,000 Are Warned as Tax Deadline Near[s]," *Toronto Daily Star,* April 17, 1949, 19; "Income Tax Collector Tough, Some Take All Delinquent's Salary," *Toronto Daily Star,* December 13, 1950, 29. The US federal government also beefed up the IRS staff after the war to investigate cases of wartime "tax evasion and black marketing"; see "U.S. May Use 10,000 in Tax Evasion Hunt," *Toronto Daily Star,* June 1, 1945, 2.

65 "Even 'Crooks' Paying Their Income Taxes, Few Evaders – McCann," *Toronto Daily Star,* September 26, 1952, 21.

66 "Higher Income Taxes Could Be Double-Edged Sword," advertisement, *Toronto Daily Star,* January 12, 1951, 18.

67 "Income Tax Crackdown[,] Raid Toronto Offices," *Toronto Daily Star,* June 6, 1961, 1; "Don't Ditch That Woman if You Have Income Tax Secrets," "How Income Tax Detectives Use Tips, Hunches to Track Cheaters," and "Real Crackdown Ahead on Foreign Tax Deals," *Financial Post,* December 2, 1961, 25–26.

68 "Idle Conversations at Cocktail Parties Help Nab Tax Evader," *Toronto Daily Star,* May 16, 1957, 8; "3 Firms Must Pay $1,200,000 in Back Taxes," *Toronto Daily Star,* April 5, 1955, 1; "Dad, Son Pay $1,400 in Fines on 7 Tax Counts," *Toronto Daily Star,* December 21, 1955, 3; "Costs Tax Evader $1,000 per Minute," *Toronto Daily Star,* April 21, 1956, 24; "Seized Books in Tax Inquiry Is Allegation," *Toronto Daily Star,* May 25, 1956, 66; "Tax Fines $102,900 for Two Men, Firms," *Toronto Daily Star,* June 20, 1956, 7; "$55,774 Tax Evasion over Seven Years Costs Firm $22,450," *Toronto Daily Star,* September 15, 1956, 21; "Call 'Floor of Mystery' Check Investors' Tax," *Toronto Daily Star,* November 6, 1957, 1; Pound, *Stikeman Elliott,* 12, 45, 64.

69 "Father and Son Fined $40,000 or 18 Months," *Toronto Daily Star,* April 3, 1947, 3.

70 The tax specialist of the Department of Finance, A.K. Eaton, described the origin of the situation rather more saltily: "Fraser Elliott took care of it [during the war] in a rather grand manner by not requiring conformance with the law." In his view, construction labour had been "getting away with murder through not paying tax on allowances." A.K. Eaton, memorandum to the Minister of Finance, July 18, 1957, LAC, Finance fonds, RG 19, vol. 4247, file 5055-03-02; *Labour Gazette* 57 (1957): 23; Canada, House of Commons, *Debates,* March 21, 1957, 2577–78; April 5, 1957, 3138–40; December 6, 1957, 2004.

71 See, for example, the ad in *Cardston* [AB] *News,* April 8, 1948, 3.

72 *Prairie Farmers Income Tax Guide and Farm Account Book* (Taxation Division, Department of National Revenue, 1947), LAC, Revenue fonds, RG 16, vol. 1006, file T1 General T1 Special T1 Farmers 1947.

73 Nikolas Rose and Peter Miller, "Political Power beyond the State: Problematics of Government," *British Journal of Sociology* 43, 2 (1992): 173–205.

74 Senate, Special Committee on the Income War Tax Act and the Excess Profits Tax Act, *Proceedings,* November 14, 1945, 13; "All Can Claim $100, 150,000 to Escape Tax," *Toronto Daily Star,* March 15, 1957, 10; Clark Davey, "Exemption of Flat $100 Aids Many," *Globe and Mail,* March 15, 1957, 1, 2; Mary Jukes, "Money Talks," *Globe and Mail,* November 19, 1958, 11.

75 George Neville, "How to Save Money on Your Income Tax," *Maclean's,* March 15, 1951, 15–19, 30–31.

76 Gifford Swartman (Indian Agent) to Department of Mines and Resources, Indian Affairs Branch, July 7, 1945, LAC, Indian Affairs fonds, RG 10, vol. 6821, file 493-1-6, part 2.

77 J.B. McKay, "Fragments," *Cornwall Standard Freeholder,* April 24, 1954. I thank Ian McKay for this reference.

78 Filler, *Farm and Ranch Review,* September 1, 1957, 26.

79 "Wage Earners ... ," classified ad, *Toronto Daily Star,* March 23, 1945, 34; "All Canadian Income Tax Payers Will Welcome This Book," display ad, *Toronto Daily Star,* February 28, 1945, 5; "Your Income Tax," display ad, *Toronto Daily Star,* January 12, 1946, 2; "At Last It's Here," classified ad, *Toronto Daily Star,* September 4, 1947, 44; "What You Should Know to Save Money on Your Income Tax," *Globe and Mail,* April 4, 1955, 10; "Need Help with Your Income Tax?" display ad, *Globe and Mail,* March 13, 1965, 11.

80 The earliest edition of the column that I have been able to find is February 10, 1945. For a sample postwar Plowman column, see February 21, 1948, 37; for a sample "Doc Tax" column, see March 20, 1965, 20. The *Star* occasionally inserted a notice soliciting questions from readers (e.g., April 19, 1947, 6). For a sample "Questions and Answers" column, see December 24, 1946, 6. New Canadians were invited to write to Dorothy Lash in "foreign" languages; see notice, *Toronto Daily Star,* January 4, 1960, 26. For a report of the annual Income Tax Forum, see "December Wedding Cuts Your Income Tax," *Toronto Daily Star,* March 15, 1961, 61; "You Can Save on Taxes," *Canadian Homes and Gardens,* April 1953, 81–82; Garfield P. Smith, "Your Taxes," *Saturday Night,* September 27, 1958, 48; J.K. Edmonds, "How to Trim Your Taxes without Actually Cheating," *Financial Post,* November 22, 1958, 34–35.

81 The *Financial Post* regularly reported the proceedings of the Canadian Tax Foundation. See, for example, November 22, 1958, 34–35.

82 "Rent Your Flat? Tax Men Seeking Income Evaders," *Toronto Daily Star,* January 16, 1960, 64.

83 Mary Jukes, "Money Talks," *Globe and Mail,* November 19, 1958, 11.

84 "Fewer than 1 in 10 Working at 2 Jobs," *Toronto Daily Star,* June 10, 1958, 53.

85 J.A.N. to Lester B. Pearson, March 1965, LAC, Pearson fonds, MG 26-N3, vol. 52, file 252–2.

86 Canada, Royal Commission on Taxation, *Report,* Appendix D, 4: 600–3; H. Heward Stikeman and Robert Couzin, "Surplus Stripping," *Canadian Tax Journal* 43, 5 (1995): 1838–50.

87 Canada, House of Commons, *Debates,* March 31, 1960, 2683.

88 Pound, *Stikeman Elliott,* 38–39; Walter Gordon, *A Political Memoir* (Toronto: McClelland and Stewart, 1977), 139, 143–44, 146; Stikeman and Couzin, "Surplus Stripping," 1850–51.

89 Pound, *Chief Justice W.R. Jackett,* 69; Margaret Conrad, *George Nowlan: Maritime Conservative in National Politics* (Toronto: University of Toronto Press, 1986), 193.

90 Gwyneth McGregor, *Business Deductions under the Income Tax* (Toronto: Canadian Tax Foundation, 1958), 9–10.

91 David Greenspan, "Expense Accounts – and the Living Is Easy," *Toronto Daily Star,* October 6, 1959, 12.

92 "Tighter Laws Asked in Taxing Expense Living," *Globe and Mail,* November 24, 1961, 22.

93 These examples are taken from Gwyneth McGregor, *Employees' Deductions under the Income Tax: A Comparative Study of Their Treatment in the United Kingdom, the United States, and Canada* (Toronto: Canadian Tax Foundation, 1960), 19–22.

94 W.S. Lloyd (Premier of Saskatchewan) to L.B. Pearson, March 24, 1964, LAC, Pearson fonds, MG 26-N3, vol. 53, file 252–212; "CLC Executive Council Decisions," *Canadian Labour* 5 (1960): n.p., June news section. The letters to finance ministers on this topic were numerous. The broken series of file numbers suggests that not all were preserved; however, in the Finance fonds is a full volume (an eight-inch stack) of letters from employees about deductions for the years 1957–64. In Pearson's fonds for 1963–65 are three files containing over 100 letters specifically on exemptions. LAC, Finance fonds, RG 19, vol. 4247, files

95055–03–3, 5055–03–8, 5055–03–9, 5055–03–10, and four files numbered 5055–03–2 dated between 1957 and 1964; LAC, Pearson fonds, MG 26-N3, vol. 53, file 252–23 (three subfiles in the series).

95 McGregor, *Employees' Deductions under the Income Tax,* 25.

96 McGregor, *Business Deductions under the Income Tax,* 20; Pound, *Stikeman Elliott,* 45.

97 According to tax scholars in 1972, recalling the early 1960s, "responsible tax practitioners" regarded surplus stripping as a "scandal." Meyer Bucovetsky and Richard M. Bird, "Tax Reform in Canada: A Progress Report," *National Tax Journal* 25, 1 (1972): 29.

98 Frederick Field to K.W. Taylor, February 27, 1959, LAC, Finance fonds, RG 19, vol. 4236, file 5020-03-04.

99 "Addresses Made at the Annual General Meeting of Shareholders of the Royal Bank of Canada," *Toronto Daily Star,* January 12, 1951, 19.

100 Memo to the Honourable Walter Gordon, "Subject: Wilful and Deliberate Evasion of Proper Taxes," June 17, 1963, LAC, Finance fonds, RG 19, vol. 4236, file 5020-03-04.

101 Doug Hartle, quoted in W. Neil Brooks, "The Royal Commission on Taxation Twenty Years Later: An Overview," in *The Quest for Tax Reform: The Royal Commission on Taxation Twenty Years Later,* ed. W. Neil Brooks (Agincourt, ON: Carswell, 1988), 3.

102 "Jail, $15,000 in Fines for Evading Taxation," *Globe and Mail,* March 16, 1961, 9.

103 See, for example, T.R. Pogue (Rainbow Chemicals) to Keith Laird (Martin, Laird, Easton, Cowan, and Chauvin), March 30, 1964, LAC, Finance fonds, RG 19, vol. 4237, file 5025-03-1, part 4.

104 James H. Smith to Lester B. Pearson, March 11, 1965, LAC, Finance fonds, RG 19, vol. 4242, file 5050-03-1 1964; G.S. Ainslie to Donald Fleming, August 16, 1961, LAC, Finance fonds, RG 19, vol. 4242, file 5050-03-1 1962.

105 Arnold L. Agnew to J.G. Diefenbaker, March 19, 1953, LAC, Diefenbaker fonds, MG 26-M, reel M-7419, doc. 12928.

106 George A. Fuller to Prime Minister Diefenbaker, May 31, 1962, LAC, Finance fonds, RG 19, vol. 4242, file 5050-03-1 1962; W. Brand to J.G. Diefenbaker, December 2, 1951, LAC, Diefenbaker fonds, MG 26-M, reel M-9312, doc. 24020–10.

107 J. Heslop to Prime Minister Diefenbaker, March 29, 1962, LAC, Finance fonds, RG 19, vol. 4242, file 5050-03-1 1962; Dr. John Dearness, "Taxation Troubles," 1944, LAC, Finance fonds, RG 19, vol. 452, file 111–14E, 4–5; Donald W. Tully to E.J. Benson, February 26, 1970, and E.D. Thompson to E.J. Benson, February 23, 1970, LAC, Finance fonds, RG 19, vol. 4778, file 5013-9 T1 Multiple. Similar macroeconomic arguments were made to Pearson on a closely related homeowners' deduction and got a thorough evaluation; see memorandum for Tom Kent from L.B.P. [Pearson], April 3, 1963, LAC, Pearson fonds, MG26-N2, vol. 7, file 252.

108 Resolution 16, Ontario Federation of Labour, submitted by the Toronto Printing Pressmen and Assistants' Union 10, cover letter dated January 13, 1962, LAC, Finance fonds, RG 19, vol. 4242, file 5050-03-1 1962; James Phelan (International Chemical Workers Union, District 4) to George Nowlan, March 18, 1963, LAC, Finance fonds, RG 19, vol. 4242, file 5050-03-1 1963. For a discussion of how tax policy could help or hurt working-class people as homeowners, see George Home (Political Education Director, CLC), circular letter to councils, federations, et cetera on Citizenship Month 1969 Taxation, December 4, 1968, 4, LAC, Canadian Labour Congress (hereafter CLC) fonds, MG 28 I 103, reel H-644.

109 Miriam Chapin, *Contemporary Canada* (New York: Oxford University Press, 1959), 175. Suzanne Morton drew my attention to this fascinating portrait by an outsider of Canada in the 1950s.

110 "Lower Indirect Taxes Said Only Tax Relief in Budget," *Toronto Daily Star,* March 11, 1950, 1. Leslie Macdonald describes discussions in the Canadian Tax Foundation in 1951–52 in

"Taxing Comprehensive Income," 81–91. The topic was also aired in Parliament, in Toronto newspapers, and in at least some western Canadian papers.

111 Canada, House of Commons, *Debates,* April 26, 1951, 2445. Sinclair's explanation of why taxing capital gains as income was a bad idea echoed some kinds of common sense, as stated in "Taxation by Stealth," editorial, *Globe and Mail,* May 23, 1950, 6, and, reporting in the United States on a Canadian Tax Foundation talk, "Capital Gain Found Difficult to Define," *New York Times,* December 2, 1951, 161.

112 Canada, House of Commons, *Debates,* April 20, 1951, 2260; April 26, 1951, 2445; May 1, 1951, 2570, 2595; May 3, 1951, 2648; May 9, 1952, 2060, 2061, 2062; March 23, 1956, 2555; "CCF Condemns Federal Budget," *Globe and Mail,* April 16, 1951, 5; "Ask Capital Gains Tax Be Imposed," *People's Weekly,* March 3, 1951, 1.

113 Fraser Robertson, "Oil for Profits: Looking into Business," *Globe and Mail,* May 22, 1957, 22; Canada, House of Commons, *Debates,* December 20, 1960, 1011; R.M. Baiden, "Canada Conversion Bonds: Powerful Propaganda for Investors," *Saturday Night,* August 16, 1958, 18–19; "More Bonds without Taxes," clipping, editorial, *Winnipeg Free Press,* June 16, 1959, 33, QUA, Dexter fonds, collection 2142, box 19, file 164 Finances 1957–60. An investment firm ad was likely one of many that offered advice on which stocks to buy in order to "Offset Higher Taxes and Increased Living Costs with Tax-Free Capital Gains," John L. Applebaum and Company ad, *Globe and Mail,* January 9, 1951, 18.

114 Canada, House of Commons, *Debates,* March 22, 1956, 2555.

115 Canada, House of Commons, *Debates,* December 5, 1949, 2732, 2737–38, 2744; March 23, 1950, 1038; Wellington Jeffers, "Is Ottawa Really Joyful at Chance to Soak Taxpayers for Capital Gains without Parliament Passing Major Policy through Crucible of Debate," *Globe and Mail,* March 22, 1950, 20.

116 Fraser Robertson, "Ottawa Double Talk: Looking into Business," *Globe and Mail,* February 27, 1957, 22; Alan Armstrong, "Surprising Tax Man Not Eyeing Stock Profits," *Toronto Daily Star,* May 25, 1958, 4; Fraser Robertson, "Queensbury Ignored by Men Who Rule on Taxation," *Globe and Mail,* November 20, 1962, B2; Devon Smith, "Fears End of Non-Taxable Capital Gains," *Globe and Mail,* November 27, 1962, B1. A letter from a constituent made explicit what Robertson hinted at: the reassessment of a capital gain several years later as income was the procedural issue on which some taxpayers felt aggrieved. See K.A. Riedeman to Arthur Maloney, MP, May 13, 1958, LAC, Finance fonds, RG 19, vol. 4236, file 5020-03-03.

117 "Taxation by Stealth," editorial, *Globe and Mail,* May 23, 1950, 6; emphasis added.

118 Donald Fleming, "Some Thoughts on the Carter Report," March 16, 1967, in *Empire Club of Canada Addresses,* http://speeches.empireclub.org.

119 *Labour Gazette* 51 (1951): 646. Summaries of annual legislative proposals and resolutions from various Canadian labour centres, federations, and particular unions on tax questions can be found in the *Labour Gazette* 48 (1948): 284, 286, 1378; 49 (1949): 553, 558, 571; 51 (1951): 646, 1472–73, 1487; 52 (1952): 158, 266, 399, 411, 860, 1199, 1320–21, 1337; 57 (1957): 23, 157, 683, 1169, 1176, 1293, 1297, 1427.

120 "Lower Indirect Taxes Said Only Tax Relief in Budget," *Toronto Daily Star,* March 11, 1950, 1. From the context of the article, the CCL meant not tax evasion but morally unacceptable tax avoidance.

121 Memorandum to the Minister (of Finance) from C.M. Isbister, April 11, 1960, LAC, Finance fonds, RG 19, vol. 4164, file T3 General.

122 *Prairie Farmers Income Tax Guide and Farm Account Book* (Taxation Division, Department of National Revenue, 1947), LAC, Revenue fonds, RG 16, vol. 1006, file T1 General T1 Special T1 Farmers 1947.

123 "CLC Brief to Taxation Commission," *Canadian Labour* 9, 2 (1964): 29.

Chapter 9: Poverty, Bureaucracy, and Taxes

1 James P. Bickerton, *Nova Scotia, Ottawa, and the Politics of Regional Development* (Toronto: University of Toronto Press, 1990), 17–19; Michael Adams, "Foreword," in Peter M. Butler, *Polling and Public Opinion: A Canadian Perspective* (Toronto: University of Toronto Press, 2007), ix–xv; Daniel Robinson, *The Measure of Democracy: Polling, Market Research, and Public Life, 1930–1945* (Toronto: University of Toronto Press, 1999).

2 Sean T. Cadigan, "The Moral Economy of Retrenchment and Regeneration in the History of Rural Newfoundland," in *Retrenchment and Regeneration in Rural Newfoundland*, ed. Reginald Byron (Toronto: University of Toronto Press, 2003), 12, 29–31; Tina Loo, "People in the Way: Modernity, Environment, and Society on the Arrow Lakes," *BC Studies* 142–43 (2004): 161–66; James L. Kenny and Andrew Secord, "Engineering Modernity: Hydroelectric Development in New Brunswick, 1945–1970," *Acadiensis* 39, 1 (2010): 3–26; Gilles Bourques et Jules Duchastel, *Restons traditionnels et progressifs: Pour une nouvelle analyse du discours politique: Le cas du régime Duplessis au Québec* (Montréal: Boreal, 1988), 220–25.

3 Pierre Elliott Trudeau, not uncontroversially, was especially scathing about what he regarded as an anti-democratic political culture in Quebec in "Some Obstacles to Democracy in Quebec," *Canadian Journal of Economics and Political Science* 24, 3 (1958): 297–311. For a more dispassionate description of the continuing pull of patron-client traditions in New Brunswick in the early 1950s, see R.A. Young, "'And the People Will Sink into Despair': Reconstruction in New Brunswick, 1942–1952," *Canadian Historical Review* 69, 2 (1988): 155–57.

4 Shirley Tillotson, "Citizen Participation in the Welfare State: An Experiment, 1945–57," *Canadian Historical Review* 75, 4 (1994): 511–42; Kevin Brushett, "Making Shit Disturbers: The Selection and Training of Company of Young Canadian Volunteers, 1965–1970," in *The Sixties in Canada: A Turbulent and Creative Decade*, ed. M. Athena Palaeologu (Montreal: Black Rose Books, 2009), 246–69; James L. Kenny, "Women and the Modernizing State: The Case of Northeast New Brunswick, 1964–72," in *Making Up the State: Women in 20th-Century Atlantic Canada*, ed. Janet Guildford and Suzanne Morton (Fredericton: Acadiensis Press, 2010), 165–78.

5 Donald V. Smiley, "Canada's Poujadists: A New Look at Social Credit," 1962, reprinted in *Forum: Canadian Life and Letters, 1920–70: Selections from the Canadian Forum*, ed. J.L. Granatstein and Peter Stevens (Toronto: University of Toronto Press, 1972), 348–51; Martin Francis, "'Set the People Free'? Conservatives and the State, 1920–1960," in *The Conservatives and British Society, 1880–1990*, ed. Martin Francis and Ina Zweiniger-Bargielowska (Cardiff: University of Wales Press, 1996), 63–64; Randle Joseph Hart, "The Truth in Time: Robert Welch, the John Birch Society, and the American Conservative Movement, 1900–1972" (PhD diss., University of Toronto, 2007), 240–45.

6 J. Harvey Perry, *A Fiscal History of Canada: The Postwar Years* (Toronto: Canadian Tax Foundation, 1989), 47.

7 James Struthers, *The Limits of Affluence: Welfare in Ontario, 1920–1970* (Toronto: University of Toronto Press, 1994), Chapters 5 and 6; Ann Porter, "Women and Income Security in the Post-War Period: The Case of Unemployment Insurance, 1945–1962," *Labour/Le travail* 31 (1993): 111–44; Alvin Finkel, "Even the Little Children Cooperated: Family Strategies, Childcare Discourse, and Social Welfare Debates 1945–1975," *Labour/Le travail* 36 (1995): 91–118; C. David Naylor, *Private Practice, Public Payment: Canadian Medicine and the Politics of Health Insurance, 1911–1966* (Montreal: McGill-Queen's University Press, 1986), Chapters 6 and 7.

8 John Porter, *The Vertical Mosaic: An Analysis of Social Class and Power in Canada* (Toronto: University of Toronto Press, 1965), 132.

9 Isaac William Martin, *Rich People's Movements: Grassroots Campaigns to Untax the One Percent* (New York: Oxford University Press, 2013), Chapter 4; Romain D. Huret, *American Tax Resisters* (Cambridge, MA: Harvard University Press, 2014), Chapter 6. Discussions of how to amend the Canadian Constitution flourished during the 1960s and 1970s, but success eluded constitutional reform until repatriation of the British North America Act and passage of the Constitution Act in 1982.

10 In this chapter and the following one, I have anonymized letters that included personal information about family budgets and small-business budgets. In letters whose authors simply expressed views or made more or less impersonal arguments for tax measures, I use the real names of the authors.

11 The problem was that, if normal deductions did not cover the tax debt, then finding the funds to pay extra in a lump sum was difficult. A.W. Kuhnle, CA, to Walter Gordon, July 1, 1964, LAC, Finance fonds, RG 19, vol. 4236, file 5020-03-2.

12 "Fred Baxter" to "Leslie" Pearson (labelled "copy," n.d.); Mary E. Macdonald (Executive Assistant to the Prime Minister) to "Fred Baxter," August 27, 1963; John R. Garland (Minister of National Revenue) to "Fred Baxter," September 12, 1963, LAC, Pearson fonds, MG 26-N3, vol. 52, file 252.211-B.

13 Canada, Royal Commission on Dominion-Provincial Relations, *A Report of the Royal Commission on Dominion-Provincial Relations*, vol. 2 (Ottawa: King's Printer, 1940), 210–15; David B. Perry, "Fiscal Figures," *Canadian Tax Journal* 18, 2 (1970): 139; William Paley, *The Principles of Moral and Political Philosophy* (1795), and W. Friend, *Principles of Taxation* (1799), quoted in Gwyneth McGregor, *Personal Exemptions and Deductions, with Special Reference to Canada, the U.S., and the U.K.* (Toronto: Canadian Tax Foundation, 1962), 7. Sometimes cited as the authority for this view is John Stuart Mill, *The Principles of Political Economy*, 7th ed. (Oxford: Oxford University Press, 1994), 171–73.

14 S.v. "Taxation," in *The New Volumes of the Encyclopaedia Britannica*, 10th ed.

15 Canada, House of Commons, *Debates*, quoted in Gwyneth McGregor, *Personal Exemptions and Deductions*, 45.

16 Walter L. Gordon, "Post-War Taxation," reprinted from the *Canadian Chartered Accountant*, December 1944, LAC, Finance fonds, RG 19, vol. 211, file 164-P; D.C. Abbott to Alex H. Jeffrey, MP, March 21, 1953, LAC, Finance fonds, RG 19, vol. 631, file 164-GR-1.

17 George Hutchens, Canadian Director, IUE, to Louis St. Laurent, July 26, 1956; W.E. Harris to C.S. Jackson, President, District 5 Council, UE, January 9, 1956 (acknowledging resolutions received); Don Doherty, Secretary of District 4 Council of the International Chemical Workers' Union, to Louis St. Laurent, November 9, 1955, LAC, Finance fonds, RG 19, vol. 631, file 164-GR-1.

18 *Labour Gazette* 49 (1949): 553, 558; 51 (1951): 646, 1472–73, 1487; 52 (1952): 399, 1320–21, 1337; 57 (1957): 683, 1169, 1293, 1297, 1427.

19 Canada, House of Commons, *Debates*, March 21, 1957, 2549; March 27, 1957, 2747; March 30, 1957, 2887; April 1, 1957, 2918, 2936.

20 This is the translation provided to the minister. The phrase "as requested by the Social Crediters" was added by the translator; there was no reference to Social Credit in the original French. J. Chevalier to Walter Harris, April 4, 1956, LAC, Finance fonds, RG 19, vol. 631, file 164-GR-1.

21 S.A. Morrison to Donald Fleming, July 13, 1958, LAC, Finance fonds, RG 19, vol. 4164, file T-3 General.

22 Anonymized to the Prime Minister, August 22, 1959, LAC, Finance fonds, RG 19, vol. 4164, file T-3 General. By "anonymized," I mean that the letter writer's name was redacted under the Access to Information and Privacy regulations.

23 "Lionel Johnson" to J.G. Diefenbaker, May 4, 1950, LAC, Diefenbaker fonds, MG 26-M, vol. 13, doc. 9566.

24 "Ease Grip on Taxpayer," clipping from Halifax newspaper dated September 4, no year, but post-1945, sent to J.G. Diefenbaker by George Drew, LAC, Diefenbaker fonds, MG 26-M, vol. 85, doc. 67821; on Toronto finance views of the exemption (keep it low), see the Royal Bank president's address to shareholders cited above. In 1965, the official poverty line was $3,000; "Labour Finds Some Hot New Issues," *Toronto Daily Star,* December 29, 1965, 6. On Burton's relationship to the King Liberals, see W.L.M. King to J.A. Robb, July 16, 1925, LAC, King fonds, MG 26-J, vol. 141, doc. 104219.

25 Bruce Burroughs to J.G. Diefenbaker, May 11, 1955, LAC, Diefenbaker fonds, MG 26-M, vol. 85, doc. 67946.

26 Mrs. R.D. Bell to Donald Fleming, December 7, 1957, LAC, Finance fonds, RG 19, vol. 4165, file T-3 General.

27 A Pearson Voter to L.B. Pearson, November 1, 1965, LAC, Pearson fonds, MG 26-N3, vol. 52, file 252.21; "Labour Finds Some Hot New Issues," *Toronto Daily Star,* December 29, 1965, 6.

28 "Annie Mae Kavan" to Lester B. Pearson, August 24, 1964; "Thelma Skerry" to Donald Fleming, December 9, 1957, LAC, Finance fonds, RG 19, vol. 4164, file T3-General.

29 "Annie Mae Kavan" to Lester B. Pearson, August 24, 1964; "Thelma Skerry" to Donald Fleming, December 9, 1957; name redacted to Dr. Gordon Chown, MP, March 14, 1960; LAC, Finance fonds, RG 19, vol. 4164, file T3-General; Joseph F. Long to L.B. Pearson, April 6, 1964, LAC, Pearson fonds, MG 26-N3, vol. 53, file 252.232; Lillian Cox to L.B. Pearson, November 12, 1964; Shirley Sullivan to Lester B. Pearson, April 21, 1964, LAC, Pearson fonds, MG 26-N3, vol. 52, file 252.2. "Extravagant" and "unnecessary" are in quotation marks to signal their role as repeated terms in this discourse.

30 See Joseph Arthur Miron to Lester B. Pearson, March 1965 (date-stamped April 1, 1965), LAC, Pearson fonds, MG 26-N3, vol. 52, file 251.2; Stuart Forester to Lester Pearson, May 12, 1965, LAC, Pearson fonds, MG 26-N3, vol. 52, file 251.21; J.S. Lavallée ("chef ouvrière") to Walter Harris (Minister of Finance), with a petition enclosed, March 27, 1956; W.E. Harris to J.S. Lavallée, April 6, 1956; J. Chevalier to Walter Harris, December 26, 1955, LAC, Finance fonds, RG 19, vol. 631, file 164GR-1 1956; James E. Rogers to Lester B. Pearson, March 21, 1962, LAC, Pearson fonds, MG 26-N2, vol. 7, file 252.

31 Canada, House of Commons, *Debates,* June 23, 1942, 3580; April 10, 1951, 1815; Perry, *Taxes, Tariffs, and Subsidies,* 2: 615. A statement of the rationale for the medical expenses deduction given to a taxpayer can be found in W.E. Harris to J.H. Schatz, May 31, 1957, LAC, Finance fonds, RG 19, vol. 4245, file 503-2-2 Medical and Funeral Expenses, 1958.

32 "Tax on Illness," *Globe and Mail,* February 21, 1957, 6.

33 W.C. Clark (Deputy Minister of Finance) to Dr. G.D.W. Cameron (Deputy Minister of National Health), personal and secret, March 30, 1951; Dr. G.D.W. Cameron to W.C. Clark, personal and secret, April 3, 1951, LAC, Finance fonds, RG 19, vol. 631, file 164-GR-2–2/95/A; Dorothy Legg to W.E. Harris (Minister of Finance), November 19, 1954; W.E. Harris to Mrs. M. Legg, December 1, 1954, LAC, Finance fonds, RG 19, vol. 631, file 164-GR-2-2-1955; E.A. Bellhouse to Income Tax Division, Department of National Revenue, July 30, 1957; Harold E. Winch, MP, to G. Nowlan, April 15, 1958; Donald M. Fleming (Minister of Finance) to Elizabeth A. Watt, May 29, 1958; George Nowlan (Minister of National Revenue) to J. Angus MacLean, MP, personal, September 10, 1957, LAC, Finance fonds, RG 19, vol. 4245, file 503-2-2 Medical and Funeral Expenses, 1958.

34 *Labour Gazette* 51 (1951): 1487; 52 (1952): 1320–21; 57 (1957): 157, 683, 1176, 1293, 1297; Audrey VanSickle (Executive Secretary, Canadian Home and School and Parent-Teacher

Federation) to Donald Fleming (Minister of Finance), April 21, 1958, LAC, Finance fonds, RG 19, vol. 4245, file 503-2-2 Medical and Funeral Expenses, 1958.

35 See, for example, "J.H. Somerset" to W. Harris (Minister of Finance), April 30, 1957, LAC, Finance fonds, RG 19, vol. 4245, file 503-2-2 Medical and Funeral Expenses, 1958.

36 Lowell A.S. Allen (Executive Assistant, Minister of Fisheries) to Donald Fleming (Minister of Finance), September 20, 1957; J. Angus MacLean to George Nowlan (Minister of Revenue), August 26, 1957; Wally Nesbitt, MP, to Donald Fleming, confidential, May 28, 1959; "Davie" (Fulton) (Minister of Justice) to Donald (Fleming), July 15, 1957, LAC, Finance fonds, RG 19, vol. 4245, file 503-2-2 Medical and Funeral Expenses, 1958.

37 Perhaps because 1957 was an election year, there are multiple examples of letters dated 1957 from disease charities and interested professional organizations in the misleadingly labelled "1958" Department of Finance file on such matters; see LAC, Finance fonds, RG 19, vol. 4245, file 503-2-2 Medical and Funeral Expenses, 1958.

38 Canada, House of Commons, *Debates,* March 31, 1960, 2682.

39 See, for example, the contents of LAC, Finance fonds, RG 19, vol. 4247, which includes files from 1957 to 1964 of letters under the general heading of Income Tax – Federal – Individuals – Employees – Budget Proposals from the Public. I have reviewed the files concerning Commuters, Students, Farmers and Fishermen, the Armed Forces, Expense Related to Employment, and Public Generally. Such letters also appear in Prime Minister Pearson's files. See, for example, W.S. Lloyd (Premier of Saskatchewan) to L.B. Pearson, March 24, 1964, LAC, Pearson fonds, MG 26-N3, vol. 53, file 252.212 Income Tax Act.

40 G. Stanley Foster to Donald Fleming, August 19, 1957, LAC, Finance fonds, RG 19, vol. 4247, file 5055-03-02 1958.

41 George Palenchuk to "Dear Sir" (Douglas Fisher, MP), March 1, 1964, LAC, Finance fonds, RG 19, vol. 4247, file 5055-03-02.

42 Eaton referenced for this observation the United Kingdom's *Report of the Royal Commission on the Taxation of Profits and Income,* paragraph 152, in his "Memorandum to the Minister re: Canadian Construction Brief, Taxation of Allowances," July 18, 1957, 4, LAC, Finance fonds, RG 19, vol. 4247, file 5055-03-02.

43 Mrs. "A.P. Lambton" to Prime Minister L. Pearson, date-stamped May 5, 1967, LAC, Pearson fonds, MG 26-N3, vol. 54, file 252.211.

44 Michael Wright, "Tax Exemption of Medical Expenses," *Globe and Mail,* February 28, 1957, 6.

45 "Tax on Illness," *Globe and Mail,* February 23, 1957, 6.

46 J.T. Place to J. Angus MacLean, MP, August 21, 1957, LAC, Finance fonds, RG 19, vol. 4245, file 503-2-2 Medical and Funeral Expenses, 1958.

47 Canada, House of Commons, *Debates,* December 10, 1951, 1724, 1725.

48 Canada, House of Commons, *Debates,* April 9, 1959, 2416; J. Harvey Perry, *A Fiscal History of Canada: The Postwar Years* (Toronto: Canadian Tax Foundation, 1989), 51; Gordon Chown, MP, to Donald Fleming, May 20, 1959, LAC, Finance fonds, RG 19, vol. 4164, file T-3 General; T.M. Brown to Donald Fleming, December 8, 1957, LAC, Finance fonds, RG 19, vol. 4165, file T-3 General.

49 Canada, House of Commons, *Debates,* April 10, 1962, 2702–3. For public responses, see "Reactions," *Toronto Daily Star,* December 21, 1960, 29.

50 A. Merkur to J.G. Diefenbaker, October 3, 1960, LAC, Finance fonds, RG 19, vol. 4237, file 5020-03-12.

51 Canada, Royal Commission on Taxation, *Report,* 1: 6; Porter, *Vertical Mosaic,* Preface and Chapter 4.

52 A married, childless breadwinner who earned $10,000 was taxable on $8,000 when the married exemption was $2,000. Increase the married exemption to $3,000, and his or her

taxable income was now only $7,000. If that reduction meant the taxpayer fell into a lower tax bracket, then his or her average rate of taxation would also be lowered.

53 Margaret Conrad, *George Nowlan: Maritime Conservative in National Politics* (Toronto: University of Toronto Press, 1986), 97; "Blames Tax Collectors," letter to the editor, *Toronto Daily Star,* August 15, 1957, 6; telegram from J. Harper Prowse (leader of the Alberta Liberal Party) to W.L.M. King, March 16, 1949, LAC, King fonds, MG 26-J, C-11050, doc. 403025.

54 John Bell to Lester B. Pearson, February 26, 1964, LAC, Pearson fonds, MG 26-N3, vol. 52, file 252.21.

55 Marion H. Bryden, *The Costs of Tax Compliance: A Report on a Survey Conducted by the Canadian Tax Foundation* (Toronto: Canadian Tax Foundation, 1961).

56 "Edwin Barnett" to F.R. Edwards (Superintendent of Administration, Department of National Revenue, Taxation Division), cc'd to J. Gear McEntyre and E.J. Benson, February 26, 1965, LAC, Pearson papers, MG 26-N3, vol. 52, file 252.211-B. Others similarly disturbed by this new regulation were Dr. E.R. Junkin to Lester B. Pearson, stamped "Seen by Prime Minister," August 27, 1965, LAC, Pearson fonds, MG 26-N3, vol. 52, file 252.211, and Sylvia Doran to Lester B. Pearson, August 30, 1967, and October 3, 1967, LAC, Pearson fonds, MG 26-N3, vol. 54, file 252.211-D.

57 Timothy Mitchell, "Economists and the Economy in the Twentieth Century," in *The Politics of Method in the Human Sciences: Positivism and Its Epistemological Others,* ed. George Steinmetz (Durham, NC: Duke University Press, 2005), 133–34.

58 "James T. Gorham" to J. Gear McEntyre (Minister of National Revenue), November 24, 1964, LAC, Pearson fonds, MG 26-N3, vol. 52, file 252.211-G.

59 I.R. Sherwood to Department of National Revenue, attention D. Hazlett, cc to Prime Minister Pearson, December 13, 1963, LAC, Pearson fonds, MG 26-N3, vol. 52, file 252.211; Robert R. Austin to Lester B. Pearson, November 25, 1963, LAC, Pearson fonds, MG 26-N3, vol. 52, file 252.211-A; J.D. McInnes, MD, FICS, FRCS(C), to Roger Mitchell, MP, cc L.B. Pearson, April 16, 1964, LAC, Pearson fonds, MG 26-N3, vol. 53, file 252.211-M; A.P. Edwards to E.J. Benson, cc to Lester B. Pearson, December 18, 1964, LAC, Pearson fonds, MG 26-N3, vol. 52, file 252.211-E; cross-reference sheet re Fred W. Webb to E.J. Benson, December 7, 1964, LAC, Pearson fonds, MG 26-N3, vol. 52, file 252.2. Several copies of a curious petition, date-stamped February 1, 1965, signed by Torontonians and residents of small-town Ontario, were "extreme" in a more left-wing direction: they denied the right of the federal government to tax the incomes of those who had no surplus while offering tax exemptions to those "able to save"; see LAC, Pearson fonds, MG 26-N3,vol. 52, file 252.2; J.G. Diefenbaker to George W. Beilhartz, March 22, 1956, LAC, Diefenbaker fonds, MG 26-M, reel M7419, doc. 12978; and Katherine Binning to J.G. Diefenbaker, June 24, 1955, LAC, Diefenbaker fonds, MG 26-M, reel M7455, doc. 67949.

60 Edith Cooper, RN, to Lester Pearson, April 27, 1964, LAC, Pearson fonds, MG 26-N3, vol. 52, file 252.211; John E. Ball to E.J. Benson, cc to Lester B. Pearson, July 11, 1964, LAC, Pearson fonds, MG 26-N3, vol. 52, file 252.21; "Mrs. G.N. Barker" to Lester B. Pearson, June 12, 1967, LAC, Pearson fonds, MG 26-N3, vol. 54, file 252.211-B.

61 For the 2015 version of the Taxpayer Bill of Rights, see http://www.cra-arc.gc.ca/. Today's legal regime has been shaped in part by the Charter of Rights and Freedoms; this context is described in Jinyan Li, "Taxpayer Rights in Canada," *Revenue Law Journal* 7, 1 (1997): 83–137.

62 "Citizens Abused by 'Little' Income Tax Officials," *Toronto Daily Star,* January 29, 1957, 17, 35.

63 Fraser Robertson, "In Fear of the Law: Looking into Business," *Globe and Mail,* May 8, 1957, 26.

64 Gwyneth McGregor, "Procedure Is Simple. Raw Deal on Income Tax? For $15 You Can Fight It in This Informal Court," *Toronto Daily Star,* September 4, 1957, 6; "Victory Hollow for Taxpayers if Crown Appeals," *Toronto Daily Star,* September 4, 1957, 6.

65 "Until Death Do Them Part," editorial, *Globe and Mail,* September 5, 1957, 6; L.J. Skalle[?], "'Until Death Do Them Part,'" letter to the editor, *Globe and Mail,* September 10, 1957, 6; H. Carrique, "'Disturbing' Tax Cases," letter to the editor, *Globe and Mail,* October 7, 1960, 6; Gwyneth McGregor, "'Disturbing' Tax Cases," *Globe and Mail,* October 15, 1960, 6; John S. Wright (a Toronto tax lawyer), "The Relationship between the Taxpayers and the Tax Collectors," *Globe and Mail,* November 22, 1960, 6.

66 Canada, House of Commons, *Debates,* August 27, 1958, 4180, 4182, 4183–84; "Checks on Returns Uncover $73,120,000, Tax Minister Says," *Globe and Mail,* March 18, 1959, 2; Conrad, *George Nowlan,* 191–94.

67 Jules Pelletier (Secretary to the Prime Minister) to Ben Quan, PEng, May 12, 1964, LAC, Pearson fonds, MG 26-N3, vol. 52, file 252.2.

68 See, for example, LAC, Finance fonds, RG 19, vol. 4236, file 5020-03-03 Interest and Penalty Assessments. This file is in the larger series Income Tax – Federal – Administration – Budget Proposals from the Public. In the same series, see also file 5050-05-A172 Canadian Institute of Chartered Accountants and Canadian Bar Association.

69 Doug Owram, "Economic Thought in the 1930s: The Prelude to Keynesianism," *Canadian Historical Review* 64, 3 (1985): 344–77.

70 John S. Morgan, "Appeals Against Administrative Decisions under Welfare Legislation," *Canadian Public Administration* 4, 1 (1961): 44–60; Struthers, *The Limits of Affluence,* 246–50.

71 For examples of this rhetoric, see sources cited in Chapter 10 describing the Canadian Chamber of Commerce 1962 campaign "Operation Freedom."

72 "Reading Matter to Be Inserted in Educational Feature for Use in Industrial Employees' Magazines" and circular letter to publishers of employees' magazines from G.W. Headly for Director of Public Information, Department of National Revenue, Taxation Division, February 26, 1952, LAC, Finance fonds, RG 19, vol. 452, file 111–14A-0–1 to 5; "Tax Troubles?," *Canadian Homes and Gardens* 28, 4 (1951): 30; Allan Fenton, "Canadians Rush for $60,000,000 Overpaid on Income Taxes, Get Rebate in Few Weeks," *Toronto Daily Star,* April 12, 1952, 12; "$60,000,000 Due Taxpayers Soon in 1951 Refunds," *Globe and Mail,* February 20, 1952, 3.

73 "Official Pocket-Picking," editorial, *Globe and Mail,* June 30, 1951, 6; reprinted from *Winnipeg Tribune,* "Income Tax Changes," *Globe and Mail,* July 9, 1951, 6; "Eager Beavers," editorial, published in sundry rural newspapers such as *Canadian Statesman* [Bowmanville, ON], July 26, 1951, 2; *Didsbury* [AB] *Pioneer,* August 1, 1951, 3; and *Crossfield* [AB] *Chronicle,* July 27, 1951, 2; "Illegal Tax Collections," editorial, *Globe and Mail,* March 11, 1952, 6.

74 "Play to Striped Pants Charged to Liberals," *Globe and Mail,* March 12, 1953, 3; "Tax Balances More Costly than Refunds," *Globe and Mail,* July 27, 1955, 20; Canada, House of Commons, *Debates,* July 26, 1955, 6832–34.

75 My translation. L.P. Demers (Secretary, Lodge 1008) to the Prime Minister, May 28, 1963, LAC, Pearson fonds, vol. 52, file 252.21; "Robert Aylward" to Prime Minister Pearson, March 26, 1968; Richard Lavoie to Prime Minister Pierson [sic], June 12, 1967; Isidore Bernatchez to Dear Sir, March 23, 1968; Mr. and Mrs. G. Lawrence to Whom it may concern, cc Prime Minister Pearson, June 15, 1967; Graham S. Boone to Taxation Data Centre, cc to Prime Minister Pearson, June 22, 1966, LAC, Pearson fonds, vol. 54, file 252.211; Matthew L. Mahoney to Lester B. Pearson, July 13, 1967, LAC, Pearson fonds, MG 26-N3, vol. 54, file 252.211-M.

76 John S. Wright, "The Relationship between the Taxpayers and the Tax Collectors," *Globe and Mail,* November 22, 1960, 6.

77 On problems created by computerization, see Conrad, *George Nowlan,* 192. Computers quickly became one of the culprits that frustrated taxpayers named in their speculations about service problems; see Paul Nadeau to Taxation Division, cc to Lester B. Pearson, date-stamped August 14, 1964, LAC, Pearson fonds, MG 26-N3, vol. 53, file 252.211-N.

78 Canada, House of Commons, *Debates,* July 26, 1955, 6832.

79 *Prairie Farmer's Income Tax Guide and Farm Account Book* (Taxation Division, Department of National Revenue, 1947), LAC, Revenue fonds, RG 16, vol. 1006, file T1 General T1 Special T1 Farmers 1947.

80 Future judge and pioneering lawyer of the interwar years Edra Sanders Ferguson, from St. Thomas, Ontario, listed a similar series of women's occupations needing the benefit of women's labour. With a feminist touch, she added that married women "are not willingly economic parasites." Edra Sanders Ferguson to Louis St. Laurent, February 20, 1951, LAC, Finance fonds, RG 19, vol. 631, file 164-GR-1.

81 Canada, House of Commons, *Debates,* May 28, 1947, 3546–47. Ross's remarks illustrate the warnings of "dire consequences" if the wartime exemption was repealed, to which Perry alludes in his mention of this exemption, among others, being removed in the 1947 budget; see Perry, *Taxes, Tariffs, and Subsidies* 2: 397. A supporter of veterans' wives working wrote in to the *Globe and Mail's* Dear Homemaker correspondence to explain the value of those contributions and got a supportive reply; see "Let Their Wives Help Veterans," *Globe and Mail,* December 18, 1946, 9.

82 *No. 68 v. Minister of National Revenue,* as reported and discussed in Rebecca Johnson, *Taxing Choices: The Intersection of Class, Gender, Parenthood, and the Law* (Vancouver: UBC Press, 2002), 23.

83 Canadian Federation of Business and Professional Women's Clubs, *Memorandum for Presentation to the Royal Commission on Taxation at Toronto, Ontario, on May 8, 1963* (Ottawa: s.n., 1963), 13–14. Support for this issue was offered in "Baby-Sitting: Business Expense," an editorial in the *Vancouver Sun,* reprinted in the *Globe and Mail,* March 2, 1953, 6.

84 "George Francis" to Lester B. Pearson, September 14, 1963, LAC, Pearson fonds, MG 26-N3, vol. 52, file 252–211. Another case of a reassessment based upon a wife's new income was described by the taxpayer in "Christopher Place" to Lester B. Pearson, February 8, 1964, LAC, Pearson fonds, MG 26-N3, vol. 52, file 252–211.

85 Carolyn C. Jones, "Split Income and Separate Spheres: Tax Law and Gender Roles in the 1940s," *Law and History Review* 6, 2 (1988): 266–69. The eight states were California, Louisiana, Texas, Idaho, Washington, Arizona, New Mexico, and Nevada.

86 I address this history in more depth in "The Family as Tax Dodge: Partnership, Individuality, and Gender in the Personal Income Tax Act, 1942 to 1970," *Canadian Historical Review* 90, 3 (2009): 391–425. For descriptions of this history in the United States, see Jones, "Split Income and Separate Spheres," 259–310; Alice Kessler-Harris, "'A Principle of Law but Not of Justice': Men, Women, and Income Taxes in the United States, 1913–1948," *Southern California Review of Law and Women's Studies* 6 (1988–89): 331–60; Canadian Tax Foundation, "Income Splitting between Husband and Wife," in *Report of Proceedings of the Tax Conference Convened by the Canadian Tax Foundation, Sixth Tax Conference* (Toronto: Canadian Tax Foundation, 1952), 47–51; Ann Shipley to Donald Fleming, March 26, 1954, Donald Fleming to Ann Shipley, April 14, 1954, and Ann Shipley to Donald Fleming, April 28, 1954, LAC, Finance fonds, RG 19, vol. 631, file 164-GR-1; and Kenneth Carter to Donald Fleming, November 22, 1957, and attached memo "Community of Property and Taxation," LAC, Finance fonds, RG 19, vol. 4164, file T3 Taxation Inquiries.

87 "Appeal Board Ruling Jars Tax Authorities," *Globe and Mail,* October 5, 1957, 2; "Ease Tax for Quebec Men," *Ottawa Journal,* October 4, 1957, 1; Cabinet Conclusions, October 9,

1957, 5, LAC, Privy Council Office fonds, RG 2, vol. 1893, series A-5-a; J.W. Glendinning (partner in Glendinning, Jarret and Campbell) to Donald Fleming, October 7, 1957, LAC, Finance fonds, RG 19, vol. 4164, file T-3 Taxation Inquiries.

88 *Minister of National Revenue v. Frank Sura,* November 3, 1959, Court Administration Services, Exchequer Court of Canada docket 142374 (contains ruling by Fisher in *Re: The Income Tax Act and Frank Sura,* October 1, 1957); *Minister of National Revenue v. Sura,* Exchequer Court of Canada, 1960 [1959] *Canada Law Reports* 92; *Sura v. Minister of National Revenue,* Supreme Court of Canada, 32 *Dominion Law Reports,* second series, 282. For a closer examination of these judgments, see Tillotson, "The Family as Tax Dodge."

89 Canada, House of Commons, *Debates,* June 20, 1961, 6662.

90 Ibid. and July 10, 1961, 7773; "Fleming Aims to Extend Personal Corporation Tax," *Toronto Daily Star,* June 22, 1961, 8; "Income Tax Act Revisions Delayed," *Ottawa Citizen,* July 10, 1961, 1. The "storm of protest" was noted in "2 Professions Urge Tax Appeal Reform," *Globe and Mail,* February 15, 1962, 26, but searches of the *Toronto Daily Star* and *Globe and Mail,* either by keyword or by browsing July 10–12, after the Liberal finance critic called Fleming's withdrawal of the personal corporation amendments "a real shocker," revealed no coverage of that story.

91 My translation. Julien Bernard to E.J. Benson (Minister of National Revenue), February 1, 1965, LAC, Pearson fonds, MG 26-N3, vol. 52, file 252.21; H.D. Langlais to L.B. Pearson, August 13, 1964, LAC, Pearson fonds, MG 26-N3, vol. 52, file 252.211. Biographical information on Langlais comes from http://www.assnat.qc.ca/fr/deputes/langlais-hormisdas-3951/biographie.html.

92 Jules Pelletier to H.D. Langlais, August 18, 1964, and "Memorandum to the Honourable the Minister of National Revenue re: H.D. Langlais," with a draft letter for the prime minister's signature, August 27, 1964, LAC, Pearson fonds, MG 26-N3, vol. 52, file 252.211.

93 Georges-William Garns to F. Simard (Quebec City National Revenue Office), cc Lester B. Pearson, July 9, 1964, LAC, Pearson fonds, MG 26-N3, vol. 52, file 252.211.

94 My translation. Armand Théroux to J.M. Laverdure, cc Lester B. Pearson, August 20, 1963, LAC, Pearson fonds, MG 26-N3, vol. 52, file 252.21.

95 Dominique Clift, "Little Result Seen in Tax Drive," *Globe and Mail,* May 9, 1960, 12.

96 My translation. Lieutenant Colonel Oscar Gilbert (President, *Le Soleil* and *L'Événement-Journal*) to J.G. Diefenbaker, January 28, 1961, LAC, Diefenbaker fonds, MG 26-M, reel M-9312, doc. 24005.

97 Maurice Boucher to District Tax Office, Quebec, re demande de renseignments, May 26, 1965, and E.J. Benson to Maurice Bourassa, copy for the Prime Minister's Office, February 19, 1965, LAC, Pearson fonds, MG 26-N3, vol. 52, file 252.211-B; George J. McIlraith to Lionel Hardy, June 26, 1964, and Lionel Hardy to George J. McIlraith, July 8, 1964, LAC, Pearson fonds, MG 26-N3, vol. 52, file 252.211-H; "Memorandum to the Honourable the Minister of National Revenue re: Mrs. Arthur Munger, Sullivan Mines, Quebec," from D.H. Sheppard, September 30, 1964, and E.J. Benson to Mrs. Arthur Munger, October 17, 1964, LAC, Pearson fonds, MG 26-N3, vol. 52, file 252.211-M; Dominique Clift, "Little Result Seen in Tax Drive," *Globe and Mail,* May 9, 1960, 12.

98 Robert Wardhaugh, *Behind the Scenes: The Life and Work of William Clifford Clark* (Toronto: University of Toronto Press, 2010), 291–94, 306–13; Ronald M. Burns, *The Acceptable Mean: The Tax Rental Agreements, 1941–1962* (Toronto: Canadian Tax Foundation, 1980), 49–52.

99 Wardhaugh, *Behind the Scenes,* 297, 308.

100 Black, *Duplessis* (Toronto: McClelland and Stewart, 1977), 414. The "power to govern" point was frequently used in Duplessis's speeches on federal-provincial relations; see 411.

101 Referring to the state's fiscal resources as the sinews of power dates back in the English tradition to at least the seventeenth century. See John Brewer, *The Sinews of Power: War,*

Money, and the English State, 1688–1783 (London: Unwin Hyman, 1989). See also Kenneth A. Schultz and Barry R. Weingast, "The Democratic Advantage: Institutional Foundations of Financial Power in International Competition," *International Organization* 57, 1 (2003): 3–42.

102 "Brief Submitted to the Hon. Maurice leNoblet Duplessis … by the Chamber of Commerce of the Province of Quebec on Federal-Provincial Relations in Matters of Taxation," November 26, 1952, QUA, Dexter fonds, collection 2142, box 18, file 154; Province of Quebec, Royal Commission of Inquiry on Constitutional Problems, *Report*, vol. 1 (Quebec: Province of Quebec, 1956), 150–54, 197–214, 291–94, 365–76; Dale C. Thomson, *Louis St. Laurent: Canadian* (Toronto: Macmillan of Canada, 1967), 377–81; Roland Parenteau, "Commentaires: Autonomie et réalisme politique," *L'actualité économique* 31, 2 (1955): 279–80.

103 F.R. Scott, "The Special Nature of Canadian Federalism," *Canadian Journal of Economics and Political Science* 13, 1 (1947): 13–14, 25.

104 Quoted in Wardhaugh, *Behind the Scenes*, 310.

105 T. Stephen Henderson, *Angus L. Macdonald: A Provincial Liberal* (Toronto: University of Toronto Press, 2007); Struthers, *The Limits of Affluence*, 113, 123–25. For a mention of Manning's views and a greater emphasis on the federal Liberals' own hesitations about the welfare state, see Alvin Finkel, "Paradise Postponed: A Re-Examination of the Green Book Proposals of 1945," *Journal of the Canadian Historical Association* 4, 1 (1993): 120–42.

106 "Labor Blasts Duplessis Report Is 'Revolutionary,'" *Toronto Daily Star*, April 18, 1956, 2.

107 Note that the income tax introduced in 1935 by the provincial government was a municipal income tax, and the province had long taxed corporation income.

108 Thomson, *Louis St. Laurent*, 371–72; "Duplessis Tax Rake-Off Fine Seen $1,000,000," *Toronto Daily Star*, March 23, 1954, 1, 2; "Duplessis' Tax Feud to Keep Out Industry 'Sorry Day' – Business," *Toronto Daily Star*, April 23, 1954, 22; "St. Laurent Answers Drew's Duplessis Plea by Quoting from Frost," *Toronto Daily Star*, May 4, 1954, 1; "Plain Talk to Mr. Duplessis. From the *Ottawa Citizen*," *Toronto Daily Star*, April 12, 1965, 6; "Drew Courts Quebec Asks Ottawa [to] Bow to Duplessis Tax Plan," *Toronto Daily Star*, May 5, 1954, 4; "National Unity at Stake," editorial, *Toronto Daily Star*, September 23, 1954, 6; "The Federal-Provincial Tax Problem," radio address by Minister of Finance Walter Harris on *The Nation's Business* (CBC), March 4, 1944, LAC, Diefenbaker fonds, MG 26-M, vol. 85, reel M7452, doc. 67909. The Montreal *Gazette* placed the responsibility on Ottawa: "Whether they will pay this increase or not will depend upon the attitude that Ottawa adopts." Quoted in "Quebec Wants Too Much," editorial, *Toronto Daily Star*, February 13, 1954, 4.

109 "St. Laurent Will Offer Duplessis Concession on Income Tax for Unity" and "St. Laurent, Duplessis Ready to Square Off in 'Battle of Taxes,'" *Toronto Daily Star*, October 4, 1954, 1; Thomson, *Louis St. Laurent*, 384.

110 Thomson, *Louis St. Laurent*, 372–73, 384; Black, *Duplessis*, 435–47, 439–41; Province of Quebec, Royal Commission of Inquiry on Constitutional Problems, *Report*, vol. 1 (Quebec: Province of Quebec, 1956), 152–53; Parenteau, "Commentaires," 274–75.

111 Hadley Cantril, *Public Opinion, 1935–1946* (Princeton, NJ: Princeton University Press, 1951), 846.

112 Black, *Duplessis*, 421.

113 Daniel Latouche, *Canada and Quebec, Past and Future: An Essay* (Toronto: University of Toronto Press, 1983), 27–34, 39–56.

114 Penny Bryden has explained the comparable contribution made by Ontario in *"A Justifiable Obsession": Conservative Ontario's Relations with Ottawa, 1943–1985* (Toronto: University of Toronto Press, 2013).

115 Six of seven federal seats were Liberal in the 1962 federal election, and all seven went Liberal in 1963. Raymond B. Blake, "Canada, Newfoundland, and Term 29: The Failure of Intergovernmentalism," *Acadiensis* 41, 1 (2012): 49–74.

116 Richard M. Bird and N. Enid Slack, *Urban Public Finance in Canada* (Toronto: Butterworth, 1983), 14–15; Enid Slack, Almos Tassonyi, and Richard Bird, "Reforming Ontario's Property Tax System: A Never-Ending Story?," Institute of Land Policy Paper 0706, September 2007, 10. Various contemporary studies testify to this stress; see New Brunswick, Royal Commission on Finance and Municipal Taxation, *Report* (Fredericton: Royal Commission on Finance and Municipal Taxation, 1963), 66–68 and Chapter 8; Saskatchewan, Committee on Provincial-Municipal Relations, *Report* (Regina: King's Printer for Saskatchewan, 1951), 35, 92; "Where a Taxpayer Revolt Is Starting," clipping, *U.S. News and World Report,* November 26, 1962, 60–62, QUA, H. Carl Goldenberg fonds, collection 3648, box 18/27, file Montreal Real Estate Tax Commission, 1963; Halifax, Commission to Investigate the Taxation System in the City of Halifax, *Report* (Halifax: privately printed, 1957), 8–16; Lawrence Sandford, City Clerk-Treasurer, Sydney, NS, "Municipal Sources of Revenue," paper presented to the twenty-first refresher course offered for municipal finance officers by the Department of Municipal Affairs, Halifax, October 24–26, 1962. A letter to the editor from "Taxpayer" in Toronto listed annual increases of his or her property tax from $110 in 1949 to $221 in 1958. He or she might well have snorted at the idea that property tax wasn't "elastic"; see "Tax Rises," *Toronto Daily Star,* March 16, 1960, 6.

117 "Taxpayers Sink Deeper in Debt as Levy Soars," *Toronto Daily Star,* October 5, 1959, 9; "Unpaid Taxes Delay Loan," *Toronto Daily Star,* February 20, 1959, 9; "Cut City Taxes on Poor Families?," *Toronto Daily Star,* March 30, 1960, 2.

118 "Parents of 27 Children Lose Home over Taxes," *Toronto Daily Star,* February 19, 1959, 1; New Brunswick, Department of Provincial Secretary-Treasurer, *Report of the Royal Commission on the Rates and Taxes Act* (Fredericton: Royal Commission on the Rates and Taxes Act, 1951), 60, 63.

119 These steps were summarized in the dossier on property taxation prepared for the CLC Citizenship Month 1968. The theme of the month was taxation. The Carter Commission report was covered, but there was also a substantial section on property taxation. See George Home, circular letter to councils, federations, et cetera on Citizenship Month 1968, LAC, CLC fonds, MG 28 I103, no box number, reel H-655.

120 D.A. Gordon to Edgar Benson, November 8, 1967, LAC, Benson fonds, R1272, vol. 7, file 7-4.

121 Mitchell Sharp, "Tax Reform: The Fiscal Context," address to the Conference of the Canadian Tax Foundation, April 26, 1967, 8–9, LAC, Finance fonds, RG 19, vol. 4389, file 1967.

122 Notes for an address by Minister of Finance Walter Gordon, to be delivered at a meeting of the Edmonton West Federal Constituency Association, Edmonton, January 28, 1964, 1, 4, 5, LAC, Finance fonds, RG 19, vol. 4389, file 1964.

123 J.G.D. (Diefenbaker) to Donald M. Fleming, March 22, 1962; T.P. Simpson to John Pratt, MP, with *Montreal Star* clipping, March 17, 1962; R. John Pratt, MP, to Donald M. Fleming, March 27, 1962; and F.I. Irwin, "Deduction of School Taxes for Purposes of Personal Income Tax," memorandum to Minister of Finance, March 30, 1962, LAC, Finance fonds, RG 19, vol. 4242, file 5050-03-1 1962–64; resolutions, National House Builders Association, January 11, 1957; Reeve and Council, United Townships of Neelon and Garson to Minister of Finance, February 12, 1957; and George Farr, Clerk-Treasurer, Township of Bertie, to Minister of Finance Harris, March 5, 1967, LAC, Finance fonds, RG 19, vol. 4242, file 5050-03-1 1957; R.H. Cooper (City Clerk), City of London, to L.B. Pearson, March 27, 1965,

LAC, Pearson fonds, MG 26-N3, vol. 53, file 252.23; Doug McKissack, Chairman, Local 535, UE Legislative Committee to Donald Fleming, March 23, 1962, LAC, Finance fonds, RG 19, vol. 4242, file 5050-03-1 1962. However much Finance argued against this idea, it would not die: during the White Paper debate in the summer of 1970, a senior member of the investment community suggested it as a help to lower-income Canadians, along with mortgage interest deductibility, and a municipal council recommended it; see W.B. McDonald (President, A.E. Ames) to Alastair Gillespie, LAC, Gillespie fonds, R1256, vol. 22, file 1.

Chapter 10: Reform and Populism in the 1960s

1   Andrée Fortin, "La participation: Des comités de citoyens au mouvement communautaire," in *La participation politique: Leçons des dernières décennies,* ed. Jacques T. Godbout (Québec: Institut québécois de la culture, 1991), 291–50; Gordon Selman, *Citizenship and the Adult Education Movement in Canada* (Vancouver: Centre for Continuing Education, University of British Columbia, 1991), Chapter 6; Peter Clancy, "Concerted Planning on the Periphery? Voluntary Economic Planning in 'the New Nova Scotia,'" *Acadiensis* 26, 2 (1997): 3–30; Shirley Tillotson, *The Public at Play: Gender and the Politics of Recreation in Post-War Ontario* (Toronto: University of Toronto Press, 2000); Ron Kuban, *Edmonton's Urban Villages: The Community League Movement* (Edmonton: University of Alberta Press, 2005).

2   John Porter, *The Vertical Mosaic: An Analysis of Social Class and Power in Canada* (Toronto: University of Toronto Press, 1965), 26–27; Eric Hoffer, *The True Believer* (New York: Harper and Brothers, 1951), 151–66; John Rawls, *A Theory of Justice* (Cambridge, MA: Harvard University Press, 1971).

3   Rawls set out the problem in *A Theory of Justice,* but many readers, including me, find his ideas more accessible in John Rawls, *Justice as Fairness: A Restatement,* ed. Erin Kelly (Cambridge, MA: Harvard University Press, 2001).

4   Rawls, *Justice as Fairness,* 91–92. There is a large literature on the process of giving public reasons that Rawls makes central to justice. This is the deliberative democracy literature summarized to 1998 in James Bohman, "The Coming Age of Deliberative Democracy," *Journal of Political Philosophy* 6, 4 (1998): 400–25. The current that particularly interests me here – the related roles of (social) science reasons and emotions – is summarized and advanced by Cheryl Hall in "Recognizing the Passion in Deliberation: Toward a More Democratic Theory of Deliberative Democracy," *Hypatia* 22, 4 (2007): 81–95.

5   Canada, House of Commons, *Debates,* June 18, 1971, 6895; "Capital Gains Tax on January 1," *Globe and Mail,* June 19, 1971, 1–2. I note here what appears to be a disagreement with Linda McQuaig, whose discussion of this episode in tax reform concludes that "the majority of voters ... ended up worse off." She might have underestimated the size of the low-income group, but in Benson's count they were in the majority. See Linda McQuaig, *Behind Closed Doors: How the Rich Won Control of Canada's Tax System ... and Ended Up Richer* (Markham, ON: Penguin Books Canada, 1987), 179.

6   One narrative of the role of taxation in state formation suggests that, the more a state relies on direct taxes (as distinct from resource rents) for revenues, the greater the development of democracy in the form of political participation of citizens in revenue-bargaining processes. See Mick Moore, "Between Coercion and Contract: Competing Narratives on Taxation and Governance," in *Taxation and State-Building in Developing Countries: Capacity and Consent,* ed. Deborah Brautigam et al. (Cambridge, UK: Cambridge University Press, 2008), 39.

7   Elections Canada, "Voter Turnout at Federal Elections and Referendums," http://www.elections.ca/content.aspx?dir=turn&document=index&lang=e&section=ele.

8 C. Joseph Muise to George Nowlan (Finance Minister), November 18, 1962, LAC, Finance fonds, RG 19, vol. 4242, file 5050–03–1. A francophone Montrealer made a similar point in 1957 that low-earning workers were "les plus nombreux voteurs" and that the Liberals had been brought down earlier that year because the personal income tax deductions had not satisfied the "petit salariés"; see J.E. Robert to Monsieur le Ministre, date-stamped December 9, 1957, LAC, Finance fonds, RG 19, vol. 4243, file 5050–03–2 1958 vol. 1.

9 A useful research project would be to compare constituency files of different MPs over time and across regions and parties to see how typical Pearson's and Diefenbaker's were in the relative quantity of tax case work. In impressionistic terms, I can say that Fielding's, King's, Bennett's, and Rhodes's included less of that type of correspondence.

10 My observation here is based upon what appears to be a full subseries of Diefenbaker's constituency files, though organization of the records does not allow me to be confident that I was able to find all of the relevant files. The examples here illustrate a pattern. J.B. and Eveline Eckel to John G. Diefenbaker, January 10, 1949, LAC, Diefenbaker fonds, MG 26-M, reel M7419, doc. 9557; John G. Diefenbaker to J.B. and Eveline Eckel, January 16, 1949, LAC, Diefenbaker fonds, MG 26-M, reel M7419, doc. 9560; John G. Diefenbaker to Mr. Hodgins, March 27, 1953, LAC, Diefenbaker fonds, MG 26-M, reel M7419, doc. 9564; John G. Diefenbaker to Leo Jackson, May 10, 1950, LAC, Diefenbaker fonds, MG 26-M, reel M7419, doc. 9567; John G. Diefenbaker to George W. Beilhartz, March 22, 1956, LAC, Diefenbaker fonds, MG 26-M, reel M7419, doc. 12978.

11 D.R.C. Bedson (private secretary to the Prime Minister) to "Joan Nielson," with a notation in Diefenbaker's handwriting, cc Minister of Finance, February 19, 1958, LAC, Finance fonds, RG 19, vol. 4545, file 503-4-2.

12 Item 25, August 29, 1962, LAC, Privy Council Office, RG2, Series A-5-a, vol. 6193, cabinet conclusions database, http://www.bac-lac.gc.ca/eng/discover/politics-government/cabinet-conclusions/.

13 My point here is based upon my reading of all the tax-related letters in Pearson's constituency files as an opposition MP, LAC, Pearson fonds, MG 26-N2, vol. 69.

14 "Dr. Richard F. Andrews" to Lester B. Pearson, November 25, 1963; L.B. Pearson to "Dr. Andrews," December 2, 1963; and John R. Garland to "Dr. Andrews," December 9, 1963, LAC, Pearson fonds, MG 26-N3, vol. 52, file 252.211-A.

15 John T. Saywell, ed., *Canadian Annual Review for 1961* (Toronto: University of Toronto Press, 1962), 79–80; John T. Saywell, ed., *Canadian Annual Review for 1962* (Toronto: University of Toronto Press, 1963), 11, 22–27.

16 J. Harvey Perry, *A Fiscal History of Canada: The Postwar Years* (Toronto: Canadian Tax Foundation, 1989), 389.

17 Daniel Leclerc to E.J. Benson, September 26, 1965, LAC, Pearson fonds, MG 26-N3, vol. 53, file 252.211-L.

18 Saywell, *Canadian Annual Review for 1962*, 26.

19 Maurice Pinard, *The Rise of a Third Party: A Study in Crisis Politics* (Englewood Cliffs, NJ: Prentice-Hall, 1971), 112–13.

20 Flyer for *Journal vers demain*, a Montreal publication linked to the Créditistes, with an attached flyer about the case of the family of Héliodore Cyr, a New Brunswick Acadian, "Pour combattre la pauvreté! Pour empêcher la vente des maisons pour les taxes! Pour faire reculer les communistes!" LAC, Diefenbaker fonds, MG 26-M, reel M9312, doc. 24035, c. 1961. One tax protester made a link specifically to the role as Créditiste organizer; see "Memorandum to the Honourable the Minister of National Revenue re: Mrs. Arthur Munger, Sullivan Mines, Quebec," from D.H. Sheppard, September 30, 1964, LAC, Pearson fonds, MG 26-N3, vol. 52, file 252.211-M.

21 A. Kenneth Eaton, *Essays in Taxation* (Toronto: Canadian Tax Foundation, 1966), 132–56. His views were well known before 1966, however. His speech at the 1961 Canadian Tax Foundation annual meeting became the subject of an editorial in the *Globe and Mail*. See "Shifting the Tax Load," *Globe and Mail*, November 27, 1961, 6.

22 "A.K. Eaton: Tax Authority Held High Post in Government," *Globe and Mail*, June 2, 1965, 2; "Eaton, Albert Kenneth (26038)," LAC, Ministry of the Overseas Military Forces of Canada fonds, RG 150, Accession 1992–93/166, vol. 2812–22, item 371833; R.B. Bryce, *Maturing in Hard Times: Canada's Department of Finance through the Great Depression* (Kingston, ON: McGill-Queen's University Press, 1986), 111.

23 Eaton, *Essays in Taxation*, 133–39.

24 Ibid., 138, 155.

25 Ibid., 25–26, 126–28, 148.

26 Ibid., 154.

27 Ibid., 30, 133.

28 For descriptions of the "operation" and a worried comment about Birchism from a business journalist, see "Canadian Chamber of Commerce Launches 'Operation Freedom,'" *Medicine Hat News*, January 10, 1962, 8; also see "Face Threats to Freedom, Nation Asked," *Globe and Mail*, January 11, 1962, 5, and Fraser Robertson, "Losing a Freedom Lurking Danger in Crusades," *Globe and Mail*, January 11, 1962, 28. For a study of John Birch Society methods, see Randle James Hart, "The Truth in Time: Robert Welch, the John Birch Society, and the American Conservative Movement, 1900–1972" (PhD diss., University of Toronto, 2007), 163–72.

29 "The Seeds of Campaign Issues," editorial, *Globe and Mail*, July 10, 1961, 6.

30 "Face Threats to Freedom, Nation Asked," *Globe and Mail*, January 11, 1962, 5.

31 "Chamber of Commerce Attacked for Campaign," *Globe and Mail*, February 19, 1962, 22.

32 "The Need Is Clear," editorial, *Kingsville Reporter*, April 19, 1962, 4.

33 "Trade Board Rejects Operation Freedom; Dislikes Methods," April 11, 1962, 20; "Chamber's Operation Freedom Is Really Blowing Up a Storm," *Brandon Sun*, May 18, 1962, 19; "Freedom Drive Called Brainwash," *Globe and Mail*, March 13, 1962, 4; "Chamber's Move Draws Criticism, *Medicine Hat News*, April 9, 1962, 5; "CCC Campaign Is Attacked," *Lethbridge Herald*, January 30, 1962, 3.

34 Park Teter, "Operation Freedom!!," *Globe and Mail*, April 11, 1962, 7; "Chamber of Commerce Freedom Seminar for City," *Brandon Sun*, March 20, 1962, 1.

35 "Trade Board Rejects Operation Freedom; Dislikes Methods," *Globe and Mail*, April 11, 1962, 20.

36 Dan Azoulay, *Keeping the Dream Alive: The Survival of the Ontario CCF/NDP, 1950–1963* (Montreal: McGill-Queen's University Pres, 1997), 190–91; Saywell, *Canadian Annual Review for 1962*, 11–12; "Chamber of Commerce Attacked for Campaign," *Globe and Mail*, February 19, 1962, 22; "Roadblocks for Operation Freedom," editorial, *Ottawa Citizen*, April 14, 1962, 6.

37 "Will Review Tax Laws, Dief Says. Main Tory Plank Revealed by PM in Keynote Speech," *Winnipeg Free Press*, May 7, 1962, 1–2; "PM Promises Review on Canadian Tax Laws," *Globe and Mail*, May 7, 1962, 1–2.

38 "Will Review Tax Laws, Dief Says. Main Tory Plank Revealed by PM in Keynote Speech," *Winnipeg Free Press*, May 7, 1962, 2; "Mr. Diefenbaker Repents," editorial, *Toronto Daily Star*, May 7, 1962, 6.

39 Leslie Macdonald, "Taxing Comprehensive Income: Power and Participation in Canadian Politics, 1962–72" (PhD diss., Carleton University, 1985), 130–34; McQuaig, *Behind Closed Doors*, 128–31.

40 "Liberal Promises Could Boost Income Tax 50 p.c. – Fleming," *Toronto Daily Star,* May 3, 1962, 21; "PM Promises Review of Canadian Tax Laws," *Globe and Mail,* May 7, 1962, 1; "PM Asks Quebec for Full Backing," *Globe and Mail,* May 8, 1962, 1; "Mike Ignored Threat of Communism – P.M.," *Toronto Daily Star,* May 15, 1962, 10; "Liberals Wallowing in Doom – Fleming," *Toronto Daily Star,* May 23, 1962, 39; Saywell, *Canadian Annual Review for 1962,* 9–10.

41 McQuaig, *Behind Closed Doors,* 138–41; J. Harvey Perry, "Background and Main Recommendations of the Royal Commission on Taxation," in *The Quest for Tax Reform: The Royal Commission on Taxation Twenty Years Later,* ed. W. Neil Brooks (Toronto: Carswell, 1988), 25–28. On Perry's role in the Canadian Foundation for Economic Education, I thank Joseph F. Clark, who responded to my queries on June 30 and July 2, 2014, in his capacity as the director of communications for that organization.

42 PC 1962–1334, as reproduced in Canada, Royal Commission on Taxation, *Report,* 1: v–vi.

43 Canada, Royal Commission on Taxation, *Report,* 6: 187–215.

44 Summary adapted from Perry, "Background and Main Recommendations of the Royal Commission on Taxation," 28–34.

45 Press release by William Mahoney, United Steelworkers of America, regarding "Memorandum to Finance Minister Mitchell Sharp on the Report of the Royal Commission on Taxation," October 27, 1967, LAC, CLC fonds, MG28-I103, reel H921, series Donald MacDonald subject files, file Royal Commission on Taxation; "MP Murphy Warns Tax Idea Could Cut Pay," clipping, *Sault Daily Star* [Sault Ste. Marie], February 22, 1969, reel H644, file Citizenship Month 1970; McQuaig, *Behind Closed Doors,* 151.

46 McQuaig, *Behind Closed Doors,* 150–51; R.B. Bryce, "Implementing the Report: Processes and Issues," in *The Quest for Tax Reform: The Royal Commission on Taxation Twenty Years Later,* ed. W. Neil Brooks (Toronto: Carswell, 1988), 39–42; Ronald Robertson, "The House of Commons Committee and the Aftermath of the Royal Commission on Taxation," in *The Quest for Tax Reform: The Royal Commission on Taxation Twenty Years Later,* ed. W. Neil Brooks (Toronto: Carswell, 1988), 44–45; Canada, Royal Commission on Taxation, *Report,* 1: 51–112, especially 60–61, 107–9.

47 Kenneth LeM. Carter, "Canadian Tax Reform and Henry Simons," *Journal of Law and Economics* 11, 2 (1968): 242.

48 Reginald Whitaker, "Reason Passion Interest," in *A Sovereign Idea: Essays on Canada as a Democratic Community* (Montreal: McGill-Queen's University Press, 1991), 154; G. Bruce Doern, "The Policy-Making Philosophy of Prime Minister Trudeau and His Advisers," in *Apex of Power: The Prime Minister and Political Leadership in Canada,* ed. T.A. Hockin (Scarborough, ON: Prentice-Hall, 1971), 127–34.

49 J.W. Pickersgill (Minister of Transport) to Ross Thatcher, personal and confidential, June 24, 1967, LAC, Sharp fonds, MG32-B41, vol. 108, file 20.

50 E.J. Benson, Minister of Finance, *Proposals for Tax Reform* (Ottawa: Queen's Printer for Canada, 1969).

51 Ibid., 9–13; McQuaig, *Behind Closed Doors,* 159–64.

52 Canada, House of Commons, *Debates,* June 18, 1971, 6893; December 16, 1971, 10534.

53 On the developments in the intervening years, see Duncan McDowall, *Sum of the Satisfactions: Canada in the Age of National Accounting* (Montreal: McGill-Queen's University Press, 2008).

54 A. Paul Pross, *Group Politics and Public Policy,* 2nd ed. (Toronto: Oxford University Press, 1992), 57–74. Although Pross argues that, for many parts of the government, organized pressure groups became important to the civil service policy function only in the mid- to late 1960s, he notes that K.W. Taylor as deputy minister of finance acknowledged in 1953 a growing interaction in his department with lobbyists at least. This accords with my sense that Finance was actively engaged in policy consultation during the 1950s.

55 Meyer Bucovetsky and Richard M. Bird, "Tax Reform in Canada: A Progress Report," *National Tax Journal* 25, 1 (1972): 39.

56 "Worst Fears of Business World Confirmed by Carter Proposals," *Globe and Mail,* February 25, 1967, 1; S.C. Legge to Eugene Forsey, June 20, 1967, LAC, CLC fonds, MG 28 I103, reel H-920, series Donald MacDonald subject files, file Royal Commission on Taxation; Bucovetsky and Bird, "Tax Reform in Canada"; Geoffrey Hale, *The Politics of Taxation in Canada* (Toronto: University of Toronto Press, 2002), 53–54.

57 David Lewis, *Louder Voices: The Corporate Welfare Bums* (Toronto: James Lewis and Samuel, 1972), 99–100; Robert Gardner, "Tax Reform and Class Interests: The Fate of Progressive Reform, 1967–72," *Canadian Taxation* 3, 4 (1981): 245–57; McQuaig, *Behind Closed Doors,* 147–50; W. Neil Brooks, "The Royal Commission on Taxation Twenty Years Later: An Overview," in *The Quest for Tax Reform: The Royal Commission on Taxation Twenty Years Later,* ed. W. Neil Brooks (Toronto: Carswell, 1988), 3–20.

58 "Carter and Tax Change," editorial, reprint, Toronto *Telegram,* February 25, 1967, LAC, Sharp fonds, MG32-B41, vol. 108, file 20 Royal Commission on Taxation 1966–67.

59 Lewis, *Louder Voices,* 99; Gardner, "Tax Reform and Class Interests," 245–57; Les Macdonald, "Why Carter Had to Be Stopped," in *The Quest for Tax Reform: The Royal Commission on Taxation Twenty Years Later,* ed. W. Neil Brooks (Toronto: Carswell, 1988), 359–63; McQuaig, *Behind Closed Doors,* Chapter 4; David G. Duff, "The Abolition of Wealth Transfer Taxes: Lessons from Canada, Australia, and New Zealand," *Pittsburgh Tax Review* 3, 1 (2005): 119.

60 Lewis, *Louder Voices,* Chapter 1.

61 Doug Owram, *The Government Generation: Canadian Intellectuals and the State, 1900–1945* (Toronto: University of Toronto Press, 1986); McDowall, *The Sum of the Satisfactions.*

62 Pierre Elliott Trudeau, "Federalism, Nationalism, and Reason," in *Federalism and the French Canadians* (Toronto: Macmillan of Canada, 1968), 182–203; John English, *Citizen of the World: The Life of Pierre Elliott Trudeau,* vol. 1 (Toronto: Vintage Canada, 2007), 391–92.

63 Macdonald, "Taxing Comprehensive Income," 571–72, 592–93.

64 The series with this title covers 1956–69 and is located in the Department of Finance fonds. As with all such collections, it is impossible to know whether the archival holdings are complete or selected. Before 1956, such letters formed part of the central registry subject files under headings such as "Taxation Inquiries."

65 Donald M. Fleming, *So Very Near: The Rising Years,* vol. 1 (Toronto: McClelland and Stewart, 1985), 483–84. Eaton, Finance's tax specialist from 1934 until his retirement in 1957, describes the process in similar terms in *Essays in Taxation,* 19–20. There is still an online version of this call for comment. Various organizations contribute proposals, as do some distinguished individual tax scholars.

66 "Text of Address by the Honourable Mitchell Sharp, Minister of Finance, at a Luncheon of the Women's Canadian Club of Ottawa, Chateau Laurier Hotel, April 21, 1966," LAC, Finance fonds, RG 19, vol. 4389, file 1966.

67 In the accessioning of these records as part of the Department of Finance fonds, the archivists preserved only three volumes – approximately a metre of records; see LAC, Finance fonds, RG 19, vols. 4778–80. These volumes contain twenty-six files of various thicknesses. Letters were filed alphabetically by last name of correspondent within these files, each of which was defined by interest or issue or under "generally." It appears that the archivists preserved only one file (e.g., the P file or R file) from each alphabetically organized topical series. An additional volume includes White Paper correspondence from the public with respect to legislation; see LAC, Finance fonds, RG 19, vol. 5222. I selected from these four volumes a sample of letters from corporate interest groups and individual industry/sectoral organizations. In addition, I read all of the files that represented public opinion: that is, letter writers not representing an industry but speaking as consumers or citizens or both. This

is not to say that they were not speaking from their own interests but that they were writing as individuals without the mediation of an industry association. They described themselves as employees, professionals, housewives, farmers, retirees, people with disabilities, owners of small businesses, and municipal politicians, to name a few. Reports from the White Paper correspondence unit during 1970 tracked the numbers of letters under various categories: those in support of or against it, by region, by issues raised, and by group (e.g., distinguishing between "citizens" and "business"); see LAC, Benson fonds, R1272, vol. 24, file 24-2.

68 Examples of budget problems and associated anger can be found in the notes to the rest of this chapter. Some examples of support for the White Paper from grateful people from low-income groups can be found in R.H. Rattray to Edgar Benson, December 1, 1969; M.L. Reynolds to Edgar Benson, date-stamped December 4, 1969; and Mr. and Mrs. R. Ritchie to Edgar Benson, date-stamped December 4, 1969, LAC, Finance fonds, RG 19, vol. 4778, file 5013-07-1 General R.

69 A record of some of these attempts to reach out to a broad public resides in the papers of Allistair Gillespie, chair of half of the parliamentary committee that toured Ontario and the west during the last two weeks of July 1970. See Michael Gillan (special assistant to Edgar Benson) to Liberal MPs, February 20, 1970, LAC, Gillespie fonds, R1526, vol. 20, file 17. In addition to the replies sent out by the Ministry of Finance, one BC MP, Minister of Fisheries Jack Davis, worked hard to consult and communicate with his constituents and to explain and defend the White Paper proposals. A dossier dated March 16, 1970, summarizing his constituents' views, his systematic and lucid responses to criticisms of the White Paper, and clippings of his "Ottawa Diary" column in the *Lions Gate Times* can be found in LAC, Gillespie fonds, R1526, vol. 22, file 2.

70 R.V. Brouillard and P.S. Elder to Edgar Benson regarding "White Paper Correspondence Unit," May 15, 1970; D.J. Orchard to Brian Huggins regarding "Details of Minister's Mail Handling by Other Departments," May 26, 1970; and D.J. Orchard to the Minister regarding "White Paper Correspondence – Cumulative Report to September 25, 1970," September 29, 1970, LAC, Benson fonds, R1272, vol. 24, file 24-41. See also a response by MP Barnett Danson to the instigator of one of these campaigns: Barnett Danson to Colin M. Brown, June 22, 1970, LAC, Benson fonds, R1272, vol. 24, file 24-28.

71 Attempting to reach the broadest possible public, Michael Gillan designed a television and radio campaign with the help of an ad agency media specialist; see Ralph Draper, Vice-President Special Projects, Vickers, and Edgar Benson to Mike Gillan, September 12, 1969, LAC, Benson fonds, R1272, vol. 24, file 24-9. Many of the letters sent to Benson in the earliest days of the debate refer to the writer having seen him on TV or having heard him on radio. The public debate began with an appearance by Benson on the public affairs program *W5* on November 7, 1969 (the day that the White Paper was tabled in Parliament), coverage in newspapers (e.g., Jack Cahill, "Tax Plans Hit $10,000 and Up," *Toronto Daily Star*, November 8, 1969, 1), and Benson's participation on CBC Radio's phone-in show *Cross-Country Check-Up* on November 10, 1969. For references to Benson's November 7 and 10 appearances, see, for example, letters from Margaret Ritchie and Joan Murphy to Edgar Benson, November 7, 1969, and Edna Y. Ross to Edgar Benson, November 10, 1969, LAC, Finance fonds, RG19, vol. 4778, file 5013-07-1; Mrs. John (Evelyn) Roeper to Edgar Benson, March 9, 1970, and Betty Rushlow to Edgar Benson, November 12, 1969, LAC, Finance fonds, RG 19, vol. 4778, file 5031-07-1. Continuing discussion of media strategy and an ad for a 1970 television show can be found in Robert Kaplan, MP, to Edgar Benson, February 10, 1970; Lloyd Francis, MP, to Edgar Benson, February 13, 1970; and an ad for a special edition in late April 1970 of CFPL London TV show *The World around Us* on the White Paper, n.d., LAC, Benson fonds, R1272, vol. 23, file 23-37.

72 Barnett J. Danson, "Suggestions Relating to the Release of the White Paper on Tax Reform," September 23, 1969, LAC, Benson fonds, R1272, vol. 24, file 24-18. The complexity of the publics that the tax reforms addressed was sketched in a *Weekend Magazine* article by Benson (or under his signature) after one by his chief populist opponent in Toronto, John Bulloch, appeared in that widely read popular magazine. They seem to have appeared in the early spring of 1970. See an undated copy of Benson's article in manuscript form and of Bulloch's article in proofs from the *Weekend Magazine,* LAC, Benson fonds, R1272, vol. 23, file 23-37.

73 See George Home, circular letter to councils, federations, et cetera, on Citizenship Month 1968, which includes the CLC statement on the Carter Commission's findings, October 31, 1967, LAC, CLC fonds, MG 28 I103, no box number, reel H-655.

74 John Hayes to Mitchell Sharp, December 4, 1967; Mike Rygus to Mitchell Sharp, December 22, 1967; Fort William Port Arthur Labour Council to Mitchell Sharp, December 8, 1967; telegram from C.P. Neale of the Vancouver and District Labour Council to Mitchell Sharp, December 13, 1967; M.E. English, Edmonton and District Labour Council, to Mitchell Sharp, December 15, 1967; R.C. Haynes of the BC Federation of Labour to Mitchell Sharp, December 5, 1967; F.C. Bodie of the Alberta Federation of Labour to Mitchell Sharp, December 4, 1967; telegram from W.L. Girey of the Veterans' Affairs component of PSAC to Mitchell Sharp, November 29, 1967, LAC, CLC fonds, MG 28 I103, reel H-920, series Donald MacDonald subject files, file Royal Commission on Taxation.

75 George Home, Director, Political Education Department, to all locals, federations, and councils, "A Social Policy for Canada," December 28, 1969, LAC, CLC fonds, MG28 I103, reel H-644, file Citizenship Month.

76 Laurent Thibodeau to Edgar Benson, November 22, 1969, LAC, Finance fonds, RG 19, vol. 4778, file 5013-9 T1 Multiple; A. Ridolpho to Edgar Benson, November 11, 1969; Clayton C. Ruby to Edgar Benson, November 18, 1969; and Rev. Roger B. Rice to Edgar Benson, January 15, 1970, LAC, Finance fonds, RG 19, vol. 4778, file 5013-07-1 General R. Eloquent support from the left was much welcomed. The text of a letter by a University of Toronto law student, Jennifer Bankier, first published in a Toronto-area Liberal Party bulletin, January 22, 1970, was circulated among Liberal MPs by MP Charles Caccia (undated marginal note), LAC, Sharp fonds, MG32-B41, vol. 72, file 72-11.

77 Mrs. Russell Rogers to Edgar Benson, November 10, 1970, LAC, Finance fonds, RG 19, vol. 4778, file 5013-07-1.

78 E.J. Rawlings to Edgar Benson, date-stamped November 12, 1969, LAC, Finance fonds, RG 19, vol. 4778, file 5013-07-1 General R.

79 Donald J. Rothwell to "Murray," photocopy made for Edgar Benson, November 18, 1969, LAC, Finance fonds, RG 19, vol. 4778, file 5013-07-1 General R.

80 Murray Rogers to Edgar Benson, February 15, 1970, LAC, Finance fonds, RG 19, vol. 4778, file 5013-07-1 General R.

81 (Miss) Agnes Roulston to Edgar Benson, November 11, 1969, LAC, Finance fonds, RG 19, vol. 4778, file 5013-07-1 General R. A recent (2013) obituary of an unmarried schoolteacher from East York, Agnes Mary Roulston, might be for this letter writer (see http://www.thestar.com).

82 Mr. and Mrs. Dieter Raatz to Edgar Benson, November 10, 1969, LAC, Finance fonds, RG 19, vol. 4778, file 5013-07-1 General R.

83 Michelle Ramsay to Edgar Benson, November 14, 1969, LAC, Finance fonds, RG 19, vol. 4778, file 5013-07-1 General R.

84 Canadian Institute of Public Opinion, *The Gallup Report* (Toronto: Canadian Institute of Public Opinion, June 25, 1966; November 19, 1966; and July 5, 1967).

85 Royal Commission on Taxation, *Hearings,* October 8, 1963 (Toronto: Angus Stonehouse and Company, 1963), 3783–86; Leslie H. Saunders, *An Orangeman in Public Life: The Memoirs of Leslie Howard Saunders* (Toronto: Brittania Printers, 1980), 209–16.

86 T. White to C.A. Dunning, May 3, 1930, QUA, Dunning fonds, collection 2121, box 9, file 7.

87 F.I. Irwin to J.R. Brown, "Additional Proposals for Tax Changes Made in Letters on Taxation, Letters Dated Early January to End of May 1970," June 23, 1970, LAC, Finance fonds, RG 19, vol. 5222, file 5490-03-1. For colourful descriptions of one of these groups, the northerners, see Tom Hennesy to Edgar Benson, November 9, 1964, LAC, Finance fonds, RG 19, vol. 4247, file 5055-03-2, and Norman Vincent to Steven Otto, MP, c. late January 1971, LAC, Finance fonds, RG 19, vol. 5222, file 5490-03-1. Another particularly vivid letter, this one from a father of young children, described the budget-balancing challenges facing a young family in an income bracket (between $10,000 and $15,000) that would bear increased income tax under the White Paper proposals: strikingly, this man's monthly mortgage payment (a "relatively small" one that he could barely afford) was just a dollar more than the $177 figure that Benson typically gave to indicate how small the additional burden on the lower-middle-class salary earner would be. The writer supported easing the burden on "the poor" but insisted that he was not among "the rich"; see Gareth M. Minnie to Edgar Benson, March 24, 1970, LAC, Finance fonds, RG 19, vol. 4780, file 5013-15-1. A Toronto local of the United Electrical, Radio, and Machine Workers of America (UERMWA) agreed with him. It argued for lowering income tax on incomes under $15,000. Other unions, such as that for steelworkers, more vaguely argued for reductions on "lower income brackets"; see Sam Gugliotta, President, UERMWA Local 514, to Pierre Trudeau, June 8, 1971, and Brian Hinkley (Recording Secretary, USWA Local 2853) to Edgar Benson, date-stamped June 21, 1971, LAC, Finance fonds, RG 19, vol. 4780, file 5013-15-1.

88 R.E. Thompson to Edgar Benson, January 12, 1970, LAC, Finance fonds, RG 19, vol. 4778, file 5013-9 T1 Multiple.

89 Betty L. Frantz to Edgar Benson and Members of the House of Commons, January 25, 1970, and petition, January 9, 1970, LAC, Sharp fonds, MG 32-B41, vol. 72, file 72-11. Her concerns about a bias in favour of big firms were echoed by, among others, the son of an independent retail lumberyard owner facing stiff competition from the national firm (Beaver Lumber); see John W. Pollock to Edgar Benson, c. February 1970, LAC, Finance fonds, RG 19, vol. 4780, file 5013-18-3.

90 Annie Thompson to Edgar Benson, February 28, 1970, LAC, Finance fonds, RG 19, vol. 4778, file 5013-9 T1.

91 L.J. Thibodeau to Edgar Benson, January 28, 1970, LAC, Finance fonds, RG 19, vol. 4778, file 5013-09 T1.

92 Vincent K. Patterson to Pierre Trudeau, January 26, 1970; A.l. Plant to Edgar Benson, January 26, 1970; and R.C. Pearce to Edgar Benson, January 19, 1970, LAC, Finance fonds, RG 19, vol. 4780, file 5013-18-3. The detailed form letter used by many of the small business letter writers (e.g., Claire Penny to Edgar Benson, January 28, 1970, LAC, Finance fonds, RG 19, vol. 4780, file 5013-18-3) included no reference to family questions, but when people from this constituency wrote their own letters, as did the three examples referenced here, family themes often appeared.

93 Robertson, "The House of Commons Committee and the Aftermath of the Royal Commission on Taxation," 51. The description of small business ownership as a personal identity is mine, not Robertson's.

94 See, for example, H.R. Drysdale to Mitchell Sharp, October 4, 1969, LAC, Sharp fonds, MG32-B41, vol. 72, file 72-9.

95 E. Bonnell to Walter Harris, February 20, 1956, LAC, Finance fonds, RG 19, vol. 4242, file 5050-03-1 1957; J.J. Walsh to Pierre Trudeau, September 6, 1969, LAC, Finance fonds, RG 19, vol. 4778, file 5005-3(70); F.T. Myles to Mitchell Sharp, October 20, 1969, LAC, Sharp fonds, MG32-B41, vol. 72, file 72-2; Annie E. Ross, Secretary of the Evening Auxiliary of the Women's

Missionary Society, Knox Presbyterian Church, to Pierre Trudeau, November 12, 1969, LAC, Finance fonds, RG 19, vol. 4778, file 5013-07-1 General R; H. Glynne Jones to Edgar Benson, December 6, 1969, and Joyce G. Jones to Edgar Benson, December 2, 1970, LAC, Finance fonds, RG 19, vol. 4780, file 5013-16-19; Doreen B. Jones to Allistair Gillespie, July 15, 1970, and M. Hall to A. Gillespie, June 12, 1970, LAC, Gillespie fonds, R1526, vol. 21, file 11.

96   A sample of the policies of Pensioners Concerned in its early days is found in L.E. Jones, City Clerk, to Pierre Trudeau, December 21, 1970, LAC, Finance fonds, RG 19, vol. 4780, file 5013-16-10.

97   Paul P. de Courval to Hon. Premier Ministre, Messieurs les Ministres, et Messieurs les Députés, October 28, 1969; Vere Spittal to Edgar Benson, January 12, 1970; and Alex Kearney to Pierre Trudeau, April 10, 1969, LAC, Sharp fonds, MG32-B41, vol. 72, file 72-9; Elgin and Ada Rowcliffe to Edgar Benson, November 8, 1969, LAC, Finance fonds, RG 19, vol. 4778, file 5013-07-1; name redacted to Gordon Chown, MP, March 14, 1960, LAC, Finance fonds, RG 19, vol. 4164, file T3-General. The attack on government extravagance, always a set-piece of anti-statism, was taken up by the younger generation, too, through themes both old and new. See Mel Walsh, "The WP Question?," clipping, *Automotive Times,* July 1970, LAC, R1272, vol. 24, file 24-4; letters from J.A. Carlson to Mitchell Sharp, January 17, 1970, and George Swift to Mitchell Sharp, February 9, 1970, LAC, Sharp fonds, MG32-B41, vol. 72, files 72–11 and 72–13; and Jack Davis, MP, "Criticisms of the White Paper," March 16, 1970, LAC, Gillespie fonds, R1526, vol. 22, file 2,.

98   John Stuart Mill, *Principles of Political Economy: And Chapters on Socialism,* ed. and introd. Jonathan Riley (Oxford: Oxford University Press, 1994), 332–34.

99   Regarding organized numbers, see John Munro (Minister of Health and Welfare) to Edgar Benson, date-stamped February 25, 1971, LAC, Finance fonds, RG 19, vol. 5222, file 5490-03-1. Munro, reporting resolutions from the National Pensioners' and Senior Citizens' Federation, noted that the federation had eight provincial branches and over 200,000 members.

100   J. Harvey Perry, "How Much Social Security Can We Stand?," in *Canadian Life Insurance Officers' Association, Yearbook, 1957–58,* 32–40; draft response to a policy accountability question on the proper level of government spending as a share of GNP to H.E. Kidd, Liberal Policy Convention 1970, LAC, Benson fonds, RG 1272, vol. 20, file 20-11.

101   "Coyne, Others May Quit if Tories Re-Elected," *Toronto Daily Star,* March 22, 1958, 7; "Denounces Tories, Criticizes Fleming for Not Knowing What Is Going On," *Toronto Daily Star,* March 25, 1958, 1, 22; "'Wreck Economy,'" *Toronto Daily Star,* March 26, 1958, 12; "Professor's Warning on Tories' Economics Is Lauded by Scholars," *Toronto Daily Star,* March 28, 1958, 1; "Coyne Fights Inflation[,] Diefenbaker Needs Cash[,] Wall Street Sees Bust-Up," *Toronto Daily Star,* June 26, 1959, 26; "Coyne Refutes Muir: Central Bank's Control over Inflation Limited," *Toronto Daily Star,* July 10, 1959, 15; "Here's the Reason for Tight Money," *Toronto Daily Star,* October 24, 1959, 18; "Coyne Offers Harsh Advice," editorial, *Toronto Daily Star,* December 16, 1959, 6; "Ashforth Attacks Sacred Cows," *Toronto Daily Star,* December 6, 1960, 14; Melville H. Watkins, "One of the 17 Anti-Coyne Professors Explains," letter to the editor, *Toronto Daily Star,* December 12, 1960, 6; "No Time for Tight Money," editorial, *Toronto Daily Star,* December 22, 1960, 6; Pierre Siklos, "Revisiting the Coyne Affair: A Singular Event that Changed the Course of Canadian Monetary History," *Canadian Economics Association* 43, 3 (2010): 994–1015.

102   Douglas G. Hartle, "Some Analytical, Political, and Normative Lessons from Carter," in *The Quest for Tax Reform: The Royal Commission on Taxation Twenty Years Later,* ed. W. Neil Brooks (Toronto: Carswell, 1988), 409.

103   Typescript of R.A. Musgrave, "The Carter Commission Report: An Evaluation," invited lecture presented at the meetings of the Canadian Political Science Association, June 2, 1967, 9, LAC, CLC fonds, MG 28 I103, reel H921, series Donald MacDonald subject files,

file Royal Commission on Taxation. The more widely cited version of Musgrave's evaluation makes the same observation; see R.A. Musgrave, "The Carter Commission Report," *Canadian Journal of Economics* 1, 1, supplement (1968): 163.

104 T.M. Brown to Donald Fleming, December 8, 1957, LAC, Finance fonds, RG 19, vol. 4165, file T-3 General; Frank H. Brickendon to D. Abbott, date-stamped September 5, 1951, LAC, Finance fonds, RG 19, vol. 3404, file 7001–7050; Mrs. William J. Lillian Clayton to J. Diefenbaker, February 7, 1963, LAC, Finance fonds, RG 19, vol. 4242, file 5050–03–1; Mrs. J.C. Stella McDonald to Minister of National Revenue, June 19, 1956, and Rodolphe Prévost to Walter Harris, January 14, 1957, LAC, Finance fonds, RG 19, vol. 4243, file 5050–03–2 1957; Anna Laberge "et tous les célibataires" to Donald Fleming, December 7, 1957, and Harry E. Todd to J. Diefenbaker, August 21, 1957, LAC, Finance fonds, RG 19, vol. 4243, file 5050–03–2 1958 vol. 1.

105 "Maurice Laframboise" to Walter Harris, February 14, 1957, LAC, Finance fonds, RG 19, vol. 4242, file 5050–03–1 1957. This CPR employee wrote to explain that, while he understood that an income tax cut might be inflationary, for a married man like himself earning between $3,000 and $3,500 ($25,852 to $30,161 in 2016 dollars), his expenses were such as to make the ten dollars a month that he was paying in income tax really better used for his family's immediate necessities. He listed his fixed expenses: telephone, life insurance, rent, pension plan, health insurance, medicines, and income tax. He reported that an ordinary winter coat for a three year old cost twenty-five dollars. "There is practically nothing left to buy clothes. I cannot even afford to go to a movie once a month." The same linking of inflation with small income tax amounts for family budgets appears in letters to Edgar Benson and Mitchell Sharp about the White Paper; see, for example, George Waring to Mitchell Sharp, November 22, 1969, LAC, Sharp fonds, MG32-B41, vol. 72, file 72-10; Mrs. William Achtemichuk to Edgar Benson, January 28, 1970, and E.L. Andrews to A. Hales, February 21, 1970, LAC, Finance fonds, RG 19, vol. 4779, file 5013-14-1.

106 K.P. Brady to Edgar Benson, November 6, 1969, LAC, Finance fonds, RG 19, vol. 4778, file 5005–03; R. Benson to Walter Harris, date-stamped August 20, 1956, LAC, Finance fonds, RG 19, vol. 4242, file 5050–03–1 1957.

107 J. Harvey Perry, *Taxes, Tariffs, and Subsidies: A History of Canadian Fiscal Development,* 2 vols. (Toronto: University of Toronto Press, 1955), 2: 455.

108 Ibid., 456.

109 D.A. Gordon to Edgar Benson, November 8, 1967, LAC, Benson fonds, R1272, vol. 7, file 7-4.

110 Ruth E. Johnson to Mitchell Sharp, Febuary 2, 1970, and Mrs. M.S. Gibb to Mitchell Sharp, n.d. (probably February 1970), LAC, Sharp fonds, MG32-B41, vol. 72, file 72-14.

111 Robert Toplin to Edgar Benson, April 6, 1970, LAC, Finance fonds, RG 19, vol. 4778, file 5013-9 T2 Multiple; Patrick H. Taylor to H.G. Chappell, MP, February 12, 1970; G.H. Taylor to Edgar Benson, November 11, 1969; W. Turner to Edgar Benson, November 10, 1969; and L.F. Taylor to Charles Turner, MP, January 13, 1970, LAC, Finance fonds, RG 19, vol. 4778, file 5013-9 T1 Multiple.

112 William H. Katerberg, "The Irony of Identity: An Essay on Nativism, Liberal Democracy, and Parochial Identities in Canada and the United States," *American Quarterly* 47, 3 (1995): 503–6.

113 Hall, "Recognizing the Passion in Deliberation," 92.

114 "The Waffle Manifesto: For an Independent Socialist Canada (1969)," points 20 and 25, http://www.socialisthistory.ca/.

115 James G. Snell, *The Citizen's Wage: The State and the Elderly in Canada, 1900-1951* (Toronto: University of Toronto Press, 1996).

116 Kevin Milligan, "The Design of Tax Policy in Canada: Thoughts Prompted by Richard Blundell's 'Empirical Evidence and Tax Policy Design,'" *Canadian Journal of Economics* 44, 4 (2011): 1189–90; Joel Slemrod and Caroline Weber, "Evidence of the Invisible: Toward a Credibility Revolution in the Empirical Analysis of Tax Evasion and the Informal Economy," *International Tax and Public Finance* 19, 1 (2012): 25–53; Joel Slemrod, "Tax Compliance and Enforcement: New Research and Its Policy Implications," working draft, November 1, 2015, presented at The Economics of Tax Policy, December 3–4, 2015, 17; Geoffrey Dunbar and Chuling Fu, "Sheltered Income: Estimating Income Under-Reporting in Canada," working paper, Bank of Canada, 2015.

117 Canada, House of Commons, *Debates,* June 18, 1971, 6894–96.

118 I am thinking here of the challenges discussed in Donald J. Savoie, *Power: Where Is It?* (Montreal: McGill-Queen's University Press, 2010).

Chapter 11: Self-Interest, Community, and the Evolution of the Citizen-Taxpayer

1 Elsbeth Heaman, "Macdonald and Fiscal Realpolitik," in *Macdonald at 200: New Reflections and Legacies* (Toronto: Dundurn, 2014), Chapter 7.

2 Marjorie E. Kornhauser, "Legitimacy and the Right of Revolution: The Role of Tax Protests and Anti-Tax Rhetoric in America," *Buffalo Law Review* 50, 3 (2002): 819–930; Dennis J. Ventry Jr., "Americans Don't Hate Taxes, They Hate *Paying* Taxes," Research Paper 251, University of California Davis Legal Studies Research Paper Series, March 2011.

3 Nicolas Delalande and Romain Huret, "Tax Resistance: A Global History," *Journal of Policy History* 25, 3 (2013): 301–30. My thanks to Delalande and Huret for organizing the 2010 colloquium "Les révoltes fiscales en Europe, aux États-Unis, et dans les empires coloniaux," in which I had a valuable opportunity to talk with tax historians from around the world. In pointing to the tax resistance among state builders, I also want to suggest a nuance to Julian E. Zelizer's framework in "The Uneasy Relationship: Democracy, Taxation, and State Building since the New Deal," in *The Democratic Experiment: New Directions in American Political History,* ed. Meg Jacobs, William J. Novak, and Julian E. Zelizer (Princeton, NJ: Princeton University Press, 2003) , 276–300.

4 Meyer Bucovetsky and Richard M. Bird, "Tax Reform in Canada: A Progress Report," *National Tax Journal* 25, 1 (1972): 34; Martha O'Brien, "Income Tax, Investment Income, and the Indian Act: Getting Back on Track," *Canadian Tax Journal* 50, 5 (2002): 1570–96.

5 Shirley Tillotson, *Contributing Citizens: Modern Charitable Fundraising and the Making of the Welfare State, 1920–66* (Vancouver: UBC Press, 2008), 34.

6 Robin Einhorn, *American Taxation, American Slavery* (Chicago: University of Chicago Press, 2006); Michael Piva, *The Borrowing Process: Public Finance in the Province of Canada, 1840–1867* (Ottawa: University of Ottawa Press, 1992); Arthur Silver, *The French Canadian Idea of Confederation, 1864–1900* (Toronto: University of Toronto Press, 1997); D.G. Creighton, *Empire of the St. Lawrence 1760–1850* (Toronto: Macmillan, 1956). E.H. Heaman's *Tax, Order, and Good Government* (Montreal: McGill-Queen's University Press, 2017) develops and refocuses this story to show what a central part taxation played in shaping the division of powers.

7 R.H. Coats to Eric Adams, May 19, 1933, quoted in Duncan McDowall, *Sum of the Satisfactions: Canada in the Age of National Accounting* (Montreal: McGill-Queen's University Press, 2008), 279n44. McDowall also describes the development of statistical capacity more generally at 30–38.

8 Isaac W. Martin, *Rich People's Movements: Grassroots Campaigns to Untax the One Percent* (Oxford: Oxford University Press, 2013).

9 W.A. Macdonald, presentation to the Toronto and District Labour Council panel, March 6, 1969, LAC, CLC fonds, MG 28 I103, reel H921, series Donald MacDonald subject files, file Royal Commission on Taxation. In research on labour councils in the 1950s and early 1960s, I did not see people of Macdonald's political stature and elite connections (Macdonald was a QC and chairman of the Canadian Bar Association in 1966) show up on the programs of Labour Council activities, though labour representatives were being included in community-wide councils of other kinds. Macdonald corresponded actively with Mitchell Sharp about Liberal Party matters and the process of circulating the Carter report. I infer his involvement in the Liberal Party from the tone and content of that correspondence; see, for example, W.A. "Bill" Macdonald to "Mike" McCabe, Executive Assistant to Mitchell Sharp, April 12, 1966; W.A. "Bill" Macdonald to Mitchell Sharp, May 25, 1966; and Mike McCabe to Bill Macdonald, June 6, 1966, LAC, Sharp fonds, MG32-B41, vol. 108, file 20. On the social and political location of labour councils in this period, see Shirley Tillotson, "'When Our Membership Awakens': Welfare Work and Canadian Union Activism, 1950–1965," *Labour/Le travail* 40 (1997): 137–70.

10 David Tough, "Broadening the Political Constituency of Tax Reform: The Visual Rhetoric of *Canadian Taxation*, 1979–81," *Journal of Canadian Studies* 46, 1 (2012): 1–20; W. Neil Brooks, ed., *The Quest for Tax Reform: The Royal Commission on Taxation Twenty Years Later* (Toronto: Carswell, 1988); Linda McQuaig, *Behind Closed Doors: How the Rich Won Control of Canada's Tax System ... and Ended Up Richer* (Markham, ON: Penguin Books Canada, 1987); Kim Brooks, ed., *The Quest for Tax Reform Continues: The Royal Commission on Taxation Fifty Years Later* (Toronto: Carswell, 2013). Going beyond Carter, but continuing the concern for social equality as well as tax fairness, a body of Canadian feminist tax scholarship has also developed, and its contours are well described in Kim Brooks, review of *Critical Tax Theory: An Introduction, Canadian Journal of Women and the Law* 22, 1 (2010): 288n11.

11 A variety of perspectives can be found in the pages of the *Canadian Tax Journal*, published by the Canadian Tax Foundation.

12 This is a colloquial phrasing of the idea of the "original position," introduced by John Rawls in *A Theory of Justice* (Cambridge, MA: Harvard University Press, 1971) and presented in *Justice as Fairness: A Restatement*, ed. Erin Kelly (Cambridge, MA: Harvard University Press, 2001), part 1, section 6. In the rest of the paragraph, I have been influenced by the discussions of kinds of consensus and means to consenus discussed in Jane Mansbridge et al., "The Place of Self-Interest and the Role of Power in Deliberative Democracy," *Journal of Political Philosophy* 18, 1 (2010): 64–100.

13 I have been influenced in my conception of this standard both by Mansbridge et al., "The Place of Self-Interest," and by a philosophical work about integrity, in particular about the threats to integrity posed by our habits of relying on the expertise of others ("epistemic dependence") and by the usefulness to integrity of appropriate ways of responding to disagreement. See Greg Scherkoske, *Integrity and the Virtues of Reason* (Cambridge, UK: Cambridge University Press, 2013), Chapter 4.

Index

286 88; modernism and, 286, 289–90; populism in consultation, 290. *See also* Royal Commission

cartoons: department of Finance, 60(f); farmer's opinions, 54(f); marketing, 54; National Government, 92(f); taxes, 89(f), 107(f); taxpayer as donkey, 93(f); used in information campaigns, 193(f), 194(f)

Catholic Church, 152, 296–97

Caughnawaga Mohawk, 121–23

CCF (Cooperative Commonwealth Federation): government and, 207, 284; living allowances for workers, 224; as official federal opposition, 112; popularity of, 186; tax evasion, 170; taxes, 185, 234

CCL (Canadian Congress of Labour), 235, 242. *See also* CLC (Canadian Labour Congress)

Chamber of Commerce, 283, 284, 315

chartered accountants, 242

cheese sold to Britain, 19–20, 32–33

cheque taxes, 110

children: Chinese workers and, 182; Conservatives and exemptions for, 101; family allowance for, 200; illegitimate, 205; income splitting with, 261; tax credit against tax owed, 178; tax exemptions, 16, 75, 81–82, 86, 87, 177; unemployed adults as, 87, 88

Chinese Canadians: disqualification of, 117; head taxes, 131, 132; income tax protests, 309; income taxes, 182; Jones Tax and, 131; union support for, 182

citizen engagement in public finance debate: on basic personal exemption, 242–45, 259–63; through bond market, 34–35, 45; towards collective life, 312; complaints about waste, 101; complaints to politicians, 280; concessions by government as a result of, 201–7; corporate taxes, 249; by diverse mass electorate, 291; and education of citizens, 78, 167, 189–94, 190, 301; during elections, 112, 279; on exceptional expenses and deductions for, 246–47; government call for, 203, 294; increase in 1960s, 293; letters to politicians, 7–8, 43, 44, 292–93;

on medical expenses as deductions, 245–46; on mortgage interest, 232; through Operation Freedom, 283; on overtime be tax free in 1940s, 180; through participatory democracy, 288; response from government in 1940s, 176, 188–90, 195–97, 199; in Tariff Commission, 53; in tax debates, 303, 304, 317; in tax protests, 101, 104, 190, 250, 352n8; in tax talks, 210, 211, 213, 237, 249, 289, 311; on taxes, 91, 94, 307; on wage tax in British Columbia, 96; on working women and income taxes in 1940s, 181–82. *See also* pocketbook politics

Citizens' Research Institute of Canada (CRIC), 64–66, 75, 190

citizenship, 99, 118, 133, 138, 208

citizenship of marginalized people, 116

Clark, Michael, 23–24, 25

Clark, W. Clifford, 149, 176, 187, 189, 190, 200, 267

CLC (Canadian Labour Congress), 210, 218, 235, 245–46, 284, 294–95. *See also* CCL (Canadian Congress of Labour)

CLTLV (Canadian League for Taxation of Land Values), 26

Cold War as seen in United States, 240

Coldwell, M.J., 185, 186, 187, 234

"Collecting Income Taxes," 140–41

collection of taxes. *See* tax collection

collectivism, 4, 5, 18, 282–83

Colonial Stock Act, 23, 97, 314

compulsory savings plan, 174–75, 199, 204–5, 310. *See also* forced savings

Confederation, 14, 310

confidence as a public finance concept, 163–65, 171

"conscience money" payments, 151–52

conscription of Indigenous men, 125

conscription of wealth, 24–25, 185

Conservative government, 47, 52, 67. *See also* Progressive Conservatives (PCs)

constitution, 14, 110, 267–68, 291

consumption taxes: alternatives to income taxes, 21, 46–47; basic vs luxury, 15, 21, 52–53; revenues from, 162; smuggling to avoid, 68

Contributing Citizens (Tillotson), 28

double taxation vs credit of provincial against federal taxes, 268–70. *See also* taxation

Doukhobors disqualification, 117

Drayton, Henry, 46, 51–52, 53, 55, 309

Duplessis, Maurice, 105, 265, 267–68, 269

East York Township, 106

Eaton, A. Kenneth (Ken): about, 282–83; education of taxpayers, 189; fiscal federalism, 69; tax exemptions, 86; tax proposals from the public, 7; tax treatment of expense allowances, 132, 246–47

economic science, 304

economy: budget speeches of 1943 and 1944, 199; data and national accounts, 289, 290; described, 167, 197, 216; federal vs provincial jurisdictions, 265, 267; impact of taxation on, 11, 233; need of foreign capital, 233; policy disagreement among economists, 299; public education about, 208, 301, 307

education of citizens and workers, 38, 40, 192–94, 193(f), 194(f)

Edwards, George, 59–60

elderly: basic exemptions, 244–45, 305; old age pension and, 304; tax reform and, 298–99

elections: confidence in politicians, 111, 271; deductions at source reduction and, 206; effect on policy decisions, 206–7, 279–80, 281; exemptions to taxes and, 86, 110–11; free enterprise vs socialism in 1962, 283; Jones tax and, 100–101; officials vs plutocrats, 111; popular masses vs intelligent class, 112; tax reforms in 1962, 285; votes won or lost on tax issues, 85–86, 250, 279–80

Elliott, C. Fraser: collection of taxes, 140, 145, 146–47; consultation about over deductions, 203; power to make judgments of tax liability, 219; public expression regarding taxpayers vs reality, 170; radio address to taxpayers, 147; tax evasion by elite, 164–65; war finance, 176

employers, 95–96, 136, 139, 177, 191–92

enfranchisement, 117, 133, 136

England. *See* United Kingdom

Equitable Income Tax Foundation, 217–18. *See also* Income Taxpayers' Association

Essays in Taxation (Eaton), 282

Exchequer Court of Canada, 62, 129, 150

exemptions from income tax, 11; budget of 1926, 74–75; budget of 1949, 212; complaints about, 88; corporate income, 162; cost of, 250; data, 325(t), 326(t); dependants, 81, 87–88; direct assistance vs medical exemptions and, 247–49; equity in the distribution of, 206; exemptions value, 87; householders vs married, 88; impact on tax revenue, 195–96; as justifications to leave subsistence income untaxed, 100, 241; lowering in 1931-32, 85; NDT and PIT, 177, 178; number of payers affected by, 80–82; other countries, 65; raising in 1926, 66; religion and, 296–97; requests from taxpayers, 87; value in current and contextualized dollars, 352n8; wages taxes, 96

exports from farmers and manufacturers, 40–41

External Affairs Department, 126, 128

fairness: business expense deductions, 230; capital gains vs tax burden, 235; care for dependants, 261; Carter Commission, 287; communist and anti-communist support for, 242; conversations about, 83, 231–32; CPF contributions, 28; data about, 317; enforcement of income taxes, 75; equalization system and transfer payments, 270; family allowances, 201; farmers' protest, 58; householder exemptions, 88; income tax vs tariffs, 48; income taxes, 49, 65, 68, 95, 197, 287, 295, 308; information campaign, 188–94; Jones tax, 99–100; loopholes and, 231; lower income earners, 248; marital exemptions, 88; progressive rates, 174; regional differences in double taxation, 90; special revenue tax in B.C., 99; subsistence needs and taxes, 242; Tax Appeal Board, 259; tax system evaluation, 167; taxes, 170, 223, 235, 236, 274, 308

families and caregiver expenses, 259–61

Family Allowances Act of 1944, 175, 199, 200–201, 282, 283, 307
family situation and income taxes, 81–82, 199
farmers: advertisements to, 225; Carter commission and, 286; Cooperative Commonwealth Federation, 158; deductible expenses, 225; evasion of income taxes, 309; exemption from wages tax, 95; help in paying, 213; indirect taxes, 50; knowledge of tax code, 225; land tax, 25–26, 55; National Policy attack on, 55–56; Quebec court case, 71–74; salaries and income tax exemptions, 352n8; Tariff Commission participation, 53; tax burdens on, 55, 76
Farmers' Platform of 1910, 24, 53, 61
fascism and tax resistance, 112–13
federal revenue system in Canada, 77
federal taxation: income taxes, 22, 24, 80–81, 241 (*see also* income taxes); indirect taxes, 21; provincial jurisdiction, 69–72, 265; regional differences, 76; sales taxes and, 76; used for payment of loan interest, 22
federalism, 266–73, 267
federal-provincial conferences, 265
Ferland, Hervé, 103–4
Fielding, W.S., 51, 63
finances, war's effect on, 174
financial capacity described, 198
Financial Counsel, 143, 144
Financial Post, 228
First Nations, 69, 129, 309. *See also* Indians; Indigenous people
flag with maple leaf, 288
Fleming, Donald: basic subsistence spending, 242–43, 245; capital gains, 235, 263; income tax reductions, 248; surplus stripping and, 229; Victory bonds and wealthy, 64
Forbes v. The Attorney General of Manitoba, 102
forced savings, 174–75, 179, 199, 204–5, 258, 310
Foyer Ouvrier and sales tax revolt in Quebec, 104
Frazer, A.W., 185, 189–90
Frazer Institute, 4

free riders, 130, 304, 308, 317
French Canadian race preservation, 87

Gagnon, Onésime, 268, 269
Gallup polls, 221–22, 296
Gillette razors and bond marketing, 40
Globe: article about Farmers and Tariff system, 55; *Caron v The King*, 72; income tax story, 31–32, 48; marketing bonds to common people, 36, 39; municipal votes for unemployed, 112; sales tax protests in Quebec, 104; tax strikes, 108. *See also Globe and Mail*
Globe and Mail: advertisements for Victory bonds, 184; bond buyers' civic duty, 183; capital gains tax, 235; collections over tax amount due, 257; forced savings, 179; medical expenses, 247; taxpayer's rights, 247–48, 255. *See also Globe*
GNP (gross national product), 162, 211, 330(t)
Gordon, Walter, 241, 272
government spending: British Columbia's taxes and, 98–99; class differences in views about, 113; debt concerns, 153; education, 94; income inequality and social spending, 249; National Government view on, 112; responsibility towards citizens vs, 113; services, 99; taxes and, 90–91, 100–1, 113; wasteful, 101, 308
governments: alliances amongst the parties, 75; businesses' relationship with, 279; centralization vs provinces, 69–74, 266–67, 270, 273; concessions in policy, 201–7; decentralization and fiscal practices, 270; direct assistance vs exemptions, 247–49; equalization system with provinces, 269, 272, 274; excuses for inaction from, 273; medical expenses debate, 247; parties support of income tax, 76–77; policies and defaults on debt, 153; problems, 92(f); size and cost of, 91; United States vs Canada's federalism, 267; wages tax, 95; welfare state, 267–68
The Great Depression, 139–73; default prevention during, 67; effect on currencies, 156, 158; financial data, 162;

public revenue need, 140; tax relief during, 135–36; taxation adjustments vs spending cuts, 99–100

Great War Veterans' Association, 27, 56

Greenspan, David, 230

Gross National Product (GNP), 162, 211, 330(t)

Hamilton United Electrical Union, 254

head taxes as poll taxes, 17

Heaman, Elsbeth, 17, 21

Home and Property Owners' Association: Winnipeg tax strike, 106

homeowners, 88, 162, 232, 271, 301, 313

Houde, Camilien, 278

House of Commons, 27, 58, 65, 79, 220

Ilsley, J.L.: anti-inflation "stabilization" project, 176, 198; complaints responses into speeches, 180; economy, 197; exemptions without creating loopholes, 206; letters from the public, 289; new tax system introduction, 175; responses to new taxpayers in 1940s, 176, 178, 188–89; speech to Trades and Labour Congress of Canada, 195–97; subsistence needs and taxes, 241

immigrants denied tax exemptions, 132

income splitting, 261–63, 273, 313

Income Tax Act of 1948, 214–16, 224, 225, 229, 255

Income Tax Act of British Columbia, 99

income tax evasion. See tax evasion

Income Tax Forum, 227

income tax payers: deduction at source, 82; diversity of, 113; poll taxes vs, 100; record keeping and, 224; regional differences, 178; statistics of men and women, 82–83; tools to protest, 84–85; unemployment effect on, 240. See also taxpayers

income taxes: administrative challenges, 59–63, 254; advocates for, 24, 25; African Canadian occupations and, 206; anti-statism, 282; arguments against, 66–68; average wages and, 212; basic personal exemptions, 240, 241, 242, 281, 287, 307; benefits and disadvantages, 67, 307; bonds and, 31, 63, 184; British North America Act of

1867 and, 69, 70; budgets and, 19–20, 51–52, 66, 80; burden for payers, 236, 240–45; capital gains and, 207, 274, 310; caregiver expenses, 205, 259–61; changes in 1926, 66; citizenship and, 99; collection (see tax collection); communication with citizens, 44, 251; complaints about, 88, 89, 180, 256; concessions by government, 201–2, 246, 310; consumption taxes vs, 21, 46, 75; court cases, 69–72, 71–74; credit of provincial against federal, 268–70; deductions, 205, 246–47, 260, 281; deductions at source, 96, 101, 177, 257, 274; defining, 48–49; direct support vs large collective refunds, 247; divorce and alimony payments, 202; double taxation, 70, 268; economy, 306; effect on rich vs poor, 34, 309; effectiveness and success, 67; elderly people tax relief, 206, 244–45; excessive during post-war 1948, 220; exemptions (see exemptions from income tax); expenditure management, 210; experts in taxes, 64; family needs, 80–81, 259–63; farmers as payers, 55, 62; federal debt payment with, 211; federal revenue portion, 77, 204; flat tax, 11; garnishing of wages, 241; higher incomes, 180, 248, 309; income splitting, 261–63; Indigenous people, 120–21, 121–22, 124, 205; interest, 73, 257; interwar years, 171; legitimacy of, 87; living allowances and, 224; lower-income earners, 125, 174, 204, 207, 300, 310; marginal rates data, 214; medical expenses as deductions, 245–46; municipal taxes as deduction from, 272; national defence tax (NDT), 177; new system in 1942, 174–209, 175; Newfoundland, 67; non-taxable income and, 224; opposition to, 12, 19–20, 21–22, 69–74; oversight commission, 60; overtime cause of increased, 180–81; payer profile during interwar years, 81–82; personal income tax (PIT), 177; Plaxton ruling and Indigenous people, 123–24; poor, 125; proportionate vs progressive, 11; protests, 66–68, 103, 164, 181–82; provincial, 94–103, 102–3, 309; public services and, 274; Quebec personal exemptions, 269; Quebec politicians, 73; raising the personal exemption, 248; rates of, 11, 61, 65, 174, 268; reasons against, 86–87, 241; record keeping, 62, 213, 251–53, 252–53; reforms, 64–66, 65, 214, 249; refunds, 95, 191, 257–58; regionalized, 76; religion and, 296–97; research, 214, 249; salaries and exemptions, 352n8; sales taxes vs, 309; Second World War and modern system, 175; senior citizens and exemptions, 244–45; social state and, 177, 198; socio-economic changes and, 251; special hardship relief from, 205; statistics, 196, 268, 277–78, 325(t), 326(t)–27(t); symbolism of payments, 135, 196, 210, 250; tariffs and excise duties vs, 74; US and Canadian, 64, 65, 69–70, 74, 313; Victory bonds as a precursor to, 43; welfare state and, 274

Income Taxpayers' Association, 217, 310
Income War Tax Act of 1917, 33–34, 80, 119, 213
Indian Act of 1875, 69, 118, 125
Indian Affairs, 120–24, 128
Indians: citizen rights and tax immunities, 120; civil rights and tax obligations, 118–19; conscription, 125; customs duties, 125–30, 128–29; discrimination, 128–29; exemptions in Jones tax, 123; income taxes and, 118–25; location and tax obligations, 118–19; status, 118–20; as taxpayers in 1940s, 178; voting rights disqualified, 117. *See also* First Nations; Indigenous people; Jay Treaty
Indigency exemption and voting rights, 136
Indigenous fisheries, 124, 203–4
Indigenous people: common-law marriages and credits, 205; concessions about fisheries income tax, 203–4; confusion in federal departments, 120; customs duties, 125–30, 126–27, 128; disqualification of, 116–17; earnings locations and income taxes, 123–24; factors in taxing, 124; income taxes and, 118–25, 182, 203–4; income taxes and living location, 119, 120–21, 123, 124;

National Revenue and Indian Affairs rulings, 121–22; P.L. (Annie) Garrow, 127–28; political privileges, 118; RCMP, 128–29; Royal Proclamation of 1763 and, 120; taxes and, 309. *See also* Indians
indirect taxation by general government, 21
industrial morale, 181, 190
Industrial provinces tax burden, 76
inflation, 156–57, 176, 198, 212, 299–301
information campaign in 1940s, 188–94, 198, 199
inheritances, 214
Institute of Chartered Accountants, 227, 231
International Woodworkers, 242
investment capital, 98–99, 207–8, 314
invisibility of indirect taxes, 20–21

Japanese people disqualification, 117
Jay Treaty, 119, 120, 127–29
JCPC (Judicial Committee of the Privy Council), 71
Jones tax, 94–103, 123, 131, 139
Judicial Committee of the Privy Council (JCPC), 71
jurisdictions, federal vs provincial, 69–70
Justice as Fairness (Rawls), 277

Kahnawake Kanien'kehá:ka, 121–23
Kanien'kehá:ka customs duties, 126–27
Kemp, H.R., 61, 63, 315
Keynesian macroeconomic theory, 176, 233, 299
Killam, Izaak Walton, 24, 32, 38, 309
King, William Lyon Mackenzie, 46; criticized by O'Leary, 91; election call advice from Fielding, 51; family allowance to House of Commons, 200; Ilsley budget speech of 1944, 199; integrity of, 303; lack of support for National Government, 112; national credit, 154; Royal Commission on Federalism, 166; taxing power shift, 265
Knowles, Stanley, 206, 247
Korean War, 300
Korean War budget of 1951, 233, 273

government, 201–7; discussed in cabinet chamber, 208; double taxation, 90;
elderly, 244; householder exemptions,
162; income taxes, 183, 309; Indigenous fisheries and income taxes, 204;
Indigenous people, 204, 205; *la Patrie*,
104–5; miners and pay deductions, 204;
new income tax systems, 181–82; railway workers, 206; response from governments, 201; sales taxes in Quebec,
104; tariffs, 68; tax evasion as, 221; tax
reporting and payment methods, 250;
taxation powers, 218; taxes, 57–58, 78,
103–5, 106, 310; unions, 90; veterans,
56; wages in Manitoba, 102; White
Paper, 295; working women, 182, 310
provinces: debt, 166; direct taxation powers, 70, 268; division of power, 69–72;
double taxation in, 70, 90; federal
employees and, 102; income taxes, 70,
102–3, 314; municipal tax arrears and,
272; revenues to cover expenses, 166;
special interests, 311; tax payment as
credit against federal taxes, 268–70;
transfer payments, 270; wartime taxation suspension agreements, 178–79
provincial taxes: bases of provincial credit,
97–98; British Columbia, 196; as credit
against federal income taxes, 268–70;
double taxation, 70, 90; Manitoba, 196;
resource-related taxes, 265; suspension
in 1941, 178
psychology of taxpayers, 5, 146
public consultations, 289, 292, 296.
   See also citizen engagement in public
   finance debate
public finances: in 1930s, 139, 165;
knowledge of Canadians about, 16–17,
172, 173; Rowell-Sirois Commission,
169, 170; science of, 170; shared burden of, 152; United States vs Canada,
165
public opinion, 23, 292, 293–94. *See also*
citizen engagement in public finance
debate
public opinion polling, 7–8, 220–21, 296
public services and regional equity, 270

Quebec: autonomism and tax dollars, 218;
charitable donations falsified, 264–65;

constitutional jurisprudence on taxing
powers, 69–72; distinct fiscal culture,
42, 364; equalization system, 269; farmers, 42; federal income tax opposition
in, 69–74; income tax exemptions,
268; Montreal collects income and sales
taxes, 103; municipal poll taxes prohibition, 131, 134; provincial personal
income taxes, 268; sales tax revolt,
103–5; special taxation deal, 269; tax
protests in 1940s, 182; taxes, 103,
263–66, 329(t)
Quebec Chronicle Telegraph, 140–41

Racey, Arthur G., 54, 259–61
racialized people, 116–17, 278
racism and discretionary enforcement of
taxes, 132–33
radio address by Elliott, 147
Ralliement des Créditistes, 280
Ralston, J.L., 174, 178
Rawls, John, 276–77, 302
RBC (Retail Bureau of Canada), campaign
to abolish federal income tax, 66–68
RCMP (Royal Canadian Mounted Police),
126, 127, 128–29, 284
Recorder's Court charges against sales tax
protesters, 104
regional cultures and taxes, 13–14, 47,
69–70
religion and taxes, 152, 296–97
residency and taxpayers, 17, 118–19
Retail Bureau of Canada (RBC), campaign
to abolish federal income tax, 66–68
retail politics, 279–80
Rhodes, E.N., 86–87; anti-tax evasion measures, 152; bond interest and income,
159; cheque tax and electoral support,
110–11; complaints for householders,
88; confidence in Canadian credit, 156;
confidence protection strategies, 163–64;
garnishing for debt payment, 164;
inflation policies, 156; letters about tax
collection, 144; London Stock Exchange
protests, 161; rhetorical style, 163; strategies during the Depression, 162
Robb, J. A., 66, 75, 88
Roosevelt, F.D., 109, 163, 170
Rowell-Sirois Commission, 168, 169, 170,
172, 216, 289

218–27; knowledge of tax code, 225; in 1940s, 179–88; opportunities, 232; overtime refusal in 1940s, 180; record keeping and, 224; strategies for, 215; surplus stripping, 229

tax collection: abuses in, 254; challenges to, 141–42, 224; confidence of citizens, 148; costs, 5, 20–21, 147, 221; cultural aspects of taxes and, 10; discretion dangers, 132–33; estate probation, 255; inefficiencies, 146; lack of qualifications, 145; local vs national, 9; methods, 20–21, 141–43, 144, 145–46, 219, 243, 251; municipal, 272; press releases about, 223; resources for, 141–42, 147, 223; simplification recommended by Carter Commission, 287; United States, 313

tax delinquencies, 82–83, 85–86

tax enforcement: change in methods, 220, 223; discrimination in, 130; improvements following, 61–62; Income Tax Act of 1948, 218–27; invoking respectability and honour, 218–20; limited during interwar years, 216; penalties, 312; police court, 82; public relations and, 222, 223; seizures, 243

tax evasion: anti-evasion provisions, 165; avoidance vs, 219, 222; bills to evaders, 73; bondholding and, 63–64; bribes, 219; capital gains and, 235; cash income of second jobs, 228–29; Catholic Church and, 152; charitable donations and, 264–65; "conscience money" payments, 151; consequences, 62–63, 139, 148–50, 222, 223, 274; corporations, 308, 310; costs of, 147; data on, 304; debates about, 61–62, 303; debt payments by garnishing, 164; Department of National Revenue, 142; enforcement, 62–63, 223–24; farmers, 213; hiding sales and income, 187; income splitting, 261–63; Income Tax Act of 1948, 218–27; Intelligence Branch, 223; judges, 164; justification to, 188, 232; legal proceedings, 149, 232; *Maclean's* story about, 222–23; methods, 150, 228–29; moonlighting, 228–29; morality of, 151–52; normal vs collective revulsion, 221–22; not declaring extra income,

187; other countries, 61; Oxford group and payments, 151–52; poll about, 221–22; publicity about, 149; rental income and, 228; risks of, 146; rumours about, 187–88; shared burden of, 152; unclear statute causing, 224; United States, 313

tax exemptions. *See* exemptions from income tax

tax experts' emergence, 64, 215, 222, 226–29, 242

tax inspectors' challenges, 141–42

tax journalism, 227–28

tax reform of 1960s, 276–305; blueprint from Carter Commission, 287; capital gains and, 305; complexity of, 304–5; discussions, 287, 288, 290, 311; education of public, 317; elderly and, 298–99; exemptions, 305; lower income earners, 296, 305; new proposals 1969, 288; Operation Freedom, 310; opposition to, 287, 288; process, 277; religion and, 296–97; results of, 290; special interests, 287, 296, 297; support of, 297–98; tax talk, 289, 311; unionists and, 295; White Paper, 312

tax reporting expense of, 96

tax research resources, 216–17

tax resistance: anti-statists and, 308; campaigns against party politics, 110; citizen participation in elections, 112; corporations, 310; fairness and, 310; hidden taxes to reduce, 309; interwar years, 78; marginalized people and, 309; in 1940s, 179–88; organizations supporting, 217–18; political action inspired by, 79; progressive taxation and, 308; responses to, 188–90. *See also* tax avoidance; tax evasion

taxation: administration of, 140, 192, 250–53, 254; appeals board, 215, 256, 274; benefits and contributors, 99, 307; bookkeepers, 225; burden during Second World War, 175; business opportunities, 215; calls for reforms, 230; capital gains, 185, 186, 207, 235; citizen responsibilities of Indians and, 129; complaints about, 180; concerns about double, 90; concessions in 1940s, 182; confidence in, 170; consultation

about, 203; cost of exemptions, 250; costs of, 140, 257; credit of provincial against federal taxes, 268–70; deception by citizens, 130; defense of, 99; documentation from tax inspectors, 213; duty to the poor, 139; encouragement from government to pay, 140; fairness, 167, 233; family needs, 259–63; farmers, 213; federal vs provincial, 310; financial capacity, 198; foreign investors and, 171; higher income untaxed, 145; income assistance and, 200; income splitting, 261–63; information about, 190, 191–92, 216–17, 249; national accounts system, 289; National Service Loan and, 158; new system introduction, 174–209, 187; peacetime tax system, 221; per capita rate in British Columbia, 98; poem about, 140–41; power to government with, 266; price stability and, 197; promotion of honour of payment, 147; protection and liabilities of, 130; protests about powers of, 218; prudent legalism, 220; racial discrimination, 130–33, 255; regional differences, 178; responsiveness of government, 201–7; Rhodes enforcement measures, 162–64; Rowell-Sirois Commission, 168, 289; rumours and new system, 187–88; service from National Revenue Department, 254; socio-economic changes and, 251; speeches about, 195–97; statistics, 216, 314, 315; Tax Appeal Board of Canada, 215; tax history for Canadians, 216; tax talk, 210, 211, 213, 249, 289; technical vulnerabilities, 231; United States, 217; voting rights and, 116–17; wealth, 185; welfare effects, 201; without citizenship, 119. *See also* Income Tax Act of 1948
taxes: anti-immigrant sentiment, 130–33; bond interest, 156; booze, 47, 75; British Columbia, 94–103; burden carried by all, 94–103; bureaucracy of, 252–54; business strategies to reduce liability of, 148; Canadian statistics, 47, 323(t), 324(t); capital gains, 233–36; charitable donations without receipts, 264–65; childcare expenses, 305; citizen participation (*see* citizen engagement

in public finance debate); citizens and, 304; civil rights and obligations of, 118–19; clarifications about statutes, 225; classes and, 78; collective obligations, 65, 311, 312; consumption, 65, 103–5, 329(t); cooperatives with privileges, 217–18; cost of elimination of some, 243; debt relief, 309; deductions of mortgage interest, 232; direct taxes, 21, 72, 183; double, 94; East York Township protests, 106; elections and, 100; evasion (*see* tax evasion); excess profits tax, 22; excise taxes, 50, 51; experts influence on, 65–66; fairness of, 26, 44; First Nations and, 69; flat rate, 177; franchise tax, 134; government restrictions to impose, 69–70; government size, 91; government spending and, 90; graduated, 177–78; head taxes, 17; hidden, 309; household expenses including, 89; householder exemptions, 88; immigrants and, 65, 132; income splitting, 261–63; income taxes (*see* income taxes); income vs capital gains, 235; increases and inflation reduction, 300; Indians living on reserve, 118; indirect vs direct, 49, 50, 66; information to taxpayers, 188–89, 222, 226, 227; interwar, 47; investment income, 50; Jay Treaty and Indigenous people and, 119; journals about, 216; as labour flow control, 131–32; land taxes, 25–26, 50; limitations on governments, 69–70; luxury taxes, 51, 52–53, 56, 309, 310; medical expenses as deductions, 280, 305; municipal (*see* municipal taxes); national defence tax (NDT), 177; number of, 89–90, 89(f); Oxford Group and, 311; Patriotic Fund, 27; personal income tax (PIT), 177; poll, 15, 43, 296, 306, 310; postwar, 47–51, 49; profits tax, 22, 24, 33, 48; progressive income, 28, 307; provincial (*see* provincial taxes); rate comparisons with Britain, 50; reform, 64–66 (*see also* tax reform of 1960); regional differences, 76, 94–103, 105; regressive, 272; relief, 46, 135, 136; religion and, 297; sales, 50, 74, 103–5, 309; single tax, 25, 26, 27; special interests and, 303;

Vancouver Board of Trade, 99, 100, 101
Vancouver Sun, 161
Verdun sales tax revolt, 103–5, 108
veterans, 49–50, 56
Victory Bonds, 310; ads in newspapers,
    37, 40–42; advertisements, 38, 41–42,
    184; budget speeches of 1943 and 1944,
    198; canvassers, 43; cashing in as protest
    in 1940s, 183; challenges during Second
    World War, 207; common project, 41;
    confidence in, 186–87; marketing statis-
    tics, 41; National Committee poster
    slogans, 40–41; protest by not buying in
    1940s, 183; Quebec businesses and, 41;
    renewal or default of, 159; small-buyers
    importance in, 183; stores accepting,
    38; tax avoidance means, 63–64; voters
    as owners of, 185
Victory Loans, 34–44; foreigners and, 130;
    marketing to all, 34–37; opposition
    to new tax system and, 176; volunteer
    canvassers, 34
voters: economic lectures to, 301; educa-
    tion of, 301; gaining, 206; income tax
    voters, 134; Indians as, 116–17; public
    consultations with, 288–89; qualifica-
    tions of, 116–17, 134–36

wages tax, 95–103
Walters, C.S., 119, 145, 219
war debt, 50, 74
war finance: argument for income tax in,
    24; bonds for, 29, 48; borrowing for,
    22, 24; budget speeches, 198; capital
    levy in Britain, 24; challenges, 183,
    205; charities, 27–28; criticism of, 176;
    critics' ideas affecting, 186; data about
    1943, 183; education of taxpayers,
    189–94; fairness of, 197; income tax
    purpose, 47–48; inflation and, 176,
    191; policy during Second World War,
    175; progressive income taxation, 28;
    steps in, 20–23

war savings certificates, 183
wartime dominion-provincial tax agree-
    ments, 101
Wartime Information Board (WIB), 180,
    193(f)
Waterous v. Minister of National Revenue,
    63
wealth taxes, 214
welfare state: building of, 175, 239;
    disabled people, 282; income tax to
    finance, 11, 12, 273, 278; opposition
    to, 282, 284, 303; Trudeau and, 303;
    unemployment insurance and, 267
White, Thomas, 19–23; advice to, 24, 29,
    289; bond strategies, 32, 33–34, 36, 40;
    borrowing in Canada, 32; conscription
    of wealth confusion, 25; income tax, 31;
    instructions to Breadner, 48; land taxes,
    27; securities dealers, 42; *Story
    of Canada's War Finance*, 23
White Paper, 278, 293, 299, 315
WIB (Wartime Information Board), 180
WIB's Rumour Clinic, 187–88
Wilson, L.A., 139, 142, 170
Winnipeg Free Press, 33, 89, 102, 108, 220
Winnipeg (MB) protests against taxes, 106
women: bonds and, 37, 41, 310; book-
    keeping duties, 228; Committees and
    Commissions on, 286, 316; Dominion
    Succession Act of 1942, 213; exemp-
    tions, 88, 100; homeowners taxation
    changes, 203; marginalized citizens,
    116, 136; organizations, 214; political
    citizenship, 117, 278; poll taxes exemp-
    tion, 137; refusal to work in 1940s,
    181–82; sales tax opposition from, 309;
    special revenue tax and, 100; tax de-
    ductible expenses, 228; tax exemptions,
    136; taxpayers, 82, 83; widows income
    taxes, 136, 213–14, 218; as wives, 16,
    65, 82
Wood Gundy, 97–98
Woodsworth, J.S., 79, 91, 158